Physics

25 Years 2025-2001

ISC

CHAPTERWISE - TOPICWISE QUESTION BANK

Physics

Class 12

Author
Ravi Raj

arihant
SUCCESS AND NOTHING LESS

arihant
SUCCESS AND NOTHING LESS

ARIHANT PRAKASHAN
(School Division Series)

ADMINISTRATIVE & PRODUCTION OFFICES

Regd. Office
'Ramchhaya' 4577/15, Agarwal Road, Darya Ganj, New Delhi -110002
Tele: 011- 47630600, 43518550

Head Office
Kalindi, TP Nagar, Meerut (UP) - 250002, Tel: 0121-7156203, 7156204

SALES & SUPPORT OFFICES

Agra, Ahmedabad, Bengaluru, Bareilly, Chennai, Delhi, Guwahati, Hyderabad, Jaipur, Jhansi, Kolkata, Lucknow, Nagpur & Pune.

PO No : TXT-XX-XXXXXXX-X-XX

Published By Arihant Publications (India) Ltd.

For further information about the books published by Arihant, log on to www.arihantbooks.com
or e-mail at info@arihantbooks.com

PRICE ₹395.00

Follow us on

Achieving 99+
Marks in Board Exams

Achieving 99+ marks in board exams is definitely an ambitious goal, but with the right approach and these 7 tips from toppers, you can definitely increase your chances of success!

Here are the 7 Topper Tips to ace your board exams:

1. Master the art of consistency

Consistency builds understanding and confidence, both crucial for excelling in exams.

2. Build a winning study strategy

Create a personalised timetable that prioritises subjects based on your strengths and weaknesses.

3. Befriend the syllabus

Focus on high-weightage topics and prioritise mastering core concepts before moving on to advanced ones.

4. Embrace active learning

Explain concepts to yourself or in study groups to solidify understanding.

5. Conquer the past

Solve Past years' papers and Sample Papers under timed conditions to practice time management and understand paper pattern.

6. Seek help, when needed!

Don't hesitate to clarify doubts with teachers, tutors, or study groups. Asking questions strengthens your understanding and prevents confusion.

7. Prioritise well-being

Eat nutritious meals, get enough sleep, regular exercise practice stress management techniques like meditation to stay calm and focused during exams.

These tips are just a starting point, and you can personalise them to fit your learning style and preferences.

Description of
Newly Added Features

01

Electric Charges and Coulomb's Law

TREND ANALYSIS 4 YEARS

Electric Charges and Coulomb's Law

Average No. of Questions Across all Sets				
Types of Questions	2024	2023	2020	2019
1 Mark	–	–	–	–
2 Marks	2	–	–	–
3 Marks	–	–	–	–
5 Marks	–	–	–	–

Trend Analysis

At the start of each chapter, Trend Analysis is given to indicate the types of questions asked from different topics of the chapter. This feature helps students to know the importance of different topics of the given chapter from exam point of view and helps them to prepare accordingly.

11. Two small, identical in size, charged metallic spheres A and B repel each other with a force F when placed at a distance r between their centres. The spheres A and B are touched by identical, but uncharged spheres C and D, respectively

12. Three charges $1\mu C$, $1\mu C$ and $2\mu C$ are kept at vertices A, B and C of an equilateral triangle ABC of 10 cm side respectively. What will the resultant force on the charge at C?

> **KEY idea**
>
> To obtain the resultant force, first calculate the force on C due to A and force on C due to B. Then, calculate resultant force,
>
> $$F_{\text{resultant}} = \sqrt{(F_{AC})^2 + (F_{BC})^2 + 2F_{AC}F_{BC}\cdot\cos\theta}$$

Key Idea

'Key Idea' is given with selected questions with the purpose to help students to get the approach 'to answer the question'. This feature help students to develop the systematic approach to answer difficult/complex questions.

14. To be the system of charges in equilibrium, force between the charge at A and B should be equal to force between the charge at A and C or B and C. For equilibrium of system of charges (i.e. net force on the system $= 0$).

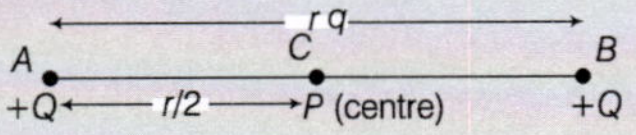

Now, sum of forces produced between the charges

$$\frac{1}{4\pi\varepsilon_0}\frac{qQ}{\left(\frac{r}{2}\right)^2} + \frac{1}{4\pi\varepsilon_0}\frac{QQ}{r^2} = 0$$

Concept Enhancer To bring the system in equilibrium put the negative charge in between the two positive charges.

Concept Enhancer

Concept Enhancer gives the brief description of the concept, which has been used to answer the question. This feature provides revision of important concept along with practice of question solving.

Most Important Topics

from each Chapter

On the basis of analysis of last 5 Years' Board Examination Papers, we have identified Important Topics from each chapter.

Chapter Name	Important Topics	Weightage in Last 5 Years' Boards				
		2025	2024	2023	2020	2019
Electric Charges and Coulomb's Law	Electric Charges and Coulomb's Law	–	2M(2Q)	–	–	–
Electric Field and Electric Dipole	Electric Field (Including Electric Field Lines)	3M	–	–	–	–
	Electric Dipole	2M	–	1M,3M	3M	–
	Gauss' Theorem	–	2M(2Q)	1M	1M	1M
Electric Potential and Potential Energy	Electric Potential and Potential Energy	–	1M	1M(2Q),2M	1M	1M,3M
Capacitance	Capacitance	2M(1Q)	3M	2M(2Q)	3M	3M
Current Electricity	Electric Current and Ohm's Law	1M,(1Q), 3M	–	1M(2Q),2M	2M	–
	Electric Cell and Their Combination	2M(2Q), 3M	1M	–	–	1M
	Kirchhoff's Laws and Their Applications	2M	1M,3M(2Q)	1M,3M(3Q)	3M(2Q)	2M,3M(2Q)
	Electric Power	–	1M	1M	2M	–
Magnetic Effect of Current: Magnetic Field	Magnetic Effect of Current : Magnetic Field	2M, 3M(2Q)	3M	1M(2Q), 3M(2Q)	1M	2M
Magnetic Force and Torque	Magnetic Force and Torque	1M(1Q), 3M,5M	1M(2Q),3M	2M(2Q)	1M,2M	1M,2M
Bar Magnet	Bar Magnet	–	–	–	–	–
Magnetic Classification of Substances	Magnetic Classification of Substances	1M(1Q)	1M(2Q)	–	–	–
Electromagnetic Induction	Electromagnetic Induction	1M(1Q), (5M)	2M,3M	1M(2Q), 2M(2Q),5M	2M,(2Q)	2M
Alternating Current Circuits	Introduction of Alternating Current	–	2M	2M	–	2M
	Basic AC Circuits(R, L and C Circuits)	–	–	–	–	–
	L-C-R, R-L and R-C Series Circuits	5M	5M	–	5M(2Q)	1M,2M,5M
Electromagnetic Waves	Electromagnetic Waves	2M	2M	2M(2Q)	2M	2M

Chapter Name	Important Topics	Weightage in Last 5 Years' Boards				
		2025	2024	2023	2020	2019
Ray Optics	Reflection and Refraction of Light	–	1M,2M	1M	1M	1M,2M
	Refraction Through a Prism	3M	3M	3M(2Q)	2M	3M
	Refraction at a Spherical Surface	1M, 3M	3M	1M	2M,3M	3M
	Dispersion	1M	1M	2M(2Q)	–	2M
Optical Instruments	Simple Microscope and Compound Microscope	–	–	1M,2M	3M	5M
	Astronomical Telescope	1M(1Q), 2M	5M	–	3M	5M
Huygens' Principle	Huygens' Principle	3M	1M,3M	1M(2Q), 3M,5M	1M	3M
Interference of Light	Interference of Light	3M	3M	1M(2Q),3M	3M	1M,5M
Diffraction of Light	Diffraction of Light	1M (1Q)	2M	1M,3M	3M	–
Photoelectric Effect	Photoelectric Effect	2M, 3M	3M	3M(2Q)	1M	1M,2M
Wave Particle Duality	Wave Particle Duality	1M(2Q)	1M	1M(2Q)	1M	–
Atomic Structure	Rutherford's Model	–	–	–	–	–
	Bohr's Model and Hydrogen Spectra	5M(2Q)	2M(2Q)	1M,2M,3M	3M	1M,3M
Atomic Mass	Atomic Mass	–	–	2M	–	–
Nuclei	Mass-Energy Equivalence	1M (Q)	1M,2M,3M	2M	1M,2M	1M
Nuclei	Nuclear Energy	5M	2M	1M,3M	1M(2Q), 3M(2Q)	–
Semiconductor Electronics	Semiconductor Electronics	1M(3Q)	–	1M(2Q),2M	1M	3M
Junction Diode	Junction Diode	5M	1M,2M,3M	3M	1M,2M	3M(2Q)

Dream, Believe, Achieve Insights from ISC Toppers

Follow all the 5P's

• Persistence • Passion • Perseverance • Purpose • Practice

MANYA GUPTA
ISC Topper (99.75%)

"Aim for high marks, that's what I was doing. I convinced myself that if I aim for 100 I will at least get a 95. That was my logic, but I ended up getting a 100. "I studied with the help of my school and tuition classes. I didn't study daily much, but before the exams, I used to pull all-nighters and study".

ARYAAN
ISC Topper (99.75%)

"Studying for 3-4 hours every day along with six hours of school helped me secure 399 out of 400 marks, scoring 99.75%."

I'm very active on all social media platforms but it has never hindered my studies. I strike a balance between hard work and fun".

The degree of toughness of any subject is merely a subjective outlook. I made sure that I incentivised myself at times when I didn't feel like sitting at my study table, especially for theoretical subjects.

I simply believe in revising the concepts which were taught at school or tuitions that very day and minimise backlogs as much as I could.

POOJA KEJRIWAL
ISC Topper (97.5%)

I believe there is no substitute to hard work. There was no fixed hours of preparation, I read a topic till the time I completely understood it. I had to be satisfied with the topic covered,"

See it is important to take breaks and everyone has their own way of entertainment. I do chat with friends on social media. I think it is fine until it becomes as addiction.

There is no secret formula as such, but one should not panic and have faith in his/her preparation.

DEVANG KUMAR
ISC Topper

DIMPLE KOTHARI
ISC Topper (97.5%)

- Don't run behind marks, crave for knowledge, experience because ultimately that's gonna help you.
- Don't let peer pressure dominate you.
- If you want to obtain good marks, leave all social media-This is a myth. I was active on Instagram & WhatsApp before my examinations, and even during my examinations. It's just that you need to remember that everyone has the same 24 hours, it's how you utilize it as well as enjoy it better than others.
- Both early morning and late night studies are best ~ you need to choose what's better for you.
- Don't hesitate to ask questions. If you have any doubts, please clarify. Everyone has different learning styles and speed, so it's nothing to be ashamed of.
- Never give up.

Please Note that all the information is collected from different websites.

Contents

ISC Chapterwise Question Bank 2025-2001

Latest Syllabus

Class XII (2026)

There will be two papers in the subject.

PAPER I : Theory	70 marks
PAPER II : Practical	15 marks
Project Work	10 marks
Practical File	5 marks

PAPER I THEORY 70 Marks

S. No.	UNIT	TOTAL WEIGHTAGE
1.	Electrostatics	14 Marks
2.	Current Electricity	
3.	Magnetic Effects of Current and Magnetism	16 Marks
4.	Electromagnetic Induction and Alternating Currents	
5.	Electromagnetic Waves	2 Marks
6.	Optics	18 Marks
7.	Dual Nature of Radiation and Matter	7 Marks
8.	Atoms and Nuclei	6 Marks
9.	Electronic Devices	7 Marks
	Total	70 Marks

Note

(i) Unless otherwise specified, only S. I. Units are to be used while teaching and learning, as well as for answering questions.

(ii) All physical quantities to be defined as and when they are introduced along with their units and dimensions.

(iii) Numerical problems are included from all topics except where they are specifically excluded or where only qualitative treatment is required.

1. ELECTROSTATICS

(i) **Electric Charges and Fields** Electric charges; conservation and quantisation of charge, Coulomb's law; superposition principle and continuous charge distribution. Electric field, electric field due to a point charge, electric field lines, electric dipole, electric field due to a dipole, torque on a dipole in uniform electric field.

Electric flux, Gauss's theorem in electrostatics and its applications to find field due to infinitely long straight wire, uniformly charged infinite plane sheet and uniformly charged thin spherical shell.

(a) Coulomb's law, SI unit of charge; permittivity of free space and of dielectric medium. Frictional electricity, electric charges (two types); repulsion and attraction; simple atomic structure-electrons and ions; conductors and insulators; quantization and conservation of electric charge; Coulomb's law in vector form; (position coordinates r_1, r_2 not necessary). Comparison with Newton's law of gravitation; Superposition principle ($\mathbf{F}_1 = \mathbf{F}_{12} + \mathbf{F}_{13} + \mathbf{F}_{14} + \ldots$).

(b) Concept of electric field and its intensity; examples of different fields; gravitational, electric and magnetic; Electric field due to a point charge $\mathbf{E} = \mathbf{F}/q_0$ (q_0 is a test charge); $\mathbf{E}$ for a group of charges (superposition principle); a point charge q in an electric field $\mathbf{E}$ experiences an electric force $\mathbf{F}_E = q\mathbf{E}$. Intensity due to a continuous distribution of charge i.e. linear, surface and volume.

(c) Electric lines of force: A convenient way to visualize the electric field; properties of lines of force; examples of the lines of force due to (i) an isolated point charge (+ve and −ve); (ii) dipole; (iii) two similar charges at a small distance;(iv) uniform field between two oppositely charged parallel plates.

(d) Electric dipole and dipole moment; derivation of the $\mathbf{E}$ at a point, (1) on the axis (end on position) (2) on the perpendicular bisector (equatorial i.e. broad side on position) of a dipole, also for $r >> 2l$ (short dipole); dipole in a uniform electric field; net force zero, torque on an electric dipole: $\tau = \mathbf{p} \times \mathbf{E}$ and its derivation.

(e) Gauss's theorem: the flux of a vector field; Q = vA for velocity vector $\mathbf{v} || \mathbf{A}$, $\mathbf{A}$ is area vector. Similarly, for electric field $\mathbf{E}$, electric flux $\phi_E = EA$ for $\mathbf{E} || \mathbf{A}$ and $\phi_E = \mathbf{E} \cdot \mathbf{A}$ for uniform $\mathbf{E}$. For non-uniform field $\phi_E = \int d\phi = \int \mathbf{E} \cdot d\mathbf{A}$. Special cases for $\theta = 0°, 90°$ and 180°. Gauss's theorem, statement: $\phi_E = q/\epsilon_0$ or $\phi_E = \oint \mathbf{E} \cdot d\mathbf{A} = q/\epsilon_0$ where ϕ_E is for a closed surface; q is the net charge enclosed, ϵ_0 is the permittivity of free space. Essential properties of a Gaussian surface.

Applications: Obtain expression for $\mathbf{E}$ due to 1. an infinite line of charge, 2. a uniformly charged infinite plane thin sheet, 3. a thin hollow spherical shell (inside, on the surface and outside). Graphical variation of E vs r for a thin spherical shell.

(ii) **Electrostatic Potential, Potential Energy and Capacitance** Electric potential, potential difference, electric potential due to a point charge, a dipole and system of charges; equipotential surfaces, electrical potential energy of a system of two point charges and of electric dipole in an electrostatic field.

Conductors and insulators, free charges and bound charges inside a conductor. Dielectrics and electric polarisation, capacitors and capacitance, combination of capacitors in series and in parallel. Capacitance of a parallel plate capacitor, energy stored in a capacitor.

(a) Concept of potential, potential difference and potential energy. Equipotential surface and its properties. Obtain an expression for electric potential at a point due to a point charge; graphical variation of E and V versus r, $V_P = W/q_0$; hence $V_A - V_B = W_{BA/q_0}$ (taking q_0 from B to A) $= (q/4\pi\varepsilon_0)(^1/r_A - 1/r_B)$; derive this equation; also $V_A = q/4\pi\varepsilon_0 \cdot 1/r_A$; for $q > 0$, $V_A > 0$ and for $q < 0$, $V_A < 0$. For a collection of charges V = algebraic sum of the potentials due to each charge; potential due to a dipole on its axial line and equatorial line; also at any point for $r >> 2l$ (short dipole). Potential energy of a point charge (q) in an electric field $\mathbf{E}$, placed at a point P where potential is

V, is given by $U = qV$ and $\Delta U = q(V_A - V_B)$. The electrostatic potential energy of a system of two charges = work done $W_{21} = W_{12}$ in assembling the system; U_{12} or $U_{21} = (1/4\pi\varepsilon_0)\, q_1 q_2 / r_{12}$. For a system of 3 charges $U_{123} = U_{12} + U_{13} + U_{23} = \frac{1}{4\pi\varepsilon_0}\left(\frac{q_1 q_2}{r_{12}} + \frac{q_1 q_3}{r_{13}} + \frac{q_2 q_3}{r_{23}}\right)$.

For a dipole in a uniform electric field, derive an expression of the electric potential energy $U_E = -\mathbf{p}\cdot\mathbf{E}$, special cases for $\phi = 0°, 90°$ and 180°.

(b) *Capacitance of a conductor C = Q/V; obtain the capacitance of a parallel-plate capacitor ($C = \varepsilon_0 A/d$) and equivalent capacitance for capacitors in series and parallel combinations. Obtain an expression for energy stored* $\left(U = \frac{1}{2}CV^2 = \frac{1}{2}QV = \frac{1}{2}\frac{Q^2}{C}\right)$ *and energy density.*

(c) *Dielectric constant $K = C'/C$; this is also called relative permittivity $K = \varepsilon_r = \varepsilon/\varepsilon_0$; elementary ideas of polarization of matter in a uniform electric field qualitative discussion; induced surface charges weaken the original field; results in reduction in* **E** *and hence, in potential difference (V); for charge remaining the same $Q = CV = C'V' = K\cdot CV'$; $V' = V/K$; and $E' = E/K$; if the capacitor is kept connected with the source of emf, V is kept constant $V = Q/C = Q'/C'$; $Q' = C'V = K\cdot CV = K\cdot Q$ increases; For a parallel plate capacitor with a dielectric in between, $C' = KC = K\cdot\varepsilon_0\cdot A/d = \varepsilon_r\cdot\varepsilon_0\cdot A/d$.*

Then $C' = \frac{\varepsilon_0 A}{(d/\varepsilon_r)}$; for a capacitor partially filled dielectric, capacitance, $C' = \varepsilon_0 A/(d - t + t/\varepsilon_r)$.

2. CURRENT ELECTRICITY

Mechanism of flow of current in conductors. Mobility, drift velocity and its relation with electric current; Ohm's law and its proof, resistance and resistivity and their relation to drift velocity of electrons; *V-I* characteristics (linear and non-linear), electrical energy and power, electrical resistivity and conductivity.

Temperature dependence of resistance and resistivity.

Internal resistance of a cell, potential difference and emf of a cell, combination of cells in series and in parallel, Kirchhoff's laws and simple applications, Wheatstone bridge, metre bridge. Potentiometer-principle and its applications to measure potential difference, to compare emf of two cells; to measure internal resistance of a cell.

(a) *Free electron theory of conduction; acceleration of free electrons, relaxation time τ; electric current $I = Q/t$; concept of drift velocity and electron mobility. Ohm's law, current density $J = I/A$; experimental verification, graphs and slope, ohmic and non-ohmic conductors; obtain the relation $I = v_d enA$. Derive $\sigma = ne^2\tau/m$ and $\rho = m/ne^2\tau$; effect of temperature on resistivity and resistance of conductors and semiconductors and graphs. Resistance R = V/I; resistivity ρ, given by $R = \rho\cdot l/A$; conductivity and conductance; Ohm's law as* $\mathbf{J} = \sigma\mathbf{E}$.

(b) *Electrical energy consumed in time t is $E = Pt = VIt$; using Ohm's law $E = \left(\frac{V^2}{R}\right)t = I^2Rt$. Potential difference $V = P/I$; $P = VI$; Electric power consumed $P = VI = V^2/R = I^2R$; commercial units; electricity consumption and billing.*

(c) *The source of energy of a seat of emf (such as a cell) may be electrical, mechanical, thermal or radiant energy. The emf of a source is defined as the work done per unit charge to force them to go to the higher point of potential (from – ve terminal to + ve terminal inside the cell) so, $\varepsilon = dW/dq$; but $dq = Idt$; $dW = \varepsilon dq = \varepsilon Idt$. Equating total work done to the work done across the external resistor R plus the work done across the internal resistance r; $\varepsilon Idt = I^2R\,dt + I^2r dt$; $\varepsilon = I(R + r)$; $I = \varepsilon/(R + r)$; also $IR + Ir = \varepsilon$ or $V = \varepsilon - Ir$ where Ir is called the back emf as it acts against the emf ε; V is the terminal potential difference. Derivation of formulae for combination for identical cells in series, parallel and mixed grouping. Parallel combination of two cells of unequal emf. Series combination of n cells of unequal emf.*

(d) *Statement and explanation of Kirchhoff's laws with simple examples. The first is a conservation law for charge and the 2nd is law of conservation of energy. Note change in potential across a resistor $\Delta V = IR < 0$ when we go 'down' with the current (compare with flow of water down a river), and $\Delta V = IR > 0$ if we go up against the current across the resistor. When we go through a cell, the – ve terminal is at a lower level and the + ve terminal at a higher level, so going from – ve to + ve through the cell, we are going up and $\Delta V = +\varepsilon$ and going from + ve to – ve terminal through the cell, we are going down, so $\Delta V = -\varepsilon$. Application to simple circuits. Wheatstone bridge; right in the beginning take $I_g = 0$ as we consider a balanced bridge, derivation of $R_1/R_2 = R_3/R_4$ [Kirchhoff's law not necessary]. Metre bridge is a modified form of Wheatstone bridge, its use to measure unknown resistance. Here $R_3 = l_1 p$ and $R_4 = l_2 p$; $R_3/R_4 = l_1/l_2$. Principle of Potentiometer: fall in potential $\Delta V \propto \Delta l$; auxiliary emf ε_1 is balanced against the fall in potential V_1 across length l_1. $\varepsilon_1 = V_1 = Kl_1$; $\varepsilon_1/\varepsilon_2 = l_1/l_2$; potentiometer as a voltmeter. Potential gradient and sensitivity of potentiometer. Use of potentiometer: to compare emfs of two cells, to determine internal resistance of a cell.*

3. MAGNETIC EFFECTS OF CURRENT AND MAGNETISM

(i) **Moving Charges and Magnetism**

Concept of magnetic field, Oersted's experiment. Biot-Savart law and its application. Ampere's Circuital law and its applications to infinitely long straight wire, straight and toroidal solenoids (only qualitative treatment). Force on a moving charge in uniform magnetic and electric fields, cyclotron. Force on a current carrying conductor in a uniform magnetic field, force between two parallel current-carrying conductors-definition of ampere, torque experienced by a current loop in uniform magnetic field; moving coil galvanometer - its sensitivity. Conversion of galvanometer into an ammeter and a voltmeter.

(ii) **Magnetism and Matter**

A current loop as a magnetic dipole, its magnetic dipole moment, magnetic dipole moment of a revolving electron, magnetic field intensity due to a magnetic dipole (bar magnet) on the axial line and equatorial line, torque on a magnetic dipole (bar magnet) in a uniform magnetic field; bar magnet as an equivalent solenoid, magnetic field lines; Diamagnetic, paramagnetic and ferromagnetic substances, with examples. Electromagnets and factors affecting their strengths, permanent magnets.

(a) *Only historical introduction through Oersted's experiment. [Ampere's swimming rule not included]. Biot-Savart law and its vector form; application; derive the expression for B (i) at the centre of a circular loop carrying current; (ii) at any point on its axis. Current carrying loop as a magnetic dipole. Ampere's circuital law: statement and brief explanation. Apply it to obtain* **B** *near a long wire carrying current and for a solenoid. Only formula of* **B** *due to a finitely long conductor.*

(b) *Force on a moving charged particle in magnetic field $\mathbf{F}_B = q(\mathbf{v}\times\mathbf{B})$; special cases, modify this equation substituting $d\mathbf{l}/dt$ for v and I for q/dt to yield $\mathbf{F} = Id\mathbf{l}\times\mathbf{B}$ for the force acting on a current carrying conductor placed in a magnetic field. Derive the expression for force between two long and parallel wires carrying current, hence, define ampere (the base SI unit of current) and hence, coulomb; from Q = It. Lorentz force.*

(c) *Derive the expression for torque on a current carrying loop placed in a uniform* **B**, *using $\mathbf{F} = I\mathbf{l}\times\mathbf{B}$ and $\tau = \mathbf{r}\times\mathbf{F}$; $\tau = NIAB\sin\phi$ for N turns $\tau = \mathbf{m}\times\mathbf{B}$, where the dipole moment $\mathbf{m} = NIA$, unit: $A\text{-}m^2$.*

A current carrying loop is a magnetic dipole; directions of current and **B** and **m** using right hand rule only; no other rule necessary. Mention orbital magnetic moment of an electron in Bohr model of H-atom. Concept of radial magnetic field. Moving coil galvanometer; construction, principle, working, theory $I = k\phi$, current and voltage sensitivity. Shunt. Conversion of galvanometer into ammeter and voltmeter of given range.

(d) *Magnetic field represented by the symbol* **B** *is now defined by the equation* $\mathbf{F} = q_0(\mathbf{v} \times \mathbf{B})$; **B** *is not to be defined in terms of force acting on a unit pole, etc.; note the distinction of* **B** *from* **E** *is that* **B** *forms closed loops as there are no magnetic monopoles, whereas* **E** *lines start from + ve charge and end on – ve charge. Magnetic field lines due to a magnetic dipole (bar magnet). Magnetic field in end-on and broadside-on positions (No derivations). Magnetic flux* $\phi = \mathbf{B} \cdot \mathbf{A} = BA$ *for B uniform and* $\mathbf{B} || \mathbf{A}$*; i.e. area held perpendicular to for* $BA(\mathbf{B}||\mathbf{A})$, $B = \phi / A$ *is the flux density [SI unit of flux is weber (Wb)]; but note that this is not correct as a defining equation as* **B** *is vector and* ϕ *and* ϕ/A *are scalars, unit of B is tesla (T) equal to* 10^{-4} *gauss. For non-uniform* **B** *field,* $\phi = \int d\phi = \int \mathbf{B} \cdot d\mathbf{A}$.

(e) *Properties of diamagnetic, paramagnetic and ferromagnetic substances; their susceptibility and relative permeability. It is better to explain the main distinction, the cause of magnetisation (M) is due to magnetic dipole moment (m) of atoms, ions or molecules being 0 for dia, > 0 but very small for para and > 0 and large for ferromagnetic materials; few examples; placed in external* **B***, very small (induced) magnetisation in a direction opposite to* **B** *in dia, small magnetisation parallel to* **B** *for para, and large magnetisation parallel to* **B** *for ferromagnetic materials; this leads to lines of* **B** *becoming less dense, more dense and much more dense in dia, para and ferro, respectively; hence, a weak repulsion for dia, weak attraction for para and strong attraction for ferro magnetic material. Also, a small bar suspended in the horizontal plane becomes perpendicular to the* **B** *field for dia and parallel to* **B** *for para and ferro. Defining equation* $H = (B/\mu_0) - M$*; the magnetic properties, susceptibility* $\chi_m = (M/H) < 0$ *for dia (as M is opposite H) and > 0 for para, both very small, but very large for ferro; hence relative permeability* $\mu_r = (1 + \chi_m) < 1$ *for dia, > 1 for para and >> 1 (very large) for ferro; further,* $\chi_m \propto 1/T$ *(Curie's law) for para, independent of temperature (T) for dia and depends on T in a complicated manner for ferro; on heating ferro becomes para at Curie temperature. Electromagnet: its definition, properties and factors affecting the strength of electromagnet; selection of magnetic material for temporary and permanent magnets and core of the transformer on the basis of retentivity and coercive force*

4. ELECTROMAGNETIC INDUCTION AND ALTERNATING CURRENTS

(i) **Electromagnetic Induction** Faraday's laws, induced emf and current; Lenz's Law, eddy currents. Self-induction and mutual induction. Transformer.

(ii) **Alternating Current** Peak value, mean value and RMS value of alternating current/voltage; their relation in sinusoidal case; reactance and impedance; *L-C* oscillations (qualitative treatment only), *L-C-R* series circuit, resonance; power in AC circuits, wattless current. AC generator.

(a) *Electromagnetic induction, magnetic flux, change in flux, rate of change of flux and induced emf; Faraday's laws. Lenz's law, conservation of energy; motional emf* $\varepsilon = Blv$*, and power* $P = (Blv)^2/R$*; eddy currents (qualitative);*

(b) *Self-Induction, coefficient of self-inductance,* $\phi = LI$ *and* $L = \dfrac{\varepsilon}{dI/dt}$*; henry = volt. Second/ampere, expression for coefficient of self-inductance of a solenoid* $L = \dfrac{\mu_0 N^2 A}{l} = \mu_0 n^2 A \times l$.

Mutual induction and mutual inductance (M), flux linked $\phi_2 = MI_1$*; induced emf* $\varepsilon_2 = \dfrac{d\phi_2}{dt} = M\dfrac{dI_1}{dt}$*. Definition of M as* $M = \dfrac{\varepsilon_2}{dI_1/dt}$ *or* $M = \dfrac{\phi_2}{I_1}$*. SI unit henry. Expression for coefficient of mutual inductance of two coaxial solenoids.* $M = \dfrac{\mu_0 N_1 N_2 A}{l} = \mu_0 n_1 N_2 A$

Induced emf opposes changes, back emf is set up, eddy currents. Transformer (ideal coupling): principle, working and uses; step up and step down; efficiency and applications including transmission of power, energy losses and their minimisation.

(c) *Sinusoidal variation of V and I with time, for the output from an AC generator; time period, frequency and phase changes; obtain mean values of current and voltage, obtain relation between RMS value of V and I with peak values in sinusoidal cases only.*

(d) *Variation of voltage and current in AC circuits consisting of only a resistor, only an inductor and only a capacitor (phasor representation), phase lag and phase lead. May apply Kirchhoff's law and obtain simple differential equation (SHM type),* $V = V_0 \sin \omega t$*, solution* $I = I_0 \sin \omega t$, $I_0 \sin(\omega t - \pi/2)$ *and* $I_0 \sin(\omega t - \pi/2)$ *for pure R, C and L circuits respectively. Draw phase (or phasor) diagrams showing voltage and current and phase lag or lead, also showing resistance R, inductive reactance* X_L*;* $(X_L = \omega L)$ *and capacitive reactance* X_C*,* $(X_C = 1/\omega C)$*. Graph of* X_L *and* X_C *versus f.*

(e) *The L-C-R series circuit: Use phasor diagram method to obtain expression for I and V, the potential difference across R, L and C; and the net phase lag/lead; use the results of 4(e), V lags I by π/2 in a capacitor, V leads I by π/2 in an inductor, V and I are in phase in a resistor, I is the same in all three; hence draw phase diagram, combine* V_L *and* V_C *(in opposite phase; phasors add like vectors) to give* $V = V_R + V_L + V_C$ *(phasor addition) and the max. values are related by* $V^2{}_m = V^2_{Rm} + (V_{Lm} - V_{Cm})^2$ *when* $V_L > V_C$ *Substituting potential difference = current × resistance or reactance, we get* $Z^2 = R^2 + (X_L - X_C)^2$ *and* $\tan\phi = (V_{Lm} - V_{Cm})/V_{Rm} = (X_L - X_C)/R$ *giving* $I = I_m \sin(\omega t - \phi)$*, where* $I_m = V_m/Z$*. Special cases for R-L and R-C circuits. [May use Kirchhoff's law and obtain the differential equation] Graph of Z versus f and I versus f.*

(f) *Power P associated with L-C-R circuit* $= \dfrac{1}{2} V_0 I_0 \cos\phi = V_{rms} I_{rms} \cos\phi = I^2_{rms} R$*; power absorbed and power dissipated; electrical resonance; bandwidth of signals and Q factor (no derivation); oscillations in an LC circuit* $(\omega_0 = 1/\sqrt{LC})$*.*
Average power consumed averaged over a full cycle $\mathbf{P} = (1/2) V_0 I_0 \cos\phi$*, power factor* $\cos\phi = R/Z$*. Special case for pure R, L and C; choke coil (analytical only),* X_L *controls current but* $\cos\phi = 0$*, hence* $\mathbf{P} = 0$*, wattless current; LC circuit; at resonance with* $X_L = X_C$*,* $Z = Z_{min} = R$*, power delivered to circuit by the source is maximum, resonant frequency* $f_0 = \dfrac{1}{2\pi\sqrt{LC}}$*.*

(g) *Simple AC generators: Principle, description, theory, working and use. Variation in current and voltage with time for AC and DC Basic differences between AC and DC.*

5. ELECTROMAGNETIC WAVES

Basic idea of displacement current. Electromagnetic waves, their characteristics, their transverse nature (qualitative ideas only). Complete electromagnetic spectrum starting from radiowaves to gamma rays: elementary facts of electromagnetic waves and their uses.

Concept of displacement current, qualitative descriptions only of electromagnetic spectrum; common features of all regions of electromagnetic spectrum including transverse nature (**E** and **B** perpendicular to **c**); special features of the common classification (gamma rays, X-rays, UV rays, visible light, IR, microwaves, radio and TV waves) in their production (source), detection and other properties; uses; approximate range of λ or f or at least proper order of increasing f or λ.

6. OPTICS

(i) **Ray Optics and Optical Instruments** Ray Optics: Reflection of light by spherical mirrors, mirror formula, refraction of light at plane surfaces, total internal reflection and its applications, optical fibres, refraction at spherical surfaces, lenses, thin lens formula, lens maker's formula, magnification, power of a lens, combination of thin lenses in contact, combination of a lens and a mirror, refraction and dispersion of light through a prism.

Optical instruments: Microscopes and astronomical telescopes (reflecting and refracting) and their magnifying powers and their resolving powers.

(a) *Reflection of light by spherical mirrors. Mirror formula: its derivation; $R = 2f$ for spherical mirrors. Magnification.*

(b) *Refraction of light at a plane interface, Snell's law; total internal reflection and critical angle; total reflecting prisms and optical fibres. Total reflecting prisms: application to triangular prisms with angle of the prism 30°, 45°, 60° and 90° respectively; ray diagrams for refraction through a combination of media, ${}_1n_2 \times {}_2n_3 \times {}_3n_1 = 1$, real depth and apparent depth. Simple applications.*

(c) *Refraction through a prism, minimum deviation and derivation of relation between n, A and δ_{min}. Include explanation of $i - \delta$ graph, $i_1 = i_2 = i$ (say) for δ_m; from symmetry $r_1 = r_2$; refracted ray inside the prism is parallel to the base of the equilateral prism. Thin prism. Dispersion; Angular dispersion; dispersive power, rainbow-ray diagram (no derivation). Simple explanation.*

(d) *Refraction at a single spherical surface; detailed discussion of one case only-convex towards rarer medium, for spherical surface and real image. Derive the relation between n_1, n_2, u, v and R. Refraction through thin lenses: derive lens maker's formula and lens formula; derivation of combined focal length of two thin lenses in contact. Combination of lenses and mirrors (silvering of lens excluded) and magnification for lens, derivation for biconvex lens only; extend the results to biconcave lens, plano convex lens and lens immersed in a liquid; power of a lens $P = 1/f$ with SI unit dioptre. For lenses in contact $1/F = 1/f_1 + 1/f_2$ and $P = P_1 + P_2$. Lens formula, formation of image with combination of thin lenses and mirrors.*

[Any one sign convention may be used in solving numericals].

(e) *Ray diagram and derivation of magnifying power of a simple microscope with image at D (least distance of distinct vision) and infinity; Ray diagram and derivation of magnifying power of a compound microscope with image at D. Only expression for magnifying power of compound microscope for final image at infinity.*

Ray diagrams of refracting telescope with image at infinity as well as at D; simple explanation; derivation of magnifying power; Ray diagram of reflecting telescope with image at infinity. Advantages, disadvantages and uses. Resolving power of compound microscope

(ii) **Wave Optics** Wave front and Huygen's principle. Proof of laws of reflection and refraction using Huygen's principle. Interference, Young's double slit experiment and expression for fringe width(β), coherent sources and sustained interference of light, Fraunhofer diffraction due to a single slit, width of central maximum.

(a) *Huygen's principle: wavefronts-different types/shapes of wavefronts; proof of laws of reflection and refraction using Huygen's theory.*

[Refraction through a prism and lens on the basis of Huygen's theory not required].

(b) *Interference of light, interference of monochromatic light by double slit. Phase of wave motion; superposition of identical waves at a point, path difference and phase difference; coherent and incoherent sources; interference: constructive and destructive, conditions for sustained interference of light waves [mathematical deduction of interference from the equations of two progressive waves with a phase difference is not required]. Young's double slit experiment: set up, diagram, geometrical deduction of path difference $\Delta x = d\sin\theta$, between waves from the two slits; using $\Delta x = n\lambda$ for bright fringe and $\Delta x = (n + \frac{1}{2})\lambda$ for dark fringe and $\sin\theta = \tan\theta = y_n/D$ as y and θ are small, obtain $y_n = (D/d)n\lambda$ and fringe width $\beta = (D/d)\lambda$.*

Graph of distribution of intensity with angular distance.

(c) *Single slit Fraunhofer diffraction (elementary explanation only). Diffraction at a single slit: experimental setup, diagram, diffraction pattern, obtain expression for position of minima, $a\sin\theta_n = n\lambda$, where n = 1, 2, 3... and conditions for secondary maxima, $a\sin\theta_n = (n + \frac{1}{2})\lambda$; distribution of intensity with angular distance; angular width of central bright fringe.*

7. DUAL NATURE OF RADIATION AND MATTER

Wave particle duality; photoelectric effect, Hertz and Lenard's observations; Einstein's photoelectric equation-particle nature of light. Matter waves-wave nature of particles, de-Broglie relation. Conclusion From Davission Germer Experiment (Qualitative Only)

(a) Photoelectric effect, quantisation of radiation; Einstein's equation $E_{max} = h\nu - W_0$; threshold frequency; work function; experimental facts of Hertz and Lenard and their conclusions; Einstein used Planck's ideas and extended it to apply for radiation (light); photoelectric effect can be explained only assuming quantum (particle) nature of radiation. Determination of Planck's constant (from the graph of stopping potential V_s *versus* frequency f of the incident light).

Momentum of photon $p = E/c = h\nu/c - h/\lambda$.

(b) de-Broglie hypothesis, phenomenon of electron diffraction (qualitative only). Wave nature of radiation is exhibited in interference, diffraction and polarisation; particle nature is exhibited in photoelectric effect. Dual nature of matter: particle nature common in that it possesses momentum p and kinetic energy *KE*. The wave nature of matter was proposed by Louis de-Broglie, $\lambda = h/p = h/mv$. Davission and Germer experiment : qualitative description of the experiment and conclusion.

8. ATOMS AND NUCLEI

(i) **Atoms** Alpha-particle scattering experiment; Rutherford's atomic model; Bohr's atomic model, energy levels, hydrogen spectrum.

Rutherford's nuclear model of atom (mathematical theory of scattering excluded), based on Geiger-Marsden experiment on α-scattering; nuclear radius r in terms of closest approach of α-particle to the nucleus, obtained by equating $\Delta K = \frac{1}{2} mv^2$ of the α-particle to the change in electrostatic potential energy ΔU of the system $U = \frac{2e \times Ze}{4\pi\varepsilon_0 r_0} = r_0 \sim 10^{-15}$ m = 1 Fermi; atomic structure; only general qualitative ideas, including atomic number Z, neutron number N and mass number A. A brief account of historical background leading to Bohr's theory of hydrogen spectrum; formulae for wavelength in Lyman, Balmer, Paschen, Brackett and Pfund series. Rydberg constant. Bohr's model of H-atom, postulates ($Z = 1$); expressions for orbital velocity, kinetic energy, potential energy, radius of orbit and total energy of electron. Energy level diagram, calculation of ΔE, frequency and wavelength of different lines of emission spectra; agreement with experimentally observed values. [Use nm and not Å for unit of λ].

(ii) **Nuclei** Composition and size of nucleus, Mass-energy relation, mass defect; binding energy per nucleon and its variation with mass number; Nuclear reactions, nuclear fission and nuclear fusion.

(a) *Atomic masses and nuclear density; Isotopes, Isobars and Isotones – definitions with examples of each. Unified atomic mass unit, symbol* u, 1u = 1/12 *of the mass of* ^{12}C *atom* = 1.66×10^{-27} *kg). Composition of nucleus; mass defect and binding energy, BE* = $(\Delta m)\, c^2$. *Graph of BE/nucleon versus mass number A, special features-less BE/nucleon for light as well as heavy elements. Middle order more stable [see fission and fusion] Einstein's equation* $E = mc^2$. *Calculations related to this equation; mass defect/binding energy, mutual annihilation and pair production as examples.*

(b) ***Nuclear Energy*** *Theoretical (qualitative) prediction of exothermic (with release of energy) nuclear reaction, in fusing together two light nuclei to form a heavier nucleus and in splitting heavy nucleus to form middle order (lower mass number) nuclei, is evident from the shape of BE per nucleon versus mass number graph. Also calculate the disintegration energy Q for a heavy nucleus* ($A = 240$) *with BE/A* $\sim$ *7.6 MeV per nucleon split into two equal halves with* $A = 120$ *each and BE/A* $\sim$ *8.5 MeV/nucleon; Q* $\sim$ *200 MeV. Nuclear fission: Any one equation of fission reaction. Chain reaction- controlled and uncontrolled; nuclear reactor and nuclear bomb. Main parts of a nuclear reactor including their functions - fuel elements, moderator, control rods, coolant, casing; criticality; utilization of energy output - all qualitative only. Fusion, simple example of* $^{1}H \rightarrow {}^{4}He$ *and its nuclear reaction equation; requires very high temperature* $\sim 10^6$ *degrees; difficult to achieve; hydrogen bomb; thermonuclear energy production in the sun and stars. [Details of chain reaction not required].*

9. ELECTRONIC DEVICES

(i) Semiconductor Electronics: Materials, Devices and Simple Circuits. Energy bands in conductors, semiconductors and insulators (qualitative ideas only). Intrinsic and extrinsic semiconductors.

(ii) Semiconductor diode: *I-V* characteristics in forward and reverse bias, diode as a rectifier; special types of junction diodes: LED, photodiode, solar cell and zener diode and its charactcristics, zener diode as a voltage regulator.

(a) *Energy bands in solids; energy band diagrams for distinction between conductors, insulators and semiconductors-intrinsic and extrinsic; electrons and holes in semiconductors.*
Elementary ideas about electrical conduction in metals [crystal structure not included]. Energy levels (as for hydrogen atom), 1s, 2s, 2p, 3s, etc. of an isolated atom such as that of copper; these split, eventually forming bands of energy levels, as we consider solid copper made up of a large number of isolated atoms, brought together to form a lattice; definition of energy bands-groups of closely spaced energy levels separated by band gaps called forbidden bands. An idealised representation of the energy bands for a conductor, insulator and semiconductor; characteristics, differences; distinction between conductors, insulators and semiconductors on the basis of energy bands, with examples; qualitative discussion only; energy gaps (eV) in typical substances (carbon, Ge, Si); some electrical properties of semiconductors. Majority and minority charge carriers-electrons and holes; intrinsic and extrinsic, doping, p-type, n-type; donor and acceptor impurities.

(b) *Junction diode and its symbol; depletion region and potential barrier; forward and reverse biasing, V-I characteristics and numericals; half wave and a full wave rectifier. Simple circuit diagrams and graphs, function of each component in the electric circuits, qualitative only. [Bridge rectifier of 4 diodes not included]; elementary ideas on solar cell, photodiode and light emitting diode (LED) as semi conducting diodes. Importance of LED's as they save energy without causing atmospheric pollution and global warming. Zener diode, V-I characteristics, circuit diagram and working of zener diode as a voltage regulator.*

Analysis of Pupil Performance:

ISC Physics

The document 'Analysis of Pupils' Performance' in ISC Class 12 Examination, is prepared by Research Development and Consultancy Division (RDCD) of the Council for the Indian School Certificate Examination (CISCE).

The purpose of this document is to provide feedback to schools in terms of strengths and weaknesses of the students in handling the examination.

TOPICS FOUND DIFFICULT/ CONFUSING BY STUDENTS

- Gauss' Theorem
- Kirchhoff's Law
- Numerical problems on Potentiometer.
- Curie temperature
- Angle of dip
- Numerical problems on alternating current.
- Ray diagrams of lenses and mirrors
- Sign convection in lenses/compound microscope
- Labelling of ray diagrams and graphs
- Diffraction
- Davisson – Germer experiment
- Mean life and Half-life of a radioactive substance
- Binding energy
- Pair production
- Modulation and demodulation
- Zener diode, common emitter amplifier their circuit diagrams and biasing, and other related topics
- Relation between "alpha" and "beta" of a transistor
- Alternating and direct current phenomena
- Phase and phase difference
- Impedance and inductance in ac circuit
- Refraction and Scattering
- Polarizer and Analyzer
- Absorption and Emission Spectrum
- Pair Production and Pair annihilation
- Forward and reverse biasing
- Numerical problems on mass defect
- Symbol of PNP / NPN transistor and Zener diode
- Communication system

SUGGESTIONS FOR STUDENTS

- Make a list of definitions, principles, and formulae.
- Memorise the technical terms / laws / key words, principles, and derivations etc. only after comprehension.
- Refer to the scope of syllabus for clarity.
- Follow the steps while doing a numerical (write the data, make conversion of units, if required in SI., write the correct formula, make correct substitution and write correct the answer with the correct unit and the direction in case of a vector quantity).Be careful with the units, such as: mm, cm, nm, μC and μF, mA, electron volt, etc. These must be converted to SI units.
- Draw a ray diagram with arrow heads.
- Draw a graph with properly labelled axes.
- Take notes in class to summarize lectures in your own words to remember the concept/ideas/derivations.
- Create Mind Maps/flow charts to consolidate your knowledge for quick revision before examinations.
- If you find it easier to recall images rather than text, associate learnt concepts with pictures, ray diagrams, graphs, and drawings.
- Practice the difficult topics regularly.

01

Electric Charges and Coulomb's Law

TREND ANALYSIS 4 YEARS

Average No. of Questions Across all Sets

Electric Charges and Coulomb's Law

Types of Questions	2024	2023	2020	2019
1 Mark	2	–	–	–
2 Marks	–	–	–	–
3 Marks	–	–	–	–
5 Marks	–	–	–	–

Electric Charge

The property of charged particles which gives rise to electric force between two charges is called **electric charge**. When two unlike objects like amber and wool are rubbed against each other, two types of charges namely positive charge and negative charge are produced, called **frictional electricity**.

These names were given by Benjamin Franklin. Transfer of electrons is the cause of frictional electricity. It is also known as electron theory of **electrification**.

Units of Charge

Unit of charge in SI system is coulomb (C)

Properties of Electric Charge

Some important properties of electric charge are discussed below,

(*i*) **Quantisation of Charge** Charge exists in discrete amount rather than continuous value and hence quantised. Mathematically, charge on an object, $q = \pm ne$ where, n is 1, 2, 3 ...... and e is the electronic charge of value 1.6×10^{-19} C.

(*ii*) **Conservation of Charge** The total charge of an isolated system is always conserved i.e. initial and final charges of the system will be same.

NOTE Charge on an electron, $e = -1.6 \times 10^{-19}$ C and charge on a proton $= +1.6 \times 10^{-19}$ C.

Conductors and Insulators

Conductors are those substances which can be used to carry or conduct electric charge from one point to other. i.e. Silver, copper, iron, etc. Insulators are those substances which cannot conduct electricity. They are also called **dielectrics**. i.e. Glass, rubber, plastic, mica, etc.

Coulomb's Law

It states that the electrostatic force of attraction or repulsion acting between two stationary point charges is directly proportional to the product of the magnitudes of the two charges and inversely proportional to the square of the distance between them. In vacuum it is given by

$$F_{\text{vacuum}} = \frac{1}{4\pi\varepsilon_0} \cdot \frac{q_1 q_2}{r^2}$$

where, q_1 and q_2 are the stationary point charges and r is the separation between them in air or vacuum and F_{vacuum} is the magnitude of force of attraction or repulsion.

Also, ε_0 = permittivity of free space
$= 8.85419 \times 10^{-12}\ C^2/N\text{-}m^2$

and $$\frac{1}{4\pi\varepsilon_0} = 9 \times 10^9\ N\text{-}m^2/C^2$$

The force between two point charges q_1 and q_2, located at a distance r in a medium other than free space or vacuum is expressed as

$$F = \frac{1}{4\pi\varepsilon} \cdot \frac{q_1 q_2}{r^2}$$

where, ε is the **absolute permittivity** of the medium.

Now, we can write $$\frac{F_{\text{vacuum}}}{F} = \frac{\varepsilon}{\varepsilon_0} = \varepsilon_r$$

where, ε_r is called **relative permittivity** of the medium also called dielectric constant (K) of the medium.

In vector form, Coulomb's law can be written as,

$$\mathbf{F} = \frac{1}{4\pi\varepsilon_0} \cdot \frac{q_1 q_2}{r^2} \hat{\mathbf{r}}$$

$$\Rightarrow \quad \mathbf{F} = \frac{1}{4\pi\varepsilon_0} \cdot \frac{q_1 q_2}{|\mathbf{r}|^3} \mathbf{r} \qquad \left[\because \hat{\mathbf{r}} = \frac{\mathbf{r}}{|\mathbf{r}|}\right]$$

where, $\mathbf{r}$ is the vector pointing from q_1 to q_2.

Direction of Electrostatic Force or Coulombic Force

The direction of electrostatic force between two point charges is along the line joining the two charges. It may be either attractive ($q_1 q_2 < 0$) or repulsive ($q_1 q_2 > 0$).

NOTE Like charges repel each other and unlike charges attract each other.

Comparing Coulomb's Law with Newton's Law of Gravitation

- Both the laws are inverse square law.
- The equations of these laws are as below,

$$F_G = \frac{G m_1 m_2}{r^2} \qquad \text{[Newton's law of gravitation]}$$

$$F_E = \frac{k q_1 q_2}{r^2} \qquad \text{[Coulomb's law]}$$

- The coulomb force is much stronger than the gravitational force between two electrons.

Electrostatic Forces are Conservative Non-Dissipative Forces

The work done during a round trip by an electrostatic force is always zero. The work does not depend on the path followed by the charge, however it depends on the initial and final positions of the charge. So, like gravitational force electrostatic force can be said as conservative force.

Principle of Superposition of Electrostatic Forces

This principle states that the net force experienced by a given charge particle q_0 due to a system of n charged particles is equal to the vector sum of the forces exerted on it due to all the other charged particles of the system.

i.e. $$\mathbf{F}_0 = \mathbf{F}_{01} + \mathbf{F}_{02} + \cdots + \mathbf{F}_{0n}$$

where, $\mathbf{F}_0$ is the net force on charge q_0 and $\mathbf{F}_{01}, \mathbf{F}_{02}, \mathbf{F}_{03}, \ldots, \mathbf{F}_{0n}$ are individual forces on charge q_0 due to charges $q_1, q_2, q_3, \ldots, q_n$ respectively.

Now, we can write net force

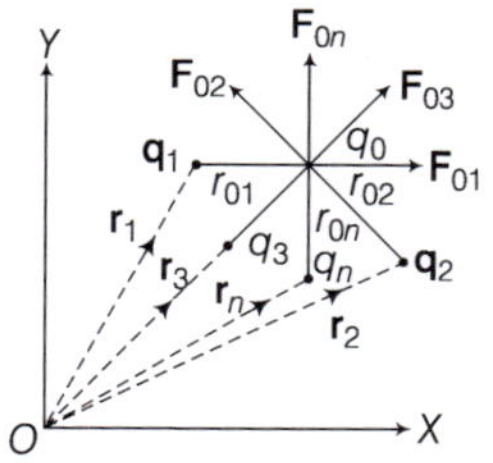

$$\mathbf{F}_0 = \frac{q_0}{4\pi\varepsilon_0}\left[\sum_{i=1}^{n} \frac{q_i}{|\mathbf{r}_0 - \mathbf{r}_i|^3}(\mathbf{r}_0 - \mathbf{r}_i)\right]$$

where, q_i and $\mathbf{r}_i$ are the magnitude and position vector respectively of the ith charge and also $(\mathbf{r}_0 - \mathbf{r}_i)$ is a vector pointing in the direction from q_i to q_0.

Electrostatic Force due to Continuous Charge Distribution

Electrostatic force on a charge q_0 due to some common continuous charge distributions are discussed below

(i) **Electrostatic Force due to Linear Charge Distribution**

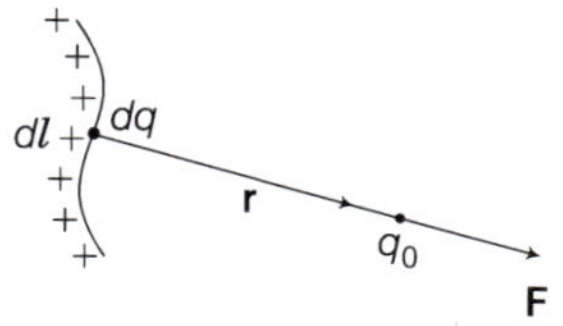

Linear charge distribution

Net force on q_0, $$\mathbf{F} = \frac{q_0}{4\pi\varepsilon_0}\int_l \frac{\lambda dl}{|\mathbf{r}|^2}\hat{\mathbf{r}}$$

(ii) **Electrostatic Force due to Surface Charge Distribution**

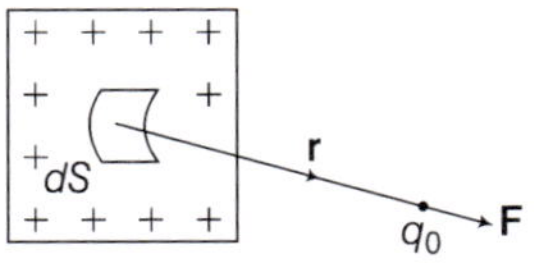

Surface charge distribution

Net force on q_0, $$\mathbf{F} = \frac{q_0}{4\pi\varepsilon_0}\int_S \frac{\sigma dS}{|\mathbf{r}|^2}\hat{\mathbf{r}}$$

(iii) **Electrostatic Force due to Volume Charge Distribution**

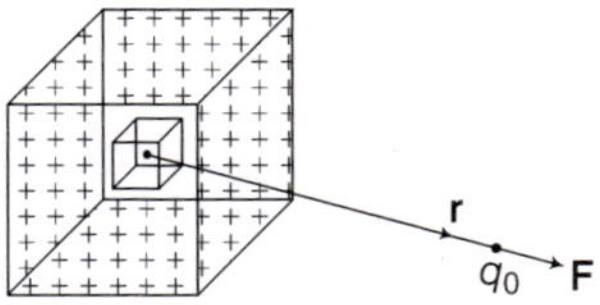

Volume charge distribution

Net force on q_0,

$$\mathbf{F} = \frac{q_0}{4\pi\varepsilon_0}\int_V \frac{\rho dV}{|\mathbf{r}|^2}\hat{\mathbf{r}}$$

PYQs Previous Years Questions

1 Mark Questions

1. Can a body be given a charge of 2.2×10^{-19} C? Given a reason for your answer. **ISC 2024**

2. Explain the statement, relative permittivity of water is 81. **ISC 2024, 2009**

3. Four charges are arranged at the corners of a square $ABCD$, as shown in the adjoining figure. The force on the charge Q kept at the centre O is, **ISC 2022 Sem-I**

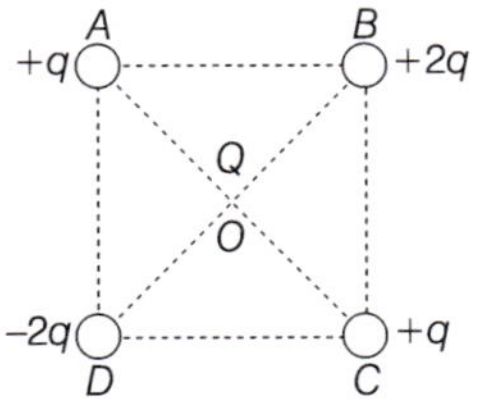

(a) zero
(b) along the diagonal AC
(c) along the diagonal BD
(d) perpendicular to side AB

4. When a soap bubble is given a positive charge, then its radius **ISC 2022 Sem-I**
   (a) decreases
   (b) increases
   (c) remains unchanged
   (d) nothing can be predicted as information is insufficient

5. The ratio of forces between two small spheres having a constant charge q when placed in air to when placed in a medium of dielectric constant K is **ISC 2022 Sem-I**
   (a) $1 : K$ (b) $K : 1$
   (c) $1 : K^2$ (d) $K^2 : 1$

6. The force between two point charges separated by a certain distance in air is F. If each of the two charges be halved and the distance between them be also halved, the new force would be **ISC 2022 Sem-I**
   (a) F (b) $2F$ (c) $3F$ (d) $4F$

7. What is meant by the term quantisation of charge? **ISC 2015**

8. Relative permittivity of water is 81. If ε_w and ε_0 are permittivities of water and vacuum respectively, then **ISC 2013**
   (a) $\varepsilon_0 = 9\varepsilon_w$ (b) $\varepsilon_0 = 81\varepsilon_w$
   (c) $\varepsilon_w = 9\varepsilon_0$ (d) $\varepsilon_w = 81\varepsilon_0$

9. A body has a positive charge of 8×10^{-19} C. It has **ISC 2012**
   (a) an excess of 5 electrons
   (b) a deficiency of 5 electrons
   (c) an excess of 8 electrons
   (d) a deficiency of 8 electrons

10. Write Coulomb's law in vector form. **ISC 2008**

11. Can 8.6×10^{-19} Coulomb of charge be given to a conductor? Explain. **ISC 2006**

3 Marks Questions
(Important Questions)

12. Two small, identical in size, charged metallic spheres A and B repel each other with a force F when placed at a distance r between their centres. The spheres A and B are touched by identical, but uncharged spheres C and D, respectively which are then removed away. The sphere B is now brought closer to A to a distance $r/2$ between their centres. What is the new force of repulsion between A and B?

13. Three charges $1\mu C$, $1\mu C$ and $2\mu C$ are kept at vertices A, B and C of an equilateral triangle ABC of 10 cm side respectively. What will the resultant force on the charge at C?

> **KEY idea**
>
> To obtain the resultant force, first calculate the force on C due to A and force on C due to B. Then, calculate resultant force,
>
> $$F_{resultant} = \sqrt{(F_{AC})^2 + (F_{BC})^2 + 2F_{AC}F_{BC} \cdot \cos\theta}$$

Case Based Question
(For Complete Chapter)

14. *Read the passage and answer the following questions*

Electrically, most of the materials can be placed in one of the two classes : conductors or insulators. Conductors are those, through which electric charge can easily flow. Metals, Human body, Earth, Mercury and Electrolytes are conductors of electricity.

In metals, only the negative charges are free to move and positive charge is immobile. The actual charge-carriers in metals are 'free electrons' and the outer electrons of the atoms leave the atoms and become 'free' to move throughout the volume of the metal. In electrolytes, both positive and negative charges move. The charges in an electrolyte are carried by ions and it is the ions that move in an electrolyte.

Those substances in which electric charge cannot flow are called insulators (or dielectrics). Glass, Hard-rubber, Plastics and Dry wood are insulators. Insulators have practically no free electrons.

An important difference between conductors and insulators is that when some charge is given to a conductor it readily gets transferred over its entire surface. On the other hand if some charge is given to an insulator it stays at the place where it is put on.

(*i*) A bird safely sits on a base high power transmission wire, while a man standing on the ground get fatal shock on touching the same. Why? **(1)**

(*ii*) Why the tyres of aircrafts are not made of ordinary rubber (which is an insulator) but of a special rubber which is slightly conducting why? **(1)**

(*iii*) By which the currents are carried in conductors? **(1)**

(*iv*) What is the major difference between the conductors and insulators? **(1)**

(*v*) What is measured by the band gap between the valence band and conduction band? **(1)**

Explanations

1. We know that, $q = ne$

$$n = \frac{2.2 \times 10^{-19}}{1.6 \times 10^{-19}} = 1.375$$

which is not possible because the conversion of electrons take place only in complete multiples.

2. Relative permittivity (ε_r) of water is the ratio of absolute permittivity (ε) and permittivity of free space (ε_0).

i.e. $$\varepsilon_r = \frac{\varepsilon}{\varepsilon_0}$$

It means that permittivity of water is 81 times that of free space.

3. (c) $\mathbf{F} = \mathbf{F}_A + \mathbf{F}_B + \mathbf{F}_C + \mathbf{F}_D$

But $\mathbf{F}_A = -\mathbf{F}_C$ and $\mathbf{F}_B = \pm \mathbf{F}_D$

$\therefore \quad \mathbf{F} = \mathbf{F}_B + \mathbf{F}_D = 2\mathbf{F}_B$ along the diagonal BD.

4. (b) Positive charges get distributed on the surface of the bubble. These positive charges repel each other because like charges repel. Hence, the surface area increase.

5. (b) Initial force when placed in air,

$$F_a = \frac{1}{4\pi\varepsilon_0} \frac{q_1 q_2}{r^2}$$

Force when placed in medium, $F_m = \dfrac{1}{4\pi\varepsilon} \dfrac{q_1 q_2}{r^2}$

$$\frac{F_a}{F_m} = \frac{\varepsilon}{\varepsilon_0}$$

$$\frac{F_a}{F_m} = K \qquad (\varepsilon = k\varepsilon_0)$$

Hence, the ratio is $K:1$.

6. (a) According to Coulomb's law, $F \propto \frac{q_1 q_2}{r^2}$

Now, $q_1' = \frac{q_1}{2}$, $q_2' = \frac{q_2}{2}$ and $r' = \frac{r}{2}$

Now, $F' \propto \frac{q_1' q_2'}{r'^2}$

Thus, $$F' \propto \frac{\frac{q_1}{2} \times \frac{q_2}{2}}{\left(\frac{r}{2}\right)^2} = F$$

Hence, option (a) is correct.

7. The total charge on an object is an integral multiple of charge of an electron, i.e. $q = ne$

where, n is the number of electrons and e is the elementary charge.

8. (d) We know that relative permittivity

$$\varepsilon_r = \frac{\varepsilon_w}{\varepsilon_0}$$

$\Rightarrow \varepsilon_w =$ absolute permittivity of water

$= (\varepsilon_r)(\varepsilon_0) = (81)(\varepsilon_0) = 81\varepsilon_0$

For water, relative permittivity, $\varepsilon_r = 81$

9. (b) Given, positive charge $= 8 \times 10^{-19}$ C

As we know from quantisation of charge, $Q = ne$

Charge on one electron, $e = 1.6 \times 10^{-19}$ C

and $n =$ number of electrons transferred

$\therefore$ Number of electrons transferred, $n = \frac{Q}{e}$

$$= \frac{8 \times 10^{-19}}{1.6 \times 10^{-19}} = 5$$

The body will have deficiency of 5 electrons, because it is having positive charge.

10. Vector form of Coulomb's law

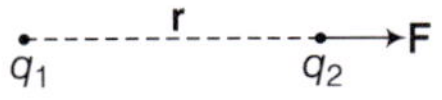

$$\mathbf{F} = \frac{1}{4\pi\varepsilon_0} \cdot \frac{q_1 q_2}{|r|^3} \mathbf{r}$$

or $$|F| = \frac{1}{4\pi\varepsilon_0} \cdot \frac{q_1 q_2}{|r|^2}$$

where, q_1 and q_2 are two charges separated by a distance r which is the displacement vector. It shows direction of force between two charges.

11. Charge on any conductor can be only an integral multiple of charge present on one electron (quantisation of charge). Then, $q = ne$

where, $n = 1, 2, 3, \ldots$

Now, $$n = \frac{8.6 \times 10^{-19}}{1.6 \times 10^{-19}} = 5.4$$

[this is a fraction and not an integer]

So, 8.6×10^{-19} C of charge cannot be given to a conductor.

12. Let q_1 and q_2 be the initial charges on spheres A and B, respectively. Then, by Coulomb's law, we have

$$F = \frac{1}{4\pi\varepsilon_0} \frac{q_1 q_2}{r^2}$$

When an identical uncharged sphere C touches A, the charges redistribute on A and C and by symmetry, each acquires a charge $q_1/2$. Similarly, when D touches B, each acquires a charge $q_2/2$. If now the distance between A and B is halved, the new force of repulsion is given by

$$F' = \frac{1}{4\pi\varepsilon_0} \frac{(q_1/2)(q_2/2)}{(r/2)^2}$$

$$= \frac{1}{4\pi\varepsilon_0} \frac{q_1 q_2}{r^2} = F$$

$\therefore$ The new force of repulsion is same as the initial force of repulsion.

13. The situation is shown as below

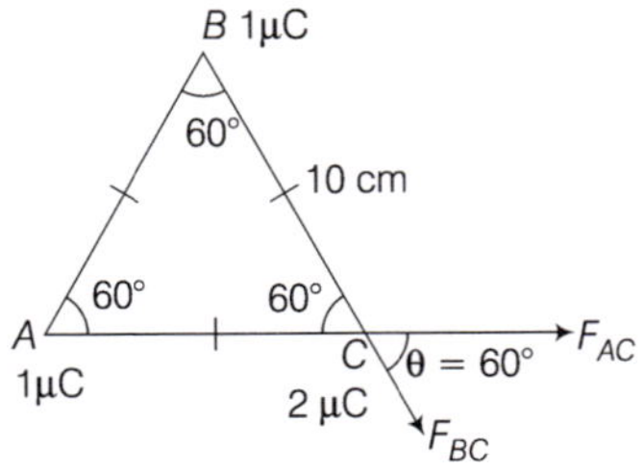

Force on C due to A

$$F_{AC} = \frac{1}{4\pi\varepsilon_0} \frac{q_A q_C}{(AC)^2}$$

$$= \frac{9 \times 10^9 \times 1 \times 10^{-6} \times 2 \times 10^{-6}}{(10 \times 10^{-2})^2} = 1.8 \text{ N}$$

Similarly, $F_{BC} = \dfrac{1}{4\pi\varepsilon_0} \dfrac{q_B\, q_C}{(BC)^2}$

$$= \frac{9\times10^9 \times 1\times10^{-6} \times 2\times10^{-6}}{(10\times10^{-2})^2} = 1.8\,\text{N}$$

∴ Resultant force on the charge at C,

$$F_{\text{resultant}} = \sqrt{F_{AC}^2 + F_{BC}^2 + 2F_{AC}F_{BC}\cos 60^\circ}$$

$$= \sqrt{(1.8)^2 + (1.8)^2 + 2\,(1.8)^2 \times \frac{1}{2}}$$

$$= 3.12\ \text{N}$$

NOTE For two equal vectors arranged at angle θ the resultant is $|F|_{\text{resultant}} = 2|F|\cos\frac{\theta}{2}$

∴ $= 2\times1.8\times\cos\theta = 3.12\ \text{N}$

14. (*i*) The circuit between the bird sitting on the live wire and the earth is not complete due to which no current flows through the body of the bird and it remains safe. However, if a man standing on ground touches the same wire, the circuit to the earth is completed through his body and a heavy current passes through his body, carrying a fatal shock.

(*ii*) The tyres of aircrafts are highly charged during landing due to friction between the tyres and the airstrip (earth). If the tyres are slightly conducting, the charge will not accumulate on them and will leak to the earth.

(*iii*) Conductor have lots of the free electrons that can carry electricity, if the potential difference is applied across them.

(*iv*) The major difference between the conductors and insulators is that when some charge is given to a conductor, it readily gets transferred over its entire, surface. On the other hand, if some charge is given to an insulator it stays at the place where it is put on.

(*v*) The more the band gap between the valence and conduction band, the worse is the conduction of the material. For conductors, there are overlapping bands. So, conductors can carry electricity. But there is a huge energy gap in the case of insulators.

CHAPTER TEST

01 Mark Questions (MCQs)

1 The number of electrons contained in 1 C of charge equals :

(a) 6.25×10^{17} (b) 6.25×10^{18}

(c) 6.25×10^{19} (d) 1.6×10^{19}

2 The SI unit of free space permittivity, ε_0 is

(a) $N\text{-}m^2C^{-2}$ (b) $N\text{-}m^{-2}C^2$

(c) $N^{-1}m^{-2}C^2$ (d) $N^{-1}m^2C^{-2}$

3 The dielectric constant K of an insulator can be

(a) -1 (b) 0

(c) 0.5 (d) 5

4 The ratio of the gravitational and the electrostatic forces between two electrons at some distance apart is

(a) 10^{42} (b) 10^{39} (c) 10^{-39} (d) 10^{-43}

01 Mark Questions (VSA)

5 Name the basic properties of electric charge.

6 Does Coulomb's formula for the force of attraction or repulsion between two point charges obey Newton's third law of motion?

7 How many electrons will have a total charge of 2C?

8 Point out right or wrong for the following statement. The mutual forces between two charges do not get affected by the presence of other charges.

02 Marks Questions

9 Plot a graph showing the variation of Coulomb's force (F) *versus* $1/r^2$, where r is the distance between the two charges of each pair of charges (1μC, 2μC) and (1μC, – 3μC). Interpret the graph, so obtained.

10 Deduce the expression for the force between two charges q_1 and q_2 with position vectors r_1 and r_2 at a point r with respect to common origin.

11 The sum of two point charges is 7μC. They repel each other with a force of 1N when kept 30 cm apart in free space. Calculate the value of each charge.

03 Marks Questions

12 (i) What do you mean by electric charge?

(ii) What are the properties of electric charge?

(iii) Differentiate between conductors and insulators.

13 (i) Discuss the comparison of Coulomb's law with Newton's law of gravitation.

(ii) Describe the principle of superposition of electrostatic forces.

05 Marks Question

14 (i) Two point charges +6μC and +2μC repel each other with a force $F = 12$N. If each is given an additional charge of – 4μC, then what will be the new force?

(ii) The charges Q and q are placed at each of the diagonally opposite corners of a square. If the net electrical force on Q is zero, then find the ratio Q/q.

Answers

1. (b) **2.** (c) **3.** (d) **4.** (a)

7. 1.25×10^{19}

11. 5μC, 2μC

14. (i) – 4 N (ii) $-2\sqrt{2}$

02

Electric Field and Electric Dipole

TREND ANALYSIS 4 YEARS

		Average No. of Questions Across all Sets			
	Types of Questions	2024	2023	2020	2019
TOPIC 01 *Electric Field (Including Electric Field Lines)*	1 Mark	–	–	–	–
	2 Marks	–	–	–	–
	3 Marks	–	–	–	–
	5 Marks	–	–	–	–
TOPIC 02 *Electric Dipole*	1 Mark	–	–	–	–
	2 Marks	–	–	–	–
	3 Marks	–	1	1	–
	5 Marks	–	–	–	–
TOPIC 03 *Gauss' Theorem*	1 Mark	–	1	1	1
	2 Marks	2	–	–	–
	3 Marks	–	–	–	–
	5 Marks	–	–	–	–

The region surrounding a charge in which it exerts a force on another charges kept around it, is called **electric field**.

Concept of Electric field

Imagine an electric charge q is located in space. If an another charge say q_0 is brought near the charge q, then the charge q_0 experiences a force (attractive or repulsive) due to the charge q. This force is said to be due to the electric field set-up by the charge q in the space surrounding it. Any other charge when placed in this field experiences an electric force.

Here, the charge q is called the **source charge** and the charge q_0 is called the **test charge**.

TOPIC 1

Electric Field (Including Electric Field Lines)

Electric Field Intensity

The electric field intensity at any point due to source charge is defined as the force experienced per unit positive test charge placed at that point without disturbing the source charge.

It is expressed as

$$\boxed{\mathbf{E} = \lim_{q_0 \to 0} \frac{\mathbf{F}}{q_0}}$$

Here, $q_0 \to 0$ i.e. the test charge q_0 must be small so that it does not produce its own electric field.

SI unit of electric field intensity (**E**) is N/C and it is a vector quantity having dimensions $[MLT^{-3}A^{-1}]$.

Electric Field Intensity (EFI) due to a Point Charge

Electric field intensity at P, $\mathbf{E} = \frac{1}{4\pi\varepsilon_0}\frac{q}{r^2}\hat{\mathbf{r}}$

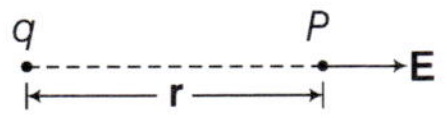

If $q > 0$, i.e. positive charge, **E** is directed away from the source charge while on the other hand, if $q < 0$ i.e. negative charge, **E** is directed towards the source charge.

The variation of E with r is shown in the graph.

$$|\mathbf{E}| \propto \frac{1}{r^2}$$

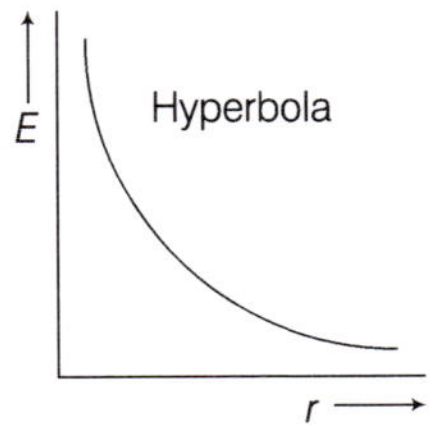

Variation of electric field intensity E due to a point charge with distance r

Electric Field Intensity due to System of Charges

This is same as the case of electrostatic force, here we will apply principle of superposition, i.e.

$$\mathbf{E} = \mathbf{E}_1 + \mathbf{E}_2 + \mathbf{E}_3 + \cdots + \mathbf{E}_n$$

$$\Rightarrow \quad \boxed{\mathbf{E} = \frac{1}{4\pi\varepsilon_0}\sum_{i=1}^{n}\frac{q_i}{|r_i|^2}\mathbf{r}_i}$$

Electric Field Intensity due to Continuous Charge Distribution

The region in which charges are closely spaced is said to have continuous distribution of charge.

The distribution of charges are of three types. Electric field associated with different types of distribution of charges are explained as below

(*i*) **Electric field due to linear charge distribution**

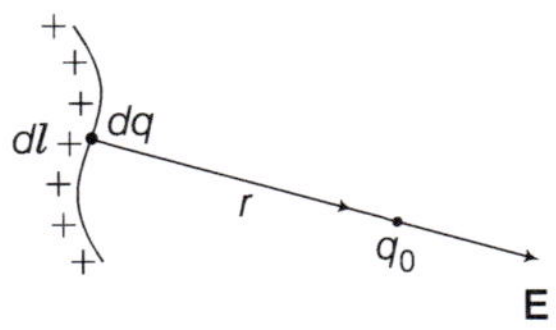

Linear charge distribution

Electric field, $\boxed{\mathbf{E} = \frac{\mathbf{F}}{q_0} = \frac{1}{4\pi\varepsilon_0}\int_l \frac{\lambda dl}{|\mathbf{r}|^2}\hat{\mathbf{r}}}$

(*ii*) **Electric field due to surface charge distribution**

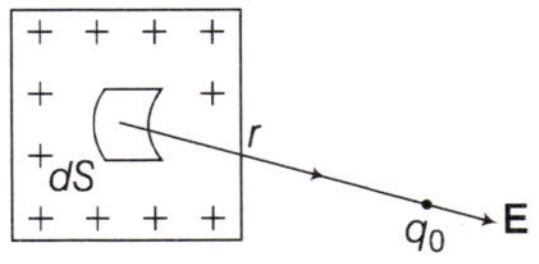

Surface charge distribution

Electric field, $\boxed{\mathbf{E} = \frac{\mathbf{F}}{q_0} = \frac{1}{4\pi\varepsilon_0}\int_S \frac{\sigma dS}{|\mathbf{r}|^2}\hat{\mathbf{r}}}$

(*iii*) **Electric field due to volume charge distribution**

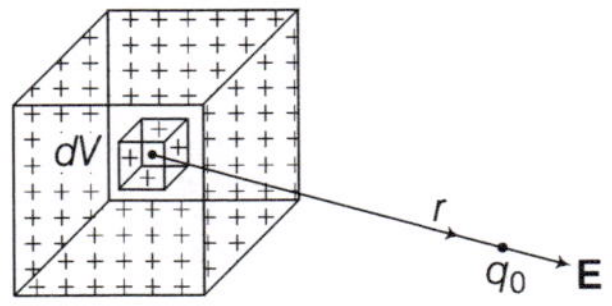

Volume charge distribution

Electric field, $\boxed{\mathbf{E} = \frac{\mathbf{F}}{q_0} = \frac{1}{4\pi\varepsilon_0}\int_V \frac{\rho dV}{|\mathbf{r}|^2}\hat{\mathbf{r}}}$

Force on a Charge in Electric Field

When a charge q is place in an electric field of intensity **E**, the force experienced by the charge is given by

$$\boxed{\mathbf{F}_E = q\mathbf{E}}$$

Electric Field Lines

Electric field lines are a way of pictorially mapping the electric field around a system of charges or distribution o charge(s).

Electric field lines due to an isolated point charge (+ve and –ve)

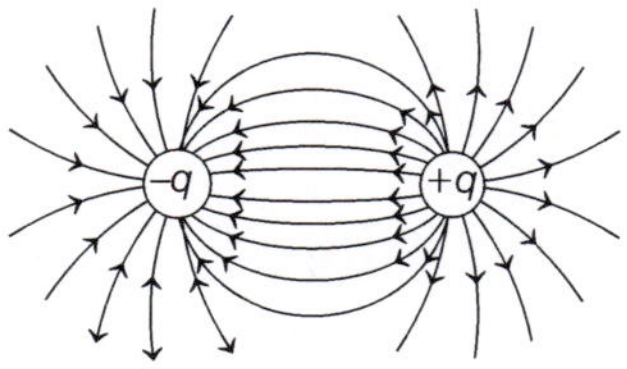

Electric field lines of an electric dipole

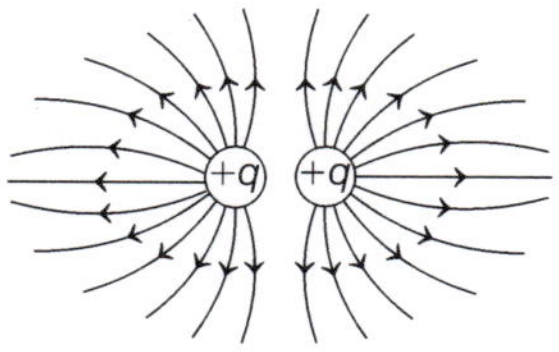

Electric field lines of two similar charge at a small distance

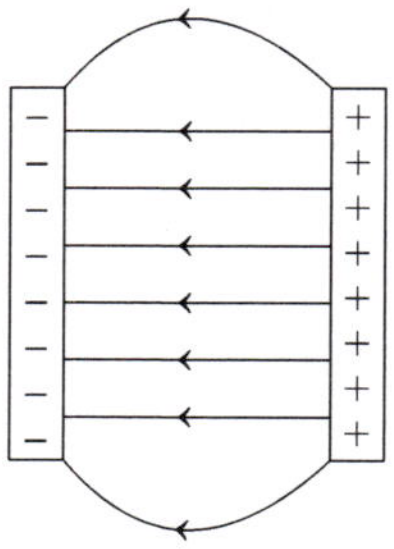

Uniform field between two oppositely charged parallel plates.

NOTE Electric field lines are also called electric lines of force.

PYQs Previous Years Questions

1 Mark Questions

1. Which one of the following is not a property of electric lines of force? **ISC 2022 Sem-I**

(a) They originate at the positive charge.

(b) They terminate at the negative charge.

(c) They intersect each other.

(d) A tangent drawn to a line of force gives the direction of electric field intensity at that point.

2. A charged oil drop weighing 1.6×10^{-15} N is found to remain suspended in a uniform electric field of intensity 2×10^{3} NC^{-1}. Find the charge on the drop. **ISC 2016**

3. Two point charges $Q_1 = 400\,\mu C$ and $Q_2 = 100\,\mu C$ are kept fixed, 60 cm apart in vacuum. Find intensity of the electric field at mid-point of the line joining Q_1 and Q_2. **ISC 2016**

4. A point charge of 5×10^{-6} C experiences a force of 2×10^{-3} N when kept in a uniform electric field of intensity E. Then, find the value of E. **ISC 2012**

5. Draw (at least three) electric lines of force due to an electric dipole. **ISC 2008**

2 Marks Questions

6. When a test charge of 2 nC is placed at the origin, it experiences a force of 8×10^{-4} N in the positive y-direction. What is the electric field at the origin? What would be the force on a charge −4 nC placed at the origin?

> **KEY idea**
>
> To calculate the force on a charge at the origin, first calculate the electric field on that charge at the origin and then force at origin with the help of formula ($F = qE$).

7. Two point charges of magnitude 2×10^{-7} C and 8.5×10^{-8} C are 0.1 m apart. Calculate the electric field intensity that each charge produces at the site of the other.

Explanations

1. (c) Electric lines of force do not intersect each other. If they do, then there will be two directions of force at a point which is not possible.

2. Here, the weight of a charged oil drop is equal to the force on the drop due to uniform electric field.

Force, $F = 1.6 \times 10^{-15}$ N

Electric field intensity, $E = 2 \times 10^{3}\ NC^{-1}$

$\because$ Force, $F = qE$

$\Rightarrow \qquad q = F/E = 1.6 \times 10^{-15}/2 \times 10^{3}$

$\Rightarrow \qquad q = 8 \times 10^{-19}$ C

3. According to the question,

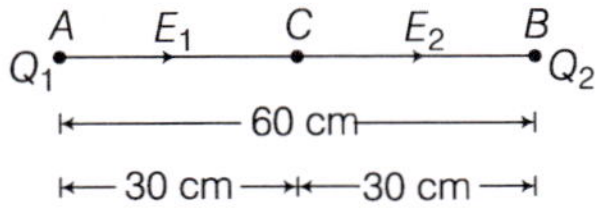

Since, two point charges $Q_1 = 400\,\mu C$ and $Q_2 = 100\,\mu C$ are kept fixed, 60 cm apart in vacuum. In the figure, C is the mid-point of AB, where we need to determine the electric field intensity.

So, net electric field,

$$E = E_1 - E_2 = \frac{kQ_1}{r^2} - \frac{kQ_2}{r^2}$$

$$= \frac{k}{r^2}(Q_1 - Q_2)$$

$$= \frac{9 \times 10^9}{(30 \times 10^{-2})^2}(400 \times 10^{-6} - 100 \times 10^{-6})$$

$$= \frac{9 \times 10^9 \times 300 \times 10^{-6}}{900 \times 10^{-4}} = 3 \times 10^7 \text{ N/C}$$

4. Electric field $(E) = \frac{F}{q} = \frac{2 \times 10^{-3}\text{ N}}{5 \times 10^{-6}\text{ C}} = 400$ N/C

5. Electric lines of force (field) start from positive charge and ends on negative charge.

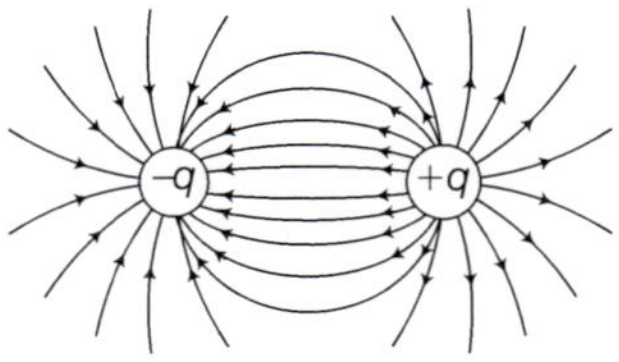

6. Charge, $q_0 = 2\text{ nC} = 2 \times 10^{-9}$ C

Force, $F = 8 \times 10^{-4}$ N

$q_1 = -4\text{ nC} = -4 \times 10^{-9}$ C

Electric field at origin, $E = \frac{F}{q_0} = \frac{8 \times 10^{-4}}{2 \times 10^{-9}}$

$= 4 \times 10^5$ N/C positive along y-direction.

Force at origin $F = q_1 E = -4 \times 10^{-9} \times 4 \times 10^5$

$= -16 \times 10^{-4}$ N

along negative y-direction.

7. Given, $q_1 = 2 \times 10^{-7}$ C,

$q_2 = 8.5 \times 10^{-8}$ C,

$r = 0.1$ m

$\therefore$ Electric field at the site of q_2,

$$E_1 = \frac{q_1}{4\pi\varepsilon_0 r^2} = \frac{2 \times 10^{-7} \times 9 \times 10^9}{(0.1)^2}$$

$= 1.8 \times 10^5$ N/C

$\therefore$ Electric field at the site of q_1,

$$E_2 = \frac{q_2}{4\pi\varepsilon_0 r^2} = \frac{8.5 \times 10^{-8} \times 9 \times 10^9}{(0.1)^2}$$

$= 7.6 \times 10^4$ N/C

TOPIC 2

Electric Dipole

Two point charges of same magnitude and opposite nature separated by a small distance altogether form an electric dipole.

Electric Dipole Moment

The strength of an electric dipole is measured by a vector quantity known as electric dipole moment (p) which is the product of magnitude of either charge (q) and separation between the two charges ($2l$). It is expressed as,

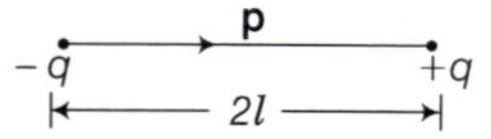

$$\mathbf{p} = q \times 2l \Rightarrow |\mathbf{p}| = q\,(2l)$$

The direction of electric dipole moment is from negative charge ($-q$) to positive charge ($+q$).

SI unit of electric dipole moment is C-m.

Electric Field Intensity at a Point on the Axial Line of Electric Dipole

Consider a point P is situated on axial line at a distance r from mid-point O of the dipole.

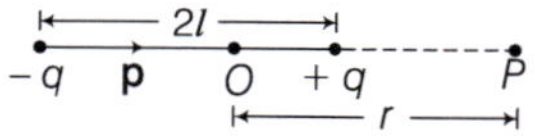

Electric field at this axial point is

$$\mathbf{E}_{\text{axial}} = \frac{1}{4\pi\varepsilon_0}\frac{2\mathbf{p}r}{(r^2 - l^2)^2}$$

When $2l << r$, $$\mathbf{E}_{\text{axial}} \approx \frac{1}{4\pi\varepsilon_0}\frac{2\mathbf{p}}{r^3}$$ $[\because r^2 - l^2 \simeq r^2]$

$$\Rightarrow \quad |\mathbf{E}_{\text{axial}}| \propto \frac{1}{r^3}$$

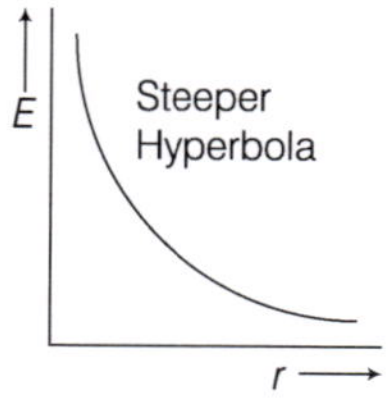

The variation of E with r

The variation of E with r is shown in the graph.

The direction of field at any point on axial line is along the direction of electric dipole moment $\mathbf{p}$.

Electric Field Intensity at a Point on Equatorial Line of Electric Dipole

Consider a point P situated on equatorial line at a perpendicular distance r from mid-point O of the dipole. Resolving electric field along two perpendicular directions, we have

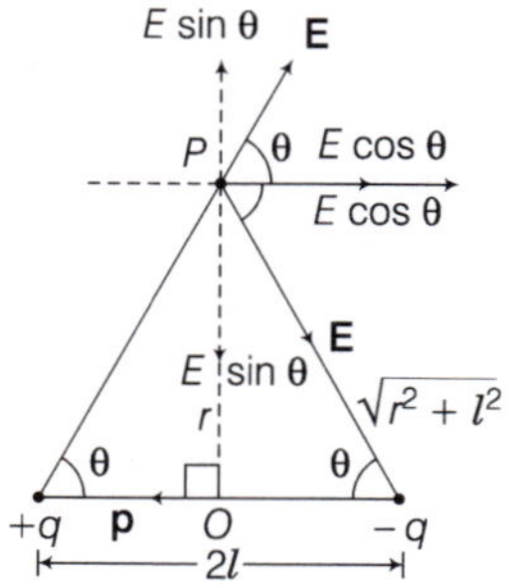

$$\mathbf{E}_{\text{equatorial}} = 2E\cos\theta = \frac{1}{4\pi\varepsilon_0}\frac{\mathbf{p}}{(r^2 + l^2)^{3/2}}$$

The direction of electric field intensity ($\mathbf{E}$) due to dipole at any point on equatorial line is opposite to the direction of dipole moment ($\mathbf{p}$).

If $\quad 2l << r,$ $$|\mathbf{E}_{\text{equatorial}}| \approx \frac{1}{4\pi\varepsilon_0}\frac{|\mathbf{p}|}{r^3}$$

Electric Field Intensity at any Point due to a Short Electric Dipole

Consider a general point $P\,(r, \theta)$ as shown in the figure. Electric field at this point due to the dipole is,

$$\mathbf{E} = \frac{1}{4\pi\varepsilon_0}\frac{\mathbf{p}}{r^3}\sqrt{3\cos^2\theta + 1} \qquad \ldots\text{(i)}$$

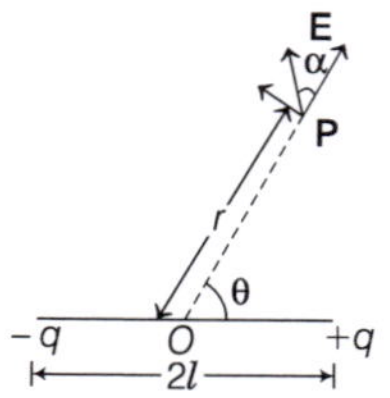

Cases

(i) For an axial point, putting $\theta = 0°$ in Eq. (i),

$$\mathbf{E}_{\text{axial}} = \frac{1}{4\pi\varepsilon_0}\frac{2\mathbf{p}}{r^3}$$

(ii) For an equatorial point, putting $\theta = 90°$ in Eq. (i),

$$\mathbf{E}_{\text{equatorial}} = \frac{1}{4\pi\varepsilon_0}\frac{\mathbf{p}}{r^3}$$

We get the same result as derived earlier

If the resultant field makes an angle α with the radial direction OP, then we have

$$\Rightarrow \quad \tan\alpha = \frac{\tan\theta}{2}$$

Torque on a Dipole in a Uniform Electric Field

When an electric dipole is placed in a uniform electric field (**E**), equal and opposite electric forces are experienced by the two charges.

Due to the couple a net torque acts on the electric dipole placed in the uniform electric field (**E**)

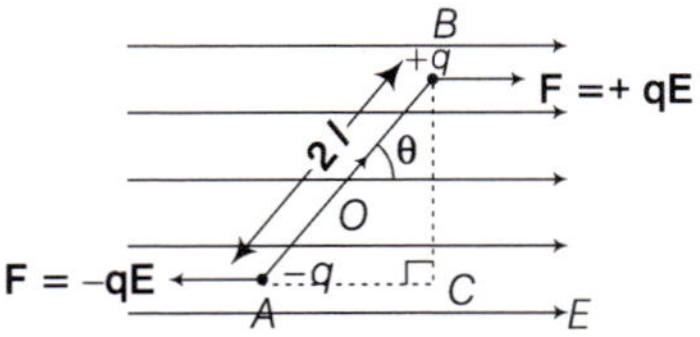

Torque on the dipole about an axis passing through the mid-point (O) of the dipole is

τ = Either force × Perpendicular distance BC between the forces $= (qE) \times (2l\sin\theta)$

$$\Rightarrow \quad \tau = (q \times 2l) \times E\sin\theta = p\,E\sin\theta$$

$\therefore$ Torque, $\tau = \mathbf{p} \times \mathbf{E} \Rightarrow \boxed{|\tau| = pE\sin\theta}$

Minimum torque experienced by electric dipole in electric field, when $\theta = 0°$ or π, then $\tau = \tau_{min} = 0$

Maximum torque, $\tau = \tau_{max}$ when $\sin\theta = 1$ i.e., $\theta = \frac{\pi}{2}$ or 90°.

$$\Rightarrow \quad \boxed{\tau_{max} = pE}$$

NOTE There exists a net force and torque on electric dipole when placed in non-uniform electric field.

PYQs Previous Years Questions

1 Mark Questions

1. In an electric dipole, what is the locus of a point having zero potential? **ISC SQP 2023**

2. A charge placed at a distance form a short electric dipole in the end on position experience a force F. If the distance is halved, then the force will become **ISC 2022 Sem-I**

(a) $4F$ (b) $8F$
(c) $F/4$ (d) $F/8$

3. An electric dipole consists of two point charges $+2$ mC and -2 mC separated by a distance of 4 cm. It is kept at an angle of 30° with an electric field intensity of 1×10^5 NC^{-1}. The torque experienced by the dipole is **ISC 2022 Sem-I**

(a) 1 N-m (b) 2 N-m
(c) 3 N-m (d) 4 N-m

4. Maximum torque acting on an electric dipole of dipole moment 3×10^{-29} C-m in a uniform electric field E is 6×10^{-25} N-m. Find the value of E. **ISC 2017**

5. What will be the net electric force acting on an electric dipole placed in a uniform electric field? **ISC 2007**

3 Marks Questions

6. Obtain an expression for intensity of electric field at a point in end-on-position i.e. on an axial line of an electric dipole. **ISC SQP 2023, 18**

7. Show that intensity of electric field **E** at a point in broadside on position is given by

$$E = \left(\frac{1}{4\pi\varepsilon_0}\right)\frac{p}{(r^2 + l^2)^{\frac{3}{2}}}$$ where the terms have their usual meanings. **ISC 2020**

8. An electric dipole of dipole moment **p** is placed in a uniform electric field **E** with its axis inclined to the field. Write an expression for the torque τ experienced by the dipole in vector form. Show diagramatically, show the dipole should be kept in the electric field so that the torque acting on it is

(*i*) maximum
(*ii*) zero **ISC 2014**

9. (*i*) Write an expression (derivation not required) for intensity of electric field in

(a) axial position.

(b) broadside position of an electric dipole, in terms of its length $(2a)$ dipole moment (p) and distance (r).

(*ii*) What is the ratio of these two intensities i.e. $E_1 : E_2$, for a short electric dipole? **ISC 2013**

10. An electric dipole is placed in a uniform external electric field **E**. Show that the torque acting on the dipole is given by $\tau = \mathbf{p} \times \mathbf{E}$, where **p** is the dipole moment. **ISC 2005**

5 Marks Questions

11. Derive an expression for intensity of electric field at a point in broadside position or on an equatorial line of an electric dipole. **ISC 2015**

12. Obtain an expression for intensity of electric field in end on position, i.e. axial position of an electric dipole. **ISC 2011**

Explanations

1. It is a straight line passing through the mid-point and perpendicular to the dipole axis (an equatorial plane).

2. (b) Electric field due to electric dipole is

$$\mathbf{E} = \frac{1}{4\pi\varepsilon_0}\frac{2\mathbf{p}}{r^3} \Rightarrow \mathbf{F} = \left(\frac{1}{4\pi\varepsilon_0}\frac{2\mathbf{p}}{r^3}\right)q$$

$$|\mathbf{E}| \propto \frac{1}{r^3} \Rightarrow \mathbf{F} \propto \frac{1}{r^3}$$

Now, distance is halved, then new force is

$$\mathbf{F}' \propto \frac{1}{\left(\frac{r}{2}\right)^3}$$

$$\mathbf{F}' \propto \frac{8}{r^3} \quad \text{or } \mathbf{F}' = 8\,\mathbf{F}$$

3. (d) Torque $(\tau) = pE\sin\theta = q \cdot 2l\,E\sin\theta$

$$= 2\times10^{-3} \times 4\times10^{-2} \times 1\times10^{5}\sin 30^\circ$$

$$= 4 \text{ N-m}$$

4. Dipole moment, $p = 3\times10^{-29}\text{Cm}$

$$\tau = 6\times10^{-25}\text{Nm}$$

$$\tau = \mathbf{p}\times\mathbf{E} = pE\sin\theta$$

For maximum value, $\theta = 90^\circ$

$$\tau = pE$$

$$\Rightarrow 6\times10^{-25} = 3\times10^{-29}\times E$$

$$\Rightarrow E = \frac{6\times10^{-25}}{3\times10^{-29}} = 2\times10^{-25+29}$$

$$= 2\times10^{+4} \text{ N/C}$$

5. Consider the diagram. Total force on the dipole placed in a uniform electric field **E** is

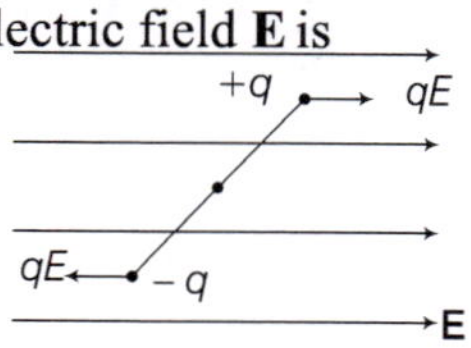

$$|\mathbf{F}| = (qE - qE) = 0$$

6. We have to calculate the field (E) at a point P on the axial line of the dipole and at a distance $OP = r$ from the centre O of the dipole.

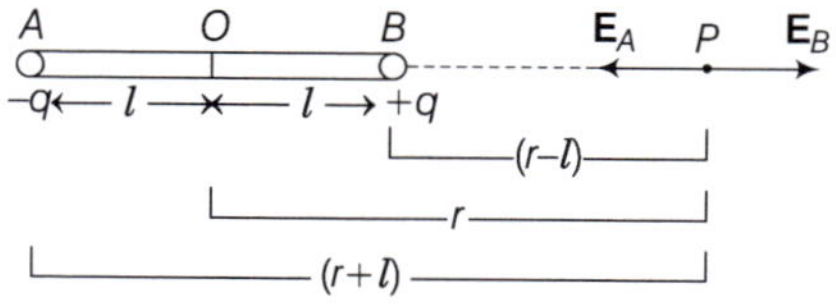

The vectors $\mathbf{E}_A$ and $\mathbf{E}_B$ are collinear and opposite, so, resultant electric field intensity at the point P,

$$|E_P| = |E_B - E_A|$$

Here, $|E_A| = \dfrac{1}{4\pi\varepsilon_o}\cdot\dfrac{q}{(r+l)^2}$

and $|E_B| = \dfrac{1}{4\pi\varepsilon_o}\cdot\dfrac{q}{(r-l)^2}$

$$\therefore \quad E_P = \frac{1}{4\pi\varepsilon_o}\left[\frac{q}{(r-l)^2} - \frac{q}{(r+l)^2}\right]$$

But $|\mathbf{p}| = q\times 2l$

$$\therefore \quad E_p = \frac{1}{4\pi\varepsilon_o}\cdot\frac{2pr}{(r^2-l^2)^2}$$

7. Consider an electric dipole, consisting of two point charges $-q$ and $+q$, separated by a small distance $AB = 2l$, with centre at O.

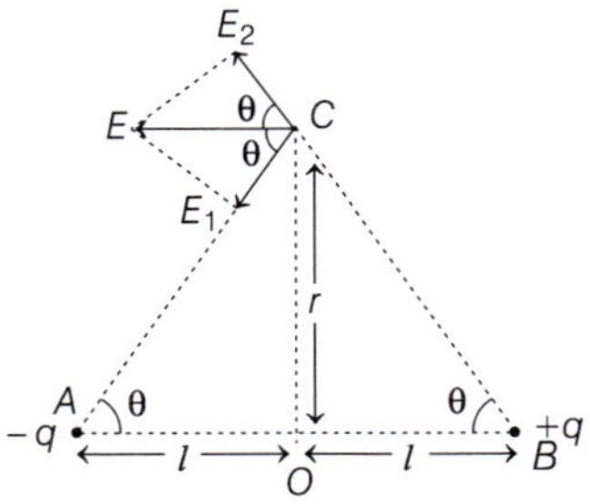

So, dipole moment, $|\mathbf{p}| = q(2l)$

Let $\quad OC = r$

Here, E_1 = Electric intensity at C due to charge $-q$ at A.

$$\therefore \quad E_1 = \frac{1}{4\pi\varepsilon_0}\frac{q}{AC^2}$$

$$\because \quad AC^2 = OC^2 + AO^2 = r^2 + l^2$$

$$\Rightarrow \quad E_1 = \frac{1}{4\pi\varepsilon_0}\frac{q}{(r^2+l^2)}$$

Similarly $E_2 = \dfrac{1}{4\pi\varepsilon_0}\dfrac{q}{r^2+l^2}$

(due to charge $+q$ at B)

$\because$ For equatorial point C,

$$\angle CAB = \angle CBA = \theta$$

Hence, the equivalent of E_1 and E_2,

$$\mathbf{E} = [(-\hat{\mathbf{i}}E_1\cos\theta - \hat{\mathbf{j}}E_1\sin\theta) + (-)\hat{\mathbf{i}}E_2\cos\theta + \hat{\mathbf{j}}E_2\sin\theta]$$

$$\Rightarrow |\mathbf{E}| = (-E_1\cos\theta - E_2\cos\theta)\hat{\mathbf{i}} \quad [E_1 = E_2]$$

Take only magnitude and remove negative sign

$$\Rightarrow \quad E = 2E_1\cos\theta \qquad (\because E_1 = E_2)$$

$$= \frac{2}{4\pi\varepsilon_0}\frac{q}{(r^2+l^2)}\cos\theta \qquad \left(\because \cos\theta = \frac{l}{\sqrt{r^2+l^2}}\right)$$

$$= \frac{2ql}{4\pi\varepsilon_0(r^2+l^2)^{3/2}} = \frac{p}{4\pi\varepsilon_0(r^2+l^2)^{3/2}}$$

$$\therefore \quad E = \frac{1}{4\pi\varepsilon_0}\frac{p}{(r^2+l^2)^{3/2}}$$

Concept Enhancer On equatorial line the electric dipole moment is opposite to the electric field direction.

8. Torque on an electric dipole placed in the uniform electric field (**E**)

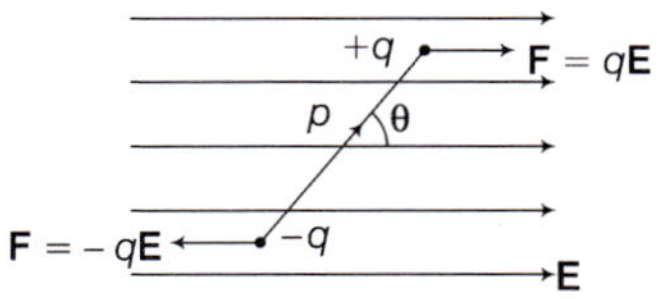

Torque, $\tau = \mathbf{p} \times \mathbf{E}$

$$\Rightarrow \quad |\tau| = pE\sin\theta$$

$$\tau = pE\sin\theta$$

(*i*) For maximum torque, $\sin\theta = 1$ or $\theta = 90°$

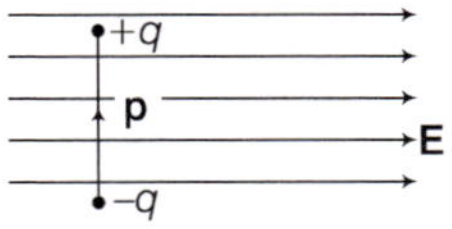

So, dipole should be kept perpendicular to the electric field.

(*ii*) Minimum torque experienced by electric dipole in electric field, when $\theta = 0°$ or π (180°)

$$\tau = \tau_{min} = 0$$

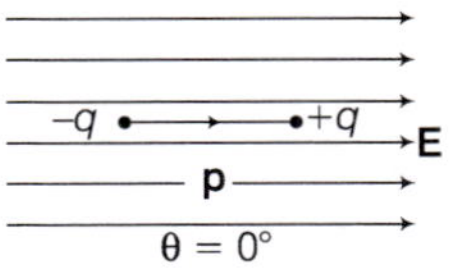

$\theta = 0°$

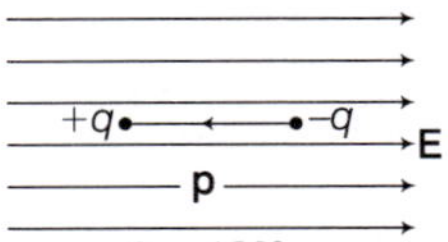

$\theta = 180°$

9. (*i*) Electric field at a general point $P(r, \theta)$ due to dipole is given by

$$E = \frac{1}{4\pi\varepsilon_0}\frac{p}{r^3}\sqrt{3\cos^2\theta + 1}$$

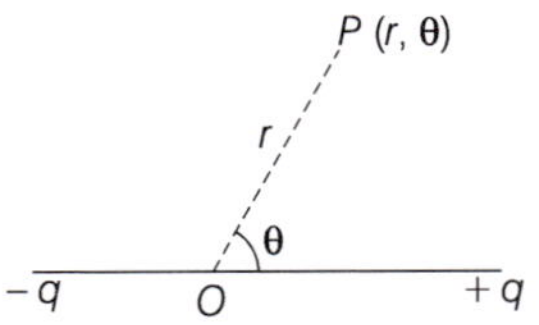

(a) For axial position $\theta = 0°$,

$$E_a = \frac{1}{4\pi\varepsilon_0}\frac{p}{r^3}\times 2 = \frac{1}{4\pi\varepsilon_0}\frac{2p}{r^3}$$

(b) For broadside on position $\theta = 90°$,

$$E_b = \frac{1}{4\pi\varepsilon_0}\frac{p}{r^3}\times 1 = \frac{1}{4\pi\varepsilon_0}\frac{p}{r^3}$$

(*ii*) The ratio of **E** at axial and broad on positions is given by

$$\frac{E_a}{E_b}=\frac{\frac{1}{4\pi\varepsilon_0}\left(\frac{2p}{r^3}\right)}{\frac{1}{4\pi\varepsilon_0}\left(\frac{p}{r^3}\right)}=\frac{2}{1}$$

$\Rightarrow \quad E_a : E_b = 2:1$

10. We can find torque by multiplying magnitude of either force by perpendicular distance between the forces.

The dipole shown in the diagram is placed in a uniform electric field **E**. The direction of electric dipole moment **p** makes an angle θ with electric field. The forces in a pair are acting on the dipole as shown in the figure.

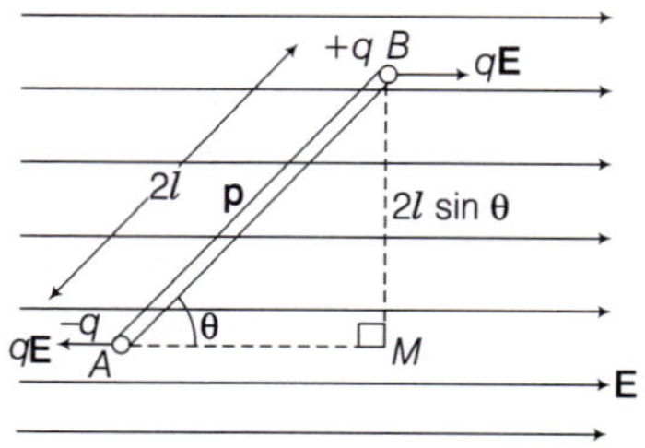

By definition,

Torque (τ) = Magnitude of either force × Perpendicular distance between the forces

$$= qE \times BM = qE \times 2l\sin\theta$$
$$= 2qlE\sin\theta = pE\sin\theta$$

$\Rightarrow \quad \boldsymbol{\tau} = \mathbf{p}\times\mathbf{E}$

Concept Enhancer Dipole is in stable equilibrium within the uniform electric field when angle between *p* and *E* is 0° and unstable equilibrium when the angle, θ = 180°.

11. Consider an electric dipole *AB* consists of two charges +*q* and −*q* separated by a distance 2*a*. We have to find electric field at point *P* on equatorial line separated by a distance *r*.

Electric field at point *P* due to charge +*q*

$$\mathbf{E}_1=\frac{1}{4\pi\varepsilon_0}\cdot\frac{q}{(\sqrt{r^2+a^2})^2}$$
$$=\frac{1}{4\pi\varepsilon_0}\cdot\frac{q}{(r^2+a^2)}, \quad \text{[along } AP]$$

Electric field at point *P* due to charge −*q*,

$$\mathbf{E}_2=\frac{1}{4\pi\varepsilon_0}\cdot\frac{q}{r^2+a^2}, \quad \text{[along } PB]$$

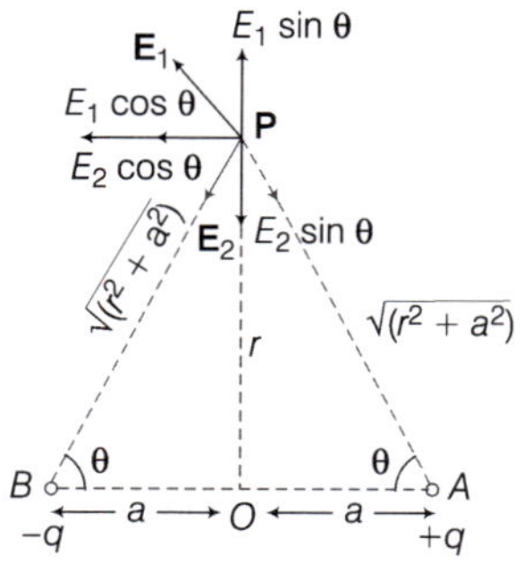

On resolving $\mathbf{E}_1$ and $\mathbf{E}_2$ into rectangular components, we get resultant electric field at point *P*,

$$E = E_1\cos\theta + E_2\cos\theta$$
$$=\frac{1}{4\pi\varepsilon_0}\cdot\frac{q}{r^2+a^2}\cos\theta+\frac{1}{4\pi\varepsilon_0}\cdot\frac{q}{(r^2+a^2)}\cos\theta$$
$$=2\times\frac{1}{4\pi\varepsilon_0}\cdot\frac{q}{(r^2+a^2)}\times\frac{a}{\sqrt{r^2+a^2}}$$
$$=\frac{1}{4\pi\varepsilon_0}\cdot\frac{q.2a}{(r^2+a^2)^{3/2}}$$

But $q\cdot 2a = p \quad \therefore \quad E=\frac{1}{4\pi\varepsilon_0}\cdot\frac{p}{(r^2+a^2)^{3/2}}$

If $r >> a$, then $E=\frac{1}{4\pi\varepsilon_0}\frac{p}{r^3}$

12. To solve this problem, we have to find electric field at *p* due to individual charges and then resultant will be calculated.

Consider a dipole *AB* made up of two charges −*q* and +*q* separated by a distance 2*l*. Let *P* be any point on the axis at a distance *r* from the mid-point *O* of the dipole. We have to determine electric field intensity at the point *P*.

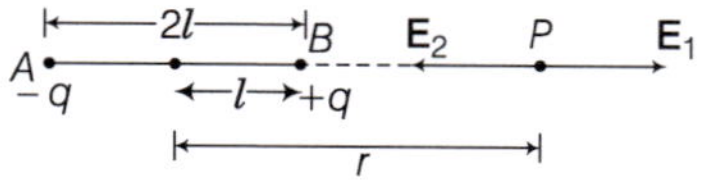

$$\mathbf{E}_1=\frac{1}{4\pi\varepsilon_0}\frac{q}{(r-l)^2}$$

[along the direction of the dipole]

$$\mathbf{E}_2=\frac{1}{4\pi\varepsilon_0}\frac{q}{(r+l)^2}$$

[opposite to the direction of dipole]

The resultant electric field intensity **E** at *P* is

$$E_{net}=\mathbf{E}_1-\mathbf{E}_2 \qquad [\text{as} E_1 > E_2]$$
$$=\frac{q}{4\pi\varepsilon_0}\left[\frac{1}{(r-l)^2}-\frac{1}{(r+l)^2}\right]$$

$$= \frac{q}{4\pi\varepsilon_0}\left[\frac{(r+l)^2-(r-l)^2}{(r-l)^2(r+l)^2}\right]$$

$$= \frac{q}{4\pi\varepsilon_0}\left[\frac{2l \times 2r}{(r^2-l^2)^2}\right]$$

$$= \frac{1}{4\pi\varepsilon_0}\frac{2ql \times 2r}{(r^2-l^2)^2} \qquad \text{[where, } p = 2ql\text{]}$$

$$\therefore \qquad \mathbf{E}_{\text{net}} = \frac{1}{4\pi\varepsilon_0}\frac{2pr}{(r^2-l^2)^2}$$

As $(l <<< r)$.

So, $(r^2 - l^2)^2 \approx (r^2)^2$

$$\therefore \qquad \mathbf{E}_{\text{net}} = \frac{1}{4\pi\varepsilon_0}\frac{2pr}{r^4}$$

$$\Rightarrow \qquad \mathbf{E}_{\text{net}} = \frac{1}{4\pi\varepsilon_0}\frac{2p}{r^3}$$

TOPIC 3

Gauss' Theorem

Area Vector

The vector associated with every area element of a closed surface is taken to be in the direction of the outward normal.

Consider the diagram below

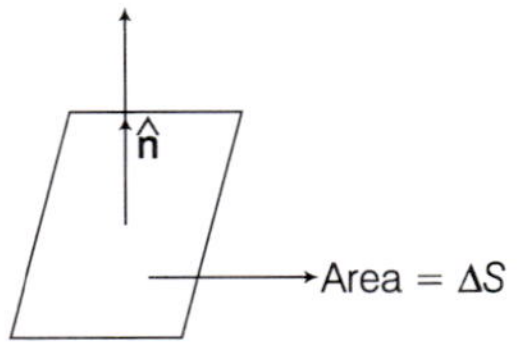

$$\boxed{\Delta \mathbf{S} = |\Delta S|\,\hat{\mathbf{n}} = (\Delta S)\hat{\mathbf{n}}}$$

Here, $\Delta\mathbf{S}$ is the area vector in the direction of the unit vector $\hat{\mathbf{n}}$, normal to the surface area ΔS.

Electric Flux

Electric flux linked with any surface is proportional to the total number of electric field lines that normally pass through that surface. It is a scalar quantity.

SI unit of electric flux is $\text{N-m}^2\,\text{C}^{-1}$ or $\text{Jm}\,\text{C}^{-1}$ or V-m.

CGS unit of electric flux is dyne-cm^2/stat-C.

NOTE The flux crossing through unit area of a surface is called flux density.

(*i*) Surface is held normal to the direction of uniform electric field $\mathbf{E}$ is

$$\Delta\phi_E = |\mathbf{E}||\mathbf{S}|\cos\theta$$

As $\theta = 0°$

So, $\Delta\phi_E = E\,\Delta S = \text{maximum}$

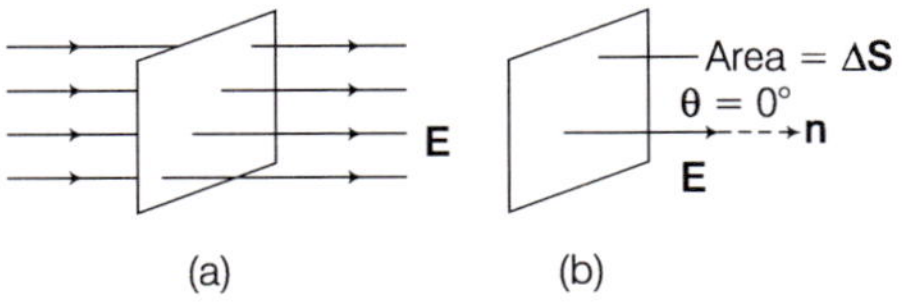

Electric flux through normal area

(*ii*) Area vector of surface makes an angle θ with the direction of uniform electric field $\mathbf{E}$,

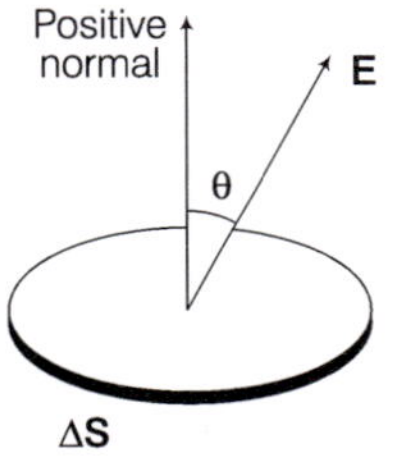

Electric field intensity and electric flux

$$\Delta\phi_E = E\Delta S\cos\theta$$

In vector form, $\Delta\phi_E = \mathbf{E}\cdot\Delta\mathbf{S}$

NOTE When $\theta = 90°$, $\phi_E = 0$ (zero).

$\theta = 180°$, $\phi_E = -E\Delta S$ = minimum.

(*iii*) Consider a closed surface S lying inside the non-uniform electric field $\mathbf{E}$.

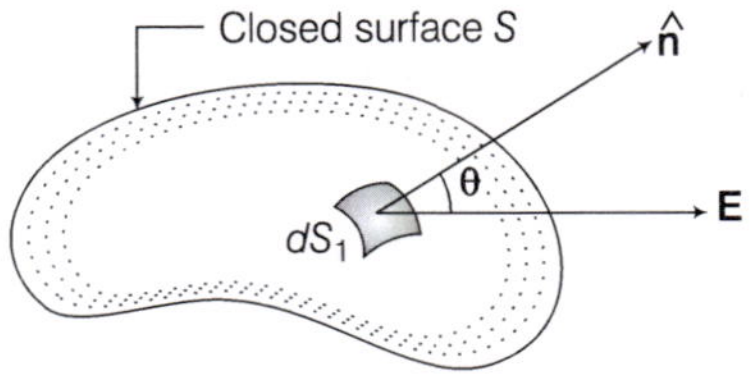

The total electric flux linked with the closed surface S is $\phi = \oint_S \mathbf{E}\cdot d\mathbf{S} = \oint E\cdot dS\cos\theta$.

The surface integral of electric field over the closed surface represents total electric flux linked with the surface.

Gauss' Theorem

The surface integral of the electric field intensity over any closed surface (called Gaussian surface) in free space is equal to $\frac{1}{\varepsilon_0}$ times the net charge enclosed within the surface.

$$\phi = \oint \mathbf{E} \cdot d\mathbf{S} = \frac{q}{\varepsilon_0}$$

where, q is the total charge enclosed by the closed Gaussian (an imaginary) surface.

NOTE On the right side of the equation of Gauss' law, charge q **present outside the Gaussian surface will not be considered.**

Coulomb's law can be deduced from Gauss' law by imagination of Gaussian surface around the charge.

Gaussian Surface

Any hypothetical closed surface enclosing a charge is called the Gaussian surface of that charge. It is chosen to evaluate the surface integral of the electric field produced by the charge enclosed by it, which in turn gives the total flux through the surface.

The Essential Properties of a Gaussian Surface

(*i*) It should be a closed surface so that a clear distinction can be made between points that are inside the surface, on the surface and outside the surface.

(*ii*) This surface must pass through the point where electric field is to be calculated.

(*iii*) The surface must have a shape according to the symmetry of the source so that the field is normal to the surface at each point and constant in magnitude.

(*iv*) For a system of charges, the Gaussian surface should not pass through any discrete charge. It is because electric field at the location of any charge is not well defined. However, the Gaussian surface can pass through a continuous charge distribution.

Applications of Gauss' Theorem (Gauss' Law)

(*i*) **Electric field due to infinitely long uniformly charged wire, with linear charged density λ**

We have considered cylindrical Gaussian surface as shown below

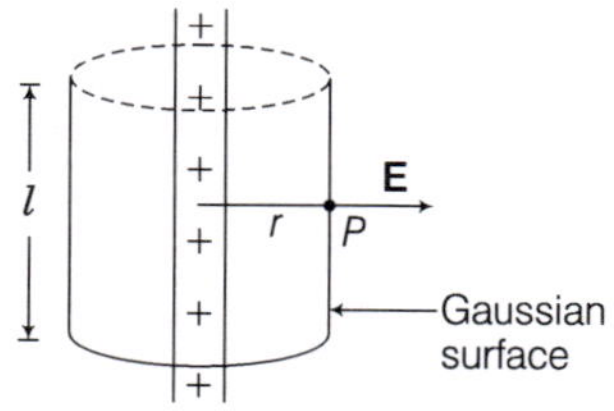

From Gauss' law, $\oint \mathbf{E} \cdot d\mathbf{S} = \frac{q}{\varepsilon_0} = \frac{\lambda l}{\varepsilon_0}$

$$\Rightarrow \boxed{E = \frac{\lambda}{2\pi\varepsilon_0 r}} \quad \text{as } \oint dS = 2\pi r l$$

where, r is the perpendicular distance from the charged wire $E \propto \frac{1}{r}$.

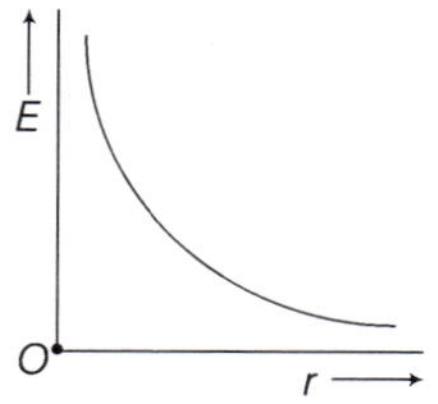

Variation of E with r for the infinitely long charged wire

(*ii*) **Electric field due to a thin infinite plane sheet of charge with uniform surface charge density σ, at any nearby point.**

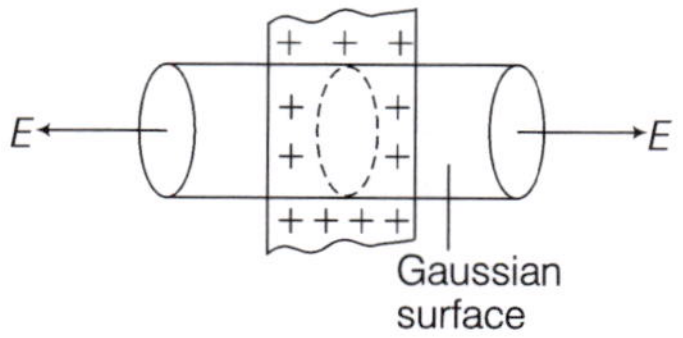

$$\boxed{E = \frac{\sigma}{2\varepsilon_0}} \quad \text{[for a plane sheet of charge]}$$

and $E = \frac{\sigma}{\varepsilon_0}$ [for a charged conducting surface]

NOTE E does not depend on r.

(*iii*) **Electric field due to a thin charged spherical shell of radius R at a distance *r* from its centre**

To find the field at a distance r from the centre of the spherical shell, we considered a spherical Gaussian surface of radius r centered at the shell and then Gauss' law is applied.

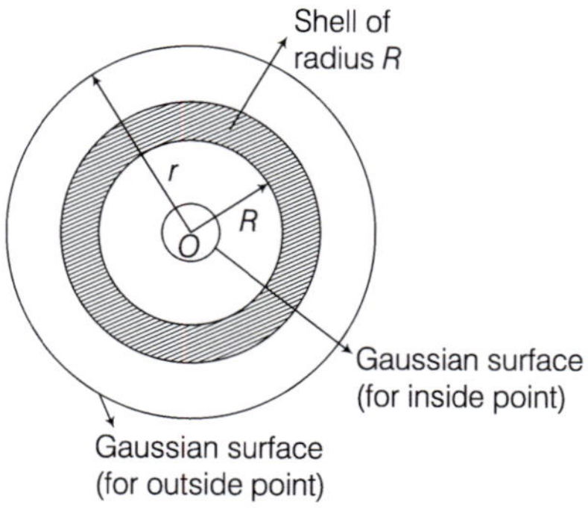

(a) **Field at an inside point** $(r < R)$

As, $q = 0 \Rightarrow \mathbf{E} = 0$

(b) **For points lie outside the shell** $(r > R)$

By Gauss' law,

$$\Rightarrow \qquad E = \frac{\sigma R^2}{\varepsilon_0 r^2} \qquad [\because r > R]$$

$$\therefore \qquad E \propto \frac{1}{r^2}$$

(c) **Field at a point on the surface** $(r = R)$

On putting $r = R$, $\Rightarrow$ $E = \dfrac{q}{4\pi\varepsilon_0 R^2} = \dfrac{\sigma}{\varepsilon_0}$

where, surface charge density, $\sigma = \dfrac{q}{4\pi R^2}$.

The variation of E *versus* r is in the diagram given below.

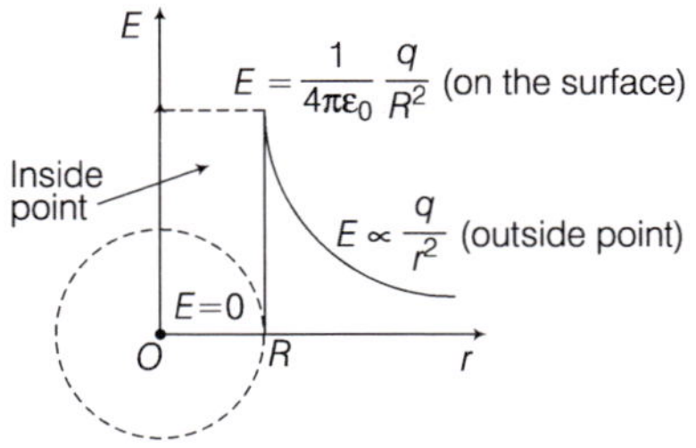

NOTE (i) Electric field inside a conductor is zero. Thus, applying Gauss' law we can say that any excess charge placed on an isolated conductor resides on the outer surface.

(ii) No charge is enclosed inside a cavity in an isolated conductor. Thus, from Gauss' law $E = 0$.

PYQs Previous Years Questions

1 Mark Questions

1. The surface charge density of a large conducting sheet is $17.7 \times 10^{-6}\,\text{Cm}^{-2}$. The electric field intensity at a point outside the sheet but close to it is **ISC SQP 2023**

(a) $1 \times 10^4\,\text{NC}^{-1}$ (b) $5 \times 10^4\,\text{NC}^{-1}$
(c) $1 \times 10^5\,\text{NC}^{-1}$ (d) $1 \times 10^6\,\text{NC}^{-1}$

2. In the figure given below, electric field intensity 'E' at a point P, at a perpendicular distance r' from an infinitely long line charge $X'X$ having linear charge density λ is given by **ISC 2022 Sem-I**

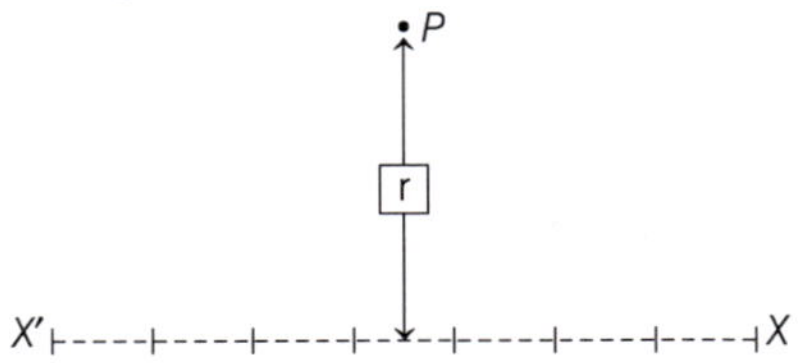

(a) $E = \left(\dfrac{1}{4\pi\varepsilon_o}\right)\dfrac{2\lambda}{r^2}$ (b) $E = \left(\dfrac{1}{4\pi\varepsilon_o}\right)\dfrac{2\lambda}{r}$

(c) $E = \left(\dfrac{1}{4\pi\varepsilon_o}\right)\dfrac{\lambda}{r^2}$ (d) $E = \left(\dfrac{1}{4\pi\varepsilon_o}\right)\dfrac{\lambda}{r}$

3. The electric flux emanating from a sphere of radius 2m is ϕ. If radius of the sphere be made four times, without changing the charge enclosed, electric flux would **ISC 2022 Sem-I**

(a) become $\phi / 4$ (b) become $\phi / 2$
(c) become 2ϕ (d) remain ϕ

4. State Gauss' theorem. **ISC 2020, 16, 07**

5. A closed surface in vacuum encloses charges $-q$ and $+3q$. The total electric flux emerging out of the surface is **ISC 2019**

(a) zero (b) $\dfrac{2q}{\varepsilon_o}$

(c) $\dfrac{3q}{\varepsilon_o}$ (d) $\dfrac{4q}{\varepsilon_o}$

6. A hollow sphere of radius R has a point charge Q at its centre. Electric flux emanating from it is ϕ. If both the charge and the radius of the sphere be doubled, electric flux emanating from the sphere will **ISC SQP 2018**

(a) remains the same
(b) becomes 2ϕ
(c) becomes 4ϕ
(d) becomes 8ϕ

7. A short electric dipole which consists of two point charges $-q$ and $+q$, is placed at the centre O and inside a large cube ($ABCDEFGH$) of length L as shown in the figure. The electric flux emanating through the cube is **ISC 2015**

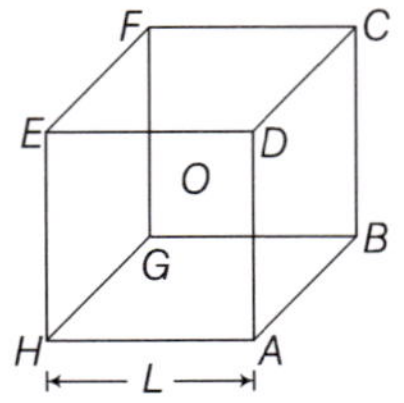

(a) $q/4\pi\varepsilon_0 L$ (b) zero
(c) $q/2\pi\varepsilon_0 L$ (d) $q/3\pi\varepsilon_0 L$

8. Intensity of electric field at a point at a perpendicular distance r from an infinite line charge, having linear charge density λ is given by **ISC 2014**

(a) $\mathbf{E}=\left(\frac{1}{4\pi\varepsilon_0}\right)\frac{\lambda}{r}$

(b) $\mathbf{E}=\left(\frac{1}{4\pi\varepsilon_0}\right)\frac{2\lambda}{r}$

(c) $\mathbf{E}=\left(\frac{1}{4\pi\varepsilon_0}\right)\frac{\lambda}{r^2}$

(d) $\mathbf{E}=\left(\frac{1}{4\pi\varepsilon_0}\right)\frac{2\lambda}{r^2}$

9. Two point charges $(+e)$ and $(-e)$ are kept inside a large metallic cube without touching its sides. Electric flux emerging out of the cube is **ISC 2011**

(a) $\frac{e}{\varepsilon_0}$ (b) $\frac{-e}{\varepsilon_0}$

(c) zero (d) $\frac{2e}{\varepsilon_0}$

2 Marks Questions

10. In case of an infinite line charge, how does intensity of electric field at a point change, if at all, when

(a) charge on it is doubled?

(b) distance of the point is halved? **ISC 2024**

11. A hollow sphere of radius R has a point charge q at its centre. Electric flux emanating from the sphere is X. How will the electric flux change, if at all, when **ISC 2024**

(a) radius of the sphere is doubled?

(b) charge q is replaced by an electric dipole?

12. Intensity of electric field at a perpendicular distance of 0.5 m from an infinitely long line charge having linear charge density (λ) is 3.6×10^3 Vm^{-1}. Find the value of λ. **ISC 2017**

3 Marks Question

13. Using Gauss' theorem, obtain and expression for intensity of electric field E at a point, which is at a distance r $(r > R)$ from the centre C of a thin spherical shell (of radius R) carrying charge Q. **ISC SQP 2018**

Case Based Question (For Complete Chapter)

14. *Read the passage and answer the following questions.*

Gauss' theorem

The Gauss' theorem in electrostatics gives a relation between the electric flux through any closed hypothetical surface (called a gaussian surface) and the charge enclosed by the surface. It states that the electric flux ϕ_E through any closed surface is equal to $1/\varepsilon_0$ times the net charge q enclosed by the surface. That is

$$\phi_E = \oint \mathbf{E}\cdot d\mathbf{A} = \frac{q}{\varepsilon_0}$$

where, ε_0 is permittivity of free space. This is the integral form of Gauss' theorem.

Gauss' theorem is very useful in computing the electric fields due to a system of charges or symmetrical continuous distribution of charge.

(*i*) What is the unit of electric flux? If the unit of electrostatic field E is volt/meter. **(1)**

(*ii*) A Gaussian surface is chosen to obtain an expression for the electric field at a point due to a given charge configuration. It is a closed surface. State one essential property of such a chosen Gaussian surface. **(1)**

(*iii*) A large hollow metallic sphere has a positive charge of 35.4 μC at its centre. Find how much electric flux emanates from the sphere. **(1)**

(*iv*) What are the applications of Gauss' theorem? **(1)**

(*v*) Is Gauss' law applicable only in the case of electric field? **(1)**

Explanations

1. (d) $E = \frac{\sigma}{2\varepsilon_0}$

$\varepsilon_0 = 8.85 \times 10^{-12}\ C^2N^{-1}m^{-2}$

σ = Surface charge density $= 17.7 \times 10^{-6}\ Cm^{-2}$

$\therefore \quad E = \frac{\sigma}{2\varepsilon_0} = \frac{17.7 \times 10^{-6}\ Cm^{-2}}{2 \times 8.85 \times 10^{-12} C^2N^{-1}m^{-2}}$

$= 1 \times 10^6\ NC^{-1}$

2. (b) $E = \left(\frac{1}{4\pi\varepsilon_0}\right)\frac{2\lambda}{r}$

3. (d) According to Gauss' law, $\phi = \frac{Q_{enclosed}}{\varepsilon_0}$

Thus, if Q remains the same, then ϕ also remains the same.

4. **Gauss' theorem** The total electric flux linked with closed surface S is equal $1/\varepsilon_0$ times the total charge inside the surface.

$$\therefore \qquad \phi = \oint \mathbf{E} \cdot d\,\mathbf{S} = \frac{q}{\varepsilon_0}$$

where, q is the total charge enclosed by the closed Gaussian (an imaginary) surface.

5. (b) Total electric flux through the closed surface,

$$\phi = \frac{1}{\varepsilon_0}(-q + 3q) = \frac{2q}{\varepsilon_0}$$

where, q is the total charge enclosed by the closed Gaussian (an imaginary) surface.

6. (b) We know that, Gauss' law, $\phi = \frac{Q_{enclose}}{\varepsilon_0}$

$\therefore \quad \phi \propto Q_{enclose}$

Thus, if $Q_{enclose}$ is double, then electric flux (ϕ) becomes 2ϕ.

7. (b) The electric flux, emanating through the cube is zero. Since, total charge inside the cube is zero.

8. (b) By applying Gauss's law, electric field due to an infinitely long line charge of line as charge density λ is,

$$E = \left(\frac{1}{4\pi\varepsilon_0}\right)\frac{2\lambda}{r}$$

where, r is the perpendicular distance from the charged wire.

9. (c) Refer to sol. 7 on page 21.

10. The intensity of electric field at a point due to infinite line charge is

$$E = \frac{\lambda}{2\pi\varepsilon_0 r}$$

where, λ is the uniform line charge density and r is the magnitude of radial distance.

(a) If charge on line charge conductor is doubled, electric field will remain same as it is independent of charge.

(b) If distance of the point is halved, the electric field will become double. i.e.,

$$E' = \frac{\lambda}{2\pi\varepsilon_0\left(\frac{r}{2}\right)} = 2\left(\frac{\lambda}{2\pi\varepsilon_0 r}\right) = 2E$$

11. (a) Using Gauss' theorem, we have

Electric flux, $\phi_E = \frac{q}{\varepsilon_0}$

So, making the radius of the sphere double does not change the electric flux emanating the sphere.

(b) Since, the total charge of an electric dipole is zero. So, if charge q is replaced by an electric dipole, then electric flux will be zero.

12. By applying Gauss' theorem, electric field due to an infinitely long straight charged wire is, $E = \frac{1}{2\pi\varepsilon_0} \cdot \frac{\lambda}{r}$

where, $\frac{1}{2\pi\varepsilon_0} = 2 \times 9 \times 10^9 mF^{-1}$.

λ = linear charge density

$r = 0.5$ m

$E = 3.6 \times 10^3 Vm^{-1}$

$$\Rightarrow \quad 3 \cdot 6 \times 10^3 = \frac{2 \times 9 \times 10^9 \times \lambda}{0 \cdot 5}$$

$$\Rightarrow \quad \lambda = \frac{3 \cdot 6 \times 10^3 \times 0 \cdot 5}{2 \times 9 \times 10^9} = 10^{-7} Cm^{-1}$$

13. Consider a shell of radius R with centre C. Let $+Q$ charge is uniformly distributed over the surface of shell, now electric field intensity at point r can be calculated by Gauss' theorem.

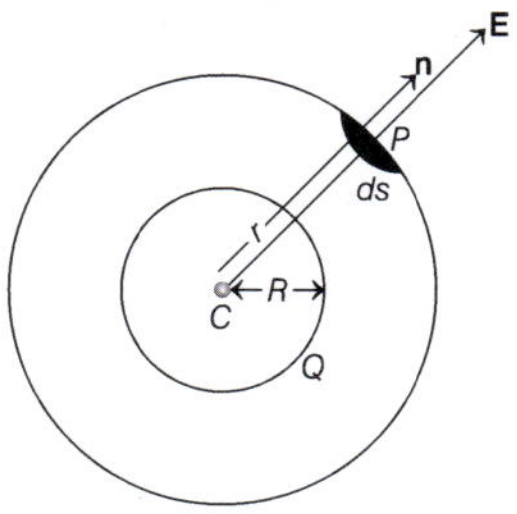

So, according to Gauss' theorem

$$\oint_S \mathbf{E}\cdot d\mathbf{s} = \oint \mathbf{E}\cdot \hat{\mathbf{n}} ds = \frac{q}{\varepsilon_0}$$

[$\because \hat{\mathbf{n}}$ = unit vector, $\mathbf{r}$ = position vector along $\mathbf{E}$]

or $$\oint E d\mathbf{s} \cos 0^\circ = \frac{q}{\varepsilon_0}$$

$$E \oint d\mathbf{s} = \frac{q}{\varepsilon_0}$$

$\Rightarrow$ $$E\,(4\,\pi r^2) = \frac{q}{\varepsilon_0} \qquad [\because \mathbf{s} = 4\,\pi r^2]$$

$$E = \frac{q}{4\pi\varepsilon_0 r^2}$$

14. (*i*) The electric flux through a plane of area A, normal to an electrostatic field $\mathbf{E}$, is given by

$$\phi_E = EA$$

$\therefore$ Unit of ϕ_E is (volt/metre) × metre^2 = volt-metre.

(*ii*) The gaussian surface should pass through the point at which electric field is required.

(*iii*) $q = 35.4 \mu C = 35.4 \times 10^{-6}$ C

As, $$\phi_E = q/\varepsilon_o = \frac{35.4 \times 10^{-6}}{8.85 \times 10^{-12}} = 4 \times 10^6 \text{ N-m}^2/\text{C}$$

(*iv*) Gauss' theorem is very useful in computing the electric fields due to a system of charges or symmetrical continuous distribution of charge.

(*v*) Gauss gave his law for the electric field only, but this rule is applicable in the case of the magnetic field also. In that case, magnetic flux lines are counted and the permittivity of the medium is replaced by the permeability of the medium. This law is also applicable for gravitational field.

CHAPTER TEST

01 Mark Questions (MCQs)

1 Two point charges $(+e)$ and $(-e)$ are kept inside a large metallic cube without touching its sides. Electric flux emerging out of the cube is

(a) e/ε_o (b) $-e/\varepsilon_o$
(c) zero (d) $2e/\varepsilon_o$

2 A rectangular frame of area 10m^2 is placed in a uniform electric field of 20NC^{-1}, with normal drawn on the surface of the frame making 60° angle with the direction of field. The electric flux through the frame is

(a) 100 Vm
(b) 200 Vm
(c) $50\sqrt{3}$Vm
(d) $100\sqrt{3}$Vm

3 A closed surface has n electric dipoles located inside it. The net electric flux emerging through the surface is

(a) ne/ε_o (b) $2e/\varepsilon_o$
(c) $2ne/\varepsilon_o$ (d) zero

4 The nucleus of hydrogen atom is a sphere of radius 10^{-15} m. The electric field at the surface of the nucleus is

(a) $14.4\times10^{4}\text{Vm}^{-1}$
(b) $14.4\times10^{10}\text{Vm}^{-1}$
(c) $14.4\times10^{19}\text{Vm}^{-1}$
(d) $14.4\times10^{20}\text{Vm}^{-1}$

01 Mark Questions (VSA)

5 A dipole of dipole moment $\mathbf{p}$ is present in a uniform electric field $\mathbf{E}$. Write the value of the angle between p and E for which the torque, experienced by the dipole is minimum.

6 Two charges of magnitudes $-2Q$ and $+Q$ are located at points $(a, 0)$ and $(4a, 0)$, respectively. What is the electric flux due to these charges through a sphere of radius $3a$ with its centre at the origin?

02 Marks Questions

7 A dipole is present in an electrostatic field of magnitude 10^6 N/C. If the work done in rotating it, from its position of stable equilibrium to its position of unstable equilibrium, 2×10^{-23} J, find the magnitude of the dipole moment of this dipole.

8 Two charges $+Q$ and $-Q$ are kept at $(-x_2, 0)$ and $(x_1, 0)$ respectively, in the XY-plane. Find the magnitude and direction of the net electric field at the origin (0, 0).

03 Marks Question

9 Define the term electric dipole moment. Is it a scalar or vector? Deduce an expression for the electric field at a point on the equatorial plane of an electric dipole of length $2a$.

05 Marks Question

10 (i) Define electric flux. Write its SI unit.

(ii) A small metal sphere carrying charge $+Q$ is located at the centre of a spherical cavity inside a large uncharged metallic spherical shell as shown in the figure. Use Gauss' law to find the expressions for the electric field at points P_1 and P_2.

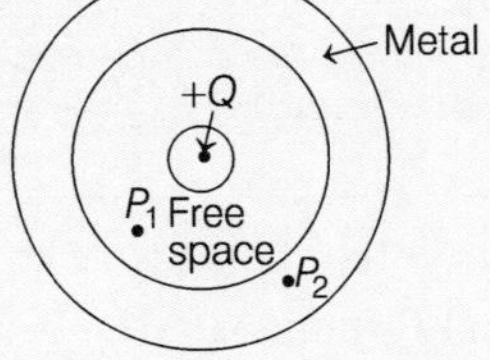

(iii) Draw the pattern of electric field lines in this arrangement. Assume that the distance of the point from the centre in each condition is r.

Answers

1. (c) **2.** (a) **3.** (d) **4.** (d)

5. 0° **6.** $\dfrac{-2Q}{\varepsilon_0}$ **7.** 2×10^{-29} C-m

03

Electric Potential and Potential Energy

TREND ANALYSIS 4 YEARS

Electric Potential and Potential Energy

Average No. of Questions Across all Sets

Types of Questions	2024	2023	2020	2019
1 Mark	1	2	1	1
2 Marks	–	1	–	–
3 Marks	–	–	–	1
5 Marks	–	–	–	–

Electrostatic Potential

The amount of work done in bringing the unit positive test charge from infinite to that point, against the electrostatic force without acceleration.

$$\text{Electrostatic potential } (V) = \frac{\text{Work done } (W)}{\text{Charge } (q)}$$

It is a scalar quantity. Its SI unit is volt (V) and $1\text{ V} = 1\text{ J/C}$ also its dimensional formula is $[ML^2T^{-3}A^{-1}]$.

NOTE Electrostatic potential is state function as electrostatic forces are conservative forces.

Electrostatic Potential Difference

The potential difference between two points in an electric field is defined as the amount of work done in moving a unit positive test charge from one point to the other.

$$V_B - V_A = \frac{W_{AB}}{q_0}$$

where, W_{AB} is work done in taking charge q_0 from A to B against electrostatic forces.

Also, the line integral of electric field from initial position A to final position B along any path is termed as potential difference between two points in the region of electric field.

$$V_B - V_A = -\int_A^B \mathbf{E} \cdot d\mathbf{l}$$

NOTE It is independent of the path, hence potential difference is same for any path between two points.

Electrostatic potential due to a point charge q

At any point P lying at a distance r from it, is given by

$$V = \frac{1}{4\pi\varepsilon_0} \cdot \frac{q}{r}$$

The potential at a point due to a positive charge is positive, while due to negative charge is negative.

Equation of electrostatic potential shows that at equal distance from a point charge q, value of V is same and hence it is spherically symmetric.

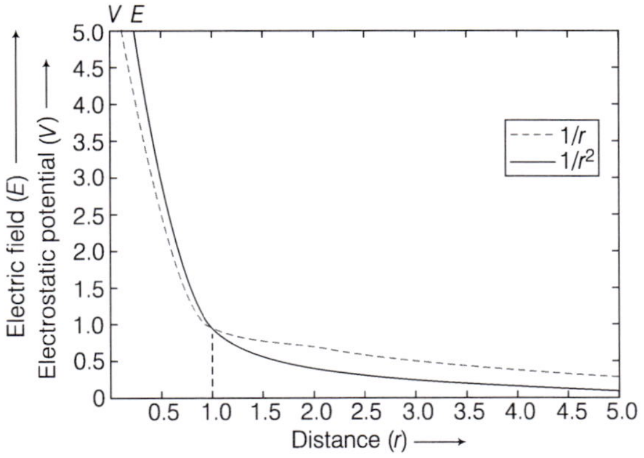

Variation of electrostatic potential V and electric field E with distance r

Electrostatic potential due to system of charges

Electrostatic potential at any point whose position vector is r due to a system or collections of point charges $q_1, q_2, \ldots, q_n$ whose position vectors are $\mathbf{r}_1, \mathbf{r}_2, \ldots, \mathbf{r}_n$ respectively, is given by

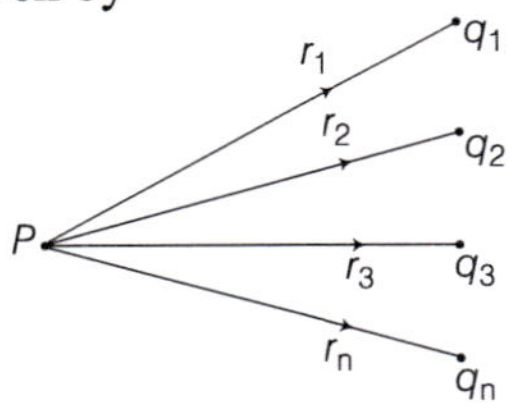

$$V = \frac{1}{4\pi\varepsilon_0} \sum_{i=1}^{n} \frac{q_i}{|\mathbf{r} - \mathbf{r}_i|}$$

where, $|\mathbf{r} - \mathbf{r}_i|$ is distance between location of charge and point of potential calculations.

Electrostatic potential due to an electric dipole At any point P whose position vector is $\mathbf{r}$ w.r.t. mid-point of the dipole is given where, θ is the angle between $\mathbf{r}$ and $\mathbf{p}$.

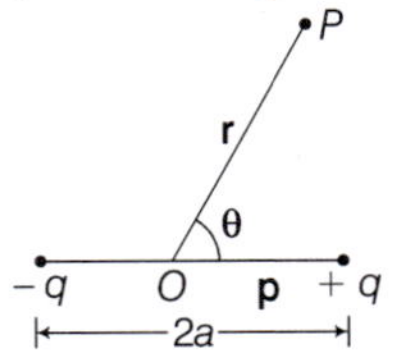

$$V = \frac{1}{4\pi\varepsilon_0} \cdot \frac{p\cos\theta}{r^2} = \frac{1}{4\pi\varepsilon_0} \frac{\mathbf{p} \cdot \mathbf{r}}{r^3}$$

$\therefore$ Electrostatic potential at point P due to a short dipole $(r >> 2a)$ is given by

$$V = \frac{\mathbf{p} \cdot \hat{\mathbf{r}}}{4\pi\varepsilon_0 r^2}$$

The **electrostatic potential at the axial point** due to an electric dipole is maximum, since $\theta = 0°$.

$$\therefore V_{\max} = \frac{1}{4\pi\varepsilon_0} \frac{p\cos 0°}{r^2} = \frac{1}{4\pi\varepsilon_0} \cdot \frac{p}{r^2}$$

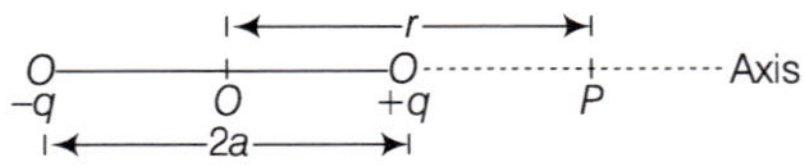

The **electrostatic potential on the perpendicular bisector or in the equatorial plane** due to an electric dipole is zero. Since, $\theta = 90°, V = 0$.

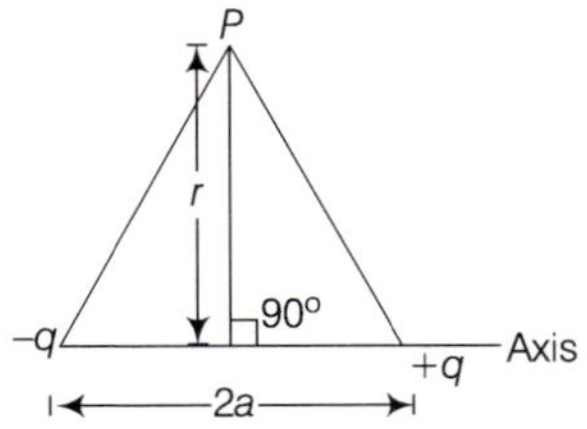

Equipotential Surface

A surface which have same electrostatic potential at every point on it, is known as equipotential surface. A perpendicular drawn on electric field lines gives the equipotential point.

Relationship between Electric Field and Electric Potential

The relation between electric field and electric potential is given as

$$dV = -\mathbf{E} \cdot d\mathbf{r} \text{ or } E = -\frac{dV}{dr}$$

If electric field is present in three dimensions, then

$$E_x = -\frac{\partial V}{\partial x}, E_y = -\frac{\partial V}{\partial y}, E_z = -\frac{\partial V}{\partial z}$$

$$[\because d\mathbf{r} = dx\,\hat{\mathbf{i}} + dy\,\hat{\mathbf{j}} + dz\,\hat{\mathbf{k}}]$$

NOTE (*i*) Electric field is in the direction in which the potential decreases steepest.

(*ii*) Its magnitude is given by the change in the magnitude of potential per unit displacement normal to the equipotential surface at the point.

Electrostatic Potential Energy

The work done against electrostatic force gets stored as potential energy. This is called electrostatic potential energy U.

$$\Delta U = U_B - U_A = W_{AB} = q_0(V_A - V_B)$$

In this case, work is done against electrostatic field while going from A to B.

- Electrostatic potential energy of a system of two point charges, q_1 and q_2 is given by, putting the values of charge with their signs

$$U = \frac{1}{4\pi\varepsilon_0} \cdot \frac{q_1 q_2}{r_{12}}$$

- Electrostatic potential energy of a system of n point charges,

$$U = \frac{1}{2}\left[\frac{1}{4\pi\varepsilon_0} \sum_{j=1}^{n} \sum_{i=1}^{n} \frac{q_j q_i}{r_{ji}}\right]$$

where, $j \neq i$ and $ij = ji$

Potential Energy in an External Field

(*i*) **Potential Energy of a Single Charge in External Field**

Potential energy of a single charge q at a point with position vector $\mathbf{r}$ in an external field is as follows

$$= q \cdot V(\mathbf{r})$$

where, $V(\mathbf{r})$ potential at that point due to the external electric field E

(*ii*) **Potential Energy of a System of Two Charges in an External Field**

$$U = q_1 . V(\mathbf{r}_1) + q_2 . V(\mathbf{r}_2) + \frac{q_1 q_2}{4\pi\varepsilon_0 r_{12}}$$

where, q_1, q_2 are two point charges at position vectors $\mathbf{r}_1$ and $\mathbf{r}_2$ respectively to origin.

$V(\mathbf{r}_1)$ = potential at $\mathbf{r}_1$ due to the external field

$V(\mathbf{r}_2)$ = potential at $\mathbf{r}_2$ due to the external field

(*iii*) **Potential energy of a system of three charges in an external field**

If three charges q_1, q_2 and q_3 be placed at three corners of a triangle, then

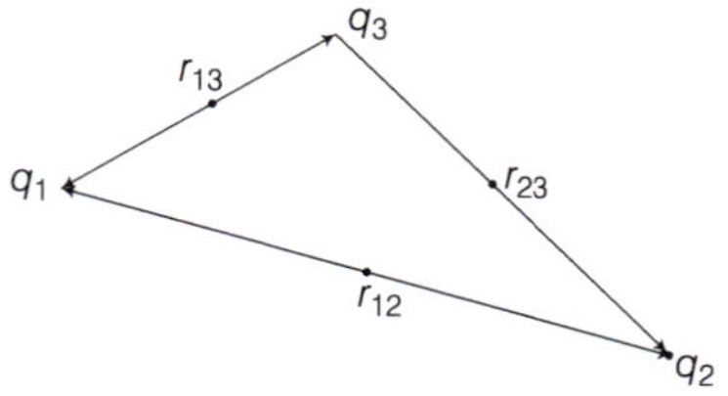

∴ The electric potential energy for the system q_1, q_2 and q_3 is

$$U = U_{12} + U_{13} + U_{23}$$

$$U = \frac{1}{4\pi\varepsilon_0}\left(\frac{q_1 q_2}{r_{12}} + \frac{q_1 q_3}{r_{13}} + \frac{q_2 q_3}{r_{23}}\right)$$

The values of q_1, q_2 and q_3 must be put with proper sign.

Potential Energy of Electric Dipole in a Uniform Electric Field

Potential energy of electric dipole when it rotates from

$$\theta_1 = 90° \text{ to } \theta_2 = \theta,$$
$$U = pE\,(\cos 90° - \cos\theta)$$
$$= -\,pE\cos\theta = -\,\mathbf{p}\cdot\mathbf{E}$$

where, $\mathbf{p}$ = dipole moment and $\mathbf{E}$ = external electric field.

PYQs Previous Years Questions

1 Mark Questions

1. In an electric dipole, what is the locus of a point having zero potential? **ISC 2024**

2. What is meant by an equipotential surface? **ISC 2023, 19**

3. Three point charges of 50 nC each are kept at the vertices of an equilateral triangle having each side = 3 m. Calculate electrostatic potential energy of the system. **ISC SQP 2023**

4. Three equal charges of 5.0μC each, are placed at the three vertices of an equilateral triangle of side 5.0cm each. The electrostatic potential energy of the system of charges is **ISC 2022 Sem-I**

(a) 13.5 J (b) 17.5 J
(c) 27 J (d) 15 J

5. Three charges $q_1 = 3\mu C$, $q_2 = 4\mu C$ and $q_3 = -7\mu C$ are placed on the circumference of a circle of radius 1.0m as shown in the figure below.

What is the value of charge q_4 placed on the same circle, if the potential at the centre, $V_0 = 0$? **ISC 2022 Sem-I**

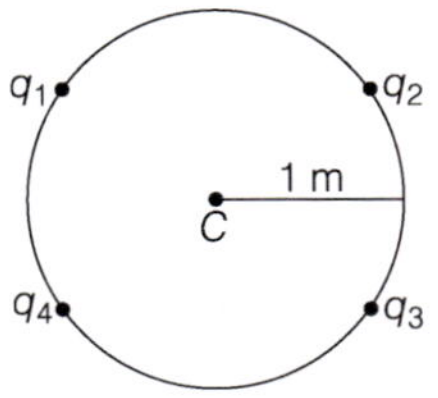

(a) $-4\mu C$ (b) $-3\mu C$
(c) $7\mu C$ (d) 0

6. An electric dipole of moment **p** is placed in a uniform electric field **E**. It has maximum (negative) potential energy when the angle between **p** and **E** is **ISC 2022 Sem-I**

(a) $\frac{\pi}{2}$ (b) zero
(c) π (d) $\frac{3\pi}{2}$

7. Electric potential at a point on the axial line of a short electric dipole is **ISC 2022 Sem-I**
(a) directly proportional to distance
(b) inversely proportional to distance
(c) inversely proportional to square of the distance
(d) directly proportional to square of the distance

8. Three point charges Q, Q and q are kept at the vertices A, B and C respectively of an equilateral triangle ABC having each side equal to a. Electrostatic potential energy of the system is zero. This is possible, if q is equal to **ISC 2022 Sem-I**
(a) Q (b) $Q/2$
(c) $-Q/2$ (d) $-Q/4$

9. Consider a point P on the perpendicular bisector dipole. At point P, **ISC 2022 Sem-I**
(a) electric field is zero
(b) electric potential is zero
(c) electric field is perpendicular to the axis of the dipole
(d) Potential gradient is zero

10. A point charge q is kept at each of the vertices of an equilateral triangle having each side a. Total electrostatic potential energy of the system is **ISC 2020**

(a) $\left(\frac{1}{4\pi\varepsilon_0}\right)\frac{3q^2}{a^2}$ (b) $\left(\frac{1}{4\pi\varepsilon_0}\right)\frac{3q}{a}$
(c) $\left(\frac{1}{4\pi\varepsilon_0}\right)\frac{3q^2}{a}$ (d) $\left(\frac{1}{4\pi\varepsilon_0}\right)\frac{3q}{a^2}$

11. The electrostatic potential energy of two point charges, 1 μC each, placed 1 metre apart in air is **ISC 2017**
(a) 9×10^3 J
(b) 9×10^9 J
(c) 9×10^{-3} J
(d) 9×10^{-3} eV

12. In the given figure below, a charge Q is fixed. Another charge q is moved along a circular arc MN of radius r around it, from the point M to the point N such that the length of the arc $MN = l$. The work done in this process is **ISC 2016**

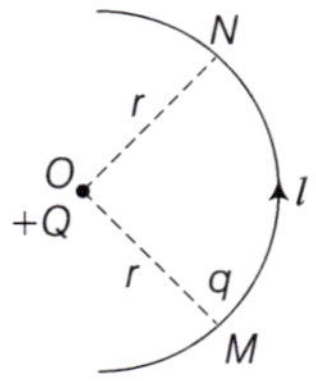

(a) zero (b) $\frac{1}{4\pi\varepsilon_0}\cdot\frac{Qq}{r^2}l$
(c) $\frac{Qq}{2\varepsilon_0 r^2}l$ (d) $\frac{Qq}{2\pi\varepsilon_0 r^2}$

13. In an electric dipole, at which point is the electric potential zero? **ISC 2016**

14. Two point charges of 10 C each, are kept at a distance of 3 m in vacuum. Calculate their electrostatic potential energy. **ISC 2015**

15. How much work is done in taking an electron around a nucleus in a circular path? **ISC 2011**

16. How much kinetic energy is gained by an electron, initially at rest, when it moves through a potential difference of 1000 V? Give your answer in joule. **ISC 2008**

2 Marks Questions

17. Calculate electric potential at a point P which is at a distance of 9 cm from a point charge of $50\mu C$. **ISC 2023**

18. The equipotential surfaces of a uniform electric field E are planes parallel to the YZ-plane.
(*i*) What is the direction of the electric field E?
(a) The electric field is along X-axis
(b) The electric field is along Y-axis
(c) The electric field is along Z-axis
(d) The electric field is along negative Y-axis.
(*ii*) An electric dipole with its charges $-q$ and $+q$, located at the points $(0, -l, 0)$ and $(0, +l, 0)$ lies in this field. Magnitude of the torque acting on the dipole is **ISC 2022 Sem-I**
(a) qlE (b) $2qlE$
(c) $4qlE$ (d) $8qlE$

19. An electron revolves around the nucleus of hydrogen atom in a circular orbit of radius 5×10^{-11} m. Calculate

(*i*) intensity of electric field of the nucleus at the position of the electron.

(*ii*) electrostatic potential energy of the hydrogen nucleus and electron system. **ISC 2010**

3 Marks Questions

20. Obtain an expression for electric potential V at a point in an end-on-position, i.e. axial position of an electric dipole. **ISC 2019**

21. Obtain an expression for electric potential 'V' due to a point charge q at a distance r. **ISC SQP 2018, 08**

Or Show that electric potential at a point P, at a distance r from a fixed point charge Q is given by **ISC 2017**

$$V=\left(\frac{1}{4\pi\varepsilon_0}\right)\frac{Q}{r}$$

22. Three equal charges of 5.0 μC each are placed at the three vertices of an equilateral triangle of side 5.0 cm each. Calculate the electrostatic potential energy of the system of charges. **ISC 2007**

4/5 Marks Question

23. Three point charges $Q_1=25\,\mu\text{C}$, $Q_2=50\,\mu\text{C}$ and $Q_3=100\,\mu\text{C}$ are kept at the corners A, B and C respectively of an equilateral ΔABC having each side equal to 7.5 m. Calculate the total electrostatic potential energy of the system. **ISC 2012**

> **KEY idea**
>
> To determine the total electrostatic potential energy, calculate the electrostatic potential energy at points A, B and C with the help of $\left(\frac{1}{4\pi\varepsilon_0}\frac{q_1q_2}{r}\right)$ and add all the indivisual electrostatic potential energy.

Case Based Question
(For Complete Chapter)

24. *Read the passage and answer the following questions.*

In definition of potential, the reference point (of zero potential) is taken at infinity (outside the field). If we take two points A and B in the electric field (figure) then potentials at A and B will be defined as above.

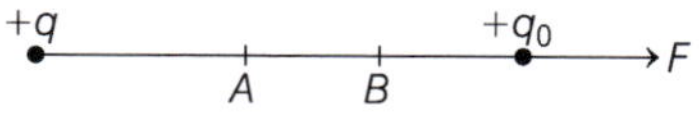

The difference in there potentials is termed as potential difference between the points A and B.

Independently, it is defined as follows

"The work done by an external agent in carrying a unit positive test charge from one point to the other point in an electric field is called the potential difference between those points."

If W be the work done in carrying the test charge q_0 from B to A, then the potential difference between A and B is given by

$$V_A-V_B=W/q_0$$

(*i*) How much work is done in taking an electron around a nucleus in a circular path? **(1)**

(*ii*) We assume the potential of earth zero. Can it be assumed +100 V? What will be the effect of it on the measurement of electric potential at a point? On the potential difference between two points? **(1)**

(*iii*) A charge of 3 C moving in a uniform electric field experiences a force of 3000N. The potential difference between two points situated in the field at a distance 1 cm from each other will be .... **(1)**

(*iv*) 2 J work is done in taking a charge of 20 C from one point to the other at a distance of 0.2 mV. What is the potential difference between the points? **(1)**

(*v*) What do you mean by 1 eV? **(1)**

Explanations

1. The locus of the point of zero potential of an electrical dipole is straight line drawn at the middle of the electric dipole.

2. Refer to text on page no. 25 (Equipotential Surface).

3.

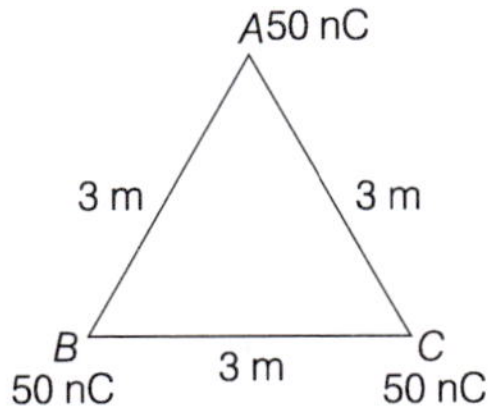

$$U = \frac{1}{4\pi\varepsilon_0}\left(\frac{q_1q_2}{r} + \frac{q_2q_3}{r} + \frac{q_3q_1}{r}\right)$$

$$= 9\times10^9 \times \left(\begin{array}{l} \dfrac{50\times10^{-9}\times50\times10^{-9}}{3} \\ +\dfrac{50\times10^{-9}\times50\times10^{9}}{3} \\ +\dfrac{50\times10^{-9}\times50\times10^{-9}}{3} \end{array}\right)$$

$$= 9\times10^9\times2.5\times10^{-15}$$

$$U = 2.25\times10^{-5}\text{ J}$$

4. (a)

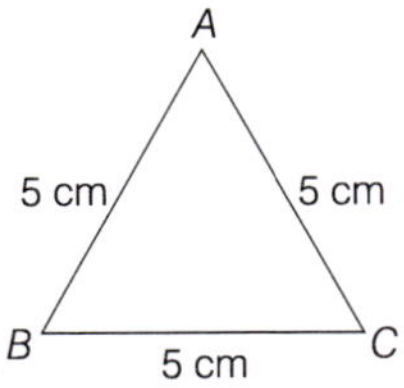

$$U = \frac{kq^2}{5\times10^{-2}} + \frac{kq^2}{5\times10^{-2}} + \frac{kq^2}{5\times10^{-2}}$$

$$= \frac{k}{5\times10^{-2}}[(5)^2 + (5.0)^2 + (5.0)^2]\times10^{-12}$$

$$= \frac{3\times9\times10^9\times25\times10^{-12}}{5\times10^{-2}} = 13.5\text{ J}$$

5. (d) According to superposition principle,

Total potential at the centre O will be given by

$$V = V_1 + V_2 + V_3 + V_4$$

$$V = (kq_1/1) + (kq_2/1) + (kq_3/1) + (kq_4/1)$$

$$V = k(q_1 + q_2 + q_3 + q_4)/1$$

$\because \quad V = 0 \quad$ (given)

$$0 = k(q_1 + q_2 + q_3 + q_4)/1$$

$$(0\times1)/k = q_1 + q_2 + q_3 + q_4$$

or $\quad 0 = 3\mu C + 4\mu C - 7\mu C + q_4$

or $\quad 0 = 7\mu C - 7\mu C + q_4$

or $\quad 0 = 0 + q_4$

$\therefore \quad q_4 = 0$

6. (c) When the angle between the dipole moment and electric field is 180°, then the potential energy of the electric dipole is maximum.

7. (c) Electric potential at a point on axial line by a short dipole is given by

$$V = \frac{\mathbf{p}\cdot\hat{\mathbf{r}}}{4\pi\varepsilon_0 r^2} \Rightarrow V \propto \frac{1}{r^2}$$

8. (c) Electrostatic potential energy due to a system of three charges is given by

$$U = k\left(\frac{q_1q_2}{r_{12}} + \frac{q_1q_3}{r_{13}} + \frac{q_2q_3}{r_{23}}\right)$$

$$\Rightarrow \quad 0 = k\left(\frac{Q^2}{a} + \frac{Qq}{a} + \frac{Qq}{a}\right)$$

$$\Rightarrow \quad -\frac{Q^2}{a} = \frac{2Qq}{a} \Rightarrow q = -\frac{Q}{2}$$

9. (b) The electric potential on the perpendicular bisector or in the equatorial plane due to an electric dipole is zero as $\theta = 90°$.

10. (c) Potential energy,

$$U = \frac{1}{4\pi\varepsilon_0}\left[\frac{q^2}{a} + \frac{q^2}{a} + \frac{q^2}{a}\right]$$

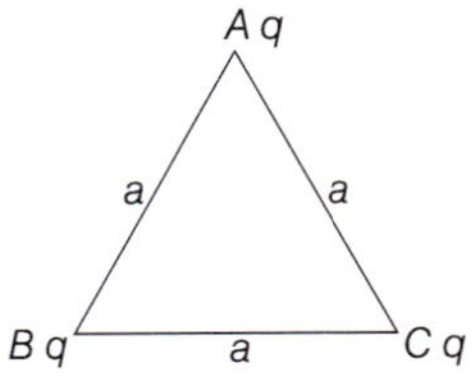

$$= \frac{1}{4\pi\varepsilon_0}\cdot\frac{3q^2}{a}$$

11. (c) The electric potential energy of two point charges 1 μC each, placed 1 metre apart in air is

$$U = \frac{1}{4\pi\varepsilon_0}\cdot\frac{q_1q_2}{r_{12}}$$

$$= 9\times10^9 \times \frac{10^{-6}\times10^{-6}}{1}$$

$$= 9\times10^9 \times 10^{-12}$$

$$= 9\times10^{-3}\text{ J}$$

12. (a)

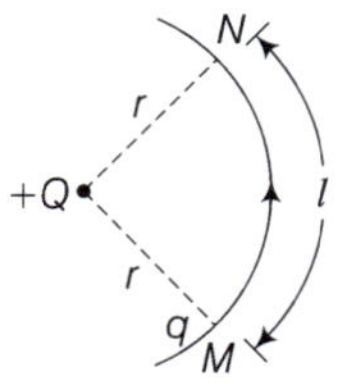

As the potential at points M and N are same and equals to $\frac{Kq}{r}$.

So, work done $= (\Delta V)q = 0$

(∵ Surface MN is equipotential so $\Delta V = 0$)

13. Electric potential at any point on the equitorial plane of dipole is zero.

14. Given, $q_1 = 10\text{ C}$, $q_2 = 10\text{ C}$, distance between charges $a = 3\text{ m}$

Electrostatic potential energy is given by

$$U = \frac{1}{4\pi\varepsilon_0}\times\frac{q_1q_2}{a} \quad \ldots\text{(i)}$$

Here, $\frac{1}{4\pi\varepsilon_0} = 9\times10^9$

Substituting the all values in Eq. (i), we get

$$U = 9\times10^9\times\frac{10\times10}{3}$$

$$\Rightarrow \quad U = 3\times10^{11}\text{ J}$$

15. The circular path around the nucleus will act as equipotential surface. Hence, work done in moving the electron around the nucleus

$$= e|\Delta V| = e(0) = 0$$

16. From conservation of mechanical energy

Change in PE = Gain in KE

$$\Delta U = \Delta K \Rightarrow eV = \frac{1}{2}mv^2$$

where, V is potential difference and e is electronic charge, m is the mass and v is the speed of the electron

$$\therefore \quad \Delta K = eV$$

$$= 1.6\times10^{-19}\times1000$$

$$= 1.6\times10^{-16}\text{ J}$$

17. Given, $r = 9\times10^{-2}$ m

$$Q = 50\times10^{-6}\text{C}$$

$$V = \frac{kQ}{r} \qquad [\because k = 9\times10^9]$$

$$V = \frac{9\times10^9\times50\times10^{-6}}{9\times10^{-2}} = 5\times10^6\text{ V}$$

18. (*i*) (a)

(*ii*) (b) Torque $(\tau) = pE\sin\theta$

$$= q\cdot 2lE \qquad (\because \theta = 90^\circ,\ p = q\cdot 2l)$$

$$= 2qlE$$

19. Given, radius of the orbit, $r = 5\times10^{-11}$ m

Charge $= +e = 1.6\times10^{-19}$ C

(*i*) Intensity of electric field,

$$E = \frac{1}{4\pi\varepsilon_0}\frac{q}{r^2}$$

$$= 9\times10^9\times\frac{1.6\times10^{-19}}{(5\times10^{-11})^2}$$

$$= 5.76\times10^{11}\text{ NC}^{-1}$$

(*ii*) Electrostatic potential energy of the system,

$$U = \frac{1}{4\pi\varepsilon_0}\frac{q_1q_2}{r}$$

$$= \frac{9\times10^9\times1.6\times10^{-19}\times(-1.6\times10^{-19})}{5\times10^{-11}}$$

$$= -4.608\times10^{-18}\text{ J}$$

20. Let the electric dipole AB is placed in a medium of dielectric constant K. The electric dipole has charges $+q$ and $-q$ separated by the distance d.

We have to determine the electric potential at point P, situated at distance r from the centre of the electric dipole.

The distance of point P from charge $+q$ is $\left(r-\frac{d}{2}\right)$ and from charge $-q$ is $\left(r+\frac{d}{2}\right)$, then potential due to $+q$ charge at point P,

$$V_1 = \frac{1}{4\pi\varepsilon_0 K}\left[\frac{q}{r-(d/2)}\right]$$

Potential due to $-q$ charge at point P,

$$V_2 = \frac{1}{4\pi\varepsilon_0 K}\left[\frac{-q}{r+(d/2)}\right]$$

$\therefore$ Resultant potential at point P, $V = V_1 + V_2$

$$V = \frac{q}{4\pi\varepsilon_0 K}\left[\frac{1}{r-(d/2)} - \frac{1}{r+(d/2)}\right]$$

$$= \frac{1}{4\pi\varepsilon_0 K}\left[\frac{q\times d}{r^2-(d/2)^2}\right]$$

If the dipole moment is p, then $p = q\times d$

$$V = \frac{1}{4\pi\varepsilon_0 K}\left[\frac{p}{r^2-(d/2)^2}\right]$$

If $\frac{d}{2} << r$, then neglecting $\left(\frac{d}{2}\right)^2$ in comparison to r^2,

$$V = \frac{1}{4\pi\varepsilon_0 K}\cdot\left(\frac{p}{r^2}\right)$$

If the electric dipole is situated in air or vacuum, then $K = 1$,

$$\therefore \quad V = \frac{1}{4\pi\varepsilon_0}\left[\frac{p}{r^2}\right]$$

21. We have to apply the relation between electric field (**E**) and potential difference dV as $dV = -\mathbf{E}\cdot d\mathbf{r}$

Let P be the point at a distance r from the origin O at which the electric field E due to charge $+q$ is required.

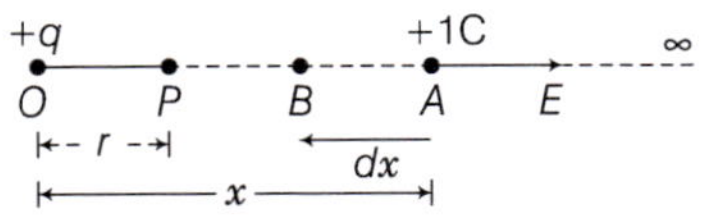

The electric potential at a point P is the amount of work done in carrying a unit positive charge from ∞ to P.

As work done is independent of the path, we choose a convenient path along the radial direction from infinity to the point P without acceleration.

Let A be an intermediate point on this path, where $OA = x$.

The electrostatic force on unit positive charge at A is $F = \frac{1}{4\pi\varepsilon_0}\frac{q}{x^2}$, along OA

Small work done in moving the charge through a distance dx from A to B

$$dW = \mathbf{F}\cdot d\mathbf{x} = F\,dx\cos 180° = -F dx$$

$[\because \cos 180° = -1]$

$$dW = -F dx$$

Total work done in moving unit positive charge from ∞ to the point P is

$$W = \int_\infty^r -F dx = \int_\infty^r -\frac{1}{4\pi\varepsilon_0}\frac{q}{x^2}dx$$

$$= -\frac{q}{4\pi\varepsilon_0}\int_\infty^r x^{-2}\,dx$$

$$= -\frac{q}{4\pi\varepsilon_0}\left[\frac{-1}{x}\right]_\infty^r$$

$$= \frac{q}{4\pi\varepsilon_0}\left[\frac{1}{r} - \frac{1}{\infty}\right] \qquad \left[\because \int x^{-2}dx = -\frac{1}{x}\right]$$

$$W = \frac{q}{4\pi\varepsilon_0 r}$$

From the definition of electric potential, this work is equal to the potential at point P.

$$V = \frac{q}{4\pi\varepsilon_0 r}$$

22. Potential energy (PE) of a system of two charges q_1 and q_2 separated by r is

$$U = \frac{1}{4\pi\varepsilon_0}\cdot\frac{q_1 q_2}{r}$$

For a system of three charges q_1, q_2 and q_3 the total potential energy U is

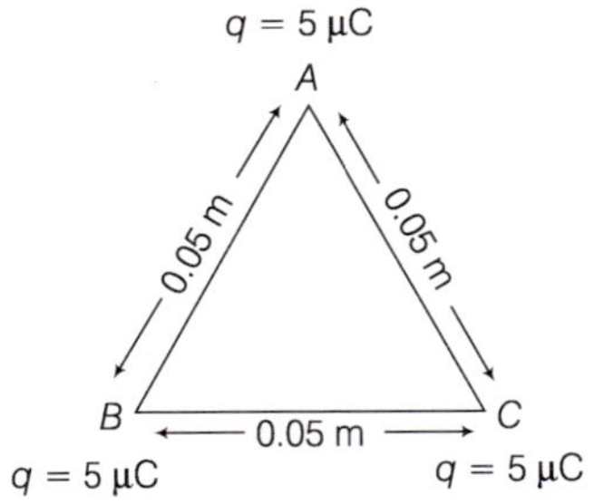

$$U = U_{AB} + U_{BC} + U_{CA}$$

$$= \frac{1}{4\pi\varepsilon_0}\left(\frac{q_1q_2}{r_{12}} + \frac{q_2q_3}{r_{23}} + \frac{q_1q_3}{r_{13}}\right)$$

$$= \frac{1}{4\pi\varepsilon_0}.3\frac{q^2}{r}$$

$[\because r_{12} = r_{23} = r_{13} = r$ and $q_1 = q_2 = q_3 = q]$

$$= 9\times10^9 \times \frac{5\times10^{-6}\times5\times10^{-6}}{5\times10^{-2}}\times 3$$

$$= 135\text{ J}$$

Common Mistake The values of charges q_1, q_2 and q_3 must be put with proper sign and units.

23. We have to find electrostatic potential energy corresponding to each pair of charge. Consider the diagram, total electrostatic potential energy of the system,

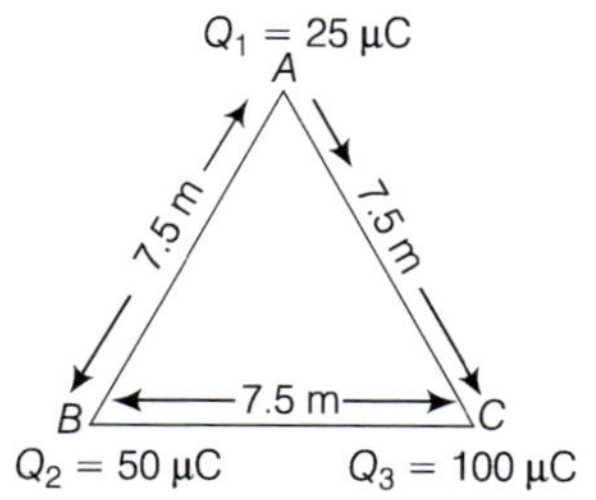

$$U = U_{AB} + U_{BC} + U_{CA}$$
$$= \frac{1}{4\pi\varepsilon_0}\frac{Q_1Q_2}{AB} + \frac{1}{4\pi\varepsilon_0}\frac{Q_2Q_3}{BC} + \frac{1}{4\pi\varepsilon_0}\frac{Q_3Q_1}{CA}$$
$$= \frac{1}{4\pi\varepsilon_0}\left(\frac{Q_1Q_2}{AB} + \frac{Q_2Q_3}{BC} + \frac{Q_3Q_1}{CA}\right)$$
$$= 9 \times 10^9\left(\frac{25 \times 50 \times 10^{-12}}{7.5} + \frac{50 \times 100 \times 10^{-12}}{7.5} + \frac{100 \times 25 \times 10^{-12}}{7.5}\right)$$
$$= \frac{9 \times 10^9 \times 10^{-12}}{7.5} \times 25 \times 50[1 + 4 + 2]$$
$$= 10.5\ \text{J}$$

24. (i) Orbit of an electron around the nucleus is equipotential, i.e. potential difference between any two points of this orbit is zero and further since work done,

$$W = q \times \Delta V$$
$$(\Delta V = 0)$$
$$W = 0$$

(ii) Yes, it can be assumed : the measurement of potential at every point will be increased by 100 V, no effect on potential difference.

(iii) Given, $F = 3000\text{N}, q = 3\text{C}$

$$E = \frac{F}{q} = \frac{3000}{3} = 1000\ \text{V/m}$$

Potential difference $(V) = Ed$

$$= 1000\ \text{V/m} \times 0.01\ \text{m} = 10\text{V}$$

(iv) $V_A - V_B = \dfrac{W}{q_0}$

$$W = 2\text{J}$$
$$q_0 = 20\text{C}$$
$$V_A - V_B = \frac{2}{20} = 0.1 = 1 \times 10^{-1}\ \text{V}.$$

(v) 1 electron-volt is the work done in taking one electron from one point to the other, when the potential difference between these points is 1 V.

$$1\text{eV} = 1.6 \times 10^{-19}\ \text{J}.$$

CHAPTER TEST

01 Mark Questions (MCQs)

1 The work done in taking a charge q once round a circle of radius r and having a charge Q at the centre is

(a) $qQ/4\pi\varepsilon_0 r$ (b) $qQ/4\pi\varepsilon_0 r^2$

(c) $qQ/4\pi\varepsilon_0(2\pi r)$ (d) zero

2 2J work is done in taking a charge of 20 C from one point to the other at a distance of 0.2 m. The potential difference between the points is

(a) 2×10^{-2} V (b) 4×10^{-1} V

(c) 8V (d) 1×10^{-1} V

3 The electric potential energy of a system of two positive point charges of $1\,\mu$ C each placed in air 1 m apart is

(a) 9×10^{3} J (b) 9×10^{9} J

(c) 9×10^{-3} J (d) 9×10^{-3} eV

4 A charge of 3 C moving in a uniform electric field experiences a force of 3000N. The potential difference between two points situated in the field at a distance 1 cm from each other will be

(a) 10 V (b) 90 V (c) 1000 V (d) 9000 V

01 Mark Questions (VSA)

5 Two charges $2\,\mu$ C and $-2\,\mu$ C are placed at points A and B, 5 cm apart. Depict an equipotential surface of the system.

6 Define the term potential energy for charge q at a distance r in an external field.

02 Marks Questions

7 Two point charges $4Q$ and Q are separated by a distance 1 m in air. At what point on the line joining the charges is the electric field intensity zero? Also, calculate the electrostatic potential energy of the system of charges. (Taking the value of charge, $Q=2\times10^{-7}$ C)

8 A dipole with its charge, $-q$ and $+q$, located at the points $(0, -b, 0)$ and $(0, +b, 0)$ is present in a uniform electric field **E**. The equipotential surfaces of the field are planes parallel to the YZ-plane.

(i) What is the direction of the electric field **E**?

(ii) How much torque would the dipole experience in this field?

03 Marks Question

9 The electric field due to a point charge at a distance r depends according to inverse square law $\left(\propto \frac{1}{r^2}\right)$.

State how the following quantities depend upon r.

(i) Potential due to a point charge.

(ii) Potential at a distance r from the centre of a charged metallic sphere of a radius R $(r < R)$.

05 Marks Question

10 An electric dipole of dipole moment **p** is oriented along X-axis as shown in the figure. Origin O is the mid-point of the dipole.

(i) Prove that no work is required to move a charged particle along Y-axis.

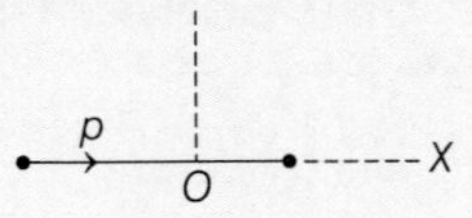

(ii) Now a uniform external electric field is switched ON along X-axis. Prove that potential energy of the dipole is minimum for this orientation.

Answers

1. (d) **2.** (d) **3.** (c) **4.** (a)

7. $x=\frac{1}{3}$ m from $+Q$ charge on the line joining the two charges, $U = 1.44$ mJ.

8. (i) Along X-axis (ii) $\tau = 2qbE$

04

Capacitance

TREND ANALYSIS 4 YEARS

Capacitance

Types of Questions	2024	2023	2020	2019
	Average No. of Questions Across all Sets			
1 Mark	–	–	–	–
2 Marks	–	2	–	–
3 Marks	1	–	1	1
5 Marks	–	–	–	–

Conductors and Insulators

A conductor contains a large number of free charge carriers to conduct electricity, while insulator does not contain any free charge carriers to conduct electricity. Examples of conductors are metals and the earth. Plastic, rubber, mica, wood, etc. are the examples of insulator.

Free Charges and Bound Charges Inside a Conductor

(*i*) In a metal, the outer (valence) electrons are free to move.

Some important results regarding electrostatic of conductors are

(*i*) Inside a conductor, electric field is zero.

(*ii*) The interior of a conductor can have no excess charge in static situation.

(*iii*) Electric field just outside a charged conductor is perpendicular to the surface of the conductor at every point.

Dielectrics and Electric Polarisation

When a conductor is placed in an external electric field, the free charge carriers adjust themself in such a way that the electric field due to induced charges and external field cancel each other and the net field inside the conductor is zero.

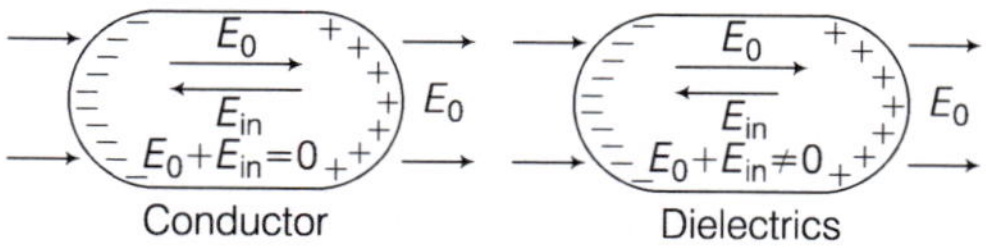

Behaviours of a conductor and dielectrics in an external electric field

A net dipole moment is developed by an external field in either case, whether polar or non-polar dielectric. The dipole moment unit volume is called polarisation and is denoted by *p*.

$$\boxed{\mathbf{p} = \chi\, \varepsilon_0 \mathbf{E}}$$

where, χ is called **electric susceptibility** of the dielectric medium.

Capacitor and Capacitance

A capacitor is a device which is used to store electrostatic potential energy or charge. It comprises of two conductors separated by an insulating medium.

Capacitance of a Conductor

If charge q is given to an isolated conductor, it leads to increase in its potential by V, such that

$$q \propto V \quad \Rightarrow \quad \boxed{q = CV}$$

where, C is known as capacitance of conductor.

- Its SI unit is farad (F).

Here, 1 Farad $= \dfrac{1 \text{ Coulomb}}{1 \text{ Volt}} \Rightarrow 1\text{F} = 1\ \text{CV}^{-1}$

- Farad is a very large unit of capacitance. So, μF is usually taken.
- The dimensions of capacitance are $[\text{M}^{-1}\text{L}^{-2}\text{T}^{4}\text{A}^{2}]$.

$$\left[\because\ 1\text{F} = \frac{1\text{C}}{1\text{V}} = \frac{1\text{C}^2}{1\text{J}} = \frac{1(\text{As})^2}{1\text{Nm}}\right]$$

Connection of Conductors

Whenever two conductors having some charges on it are connected by a conducting wire, then potential of each conductor will be same after the connection.

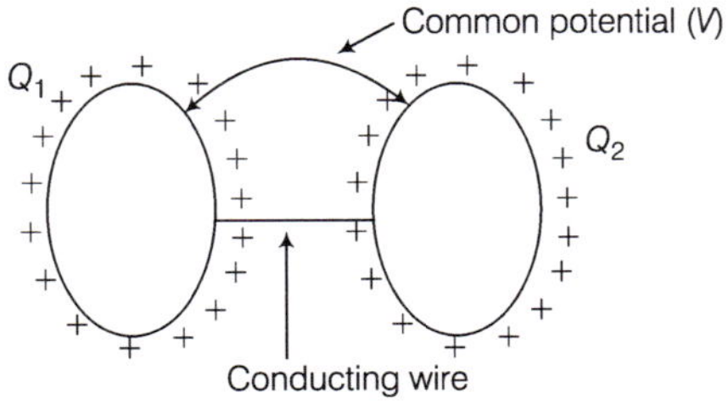

Two conductors connected by a wire

Parallel Plate Capacitor

The most common among all capacitors is parallel plate capacitor.

The capacitance of a parallel plate capacitor partially filled with a dielectric medium of dielectric constant K is given by

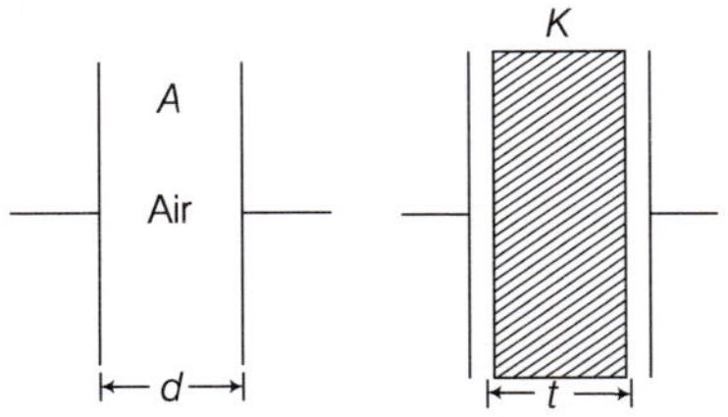

Air filled capacitor　Dielectric filled capacitor

$$C = \frac{\varepsilon_0 A}{(d - t + t/K)}$$

where, A = area of each plate
d = separation between two plates
t = thickness of dielectric medium
K = dielectric constant of dielectric medium.

Special Cases

- The capacitance of air filled (i.e., $K = 1$) parallel plate capacitor is given by

$$C_0 = \frac{\varepsilon_0 A}{d}$$

- When a dielectric or insulator of dielectric constant K is filled fully between the plates, $t = d$, then

$$C = \frac{KA\varepsilon_0}{d} = KC_0$$

- If there is a slab of metal ($K = \infty$) of thickness t between the plates, then capacitance is given by,

$$C = \frac{\varepsilon_0 A}{d - t}$$

So, we can say that capacitance of parallel plate capacitor increases on the insertion of insulator inside it.

Dielectric Constant

If C_{vacuum} be capacity of a capacitor with vacuum or air between its plates and $C_{\text{dielectric}}$ be the capacity with dielectric between the plates, the dielectric constant K is defined as $K = \dfrac{C_{\text{dielectric}}}{C_{\text{vacuum}}}$.

Dielectric constant is also known as **relative permittivity** ($\varepsilon_r = \varepsilon / \varepsilon_0$) of the dielectric.

Hence, net electric field inside the dielectric gets reduced to $E_0 - E_p$, where, E_0 is external electric field. This process is called **electric polarisation**.

$$K = \frac{E_0}{E_0 - E_p}$$

- The introduction of dielectric medium into the parallel plate capacitor (battery disconnected) leads to change in physical quantities are as listed below.

Before Introduction of Dielectric Slab	After Introduction of Dielectric Slab
Charge (q)	No change (charge q)
Electric field (E)	Decreases $\left(E' = \dfrac{E}{K}\right)$
Potential difference (V)	Decreases $\left(V' = \dfrac{V}{K}\right)$
Capacitance (C)	Increases ($C' = KC$)
Electrostatic energy (U)	Decreases $\left(U' = \dfrac{U}{K}\right)$

- The introduction of dielectric medium in charged capacitor connected with a battery leads to change in physical quantities are as listed below

Before Introduction of Dielectric Slab	After Introduction of Dielectric Slab
Potential difference (V)	No change in potential difference (V)
Capacitance (C)	Increases capacitance ($C' = KC$)
Charge (q)	Increases charge ($q' = qK$)
Electric field(E)	No change in electric field ($E' = E$)
Electrostatic potential energy (U)	Increases electrostatic energy ($U' = KU$)

Combination of Capacitors

(i) Series Combination of Capacitors

The charge on each capacitor is same for any value of capacitance and equal to the charge across the combination.

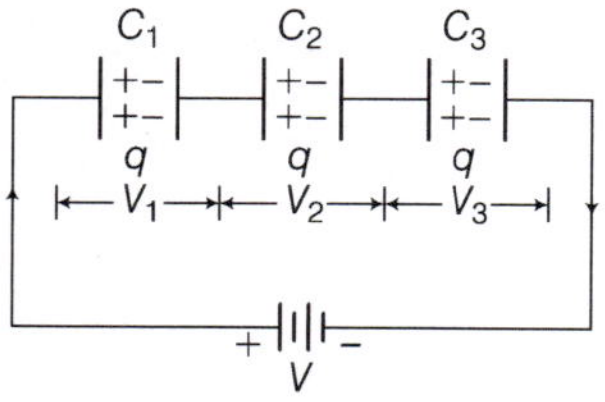

A series combination of capacitors

(i) $V = V_1 + V_2 + V_3$

(ii) $V_1 : V_2 : V_3 = \frac{1}{C_1} : \frac{1}{C_2} : \frac{1}{C_3}$

(*iii*) The equivalent capacitance is given by

$$\frac{1}{C} = \frac{1}{C_1} + \frac{1}{C_2} + \frac{1}{C_3}$$

NOTE For two capacitors, $C = \frac{C_1 C_2}{C_1 + C_2}$.

(*iv*) The equivalent capacitance of n identical capacitors connected in series each of capacitance C is given by $C_s = \frac{C}{n}$.

(ii) Parallel Combination of Capacitors

The potential difference across each capacitor is same for any value of capacitance and equal to the potential difference across the combination.

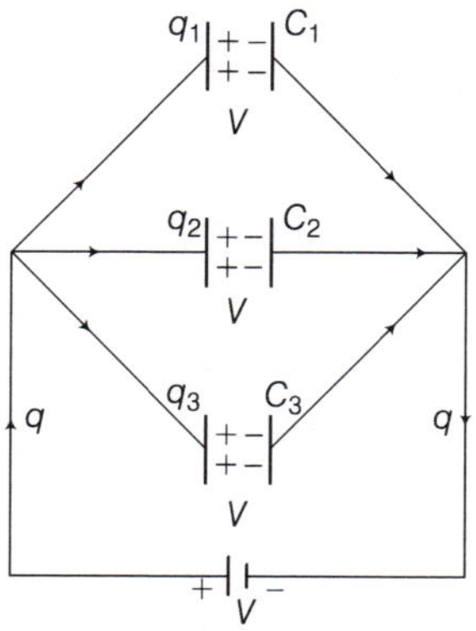

A parallel combination of capacitors

(*i*) $q = q_1 + q_2 + q_3$

(*ii*) The equivalent capacitance (C) is given by

$$C = C_1 + C_2 + C_3$$

(*iii*) The total charge on the capacitors is divided in the ratio of their capacitances i.e.,

$$q \propto C$$

$$\Rightarrow \quad q_1 : q_2 : q_3 = C_1 : C_2 : C_3$$

(*iv*) The equivalent capacitance of n identical capacitors connected in parallel combination is $C_p = nC$.

Energy Stored in a Capacitor

The electrostatic energy stored in a capacitor (parallel plate) is given by,

$$U = \frac{1}{2} CV^2 = \frac{1}{2} qV = \frac{q^2}{2C}$$

where, q = charge on capacitor, C = capacitance, V = potential difference across capacitor.

Energy Density

The energy stored per unit volume in an electric field E is known as energy density.

i.e. $$U_E = \frac{U}{Ad}$$

$$U_E = \frac{1}{2} \varepsilon_0 E^2$$

PYQs Previous Years Questions

1 Mark Questions

1. Three capacitors $C_1 = 3\mu F, C_2 = 6\mu F$ and $C_3 = 10\mu F$ are connected to a 50V battery as shown in the figure below.

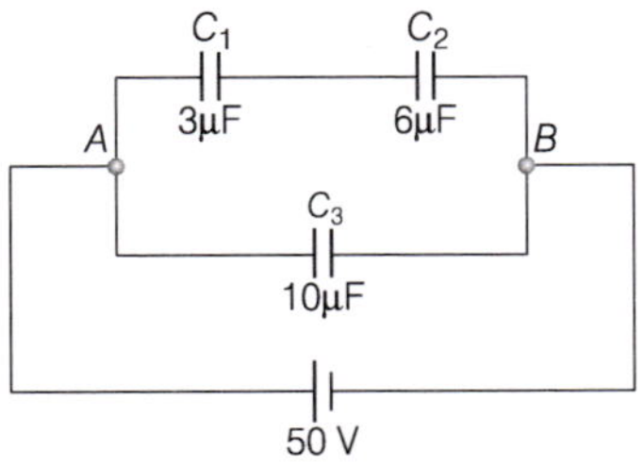

The equivalent capacitance of the circuit between point A and B and the charge on C_1 are ...... **ISC 2022 Sem-I**

(a) $12\mu F, 150\mu C$
(b) $4.75\mu F, 100\mu C$
(c) $12\mu F, 100\mu C$
(d) $4.75\mu F, 150\mu C$

2. Three capacitors, each of capacitance C, are connected in series. Their equivalent capacitance is C_s. The same three capacitors are now connected in parallel. Their equivalent capacitance becomes C_p. The ratio of C_p to C_s is **ISC 2022 Sem-I**

(a) 9 : 1 (b) 1 : 9
(c) 3 : 1 (d) 1 : 3

3. Consider 10 identical capacitors each of capacitance 5 μF. The ratio of the minimum and the maximum possible values of the capacitance that can be obtained from them, is **ISC 2022 Sem-I**

(a) 1 : 50 (b) 1 : 100
(c) 50 : 1 (d) 100 : 1

4. The capacitance of a parallel plate capacitor does not depend on **ISC 2022 Sem-I**

(a) area of each plate
(b) potential difference between the two plates
(c) nature of the medium between the two plates
(d) distance between the two plates

5. A parallel plate air capacitor has a capacitance of 5 μF. It becomes 50 μF when a dielectric medium occupies the entire space between its two plates. What is the dielectric constant of the medium? **ISC 2014**

2 Marks Questions

6. Calculate equivalent capacitance of the circuit shown in figure given below.

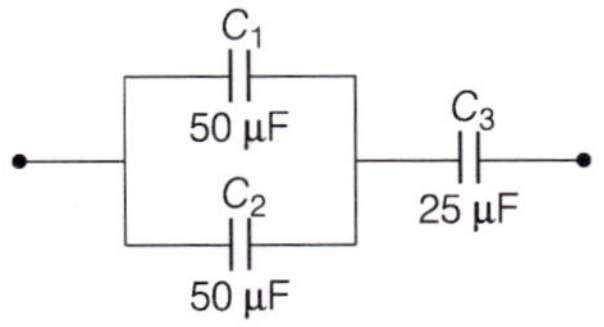

ISC 2023

7. You are provided with many identical capacitors each of capacitance $100\mu F$. How will you connect a minimum number of them to obtain a capacitance of $75\mu F$?

Draw a diagram in support of your answer. **ISC SQP 2023**

8. A parallel plate capacitor of plate area $A = 600\ cm^2$ and plate separation $d = 2.0$ mm is connected to DC source of 200V. **ISC 2022 Sem-I**

(i) What is the magnitude of the uniform electric field E between the plates?

(a) $E = 1.0 \times 10^5$ V/ m, (b) $E = 1.0 \times 10^7$ V/ m,
(c) $E = 0.5 \times 10^5$ V/ m, (d) $E = 0.5 \times 10^7$ V/ m,

(ii) What is the charge density σ on any one of the two plates?

(a) $\sigma = 8.85 \times 10^{-7}\ C/m^2$
(b) $\sigma = 8.85 \times 10^{-9}\ C/m^2$
(c) $\sigma = 4.45 \times 10^{-7}\ C/m^2$
(d) $\sigma = 4.45 \times 10^{-9}\ C/m^2$

KEY idea

To calculate the surface charge density (σ). First calculate the uniform electric field (E) between the plates with the help of formula ($E = V/d$), then apply formula $E = \frac{\sigma}{\varepsilon_0}$.

9. A capacitor of capacitance $10\mu F$ is charged to a potential difference of 1000 V. **ISC 2022 Sem-I**

(i) Electrostatic potential energy stored in the capacitor is

(a) 0.005 J (b) 0.25 J
(c) 0.5 J (d) 5.0 J

(ii) If a slab of dielectric constant $K = 5$ is introduced between its two plates in order to occupy the space completely, capacitance of the capacitor becomes

(a) $2\mu F$ (b) $10\mu F$
(c) $50\mu F$ (d) $100\mu F$

10. Three capacitors $C_1 = 3\mu F$, $C_2 = 6\mu F$ and $C_3 = 10\mu F$ are connected to a 50 V battery as shown in the figure below.

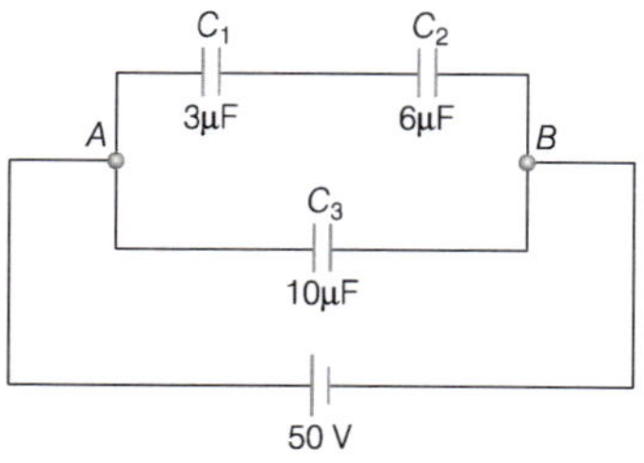

Calculate

(*i*) the equivalent capacitance of the circuit between points A and B.

(*ii*) the charge on C_1. **ISC 2017**

11. Obtain an expression for equivalent capacitance C when three capacitors having capacitance C_1, C_2 and C_3 are connected in series. **ISC 2016, 2012**

12. You are provided with $8\mu F$ capacitors. Show with the help of a diagram how you will arrange minimum number of them to get a resultant capacitance of $20\ \mu F$. **ISC 2014**

13. Three capacitors $C_1 = 6\mu F$, $C_2 = 12\mu F$ and $C_3 = 20\mu F$ are connected to a 100 V battery as shown in figure below.

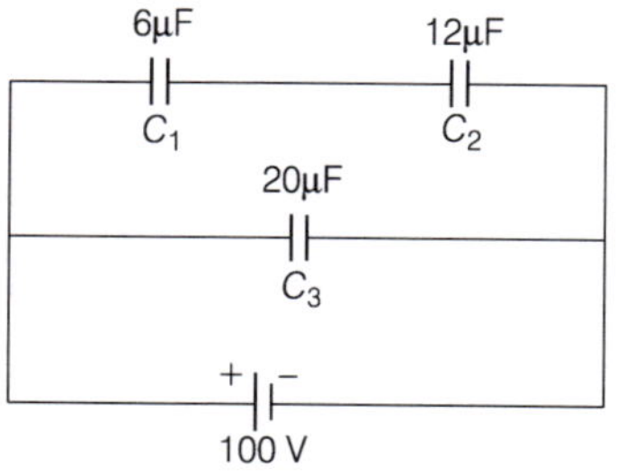

Calculate

(*i*) charge on each plate of capacitor C_1.

(*ii*) electrostatic potential energy stored in capacitor C_3. **ISC 2013**

14. Three capacitors each of capacitance C are connected in series. Their equivalent capacitance is C_s. The same three capacitors are now connected in parallel. Their equivalent capacitance becomes C_p. Find the ratio (C_p / C_s). **ISC 2011**

15. An isolated $16\ \mu F$ parallel plate air capacitor has a potential difference of 1000 V [shown in Fig. (a)]. A dielectric slab having relative permittivity (i.e., dielectric constant) = 5 is introduced to fill the space between the two plates completely [shown in Fig. (b)]. Calculate

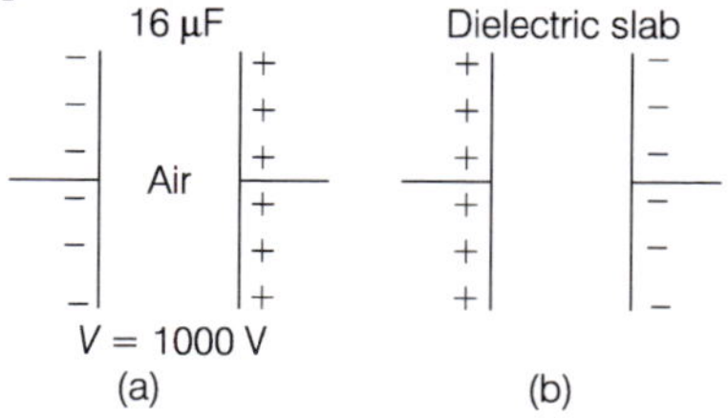

(*i*) the new capacitance of the capacitor.

(*ii*) the new potential difference between the two plates of the capacitor. **ISC 2010**

16. Find the electric charge Q_1 on plates of capacitor C_1, shown in figure below. **ISC 2009**

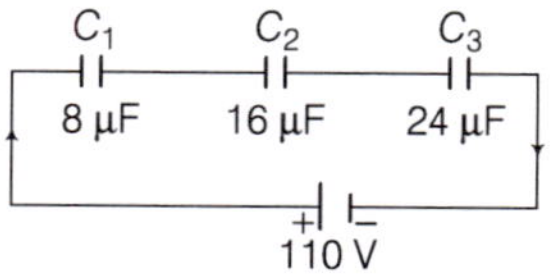

17. Find the equivalent capacitance of the following circuit between the junctions A and B given $C_1 = C_2 = C_3 = C_4 = 10\mu F$ and $C_5 = 5\mu F$. **ISC 2008**

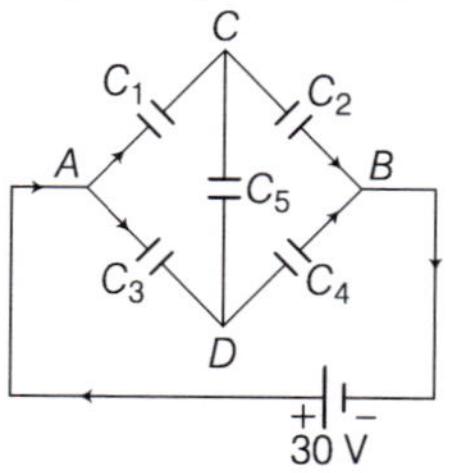

3 Marks Questions

18. Obtain an expression for equivalent capacitance C with three capacitors C_1, C_2 and C_3 are connected in series. **ISC 2024**

19. A parallel plate capacitor is charged by a battery, which is then disconnected. A dielectric slab having dielectric constant (relative permittivity) K, is now introduced between its two plates in order to occupy the space completely. **ISC 2020**

State, in terms of K, its effect on the following

(*i*) the capacitance of the capacitor.

(*ii*) the potential difference between its plates.

(*iii*) the energy stored in the capacitor.

20. Three capacitors of capacitance $C_1 = 3\mu F, C_2 = 6\mu F$ and $C_3 = 10\mu F$ are connected to a 10V battery as shown in the figure given below.

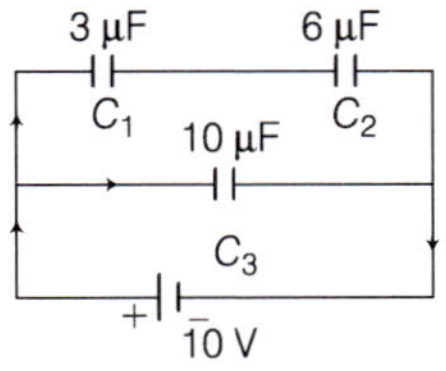

ISC 2019

Calculate

(*i*) equivalent capacitance.

(*ii*) electrostatic potential energy stored in the system.

21. Deduce an expression for equivalent capacitance C when three capacitors C_1, C_2 and C_3 are connected in parallel. **ISC 2018**

22. A parallel plate capacitor is charged by a battery, which is then disconnected. A dielectric slab is now introduced between the two plates to occupy the space completely. State the effect on the following. **ISC SQP 2018**

(*i*) the capacitance of the capacitor

(*ii*) potential difference between the plates

(*iii*) the energy stored in the capacitor

Case Based Question (For Complete Chapter)

23. Direction *Read the passage given below and answer the following questions.*

Dielectrics

A dielectrics is an insulating material in which all the electrons are tightly bound to the nuclei of the atoms. Thus, there are no free electrons to carry current. Hence, the electrical conductivity of a dielectric is very low. (The conductivity of an ideal dielectric is zero). Glass, plastic, mica, oil, etc. are examples of dielectrics.

It is found experimentally that when a dielectric material is placed between the plates of a capacitor, the capacitance of the capacitor increases by a dimensionless factor K which is called the "dielectric constant" or "Specific Inductive capacity of the material." Thus,

$$C = KC_0$$

or $$K = \frac{C}{C_0}$$

(*i*) Will a dielectric-filled capacitor store more charge or less charge than a similar air capacitor at the same potential differences? **(1)**

(*ii*) How is dielectric constant (or relative permittivity of a dielectric expressed in terms of capacitance? **(1)**

(*iii*) What may be a possible reason of water having a much greater dielectric constant (=80) than say mica (6)? **(1)**

(*iv*) In a parallel-plate capacitor, the capacitance increases from 4μF to 80μF on introducing a dielectric medium between the plates. What is the dielectric constant of the medium. **(1)**

(*v*) If the dielectric medium is a solid substance, then is there any other advantages of it in addition to an increase in the capacitance? **(1)**

Explanations

1. (c) $\frac{1}{C_{eq}} = \frac{1}{C_1} + \frac{1}{C_2} = \frac{1}{3} + \frac{1}{6}$

$C_{eq} = 2\mu F$

C_{eq} is in parallel with C_3, hence equivalent capacitance of the circuit between points A and B will be $10 + 2 = 12\mu F$.

Charge on $C_1 = q_1 = (C_{eq})(V) = (2\mu F)(50\ V) = 100\ \mu C$

2. (a) Three capacitors are in series

$$\frac{1}{C_s} = \frac{1}{C_1} + \frac{1}{C_2} + \frac{1}{C_3}$$

$$\Rightarrow \quad \frac{1}{C_s} = \frac{1}{C} + \frac{1}{C} + \frac{1}{C}$$

$$\Rightarrow \quad \frac{1}{C_s} = \frac{3}{C} \Rightarrow C_s = \frac{C}{3}$$

Three capacitors are in parallel

$$C_p = C_1 + C_2 + C_3$$
$$= C + C + C = 3C$$

$$\text{ratio} = \frac{C_p}{C_s} = \frac{3C}{\frac{C}{3}} = \frac{9C}{C} = 9:1$$

3. (b) Minimum capacitance $=\frac{1}{10}\times 5=\frac{1}{2}\mu F$

Maximum capacitance $=10\times 5=50\,\mu F$

Ratio of minimum to maximum value of capacitance

$$=\frac{\frac{1}{2}}{50}=\frac{1}{100} \text{ or } 1:100$$

4. (b) Potential difference between the plate $C=\frac{Q}{V}$ but the capacitance of a parallel plate capacitor neither depends on ϕ nor on V.

5. Given, capacitance in air, $C_0=5\mu F$

Capacitance with dielectric, $C=50\mu F$

$\therefore$ Dielectric constant, $K=\frac{C}{C_0}=\frac{50}{5}=10$

6. From the given circuit,

C_1 and C_2 are in parallel and C_3 is in series with C_1 and C_2.

$$C_1+C_2=50\,\mu F+50\mu F=100\mu F$$

Now, (C_1+C_2) is in series with C_3

$$\frac{(C_1+C_2)C_3}{(C_1+C_2)+C_3}=\frac{100\mu F\times 25\mu F}{100\mu F+25\mu F}\Rightarrow\frac{2500\mu F}{125}\Rightarrow 20\mu F$$

7. Capacitance $=100\mu F$

Capacitors are used to store energy between the plates when current is applied.

When the identical n capacitors are connected in series then net capacitance is, $C_n=C/n$.

If the n identical capacitors are connected in parallel then the net capacitance is, $C_n=nC$.

From the above information, we can construct the circuit connection to obtain a capacitance of $75\mu F$.

4 capacitors of capacitance $100\mu F$ are connected in the series which has net capacitance, $C_1=C/4$.

The value of C is $100\mu F$.

$$C_s=100/4=25\mu F.$$

2 capacitors are connected in series which has net capacitance, $C_2=C/2$.

$$C_2=100/2=50\mu F$$

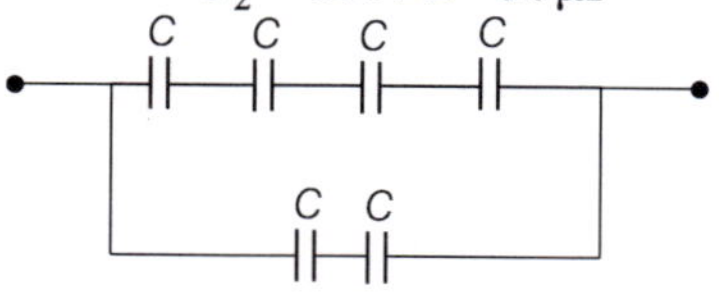

Then, both C_1 and C_2 are connected parallel in the connection.

Now, the net connection is $C_n=C_1+C_2$

$$C_n=25+50=75\,\mu F$$

6 capacitors is needed to obtain a capacitance of $75\mu F$.

8. (*i*) (a) $A=600\text{cm}^2=600\times 10^{-4}\text{ m}^2$

$$d=2.0\text{ mm}$$
$$V=200\text{ V}$$
$$E=V/d$$
$$=\frac{200\text{ V}}{0.002\text{ m}}$$
$$=1\times 10^5\text{ V/m}$$

(*ii*) (a) $E=\frac{\sigma}{\varepsilon_0}$

$$1\times 10^5\text{ V/m}=\frac{\sigma}{8.85\times 10^{-12}}$$

$$\sigma=1\times 10^5\text{ V/m}\times 8.85\times 10^{-12}$$
$$=8.85\times 10^{-7}\text{ C/m}^2$$

9. (*i*) (d) Electrostatic potential energy

$$E=\frac{1}{2}CV^2$$
$$=\frac{1}{2}\times 10\times 10^{-6}\times(1000)^2=5\text{ J}$$

(*ii*) (c) Initially, $C_0=10\mu F$

After inserting a slab,

$$C'=C_0K$$
$$=10\times 5$$
$$=50\mu F$$

10. (*i*)

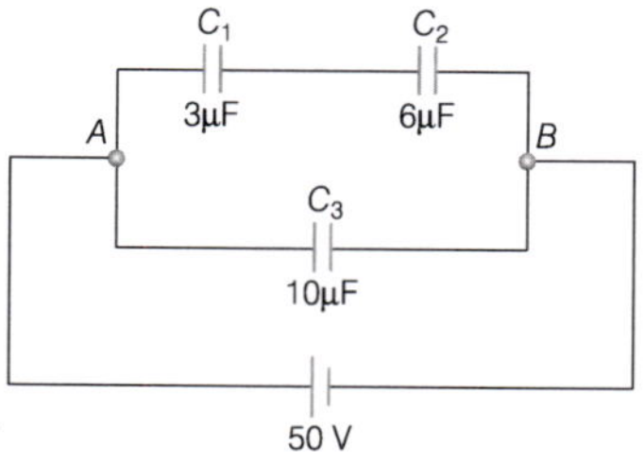

From the above figure, as C_1 and C_2 are connected in series,

Hence, $\frac{1}{C_{eq}}=\frac{1}{C_1}+\frac{1}{C_2}$

$\Rightarrow \frac{1}{C_{eq}}=\frac{1}{3}+\frac{1}{6}$

$\Rightarrow C_{eq}=2\mu F$

Now, C_{eq} is in parallel with C_3, hence equivalent capacitance of the circuit between points A and B will be $10+2=12\mu F$

(*ii*) Capacitors C_1 and C_2 are in series. Thus, charge on equivalent capacitance of C_1 and C_2 will be same as individual charge on C_1 and C_2

$\therefore$ Charge on $C_1 = q_1 = (C_{eq})(V)$

$$= (2\mu F)(50\,V) = 100\,\mu C$$

11. In series combination, charge on each capacitor will be same. The potential will be divided across the individual capacitors.

Let a battery of emf V is connected with the series combination of capacitors and let V_1, V_2 and V_3 are potential difference across each capacitor, then

$$V_1 = \frac{Q}{C_1}, \quad V_2 = \frac{Q}{C_2} \quad \text{and} \quad V_3 = \frac{Q}{C_3}$$

But, $\quad V = V_1 + V_2 + V_3$

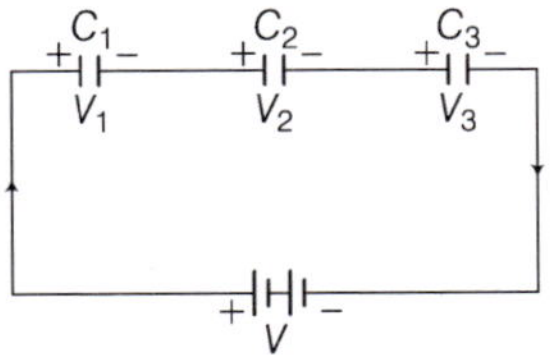

$$\Rightarrow \quad V = \frac{Q}{C_1} + \frac{Q}{C_2} + \frac{Q}{C_3}$$

$$\Rightarrow \quad V = Q\left(\frac{1}{C_1} + \frac{1}{C_2} + \frac{1}{C_3}\right)$$

But $\quad V = \frac{Q}{C_{eq}}$

where, C_{eq} is equivalent capacitance of the combination.

$$\Rightarrow \quad \frac{1}{C_{eq}} = \frac{1}{C_1} + \frac{1}{C_2} + \frac{1}{C_3}$$

> **Concept Enhancer** The capacitance depends on shape, size and geometry of conductor, nature of surrounding medium and presence of other conductors in the neighbourhood of it.

12. For getting a capacitance of $20\,\mu F$, the combination should be as shown in the diagram.

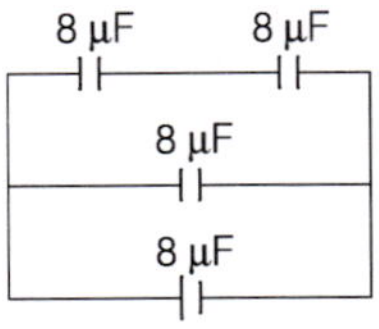

The series combination of $8\,\mu F$ capacitors will give equivalent capacitance of $4\,\mu F$.

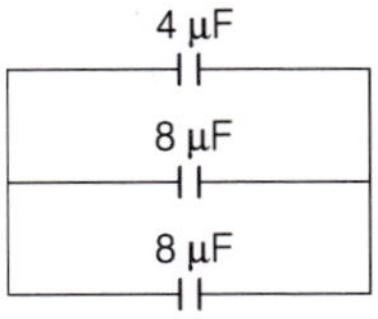

Now, capacitors $4\mu F$, $8\mu F$ and $8\mu F$ are in parallel.

Hence, $C_{eq} = 4\mu F + 8\mu F + 8\mu F = 20\mu F$

13. We have to apply the concept of series and parallel combination to find equivalent capacitance.

(*i*) It is clear from the diagram that C_1 and C_2 are in series.

$$\frac{1}{C_{eq}} = \frac{1}{C_1} + \frac{1}{C_2} = \frac{1}{6} + \frac{1}{12}$$

$$= \frac{2+1}{12} = \frac{3}{12} = \frac{1}{4}$$

$$\therefore \quad C_{eq} = 4\,\mu F$$

Charge on $4\,\mu F$ capacitor,

$$q = CV = 4 \times 10^{-6} \times 100$$

$$= 4 \times 10^{-4}\,C$$

Charge on positive plate of C_1 is $+4 \times 10^{-4}$ C.

and on negative plate of C_1 is -4×10^{-4} C.

Note that charge on C_1 and C_2 will be same.

(*ii*) Electric potential difference across the plate of C_3 capacitor $= 100$ V

$\therefore$ Electrostatic energy,

$$= \frac{1}{2}CV^2$$

$$= \frac{1}{2} \times 20 \times 10^{-6} \times 100 \times 100$$

$$= 10^{-1} = 0.1\ J$$

14. Let n capacitors each of capacitance C are connected in series to a battery of voltage V as shown below.

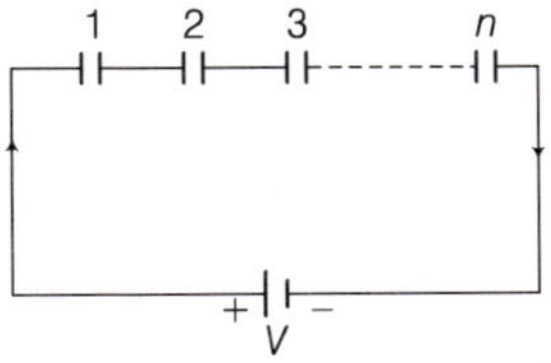

Let C_P and C_S be the equivalent capacitance in parallel and series combination respectively. The equivalent capacitance of the series combination

$$C_s = \frac{C}{n}$$

For the parallel combination,

$$C_p = nC = \frac{C_p}{C_s} = \frac{nC}{C/n} = n^2$$

According to the question, $n = 3$

$$\Rightarrow \quad \frac{C_p}{C_s} = n^2 = (3)^2 = 9$$

15. Given, $V_0 = 1000$ V, $C_0 = 16\mu$F

$$= 1.6 \times 10^{-5}\,\text{F}, K = 5$$

(*i*) We know that $C_0 = \frac{\varepsilon_0 A}{d}$

The new capacitance

$$C = KC_0 = 5 \times 1.6 \times 10^{-5}$$
$$= 8 \times 10^{-5}\ \text{F}$$

(*ii*) New potential

$$V = \frac{V_0}{K} = \frac{1000}{5} = 200\ \text{V}$$

16. According to the diagram, capacitors are in series.

$$\frac{1}{C_{eq}} = \frac{1}{C_1} + \frac{1}{C_2} + \frac{1}{C_3}$$

$$\Rightarrow \quad \frac{1}{C} = \frac{1}{8} + \frac{1}{16} + \frac{1}{24}$$

$$\Rightarrow \quad \frac{1}{C} = \frac{6+3+2}{48} = \frac{11}{48}$$

$$\therefore \quad C = \frac{48}{11}\,\mu\text{F}$$

Charge on each capacitor,

$$Q = CV = \frac{48}{11} \times 110 = 480\,\mu\text{C}$$

17. For a Wheatstone bridge to be balanced, the ratio of capacitances of adjacent arms must be equal.

Clearly, from the given circuit

$$C_1 C_4 = 100\mu\text{F}$$

and $\quad C_3 C_2 = 100\mu\text{F}$

$$\Rightarrow \quad C_1 C_4 = C_2 C_3$$

$$\Rightarrow \quad \frac{C_1}{C_2} = \frac{C_3}{C_4}$$

So, it is a balanced Wheatstone bridge.

Now, we can remove C_5 from the given circuit.

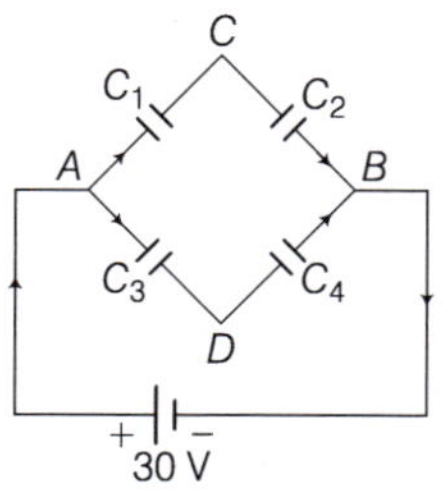

So, C_1 and C_2 are in series,

$$\frac{1}{C'} = \frac{1}{10} + \frac{1}{10} = \frac{1}{5}$$

$$\Rightarrow \quad C' = 5\,\mu\text{F}$$

and C_3 and C_4 are in series, $C'' = 5\,\mu$F

Now, C' and C'' are in parallel,

$\therefore$ Net capacitance,

$$C = C' + C'' = 5 + 5 = 10\mu\text{F}$$

Caution The capacitor C_5 is removed because potential of its terminals is same and hence, potential difference is zero across it.

18. Refer to text on page no. 36. (Combination of capacitors)

19. (*i*) Let the initial capacitance, $C_0 = \varepsilon_0 \frac{A}{d}$

So, the final capacitance, after the insertion of dielectric medium

$$C = K\varepsilon_0 = \frac{A}{d} = KC_0$$

(*ii*) Initial potential difference, $V_0 = \frac{Q_0}{C_0}$

New potential difference, $V = \frac{Q_0}{C} = \frac{Q_0}{KC_0} = \frac{V_0}{K}$

(*iii*) Also, initial energy stored in capacitor, $E_0 = \frac{Q_0^2}{2C_0}$

New energy stored,

$$E = \frac{Q_0^2}{2C} = \frac{Q_0^2}{2(KC_0)} = \frac{E_0}{K}$$

20. (*i*) C_1 and C_2 are in series combination.

Then, equivalent capacitance, $C' = \frac{3 \times 6}{3+6} = 2\mu$F

Now C' and C_3 are in parallel combination.

Then, equivalent capacitance

$$C = C' + C_3 = 2 + 10 = 12\,\mu\text{F}$$

(*ii*) Total charge,

$$Q = CV = 12 \times 10 = 120\mu\text{C}$$

Potential energy stored in the system,

$$U = \frac{1}{2}QV = \frac{1}{2} \times 120 \times 10^{-6} \times 10$$
$$= 600 \times 10^{-6} = 6 \times 10^{-4} J$$

21. **Capacitors in parallel** Suppose $+Q$ charge is given to the point A by means of an electric source. This charge is distributed on all the three capacitors according to their capacitances.

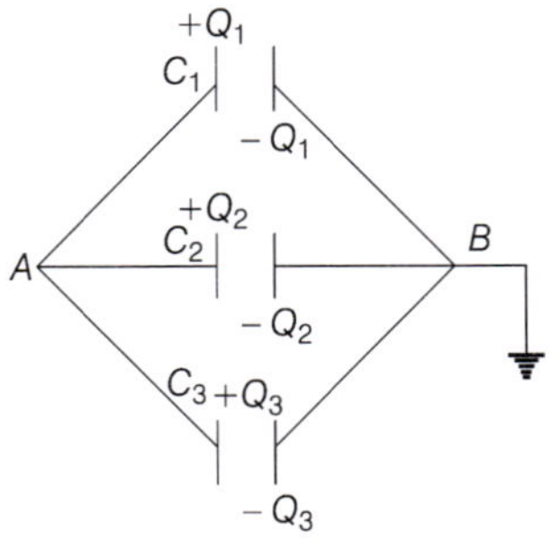

If the charges on the capacitors C_1, C_2 and C_3 be Q_1, Q_2 and Q_3 respectively, then

$$Q_1 = C_1V, Q_2 = C_2V \text{ and } Q_3 = C_3V$$

The total charge on all the three capacitors is

$$Q = Q_1 + Q_2 + Q_3$$
$$= C_1V + C_2V + C_3V$$
$$= V(C_1 + C_2 + C_3) \quad \dots \text{(i)}$$

If the capacitor of this combination be C, then

$$Q = CV \quad \dots \text{(ii)}$$

Combining Eqs. (i) and (ii), we obtain

$$CV = V(C_1 + C_2 + C_3)$$
$$C = C_1 + C_2 + C_3$$

The equivalent capacitance of the capacitors connected in parallel is equal to the sum of their individual capacitance.

22. (*i*) When capacitor is fully charged, then capacitance of capacitor can be given as

$$C_0 = \frac{\varepsilon_0 A}{d}$$

Let a dielectric slab having dielectric constant (K) inserted in the capacitor, then we know that

$$K = \frac{\varepsilon_m}{\varepsilon_0}$$

$$\Rightarrow \quad \varepsilon_m = \varepsilon_0\varepsilon_r = K\varepsilon_0$$

Then capacitance of new capacitor with dielectric slab is, $C_m = K\frac{\varepsilon_0 A}{d}$

$$C_m = KC_0$$

(*ii*) $V = \frac{Q}{C_m} = \frac{Q}{KC_0} \qquad \left[\because C_0 = \frac{C_m}{K}\right]$

Hence, potential difference decreases by factor of $\left(\frac{1}{K}\right)$.

(*iii*) Energy of capacitor $= \frac{1}{2}C_0V^2$

For dielectric medium

$$E = \frac{1}{2}C_mV^2 = \frac{KC_0V^2}{2}$$
$$E = K\left(\frac{1}{2}C_0V^2\right)$$

Here, energy increases by the factor K times.

23. (*i*) More charge, because the capacitance of a dielectric filled capacitor is larger than an air filled capacitor and $Q = CV$.

(*ii*) $K = C / C_0$, where C is the capacitance of a capacitor filled completely with the dielectric and C_0 that of the same capacitor with vacuum (or air) between the plates.

(*iii*) Water molecules have permanent dipole moments. That's why water having a much greater dielectric constant (= 80) than say mica (= 6).

(*iv*) $K = \frac{C}{C_0} = \frac{80\mu F}{4\mu F} = 20$

(v) Yes, it helps in keeping the plates of the capacitor very close to each other without touching.

CHAPTER TEST

01 Mark Questions (MCQs)

1 The real seat of charge in a capacitor is
(a) metal plates
(b) battery
(c) dielectric material
(d) None of the above

2 1 Farad is equivalent to
(a) 1 C / 1 V (b) 1 V / 1 C
(c) 1 J /1 C (d) None of these

3 The equivalent capacitance between points A and B in the given figure would be

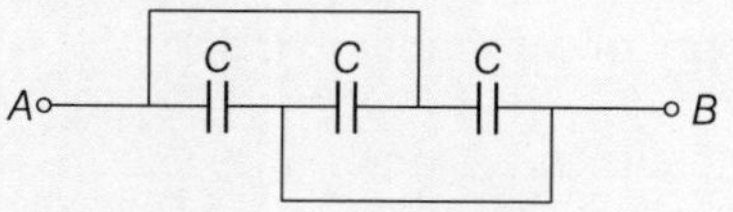

(a) 3 C (b) C/3
(c) 3C/2 (d) None of these

4 The equivalent capacitance between points A and B in the given figure would be

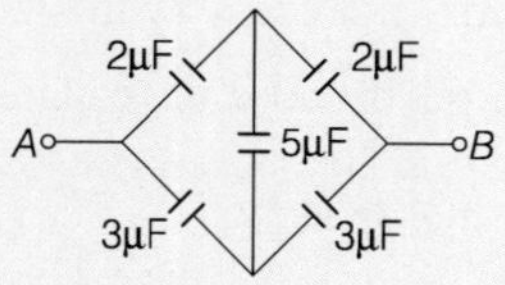

(a) 2.5μF (b) 15μF
(c) 2.4μF (d) None of these

01 Mark Questions (VSA)

5 A capacitor has no charge. Is its capacitance zero?

6 What is the function of second plate in parallel plate capacitor?

7 The following graph shows the variation of charge Q with voltage V for two capacitors K and L, which capacitor stores more electrostatic energy?

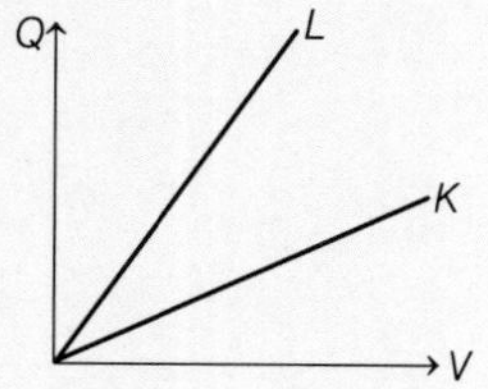

02 Marks Questions

8 Determine the potential difference across the plates of the capacitor C_1 of the network shown in the figure (assume $E_1 > E_2$).

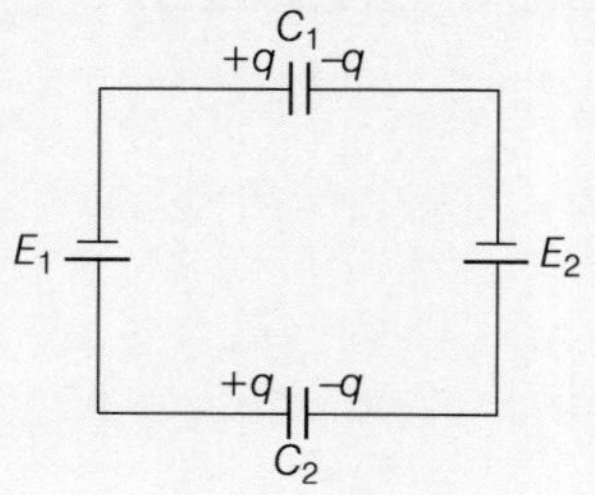

9 A slab of material of dielectric constant K has the same area as that of the plates of a parallel plate capacitor but has the thickness $d/2$, where d is the separation between the plates. Find out the expression for its capacitance when the slab is inserted between the plates of the capacitor.

03 Marks Questions

10 The two plates of a parallel plate capacitor are 4 mm apart. A slab of dielectric constant 3 and thickness 3 mm is introduced between the plates with its faces parallel to them. The distance between the plates is so adjusted that the capacitance of the capacitor becomes (2/3)rd of its original value. What is the new distance between the plates?

11 (i) Deduce the expression for the energy stored in a charged capacitor.
(ii) Show that the effective capacitance C of a series combination of three capacitors C_1, C_2 and C_3 is given by

$$C = \frac{C_1C_2C_3}{(C_1C_2 + C_2C_3 + C_3C_1)}$$

Answers

1. (c) **2.** (a) **3.** (a) **4.** (a)
7. L

8. $E_1 - E_2 = q\left(\frac{1}{C_1} = \frac{1}{C_2}\right)$

10. 5 mm **11.** (i) $\frac{q^2}{2C}$

05

Current Electricity

TREND ANALYSIS 4 YEARS

Average No. of Questions Across all Sets

Topic	Types of Questions	2024	2023	2020	2019
TOPIC 01 Electric current and Ohm's Law	1 Mark	–	2	–	–
	2 Marks	–	1	1	–
	3 Marks	–	–	–	–
	5 Marks	–	–	–	–
TOPIC 02 Electric Cell and Their Combination	1 Mark	1	–	–	–
	2 Marks	–	–	–	1
	3 Marks	–	–	–	–
	5 Marks	–	–	–	–
TOPIC 03 Kirchhoff's Laws and Their Applications	1 Mark	1	–	–	–
	2 Marks	–	1	–	1
	3 Marks	2	2	2	2
	5 Marks	–	–	–	–
TOPIC 04 Electric Power	1 Mark	1	1	–	–
	2 Marks	–	–	1	–
	3 Marks	–	–	–	–
	5 Marks	–	–	–	–

TOPIC 1

Electric Current and Ohm's Law

Electric Current

It is defined as the rate of flow of electric charge through any cross-section of a conductor.

If ΔQ charge flows in time Δt, then current at any time t is

$$I = \lim_{\Delta t \to 0} \frac{\Delta Q}{\Delta t} = \frac{dQ}{dt}$$

Charge can be written as

$$\Delta Q = ne \quad \text{[quantisation of charge]}$$

where, n = number of free electrons

e = charge on an electron

$= 1.6 \times 10^{-19}\text{C}$

Current is a scalar quantity. It is in the direction of flow of positive charge and opposite to the direction of flow of negative charge.

The SI unit of current is ampere and is represented by A.

We can write

$$1 \text{ ampere} = \frac{1 \text{ coulomb (C)}}{1 \text{ second (s)}} = 1 \text{ C/s}$$

NOTE Although electric current has both magnitude and direction yet is a scalar quantity, because the laws of ordinary algebra are used to add electric currents instead of laws of vector addition.

Current Density

Current density at a point in a conductor is the ratio of the current at that point in the conductor to the area of cross-section of the conductor at that point, provided area is held normal to the direction of flow of current.

Current density, $J = \frac{\Delta I}{\Delta A} \Rightarrow J = \frac{dI}{dA}$,

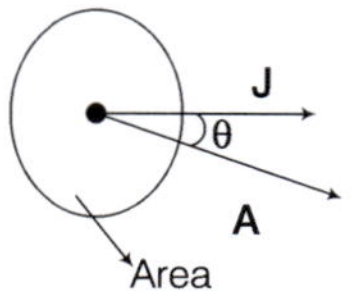

Also, $dI = \mathbf{J} \cdot d\mathbf{A}$

$$I = \int \mathbf{J} \cdot d\mathbf{A} = \int J \, dA \cos\theta \quad [\because \Delta A \to 0]$$

Current density is a vector quantity.

Mechanism of Flow of Current in Conductor

Flow of current in conductors can be explained on the basis of electron theory. In an atom, the electrons far from the nucleus experience a very feeble force. Hence, the outer electrons can be removed easily from the atom. These electrons are called **free electrons** or **conduction electrons**.

There are some other materials in which the electrons will be bound and they will not be accelerated, even if the electric field is applied, i.e., **no current on applying electric field**. Such materials are called **insulators**. e.g. Wood, plastic, rubber, etc.

NOTE Conductivity of semiconductors (Ge, Si) lies between conductor and insulator.

Some related terms with flow of electrons are discussed below.

(i) Drift Velocity

It is defined as the average velocity with which the free electrons in a conductor get drifted towards the positive end of the conductor under the influence of an electric field applied across the conductor. It is denoted by v_d.

The drift velocity of an electron is of the order 10^{-4} ms^{-1}.

(ii) Relaxation Time

The average time difference between two successive collisions of drifting electrons inside the conductor under the influence of electric field applied across the conductor, is known as relaxation time (τ).

Relation between Drift Velocity and Relaxation Time

Average drift velocity, $v_d = \frac{eE}{m}\tau$

(iii) Electric Current

$$I = \frac{q}{t} = \frac{nAle}{t} = \frac{nAle}{l/v_d}$$

Hence, electric current in terms of drift velocity

$$I = neAv_d$$

where, n = number density of free electrons,
e = electronic charge
A = cross-sectional area
v_d = drift velocity of an electron.
and l = length of the conductor.

(iv) Current Density

Current density at any point of conductor

$$J = nev_d \qquad \left[\text{where, } J = \frac{I}{A}\right]$$

(v) Mobility

It is defined as the magnitude of drift velocity per unit electric field. It is expressed as

$$\mu = \frac{\text{Drift velocity } (v_d)}{\text{Electric field } (E)} = \frac{qE\tau/m}{E} = \frac{q\tau}{m}$$

where, τ is the average relaxation time of the charge while drifting towards the opposite electrode and m is the mass of the charged particle.

The SI unit of mobility is $\text{m}^2\text{s}^{-1}\text{V}^{-1}$ or $\text{ms}^{-1}\text{N}^{-1}\text{C}$.

Ohm's Law

At constant temperature and other physical conditions (like mechorincal strain etc remaining same) the potential difference V across the ends of a given metallic wire (conductor) in a circuit (electric) is directly proportional to the current flowing through it.

$$V \propto I$$

The variation of current w.r.t. applied potential difference is shown with the help of the given graph.

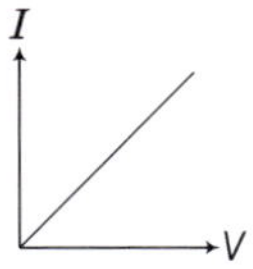

$$\boxed{V = IR}$$

where, R = resistance of the conductor.

Relation among J, σ and E

It is a microscopic form of Ohm's law.

$\Rightarrow$ $$\boxed{J = \sigma E}$$

NOTE The device which do not obey Ohm's law are called non-ohmic devices such as vacuum tubes, semiconductor diode etc. But the relation $\left(\frac{V}{I} = R\right)$ is valid for both, ohmic and non-ohmic devices.

Resistance of a Conductor

It is defined as the ratio of the potential difference applied across the conductor to the current flowing through it

$$\left(R = \frac{V}{I}\right)$$

The resistance of a conductor is given by

$$\boxed{R = \rho \frac{l}{A}}$$

where, ρ is a constant, known as resistivity of the material. It depends upon nature of the material and temperature.

SI unit of resistance ohm (Ω) and SI unit of resistivity (ρ) is Ω-m.

Relationship between resistivity (ρ) and relaxation time (τ) is given by $\rho = \frac{m}{ne^2\tau}$

where, m = mass of electron, n = number of electrons and e = charge on an electron.

Conductance and Conductivity

Conductance is the reciprocal of resistance of a conductor expressed as $G = \frac{1}{R}$.

Its SI unit is mho(Ω^{-1}) or siemen (S).

Conductivity is defined as the reciprocal of resistivity of a conductor. It is expressed as

$\sigma = \frac{1}{\rho}$. Its SI unit is **mho per metre** (Ω^{-1}/m).

Temperature Coefficient

- **Temperature coefficient** of resistances is given by

$$\boxed{\alpha = \frac{R_2 - R_1}{R_1(t_2 - t_1)}}$$

  where, R_1 and R_2 are the resistance at t_1°C and t_2°C, respectively.

  SI unit of α is per degree celsius or/°C.

- **For metals,** the value of α is **positive**, therefore resistance of the metal increases with rise in temperature.
- **For semiconductors**, the value of α is negative, therefore resistance of semiconductor decreases with rise in temperature.
- **For insulator**, α is high and repositive.
- **For alloys**, the value of α is very small.

The graphs showing resistivity as a function of temperature for metals, semiconductor and alloys are as follows

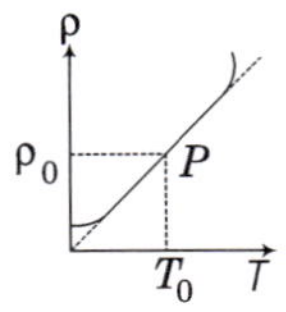

Resistivity as a function of temperature for metals

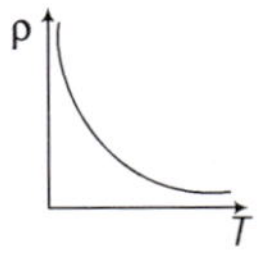

Resistivity as a function of temperature for semiconductors

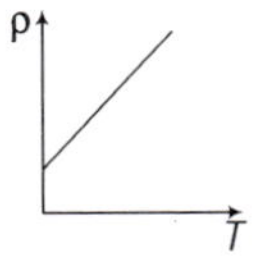

Resistivity as a function of temperature for alloys

- If conductor is stretched or compressed to n times of original length, then

$$l' = nl \qquad \left[\because R' = \frac{\rho \cdot nl}{A/n} = n^2 \frac{\rho l}{A} = n^2 R\right]$$
$$R' = n^2 R$$

where, R' is the new resistance and R is the original resistance.

PYQs Previous Years Questions

1 Mark Questions

1. An electric current (I) flowing through a metallic wire is gradually increased. The graph of heating power (P) developed in it *versus* the current (I) is **ISC 2023**

(a) 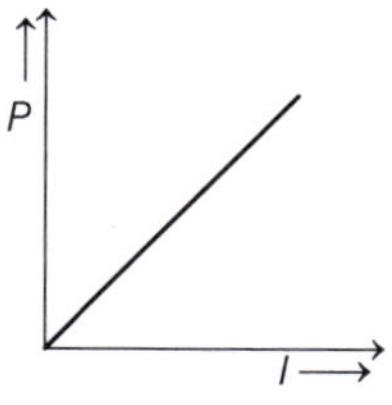

(b) 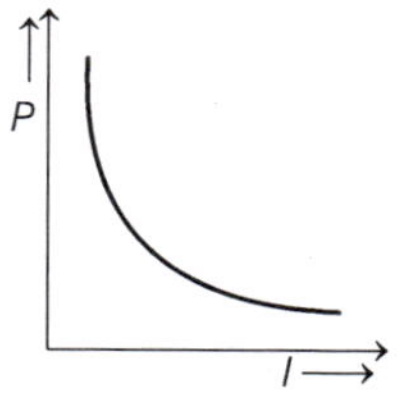

(c) 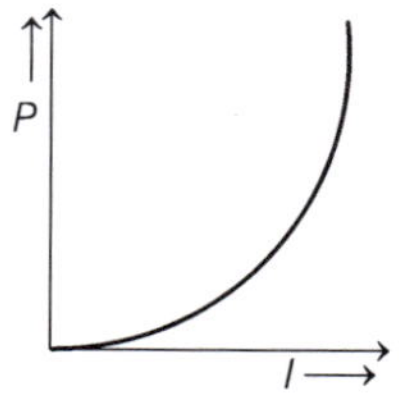

(d) 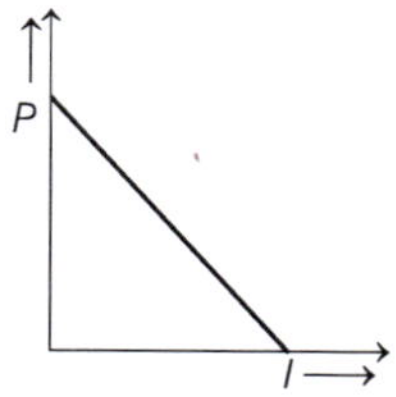

2. In case of metals, what is the relation between current density (J), electrical conductivity (σ) and electric field intensity (E)? **ISC 2023**

3. The resistance of a wire is 10 Ω. It is stretched so that its length becomes four times. What will be the new resistance of the wire? **ISC 2022 Sem-I**

(a) 40 Ω (b) 160.0 Ω
(c) 120 Ω (d) 80.0 Ω

4. If m, e, τ and n respectively represent the mass, charge, average relaxation time and density of the electron, then what will be the resistance of a wire of length l and area of cross-section A? **ISC 2022 Sem-I**

(a) $\frac{ml}{ne^2\tau A}$ (b) $\frac{m\tau^2 A}{ne^2 l}$
(c) $\frac{ne^2\tau A}{2ml}$ (d) $\frac{ne^2 A}{2m\tau l}$

5. The drift velocity of a current carrying conductor is v. What will be the drift velocity if the current flowing through the wire is doubled? **ISC 2022 Sem-I**

(a) $v/4$ (b) $v/2$
(c) $2v$ (d) $4v$

6. If a variable resistance is connected to a cell of constant emf, then the graph which represents the correct relationship between current I and resistance R is **ISC 2022 Sem-I**

(a) 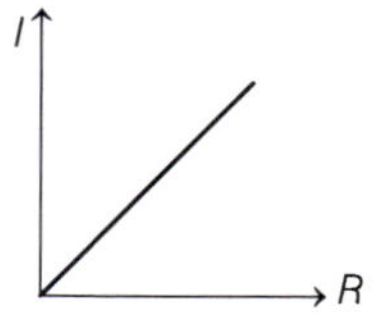

(b) 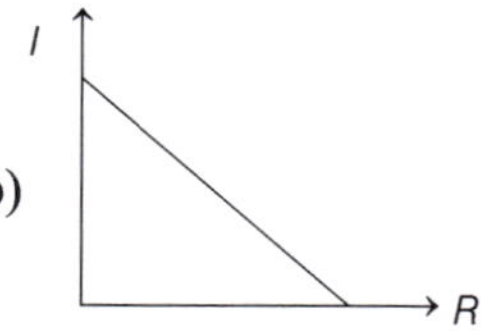

(c) 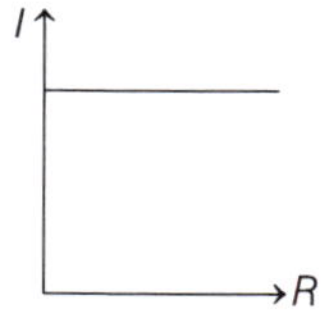

(d) 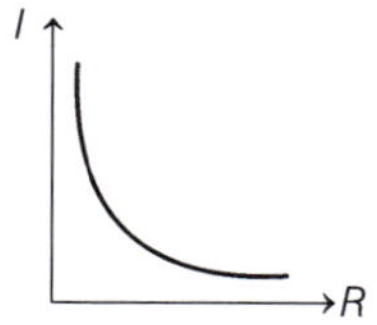

7. A metallic wire of resistance R is stretched slowly and uniformly (keeping its temperature constant) till its new radius becomes half. Its resistance, then becomes **ISC 2022 Sem-I**

(a) $16R$ (b) $8R$ (c) $4R$ (d) R

8. Specific resistance of the material of a wire depends on **ISC 2022 Sem-I**

(a) length of the wire
(b) area of cross-section of the wire
(c) volume of the wire
(d) temperature of the wire

9. When a potential difference of 2 V is applied between the two ends of a 1m long and uniform metallic wire, current density in it is found to be 4×10^6 Am^{-2}. Resistivity of the material of the wire is **ISC 2022 Sem-I**

(a) 5×10^{-7} Ω-m (b) 5×10^{-8} Ω-m
(c) 5×10^{6} Ω-m (d) 5×10^{8} Ω-m

10. SI unit of electrical conductivity is **ISC 2022 Sem-I**

(a) $\Omega\,m^{-1}$ (b) $\Omega\,m^{-2}$
(c) $\Omega^{-1}m^{-1}$ (d) $\Omega^{-1}m^{-2}$

11. Ohm's law in vector form is **ISC SQP 2018**

(a) $V = IR$ (b) $\mathbf{J} = \sigma\,\mathbf{E}$
(c) $\mathbf{J} = \rho\mathbf{E}$ (d) $\mathbf{E} = \sigma\,\mathbf{J}$

12. What is meant by drift speed of free electrons? **ISC 2017**

13. For a metallic conductor, what is the relation between current density (J), conductivity (σ) and electric field intensity (E)? **ISC 2016**

14. Define temperature coefficient of resistance of the material of a conductor. **ISC 2014**

15. A current I flows through a metallic wire of radius r and free electrons in it drift with a velocity v_d. Calculate the drift velocity of the free electrons through the wire of the same material, having double the radius, when same current flows through it. **ISC 2014**

16. In current electricity, Ohm's law is obeyed by all **ISC 2011**

(a) solids (b) metals (c) liquids (d) gases

17. Explain the statement 'temperature coefficient of resistance of metal is $4 \times 10^{-3}/°C$. **ISC 2010**

18. A wire of resistivity ρ is stretched uniformly, so that its length becomes four times. What is its new resistivity? (assume temperature of the wire remains constant during stretching of the wire.) **ISC 2008**

19. Show graphically how electrical resistance of a piece of silicon or germanium varies when its temperature is varied. **ISC 2008**

20. Calculate the electric current density in a uniform wire connected to a battery of emf 3.5 V and negligible internal resistance. The resistance of the wire is 2.0 Ω and its area of cross-section is 0.70×10^{-6} m^2. **ISC 2007**

> **KEY idea**
>
> In the given problem as internal resistance is zero (negligible) firstly find the current by the formula $i = \frac{E}{R}$
>
> and then find the electric current density $j = \frac{i}{A}$

21. State the physical condition in which Ohm's law is not valid for a conductor. **ISC 2002**

22. If the potential difference applied across a variable resistor is constant, draw a graph between the current in the resistor and the resistance. **ISC 2000**

2 Marks Questions

23. With reference to free electron theory of conductors, define. **ISC 2023**

(a) Drift velocity.

(b) State any one use of a potentiometer.

24. With reference to the free electron theory of conductors, **ISC 2022 Sem-I**

(*i*) Drift velocity is

(a) the average velocity of free electrons with which they move towards the positive terminal

(b) the velocity of free electrons with which they move towards the positive terminal

(c) the average speed of free electrons with which they move towards the negative terminal

(d) the speed of free electrons with which they move towards the negative terminal

(*ii*) Relaxation time is

(a) the time interval between number of collisions of a free electron in a conductor

(b) the average time interval between two successive collisions of a free electron with metallic ions in a conductor

(c) the time interval between number of collisions of metal ions in a conductor

(d) the time interval between collision of free electrons with each other

25. A uniform copper wire having a cross-sectional area of 1 mm^2 carries a current of 5A. Calculate the drift speed of free electrons in it. **ISC 2020**

(Free electron number density of copper $= 2 \times 10^{28}/m^3$)

26. Define current density. Write an expression which connects current density with drift speed. **ISC 2018**

27. Define drift velocity and relaxation time, with reference to the free electron theory of conductors. **ISC SQP 2018**

28. A metallic wire has a resistance of 3.0 Ω at 0°C and 4.8Ω at 150°C. Find the temperature coefficient of resistance of its material. **ISC 2016**

29. Draw labelled graphs to show how electrical resistance varies with temperature for **ISC 2015**

(*i*) a metallic wire (*ii*) a piece of carbon

30. When a potential difference of 3 V is applied between the two ends of a 60 cm long metallic wire, current density in it is found to be 1×10^{-7} Am^{-2}. Find conductivity of the material of the wire in SI system. **ISC 2012**

31. What is current density? Write the vector equation connecting current density J with electric field intensity E, for an ohmic conductor. **ISC 2010**

32. Two wires A and B of equal masses and of the same material are taken. The diameter of wire A is half the diameter of wire B. If the resistance of wire A is 24 Ω, calculate the resistance of wire B. **ISC 2006**

33. A potential difference of V volt is applied across a copper wire of length l and diameter d. How will the drift velocity be affected, if **ISC 2005**

(*i*) V is doubled.

(*ii*) l is doubled.

34. Name one material whose resistivity decreases with rise in temperature. Explain briefly on the basis of free electron theory why the resistivity decreases. **ISC 2000)**

3 Marks Questions

35. (*i*) What is meant by

(a) drift velocity (b) relaxation time?

(*ii*) A metallic plug AB is carrying a current I (see figure below). State how the drift velocity of free electrons varies from end A to B. **ISC 2009**

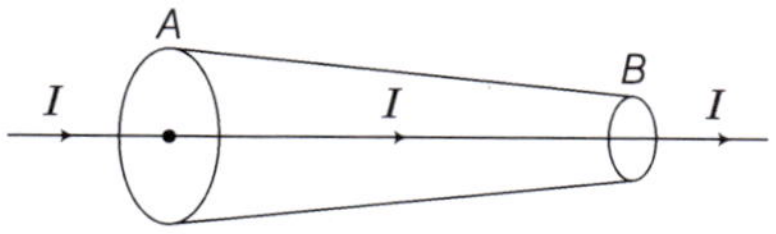

36. Write down a simple relationship to show the variation of resistance with temperature. Define temperature coefficient of resistance. In what way the temperature coefficient of carbon is different from that of the common conductors? **ISC 2001**

4/5 Marks Question

37. The current flowing through a conductor is given by $I = neAv_d$.

(*i*) Identify each term in the equation.

(*ii*) Obtain an expression for V_d, if the current flowing through the conductor of length l has its ends maintained at a potential difference V volt. **ISC 2006**

Explanations

1. (c) Heating power (P) is directly proportional to I^2

As, $H = VIt$

Applying ohm's law, $H = I^2Rt$. From this equation, we can conclude that the heat produced is directly proportional to the square of electric current.

2. $I = nAev_d = nAe\left(\frac{eE}{m}\tau\right)$

$$\frac{I}{A} = \frac{ne^2\tau E}{m}$$

$$J = \frac{1}{P}E \qquad \left[\because J = \frac{I}{A} \text{ and } P = \frac{m}{ne^2T}\right]$$

$$J = \sigma E$$

3. (b) $R = 10\,\Omega$

As, $R = L/A$

From volume $AL = A'L'$ ... (i)

$L' = 4L$

From Eq. (i), $A' = A/4$

So, new resistance,

$$R' = \frac{\rho L'}{A'} \Rightarrow R' = \frac{\rho 4L}{A/4} = 16R$$

So, new resistance $= 16R = 16 \times 10 = 160\,\Omega$

4. (a) $R = \rho\frac{l}{A} = \frac{1}{\sigma A}$

$$\sigma = \frac{ne^2\tau}{m} \Rightarrow R = \frac{1}{\sigma A} = \frac{ml}{ne^2\tau A}$$

5. (c) $I = neAv_d$

$v_d \propto I$

If current is doubled then v_d will become double.

6. (d) According to the Ohm's law,

$$V = IR$$

Now, if $V =$ constant

So, $I \propto \frac{1}{R}$

where, $I =$ current and $R =$ variable resistance.

The variation is shown in the graph.

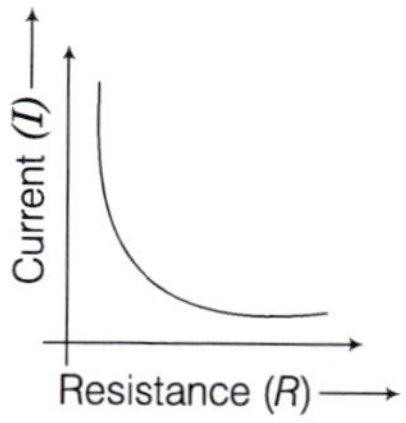

7. (a) As, $R = \rho \cdot \frac{l}{A} = \rho \cdot \frac{l \cdot A}{A^2} = \rho \cdot \frac{V}{A^2} = \rho \cdot \frac{V}{(\pi r^2)^2}$

$\therefore \quad R \propto \frac{1}{r^4}$

$\therefore \quad \frac{R'}{R} = \left(\frac{r}{r'}\right)^4 = \left(\frac{r}{r/2}\right)^4 = (2)^4 = 16 \qquad \left[\because r' = \frac{r}{2}\right]$

$\therefore \quad R' = 16R$

8. (d) Temperature of the wire.

9. (a) $J = 4 \times 10^6 \text{ Am}^{-2}, l = 1 \text{ m}, V = 2 \text{ V}$

$$J = \frac{i}{A} = \frac{1}{A}\left(\frac{V}{R}\right) = \frac{V}{A} \cdot \frac{A}{\rho l} = \frac{V}{\rho l}$$

$$\therefore \quad \rho = \text{resistivity} = \frac{V}{Jl} = \frac{2}{4 \times 10^6 \times 1} = 5 \times 10^{-7} \ \Omega\text{-m}$$

10. (c) Electrical conductivity, $(\sigma) = \frac{1}{\rho}$

$$\therefore \text{SI unit} = \frac{1}{\Omega\text{-m}} = \Omega^{-1} \text{ m}^{-1}$$

11. (b) As we know, $I = Anev_d$

$$I = nAe\left(\frac{eE\tau}{m}\right) \qquad \left[\because v_d = \frac{eE\tau}{m}\right]$$

$$I = \frac{nAe^2\tau E}{m}$$

$$\frac{I}{A} = \frac{ne^2\tau E}{m}$$

$$\mathbf{J} = \frac{ne^2\tau \mathbf{E}}{m} \qquad \left[\because J = \frac{I}{A}\right]$$

$$\mathbf{J} = \left(\frac{1}{\rho}\right)\mathbf{E} \qquad \left[\because \rho = \frac{m}{ne^2\tau}\right]$$

$$\mathbf{J} = \sigma\mathbf{E} \qquad \left[\because \sigma = \frac{1}{\rho}\right]$$

12. Refer to text on page no. 46 (Drift Velocity).

Average drift velocity, $v_d = \frac{eE}{m}\tau$

$v_d = \tau =$ average relaxation time

$E =$ electric field

$e =$ charge on electron

13. For a metallic conductor, the relation between current density (J), conductivity (σ) and electric field intensity (E) can be given as $\mathbf{J} = \sigma\,\mathbf{E}$

14. Change in resistance per unit original resistance per unit rise in temperature is called temperature coefficient of resistance.

i.e $$\alpha = \frac{R_2 - R_1}{R_1(t_2 - t_1)}$$

R_1, R_2 are resistances at t_1°C, t_2°C

15. We know that,

$$J = nev_d$$

$$\Rightarrow \quad \frac{I}{A} = nev_d$$

$$\Rightarrow \quad v_d = \frac{I}{neA} \qquad \ldots\text{(i)}$$

As radius is doubled $A' = 4A$ $\quad \left[\begin{matrix}\text{as } A = \pi r^2 \\ A' = \pi(2r)^2\end{matrix}\right]$

$$\text{As} \quad v'_d = \frac{1}{ne4A} \qquad \ldots\text{(ii)}$$

$\Rightarrow$ So, from Eqs. (i) and (ii),

$$\frac{v'_d}{v_d} = \frac{A}{A'} = \frac{A}{4A}$$

$$\Rightarrow \quad v'_d = \frac{1}{4}v_d$$

16. (b) Ohm's law is obeyed by all metals, provided temperature remains unchanged.

Hence, option (b) is correct.

17. As given temperature coefficient of resistance of a metal is 4×10^{-3}/°C, it represents the increase in resistance by $4 \times 10^{-3}\ \Omega$ for rise of temperature by unit degree celsius. (1°C)

18. Resistivity, $\rho = \frac{m}{ne^2\tau}$

where, $n =$ number of electrons $=$ constant

$e =$ electron charge $=$ constant

$\tau =$ relaxation time $=$ constant

$m =$ mass of electron $=$ constant

$\Rightarrow \rho$ is independent of dimension

So, resistivity remains unchanged when the wire is stretched.

19. While temperature increases, resistance of semiconductor decreases as shown below.

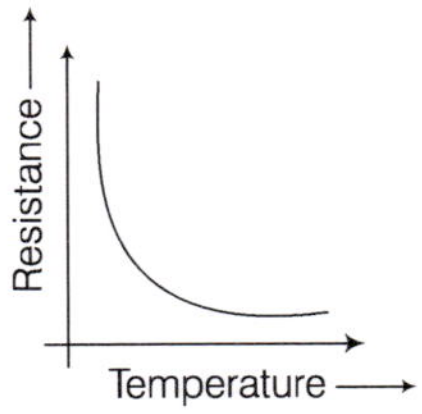

20. Given, $R =$ resistance of wire $= 2\,\Omega$

$A =$ area of cross-section $= 0.70 \times 10^{-6}\text{ m}^2$

$E =$ voltage of battery $= 3.5$ V

$r =$ internal resistance $= 0$

$$i = \frac{E}{R + r} = \frac{3.5}{2 + 0} = 1.75 \text{ A}$$

$\therefore \quad J = \frac{i}{A}$

$\therefore \quad J = \frac{1.75}{0.70 \times 10^{-6}} = 2.50 \times 10^6 \text{ A/m}^2$

21. We know that, Ohm's law is

$$V = RI$$

where, R is resistance of the conductor which is constant at a given temperature

$\Rightarrow \quad V \propto I$

But when temperature changes, R changes, so potential difference (V) will not be proportional to the current (I), thus Ohm's law is not valid in this case.

22. According to the Ohm's law, $V = IR$

Now, if V = constant

So, $\quad I \propto \frac{1}{R}$

where, I = current, R = variable resistance

The variation is shown in the diagram.

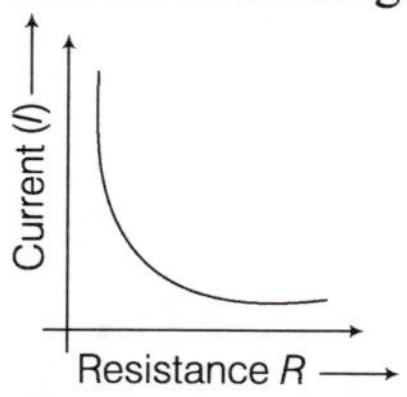

23. (a) Refer to text on page 46. (Topic -1) (Drift velocity)

(b) Refer to text on page 62. (Topic - 3) (Sensitivity of Potentiometer)

24. (i) (a), (ii) (b)

25. Given, cross-sectional area of a copper wire,

$A = 1 \text{ mm}^2 = 1 \times 10^{-6} \text{ m}^2$,

Current, $I = 5$ A

Free electron number density, $n = 2 \times 10^{28}/\text{m}^3$

Drift velocity, $v_d = ?$

As we know that, $I = nAev_d$

$$\Rightarrow \quad v_d = \frac{I}{neA}$$

$$= \frac{5}{2 \times 10^{28} \times 1.6 \times 10^{-19} \times 1 \times 10^{-6}}$$

$$= 1.56 \times 10^{-3} \text{ ms}^{-1}$$

26. The ratio of current flowing at any point in a conductor to the area of cross-section at that place is defined as current density.

$$J = \frac{I}{A}$$

The current density at any point of conductor in terms of drift velocity is, $J = nev_d$

where, v_d = drift velocity.

27. **Drift velocity** It is defined as the average velocity with which the free electron get drifted towards the positive end of the conductor under the influence of an external electric field applied.

Relaxation time The average time that has been elapsed since each electron suffered its last collision with ion/atom of conductor is called relaxation time.

28. At temperature t_0 (0°C), resistance $R_0 = 3\Omega$

At temperature t (150 °C),
resistance $R_t = 4.8\,\Omega$

$\because$ Temperature coefficient of resistance,

$$\alpha = \frac{R_t - R_0}{R_0 \times \Delta t}$$

$$\alpha = \frac{4.8 - 3.0}{3 \times 150} \qquad [\because \Delta t = 150 - 0]$$

$$\alpha = \frac{1.8}{3 \times 150} = \frac{0.6}{150}$$

$$= \frac{6}{1500} = \frac{2}{500}$$

$$\alpha = 0.004 \text{ °C}^{-1}$$

29. (*i*) The resistance of metal increases exponentially with temperature as shown in the graph.

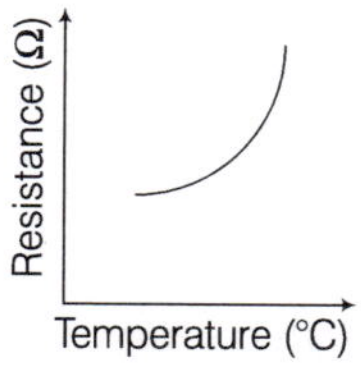

Graph for metallic wire

(*ii*) The resistance of carbon decreases exponentially with temperature as shown in the graph.

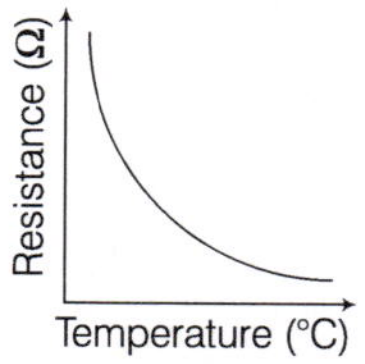

Graph for a piece of carbon

30. We have to apply Ohm's law for current density

$$\mathbf{J} = \sigma\, \mathbf{E}$$

Given, potential difference $V = 3$ V,

Length, $l = 60$ cm $= 0.6$ m ,

Current density, $J = 1 \times 10^{-7}$ Am^{-2}

We know that,

Conductivity,

$$\sigma = \frac{J}{E} = \frac{J \cdot l}{V} = \frac{1 \times 10^{-7} \times 0.6}{3}$$

$$= 2 \times 10^{-8}\ (\Omega\text{-m})^{-1} \qquad \left[\text{as, } E = \frac{V}{l}\right]$$

31. The ratio of current flowing at any point in a conductor to the area of cross-section at that place is defined as current density.

$$|\mathbf{J}| = \frac{I}{|\mathbf{A}|}$$

In vector form, current density $\mathbf{J} = \sigma\, \mathbf{E}$

where, $\sigma =$ conductivity.

$E =$ electric field across the conductor.

32. We know that, resistance

$$R = \rho \frac{l}{A} \Rightarrow R_A = \frac{\rho l_A}{\pi r_A^2}, R_B = \frac{\rho l_B}{\pi r_B^2}$$

where, symbols having their usual meaning.
Given, same mass and same material. Let d be the density of both wires respectively. Then, according to the question

$$M_A = M_B$$

[where, M_A, M_B masses of A and B]

$$\pi r_A^2 l_A d = \pi r_B^2 l_B d$$

$$\frac{\pi r_B^2}{4} l_A d = \pi r_B^2 l_B d \qquad \left[\because r_A = \frac{r_B}{2}\right]$$

$$\therefore \quad l_A = 4 l_B$$

[where, l_A, l_B are the lengths of the two wires]

$$\therefore \quad \frac{R_B}{R_A} = \frac{\rho l_B}{4\pi r_A^2} \cdot \frac{\pi r_A^2}{\rho l_A}$$

[where, R_A, R_B are the resistances of the wires A and B and ρ is the resistivity]

$$\frac{R_B}{R_A} = \frac{l_B}{4 l_A} = \frac{1}{16}$$

$$\therefore \quad R_B = \frac{24}{16} = 1.5\ \Omega$$

33. We know that, drift velocity

$$v_d = \frac{eV}{ml} \times \tau$$

where, $V =$ potential difference

$m =$ mass of the electron

$l =$ length of the wire

$\tau =$ relaxation time

(*i*) If V is doubled, then drift velocity will also be double.

(*ii*) If l is doubled, then drift velocity will be half.

34. Resistivity in semiconductors like germanium or silicon decreases with rise in temperature i.e., their temperature coefficient of resistance is negative.

The reason is that, for such substance e.g., silicon, the value of n (the number of free electrons in unit volume) is very small compared to the metals; but with rise in temperature the number of free electrons i.e., the value of n goes on increasing in the conduction band. Therefore, the resistance $R = \left(\frac{ml}{\tau e^2 nA}\right)$ goes on decreasing. Although in these substances also the relaxation time τ decreases with rise in temperature but the increase in the value of n is large compared to the decrease in τ. Hence, the net effect of rise in temperature is that the resistance decreases.

35. (*i*) Refer to solution 27

(*ii*) We know that, $J = nev_d$

$$\Rightarrow \quad \frac{I}{A} = nev_d \Rightarrow v_d \propto \frac{1}{A}$$

[$\because n, e, I$ and v_d are constants]

where, $n =$ no. of free electrons

$e =$ electron charge

$v_d =$ drift speed

$A =$ area of cross-section

So, drift velocity (v_d) at A is smaller than at B.
Because area of cross-section A is larger than B.

36. The variation of resistance with temperature is given by the relation

$$R_t = R_0\ (1 + \alpha t) \qquad \ldots\text{(i)}$$

where, R_t and R_0 are the resistance of the conductor at t °C and 0°C respectively and α is the temperature coefficient of the resistance.

Using Eq. (i), we get

$$\alpha = \frac{R_t - R_0}{R_0 t}$$

then temperature coefficient of resistances is defined as the change in resistance per unit original resistance for each degree rise in temperature. The temperature coefficient of carbon (a semiconductor) is negative whereas for metals, it is positive. Thus, the resistance of carbon falls when its temperature increases.

37. Drifting occurs due to application of external electric field. When no external field is applied there is no drift of electrons in the conductor.

(*i*) The given expression is

$$I = neAv_d$$

where, I = current flowing through the conductor

n = number of free electrons per unit volume

e = charge of an electron

A = area of cross-section

v_d = drift velocity

(*ii*) When a conductor of length l is subjected to the potential difference of V, each electron experiences

a force $$F = -e\frac{V}{l}$$

and free electron acquires an acceleration

$$a = \frac{F}{m} = -\frac{eE}{m} = \frac{-eV}{ml} \quad \left[\text{as, } E = \frac{V}{l}\right] \quad \ldots\text{(i)}$$

where, m = mass of electron, e = electronic charge and E = electric field. Free electrons starts accelerating in the conductor.

The average time difference between two consecutive collisions is known as relaxation time of electron and

$$\bar{\tau} = \frac{\tau_1 + \tau_2 + \cdots + \tau_n}{n} \quad \ldots\text{(ii)}$$

where, $\tau_1, \tau_2, \cdots, \tau_n$ are the average time differences between 1st, 2nd, ..., n th collisions.

$\therefore v_1, v_2, \ldots, v_n$ are velocities gained by electron in 1st, 2nd, ..., n th collisions with initial thermal velocities $u_1, u_2, \ldots, u_n$ respectively.

$$\therefore \quad v_1 = u_1 + a\tau_1$$

$$v_2 = u_2 + a\tau_2$$

$$\vdots \quad \vdots \quad \vdots$$

$$v_n = u_n + a\tau_n$$

The drift speed v_d may be defined as

$$v_d = \frac{v_1 + v_2 + \cdots + v_n}{n}$$

$$v_d = \frac{(u_1 + u_2 + \cdots + u_n) + a(\tau_1 + \tau_2 + \cdots + \tau_n)}{n}$$

$$v_d = \frac{(u_1 + u_2 + \cdots + u_n)}{n} + \frac{a(\tau_1 + \tau_2 + \cdots + \tau_n)}{n}$$

$$v_d = 0 + a\tau \quad [\because \text{average thermal velocity} = 0]$$

$$v_d = -\left(\frac{eV}{ml}\right)\tau \quad [\text{from Eq. (i)}]$$

This is the required expression of drift speed of free electrons.

$$\Rightarrow \quad |v_d| = \frac{eV}{lm}\tau \quad \left[\because E = \frac{V}{l}\right]$$

TOPIC 2

Electric Cell and Their Combination

An **electric cell** is a source of electrical energy which maintains a continuous flow of charge in a circuit.

It has two electrodes (*i*) positive (P) and (*ii*) negative (N) as shown below.

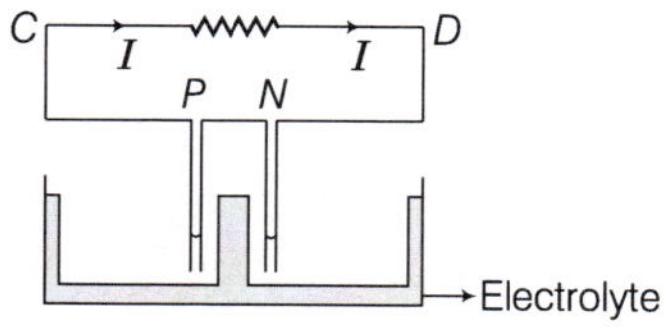

NOTE In a standard cell there is no chemical reaction except when current is passing.

Electromotive Force (EMF) of a Cell

The work done by cell in moving unit positive charge through the whole circuit (including the cell) is called electromotive force (emf) of the cell.

EMF of the cell $\boxed{E = W/q}$

Its SI unit is joule/coulomb or volt.

If $W = 1$ J and $q = 1$ C, then $E = 1$ V

i.e., if in the flow of 1 C of charge, the work done by the cell is 1 J, then the emf of the cell is 1 V.

Internal Resistance (r)

Internal resistance of a cell is defined as the resistance offered by the electrolyte of the cell, to the flow of current through it. It is denoted by r. Its SI unit is ohm (Ω).

Back EMF

When a steady current i is established in the circuit, a charge dq flows in the circuit in time dt. By the definition of emf, the work done by the cell is given by

$$dW = Edq = Eidt \qquad [\because dq = idt]$$

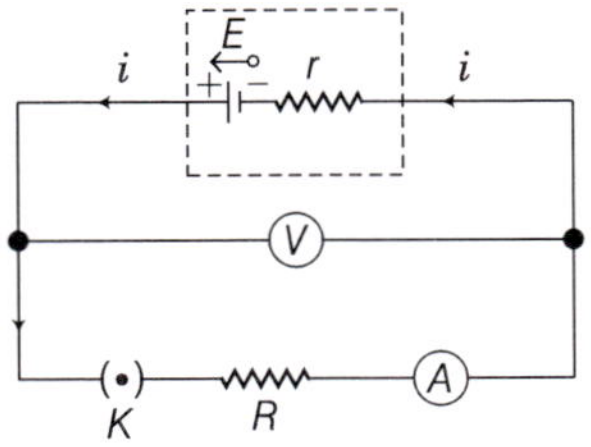

$$\Rightarrow \qquad E = V + ir \Rightarrow \boxed{V = E - ir}$$

Thus, the significant current from a cell can be drawn only when the potential difference across its terminals is greater than ir. $(E > ir)$

This product ir opposes the flow of current through the cell so, it is called back EMF.

Terminal Potential Difference (V)

Terminal potential difference of a cell is defined as the potential difference between the two terminals of the cell in a closed circuit (i.e., when current is drawn from the cell). It is represented by V and its unit is volt.

The Relation among r, R, E and V

Internal resistance, $r = R\left(\frac{E}{V} - 1\right)$ ...(i)

where, $R =$ external resistance,

$E =$ emf of cell

$V =$ terminal voltage of cell

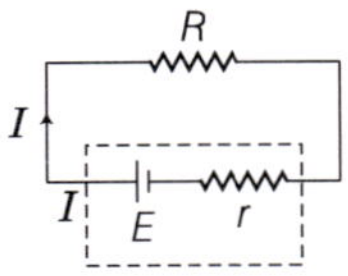

Also, $V = E - Ir$ ...(ii)

and $V = \left(\frac{E}{R + r}\right)R$

or $$\boxed{V = \frac{E}{\left(1 + \frac{r}{R}\right)}}$$ ...(iii)

The terminal voltage increases with the increase of external resistance R.

The graphical representation of variation of terminal voltage (V) with the external resistance (R) is shown below.

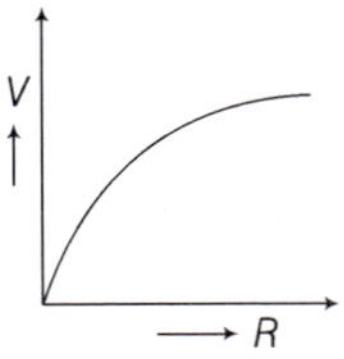

Variation of terminal voltage with external resistance

During charging of the cell, $V = E + Ir$

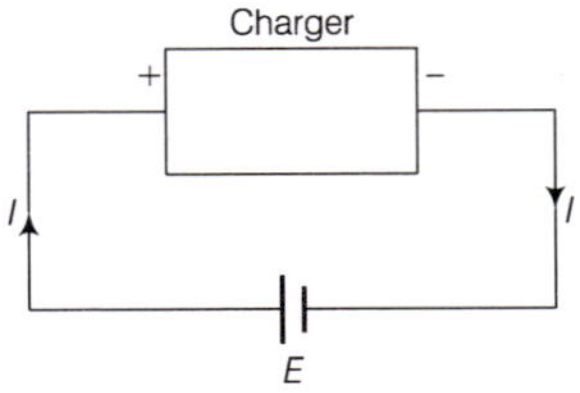

So, $V < E$ when the current is drawn from the cell (i. e., discharging) and $V > E$ when the charging of cell takes place.

The variation of terminal voltage with the current drawn from the cell is shown graphically.

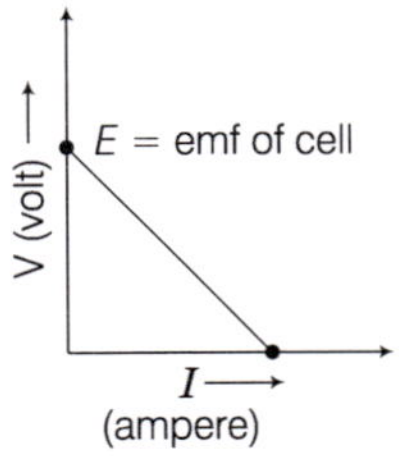

Variation of terminal voltage *versus* current

Combination of Cells

The combination of cells is called battery.

Cells can be combined in three ways

(*i*) In series

(*ii*) In parallel

(*iii*) In mixed grouping

(i) Series Combination

The equivalent emf of battery

$$E = E_1 + E_2$$

Equivalent internal resistance, $r = r_1 + r_2$

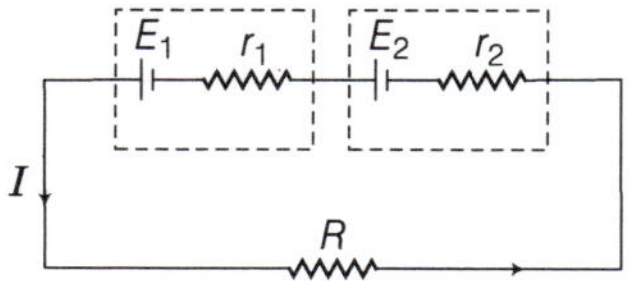

Series combination of cells

If polarity of one of the batteries is reversed, then equivalent emf $|E_1 - E_2|$ and net internal resistance continue to be the same i.e.,

$$r_{eq} = r_1 + r_2$$

(ii) Parallel Combination

The equivalent emf of parallel combination of cells is given by $$E_{eq} = \frac{E_1 r_2 + E_2 r_1}{r_1 + r_2}$$

and equivalent internal resistance of combination

$$r_{eq} = \frac{r_1 r_2}{r_1 + r_2}$$

(iii) Mixed Grouping

It consists of m rows in parallel combination such that each row contains n cells of each of the emf E and internal resistance r.

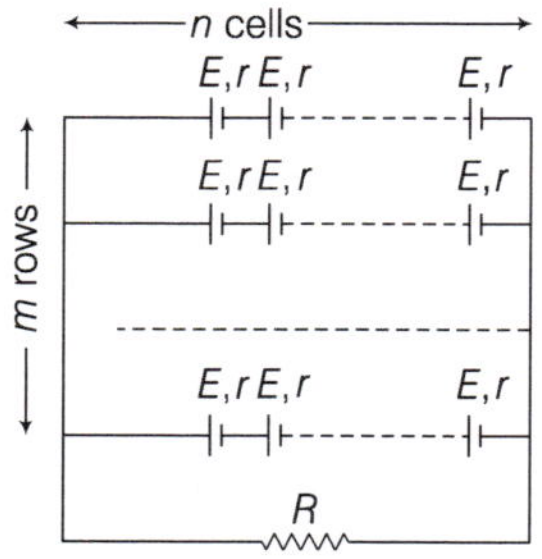

Mixed grouping of cells

Then, current in the circuit is given by $I = \frac{mnE}{mR + nr}$

Net internal resistance is given by, $r_0 = \frac{nr}{m}$

Also, maximum current is drawn from the battery, when external resistance matches with the net internal resistance i.e.

$$R = \frac{nr}{m}$$

$$\therefore \quad I_{max} = \frac{mE}{2r}$$

PYQs Previous Years Questions

1 Mark Questions

1. Three identical cells each of emf e are connected in parallel to form a battery. What is the emf of the battery? **ISC 2024**

2. A cell of emf E is connected to an external resistance R. The potential difference across cell is V. The internal resistance of cell will be **ISC 2022 Sem-I**

(a) $\frac{(E-V)R}{E}$ (b) $\frac{(E-V)R}{V}$

(c) $\frac{(V-E)R}{V}$ (d) $\frac{(V-E)R}{E}$

3. n identical cells each of emf E and internal resistance r are connected in parallel. An external resistance R is connected in series to this combination. The current through R is **ISC 2022 Sem-I**

(a) $\frac{nE}{R+nr}$ (b) $\frac{nE}{nR+r}$ (c) $\frac{E}{R+nr}$ (d) $\frac{nE}{R+r}$

4. Four identical cells each having an emf of 4 V are connected in parallel. What will be the emf of this combination? **ISC 2022 Sem-I**

(a) 1 V (b) 16 V (c) 1/4 V (d) 4 V

5. A battery sends a current of 1.5 A through an external resistance of 1.0 Ω. If internal resistance of the battery is 0.5 Ω, its emf is **ISC 2022 Sem-I**

(a) 2.00 V (b) 2.25 V
(c) 2.50 V (d) 2.75 V

6. N identical cells each of emf e and internal resistance r are connected in series to form a row. M such rows are connected in parallel to form a battery. When an external resistance R is connected to the battery, current flowing through it is **ISC 2022 Sem-I**

(a) $MNe/(R+r)$ (b) $MNe/(NR+Mr)$
(c) $MNe/(MR+Nr)$ (d) $Ne/(MR+Nr)$

7. A resistor R is connected to a cell of emf e and internal resistance r. Potential difference across the resistor R is found to be V. State the relation between e, V, R and r. **ISC 2015**

8. Three identical cells each of emf 2 V and internal resistance 1 Ω are connected in series to form a battery. The battery is then connected to a parallel combination of two identical resistors, each of resistance 6 Ω. Find the current delivered by the battery. **ISC 2015**

9. Find the emf of the battery shown in the figure. **ISC 2014**

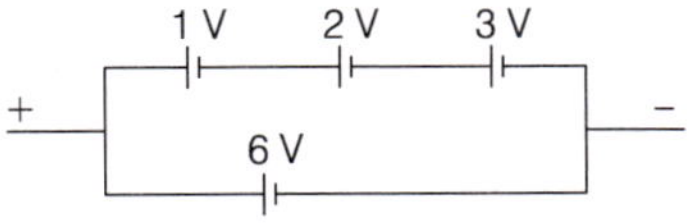

10. Figure below shows five DC sources (cells). Their emfs are shown in the figure.

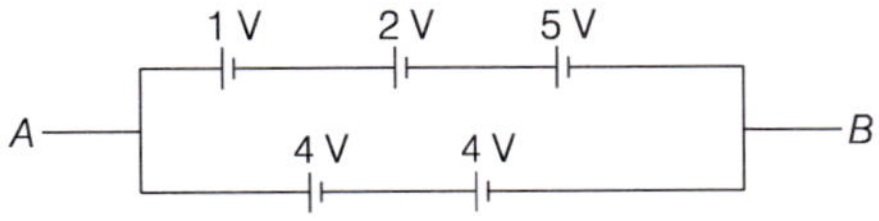

Emf of the battery AB is **ISC 2012**

(a) 8 V (b) 16 V
(c) 4 V (d) 2 V

2 Marks Question

11. Calculate the net emf across A and B as shown in the figure below **ISC 2019**

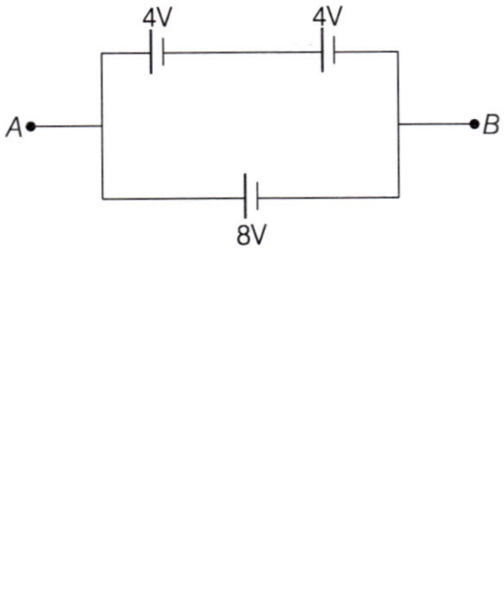

3 Marks Questions

12. n cells, each of emf e and internal resistance r are joined in the series to form a row. m such rows are connected in parallel to form a battery of $N = mn$ cells. This battery is connected to an external resistance R.

(i) What is the emf of this battery and how much is its internal resistance?

(ii) Show that current I flowing through the external resistance R is given by

$$I = \frac{Ne}{mR + nr}$$

ISC 2013

13. Define the emf of a cell in terms of the work done in moving a charge through the cell.

Using Joule's law obtain the equation, emf $= I\,(R + r)$. (The symbols have their usual meaning). **ISC 2007**

4/5 Marks Question

14. Two cells of same emf E, but different internal resistances r_1 and r_2 are connected to an external resistance R as shown in the figure given below.

The voltmeter V reads zero. Obtain an expression for R in terms of r_1 and r_2. Calculate the voltage across the cell of internal resistance r_2. (Assume that the voltmeter V is of infinite resistance). **ISC 2005**

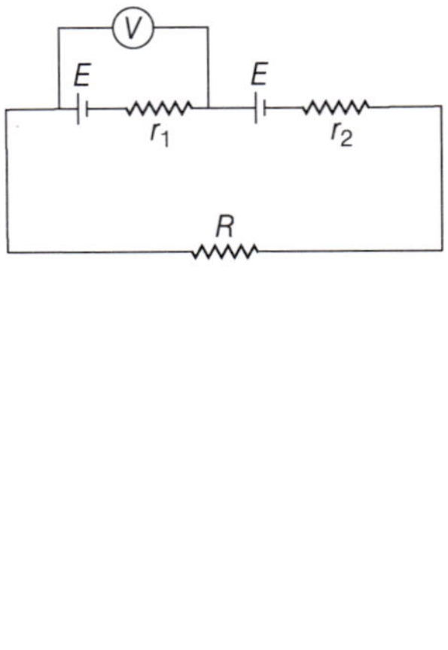

Explanations

1.

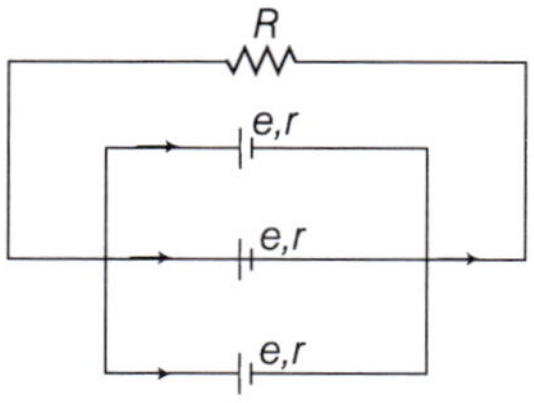

Current in the resistance R is the given by

$$I = \frac{E}{\left(R + \frac{r}{m}\right)} \text{ or } E = \frac{I}{R + \frac{R}{m}}$$

2. (b) Let the current in the circuit,

$$I = \frac{V}{R}$$

Across the cell, $E = V + Ir$

$$\Rightarrow \quad r = \frac{E - V}{I} = \frac{E - V}{\frac{V}{R}} = \left(\frac{E - V}{V}\right)R$$

3. (b) Total resistance of circuit

$$= R + \frac{r}{n}$$

Current, $I = \dfrac{E}{R + \frac{r}{n}} = \dfrac{nE}{nR + r}$

4. (d) In the parallel combination difference or emf are same. The combined emf is 4 V.

5. (b) $I = 1.5$ A

$R = 1.0\,\Omega$, $r = 0.5\,\Omega$

emf $= E = ?$

As we know, $I = \dfrac{E}{R + r}$

$\Rightarrow \; E = I\,(R + r) = 1.5\,(1.0 + 0.5) = 2.25$ V

6. (c) $E_{eq} = Ne$

$$\frac{1}{r_{eq}} = \frac{1}{Nr} + \frac{1}{Nr} \;..... + \text{upto } M \text{ terms} = \frac{M}{Nr}$$

$$\therefore \quad r_{eq} = \frac{Nr}{M}$$

$$\therefore \quad I = \frac{E_{eq}}{r_{eq} + R} = \frac{Ne}{\frac{Nr}{M} + R} = \frac{MNe}{MR + Nr}$$

7. The relation between e, V, R and r is that $e = IR + Ir$

where, $e =$ emf of cell,

$IR =$ potential drop across external resistance R

and $Ir =$ potential drop across internal resistance r.

8. According to the figure, all $1\,\Omega$ resistors are in the series combination and $6\,\Omega$ resistors are in parallel combination. So, the equivalent resistance of the circuit,

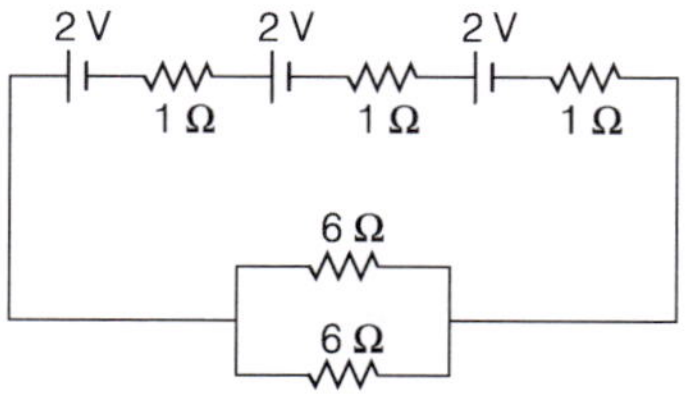

$$R_T = 1 + 1 + 1 + \frac{6 \times 6}{6 + 6}$$

$$\Rightarrow \quad R_T = 3 + \frac{36}{12}$$

$$\Rightarrow \quad R_T = 6\,\Omega$$

Total voltage of the circuit, $V_T = 2 + 2 + 2 = 6$ V

Now current in the circuit, $I = \dfrac{V_T}{R_T} = \dfrac{6}{6} = 1$ A

9. Consider the circuit. Let the emf of the battery is E_{eq}.

It is clear from the figure that the cells E_1, E_2 and E_3 are in series.

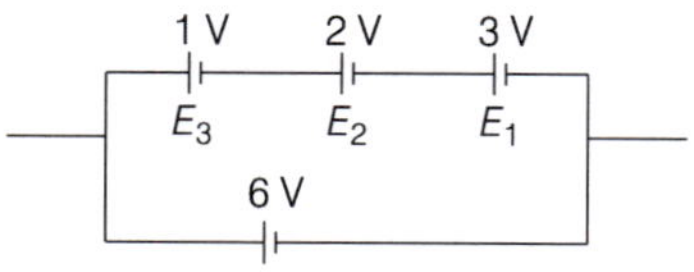

So, equivalent emf $\quad E_4 = E_1 + E_2 + E_3$

$$= 3\text{ V} + 2\text{ V} + 1\text{ V} = 6\text{ V}$$

As the two cells are in parallel

10. Consider the diagram

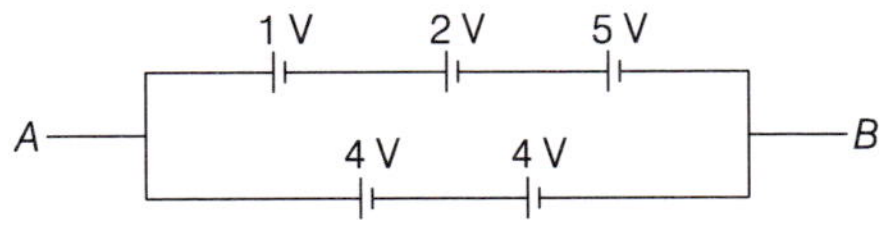

The cells connected in series will be added up for the calculation of equivalent emf.

Now, the two cells are in parallel.

So, the equivalent emf will be

V_e = emf of each cell = 8 V.

The correct option is (a)

11. 4V and 4V cells are in series so their combined emf, $E_1 = 4 + 4 = 8$V. Now E_1 and 8V cells are in parallel, so the combined emf of the battery is 8V.

12. In mixed grouping of cells the equivalent emf can be calculated by first calculating emf for the series combination and then find equivalent emf for the parallel combination. Let $E_1, E_2, \ldots, E_n$ are emf's and $r_1, r_2, \ldots, r_n$ are the internal resistances of n cells.

(*i*) For I cell, $E_1 = V_1 + ir_1$

$\Rightarrow \quad V_1 = E_1 - ir_1$

For II cell, $V_2 = E_2 - ir_2$

For n th cell, $V_n = E_n - ir_n$

Total voltage difference

$V = V_1 + V_2 + V_3 + \cdots + V_n$

$V = (E_1 + E_2 + \cdots + E_n) - i(r_1 + r_2 + \cdots + r_n)$

$V = E_{eq} - ir_{eq}$

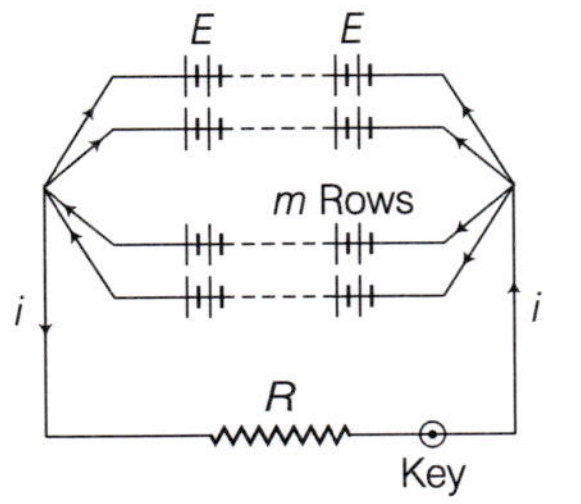

where, $\quad E_{eq} = E_1 + E_2 + \cdots + E_n$

$r_{eq} = r_1 + r_2 + \cdots + r_n$

If $\quad E_1 = E_2 = \cdots = E_n = E$

and $\quad r_1 = r_2 = \cdots = r_n = r$

Then, $\quad E_{eq} = nE \Rightarrow r_{eq} = nr$

If m rows of series of n cells are connected in parallel, then

Total emf of battery i.e., equivalent emf = nE

Total internal resistance = $\frac{nr}{m}$

(*ii*) The electric current flow in the circuit

$$I = \frac{\text{Total emf}}{\text{Total resistance}}$$

$$I = \frac{nE}{\frac{nr}{m} + R} = \frac{mn\,E}{nr + mR}$$

According to the question, $E = e$

$$I = \frac{mne}{mR + nr} = \frac{Ne}{mR + nr} \qquad [\because N = mn]$$

13. Work done by a battery of emf E, when charge dq passes through the battery is (dqE). Work done in carrying a unit positive charge in a circuit is defined as emf of a cell.

Suppose, when a steady current I is established in a circuit containing a cell of emf E, internal resistance r and an external resistance R, a charge dq flows in the circuit in time dt. By the definition of emf and according to Joule's law, the work done by the cell is given by

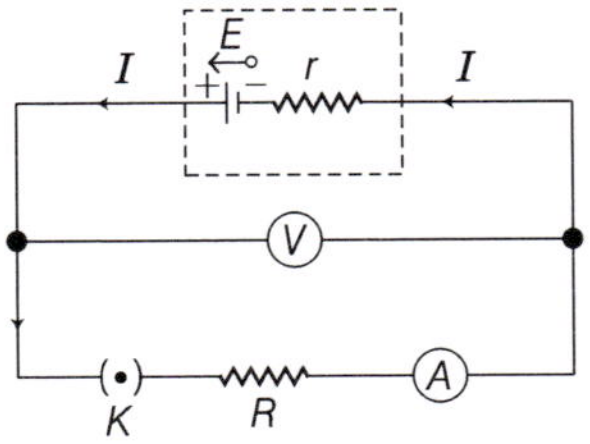

$$dW = E\,dq = EI\,dt \qquad [\because dq = I\,dt]$$

If $V = IR$ be the potential difference across R, then the external work done by the cell is given by

$$dW_{ext} = V\,dq = VI\,dt$$

$$= I^2R\,dt \qquad \text{[by Joule's law]}$$

If $V = Ir$ be the potential drop across the internal resistance r, the internal work done by the cell is given by

$$dW_{int} = VIdt = I^2rdt \qquad \text{[by Joule's law]}$$

By the law of conservation of energy,

$$dW = dW_{ext} + dW_{int}$$

$$EI\,dt = I^2R\,dt + I^2r\,dt$$

$$E = I(R + r)$$

14. Find effective emf of the series combination of the cell. Then, current through the circuit can be calculated using $i = \frac{E_{net}}{r_{net}}$.

As the two cells are in series, the effective emf is $2E$ and the total resistance is $r_1 + r_2 + R$.

Therefore, the current in the circuit is

$$i = \frac{2E}{r_1 + r_2 + R} \quad \text{...(i)}$$

The voltage across the cell of internal resistance r_1 is

$$V = E - ir_1 = 0 \quad [\because \text{voltmeter } V \text{ reads zero}]$$

$$i = \frac{E}{r_1} \quad \text{...(ii)}$$

From Eqs. (i) and (ii), we get

$$\frac{E}{r_1} = \frac{2E}{r_1 + r_2 + R}$$

$$\Rightarrow \quad R = r_1 - r_2$$

This is required relation.

The voltage across the cell of internal resistance r_2 is

$$V' = E - ir_2$$

TOPIC 3

Kirchhoff's Laws and Their Applications

Ohm's law was not sufficient to study of the circuits containing more than one source of emf. Kirchhoff has given two rules based on conservation of the electric charge and conservation of energy. These are known as Kirchhoff's laws.

Kirchhoff's First Law/Junction Law/Current Law

The algebraic sum of electric current at any junction of the electric circuit is equal to zero i.e., the sum of current entering into a junction is equal to the sum of current leaving the junction.

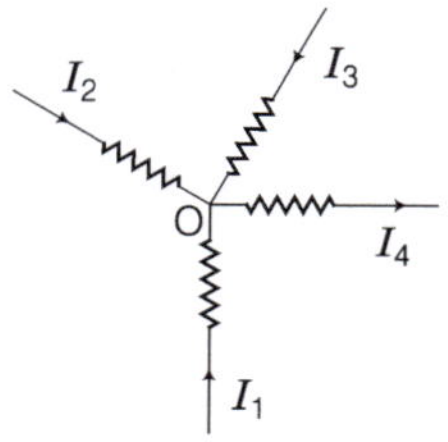

$$\Sigma I = 0, I_4 = I_1 + I_2 + I_3$$

Junction law supports the **law of conservation** of charge, because junction is a point in a circuit which cannot act as a source or sink of charge(s).

Junction law supports the **law of conservation** of charge, because junction is a point in a circuit which cannot act as a source or sink of charge(s).

Kirchhoff's Second Law/Loop Law/Voltage Law

In any closed mesh of electrical circuit, the algebraic sum of emfs of cell and product of current and resistance is always equal to zero.

$$\Sigma E + \Sigma IR = 0$$

Kirchhoff's second law supports **the law of conservation of energy**. Because the net change in the energy of a charge, after the charge complete a closed path must be zero.

Sign convention for Kirchhoff's second law

(*i*) Emf from negative to positive of the battery is taken to be positive i.e. + E.

(*ii*) Emf from positive to negative of the battery is taken to be negative i.e. – E.

(*iii*) The potential drop in the direction of current is taken to be negative i.e. $V = -IR$.

(*iv*) The potential drop opposite to the flow of current is taken to be positive i.e. $V = +IR$

Differences between Kirchhoff's I and II Laws

First law	Second law
This law can be used in open and closed circuits.	This law can be used in closed circuits only.
This law supports the law of conservation of charge.	This law supports the law of conservation of energy.
According to this rule, $\Sigma I = 0$	According to this rule, $\Sigma E = \Sigma IR$

Wheatstone Bridge

It is an arrangement of four resistances P, Q, R and S connected to form the arms of quadrilateral $ABCD$ as shown in figure given below.

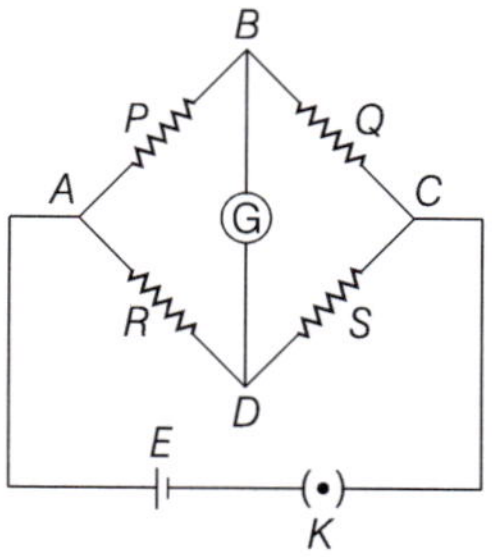

A battery with key and galvanometer are connected along its two diagonals, respectively.

The bridge is said to be **balanced**, when

(i) $V_B = V_D$

(ii) there is no flow of current through the galvanometer.

In the balanced condition, ratio of resistances of adjacent arms are equal.

i. e. $\frac{P}{Q} = \frac{R}{S} \Rightarrow PS = QR$

The Wheatstone bridge is said to be sensitive, if it gives ample deflection in the galvanometer even on slight change of resistance.

For sensitivity of galvanometer, the magnitude of four resistanes P, Q, R and S should be of same order.

Meter Bridge

It is an electrical device used to determine the resistance and hence specific resistance of material of the given wire/conductor.

It is based on the principle of balanced Wheatstone bridge. Resistance of a uniform wire ∝ Length of conductor.

At balanced situation of bridge,

$$\frac{P}{Q} = \frac{R}{S} \text{ or } \frac{l}{100 - l} = \frac{R}{S}$$

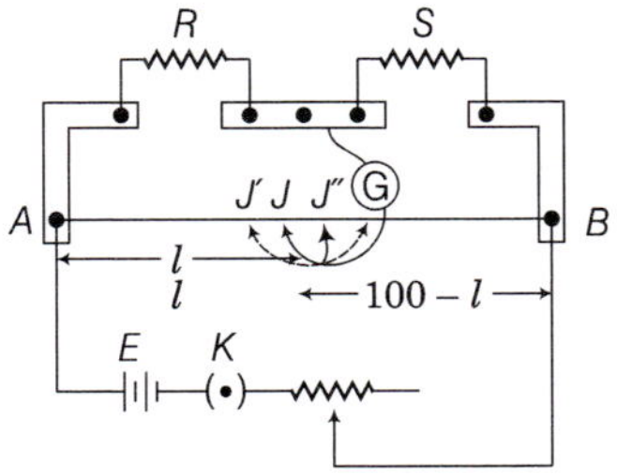

Meter bridge

$$S = \left(\frac{100 - l}{l}\right) \times R$$

where, l is the balancing length.

where, P, Q, R and S are the arm resistances of a balanced Wheatstone bridge.

Potentiometer

It is an electrical device which can be used for the following purposes.

- Measure the potential difference with greater accuracy.
- Compare the emfs of two cells.
- Measure the emf of a cell.
- Used to determine the internal resistance of a primary cell.

The potentiometer works on the principle that the potential difference across any two points of uniform current carrying conductor is directly proportional to the length between the two points of the wire of potentiometer i.e.,

$$V \propto l$$

$$\Rightarrow \quad V = kl$$

where k = constant of proportionality called the potential gradient.

$$\therefore \quad k = \frac{V}{l}$$

So the potential gradient is defined as the potential drop per unit length of potentiometer wire.

Measurement of Potential Difference Using Potentiometers

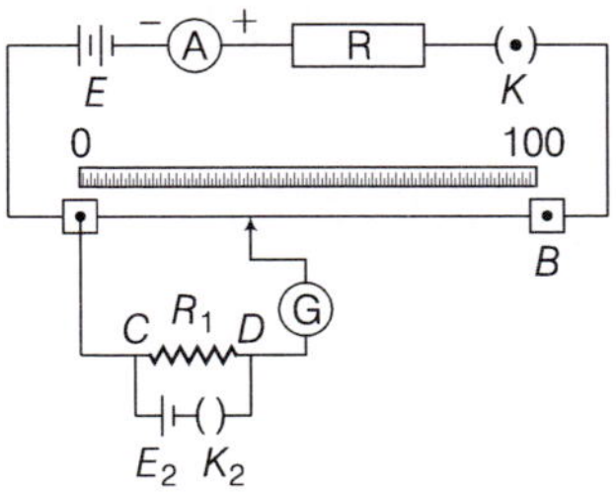

Potentiometer

If r is the resistance of potentiometer wire of length L, then potential gradient of potentiometer wire is given by

$$k = \left(\frac{E}{R + r}\right)\frac{r}{L}$$

∴ Potential drop across potentiometer wire

$$V = kl = \left(\frac{E}{R + r}\right)\frac{r}{L} l$$

Comparison of EMF of Two Cells

The emfs of two primary cells can be compared using potentiometer as

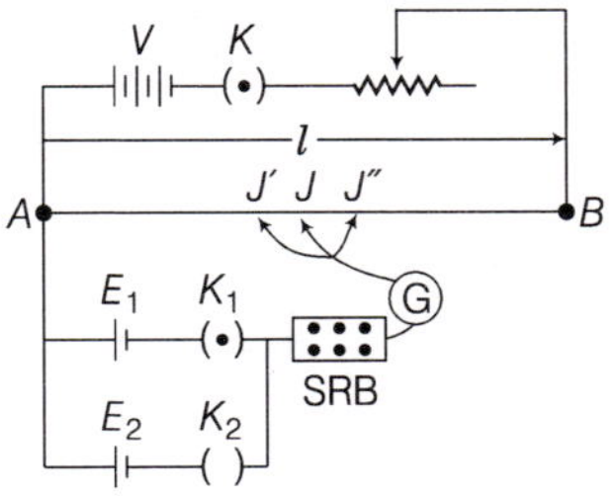

$$\frac{E_1}{E_2} = \frac{l_1}{l_2}$$

where, l_1 and l_2 are the balancing lengths corresponding to the cells of emfs E_1 and E_2 respectively.

Determination of Internal Resistance of Cell

The internal resistance can be determined using potentiometer.

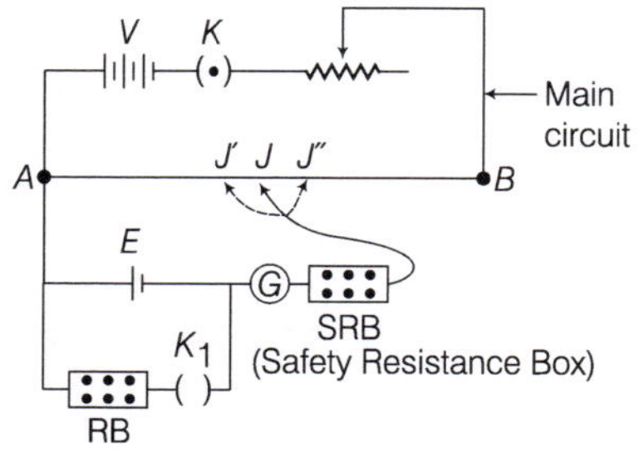

Resistance box

$$r = R\left(\frac{l_1}{l_2} - 1\right)$$

Sensitivity of Potentiometer

The sensitivity of a potentiometer refers to the capability of measuring very small potential difference and exhibit change in balancing length even on very small change in potential difference. It can also be used to calibrate a voltmeter or an ammeter. The sensitivity of potentiometer can be increased by increasing the number of wires of potentiometer and decreasing the value of potential gradient.

NOTE The potentiometer is a better device to measure potential difference, than a voltmeter as null point method is used and hence it can measure even the emf of cell but voltmeter cannot.

PYQs Previous Years Questions

1 Mark Questions

1. A meter bridge is balanced with a known resistance (R) in the left hand gap and an unknown resistance (S) in the right hand gap. Balance point is found to be at a distance of l cm from the left hand side. When the battery and the galvanometer are interchanged, balance point will **ISC 2024**

(a) shift towards left
(b) shift towards right
(c) remain same
(d) shift towards left or right depending on the values of R and S

2. The current in the circuit shown in figure below, will be **ISC 2022 Sem-I**

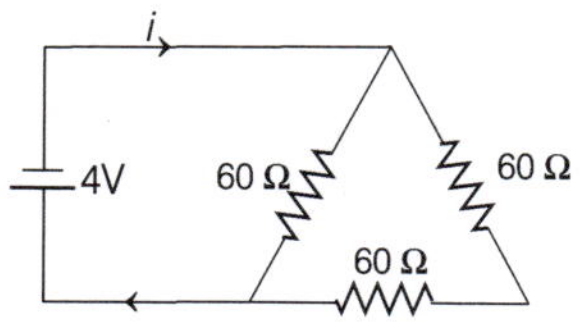

(a) (1/45) A
(b) (1/15) A
(c) (1/10) A
(d) (1/5) A

3. The figure given below shows currents in a part of an electric circuit. The current i is **ISC 2022 Sem-I**

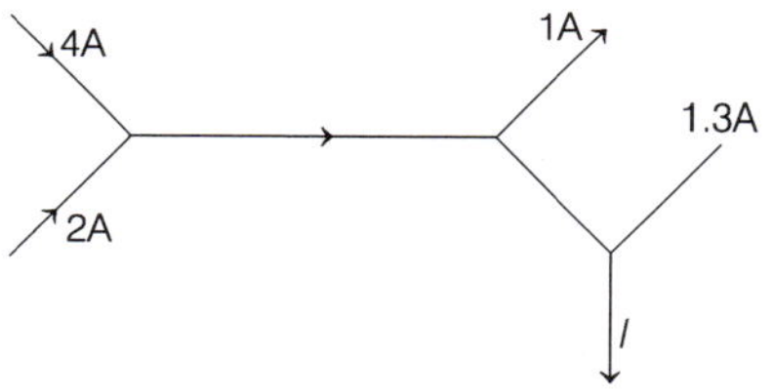

(a) 1.7 A
(b) 3.7 A
(c) 2.7 A
(d) 4.7 A

4. The circuit shown in figure below is used to compare the emf of two cells E_1 and E_2 where $E_2 > E_1$. The null point is at C when the galvanometer is connected to E_1. When the galvanometer is connected to E_2, the null point will be **ISC 2022 Sem-I**

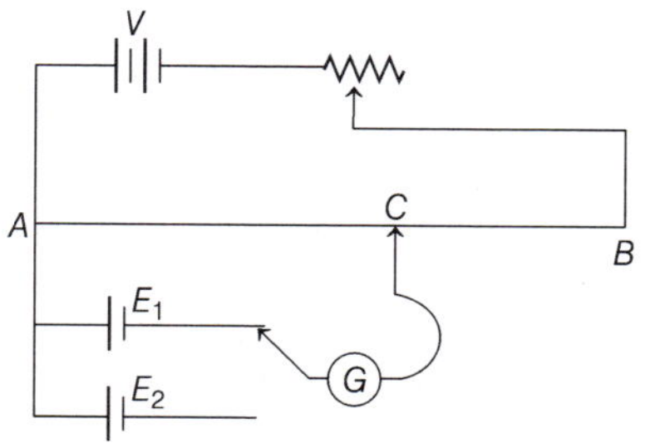

(a) to the left of C
(b) to the right of C
(c) at C itself
(d) no where on AB

5. A 2 V battery, a 15 Ω resistor and a potentiometer of 100 cm length, all are connected in series. If the resistance of potentiometer wire is 5 Ω, then the potential gradient of the potentiometer wire is .... **ISC 2022 Sem-I**

(a) 0.005 V/cm (b) 0.05 V/cm
(c) 0.02 V/cm (d) 0.2 V/cm

6. In an experiment of meter bridge, a null point is obtained at the centre of the bridge wire. When a resistance of 5 is connected in one gap, what is the value of resistance in the other gap? **ISC 2022 Sem-I**

(a) 10 Ω (c) 5 Ω
(b) 1/5 Ω (d) 500 Ω

7. The potential gradient along the length of a uniform wire is 20 V/m. B and C are the two points at 40 cm and 70 cm point on a meter scale fitted along the wire. What is the potential difference between B and C? **ISC 2022 Sem-I**

(a) 6 V (b) 0.4V (c) 0.6 V (d) 4 V

8. Kirchhoff's junction rule is based on the principle of conservation of **ISC 2022 Sem-I**

(a) energy (b) charge
(c) momentum (d) momentum and energy

9. Wheatstone bridge principle is used to measure **ISC 2022 Sem-I**

(a) resistance of a wire
(b) potential difference across a resistor
(c) current flowing through a wire
(d) emf of a cell

10. In the Wheatstone bridge circuit shown below, $P = 10\ \Omega$, $Q = 20\ \Omega$, $R = 200\ \Omega$, $S = 100\ \Omega$ and emf of the battery being 2V. The current flowing through the galvanometer is **ISC 2022 Sem-I**

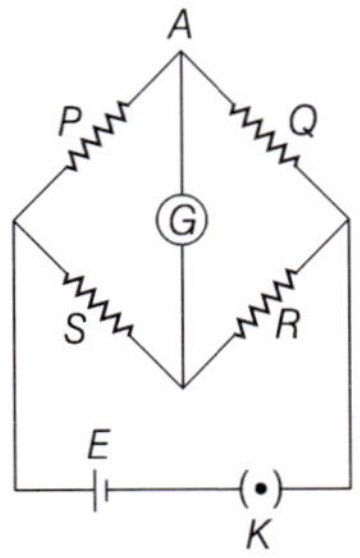

(a) 0 (b) 1 A (c) 2 A (d) 3 A

11. If potential difference across 80 cm of a potentiometer wire is 2V, potential gradient across the wire is **ISC 2022 Sem-I**

(a) $0.025\ Vm^{-1}$ (b) $0.050\ Vm^{-1}$
(c) $0.075\ Vm^{-1}$ (d) $2.50\ Vm^{-1}$

12. In a potentiometer, balancing length with a standard cell of emf 1.08 V is 21.6 cm. Balancing length with a cell of emf 1.50V will be **ISC 2022 Sem-I**

(a) 21.6 cm (b) 30.0 cm (c) 45.0 cm (d) 60.0 cm

13. In a potentiometer experiment, balancing length is found to be 120 cm for a cell ε_1 of emf 2 V. What will be the balancing length for another cell ε_2 of emf 1.5 V? No other changes are made in the experiment. **ISC 2018**

14. How will be the sensitivity of a potentiometer change with increase in current flowing through its wire? **ISC SQP 2018**

15. Name the two conservation laws implied in Kirchhoff's laws for electric circuits. **ISC 2017, 07, 02**

16. In figure given below, find the value of resistance X for which points A and B are at the same potential. **ISC 2016**

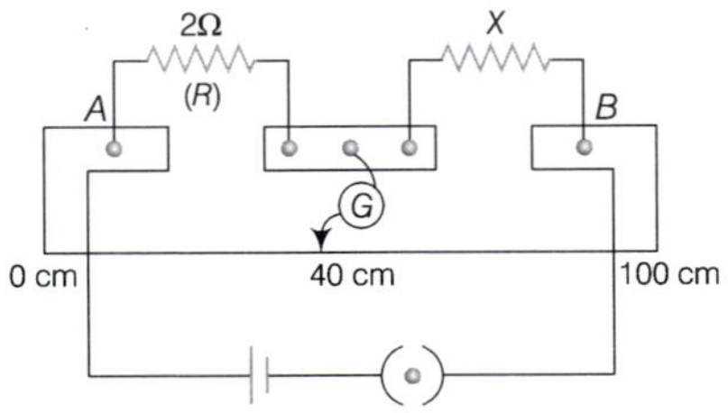

17. Five resistors are connected as shown in the figure.

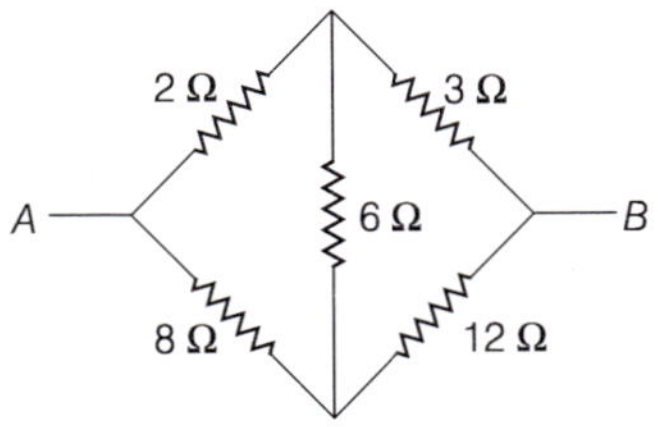

The effective resistance i.e., equivalent resistance between the points A and B is **ISC 2013**

(a) 4 Ω (b) 5 Ω (c) 15 Ω (d) 20 Ω

18. A 10 m long potentiometer wire carries a steady current. A standard cell of emf 1.018 V is balanced against a length of 254.5 cm of the wire. What is the potential gradient across the potentiometer wire? **ISC 2011**

19. A moving coil galvanometer can be converted into a voltmeter by connecting

(a) a low resistance in series with its coil
(b) a low resistance in parallel with its coil
(c) a high resistance in parallel with its coil
(d) a high resistance in series with its coil **ISC 2010**

20. A part of an electric circuit is shown below.

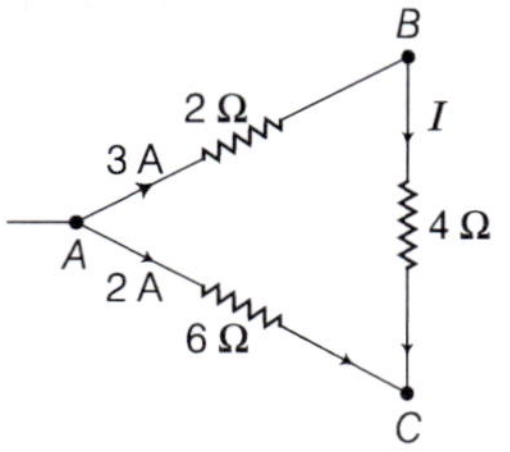

Using Kirchhoff's 2nd law, find the current I flowing through the 4Ω resistor. **ISC 2010**

21. Find the value of resistance X in the circuit below so that the junctions M and N are at the same potential. **ISC 2009**

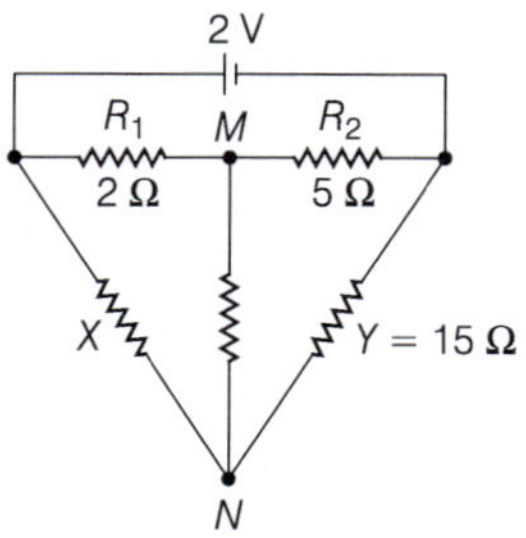

22. Why is a potentiometer preferred over a voltmeter in measuring the emf of a cell? **ISC 2007**

23. In the circuit (given figure below) the length of the wire $AB = 400$ cm. Where should the jockey J be placed, so that the galvanometer shows a zero deflection? **ISC 2006**

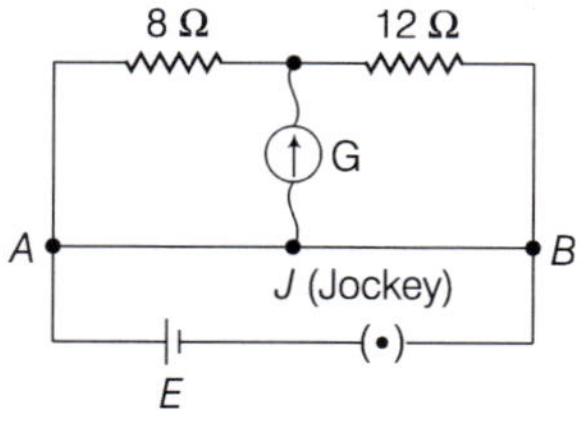

2 Marks Questions

24. (*i*) Write balancing condition of a Wheatstone brigde.

(*ii*) Current I flowing through a metallic wire is related to drift speed v_d of free electrons as follows.

$$I = nAev_d$$

State what the symbol n stands for. **ISC 2023**

25. In a potentiometer experiment, the balancing length with a resistance of $2\,\Omega$ is found to be 100 cm, while that of an unknown resistance is 500 cm. Calculate the value of the unknown resistance. **ISC 2019**

26. You are provided with one low resistance R_L and one high resistance R_H and two galvanometers. One galvanometer is to be converted to an ammeter and the other to a voltmeter. Show how you will do this with the help of simple, labelled diagrams. **ISC 2013**

27. A galvanometer with a resistance of 75 Ω produces a full scale deflection with a current of 5 mA. How can this galvanometer be converted into an ammeter which has a range of 0–5 A? **ISC 2011**

28. Draw a circuit diagram for the determination of the internal resistance of a cell using a potentiometer. Derive the formula to be used. **ISC 2002**

29. The resistance of a galvanometer is 50 Ω. It is converted into

(*i*) a voltmeter using a 10 kΩ resistor.

(*ii*) an ammeter using a 10 mΩ resistor.

Calculate the resistance of the voltmeter and the ammeter to an accuracy of 2 significant figures only. **ISC 2003**

3 Marks Questions

30. Figure below shows two batteries E_1 and E_2 having emfs of 18V and 10V and internal resistances of $1\,\Omega$ and 2Ω respectively. W_1, W_2 and W_3 are uniform metallic wires AC, FD and BE having resistance of $8\,\Omega$, $6\,\Omega$ and $10\,\Omega$ respectively. B and E are mid-points of the wires W_1 and W_2. Using Kirchhoff's laws of electrical circuits, calculate the current flowing in the wire W_3. **ISC 2024**

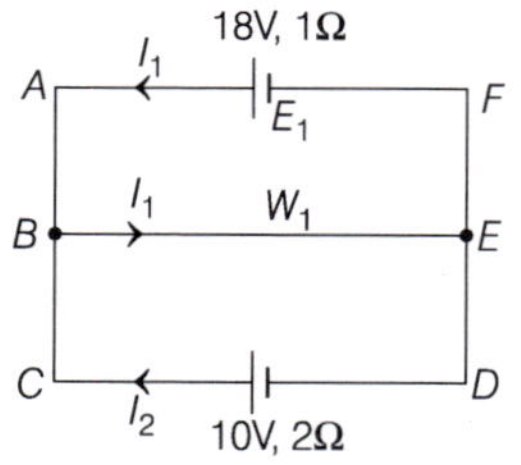

31. Figure below shows a potentiometer circuit in which the driver cell D has an emf of 6 V and internal resistance of 2Ω. The potentiometer wire AB is 10m long and has a resistance of $28\,\Omega$. The series resistance R, is of $20\,\Omega$. **ISC 2024**

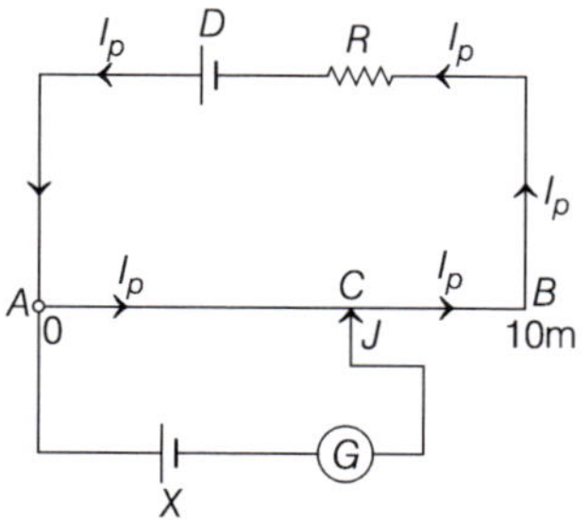

Calculate

(a) The current I_p flowing in the potentiometer wire AB when the jockey (J) does not touch the wire AB.

(b) emf of the cell X, if the balancing length AC is 4.5 m.

32. (*i*) Eight identical cells, each of emf 2V and internal resistance 3Ω, are connected in series to form a row. Six such rows are connected in parallel to form a battery. This battery is now connected to an external resistor R of resistance 6Ω. Calculate.

(a) emf of the battery.

(b) internal resistance of the battery

(c) current flowing through R.

Or

(*ii*) In the circuit shown in figure below, E_1 and E_2 are batteries having emfs of 25 V and 26V. They have an internal resistance of 1Ω and 5Ω, respectively. Applying Kirchhoff's laws of electrical networks, calculate the currents I_1 and I_2.

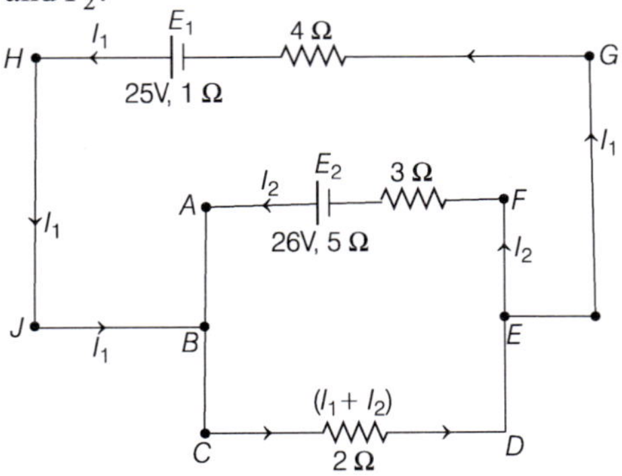

ISC 2023

33. (*i*) In a meter bridge circuit, resistance in the left gap is 4 Ω and an unknown resistance R is in the right-hand gap as shown in figure below. The null point is found to be 40 cm from the left end of the wire.

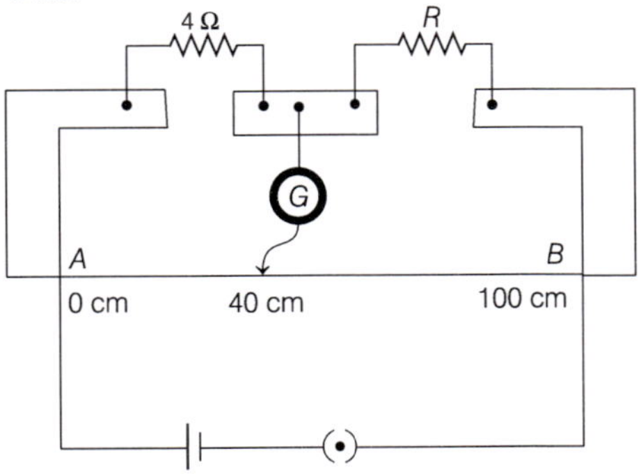

(a) Calculate the value of the unknown resistance R.

(b) What change will you make in R to bring the null point to the midpoint of the wire AB?

ISC SQP 2023

Or

(*ii*) A circuit is used to determine the internal resistance and the emf of a cell. It consists of the cell, a variable resistor, an ideal ammeter A and an ideal voltmeter V. Figure shows part of the circuit with the ammeter and voltmeter missing.

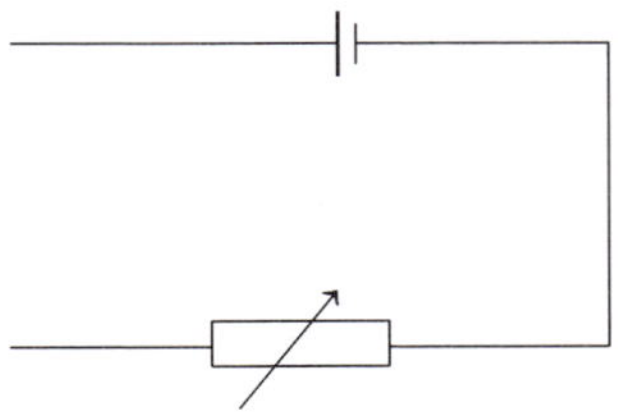

The variable resistor is set to be 1.5 Ω. When the cell converts 7·2 mJ of energy, 5.8 mC of charge moves completely around the circuit. The potential difference across the variable resistor is 0.55 V.

(a) Redraw the diagram showing the positions of the ammeter and the voltmeter.

(b) Calculate the emf of the cell.

34. The circuit diagram given below is that of a potentiometer used to measure internal resistance r of a cell. **ISC 2022 Sem-I**

(*i*) To find out the first balancing length l_1,

(a) both the keys K_1 and K_2 are closed together

(b) both the keys K_1 and K_2 are kept open

(c) K_1 is closed and K_2 is kept open

(d) K_2 is closed and K_1 is kept open

(*ii*) Working formula to calculate the internal resistance of a cell is

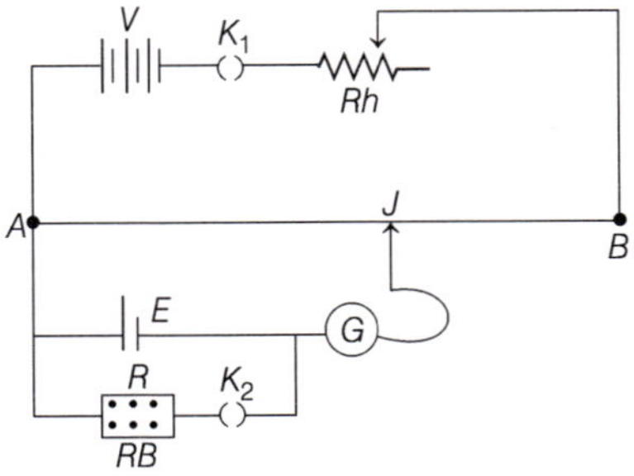

(a) $r = R\left(\dfrac{l_1}{l_2} - 1\right)$ (b) $r = R\left(\dfrac{l_2}{l_1} - 1\right)$

(c) $R = r\left(\dfrac{l_2}{l_1} - 1\right)$ (d) $R = r\left(\dfrac{l_1}{l_2} - 1\right)$

(*iii*) If the value of R is increased, balancing length

(a) l_1 increases (b) l_2 increases

(c) l_2 decrease (d) l_2 remains unchanged

35. A potentiometer circuit is shown in figure below. AB is a uniform metallic wire having length of 2m and resistance of 8Ω. The batteries E_1 and E_2 have emfs of 4V and 1.5 V and their internal resistances are 1Ω and 2Ω respectively. **ISC 2020**

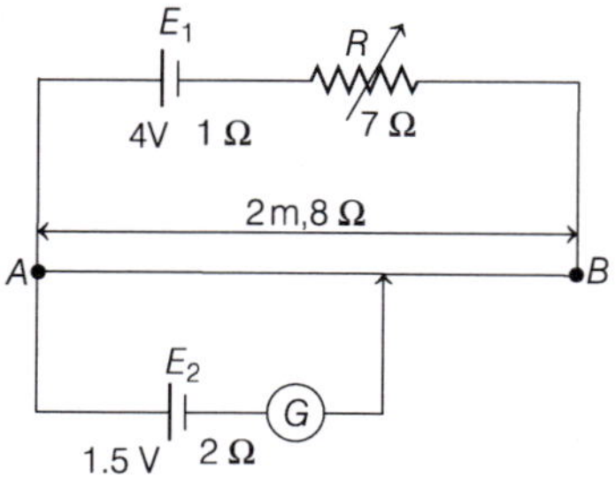

(*i*) When the jockey J does not touch the wire AB, calculate

(a) the current flowing through the potentiometer wire AB.

(b) the potential gradient across the wire AB.

(*ii*) Now the jockey J is made to touch the wire AB at a point C such that the galvanometer G shows no deflection. Calculate the length AC.

36. E_1 and E_2 are two batteries having emfs of 3V and 4V and internal resistances of 2Ω and 1Ω, respectively. They are connected as shown in figure below. Using Kirchhoff's laws of electrical circuits, calculate the currents I_1 and I_2. **ISC 2020**

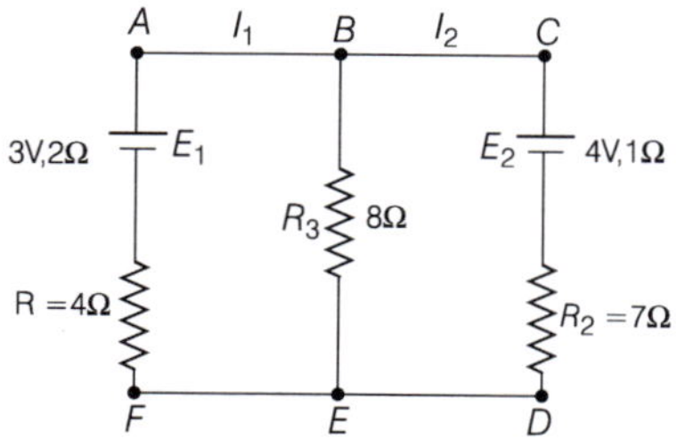

37. Obtain the balancing condition for the Wheatstone bridge arrangement as shown in the figure given below. **ISC 2019**

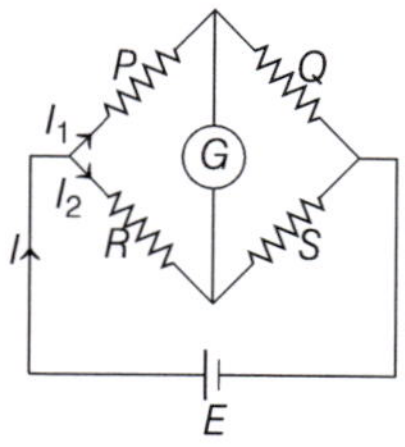

38. Draw a labelled circuit diagram of a potentiometer to measure the internal resistance r of a cell. Write the working formula (derivation not required). **ISC 2019**

39. ε_1 and ε_2 are two batteries having emf of 34 V and 10 V respectively and internal resistance of $1\,\Omega$ and $2\,\Omega$, respectively. They are connected as shown in figure below. Using Kirchhoff's laws of electrical networks, calculate the currents I_1 and I_2. **ISC 2018**

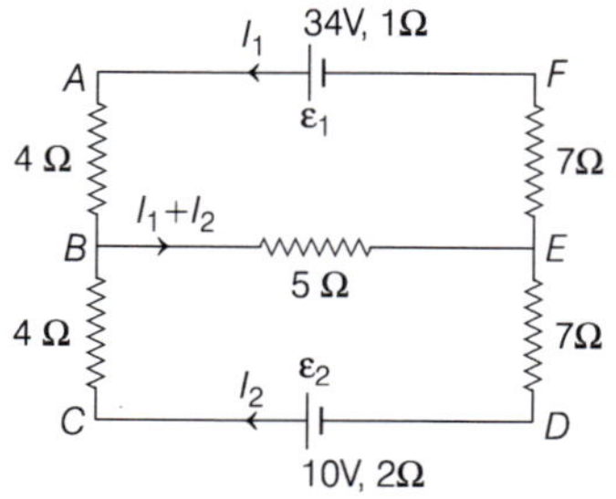

40. Using Kirchhoff's laws of electrical networks, calculate the current I_1, I_2 and I_3 in the circuit shown below **ISC SQP 2018**

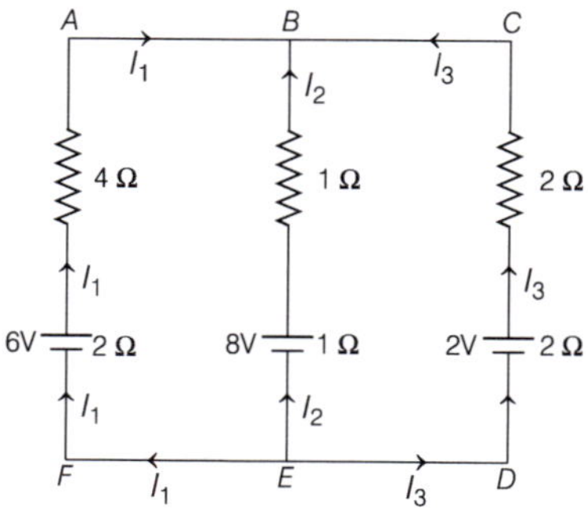

41. With the help of a neatly drawn and labelled diagram, obtain balancing condition of a Wheatstone bridge. **ISC 2015, 12, 02**

42. A 10 m long uniform metallic wire having a resistance of $20\ \Omega$ is used as potentiometer wire. This wire is connected in series with another resistance of $480\ \Omega$ and a battery of emf 5V having negligible internal resistance. If an unknown emf e is balanced across 6 m of the potentiometer wire, calculate **ISC 2015**

(*i*) the potential gradient across the potentiometer wire.

(*ii*) the value of the unknown emf e.

43. The figure below shows a uniform manganin wire XY of length 100 cm and resistance $9\ \Omega$, connected to an accumulator D of emf 4 V and internal resistance $1\ \Omega$ through a variable resistance R. E is a cell of emf 1.8 V connected to the wire XY *via* jockey J and a galvanometer G. It is found that the galvanometer shows no deflection when $XJ = 80$ cm. Find the value of R.

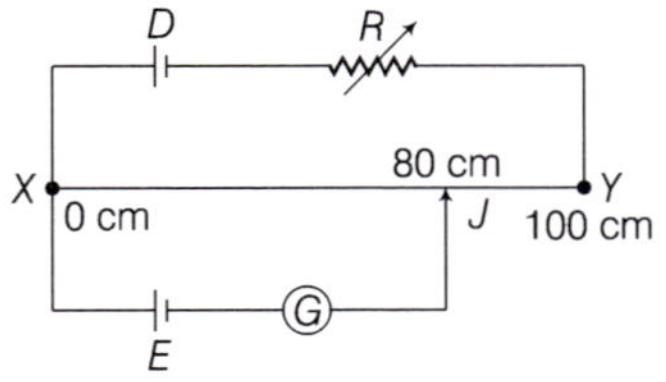

ISC 2009

44. A galvanometer with a coil of resistance 100 Ω and a scale having 100 divisions has a current sensitivity of 25 μA/division. How will you convert it into an ammeter of range 0 to 5 A? ISC 2008

45. In the circuit given alongside, E_1 and E_2 are two cells of emfs 4 V and 6 V respectively, having negligible internal resistances. Applying Kirchhoff's laws of electrical networks, find the values of I_1 and I_2.

ISC 2008

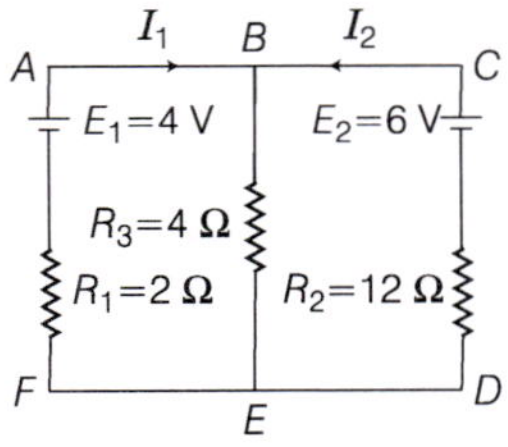

46. Given that the resistance of the voltmeter is 400 Ω. Find the voltmeter's reading. ISC 2004

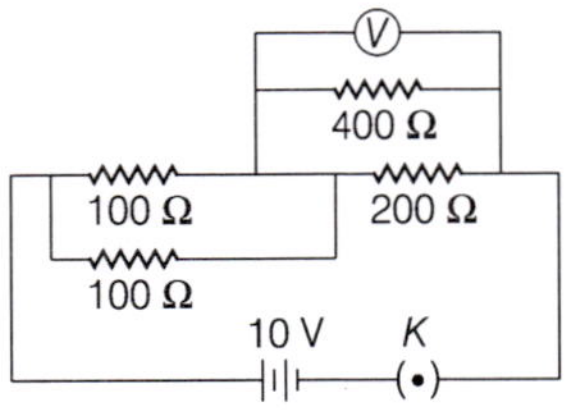

KEY idea

Calculate the equivalent resistance first, then after calculate the current through voltmeter. Both of these will help in knowing the voltmeter reading through $V = IR$

4/5 Marks Questions

47. In a meter bridge circuit, resistance in the left hand gap is 2 Ω and an unknown resistance X is in the right hand gap as shown in figure below. The null point is found to be 40 cm from the left end of the wire. What resistance should be connected to X so that the new null point is 50 cm from the left end of the wire?

ISC 2017

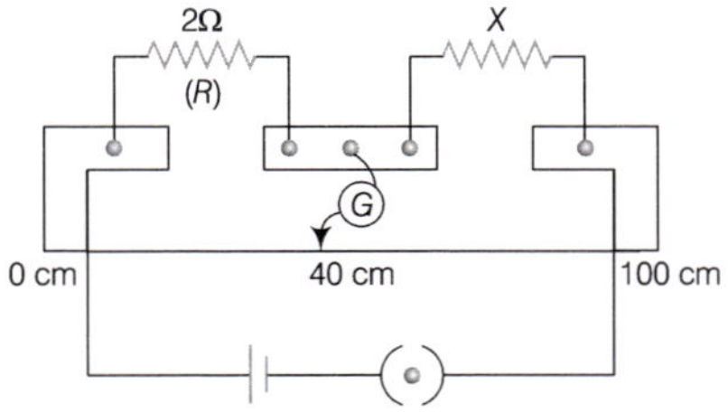

48. (*i*) Figure below shows two resistors R_1 and R_2 connected to a battery having an emf of 40V and negligible internal resistance. A voltmeter having a resistance of 300 Ω is used to measure potential difference across R_1. Find the reading of the voltmeter.

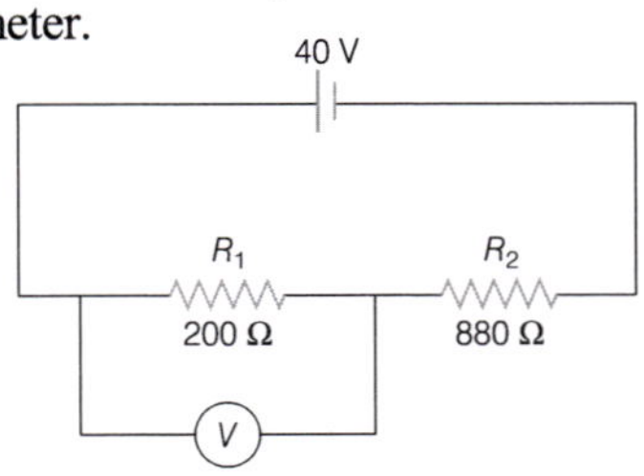

(*ii*) A moving coil galvanometer has a coil of resistance 59 Ω. It shows a full scale deflection for a current of 50 mA. How will you convert it to an ammeter having a range of 0 to 3A? ISC 2017

49. (*i*) In the circuit shown in figure below, E_1 and E_2 are cells having emfs 2V and 3V respectively and negligible internal resistances. Applying Kirchhoff's laws of electrical networks, find the values of currents I_1 and I_2.

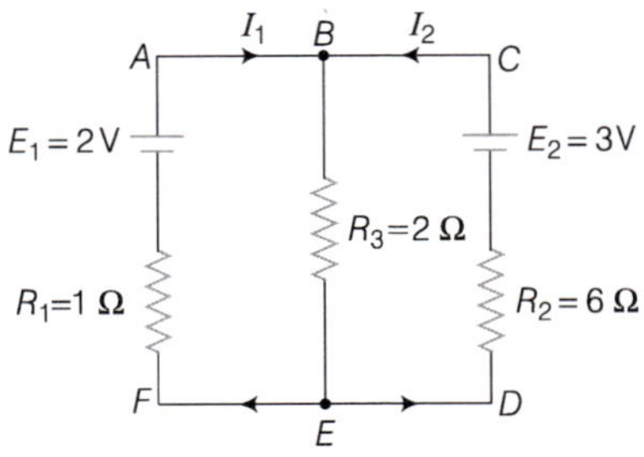

(*ii*) State how a moving coil galvanometer can be converted into an ammeter. ISC 2016

50. Draw a labelled circuit diagram of a potentiometer to measure internal resistance of a cell. Write the working formula. (Derivation not required). ISC 2016

51. In the circuit shown in figure, $E_1 = 17$ V, $E_2 = 21$ V, $R_1 = 2\ \Omega$, $R_2 = 3\ \Omega$ and $R_3 = 5\ \Omega$. Using Kirchhoff's laws, find the currents flowing through the resistors R_1, R_2 and R_3. (Internal resistance of each of the batteries is negligible.) ISC 2013

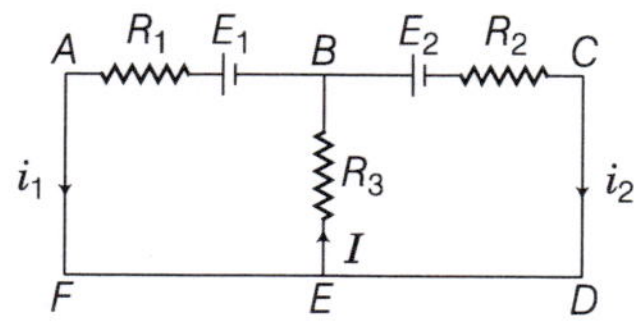

52. In the circuit shown in figure given alongside, E is a battery of emf 6 V and internal resistance 1 Ω. Find the reading of the ammeter A, if it has negligible resistance.

ISC 2012

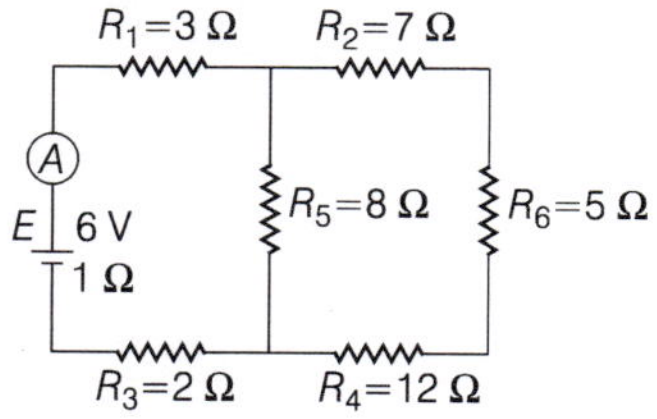

53. In the circuit shown in figure, E_1 and E_2 are batteries having emfs 4.0 V and 3.5 V respectively and internal resistances 1 Ω and 2 Ω respectively. Using Kirchhoff's laws, calculate currents I_1, I_2 and I_3.

ISC 2011

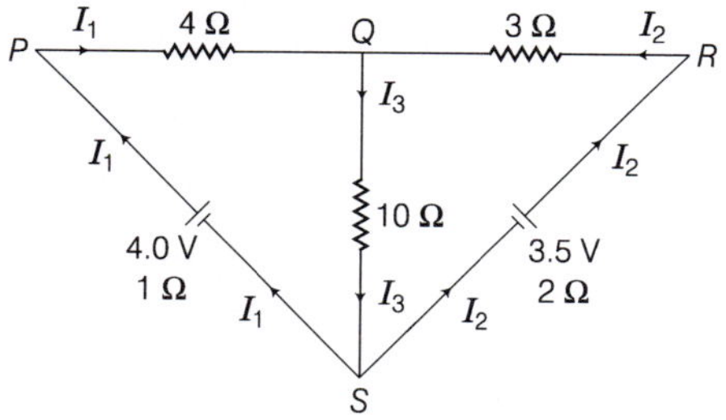

54. In the circuit shown alongside, PQ is a uniform metallic wire of length 4 m and resistance 20 Ω. Battery B has an emf of 10 V and internal resistance of 1 Ω. J is a jockey or slide contact. Resistance of the ammeter A and connecting wires is negligible.

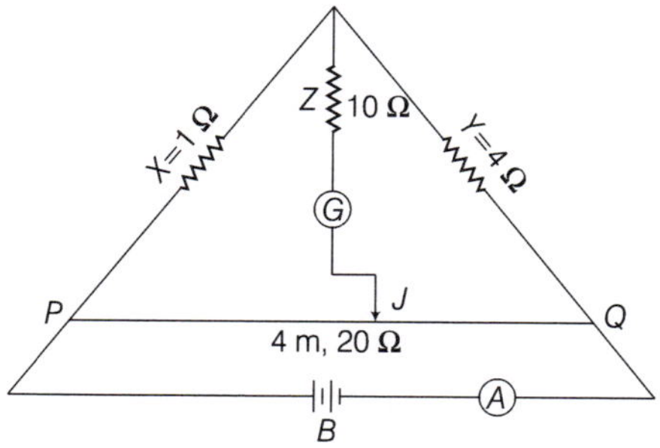

(*i*) When the jockey J does not touch the wire PQ, what is the reading of ammeter A?

(*ii*) Where should the jockey J be pressed on the wire PQ, so that the galvanometer G shows no deflection?

ISC 2010

55. State and explain Kirchhoff's law for electric circuits. What are the conservation laws implied in each law? State the sign convention for current and emf. Use the figure given along side for your explanation.

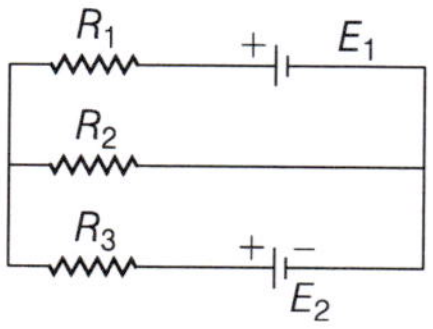

ISC 2000

Explanations

1. (c) If the galvanometer and battery are interchanged, the position of balance point remains unchanged. Hence, the galvanometer will show no current. Interchanging the resistors R and S can change the balance point.

2. (c) $R_s = 60 = 60 = 120\ \Omega$

R_s and R_3 are in parallel.

$$R_{eq} = \frac{R_s R_3}{R_s + R_3} = \frac{120 \times 60}{120 + 60} = \frac{120 \times 60}{180} = 40\ \Omega$$

$$i = \frac{V}{R} = \frac{4}{40} = \frac{1}{10}\ \text{A}$$

3. (b) $I = 4 + 2 - 1 - 1.3 = 3.7$ A

4. (a) The left of C since $E \propto I$. So, for $E_1 > E_2$.

We have $I_1 > I_2$ and hence null point will be obtained at shorter length i.e., to the left of C.

5. (a) Potential gradient $= \dfrac{e}{(R + R_w + r)} \times \dfrac{R}{L}$

$$= \frac{2}{(15 + 5 + 0)} \times \frac{5}{1} = 0.5 \frac{\text{V}}{\text{m}}$$

$$= 0.005\ \text{V/cm}$$

6. (b) $\dfrac{P}{Q} = \dfrac{R}{S}$

As, $P = Q \Rightarrow 1 = \dfrac{R}{S} \Rightarrow S = 5\ \Omega$

7. (a) 6 V

Two points at 40 cm and 70 cm point on meter scale fitted along the wire.

Let potential difference between B and C is

$$\therefore \quad K = \frac{E}{L} = 20 \text{ V/m}$$

$$\therefore \quad E = K.L = 20 \times (0.70 - 0.40)$$

$$= 20 \times 0.3 = 6 \text{ V}$$

8. (b) **9.** (a)

10. (a) $P = 10\,\Omega, Q = 20\,\Omega$

$S = 100\,\Omega, R = 200\,\Omega$

As $\quad \frac{P}{Q} = \frac{10}{20} = \frac{1}{2}, \frac{S}{R} = \frac{100}{200} = \frac{1}{2}$

$$\therefore \quad \frac{P}{Q} = \frac{S}{R}$$

Hence, it is a balanced Wheatstone bridge.

$\therefore I_g$ = current through galvanometer $= 0$

11. (d) $E = 2$ V, $l = 80$ cm $= 0.8$ m

$\therefore$ Potential gradient $(K) = \frac{E}{l} = \frac{2}{0.8} = 2.5 \text{ Vm}^{-1}$

12. (b) $E_1 = 1.08$ V, $l_1 = 21.6$ cm

$E_2 = 1.50$ V, $l_2 = ?$

At the balancing point in a potentiometer,

$$\frac{E_2}{E_1} = \frac{l_2}{l_1}$$

$$\therefore \quad l_2 = \left(\frac{E_2}{E_1}\right) l_1 = \left(\frac{1.50}{1.08}\right) \times 21.6 = 30 \text{ cm}$$

13. If l_1 and l_2 are the balancing lengths corresponding to emfs ε_1 and ε_2, then

$$\frac{\varepsilon_1}{\varepsilon_2} = \frac{l_1}{l_2}$$

$$\frac{2}{1.5} = \frac{120}{l_2}$$

$\therefore$ Balancing length, $l_2 = \frac{120 \times 1.5}{2} = 90 \text{ cm}$

14. Sensitivity of potentiometer means smallest potential difference that can be measured with the help of it. It can be increased by decreasing its potential gradient (K) i.e. sensitivity $\propto \frac{1}{K}$

$\therefore$ By increasing the current through the wire, sensitivity of the potentiometer decreases.

15. Kirchhoff's first law is based on conservation of charge and second law is based on conservation of energy.

16. Applying the Wheatstone bridge condition (balanced)

$$\frac{R}{X} = \frac{l}{100 - l}$$

$R = 2\Omega$ $X = ?$ $l = 40$ cm

$$\frac{2}{X} = \frac{40}{100 - 40}$$

$$\Rightarrow \quad \frac{2}{X} = \frac{40}{60}$$

$$\Rightarrow \quad X = \frac{2 \times 60}{40} = 3\Omega$$

17. (a) The given combination will act as balanced Wheatstone bridge. The resistance of the middle branch can be removed.

Clearly,

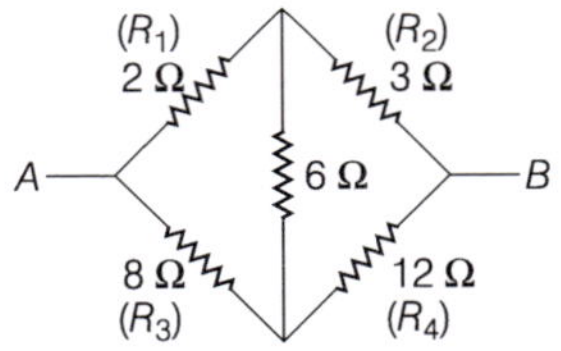

$$R_1 R_4 = (2\,\Omega)(12\,\Omega) = 24\,\Omega$$

$$R_2 R_3 = (3\,\Omega)(8\,\Omega) = 24\,\Omega$$

$R_1 R_4 = R_2 R_3$ online hence bridge is balanced

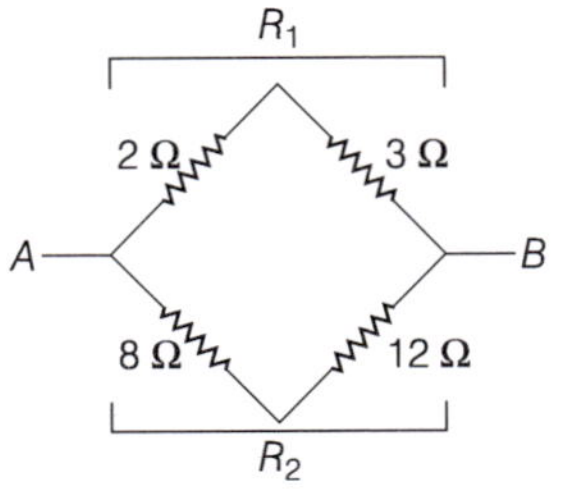

$$R_1 = 5\,\Omega, R_2 = 20\,\Omega$$

$$R_{eq} = \frac{R_1 R_2}{R_1 + R_2} = \frac{5 \times 20}{25} = \frac{100}{25} = 4\,\Omega$$

Hence, option (a) is correct.

18. Given, $\quad l = 254.5$ cm, $E = 1.018$ V

where, $\quad E =$ emf of the cell

$l =$ balancing length

Potential gradient $k = E/l$

$$= \frac{1.018}{254.5} = 0.004 \text{ V/cm}$$

19. (d) A moving coil galvanometer can be converted into a voltmeter by connecting a high resistance in series with its coil.

Hence, option (d) is correct.

20. Applying Kirchhoff's 2nd law in the given loop $ABCA$, i.e., net voltage across this loop must be equals to zero.

$$-3\times2 - I\times4 + 6\times2 = 0$$

$$\Rightarrow \quad -6 - 4I + 12 = 0 \quad \Rightarrow \quad 4I = 6$$

$$\therefore \quad I = \frac{6}{4} = 1.5\text{ A}$$

21. For balanced condition of Wheatstone bridge,

$$\frac{P}{Q} = \frac{R}{S} \quad \Rightarrow \quad \frac{R_1}{R_2} = \frac{X}{Y}$$

$$\Rightarrow \quad \frac{2}{5} = \frac{X}{15} \quad \Rightarrow \quad X = 6\,\Omega$$

where, P, Q, R and S are arm resistances of the Wheatstone bridge.

22. Potentiometer works on the principle of null deflection and it does not draw any current from the cell whose actual emf is to be measured whereas voltmeter measures the potential difference, because it draws some current from the cell. So, potentiometer is preferred over voltmeter.

23. By Wheatstone's bridge principle,
Resistance $(R) \propto$ Length (l)

$$\Rightarrow \quad \frac{R_1}{R_2} = \frac{l_1}{l_2}$$

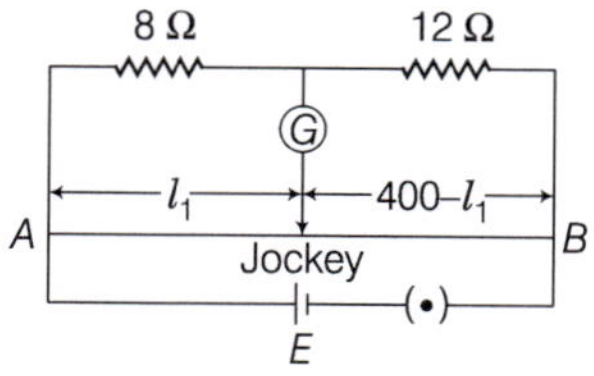

According to the figure,

$$\Rightarrow \quad \frac{8}{12} = \frac{l_1}{400 - l_1}$$

$$\Rightarrow \quad 3200 - 8l_1 = 12\,l_1$$

$$\therefore \quad l_1 = \frac{3200}{20} = 160\text{ cm from end } A$$

24. (*i*) A Wheatstone bridge is said to be in a balanced condition when no current flow through the galvanometer. This condition can be achieved by adjusting the known resistance and variable resistance.

(*ii*) Electric current

$$I = \frac{q}{t} = \frac{nALe}{t} = \frac{nALe}{L/v_d}$$

drift velocity's electric current,

$$I = neAv_d$$

where, n = number density of free electrons,
e = electronic charge,
A = cross-sectional area,
v_d = drift velocity of an electron
and L = length of the conductor.

25. If l_1 and l_2 are the balancing lengths corresponding to resistance R and X respectively,

$$\frac{X}{R} = \frac{l_2}{l_1}$$

Unknown resistance, $X = \frac{l_2}{l_1}R = \frac{500}{100}\times 2$

$$X = 10\,\Omega$$

26. For conversion of galvanometer into ammeter a low resistance is shunted.

Similarly to convert to voltmeter a high resistance is connected in series.

Conversion of galvanometer into ammeter

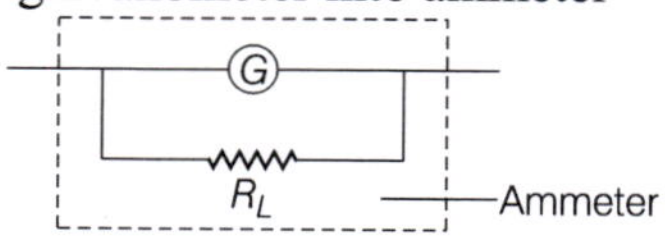

R_L = low resistance or shunt resistance

Conversion of galvanometer into voltmeter

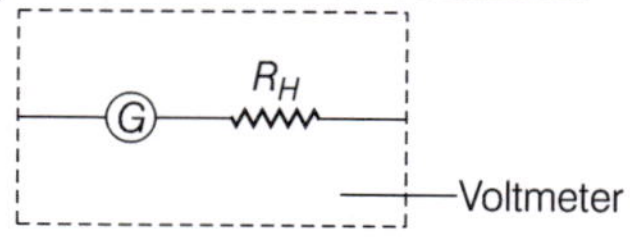

R_H = high resistance

27. Given, $i_g = 5\text{ mA} = 5\times10^{-3}\text{ A} = 0.005\text{ A}$

$i = 5\text{A}, \ G = 75\ \Omega$

i_g = galvanometer current
G = galvanometer resistance
i = net current

Shunt resistance, $S = \left(\frac{i_g}{i - i_g}\right)G = \left(\frac{5\times10^{-3}}{5 - 0.005}\right)\times 75$

$$= 0.075\,\Omega$$

By adding a shunt resistance of $0.075\,\Omega$ a galvanometer can be converted to ammeter having range 0.5 A.

28. Consider the diagram

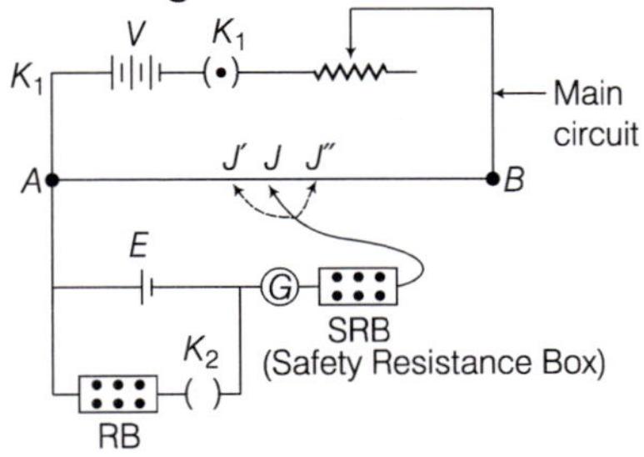

Let E is potential difference across l_1.

As ($E \propto l_1$). So, $\quad E = kl_1 \qquad$ ...(i)

V is potential difference across l_2,

So, $\quad V = Kl_2 \qquad$ ...(ii)

On dividing Eq. (i) by Eq. (ii), we get

$$\frac{E}{V} = \frac{kl_1}{kl_2} \Rightarrow \frac{E}{V} = \frac{l_1}{l_2}$$

Let r be the internal resistance of the cell. If current I flows through the cell when it is shunted with resistance R from safety box then from ohm's law

$$E = I(R + r) \text{ and } V = IR$$

$$\frac{E}{V} = \frac{R + V}{R} \Rightarrow r = R\left(\frac{l_1}{l_2} - 1\right)$$

29. (*i*) Total resistance of voltmeter

$$10\text{k}\Omega = 10 \times 10^3\,\Omega$$
$$= 50 + 10000 = 10050 = 1.01 \times 10^4\,\Omega.$$
$$= 1.0 \times 10^4\,\Omega$$
$$10\text{M}\Omega = 10 \times 10^{-3}\,\Omega$$

(*ii*) Resistance of ammeter $= \frac{1}{R} = \frac{1}{50} + \frac{1}{10^{-2}} = \frac{1}{50} + 100$

$$= 0.02 + 100 = 100.02\ \Omega$$

$$\therefore \quad R = \frac{1}{100.02} = 0.009998$$
$$= 9.99 \times 10^{-3}\ \Omega$$
$$= 10 \times 10^{-3}\ \Omega$$

30.

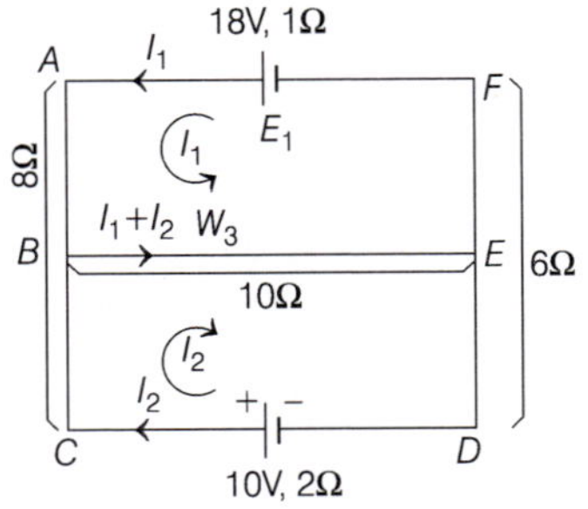

Loop equation,

Loop ***AFEB***

$$3I_1 + 4I_1 + 1I_1 + 10(I_1 + I_2) = 18 \qquad \text{...(i)}$$

Loop *BCDE*,

$$3I_2 + 2I_2 + 4I_2 + 10(I_1 + I_2) = 10 \qquad \text{...(ii)}$$

from equation (i) and (ii),

$$18I_1 + 10I_2 = 18 \qquad \text{...(iii)}$$
$$10I_1 + 19I_2 = 10 \qquad \text{...(iv)}$$

from Eq. (iv) thus, $I_1 = \frac{10 - 19I_2}{10}$

Substitute in Eq. (iii)

Here, $\frac{18}{10}(10 - 19I_2) + 10I_2 = 18$

$$\Rightarrow \quad \frac{180}{10} - \frac{342}{10}I_2 + 10I_2 = 18$$

$$\Rightarrow \quad \frac{(-342 + 100)}{10}I_2 = 18 - \frac{180}{10}$$

$$I_2 = 0$$

from I_1, $\frac{10 - 19I_2}{10} = \frac{10}{10} = 1\text{A}$

31.

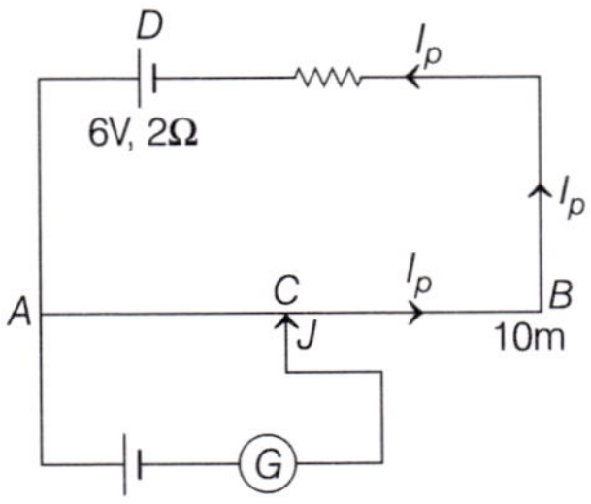

(a) The current I_p flowing in the potentiometer wire AB when the jockey (J) does not touch the wire AB, is $I_p = \frac{V}{R_{\text{net}}} = \frac{6\text{V}}{R_{AB} + R_s + r}$

$$= \frac{6}{28 + 20 + 2} = \frac{6}{50} = 0.12\text{ A}$$

(b) When the jockey is moved to point B, potential drop will be

$$V_{AB} = 28 \times 0.12 = 3.36\text{ V}$$

Length of the wire AB is 10 m, so potential gradient,

$$K = \frac{V_{AB}}{L} = \frac{3.36}{10} = 0.336\ \Omega/\text{m}$$

The length of the wire AC is 4.5 in the null deflection position or balancing position, then potential difference between points A and C,

$$V_{AC} = 0.336 \times 4.5 = 1.512\text{ V}$$

$\therefore$ The emf of cell X is 1.512 V.

32. (*i*) (a) The emf of each cell is 2V, so the emf of battery consisting of six rows connected in parallel is

$E - \text{battery} = 6 \times 2\text{ V} = 12\text{ V}$

(b) The internal resistance of a single cell is 32 Ω. When six rows of cells are connected in parallel the equivalent internal resistance of the battery is

$$\frac{1}{R_{\text{internal}}} = \frac{1}{32} + \frac{1}{32} + \frac{1}{32} + \frac{1}{32} + \frac{1}{32} + \frac{1}{32} = \frac{6}{32}$$

$$R_{\text{internal}} = \frac{32}{6} = 5.33\,\Omega$$

(c) To calculate the current flowing through R, first we need to calculate the total resistance of the circuit;

$$R_{\text{total}} = R + R_{\text{internal}}$$

$$R_{\text{total}} = 62 + 5.33 = 67.33\Omega$$

Using Ohm's law, the current flowing through R is

$$I = \frac{\varepsilon}{R_{\text{total}}}$$

$$I = \frac{12\text{ V}}{67.33\,\Omega}$$

$$I = 0.178\text{ A}$$

Therefore, the current flowing through R is 0.178 A.

Or

(*ii*) Considering loop $ABCDEF$ in the same order and applying Kirchhoff's voltage law,

$$3I_2 + 2(I_1 + I_2) - (25 - I_1) = 0$$

$$2I_1 + 10I_2 = 26 \quad \text{...(i)}$$

Considering loop $HICDGH$ in the same order and applying Kirchhoff's voltage law,

$$4I_1 + 2(I_1 + I_2) - (25 - I_1) = 0$$

$$7I_1 + 2I_2 = 25 \quad \text{...(ii)}$$

Solving Eqs. (i) and (ii), we get

$$I_1 = 3\text{A}$$

Putting this in Eq. (i), we get

$$I_2 = 2\text{A}$$

33. (*i*) (a) From formula

$$\frac{P}{Q} = \frac{R}{S} \Rightarrow \frac{40}{60} = \frac{4}{R}$$

$$R = 6\,\Omega$$

(b) If the null point to the midpoint of the wire AB, then $P = Q = 50$ cm

$$\frac{P}{Q} = \frac{R}{S}$$

$$\frac{50}{50} = \frac{6}{R}$$

$$R = 6\,\Omega$$

Or

(*ii*) (a)

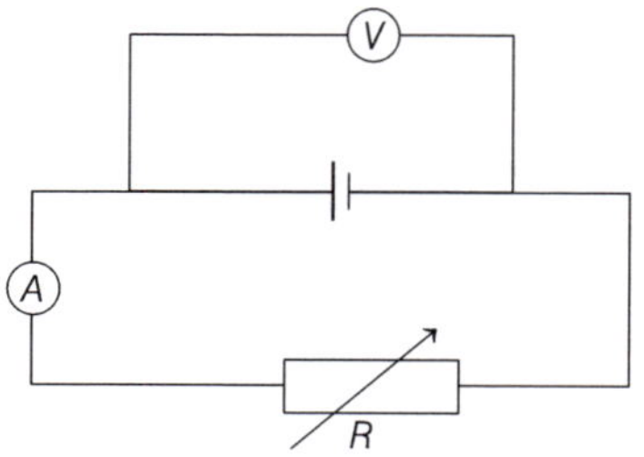

(b) $P = VI$

$$E = VIt$$

$$E = V\frac{q}{t}t$$

$$E = V\,q$$

$$V = E / q = \frac{7.2 \times 10^{-3}}{5.8 \times 10^{-3}} = 1.24\text{ V}$$

34. (*i*) (c)

(*ii*) (a) Length of wire $= l$

At balance point, when K_2 is open, $E = kl_1$

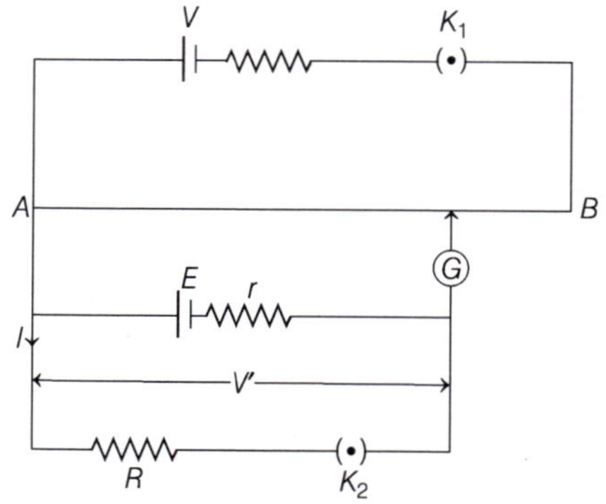

When K_2 is closed,

$$V' = IR = E - Ir = kl_2$$

$$\Rightarrow \quad Ir = E - V'$$

$$\Rightarrow \quad \frac{V'}{R} \cdot r = E - V'$$

$$\Rightarrow \quad r = (E - V') \cdot \frac{R}{V'}$$

$$= \left(\frac{E}{V'} - 1\right) \cdot R$$

As, $\frac{E}{V} = \frac{kl_1}{kl_2} = \frac{l_1}{l_2}$

$\therefore \quad r = \left(\frac{l_1}{l_2} - 1\right) \cdot R$

(*iii*) (b)

35. (*i*) (a) According to the circuit diagram given, current in the circuit or through the potentiometer wire is

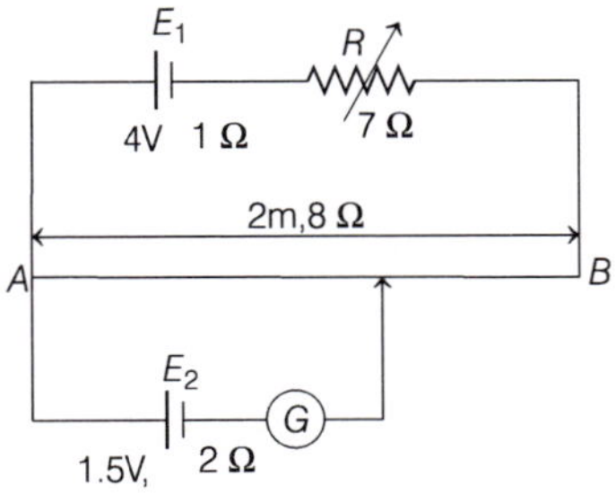

$$I = \frac{E_1}{R_{AB} + R + r_1}$$

$$= \frac{4}{(8+7+1)}$$

$$= \frac{4}{16}\text{A} = 0.25\text{A}$$

(b) The potential gradient across the wire *AB* can be calculated as follows

Resistance of potentiometer wire,

$$R_{AB} = 8\,\Omega$$

$\therefore$ Potential difference across the wire,

$$V = IR_{AB} = \frac{4}{16} \times 8 = \frac{32}{16} = 2\text{ V}$$

Length of potentiometer wire

$$= 2\text{ m} = 200\text{ cm}$$

$\therefore$ Potential gradient, $K = \frac{V}{l}$

$$= \frac{2}{200} = 0.01\text{ Vcm}^{-1}$$

(ii) The length *AC* which is to be calculated for the emf 1.5 V at the balanced point will be

As, $\varepsilon = Kl$

$$\Rightarrow l = \frac{\varepsilon}{K} = \frac{1.5}{0.01} = 150\text{ cm}$$

36. Considering the figure given in the question, when we consider the loop *ABEFA* and apply Kirchhoff's second law to it, then

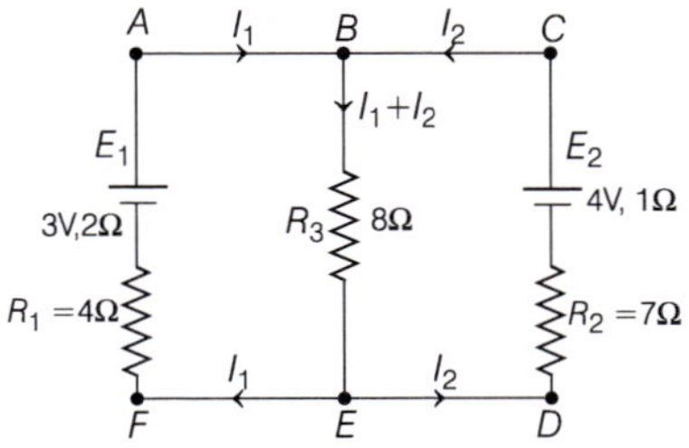

$$8(I_1 + I_2) + I_1 \times 4 + I_1 \times 2 = 3$$

$$8I_1 + 8I_2 + 4I_1 + 2I_1 = 3$$

$$14I_1 + 8I_2 = 3 \quad \text{...(i)}$$

If we consider the loop *BEDCB* and apply Kirchhoff's second law,

$$8(I_1 + I_2) + I_2 \times 7 + I_2 \times 1 = 4$$

$$8I_1 + 8I_2 + 7I_2 + I_2 = 4$$

$$8I_1 + 16I_2 = 4$$

$$2I_1 + 4I_2 = 1 \quad \text{...(ii)}$$

Equating Eqs. (i) and (ii), we get

$$28I_1 + 16I_2 = 6 \quad \text{...(iii)}$$

$$28I_1 + 56I_2 = 14 \quad \text{...(iv)}$$

After solving Eqs. (iii) and (iv), we get

$$40I_2 = 8 \Rightarrow I_2 = \frac{1}{5}\text{A}$$

and $\quad I_1 = \frac{1}{10}\text{A} \quad$ [from Eq. (i)]

37. In figure, four resistances *P, Q, R* and *S* are connected in the four arms of a parallelogram *ABCD*. Between *B* and *D* there is a sensitive galvanometer and a cell is connected between *A* and *C*. A current *I* is allowed to flow from the cell. At the point *A*, the current *I* is divided into two parts.

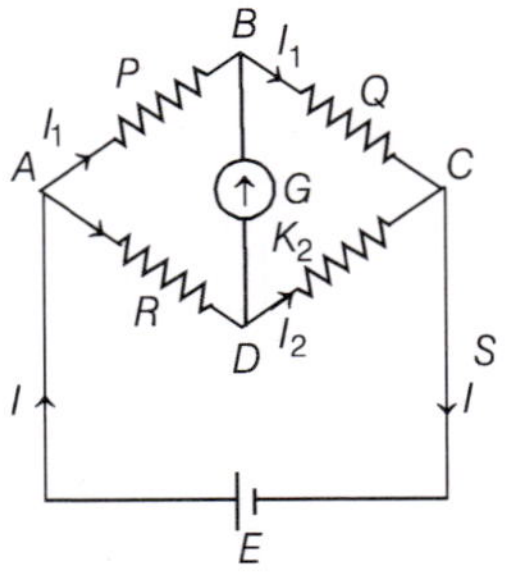

One part I_1 flows in the arm *AB* and the other part I_2 flows in the arm *AD*. The resistances *P, Q, R* and *S* are so adjusted that there is no deflection in the galvanometer *G*. i.e., there is no current in the diagonal *BD*. Thus, the same current I_1 will flow in the arm *BC* as in the arm *AB* and the same I_2 will flow in the arm *DC* as in the arm *AD*.

Applying Kirchhoff's second law for the closed loop *BADB*, we have

$$PI_1 = RI_2 \quad \text{...(i)}$$

Similarly, for the closed loop *CBDC*, we have

$$QI_1 = SI_2 \quad \text{...(ii)}$$

Dividing Eq. (i) by Eq. (ii), we get

$$\frac{I_1 P}{I_1 Q} = \frac{I_2 R}{I_2 S}$$

or

$$\frac{P}{Q} = \frac{R}{S}$$

Concept Enhancer Wheatstone bridge is said to be in a balanced condition when no current flows through the galvanometer.

38. Let E' be emf of the battery. A constant current i is maintained through the potentiometer wire with the help of rheostat.

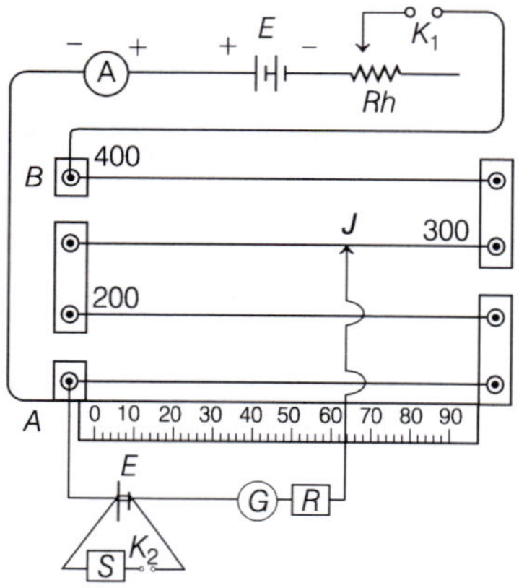

The plug key K_2 is kept out and the jockey J is moved on the potentiometer wire to balance the emf E of the cell, whose internal resistance r is to be determined.

The internal resistance of the cell is given by

$$r = \left(\frac{l_1}{l_2} - 1\right) S$$

where, l_1 is the balancing length of potentiometer wire without resistance box, l_2 is the balancing length with resistance box and S is the resistance of the resistance box.

39. In loop *BEFAB*,

$$-5(I_1 + I_2) - 7I_1 - I_1 + 34 - 4I_1 = 0$$

$$17I_1 + 5I_2 = 34 \quad \text{...(i)}$$

In loop *BEDCB*,

$$-5(I_1 + I_2) - 7I_2 - 2I_2 + 10 - 4I_2 = 0$$

$$18I_2 + 5I_1 = 10 \quad \text{...(ii)}$$

Solving Eqs. (i) and (ii), we get

$$I_1 = 2\,\text{A and } I_2 = 0$$

40. According to the question,

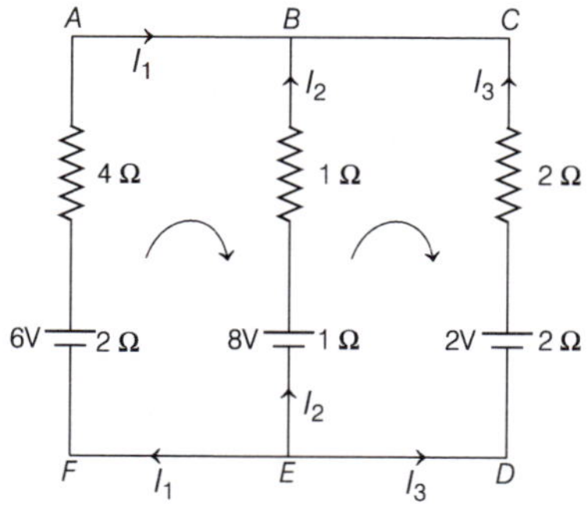

Applying Kirchhoff's law in loop 1 (*ABEFA*),

$$-6I_1 + 2I_2 - 8 + 6 = 0$$

$$\Rightarrow \quad -6I_1 + 2I_2 - 2 = 0$$

$$\Rightarrow \quad -6I_1 + 2I_2 = 2$$

$$\Rightarrow \quad -3I_1 + I_2 = 1 \quad \text{...(i)}$$

Applying Kirchhoff's law in loop 1 (*BCDEB*),

$$+4I_3 - 2 + 8 - 2I_2 = 0$$

$$\Rightarrow \quad 4I_3 - 2I_2 + 6 = 0$$

$$\Rightarrow \quad 2I_2 - 4I_3 = 6$$

$$\Rightarrow \quad I_2 - 2I_3 = 3 \quad \text{...(ii)}$$

Applying KCL, $I_1 + I_2 + I_3 = 0$

$$\Rightarrow \quad I_1 + I_2 = -I_3$$

Substituting I_3 in Eq. (ii), we get

$$I_2 - 2(I_1 + I_2) = 3$$

$$\Rightarrow \quad I_2 - 2I_1 - 2I_2 = 3$$

$$-2I_1 - I_2 = 3 \quad \text{...(iv)}$$

Solving Eqs. (i) and (iv), we get

$$-3I_1 + I_2 = 1$$

$$-2I_1 - I_2 = 3 \Rightarrow -5I_1 = 4$$

$$\Rightarrow \quad I_1 = -\frac{4}{5}\,\text{A}$$

$$I_2 = 2I_1 - 3$$

$$= 2\left(-\frac{4}{5}\right) - 3$$

$$= \frac{-8}{5} - 3 = \frac{-23}{5}\,\text{A}$$

And $I_3 = -(I_1 + I_2) = \frac{+23}{5} + 4/5 = \frac{27}{5}$ A

Negative sign implies I_1 and I_2 are in opposite direction of what we have assumed.

41. In case of balanced Wheatstone bridge the current through the galvanometer is zero. The labelled diagram of Wheatstone bridge is given

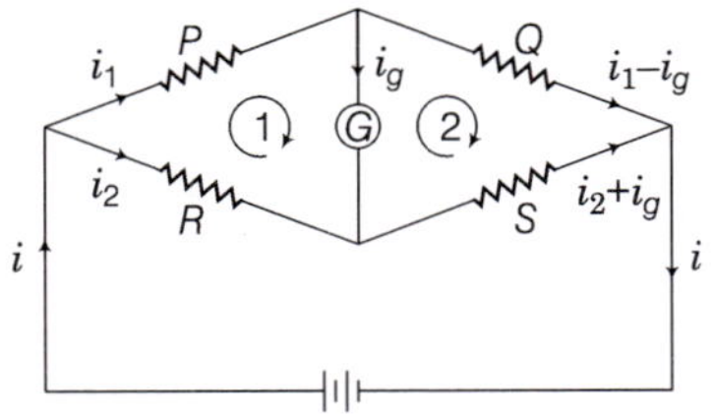

P, Q, R and S are the arm resistances of Wheatstone bridge.

Proof By Kirchhoff's law

In loop 1,

$$-i_1P - i_gG + i_2R = 0 \quad \ldots\text{(i)}$$

In loop 2,

$$-(i_1 - i_g)Q + (i_2 + i_g)S + i_gG = 0 \quad \ldots\text{(ii)}$$

If there is no current in galvanometer i.e., $i_g = 0$, then Wheatstone bridge will be balance, then Eqs. (i) and (ii) gives

$$i_1P - i_2R = 0$$

$$i_1P = i_2R \quad \ldots\text{(iii)}$$

$$i_1Q - i_2S = 0$$

$$i_1Q = i_2S \quad \ldots\text{(iv)}$$

On dividing Eq. (iii) by Eq. (iv), we get

$$\frac{P}{Q} = \frac{R}{S}$$

$$\Rightarrow \quad PS = QR$$

i.e., product of resistances of opposite arms are equal.

42. Given, $l_1 = 10$ m, $R = 20\,\Omega$, $R_1 = 480\,\Omega$, $E_1 = 5$ V, balancing length $l_2 = 6$ m

(*i*) The potential gradient across the potentiometer wire is given by

$$K = \frac{V}{l} = \frac{5}{6} = 0.83 \text{ V/m}$$

(*ii*) We know that $\frac{E_1}{E_2} = \frac{l_1}{l_2}$

Substituting the all values,

$$\frac{5}{E_2} = \frac{10}{6} \Rightarrow E_2 = \frac{6 \times 5}{10} = 3\text{ V}$$

43. For no deflection in the galvanometer balanced condition should be achieved that a null point is obtained by the jockey (J).

Given, The cell E is balanced at $l = 80$ cm

Let k is potential gradient.

$$E = kl \Rightarrow 1.8 = k \times 0.80$$

$$\therefore \quad k = 2.25 \text{ Vm}^{-1}$$

Potential gradient along the wire XY,

$$k = \frac{V}{l}$$

[$\because l$ = length of the wire = 100 cm = 1m]

$$\therefore \quad 2.25 = \frac{V}{1} \Rightarrow V = 2.25 \text{ V}$$

Current in the potentiometer wire XY is

$$I = \frac{4}{1 + R + 9}$$

Now, $V = I \times$ Resistance of wire

$$2.25 = \frac{4}{1+R+9} \times 9 \Rightarrow 2.25 = \frac{36}{10+R}$$

$$\Rightarrow \quad 10 + R = \frac{36}{2.25} = 16$$

$$\therefore \quad R = 16 - 10 = 6\,\Omega$$

44. Given, resistance of the galvanometer

$G = 100\,\Omega$, $i_g = 100 \times 25\,\mu\text{A} = 0.0025$ A

Shunt resistance is given by

$$S = \left(\frac{i_g}{i - i_g}\right) G \quad [\because i = 5\text{A}]$$

where, i_g = galvanometer current

G = galvanometer resistance

i = current to which shunt resistance is to added

$$= \frac{2.5 \times 10^{-3}}{5 - 0.0025} \times 100$$

$$S \approx 0.05\,\Omega \quad \text{[in parallel]}$$

45. Currents and emfs are shown in the given circuit. Now, applying Kirchhoff's second law, in closed loop $ABEFA$,

$$4 = (I_1 + I_2)4 + I_1 \times 2$$

$$\Rightarrow \quad 4 = 4I_1 + 4I_2 + 2I_1$$

$$\Rightarrow \quad 4 = 6I_1 + 4I_2 \quad \ldots\text{(i)}$$

Similarly, in closed loop $BCDEB$,

$$6 = 4(I_1 + I_2) + 12I_2$$

$$6 = 4I_1 + 16I_2 \quad \ldots\text{(ii)}$$

On solving Eqs. (i) and (ii), we get

$$6I_1 + 4I_2 = 4$$

and $$I_1 + 4I_2 = 3/2$$

$$5I_1 = \frac{5}{2}$$

$\Rightarrow$ $$I_1 = 0.5\text{ A}$$

Substituting $I_1 = 05\text{ A}$ in Eq. (i), we get

$\therefore$ $$I_2 = 0.25\text{ A}$$

46. Let, R_V is the resistance of the voltmeter. This R_V is in parallel with 200 Ω resistance, The equivalent resistance of 200 Ω and 400 Ω is

$$\frac{1}{R'} = \frac{1}{400} + \frac{1}{200}$$

or $$R' = 133.33\,\Omega$$

Again from the figure two resistances of 100 Ω each are in parallel to each other. Their equivalent resistance is R'', then

$$\frac{1}{R''} = \frac{1}{100} + \frac{1}{100} \Rightarrow R'' = 50\,\Omega$$

Now, according to the question, R' and R'' are in series, therefore their equivalent resistance R will be

$$R = 133.33 + 50 = 183.33\,\Omega$$

$$V = 10\text{ V}$$

Total current through voltmeter

$$I = \frac{V}{R} = \frac{10}{183.33} = 0.054\text{ A}$$

Voltmeter reading, $V = IR'$

$$= 0.054 \times 133.33$$

$$= 7.19\text{ V}$$

47.

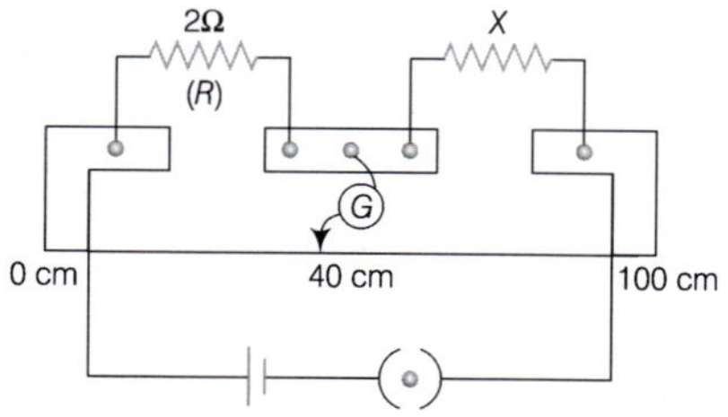

Applying the condition of balanced Wheatstone bridge,

$$\frac{R}{X} = \frac{l}{100 - l}$$

According to the question, $R = 2\Omega$

$$X = ?$$

$$l = 40\text{ cm}$$

$$\frac{2}{X} = \frac{40}{100 - 40}$$

$$\frac{2}{X} = \frac{40}{60} \Rightarrow X = \frac{2 \times 60}{40} = 3\,\Omega$$

The equivalent resistance of 3 Ω and 5 Ω in parallel is $\frac{3S}{3+S}\,\Omega$

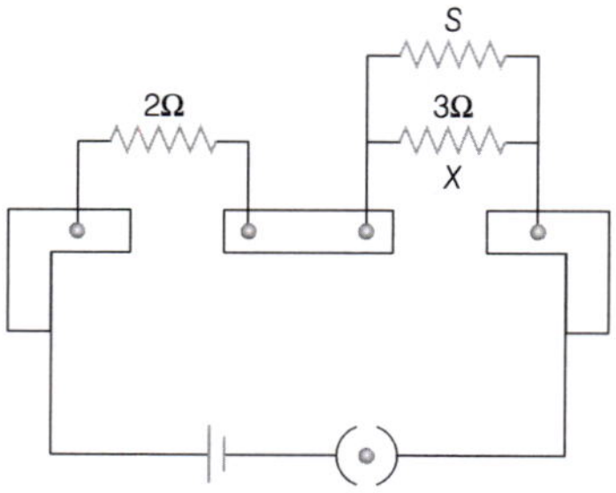

Again applying the condition of balanced Wheatstone bridge,

$$\Rightarrow \quad \frac{2}{\frac{3S}{3+S}} = \frac{50}{50} = 1$$

$$\Rightarrow \quad 2 = \frac{3S}{3+S}$$

$$\Rightarrow \quad 2(3+S) = 3S$$

$$\Rightarrow \quad 6 + 2S = 3S$$

$$\Rightarrow \quad 3S - 2S = 6$$

$$\Rightarrow \quad S = 6\,\Omega$$

48. (*i*)

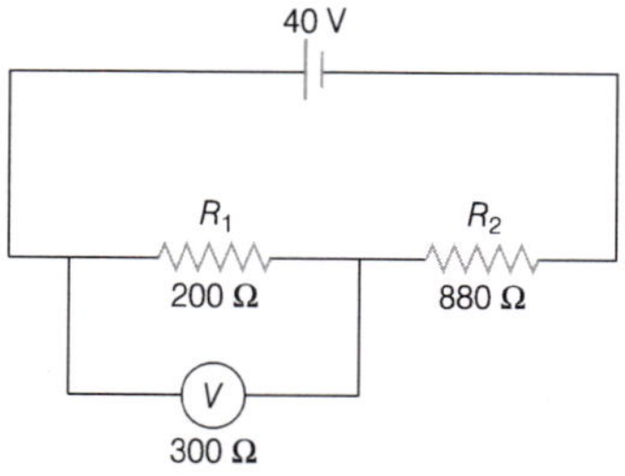

Total current $= I$

According to Ohm's law,

$$V = IR$$

$$I = \frac{V}{R} = \frac{40}{1080}$$

$$\left[\begin{aligned} R_s &= R_1 + R_2 \\ &= 200 + 880 \\ &= 1080\,\Omega \end{aligned}\right]$$

$$= \frac{1}{27}\text{ A}$$

Now, for R_1, potential difference $V = IR_1$

$$= \frac{1}{27} \times 200 = 7.40\text{ V}$$

(*ii*) $R = 59\,\Omega$

According to the formula,

$$S = \left(\frac{I_g}{I - I_g}\right)G$$

$$G = 59\,\Omega$$

$$I_g = 50\text{ mA} = 50 \times 10^{-3}\text{ A}$$

$$I = 3\text{A}$$

$\therefore$ Shunt resistance

$$S = \frac{I_g G}{I - I_g} = \frac{50 \times 10^{-3} \times 59}{(3 - 50 \times 10^{-3})}$$

$$= \frac{50 \times 59}{1000 \times \frac{59}{20}} = \frac{50 \times 59 \times 20}{1000 \times 59} = 1\,\Omega$$

Hence, to convert galvanometer into ammeter, a shunt of $1\,\Omega$ is connected in parallel with the galvanometer.

49. (*i*) Consider the figure given in the question,

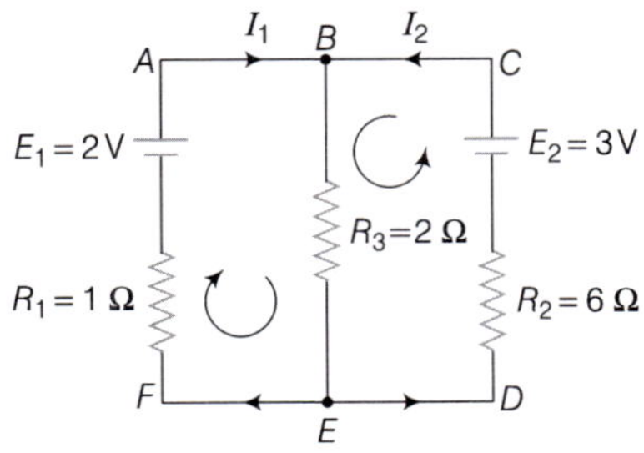

Consider the loop *ABEFA* and apply Kirchhoff's second law to it.

$$2\,(I_1 + I_2) + I_1 \times 1 = 2$$

$$\Rightarrow \quad 2I_1 + 2I_2 + I_1 = 2$$

$$\Rightarrow \quad 3I_1 + 2I_2 = 2 \quad \text{...(i)}$$

Consider the loop *BCDEB* and apply Kirchhoff's second law to it.

$$2(I_1 + I_2) + 6I_2 = 3$$

$$\Rightarrow \quad 2I_1 + 2I_2 + 6I_2 = 3$$

$$\Rightarrow \quad 2I_1 + 8I_2 = 3 \quad \text{...(ii)}$$

On multiplying Eq. (i) by 4, we get

$$12I_1 + 8I_2 = 8 \quad \text{...(iii)}$$

On solving Eqs. (ii) and (iii), we get

$$12I_1 + 8I_2 = 8$$

$$2I_1 + 8I_2 = 3$$

$$\underline{- \quad - \quad -}$$

$$10I_1 = 5$$

$$\Rightarrow \quad I_1 = \frac{5}{10} = 0.5\text{ A}$$

On substituting the value of I_1 in Eq. (i), we get

$$I_2 = 0.25\text{ A.}$$

$$\therefore \quad I_1 = 0.5\text{ A}$$

$$I_2 = 0.25\text{ A}$$

(*ii*) A moving coil galvanometer can be converted into an ammeter by using a low resistance wire in parallel with it.

50.

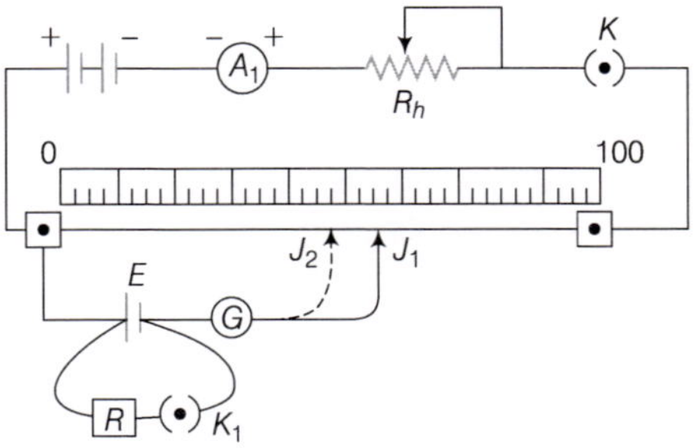

The working formula is $r = \left(\frac{l_1}{l_2} - 1\right) R$

Thus, knowing the values of l_1, l_2 and R, the internal resistance r of the cell can be determined.

51. Apply Kirchhoff's current and voltage rule for each loop.

Given, according to the figure

$$E_1 = 17\text{ V}, E_2 = 21\text{ V}$$

$$R_1 = 2\,\Omega, R_2 = 3\,\Omega \quad \text{and} \quad R_3 = 5\,\Omega$$

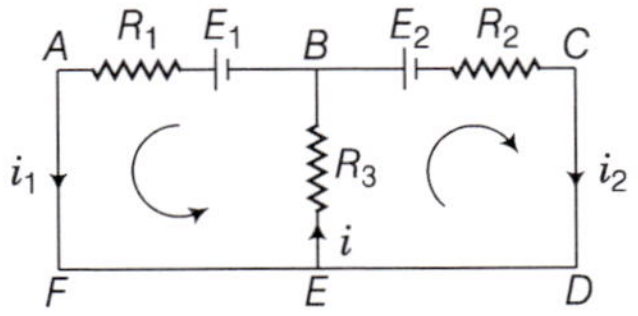

In loop *AFEBA*

$$E_1 - i_1 R_1 - iR_3 = 0$$

$$\Rightarrow \quad 17 = 2i_1 + 5i \quad \text{...(i)}$$

In loop *BCDEB*

$$E_2 - i_2 R_2 - iR_3 = 0$$

$$\Rightarrow \quad E_2 = i_2 R_2 + iR_3$$

$$21 = 3i_2 + 5i \quad \text{...(ii)}$$

By Kirchhoff's I law

$$i_1 + i_2 = i \quad \text{...(iii)}$$

From Eqs. (i) and (ii), we get

$$17 = 2i_1 + 5\,(i_1 + i_2) = 2i_1 + 5i_1 + 5i_2$$

$$17 = 7i_1 + 5i_2 \quad \text{...(iv)}$$

From Eqs. (ii) and (iii), we get

$$21 = 3i_2 + 5\,(i_1 + i_2) = 3i_2 + 5i_1 + 5i_2$$

$$21 = 5i_1 + 8i_2 \quad \text{...(v)}$$

On solving Eqs. (iv) and (v), we get

$$i_1 = 1\text{A}, \; i_2 = 2\text{ A}$$

$$i = i_1 + i_2 = 1 + 2 = 3\text{ A}$$

52. We have to find equivalent resistance in the circuit and then current can be calculated using $V = IR$.

According to the given circuit diagram,

$$R_{eq_1} = R_2 + R_6 + R_4$$

[since R_2, R_6 and R_4 are in series]

$$= 7 + 5 + 12 = 24\,\Omega$$

Now, R_{eq_1} and R_5 are in parallel, so

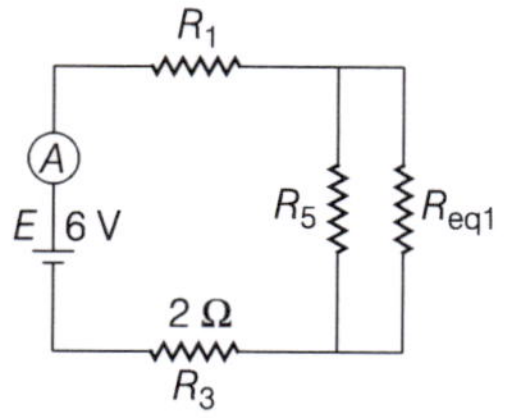

$$\frac{1}{R_{eq_2}} = \frac{1}{R_5} + \frac{1}{R_{eq_1}}$$

$$= \frac{1}{8} + \frac{1}{24} = \frac{3+1}{24} = \frac{4}{24} = \frac{1}{6}$$

$\therefore \quad R_{eq_2} = 6\,\Omega$

Now, R_{in}, R_{eq_2}, R_1 and R_3 are in series, so

$$R_{eq} = R_{eq_2} + R_1 + R_3 + R_{in}$$

$$= 6 + 3 + 2 + 1 = 12\,\Omega$$

The current measured by ammeter

$$I = \frac{V}{R} = \frac{6}{12} = \frac{1}{2} = 0.5 \text{ A}$$

53. To solve this problem, we have to apply Kirchhoff's first law for current division and Kirchhoff's second law for potential differences in each loop. Applying Kirchhoff's second law for closed mesh *PQSP*,

$$1I_1 + 4I_1 + 10(I_1 + I_2) = 4$$

as $\quad I_3 = I_1 + I_2$

[by applying Kirchhoff's I law at point *Q*]

$$\therefore \quad 15I_1 + 10I_2 = 4 \quad \ldots\text{(i)}$$

Similarly, for closed loop *RQSR*,

$$2I_2 + 3I_2 + 10(I_1 + I_2) = 3.5$$

$$10I_1 + 15I_2 = 3.5 \quad \ldots\text{(ii)}$$

On solving Eqs. (i) and (ii), we get

$$I_1 = 0.2 \text{ A and } I_2 = 0.1 \text{ A}$$

$$I_3 = I_1 + I_2 = 0.3 \text{ A}$$

Currents I_1, I_2 and I_3 are shown in the circuit diagram.

Common Mistake We should not confuse with signs while applying Kirchhoff's laws, specially about signs of incoming and outgoing currents.

54. For no deflection in the galvanometer the bridge should be balanced.

(*i*) When jockey does not touch the wire *PQ*, 10 Ω is not connected.

In upper arm of *PQ*,

Resistances $X + Y = 1 + 4 = 5\,\Omega$

[for series combination]

20 Ω and 5 Ω are in parallel.

$$\therefore \quad R_{\text{Total}} = \frac{20 \times 5}{20+5} = \frac{100}{25} = 4\,\Omega$$

$\therefore$ Current in circuit,

$$I = \frac{E}{r + R_{\text{Total}}} = \frac{10}{1+4} = 2\text{A}$$

(*ii*) Let the distance of the jockey (*J*) be *x*.

Then, by Wheatstone bridge under balanced condition,

$$\frac{X}{Y} = \frac{x}{4-x}$$

$$\Rightarrow \quad \frac{1}{4} = \frac{x}{4-x}$$

$$4 - x = 4x$$

$$\Rightarrow \quad 4 = 5x$$

$$\therefore \quad x = 0.8 \text{ m}$$

55. Kirchhoff has given two rules based on conservation of electric charge and of energy these are known as Kirchhoff's laws.

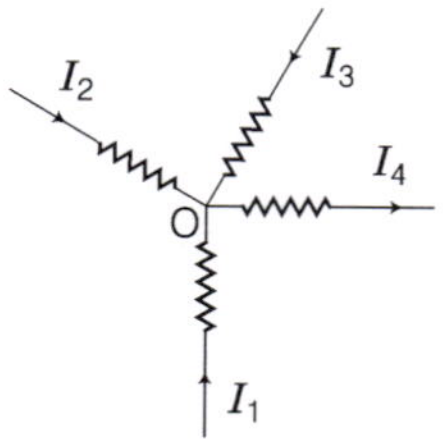

Kirchhoff's first law or junction rule The algebraic sum of electric currents at any junction of electric circuit is equal to zero i.e., the sum of current entering into a junction is equal to the sum of current leaving the junction, i.e.

$$\Sigma I = 0, I_4 = I_1 + I_2 + I_3$$

Junction law supports law of conservation of charge, because this is a point in circuit which cannot act as a source or sink of charge(s).

Kirchhoff's second law or voltage rule In any closed mesh of electrical circuit, the algebraic sums of emf of cell and the product of currents and resistance is always equal to zero i.e.,

$$\Sigma E + \Sigma IR = 0$$

Kirchhoff's second law supports the law of conservation of energy. Because the net change in the energy of a charge, after the charge complete a closed path must be zero.

NOTE Sign convention for Kirchhoff's second law

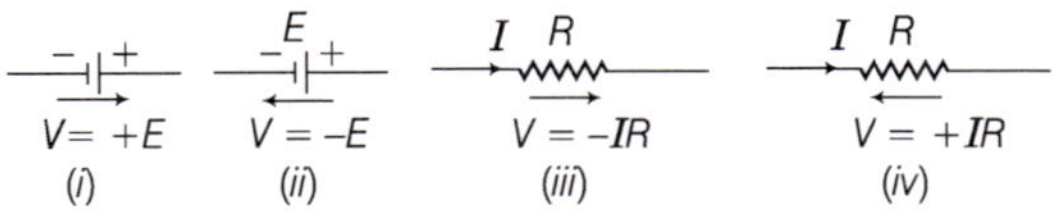

Consider the circuit diagram shown alongside. The second law can be expressed as, $\Sigma E + \Sigma IR = 0$

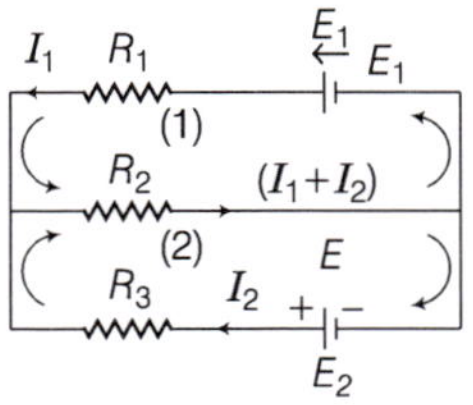

As given in the diagram, applying this law for mesh (1)

For mesh or loop (1), $-I_1 R_1 - (I_1 + I_2) R_2 = E_1 = 0$

$\therefore \quad I_1 R_1 + (I_1 + I_2) R_2 = E_1$

For mesh (2), $\quad -I_2 R_3 - (I_1 + I_2) R_2 + E_2 = 0$

$\therefore \quad I_2 R_3 + (I_1 + I_2) R_2 = E_2$

TOPIC 4

Electric Energy and Power

Electrical Energy

It is defined as the total work done (W) by the source of emf in maintaining the electric current (I) in the given circuit for a specified time (t).

Total charge that crosses the resistor is given by $q = It$

Energy gained is given by,

$$W = Vq = V\,(It) = VIt \qquad \left[\because V = \frac{W}{q}\right]$$

$$= [IR]\,It = I^2 R\,t \qquad [\because V = IR]$$

$$= \left[\frac{V}{R}\right]^2 Rt = \frac{V^2 t}{R} = Pt \qquad \left[\because P = \frac{V^2}{R}\right]$$

SI unit of electric energy is joule.

Commercial Units of Electricity Consumption

To measure the electric energy consumed commercially, joule is not sufficient. So, to express electric energy consumed commercially a special unit kilo-watt-hour is used in place of joule. It is also called 1 unit of electric energy or board of trade unit (BTU).

1 kWh or 1 unit of electric energy is the amount of energy dissipated in 1 h in a circuit when the electric power in the circuit is 1 kW.

$$1\ \text{kWh} = 3.6 \times 10^6\ \text{J}$$

Billing The billing of electricity is done by calculating number of units consumed as below

$$\text{Number of units} = \frac{\text{watt} \times \text{hours}}{1000}$$

Production of Heat

The amount of heat produced in a current carrying conductor, H is given by

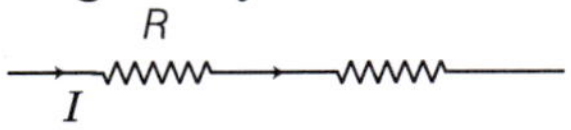

$$\boxed{H = I^2 Rt} \qquad \begin{bmatrix} R = \text{resistance} \\ I = \text{current} \end{bmatrix}$$

$$\Rightarrow \quad \boxed{H = \frac{V^2}{R} t} \quad \text{where, } t = \text{time} \qquad [\because V = IR]$$

Electric Power

The rate of consumption of electrical energy or production of heat energy is known as electric power. SI unit of electric power is watt (W).

Electric power, $P = I^2 R = \dfrac{V^2}{R} = VI$

Hence, $\boxed{P = VI}$

If V_s = specified voltage and W is wattage of a bulb or appliance, then resistance of bulb of appliance $R = \dfrac{V_s^2}{W}$.

If V_a is applied voltage, then actual power consumed

$$P_a = \frac{V_a^2}{R} = \frac{V_a^2}{V_s^2} W$$

Illumination of Electric Bulbs

Electric bulbs are illuminated in parallel and in series. On electric bulbs wattage and voltage are marked. If we have 40 W, 220 V bulb, then it means that on operating the bulb at 220 V, the power dissipated will be 40 W.

When bulbs of different ratings are connected in parallel, the bulb rated with maximum watt will give maximum illumination on the other hands, if the same bulbs are connected in series, then the bulb of lowest power will give maximum illumination.

PYQs Previous Years Questions

1 Mark Questions

1. Three bulbs B_1 (230V, 40W), B_2 (230V, 60W) and B_3(230V, 100W) are connected in series to a 230V supply. Which bulb glows the brightest? **ISC 2024**

2. If R_1 and R_2 are filament resistances of a 100 W bulb and a 50 W bulb respectively, designed to operate on the same voltage, then **ISC SQP 2023**

   (a) $R_1 = R_2$ (b) $R_1 = 4R_2$ (c) $R_2 = 4R_1$ (d) $R_2 = 2R_1$

3. An electric bulb is marked 200 V, 50 W. If it is used on a 400 V supply, it will draw a current of **ISC 2022 Sem-I**

   (a) 0.25 A (b) 0.40 A (c) 0.50 A (d) 0.80 A

4. If R_1 and R_2 are filament's resistances of a 200 W and a 100 W bulb respectively, designed to operate on the same voltage, then **ISC 2014**

   (a) $R_1 = R_2$ (b) $R_2 = 2R_1$ (c) $R_2 = 4R_1$ (d) $R_1 = 4R_2$

5. Three bulbs of specifications 60 W/220 V, 100 W/220 V and 1000 W/220 V are connected in series. Which one will glow the brightest? **ISC 2004**

6. The maximum power dissipated in a 10000 Ω resistor is 10 W. What is the maximum current? **ISC 2001**

2 Marks Questions

7. A torch bulb rated as 4.5 W, 1.5 V is connected as shown in figure given below. **ISC 2022 Sem-I**

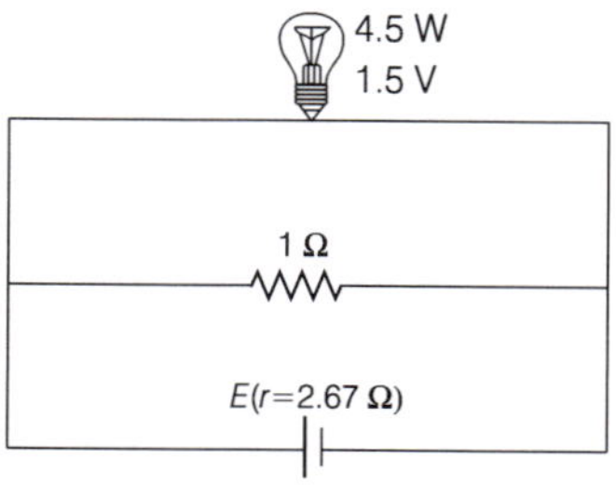

   (i) What should be the emf of the cell required to make this bulb glow at full intensity?

   (a) 4.5 V (b) 1.5 V
   (c) 2.67 V (d) 13.5 V

   (ii) What is the current passing through 1 Ω resistor?

   (a) 4.5 A (b) 1.5 A
   (c) 2.67 A (d) 13.5 A

8. An electric bulb is rated as 250 V, 750 W. Calculate the **ISC 2020**

   (i) electric current flowing through it, when it is operated on a 250 V supply and

   (ii) resistance of its filament.

9. Two resistors $R_1 = 60\ \Omega$ and $R_2 = 90\ \Omega$ are connected in parallel. If electric power consumed by the resistor R_1 is 15 W, calculate the power consumed by the resistor R_2. **ISC 2017**

3 Marks Questions

10. Two bulbs B_1 and B_2 are connected in series with a source of emf 250V as shown in the figure below. The labels on the bulbs read 250V, 80W and 250V, 100W respectively. **ISC 2022**

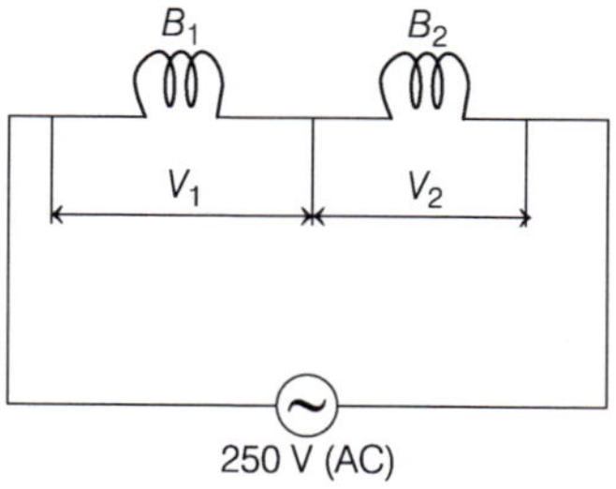

   (i) What will be the ratio of the resistance of the bulbs R_1 / R_2?

   (a) 5 : 4 (b) 4 : 5
   (c) 1 : 1 (d) 5 : 3

(ii) What will be the ratio of the power consumed (P_1 / P_2) when connected in series?

(a) 5:4 (b) 4 : 5

(c) 1: 1 (d) 5 : 3

(iii) What is the ratio of the pd across the bulbs (V_1 / V_2)?

(a) 5:4 (b) 4 : 5

(c) 1: 1 (d) 5 : 3

11. An electric bulb is marked 200 V, 100 W. Calculate electrical resistance of its filament. If five such bulbs are connected in series to a 200 V supply, how much current will flow through them? **(2018)**

KEY idea

In the given problem first we have to calculate the resistance with the help of $P = \frac{V^2}{R}$ and then calculate the current by the formula $i = \sqrt{P / R}$.

Case Based Question
(For Complete Chapter)

12. Direction *Read the passage given below and answer the questions that follow.*

Meter bridge is a sensitive device based on the principle of Wheatstone's bridge, for the determination of the resistance of a conductor (wire). Its sensitivity is much more than that of the post-office box.

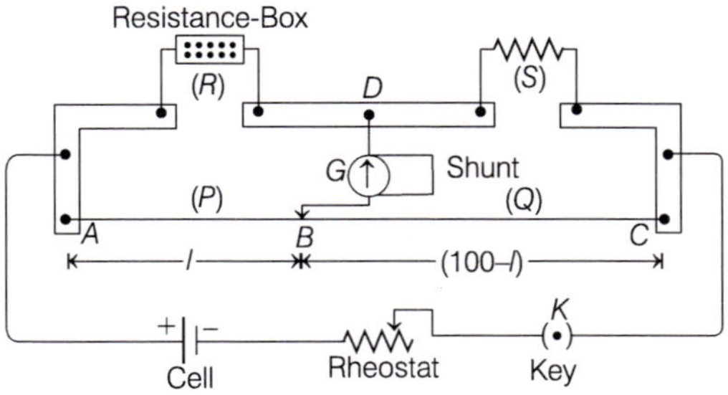

Meter bridge AC is a 1 metre wire of manganin or constantan which is fixed along a scale on a wooden base. The area of cross-section of the wire is same at all places. The ends A and C of the wire are joined to two L-shaped copper strips carrying binding-screws as shown. In between these strips, leaving a gap on either side, there is a third copper strip having three binding screws. The middle screw D is connected to a sliding jockey B through a shunted-galvanometer G. The knob of the jockey can be made to touch at any point on the wire.

(i) What do you mean by Meter bridge? **(1)**

(ii) At which condition the value of R and S becomes same? **(1)**

(iii) Write the construction of Meter bridge. **(1)**

(iv) What are the applications of Meter bridge? **(1)**

(v) What are the advantages of Meter bridge? **(1)**

Explanations

1. Electric power, $P = \frac{V^2}{R}$

Since, $V = 230$ V, the resistance of 40 W bulb is the high.

In series, electric power $= i^2 R$

Hence, the bulb with the high resistance i.e., 40 W bulb will glow the brightest.

2. (d) Power of bulb is inversely proportional to the resistance of filament wire of bulb.

$$\frac{P_1}{P_2} = \frac{R_2}{R_1}, \quad \frac{100}{50} = \frac{R_2}{R_1}$$

$$\Rightarrow \quad \frac{R_2}{R_1} = 2$$

$$\therefore \quad R_2 = 2R_1$$

3. (c) Bulb rating = 200 V, 50 W

$$\therefore \quad R = \frac{V^2}{P} = \frac{200 \times 200}{50} = 800\,\Omega$$

$$\text{Now, } I = \frac{V'}{R} = \frac{400}{800} = \frac{1}{2} = 0.50 \text{ A}$$

4. (b) We know that, power $P = \frac{V^2}{R}$

$$\Rightarrow \quad P_1 = \frac{V_1^2}{R_1} = \frac{V^2}{R_1}$$

[let common voltage be V] ...(i)

$$P_2 = \frac{V_2^2}{R_2} = \frac{V^2}{R_2} \quad \text{...(ii)}$$

From Eqs. (i) and (ii), we get

$$P_1R_1 = P_2R_2$$

$$\Rightarrow \quad 200 \times R_1 = 100 \times R_2$$

$$\Rightarrow \quad R_2 = 2R_1$$

5. We know that, resistance is given by

$$R = \frac{V^2}{P}$$

$$\Rightarrow \quad R \propto \frac{1}{P}$$

P is power. The resistance of 60 W/220 V bulb will be greater than any other given bulbs.

Brightness depends upon the power consumed.

In series, $P = I^2R$.

Hence, 60 W/220 V bulb will glow brighter.

6. Given, maximum power $= 10$ W, Resistance $= 10000\ \Omega$

Since, $P = i^2R$

$$\Rightarrow \quad i^2 = \frac{P}{R} = \frac{10}{10000}$$

$$= \frac{1}{1000}$$

$$\Rightarrow \quad i = \frac{1}{10\sqrt{10}}$$

$$= 0.0316 \text{ A}$$

7. (*i*) (d) When bulb glows with full intensity, potential difference across it is 1.5 V. So, current through the bulb and resistance of 1 Ω are 3A and 1.5 A respectively. So, main current from the cell

$$i = 3 + 1.5 = 4.5 \text{ A}$$

By using, $E = V + IR$

$$\Rightarrow \quad E = 1.5 + 4.5 \times 2.67 = 13.5 \text{ V}$$

(*ii*) (b) Voltage across 1Ω resistor $= 1.5$ V

$$\therefore \quad I = \frac{1.5}{1} = 1.5 \text{ A}$$

8. (*i*) Given, voltage,

$V = 250$ V and power, $P = 750$ W

Power, $P = VI$

$$750 = 250 \times I$$

$$\Rightarrow \text{Current,} \quad I = \frac{750}{250} = 3 \text{ A}$$

(*ii*) Now, from Ohm's law,

$$V = IR$$

$$\Rightarrow \quad R = \frac{V}{I} = \frac{250}{3} = 83.33\,\Omega$$

Hence, resistance of filament $= 83.33\,\Omega$

9.

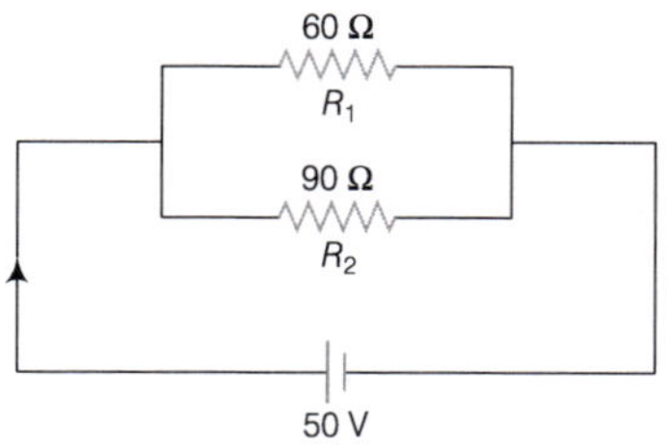

Equivalent resistance of the circuit $= R_{eq}$

$$\frac{1}{R_{eq}} = \frac{1}{R_1} + \frac{1}{R_2}$$

$$= \frac{1}{60} + \frac{1}{90} = \frac{3+2}{180} = \frac{5}{180}$$

$$R_{eq} = 36\Omega$$

Now, given $P_1 = 15$ W

$$R_1 = 60\Omega$$

Hence applying $P_1 = \dfrac{V^2}{R_1}$

$$V^2 = P_1R_1 = 15 \times 60$$

$$V^2 = 900$$

$$V = \sqrt{900} = 30 \text{ V}$$

Same V is applied for both R_1 and R_2,

$$\text{Total power, } P_{Total} = \frac{V^2}{R_{eq}} = \frac{(30)^2}{36}$$

$$= \frac{30 \times 30}{36} = 25 \text{ W}$$

Hence, P_2(Power consumed by resistance R_2)

$$= P_{Total} - P_1 = 25 - 15 = 10 \text{ W}$$

10. (*i*) (a) $R_1 = \dfrac{(250)^2}{80}$, $R_2 = \dfrac{(250)^2}{100}$

$$\frac{R_1}{R_2} = \frac{\frac{(250)^2}{80}}{\frac{(250)^2}{100}} = \frac{100}{80} = 5:4$$

(*ii*) (a) $\dfrac{P_1}{P_2} = \dfrac{I^2R_1}{I^2R_2} = \dfrac{R_1}{R_2} = 5:4$

(*iii*) (a) $\dfrac{V_1}{V_2} = \dfrac{IR_1}{IR_2} = 5:4$

11. We have, power, $P = \dfrac{V^2}{R}$

$$\text{Resistance, } R = \frac{V^2}{P} = \frac{(200)^2}{100}$$

$$= \frac{200 \times 200}{100} = 400\,\Omega$$

When five bulbs are joined in series, the same current will flow through the each bulb.

Current, $i = \sqrt{\frac{P}{R}} \Rightarrow i = \sqrt{\frac{100}{400}}$

$$\Rightarrow \qquad i = \frac{1}{2} = 0.5\text{ A}$$

12. (*i*) A meter-brid ge is an instrument that works on the principle of a Wheatstone bridge. It is also known as slide wire bridge.

(*ii*) The value of resistance R and resistance S is same when the length of AB and BC both are same.

$$\frac{P}{Q} = \frac{R}{S}$$

As, P and Q are same

$$\Rightarrow \qquad 1 = \frac{R}{S}$$

$$\therefore \qquad S = R$$

(*iii*) In metre-bridge AC is a 1 m wire of maganin or constantan which is fixed along a scale on a wooden base. The area of cross-section of the wire is same at all places. The ends A and C of the wire are joined to two L-shaped copper strips carrying binding-screws as shown in figure.

(*iv*) Finding the unknown resistance of a conductor as that of in a wheatstone bridge.

(*v*) Advantages of meter-bridge are following

(a) To find the unknown resistance very-very accurately.

(b) Directly applied in ammeter or voltmeter. So, resistance offered by ammeter and voltmeter do not effect the readings.

CHAPTER TEST

01 Mark Questions (MCQs)

1 The drift velocity of the free electrons in a conducting wire carrying a current I is v. If in a wire of the same metal, but of double the radius, the current be $2I$, then the drift velocity of the electrons will be

(a) $v/4$ (b) $v/2$
(c) v (d) $4\ v$

2 P and Q are two square plates of copper having the same thickness. The current is flowing through them as shown. The side of Q is twice the side of P, then

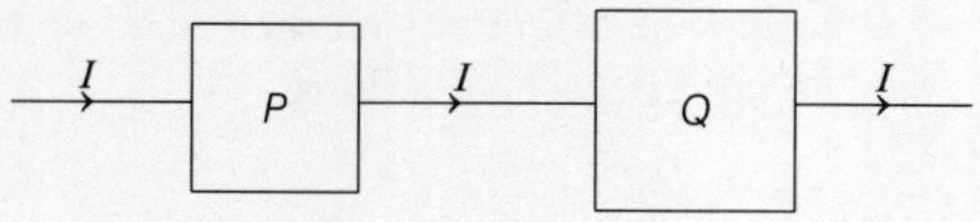

(a) the resistance of P is twice that of Q
(b) the resistance of P is half that of Q
(c) both have equal resistances
(d) the resistance of P is one-fourth that of Q

3 Five DC sources (cells)s of given emf are shown in the figure below. Emf of the battery AB is

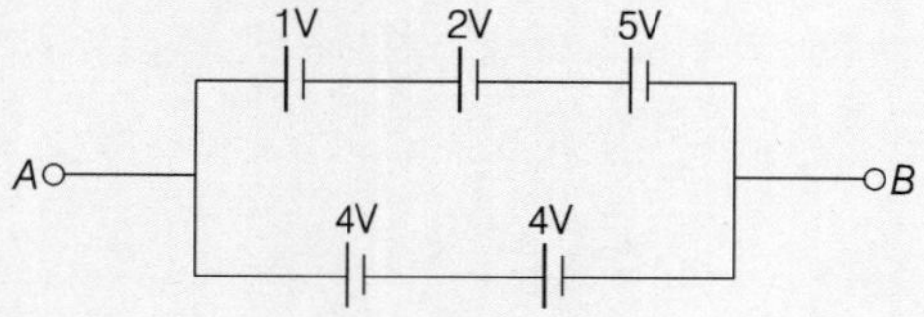

(a) 8 V (b) 16 V
(c) 4 V (d) 2 V

4 A cell of emf 1.5 V gives a current of 15 A when connected directly to an ammeter of 0.04 Ω resistance. The internal resistance of the cell is

(a) 0.04 Ω (b) 0.06 Ω
(c) 0.1 Ω (d) 1.0 Ω

5 A current of 2.0 A passes through a cell of emf 1.50 V and internal resistance 0.15 Ω from the negative to the positive terminal. The terminal voltage of the cell will be

(a) 1.35 (b) 1.50
(c) 1.00 (d) 1.20

01 Mark Questions (VSA)

6 What do you mean by back EMF?

7 What do you mean by internal resistance (r) ?

8 Write the relation between r, R, E and V.

03 Marks Questions

9 A galvanometer with a coil of resistance 100 Ω and a scale having 10 divisions has a current sensitivity of 25μA/div. How will you convert it into an ammeter of range 0 to 5A?

10 (i) Describe the working and construction of potential meter.

(ii) What do you mean by Wheatstone bridge? Explain.

05 Marks Questions

11 Using Kirchhoff''s rules in the given circuit, determine

(i) the voltage drop across the unknown resistor R and

(ii) the current I_2 in the arm EF.

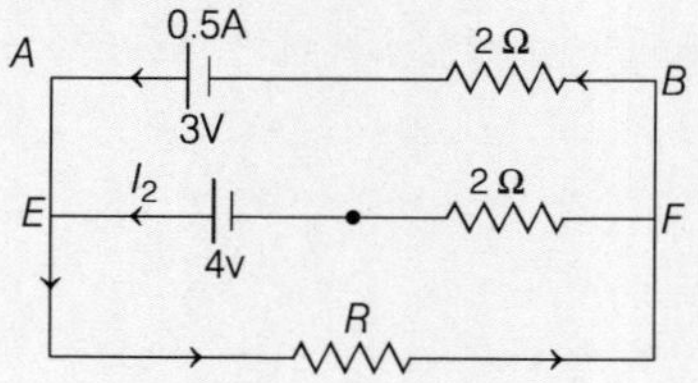

12 (i) State with the help of a circuit diagram, the working principle of a meter bridge. Obtain the expression used for determining the unknown resistance.

(ii) What happens if the galvanometer and cell are interchanged at the balance point of the bridge?

(iii) Why is it considered important to obtain the balance point near the mid-point of the wire?

Answers

1. (b) **2.** (a) **3.** (a) **4.** (c) **5.** (c)

9. 0.05 Ω

11. (i) $V_{AB} = 4\text{ V}, V_{CB} = 8\text{V}$ (ii) 8 A

06

Magnetic Effect of Current : Magnetic Field

TREND ANALYSIS 4 YEARS	Average No. of Questions Across all Sets				
	Types of Questions	2024	2023	2020	2019
Magnetic Effect of Current : Magnetic Field	1 Mark	–	2	1	–
	2 Marks	–	–	–	1
	3 Marks	1	2	–	–
	5 Marks	–	–	–	–

Magnetic Field

The space in the surroundings of a magnet or a current carrying conductor in which its magnetic influence can be experienced is called magnetic field. It is expressed as **B**.

The SI unit of magnetic field is tesla (T) and its CGS unit is gauss (G).

$$1 \text{ tesla} = 10^4 \text{ gauss}$$
$$1\,\text{T} = 1\,\text{Wb/m}^2 = 1\,\text{NA}^{-1}\text{m}^{-1}$$

In the CGS system, the magnetic field is expressed in gauss (G). $1\,\text{T} = 10^4\,\text{G}$

The dimensions of B are $[\text{MT}^{-2}\text{A}^{-1}]$.

Oersted's Experiment

Oersted experimentally demonstrated that the current carrying conductor produces magnetic field around it. His experimental arrangement is shown in the figure below

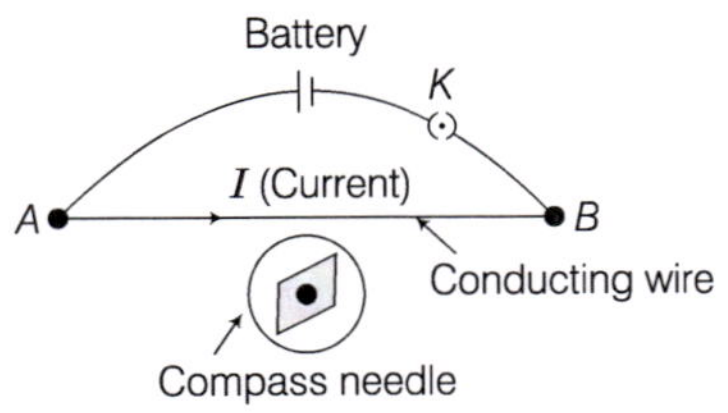

Biot-Savart's Law

According to this law, the magnetic field due to the small current carrying element at any nearby point P is given by

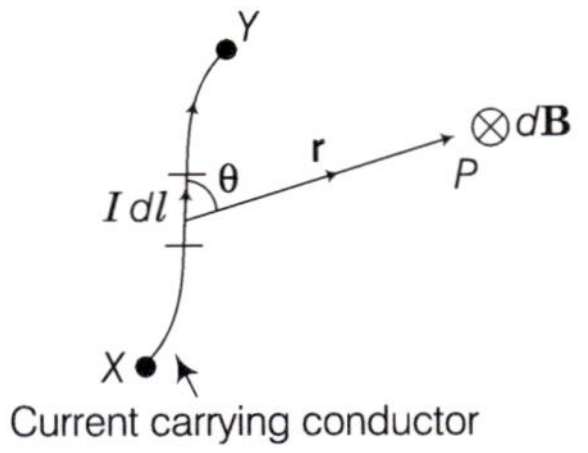

$$d\mathbf{B} = \frac{\mu_0}{4\pi} \cdot \frac{I\,dl \times \mathbf{r}}{|r|^3} \quad \text{or} \quad d\mathbf{B} = \frac{\mu_0}{4\pi} \cdot \frac{Idl \sin\theta}{r^2}$$

where, $I\,dl$ = current element (vector quantity)

r = displacement vector from current element to the point P.

The SI unit of magnetic field is tesla. Here,

$$\frac{\mu_0}{4\pi} = 10^{-7}\ \text{T-m/A}$$

where, μ_0 = permeability of free space.

Direction of Magnetic Field is given by Right Hand Thumb Rule

According to this rule, if we grab the straight conductor in our right hand such that the thumb points in the direction of current, then curling of fingers indicates the direction of magnetic field **B** as shown in the figure below.

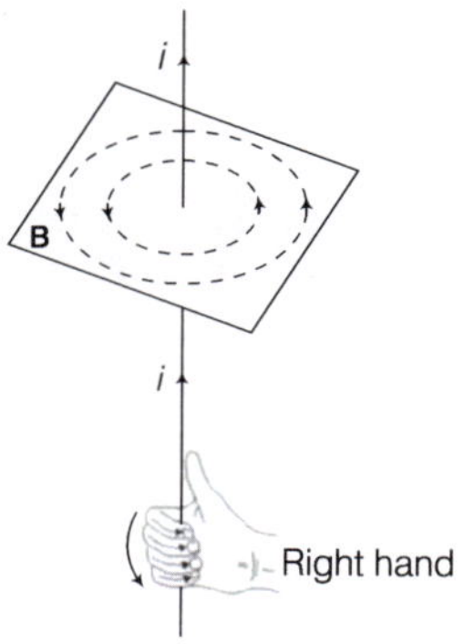

Relation between c, μ_0 and ε_0

The relation between speed of light in vacuum (c), permeability of free space (μ_0) and permittivity of free space (ε_0) is given by

$$\boxed{c = \frac{1}{\sqrt{\mu_0 \varepsilon_0}}}$$

Magnetic Field Near a Long Straight Wire

The magnetic field due to a long infinite straight current carrying conductor at any point P at a distance r from the wire is given by

$$B = \frac{\mu_0}{4\pi} \cdot \frac{2I}{r} = \frac{\mu_0 I}{2\pi r}$$

$\Rightarrow$ $$\boxed{B \propto \frac{1}{r}}$$

Magnetic Field at the Centre of a Circular Loop is given by

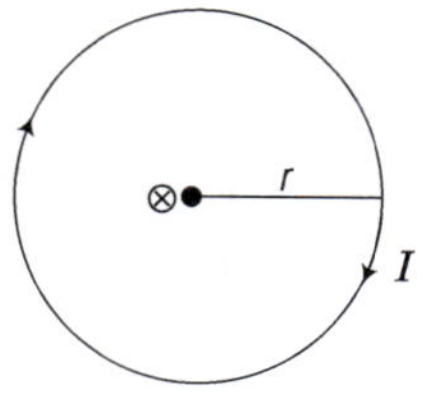

$$B = \frac{\mu_0 I}{2r}$$

For N turns of coil, $$\boxed{B = \frac{\mu_0 NI}{2r}}$$

The magnetic field at the centre of semi-circular loop is given by

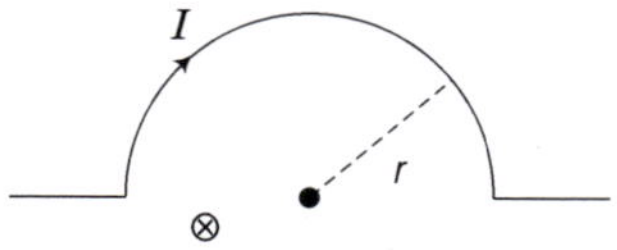

$$\boxed{B = \frac{\mu_0 I}{4r}}$$

The magnetic field at the centre of an arc of circular loop is given by

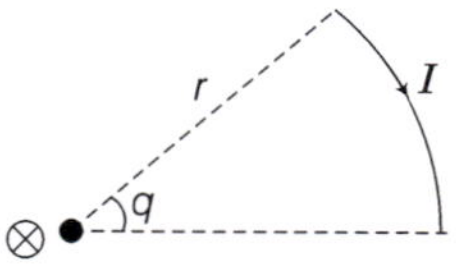

$$\boxed{B = \frac{\mu_0}{4\pi} \cdot \frac{I\theta}{r}}$$

where, θ is taken in radian.

Direction of the Magnetic Field at the Centre of Circular Loop is given by Right Hand Rule

(*i*) If the current is clockwise, the magnetic field is perpendicular to the plane downward.

(*ii*) If the current is anti-clockwise, the magnetic field is perpendicular to the plane upward.

Magnetic Field on the Axis of Circular Loop

The magnetic field at any point $P(r)$ lie on the axis of a circular current (I) carrying conductor (loop) of radius a is given by

$$\boxed{B = \frac{\mu_0 NIa^2}{2(r^2 + a^2)^{3/2}}}$$

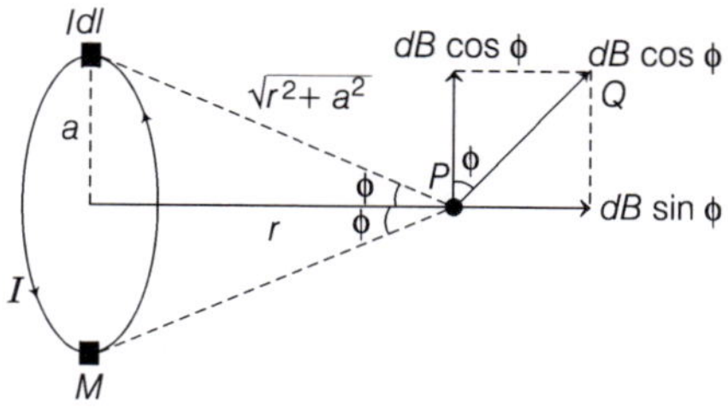

where, N = number of turns in the loop.

In the situation shown in the figure, the direction of the field is away from the centre.

Cases

(*i*) At the centre of loop, $r = 0$

$$B = \frac{\mu_0 NI}{2a}$$

(*ii*) At the axial points lying far away from the unit, $r >> a$, $B = \frac{\mu_0 NIa^2}{2r^3}$

(*iii*) At an axial point at a distance equal to the radius of the unit, $r = a$

$$B = \frac{\mu_0 NI^2}{2^{5/2} a}$$

Ampere's Circuital Law

The line integral of the magnetic field **B** around any closed plane curve is equal to μ_0 times the net current (I) passing through the loop. It is expressed as $\oint \mathbf{B} \cdot d\mathbf{l} = \mu_0 I$

where, μ_0 is permeability of free space.

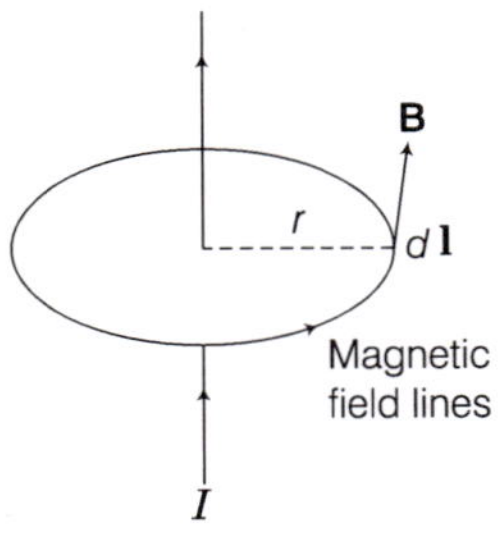

NOTE In the right hand of above equation, current is only inside the closed curve. Outside current is not considered.

The magnitude of magnetic field of a long straight wire using Ampere's law [$\because$ **B** and dl are in same direction]

$$\Rightarrow \quad \boxed{B = \frac{\mu_0 I}{2\pi r}}$$

Magnetic Field Due to a Straight Solenoid

A solenoid is a long cylindrical helix. It is made by winding closely a large number of turns of insulated copper wire over a tube of cardboard or China-clay.

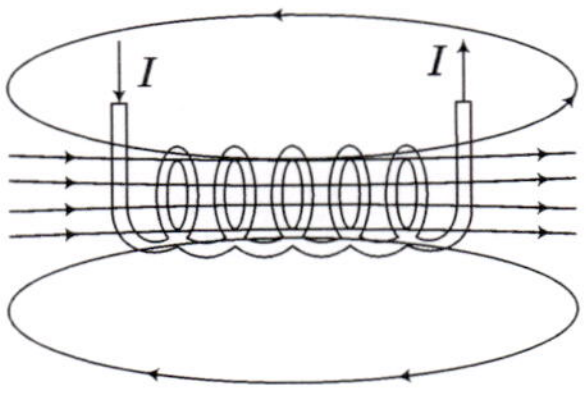

The magnetic field at any point inside the solenoid is given by

$$\boxed{B = \mu_0 nI}$$

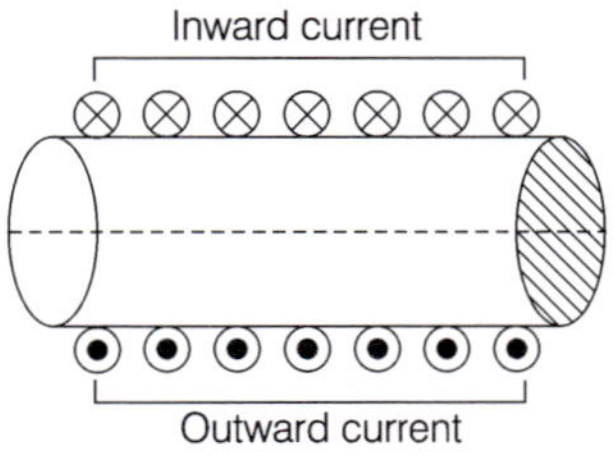

The magnetic field at the ends of solenoid is given by

$$\boxed{B = \frac{1}{2}\mu_0 nI}$$

where, n = number of turns per unit length
I = current flowing through the solenoid
and μ_0 = permeability of free space.

The magnetic field (**B**) at any point outside the solenoid is zero.

Current Carrying Loop as a Magnetic Dipole

A current loop behaves as a magnetic dipole.

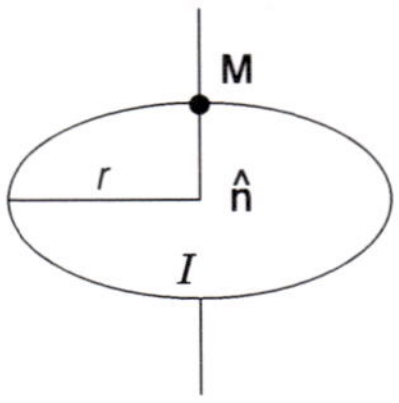

Magnetic dipole moment of the loop, $\mathbf{M} = I\mathbf{A}$

where, I = current in loop,
and $\mathbf{A}$ = area vector (of the loop).

$$|\mathbf{M}| = I\pi r^2$$

If loop has N turns, then $\mathbf{M} = NI\mathbf{A}$

Magnetic moment **M** is a vector quantity and its SI unit is A-m^2.

The direction of the magnetic dipole moment is perpendicular to the plane outward when current is anti-clockwise and perpendicular to the plane downward when current is clockwise.

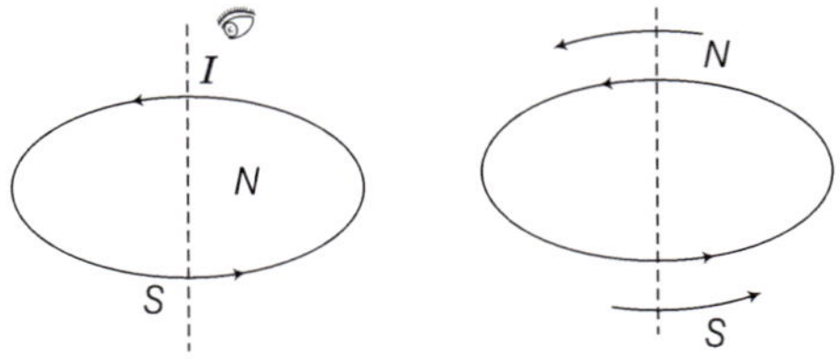

In the situation shown in the above diagram, the plane facing the observer behaves as north pole and opposite plane as south pole.

Magnetic Dipole Moment of a Revolving Electron

An electron being a charged particle, constitutes a current while moving in its circular orbit around the nucleus, so it also constitutes magnetic field.

As, $I = \frac{e}{T} = \frac{e}{\frac{2\pi r}{v}} = \frac{ev}{2\pi r}$ or $\boxed{I = \frac{ev}{2\pi r}}$

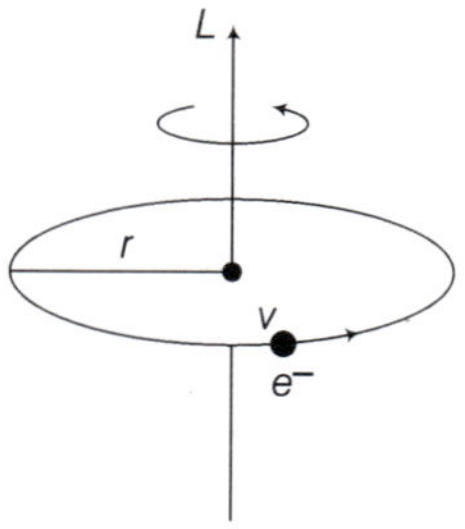

where, T = Time period of revolution

$$= \frac{2\pi r}{v}$$

Magnetic dipole moment of a revolving electron is given by

$$M = I \cdot \pi r^2 = \frac{evr}{2}$$

or $$M = \frac{e}{2m_e} L$$

where, v = speed of electron in a circular path of radius r, L is the angular momentum and given as $L = m_e vr$, where m_e is mass of electron.

Dipole moment can also be written as

$$\boxed{M = \frac{e}{4\pi m_e} nh}$$

As angular moment of an electron revolving around a nucleus is $\frac{nh}{2\pi}$, where h = Planck's constant and $n = 1, 2, 3, \ldots$.

PYQs Previous Years Questions

1 Mark Questions

1. A circular coil has radius r, number of turns N and carries a current I, magnetic flux density B at its centre is **ISC 2023**

(a) $\mu_0 NI$ (b) $\mu_0 NI / 2r$
(c) $\mu_0 NI / 4\pi r$ (d) $\mu_0 NI / 4r$

2. Magnetic flux density of the magnetic field at a point on the axis of a long straight solenoid is given by **ISC SQP 2023**

(a) $B = \mu_0 nI$ (b) $B = \frac{\mu_0 I}{2r}$
(c) $B = \frac{\mu_0 I}{4\pi r}$ (d) $B = \mu_0 I$

3. A straight long wire is turned into a loop of radius $R = 10$ cm, as shown in figure below. If a current $I = 16$ A is passed through the wire, then the magnetic field at the centre of the loop is **ISC 2022 Sem-I**

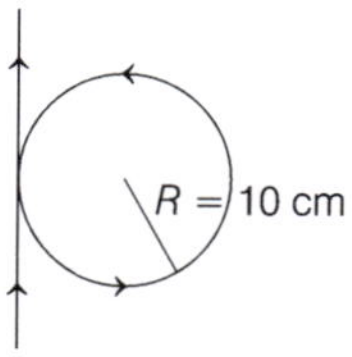

(a) 3.4×10^{-5} T (b) 6.8×10^{-5} T
(c) 1.7×10^{-5} T (d) 5.1×10^{-5} T

4. What is the angle between the current element $d\mathbf{l}$ and the magnetic flux density $\mathbf{B}$ at point P in the figure given below? **ISC 2022 Sem-I**

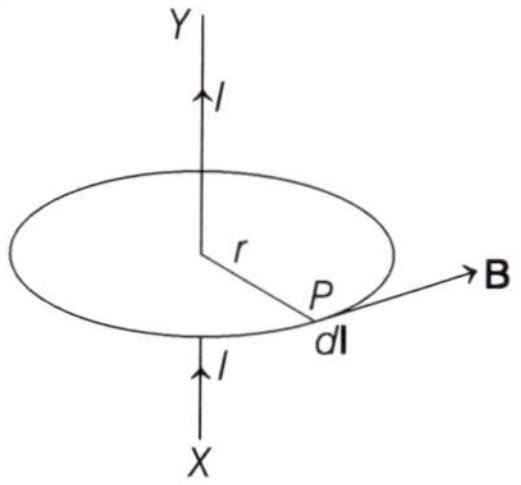

(a) Parallel to each other
(b) Perpendicular to each other
(c) Normal to each other
(d) Any angle between them is possible

5. What is the SI (base unit) unit of permeability? **ISC 2022 Sem-I**

(a) kg-ms^{-2}A^{-2} (b) kg-m^{2}s^{-2}A^{-2}
(c) kg-m^{2}sA^{-2} (d) kg-m s^{2}A^{-2}

6. What is the locus of an electron, projected perpendicular to a uniform magnetic field? **ISC 2022 Sem-I**

(a) Circle (b) Right bisector
(c) Parabola (d) Straight line

7. The point P is at a perpendicular distance of 0.2 m from a long straight wire YY', which carries a current of 1.6 A, as shown in figure.

Magnetic flux density of the magnetic field at point P is **ISC 2022 Sem-I**

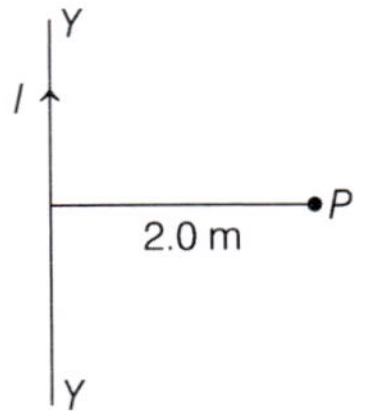

(a) 1.6×10^{-6} T directed into the paper
(b) 1.6×10^{-6} T coming out of the paper
(c) 0.8×10^{-6} T directed into the paper
(d) 0.8×10^{-6} T coming out of the paper

8. Magnetic field B at a point on the axis of (and inside) a long current carrying solenoid is given by **ISC 2022 Sem-I**

(a) $2\mu NI/l\pi$ (b) $\mu NI/l\pi$
(c) $\mu NI/l$ (d) $\mu NI/2l$

9. Write Biot-Savart's law in vector form. **ISC 2020**

10. A circular coil carrying a current I has radius R and the number of turns N. All the three, i.e. the current I, radius R and number of turns N are doubled, then magnetic field at its centre becomes **ISC 2018**

(a) double (b) half
(c) four times (d) one-fourth

11. Current flowing through a long solenoid is varied, then magnetic flux density of the magnetic field inside it varies **ISC SQP 2018**

(a) inversely with I (b) inversely with I^2
(c) directly with I (d) directly with I^2

12. Choose the correct option of : The Biot-Savart's law in vector form is **ISC 2013**

(a) $d\mathbf{B} = \frac{\mu_0}{4\pi}\frac{dl\,(I\times r)}{\mathbf{r}^3}$ (b) $d\mathbf{B} = \frac{\mu_0}{4\pi}\frac{I(dl\times \mathbf{r})}{\mathbf{r}^3}$

(c) $d\mathbf{B} = \frac{\mu_0}{4\pi}\frac{I\,(\mathbf{r}\times dl)}{\mathbf{r}^3}$ (d) $d\mathbf{B} = \frac{\mu_0}{4\pi}\frac{I\,(dl\times \mathbf{r})}{\mathbf{r}^2}$

13. Figure shows a point P near a long conductor XY carrying a current I.
MN is a short current conductor, kept at the point P, parallel to the conductor XY. What is the direction of magnetic flux density B at the point P due to the current flowing through XY? **ISC 2012**

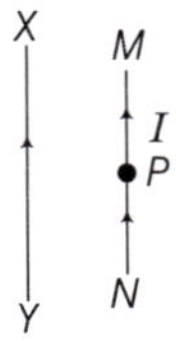

14. Calculate the magnetic field (in SI unit) at the centre of a tangent galvanometer coil of 50 turns and radius 10 cm when a current of 1.0 A passes through it. **ISC 2007**

15. State Ampere's circuital law. **ISC 2005**

2 Marks Questions

16. An electric current I flows through an infinitely long conductor as shown in the figure given alongside. Write an expression and direction for the magnetic field at point P.

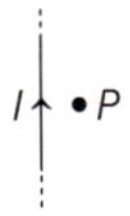

Or

An electric current I flows through a circular loop as shown in the figure given below. Write an expression and direction for the magnetic field at the centre of the loop at point P. **ISC 2019**

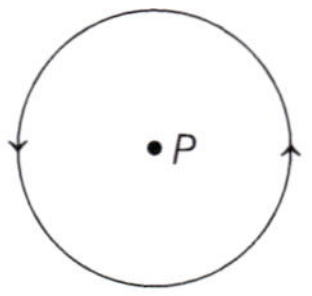

17. A long straight wire is bent as shown in the adjacent figure. Find the resultant magnetic field B at the centre C of the circular path of radius 2 cm, if a current I of 5 A is passed through the wire as shown in figure. **ISC SQP 2018**

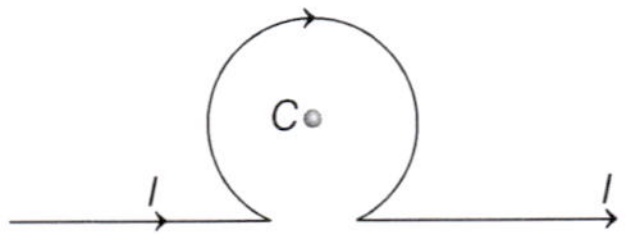

18. Using Ampere's circuital law, obtain an expression for the magnetic flux density B at a point P at a perpendicular distance r from a long current carrying conductor. (Statement of the law is not required)
ISC 2017

3 Marks Questions

19. Using Biot-Savart law, show that magnetic flux density B at the centre of a current carrying circular coil of radius R is given by **ISC 2024**

$$B = \frac{\mu_0 I}{2R}$$

where, the terms have their usual meanings.

20. Using Ampere's circuital law, obtain an expression for magnetic flux density B at a point near an infinitely long and straight conductor, carrying a current I.
ISC 2023

21. Obtain an expression for magnetic flux density B at the centre of a current carrying circular coil.
ISC SQP 2023

22. Obtain an expression for magnetic flux density B at the centre of a circular coil of radius R having N turns and carrying a current I. **ISC 2015**

23. Find magnetic flux density at a point on the axis of a long solenoid having 5000 turns/m when it is carrying a current of 2 A. **(2014)**

24. Using Ampere's circuital law or Biot-Savart's law, show that magnetic flux density B at a point P at a perpendicular distance a from a long current carrying conductor is given by $B = \left(\frac{\mu_0}{4\pi}\right)\frac{2I}{a}$. [Statement of the laws not required]. **ISC 2011, 05**

25. Obtain an expression for magnetic flux density B at the centre of a circular coil of radius R and having N turns, when a current I is flowing through it.
ISC 2009, 01

4/5 Marks Questions

26. (*i*) Two infinitely long current carrying conductors X and Y are kept parallel to each other, 24 cm apart in vacuum. They carry currents of 5A and 7A respectively, in the same direction, as shown in figure below. Find the position of a neutral point, i.e. a point where resultant magnetic flux density is zero. (Ignore earth's magnetic field)

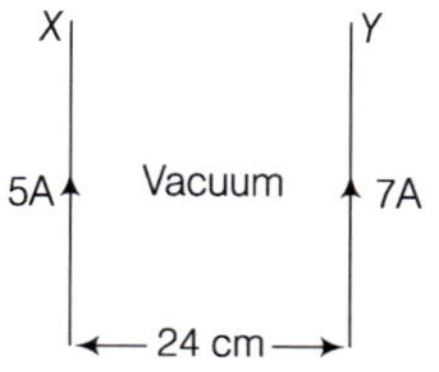

(*ii*) If current through the conductor Y is reversed in direction, will neutral point lie between X and Y, to the left of X or to the right of Y?
ISC 2016

27. (*i*) Write an expression for Biot-Savart's law in the vector form. Write an expression for the magnetic field at the centre of a circular coil of radius R, with N turns and carrying a current I.

(*ii*) A helium nucleus completes one round of a circle of radius 0.8 m is 2 s. Find the magnetic field at the centre of the circle. **ISC 2006**

28. A circular coil of N turns and radius R carries a current I. It is unwound and rewound to make another coil of radius $R/2$, current I remaining the same. Calculate the ratio of the magnetic moments of the new coil and the original coil. **ISC 2003**

Case Based Question
(For Complete Chapter)

29. Direction *Read the passage given below and answer the questions that follow.*

X and Y are two concentric and coplanar circular coils carrying currents of 6A and 2 A in opposite directions as shown in figure below. Their radii are $R_X = 8\pi$ cm and $R_Y = 4\pi$ cm, whereas number of turns in X and Y are 50 and 100, respectively. **ISC 2022 Sem-I**

Answer the following on basis of above information.

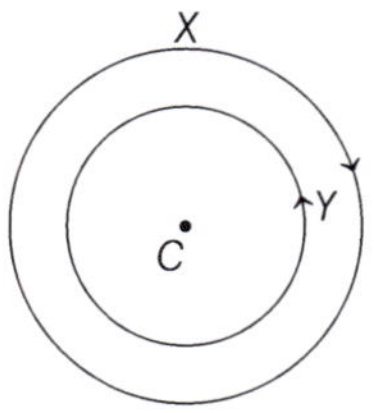

(i) Magnetic field at the common centre C due to current in the coil X is

(a) 7.5×10^{-4} T b) 7.5×10^{-6} T
(c) 1.0×10^{-4} T (d) 2.0×10^{-4} T

(ii) Magnetic field at the common centre C due to current in the coil Y is

(a) 1×10^{-5} T (b) 2×10^{-4} T
(c) 2×10^{-3} T (d) 1×10^{-3} T

(iii) Resultant magnetic field at the common centre C due to the current in the coils X and Y is

(a) 2.5×10^{-3} T (b) 2.5×10^{-4} T
(c) 2.5×10^{-5} T (d) 2.5×10^{-6} T

Explanations

1. (b) Magnetic flux density $B = \frac{\mu_0 NI}{2r}$

2. (a) For a long solenoid magnetic flux density $B = \mu_0 nI$

3. (b) $B = \frac{\mu_0}{4\pi} \cdot \frac{2I}{r} = \frac{\mu_0 I}{2\pi r}$

$$= \frac{\mu_0 i}{2r}\left(\frac{1}{\pi} - 1\right) = \frac{4\pi \times 10^{-7}}{2 \times 10^{-1}} \times \left(\frac{1}{3.14} - 1\right)$$

$= 6.8 \times 10^{-5}$ T (outward direction)

4. (a) The current element $d\mathbf{l}$ and magnetic flux density $\mathbf{B}$ at any point P are always tangential to each other.

5. (a) Here, $\mu_0 = \frac{\text{Newton}}{\text{Ampere}^2} = \frac{\text{kg-ms}^{-2}}{\text{A}^2} = \text{kg-m s}^{-2}\text{A}^{-2}$

6. (a)

7. (a) Given, $i = 1.6$ A, $d = 0.2$ m

Magnetic field due to long straight wire,

$$B = \frac{\mu_0}{4\pi} \cdot \frac{i}{d} \times 2 = 10^{-7} \times \frac{1.6}{0.2} \times 2$$

$= 1.6 \times 10^{-6}$ T, directed into the paper

8. (c) Magnetic field at a point inside on the axis of a solenoid in a given medium is

$B = \mu nI$, where n = number of turns per unit length $= \frac{N}{l}$

$\therefore \quad B = \mu NI/l$

9. Refer to text on page 85. (Biot Savart's Law)

10. (a) Magnetic field at the centre of a current carrying coil is given by $\quad B = \frac{\mu_0 NI}{2R} \quad$ ...(i)

If $I' = 2I$, $R' = 2R$, $N' = 2N$, then

Magnetic field, $B' = \frac{\mu_0 N' I'}{2R'} = \frac{\mu_0 (2N)(2I)}{2(2R)}$

$$B' = 2\left(\frac{\mu_0 NI}{2R}\right)$$

$B' = 2B$ [from Eq. (i)]

11. (c) Let a rectangular amperian loop $PQRS$ is taken in a solenoid. Now, applying Ampere's circuital law in this loop

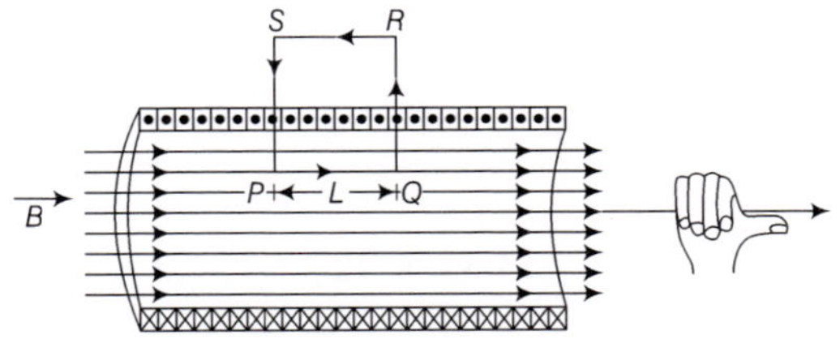

$$\oint_{PQRS} \mathbf{B} \cdot d\mathbf{l} = \int_P^Q \mathbf{B} \cdot d\mathbf{l} + \int_Q^R \mathbf{B} \cdot d\mathbf{l} + \int_R^S \mathbf{B} \cdot d\mathbf{l}$$

$$+ \int_S^P \mathbf{B} \cdot d\mathbf{l} = \mu_0 nLI \quad \text{... (i)}$$

On remaining three sides i.e. RQ, SR and PQ, $\mathbf{B} \cdot d\mathbf{l}$ is zero as $\mathbf{B}$ is either zero or perpendicular to $d\mathbf{l}$. Thus,

$$\int_P^Q \mathbf{B} \cdot d\mathbf{l} = BL$$

Hence, Eq. (i) becomes

$BL = \mu_0 nLI$

$B = \mu_0 nI$ or $B \propto I$

12. (b) Biot-Savart's law in vector form is

$$d\mathbf{B} = \frac{\mu_0}{4\pi} \frac{I(d\mathbf{l} \times \mathbf{r})}{r^3}$$

13. According to Biot-Savart's law, we can say that the direction of magnetic flux density at the point P due to the current flowing through the conductor XY is perpendicular to the plane of the paper directed into the page, as shown in the diagram.

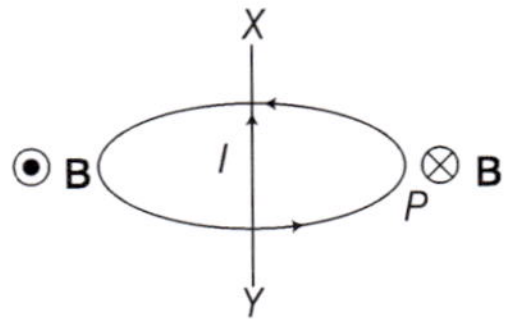

14. Magnetic field at the centre of tangent galvanometer is given by

$$B = \frac{\mu_0 NI}{2r}$$

Given, $N = 50$, $r = 10$ cm $= 0.1$ m, $I = 1$ A

Also, $\mu_0 = 4\pi \times 10^{-7}$

So, $B = \dfrac{4 \times 3.14 \times 10^{-7} \times 50 \times 1}{2 \times 0.1}$

$= 3.14 \times 10^{-4}$ T

15. **Ampere's circuital law** The line integral of the magnetic field **B** around any closed loop is equal to μ_0 times the total current passing through the loop. i.e.

$\oint \mathbf{B} \cdot d\mathbf{l} = \mu_0 I$

where, I = total current inside the closed path.

16.

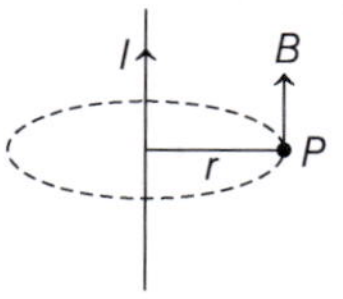

The magnitude of the magnetic field at a point P,

$$B = \frac{\mu_0 I}{2\pi r}$$

Its direction at point P is along the tangent to a circle of radius r centred on the conductor.

Or

The magnitude of the magnetic field at point P,

$$B = \frac{\mu_0 I}{2a}$$

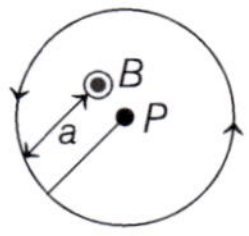

The magnetic field **B** is perpendicular to the plane of the coil, directed upward.

17. Here, $B_1 = \dfrac{\mu_0 I}{4\pi r} \odot \Rightarrow B_2 = \dfrac{\mu_0 I}{2r} \otimes \Rightarrow B_3 = \dfrac{\mu_0 I}{4\pi r} \odot$

$\Rightarrow \quad B_C = B_2 - (B_1 + B_3) = \dfrac{\mu_0 I}{2r} - \dfrac{\mu_0 I}{2\pi r}$

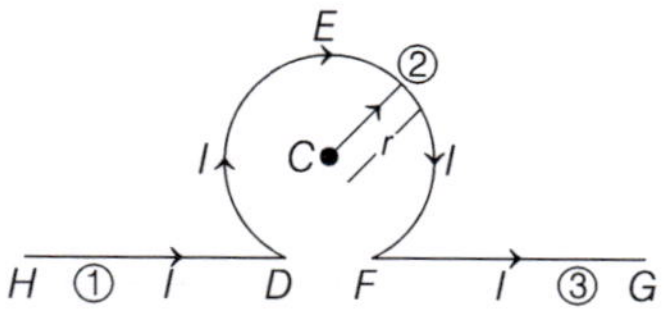

$$= \frac{\mu_0 I}{2r}\left[\frac{1}{\pi} - 1\right]\hat{\mathbf{n}}$$

or $\quad B_C = \dfrac{\mu_0 I}{2r}\left[\dfrac{1}{\pi} - 1\right]$, upward

Using $I = 5$A, $r = 2$ cm $= 2 \times 10^{-2}$ m,

then $B_C = \dfrac{4\pi \times 10^{-7} \times 5}{2 \times 2 \times 10^{-2}}\left[\dfrac{1-\pi}{\pi}\right]$

$= 5 \times 10^{-5}\,[1 - \pi] = 10.7 \times 10^{-5}$T, upward direction.

Concept Enhancer Apart from circular loop, we can also calculate the magnetic field at the centre of the circular arc by the relation

$$B = \frac{\mu_0}{4\pi} \cdot \frac{i}{r} \cdot \theta$$

where, θ = angle at the centre of the circular arc.

18. To find magnetic field at a point, consider Amperian loop around an infinitely long conducting wire as shown.

Here,we have to determine the magnetic field at point P, which is situated at a distance a from the centre of the circular loop around the conducting wire. The magnetic field (**B**) is tangential to the circumference of the loop.

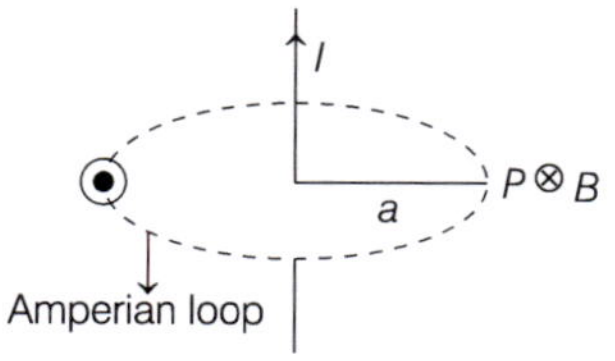

As we know that from Ampere's circuital law,

$$\oint \mathbf{B} \cdot dl = \mu_0 I$$

As $\quad \oint dl = 2\pi a$

So, $\quad B \cdot 2\pi a = \mu_0 I$

$$B = \frac{\mu_0 I}{2\pi a} \times \frac{2}{2}$$

$\Rightarrow \quad B = \dfrac{\mu_0}{4\pi}\dfrac{2I}{a}$

The direction of magnetic field will be determined by right hand thumb rule.

19. Consider a circular coil of radius R and carrying a current I in the direction as shown in figure. Suppose the entire circular coil is divided into a large number of current elements, each of length dl.

According to Biot-Savart's law, the magnetic field dB at the centre O of the coil due to the current element Idl is given by

$$B = \frac{\mu_0}{4\pi}\frac{I(d\mathbf{l} \times \mathbf{R})}{R^3} \qquad \text{...(i)}$$

The magnitude of dB at the centre O is

$$dB = \frac{\mu_0}{4\pi} \frac{Idl \times R \sin\theta}{R^3}$$

$$\Rightarrow \quad dB = \frac{\mu_0}{4\pi} \frac{Idl \sin\theta}{R^2}$$

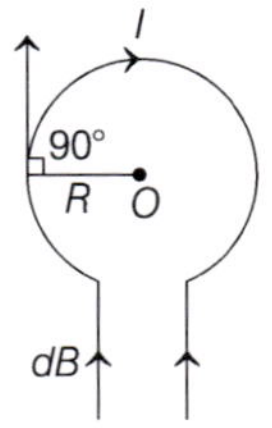

$$\therefore \quad B = \int dB = \int \frac{\mu_0}{4\pi} \frac{Idl \sin\theta}{R^2}$$

$$\theta = 90° \quad \Rightarrow \quad \sin 90° = 1$$

$$\therefore \quad B = \frac{\mu_0}{4\pi} \frac{I}{R^2} \int dl$$

$$\int dl = \text{Total length of the coil} = 2\pi r$$

$$B = \frac{\mu_0}{4\pi} \frac{I}{R^2} (2\pi R) = \frac{\mu_0 I}{2R}$$

20. Refer to text on page 87 (Ampere's Circuital Law).

21. Let there be a loop of radius a, carrying a current I and O be the centre of the loop, at which the field is required.

By Biot-Savart's law, the magnitude of the magnetic field at O due to a small element δl of the loop is

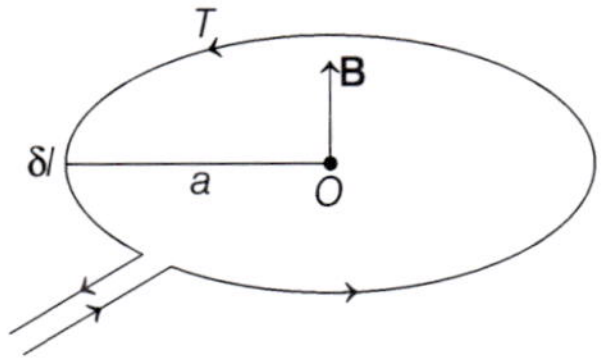

$$\delta B = \frac{\mu_0}{4\pi} \frac{I\,\delta l \sin\theta}{a^2}$$

where, θ is the angle between the length of the element (δl) and the line joining the element to the point O. Here, $\theta = 90°$ (every element of a circle is perpendicular to the radius). Therefore, $\delta B = \frac{\mu_0}{4\pi} \frac{I\delta l}{a^2}$.

The direction of the field will be the same for all elements of the coil. Therefore, the magnitude of the magnetic field **B** at O due to the entire coil is

$$B = \frac{\mu_0}{4\pi} \frac{I}{a^2} \Sigma\delta l$$

But $\Sigma\delta l = 2\pi a$ (the length of the circumference of the coil).

$$\therefore \quad B = \frac{\mu_0}{4\pi} \frac{I}{a^2} (2\pi a) \quad \text{or} \quad B = \frac{\mu_0 I}{2a}$$

If the circular coil has N turns, then the field at the centre would be $B = \frac{\mu_0 NI}{2a}$

The magnetic field **B** is perpendicular to the plane of the coil, directed upwards. If the current in the coil be reversed, the field will be directed downwards.

22. Consider a circular coil of radius R and carrying a current I in the direction as shown in figure. Suppose, the entire circular coil is divided into a large number of current elements, each of length dl.

According to Biot-Savart's law, the magnetic field $d\mathbf{B}$ at the centre O of the coil due to the current element Idl is given by

$$\mathbf{B} = \frac{\mu_0}{4\pi} \frac{I(d\mathbf{l} \times \mathbf{R})}{R^3}$$

The magnitude of $d\,\mathbf{B}$ at the centre O is

$$dB = \frac{\mu_0}{4\pi} \cdot \frac{Idl \times R \sin\theta}{R^3}$$

$$\Rightarrow \quad dB = \frac{\mu_0}{4\pi} \frac{Idl \sin\theta}{R^2}$$

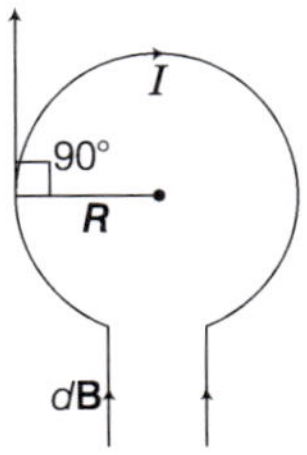

$$\therefore \quad B = \int dB = \int \frac{\mu_0}{4\pi} \frac{Idl \sin\theta}{R^2}$$

$$\theta = 90° \quad \Rightarrow \quad \sin 90° = 1$$

$$\therefore \quad B = \frac{\mu_0}{4\pi} \frac{1}{R^2} \int dl$$

$$\int dl = \text{total length of the coil} = 2\pi r$$

$$B = \frac{\mu_0}{4\pi} \frac{1}{R^2} (2\pi R) = \frac{\mu_0 I}{2R}$$

If the coil has N turns, then

$$B = \frac{\mu_0 NI}{2R}$$

23. To find magnetic flux density at the centre of a solenoid, we have to find the magnetic field at the centre.

Magnetic flux density at the centre

= Magnetic field at the centre

$$B = \mu_0 ni$$

where, i = current through the solenoid

μ_0 = permeability of free space $= 4\pi \times 10^{-7}$

$n =$ number of turns per unit length

$\therefore \quad B = 4\pi \times 10^{-7} \times 5000 \times 2$

$[\because n = 5000 \text{ turns / m}, i = 2\text{ A}]$

$= 8\pi \times 10^{-4} \times 5 = 4\pi \times 10^{-3}$

$= 1.256 \times 10^{-2}$ T

24. In such cases where symmetry exist it is easier to find field by Ampere's circuital law.

To find magnetic field at a point, consider Amperian loop around an infinitely long conducting wire as shown.

In order to determine the magnetic field at point P, which is situated at a distance a from the centre of the circular loop around the conducting wire. The magnetic field (B) is tangential to the circumference of the loop.

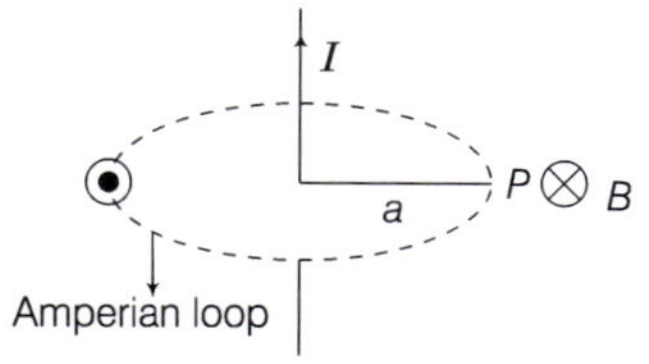

As we know that, from Ampere's circuital law,

$$\oint \mathbf{B} \cdot dl = \mu_0 I$$

As $\quad \oint dl = 2\pi a$

So, $\quad \mathbf{B} \cdot 2\pi a = \mu_0 I$

$$\mathbf{B} = \frac{\mu_0 I}{2\pi a} \times \frac{2}{2}$$

$\Rightarrow \quad \mathbf{B} = \dfrac{\mu_0}{4\pi} \dfrac{2I}{a}$

The direction of magnetic field will be determined by right hand thumb rule.

25. Take a small current element in the circular coil and find **B** due to it. After that integrate it for whole length of the loop.

Consider a small element dl on circular coil of radius R carrying current I.

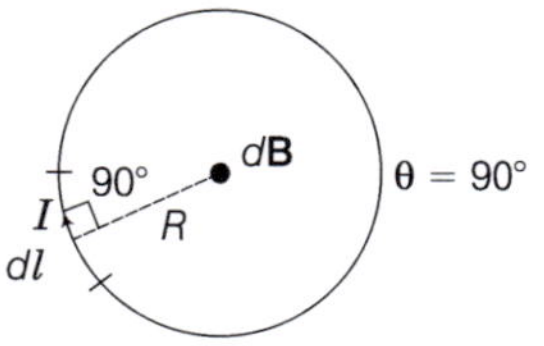

$\therefore$ By Biot-Savart's law, magnetic field at the centre due to element of coil.

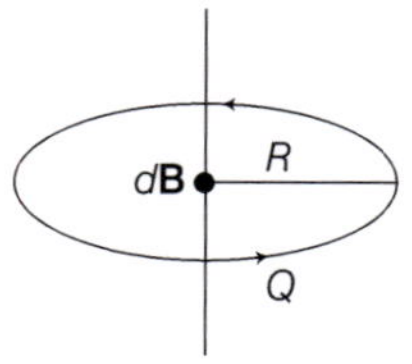

$$dB = \frac{\mu_0}{4\pi} \cdot \frac{I\, dl \sin 90°}{R^2}$$

$\Rightarrow \quad dB = \dfrac{\mu_0}{4\pi} \cdot \dfrac{I}{R^2} dl$

$$B = \oint \frac{\mu_0}{4\pi} \frac{I}{R^2} dl$$

$$= \frac{\mu_0}{4\pi} \frac{I}{R^2} \oint dl$$

$$= \frac{\mu_0}{4\pi} \frac{I}{R^2} \times 2\pi R$$

$$B = \frac{\mu_0 I}{2R} \qquad [\because \oint dl = 2\pi R]$$

For N turns of coil, $B = \dfrac{\mu_0 NI}{2R}$.

Common Mistake In this case, we cannot apply Ampere's law.

26. (*i*) According to the question,

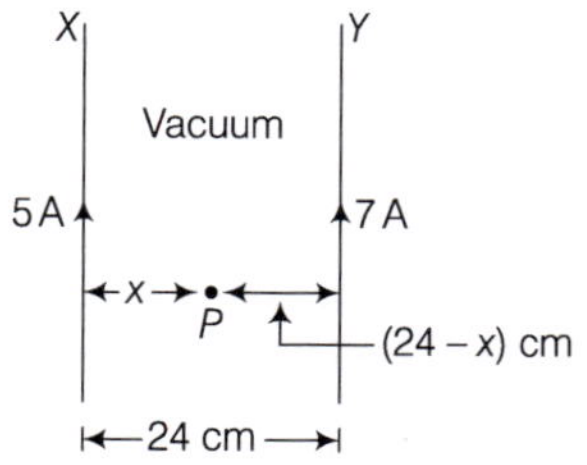

Let at point P, the magnetic flux density be zero.

So, magnetic field due to 5 A wire at point P is

$$\frac{\mu_0 5}{2\pi x}(-\hat{\mathbf{k}}) \qquad \text{... (i)}$$

Magnetic field due to 7A wire at point P is

$$\frac{\mu_0 7}{2\pi(24 - x)}(+\hat{\mathbf{k}}) \qquad \text{... (ii)}$$

We know that, P is a neutral point so, from Eqs. (i) and (ii)

$$\frac{5\mu_0}{2\pi x} = \frac{7\mu_0}{2\pi(24 - x)}$$

$$\Rightarrow \quad \frac{5}{x} = \frac{7}{24-x}$$

$\Rightarrow$ $120 - 5x = 7x \Rightarrow 12x = 120$

$\Rightarrow$ $x = 10$ cm (from current carrying wire X)

Thus, the position of a neutral point is 10 cm.

(*ii*) No, on reversing the current in the wire Y, neutral point will not lie between X and Y. It will lie on the left of wire X.

Common Mistake Generally, here is a confusion for two parallel current carrying wire in same direction repel like the similar poles of a bar magnet but they will be attract each other.

27. (*i*) Refer to solution no. 12 and 25 on pages 91 and 94.

(*ii*) We know that, magnetic field at the centre of a coil carrying current I is

$$B = \frac{\mu_0 NI}{2R}$$

In this case, revolving of helium nucleus will constitute the current.

For $N = 1$, [i.e. only one turn]

$$B = \frac{\mu_0 \times N}{2R} \times \frac{2e}{t}$$

[For helium, $I = \frac{Q}{t} = \frac{2e}{t}$, as the nucleus has $+2e$ charge]

$$\Rightarrow \quad B = \frac{4\pi \times 10^{-7} \times 1 \times 2 \times 1.6 \times 10^{-19}}{2 \times 0.8 \times 2}$$

$$= 1.256 \times 10^{-25} \text{ T}$$

28. The length of wire will be same in two cases as the same coil is unwound and rewound.

Length of the wire is same.

$$\therefore \quad N_1 \times (2\pi R) = N_2 \times 2\pi \left(\frac{R}{2}\right)$$

[N_1 and N_2 = number of turns in two coils]

$$N_2 = 2N_1$$

Now, the ratio of magnetic moments is given by

$$\frac{M_1}{M_2} = \frac{N_1 I A_1}{N_2 I A_2} = \frac{N_1 \times \pi R_1^2}{N_2 \times \pi R_2^2}$$

$$\frac{M_1}{M_2} = \left(\frac{N_1}{2N_1}\right) \times \left(\frac{R}{R/2}\right)^2 = \frac{1}{2} \times 4 = 2$$

$$M_1 : M_2 = 1:2$$

29. Magnetic field at the centre of circular loop is

$$B = \frac{\mu_0 NI}{2R}$$

(*i*) (a) $B_X = \dfrac{4\pi \times 10^{-7} \times 50 \times 6}{2 \times 8\pi \times 10^{-2}}$

$= 7.5 \times 10^{-4}$ T

(*ii*) (d) $B_Y = \dfrac{4\pi \times 10^{-7} \times 100 \times 2}{2 \times 4\pi \times 10^{-2}}$

$= 1 \times 10^{-3}$ T

(*iii*) (b) $B_{\text{net}} = B_Y - B_X$

$= (10 - 7.5) \times 10^{-4}$

$= 2.5 \times 10^{-4}$ T

CHAPTER TEST

01 Mark Questions (MCQs)

1 The magnetic field strength at a point due to a long straight conductor

(a) obeys the inverse square law

(b) varies inversely as the distance from conductor

(c) varies as the inverse of the cube of the distance from the conductor

(d) None of the above

2 Magnetic induction vector **B** in terms of base units of SI would be

(a) $kg\, s^{-1} A^{-1}$ (b) $kg\, s^{-2} A^{-1}$

(c) $kg\, s^{-2} A^{-2}$ (d) $kg^2\, s^{-2} A^{-1}$

3 Which graph represents the variation of magnetic field B with distance a from a long straight current carrying conductor?

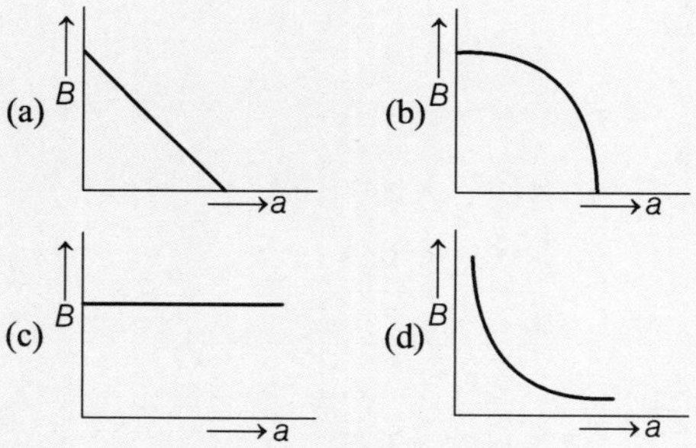

01 Mark Questions (VSA)

4 Draw the magnetic field lines due to a current carrying loop.

5 A circular coil of closely wound N turns and radius r carries a current I. Write the expression for the magnetic momentum of this coil.

6 Find the magnetic moment of a square coil of radius a and current flowing through the coil is I and number of turns is N.

02 Marks Questions

7 Two identical circular loops P and Q, each of radius r and carrying equal currents are kept in the parallel planes having a common axis passing through O. The direction of current in P is clockwise and in Q is anti-clockwise as seen from O which is equidistant from the loops P and Q. Find the magnitude of the net magnetic field at O.

8 A long solenoid of length L having N turns carries a current I. Deduce the expression for the magnetic field in the interior of the solenoid.

03 Marks Questions

9 (i) Explain the Oersted's experiment.

(ii) Explain in detail about the Biot-Savart's law.

10 (i) Describe the magnetic field on the axis of circular loop.

(ii) Explain in detail on Ampere's circuital law.

05 Marks Questions

11 Figure shows a long straight wire of circular cross-section of radius a carrying steady current I. The current I is uniformly distributed across this cross-section. Derive the expressions for the magnetic field in the region $r < a$ and $r > a$.

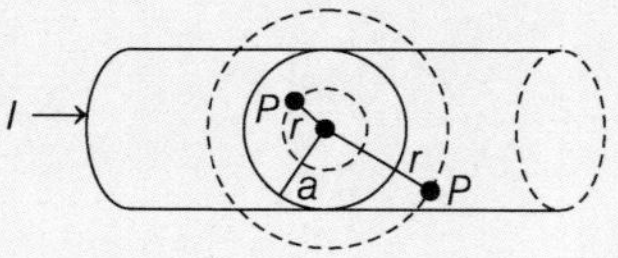

12 A solenoid of length 1.0 m, has a radius of 1 cm and has a total of 1000 turns wound on it. It carries a current of 5 A. Calculate the magnitude of axial magnetic field inside the solenoid. If an electron was to move with a speed of 10^4 m/s along the axis of this current carrying solenoid, what would be the force experienced by this electron?

13 The magnetic moment vectors μ_s and μ_L associated with the intrinsic spin angular momentum s and orbital angular momentum L respectively, of an electron are predicted by quantum theory (and verified experimentally to a high accuracy) to given by

$\mu_s = -(e/m)s, \mu_L = -(e/2m)L$. Which of these relations is in accordance with the result expected classically? Outline the derivation of the classical result.

Answers

1. (b) **2.** (a) **3.** (d) **5.** $M = \pi N I r^2$

6. $\mu_0 N I a^2$ **7.** $B = \dfrac{\mu_0 I}{2^{3/2} r}$ **8.** $B = \mu_0 n i$

11. $B = \dfrac{\mu_0 I r}{2\pi a^2}, B = \dfrac{\mu_0 I}{2\pi r}$ **12.** $B = 6.28 \times 10^{-3}$ T, $F = 0$

07

Magnetic Force and Torque

TREND ANALYSIS 4 YEARS

Magnetic Force and Torque

Average No. of Questions Across all Sets

Types of Questions	2024	2023	2020	2019
1 Mark	2	–	1	1
2 Marks	–	2	1	1
3 Marks	1	–	–	–
5 Marks	–	–	–	–

Definition of Magnetic Field (B) : Magnetic Force

If a charged particle carrying a positive charge q and moving with velocity $\mathbf{v}$ through a particular point in a magnetic field $\mathbf{B}$ experiences a deflecting force $\mathbf{F}$, then

$$\boxed{\mathbf{F} = q(\mathbf{v} \times \mathbf{B})}$$

The force $\mathbf{F}$ on the charged particle is perpendicular to the plane containing $\mathbf{v}$ and $\mathbf{B}$ and is also called as **Lorentz force**.

Derivation for SI Unit of Magnetic Field

The magnitude of the force on the charged particle is

$$|\mathbf{F}| = q|\mathbf{v}||\mathbf{B}|\sin\theta$$

where, θ is the angle between $\mathbf{v}$ and $\mathbf{B}$.

$$F = qvB\sin\theta \Rightarrow B = \frac{F}{qv\sin\theta}$$

If $\mathbf{v}$ is the velocity, q is positive charge and $\mathbf{B}$ is the magnetic field, then

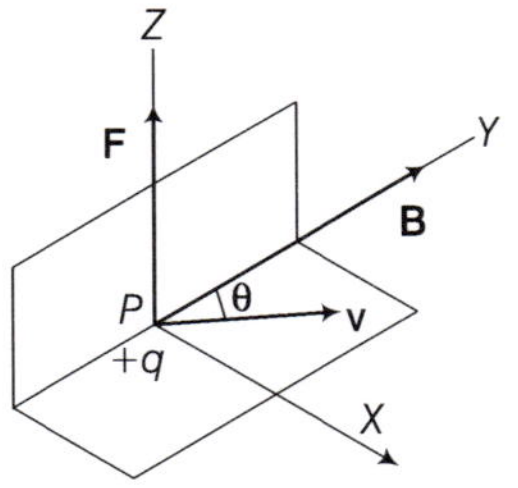

$$F = 1\,\text{N}, q = 1\,\text{C}, v = 1\,\text{m/s}$$

$$\sin\theta = 1 \Rightarrow \theta = 90°$$

$$\text{then } B = \frac{1\,\text{N}}{(1\,\text{C})(1\,\text{m/s})} = 1\,\text{NA}^{-1}\text{m}^{-1} = 1\,\text{T}$$

So, SI unit of B is **tesla** (T).

- In CGS system, the magnetic field is expressed in **gauss (G)** and $\mathbf{1\,T} = 10^{-4}$ G.
- Work done by the magnetic force on a charge particle is zero as force acting on the particle is perpendicular to the displacement ($\mathbf{F} \perp \mathbf{v}$).
- Magnetic force cannot increase the kinetic energy of charge particle.

NOTE The trajectory/path traversed by the charged particle is

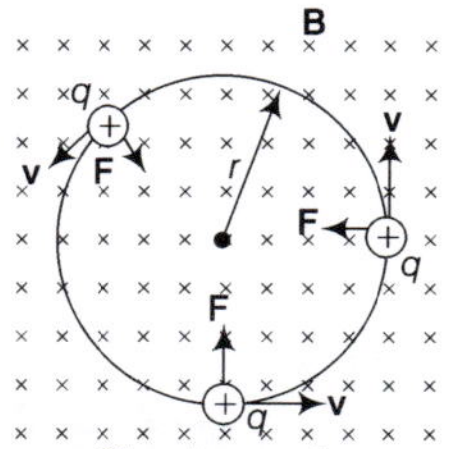

Circular motion

(*i*) straight line when angle between **v** and **B** is 0° or 180°.

(*ii*) circle when angle between **v** and **B** is 90°.

(*iii*) helix when angle between **v** and **B** is an acute angle.

Force on a moving charge in a uniform magnetic field and important formulae associated with it

When charge particle enters in a magnetic field perpendicularly, then it goes on a circular path, then

(*i*) $\frac{mv^2}{r} = qvB$ (*ii*) $r = \frac{mv}{qB} = \frac{\sqrt{2mK}}{qB}$

(*iii*) $T = \frac{2\pi m}{qB}$ (*iv*) $f = \frac{qB}{2\pi m}$ (*v*) $\text{KE} = \frac{q^2B^2r^2}{2m}$

where, q is charge, $\mathbf{B}$ is magnetic field, r is radius of circular path, v is speed, T is time period, f is frequency and KE is kinetic energy.

When angle between v and B is θ ($<90°$), then path traversed is helical

(*i*) The velocity can be resolved in parallel ($v_{\parallel}$) and perpendicular ($v_{\perp}$) components.

(*ii*) Parallel component helps in covering the pitch and perpendicular component helps in circular motion.

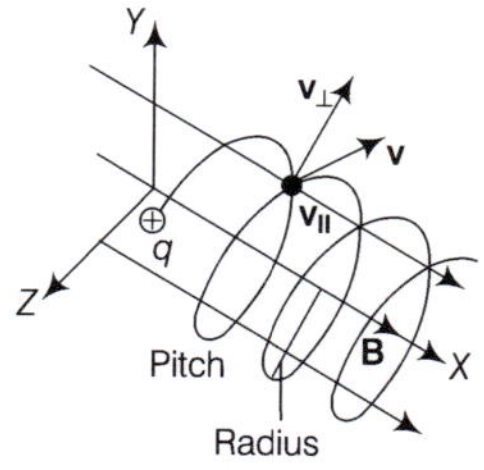

Helical motion

- Radius of helical path,
  $r = \frac{mv\sin\theta}{qB} = \frac{mv_{\perp}}{qB} = \frac{p}{qB}$

  where, p = momentum, $v_{\perp} = v\sin\theta$ = perpendicular component of the velocity.

- Time period, $T = \frac{2\pi m}{qB}$

- Frequency, $f = \frac{qB}{2\pi m}$

- Pitch $= \frac{2\pi mv\cos\theta}{qB} = \frac{2\pi mv_{\parallel}}{qB}$

  where, $v_{\parallel} = v\cos\theta$ = parallel component of velocity.

Lorentz Force

When a particle carrying a charge q is moving in space, where both an electric field $\mathbf{E}$ and a magnetic field $\mathbf{B}$ are present, then the net force on the particle is called Lorentz force.

$$\mathbf{F} = q\mathbf{E} + q(\mathbf{v} \times \mathbf{B})$$

Magnetic Force on a Current Carrying Conductor in a Uniform Magnetic Field

When a current carrying conductor is placed in a uniform magnetic field, then due to motion of free electrons inside the conductor, a magnetic force is applied on it.

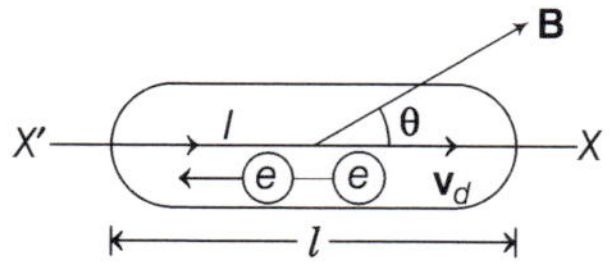

Total force on the wire can be calculated by summing all the forces on all electrons of a wire of length l or due to current by that number of electrons is given by

$$\therefore \quad F = IlB\sin\theta = I\mathbf{l} \times \mathbf{B}$$

where Idl is the current element whose direction is towards the direction of current, $\mathbf{B}$ is magnetic field and θ is the angle between current element and magnetic field.

If $\theta = 0°$ or $180°$, then $F = 0$, hence no force on a current carrying conductor.

If $\theta = 90°$, then $F = IlB$, hence maximum force on a current carrying conductor.

Force between Two Straight Parallel Current Carrying Conductors

Magnetic force per unit length between two straight parallel current carrying conductors is given by

$$f = \frac{F}{l} = \frac{\mu_0}{4\pi} \cdot \frac{2I_1I_2}{r} = \frac{\mu_0 I_1 I_2}{2\pi r}$$

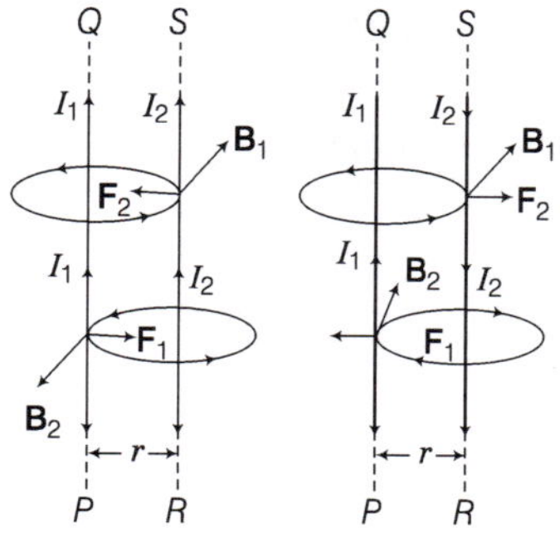

Parallel currents attract

Anti-parallel currents repel

where, I_1 and I_2 are current in the wires, r is the distance between wires and l is the length of each conductor.

Definition of the Ampere

One ampere is that value of current which flows through two straight, parallel infinitely long current carrying conductors placed in air or vacuum or in free space at a distance of 1 m and they experience a force of attractive or repulsive in nature of magnitude 2×10^{-7} N/m on their unit length.

If $\quad I_1 = I_2 = 1\,\text{A}$ and $\quad r = 1\,\text{m}$

Then $\quad f = \dfrac{\mu_0}{2\pi} = \dfrac{4\pi \times 10^{-7}}{2\pi} = 2 \times 10^{-7}\ \text{N/m}$

Torque on a Current Loop

Torque experienced by a current carrying loop placed in the uniform external magnetic field **B** is given by

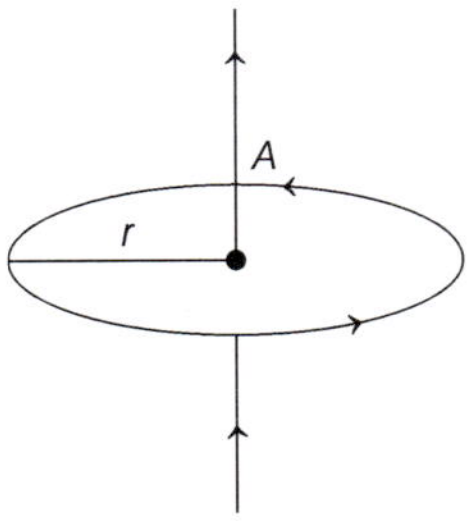

$$\boxed{\tau = \mathbf{M} \times \mathbf{B}}$$

where, $\quad \mathbf{M} = NI\mathbf{A}$

As discussed earlier here, **M** is **magnetic dipole moment** of the loop and its SI unit is A-m^2.

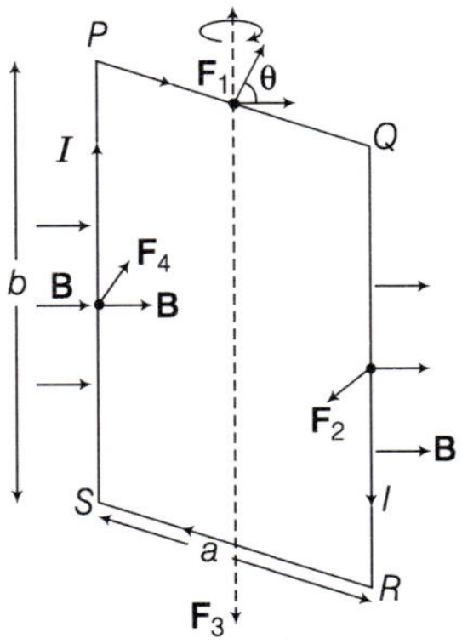

Area vector of the loop

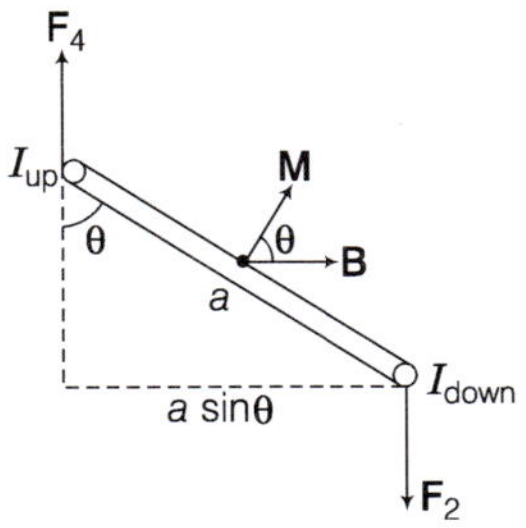

Top view of the loop

$\Rightarrow \quad |\tau| = BINA \sin\theta$

where, θ is the angle between the direction of **B** and the normal drawn on the plane of coil along the area vector **A** or **M**.

- Net force on a current carrying loop in a uniform magnetic field is always zero.
- **Radial Magnetic Field** When plane of the coil is parallel to the magnetic field such that the area vector of the coil is perpendicular to the magnetic field, the field is called radial magnetic field.

Moving Coil Galvanometer

It is a device used to detect the current in an electrical circuit.

- In equilibrium torque or moment of the coil of a galvanometer is given by

$$\tau = k\theta = NIBA$$

where, N = number of turns of the coil,
θ = angle of twist or deflection of the coil of galvanometer,
B = magnetic field,
A = area of the coil and k = torsional constant of the spring.

The coil shown remains suspended in radial magnetic field, so that it always experiences the maximum torque.

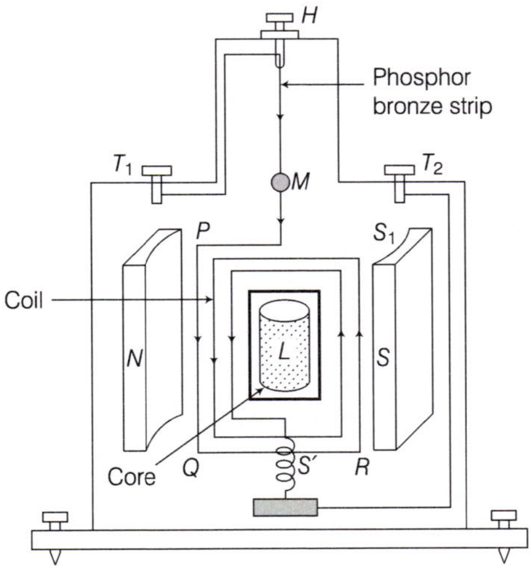

Current sensitivity,

$$I_s = \frac{\theta}{I} = \frac{NBA}{k}$$

Its SI unit is rad/A or div/A.

Voltage sensitivity,

$$V_s = \frac{\theta}{V} = \frac{\theta}{IR} = \frac{I_s}{R} = \frac{NBA}{kR}$$

Its SI unit is rad/V or div/V.

Torque or moment of galvanometer,

$$\frac{1}{G} = \frac{\theta}{I} = \frac{NBA}{k}$$

where, G is galvanometer constant.

Conversion of a Galvanometer into Ammeter

To convert a galvanometer into ammeter, its resistance needs to be lowered, so that maximum current can pass through it and it can give exact reading.

A shunt (low resistance) is connected in parallel with the galvanometer.

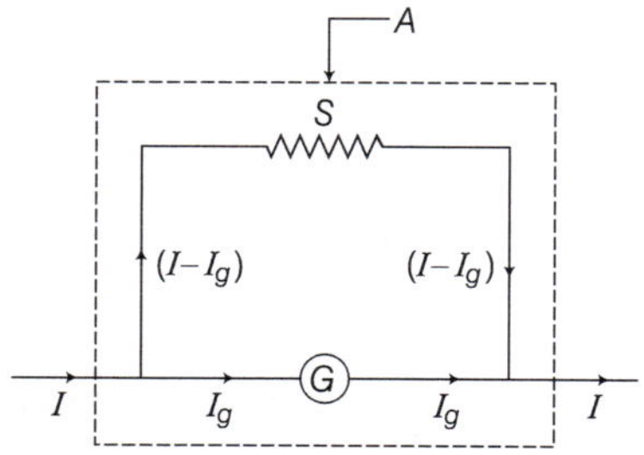

$$S = \left(\frac{I_g}{I - I_g}\right) G$$

where, I = total current in circuit,
G = resistance of the galvanometer
S = resistance of the shunt (low resistance)
I_g = current through the galvanometer.

Conversion of a Galvanometer into Voltmeter

To convert a galvanometer into voltmeter, its resistance needs to be increased, so that there is no potential drop across it because with high resistance no current passes through it. A high resistance is connected in series with the galvanometer, then the value of R is given by

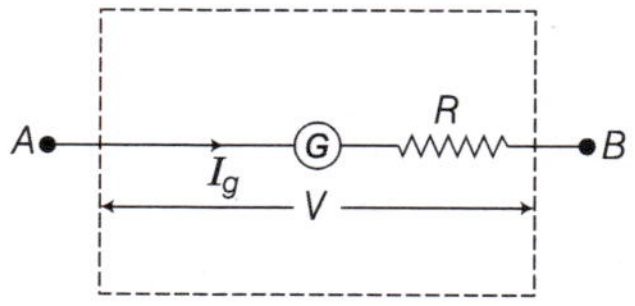

$$R = \frac{V}{I_g} - G$$

where, V = potential difference across the terminals A and B
I_g = current through the galvanometer (full scale deflection current)
R = high resistance
G = resistance of the galvanometer.

PYQs Previous Years Questions

1 Mark Questions

1. Lorentz force in vector form is **ISC 2024**
(a) $F = Bqv \sin\theta$
(b) $\mathbf{F} = q(\mathbf{v} \times \mathbf{B})$
(c) $\mathbf{F} = q(\mathbf{B} \times \mathbf{v})$
(d) $\mathbf{F} = \mathbf{v}(q \times \mathbf{B})$

2. **Assertion** When an electric current is passed through a moving coil galvanometer, its coil gets deflected.
Reason A circular coil produces a uniform magnetic field around itself when an electric current is passed through it. **ISC 2024**
(a) Both Assertion and Reason are true and Reason is the correct explanation for Assertion.
(b) Both Assertion and Reason are true but Reason is not the correct explanation for Assertion.
(c) Assertion is true and Reason is false.
(d) Assertion is false and Reason is true.

3. Which of the following is the right expression to define the magnetic field B ? **ISC 2022 Sem-I**
(a) $\mathbf{F} = q(\mathbf{v} \times \mathbf{B})$
(b) $\mathbf{F} = B\,(\mathbf{I} \times \mathbf{l})$
(c) $\frac{\mathbf{F}}{l} = \frac{\mu_0}{2\pi}\frac{I^2}{a}$
(d) $B = \mu_0 ni$

4. A proton is moving in a uniform magnetic field B with a velocity v at an angle θ with the field. The force acting on the proton is minimum, when θ is **ISC 2022 Sem-I**
(a) 120° (b) 90° (c) 60° (d) 0°

5. Two long straight wires P and Q are parallel to each other. They carry currents in the same direction as shown in the figure.

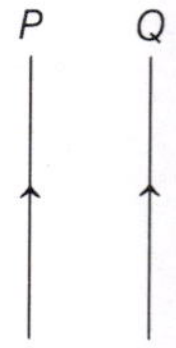

The wire P is kept fixed, then the wire Q will
(a) also remain at rest **ISC 2022 Sem-I**
(b) move towards the wire P
(c) move away from the wire P
(d) come out of the plane of this paper

6. How can a moving coil galvanometer be converted into a voltmeter? **ISC 2020, 18**

7. Why are the pole pieces of a horseshoe magnet in a moving coil galvanometer made cylindrical in shape? **ISC 2019**

8. Which of the two, an ammeter or a voltmeter has a greater resistance? **ISC SQP 2018**

9. When would a moving charged particle travel undeviated in a uniform magnetic field? **ISC SQP 2018**

10. Write the expression for the Lorentz force **F** in vector form. **ISC 2016**

11. State how a moving coil galvanometer can be converted into an ammeter. **ISC 2016**

12. A moving electron enters a uniform and perpendicular magnetic field. Inside the magnetic field, the electron travels along **ISC 2016**

(a) a straight line (b) a parabola
(c) a circle (d) a hyperbola

13. When does a moving charged particle not experience any force while moving through a uniform magnetic field? **ISC 2014**

14. In a moving coil galvanometer, what is meant by a radial magnetic field? **ISC 2012**

15. An electron is moving with a velocity of 5×10^7 ms^{-1}, enters in a magnetic field of 1 Wb m^{-2} at an angle of 30°. Calculate the force on the electron. **ISC 2006, 01**

16. State two factors on which the sensitivity of a moving coil galvanometer depends. **ISC 2006**

17. A wire of length 10 cm, carrying 10 A of current is placed at an angle of 53° with respect to a magnetic field B of strength 0.1 T. Find the force experienced by the wire. $\left[\text{Use, } \sin 53° = \frac{4}{5}\right]$ **ISC 2004**

2 Marks Questions

18. (*i*) A long straight wire *AB* carries a current of 5A. *P* is a proton travelling with a velocity of 2×10^6 m/s, parallel to the wire, 0.2 m from it and in a direction opposite to the current, as shown in figure below. Calculate the force which magnetic field of the current carrying conductor *AB* exerts on the proton.

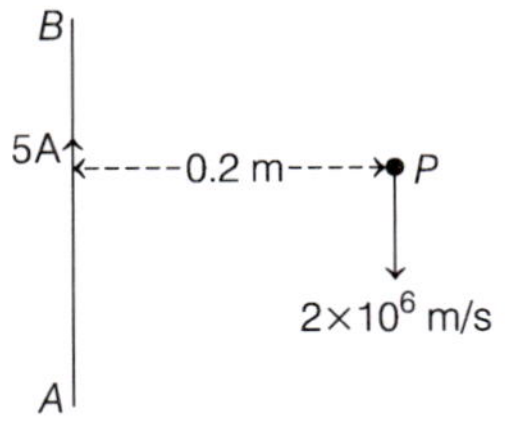

(*ii*) A moving coil galvanometer of resistance 55 Ω produces a full scale deflection for a current of 250 mA. How will you convert it into an ammeter having a range of 0 – 3 A? **ISC 2023**

19. (*i*) Two long straight wires *A* and *B* are kept parallel to each other, 5 cm apart, in vacuum. They carry currents of 5A and 10A respectively in the same direction as shown in figure below. Calculate the force per unit length acting on the wire *B* due to the current flowing in the wire *A*. **ISC SQP 2023**

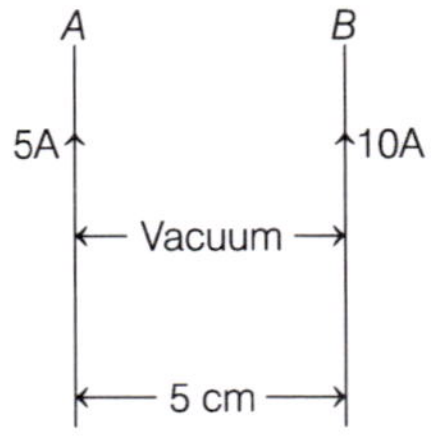

Or

(*ii*) An electron moving with a velocity of 8×10^6 m/s enters a uniform and transverse magnetic field of 3×10^{-3}T. Calculate the radius of the circular path described by it.

20. The resistance of a galvanometer is 50 Ω. It is converted into a voltmeter and ammeter. Calculate the resistance of the voltmeter and ammeter to an accuracy of 2sf. Only with the mention below in the subparts.

(*i*) A voltmeter using a 10 kΩ resistor is **ISC 2022 Sem-I**

(a) 10050 Ω (b) 10.050 Ω
(c) 0.0999 Ω (d) 10 kΩ

(*ii*) An ammeter using a 10 m Ω resistor is

(a) 50 Ω (b) 10 m Ω
(c) 0.0999 Ω (d) 50.0999 Ω

21. Consider a moving coil galvanometer *G* and two resistors $R_1 = 5000\ \Omega$ and $R_2 = 0.1\ \Omega$.

(*i*) To convert the given galvanometer *G* into an ammeter, **ISC 2022 Sem-I**

(a) R_1 is connected in series with *G*
(b) R_1 is connected in parallel with *G*
(c) R_2 is connected in series with *G*
(d) R_2 is connected in parallel with *G*

(*ii*) To convert the given galvanometer *G* into a voltmeter,

(a) R_1 is connected in series with *G*
(b) R_1 is connected in parallel with *G*
(c) R_2 is connected in series with *G*
(d) R_2 is connected in parallel with *G*

22. Write an expression for force per unit length between two long current carrying wires, kept parallel to each other, in vacuum and hence define an ampere, the SI unit of current. **ISC 2020**

23. A rectangular loop of area 5 m^2, has 50 turns and carries a current of 1 A. It is held in an uniform magnetic field of 0.1T, at an angle of 30°. Calculate the torque experienced by the coil. **ISC 2019**

24. A long horizontal wire P carries a current of 50 A. It is rigidly fixed. Another wire Q is placed directly above and parallel to P, as shown in figure. The weight per unit length of the wire Q is 0.025 Nm^{-1} and it carries a current of 25 A. Find the distance r of the wire Q from the wire P, so that the wire Q remains at rest. **ISC 2018**

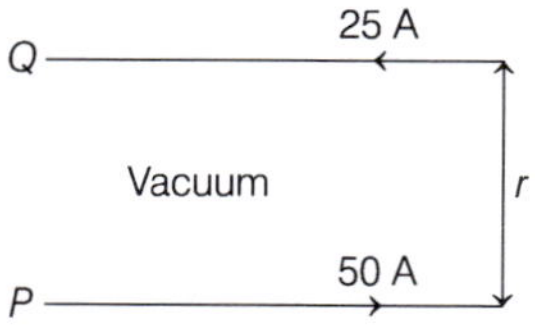

25. Calculate force per unit length acting on the wire **B** due to the current flowing in the wire A as shown in figure below. **ISC 2018**

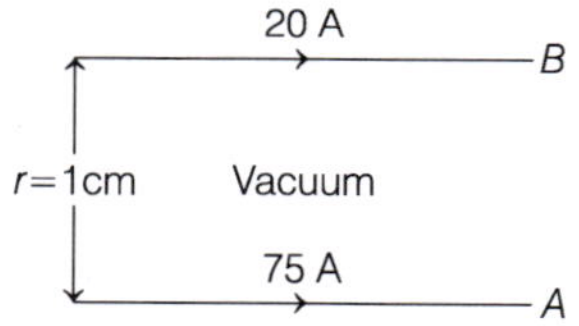

26. A moving charged particle q travelling along the positive X-axis enters a uniform magnetic field **B**. When will the force acting on q be maximum? **ISC 2018**

27. PQ is a long straight conductor carrying a current of 3A as shown in figure below. An electron moves with a velocity of 2×10^7 ms^{-1} parallel to it. Find the force acting on the electron. **ISC 2017**

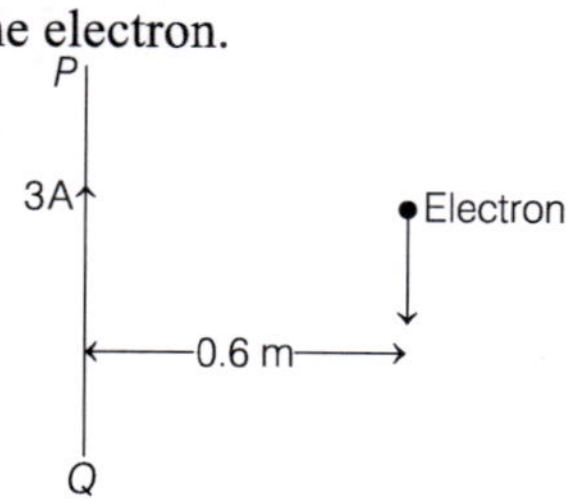

> **KEY idea**
>
> To calculate the force, first calculate the magnetic field B and then calculate force $F = Bil$.

28. A moving coil galvanometer has a coil of resistance 59 Ω. It shows a full scale deflection for a current of 50 mA. How will you convert it to an ammeter having a range of 0 to 3A? **ISC 2017**

29. Define ampere in terms of force between two current carrying conductors. **ISC 2016**

30. Figure below shows two infinitely long and thin current carrying conductors X and Y kept in vacuum, parallel to each other at a distance a.

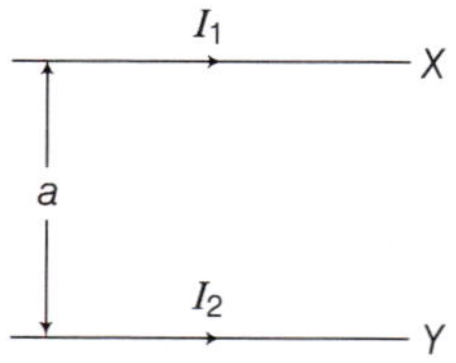

(*i*) How much force per unit length act on the conductor Y due to the current flowing through X? Write your answer in terms of $\left(\frac{\mu_0}{4\pi}\right)$, I_1, I_2 and a.
[Derivation of formula is not required]

(*ii*) Define ampere in terms of force between two current carrying conductors. **ISC 2016, 13, 11, 08**

31. Show that the radius of a charged particle entering perpendicularly in a magnetic field is directly proportional to its momentum. **ISC 2004**

3 Marks Questions

32. Figure given below shows an infinitely long metallic wire YY' which is carrying a current I'. P is a point at a perpendicular distance r from it. **ISC 2024**

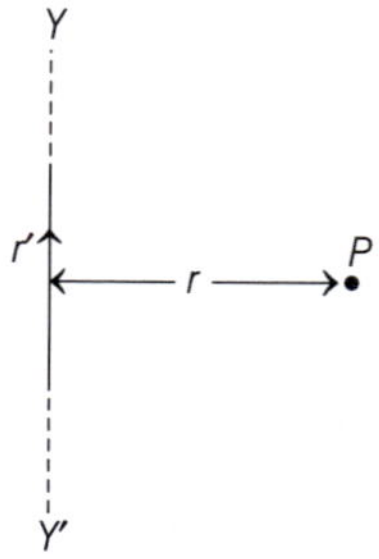

(i) What is the direction of magnetic flux density B of the magnetic field at the point P ?

(ii) What is the magnitude of magnetic flux density B of the magnetic field at the point P ?

(iii) Another metallic wire MN having length l and carrying a current I is now kept at the point P. If the two wires are in vacuum and parallel to each other, how much force acts on the wire MN due to the current I' flowing in the wire YY'?

33. A small magnetic needle NS having magnetic dipole moment P_m is kept in two uniform and perpendicular magnetic fields B_F and B_H as shown below.

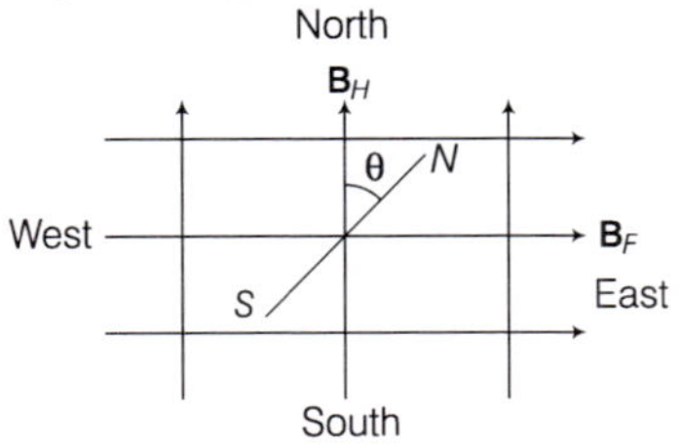

(*i*) What is the effect of each of the magnetic fields B_F and B_H on the needle?

(*ii*) When the needle is in equilibrium, obtain an expression for angle θ made by the needle with $\mathbf{B}_H$ in terms of $\mathbf{B}_F$ and $\mathbf{B}_H$ only. **ISC 2010**

34. Obtain the formula, $I = k\theta$ for a moving coil galvanometer given the deflecting torque $\tau = \mathbf{M} \times \mathbf{B}$, where $\mathbf{M}$ is the magnetic dipole moment of the coil placed in the magnetic field $\mathbf{B}$, I is the current in the galvanometer and θ is the deflection. **ISC 2008**

35. Two very long conductors carrying currents I_1 and I_2 are separated by a distance d as shown in the figure. Give the expressions (do not derive) for the magnetic fields $\mathbf{B}_{12}$ and $\mathbf{B}_{21}$ at P and Q respectively produced by the electric currents I_2 and I_1. What are the directions of these fields?

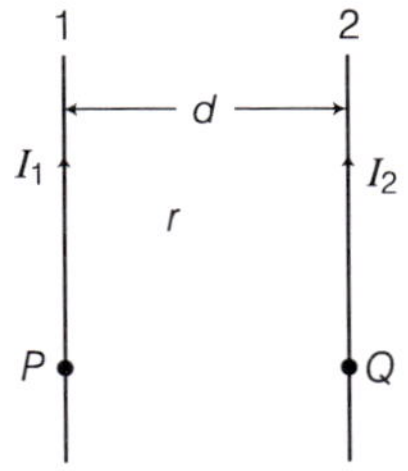

Define the SI unit of currents using the alongside set-up. **ISC 2007**

4/5 Marks Questions

36. (i) Using Ampere's circuital law, obtain an expression for the magnetic flux density B at a point X at a perpendicular distance r from a long current carrying conductor. (Statement of the law is not required).

> **KEY idea**
>
> To calculate the force acting on electron first calculate the magnetic field then calculate the force by the relation $F = Bev$.

(ii) PQ is a long straight conductor carrying a current of 3A as shown in figure iv below. An electron moves with a velocity of 2×10^7 ms^{-1} parallel to it. Find the force acting on the electron. **ISC 2017**

Case Based Question
(For Complete Chapter)

37. Direction *Read the passage given below and answer the questions that follow.*

It is an easy and sensitive instrument to detect and measure electric current. Its action is based upon the principle that when electric current flows in a coil placed in a magnetic field, a deflecting torque acts upon the coil whose magnitude depends upon the strength of the current. From the measurement of the deflection of the coil, the strength of the current can be computed.

Moving-coil galvanometers are of two types: suspended-coil galvanometer and pivoted-coil (or weston) galvanometer. The principle and working of the two types of galvanometers are the same, only there is some difference in their constructions. In suspended-coil galvanometer, the coil is suspended by a thin phospher-bronze strip and the deflection of the coil is measured by a lamp and scale arrangement. In pivoted-coil galvanometer, the coil swings between two pivots and the deflection of the coil is read by a pointer on a circular scale. The pivoted-coil galvanometer is less sensitive than the suspended-coil galvanometer, but can be taken easily from one place to another.

(*i*) What do you mean by moving coil galvanometer ? **(1)**

(*ii*) On which principle the moving coil galvanometer is based on? **(1)**

(*iii*) Write the types of moving coil galvanometer **(1)**

(*iv*) What are the difference between the types of galvanometer? **(1)**

(*v*) From the suspended coil galvanometer and the pivoted-coil galvanometer. Which galvanometer is more sensitive? **(1)**

Explanations

1. (*b*) Expression for Lorentz force is given as

$$\mathbf{F} = q(\mathbf{v} \times \mathbf{B})$$

where, q is charge of the particle,

$\mathbf{v}$ is velocity of the particle,

and $\mathbf{B}$ is the magnetic field in which the particle is moving.

2. (*a*) Both Assertion and Reason are true and Reason is the correct explanation for Assertion.

The moving coil galvanometer consists of a coil with many turns free to rotate about a fixed axis and in this way, coil gets deflected in a uniform radial magnetic field. When a current flows through the coil, a torque acts on it.

3. (a)

4. (d) $\mathbf{F} = q(\mathbf{v} \times \mathbf{B})$

$\therefore \quad F = qvB \sin\theta$

For F to be minimum, $F = 0$

i.e., $\sin\theta = 0$

$\therefore \quad \theta = 0°$

5. (b)

6. A moving coil galvanometer can be converted into a voltmeter by using a high resistance is connected in series with the galvanometer.

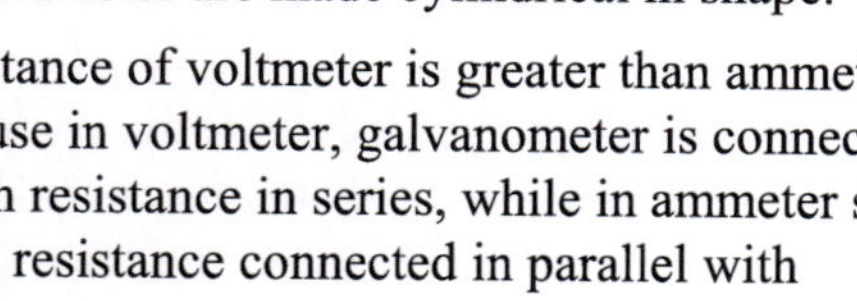

7. For increasing the strength of the magnetic field, the pole pieces of a horseshoe magnet in a moving coil galvanometer are made cylindrical in shape.

8. Resistance of voltmeter is greater than ammeter, because in voltmeter, galvanometer is connected with a high resistance in series, while in ammeter small shunt resistance connected in parallel with galvanometer.

9. When a charged particle is moving parallel to the magnetic field force exerted by the field on the particle is, $F = qvB\sin\theta = 0$. Hence, the path of charged particle, remains unchanged i.e. straight line.

10. In vector form, expression for Lorentz force can be given as

$$\mathbf{F} = \mathbf{F}_e + \mathbf{F}_m = q\mathbf{E} + q(\mathbf{v} \times \mathbf{B})$$

$$\mathbf{F} = q(\mathbf{E} + \mathbf{v} \times \mathbf{B})$$

11. A moving coil galvanometer can be converted into an ammeter by using a low resistance wire in parallel with it.

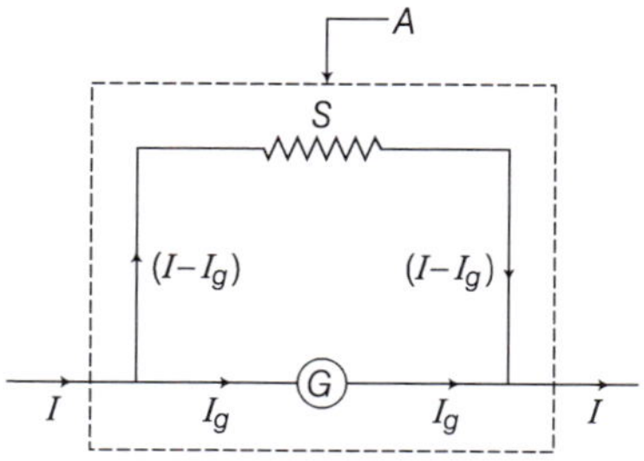

12. (c) According to right hand thumb rule, the electron travels along a circle. Since, the right hand thumb rule states that " when a force is perpendicular to velocity and hence it changes its path continuously and this force acts as a centripetal force and produces a circular motion perpendicular to the magnetic field.

13. Force experienced by a moving charged particle is $|\mathbf{F}| = qvB\sin\theta$

where, θ = angle between $\mathbf{v}$ and $\mathbf{B}$

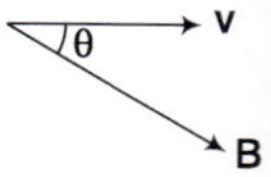

$$|\mathbf{F}| = 0$$

$$\Rightarrow \quad qvB\sin\theta = 0$$

$$\therefore \quad \theta = 0 \text{ or } \pi$$

So, for the angle $\theta = 0$ or π force experienced by moving charge is zero.

14. Radial magnetic field When plane of the coil is parallel to the magnetic field such that the area vector of the coil is perpendicular to the magnetic field, the field is called radial magnetic field.

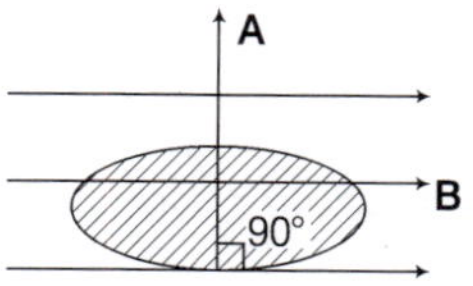

15. According to the question,

$$q = 1.6 \times 10^{-19} \text{ C}$$

$$v = 5 \times 10^7 \text{ m/s}$$

$$\theta = 30°, B = 1 \text{ Wb m}^{-2}$$

$$F = qvB\sin\theta$$

$= 1.6\times 10^{-19}\times 5\times 10^{7}\times 1\times \sin 30°$
$= 4\times 10^{-12}$ N

16. The current sensitivity and voltage sensitivity of the galvanometer depend on the number of turns of coil, magnetic field **B**, area A of the coil and torsion constant k of the spring or suspension wire.

17. Given, length of the wire, $l = 10\text{ cm} = 0.1$ m, $i = 10$ A, $\theta = 53°$, $B = 0.1$ T

$F = ?$

As, $F = iBl\sin\theta = 10\times 0.1\times 0.1\times \sin 53°$

$\therefore \quad F = 0.08$ N $\quad \left[\because \sin 53° = \frac{4}{5}\right]$

18. $I = 5$A

$v = 2\times 10^{6}$ m/s

$r = 0.2$ m

$$B = \frac{\mu_0}{4\pi}\frac{2I}{r} = \frac{10^{-7}\times 2\times 5}{0.2}$$

$= 5\times 10^{-6}$

Now,

Force $(F) = qvB\sin 90°$

$= (1.6\times 10^{-19})(2\times 10^{6})(5\times 10^{-6})$

$= 16\times 10^{-19}$

(*ii*) $I_g = 250\times 10^{-3}$ A

$R_g = 55\,\Omega$

$I = 3$ A

$R_s = ?$

$$R_s = \frac{I_g R_g}{I - I_g} = \frac{250\times 10^{-3}\times 55}{3 - 250\times 10^{-3}}$$

$$= \frac{250\times 10^{-3}\times 55}{2.75} = \frac{25\times 55}{275} = 5$$

$R_s = 5\,\Omega$

To convert a galvanometer into an ammeter. Connect a 5 Ω resistance in parallel to it.

19. (*i*) Force per unit length between the wires

$$(F) = \frac{\mu_0 I_1 I_2}{2\pi d} = \frac{4\pi\times 10^{-7}\times 5\times 10}{2\times\pi\times 5\times 10^{-2}}$$

$= 20\times 10^{-5} = 2\times 10^{-4}$ N/m

(*ii*) $m_e = 9\times 10^{-31}$ kg, $v = 8\times 10^{6}$ m/s

$e = 1.6\times 10^{-19}$ C, $B = 3\times 10^{-3}$ T

$$r = \frac{mv}{|e|B}$$

$$= \frac{(9\times 10^{-31})(8\times 10^{6})}{(1.6\times 10^{-19})(3\times 10^{-3})}$$

$$= \frac{9\times 10^{-31}\times 8\times 10^{6+19+3}}{1.6\times 3} = 1.5\times 10^{-2}\text{m}$$

20. (*i*) (d) 10 k Ω resistor

$R_V = G + R$

$= 50\,\Omega + 10\,\text{k}\Omega$

$= 10.05\,\text{k}\,\Omega = 10\,\text{k}\,\Omega$

(*ii*) (b) 10 m Ω resistor

$$R_A = \frac{50\,\Omega\times 10\,\text{m}\Omega}{50\,\Omega + 10\,\text{m}\Omega}$$

$$= \frac{50000\,\text{m}\Omega\times 10\,\text{m}\Omega}{50000\,\text{m}\Omega + 10\,\text{m}\Omega}$$

$$= \frac{500000\,(\text{m}\Omega)^2}{50010\,\text{m}\Omega} = 9.998\,\text{m}\Omega$$

$= 10\,\text{m}\Omega$

21. (*i*) (d), (*ii*) (a)

22. Refer to text on page 98 (Force between Two Straight Parallel Current Carrying Conductors) and page 99 (Definition of the Ampere).

23. Given, area of rectangular loop, $A = 5\text{ m}^2$

Number of turns, $N = 50$

Current, $I = 1$ A

Magnetic field, $B = 0.1$ T

Angle, $\theta = 30°$

Torque experienced by the coil,

$\tau = NIAB\sin(90° - \theta)$

$= 50\times 1\times 5\times 0.1\times \sin(90° - 30°)$

$= 50\times 1\times 5\times 0.1\times \sin 60°$

$$= \frac{25\sqrt{3}}{2} = 12.5\sqrt{3}\text{ N-m}$$

24. The magnetic force per unit length on the wire Q due to the current in the wire P is

$$\frac{F}{l} = \frac{\mu_0}{2\pi}\cdot\frac{i_1 i_2}{r}$$

Here, $\frac{F}{l} = 0.025$ N/m, $i_1 = 50$ A

and $i_2 = 25$ A

$\therefore \quad 0.025 = 2\times10^{-7} \times \dfrac{50\times25}{r}$

$\Rightarrow \quad r = \dfrac{2\times10^{-7}\times50\times25}{0.025}$

$\therefore \quad r = 0.01\,\text{m}$

25. Here, $i_1 = 20$ A, $i_2 = 75$ A,

$r = 1\,\text{cm} = 1\times10^{-2}$ m

$\therefore$ Force per unit length,

$$\frac{F}{l} = \frac{\mu_0}{2\pi}\cdot\frac{i_1 i_2}{r}$$

$$\frac{F}{l} = \frac{2\times10^{-7}\times20\times75}{1\times10^{-2}}$$

$$\frac{F}{l} = 0.03\ \text{N/m}$$

26. Force experienced by a moving charged particle is given by $F = qvB\sin\theta$

where, θ is the angle between **v** and **B**.

If $\theta = 90°$, then $\sin\theta = 1$ (maximum)

$\therefore \quad F_{\text{max}} = qvB$ (maximum)

Hence, if charged particle is moving perpendicular to the direction of magnetic field **B**, it experiences a maximum force which acts perpendicular to the direction of **B** and **v**.

27. We have to calculate force on a long straight conductor.

Force acting on the electron

$$F = qvB$$

Due to wire, the field created is

$$B = \frac{\mu_0 I}{2\pi R} = \frac{\mu_0\times3}{2\times\pi\times0.6}$$

$$= \frac{4\pi\times10^{-7}\times3\times10}{2\times\pi\times6} = 10^{-6}\ \text{T}$$

Now, $F = 1.6\times10^{-19}\times2\times10^{7}\times10^{-6}$

$$F = 32\times10^{-19}\ \text{N}$$

28. $R = 59\,\Omega$

According to the formula, $S = \left(\dfrac{I_g}{I - I_g}\right)G$

$$G = 59\,\Omega$$

$$I_g = 50\ \text{mA} = 50\times10^{-3}\ \text{A}$$

$$I = 3\text{A}$$

$\therefore$ Shunt resistance

$$S = \frac{I_g G}{I - I_g} = \frac{50\times10^{-3}\times59}{(3-50\times10^{-3})}$$

$$= \frac{50\times59}{1000\times\frac{59}{20}} = \frac{50\times59\times20}{1000\times59} = 1\,\Omega$$

Hence, to convert galvanometer into ammeter, a shunt of $1\,\Omega$ is connected in parallel with the galvanometer.

29. One ampere is that value of steady current which on flowing in each of two parallel infinitely long conductors of negligible cross-section placed in vacuum at a distance of 1m from each other, produces a force of 2×10^{-7} newton per metre between them.

30. First, we have to find force between the wires by assuming that one of the wires is of finite length. Then, force is divided by length to find force per unit length.

(*i*) Let length of the wire Y be l.

Force on Y, $F_Y = \dfrac{\mu_0 I_1}{2\pi a}(I_2 l)$, towards X.

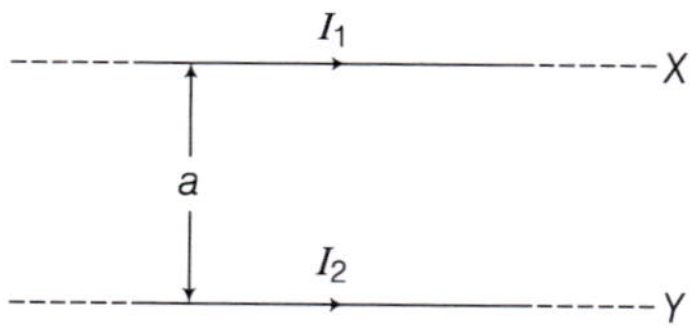

Force per unit length, $\dfrac{F_Y}{l} = \dfrac{\mu_0 I_1 I_2}{2\pi a}$

NOTE If wires are carrying current in same direction, force is attractive and for currents in opposite direction the force will be repulsive in nature.

(*ii*) Refer to Ans 29 text on page 106.

31. When a charged particle enters in a uniform magnetic field perpendicularly, central force acts on the particle which provides centripetal force for the circular motion of the particle.

Situation is shown in figure

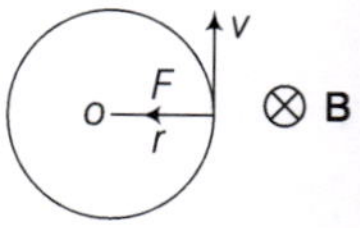

Centripetal force, $F = \dfrac{mv^2}{r}$

As magnetic force will provide the necessary centripetal force to the charged particle.

$$\Rightarrow \quad \frac{mv^2}{r} = qvB$$

$$\Rightarrow \quad \frac{mv}{r} = qB$$

$$\Rightarrow \quad p = mv = rqB$$

$$\Rightarrow \qquad r = \frac{p}{qB} \Rightarrow r \propto p$$

where, $p = mv$ = momentum.

Common Mistake To have a circular motion, particle must enter perpendicularly into the magnetic field.

32. (i) The direction of magnetic flux density B of the magnetic field at point P is downward and into the paper.

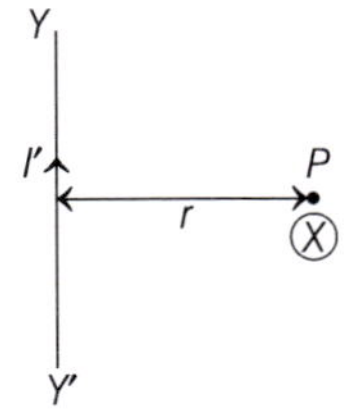

(ii) Magnitude of magnetic flux density B of the magnetic field at the point P is

$$B = \frac{\mu_0 I}{2\pi r}$$

(iii) Force on wire MN having length l and carrying a current I due to long metallic wire YY',

$$F = \frac{\mu_0}{4\pi} \frac{2I'I}{r} l$$

33. As the magnetic needle is placed in a two mutually perpendicular fields, both the fields will try to rotate the magnet in opposite directions.

(*i*) We know that torque on a magnetic dipole placed in a uniform magnetic field **B** is$\tau = \mathbf{M} \times \mathbf{B}$, where,

M = magnetic dipole moment and **B** is magnetic field.

The diagram (below) shows the situation given in question.

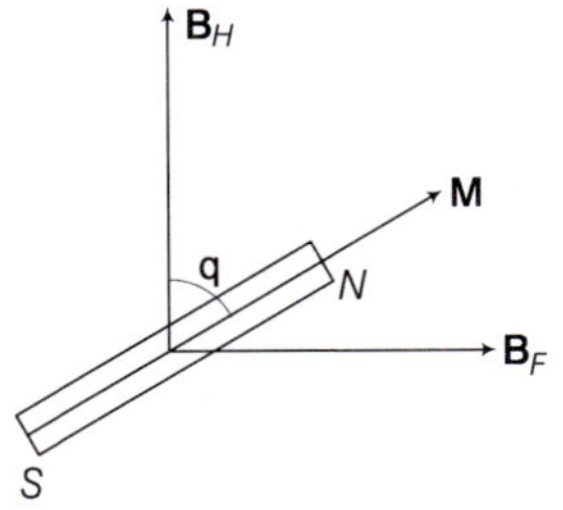

Torque due to $\mathbf{B}_H$ is anti-clockwise and torque due to $\mathbf{B}_F$ is clockwise.

(*ii*) In equilibrium, $|\tau_{B_H}| = |\tau_{B_F}|$

$$\Rightarrow MB_H \sin\theta = MB_F \sin(90 - \theta)$$

$$\Rightarrow \qquad \tan\theta = \frac{B_F}{B_H}$$

$$\Rightarrow \qquad \theta = \tan^{-1}\left(\frac{B_F}{B_H}\right)$$

Here, **M** represents the magnetic moment.

34. The working of a moving coil galvanometer is based on the fact that when a current carrying coil is placed in a magnetic field, it experiences a net torque.

Consider the diagram, where the coil $PQRS_1$, is suspended freely in the magnetic field.

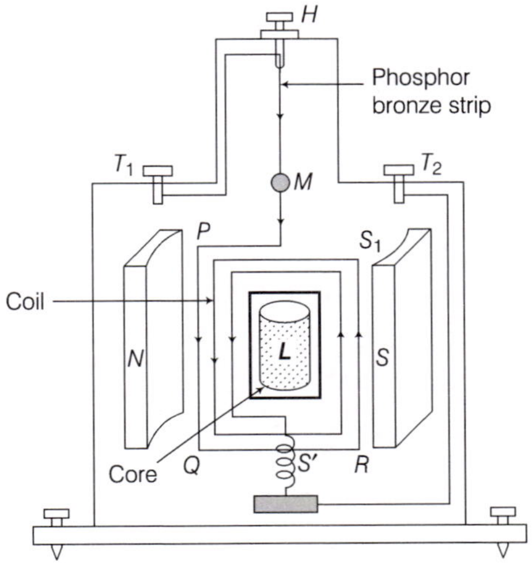

Let $\quad l$ = length PQ or RS_1 of the coil

b = breadth QR or SP of the coil

N = number of turns in the coil

Area of each turn of the coil $A = l \times b$

Let $\quad B$ = strength of the magnetic field in which coil is suspended

I = current passing through the coil in the direction of $PQRS_1$

Let at any instant of time, α be the angle which the normal drawn to the plane of the coil makes with the direction of magnetic field.

The rectangular current carrying coil when placed in the magnetic field experiences a torque whose magnitude is given by, $\tau = NIBA \sin\alpha$

Due to this torque, the coil rotates and suspension wire gets twisted. A restoring torque is set up in the suspension wire.

Let θ be the twist produced in the phosphor bronze strip due to rotation of the coil and k be the restoring torque per unit twist of the phosphor bronze strip.

Then, total restoring torque produced $= k\theta$

In equilibrium position of the coil,

Deflection torque = Restoring torque

$\therefore \quad NIBA = k\theta \quad [\because \alpha = 90°]$

or $\quad I = \frac{k}{NBA}\theta = G\theta$

where, $\quad \frac{k}{NBA} = G$

It is known as galvanometer constant.

$\Rightarrow \quad I \propto \theta$

$\therefore$ Current is directly proportional to the deflection produced in the coil.

35. $\mathbf{B}_{12} = \frac{\mu_0 I_2}{2\pi d}, \mathbf{B}_{21} = \frac{\mu_0 I_1}{2\pi d}$

The direction of field at P is perpendicular to the plane of the paper and outwards. The direction of field at Q is perpendicularly inwards to the plane of paper.

Refer text on page 98. (Force Between Two Straight Parallel Current Carrying Conductors)

Concept Enhancer When currents in two parallel wires flow in same direction, then they will attract each other and *vice-versa*.

36. To find magnetic field at a point, consider Amperian loop around an infinitely long conducting wire as shown.

(*i*) In order to determine the magnetic field at point P, which is situated at a distance a from the centre of the circular loop around the conducting wire. The magnetic field (**B**) is tangential to the circumference of the loop.

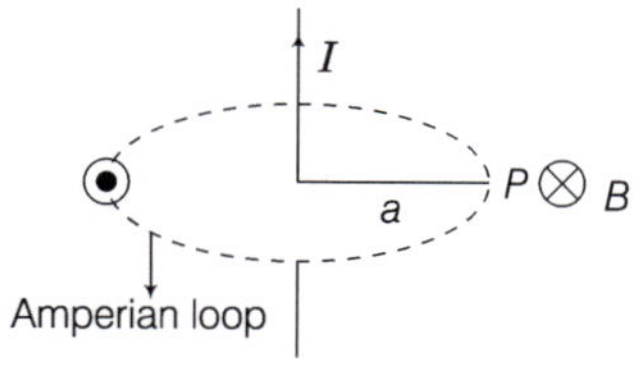

As we know that from Ampere's circuital law,

$$\oint \mathbf{B} \cdot dl = \mu_0 I$$

As $\quad \oint dl = 2\pi a$

So, $\quad \mathbf{B}\, 2\pi a = \mu_0 I$

$$\mathbf{B} = \frac{\mu_0 I}{2\pi a} \times \frac{2}{2}$$

$$\Rightarrow \quad \mathbf{B} = \frac{\mu_0}{4\pi}\frac{2I}{a}$$

The direction of magnetic field will be determined by right hand thumb rule.

(*ii*)

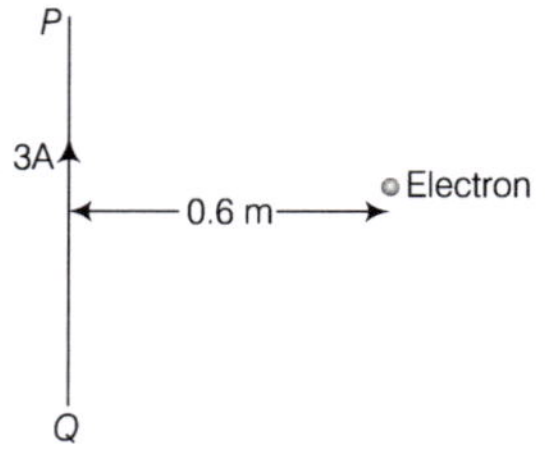

From the given figure, if we have to calculate force on a long straight conductor.

Force acting on the electron is as follows

$$F = qvB$$

Due to wire, the field created is

$$B = \frac{\mu_0 I}{2\pi R} = \frac{\mu_0 \times 3}{2 \times \pi \times 0.6}$$

$$= \frac{4\pi \times 10^{-7} \times 3 \times 10}{2 \times \pi \times 0.6} = 10^{-6} \text{ T}$$

$$F = Bqv$$

Now, $F = 1.6 \times 10^{-19} \times 2 \times 10^7 \times 10^{-6}$

$$= \frac{16}{10} \times 10^{-19} \times 2 \times 10^7 \times 10^{-6}$$

$$= 16 \times 2 \times 10^{-19+6-6}$$

$$F = 32 \times 10^{-19} \text{ N}$$

37. (*i*) Moving-coil galvanometer is an easy and sensitive instrument to detect and measure electric current.

(*ii*) Moving-coil galvanometer is based upon the principle that when electric current flows in a coil placed in a magnetic field, a deflecting torque acts upon the coil whose magnitude depends upon the strength of the current.

(*iii*) Moving coil galvanometer are of two types:

(a) Suspended-coil galvanometer

(b) Pivoted-coil (or weston) galvanometer

(*iv*) In suspended-coil galvanometer, the coil is suspended by a thin phospher-bronze strip and the deflection of the coil is measured by a lamp and scale arrangement and in pivoted-coil galvanometer, the coil swing between two pivots and the deflection of the coil is read by pointer on a circular scale.

(*v*) Pivoted coil galvanometer is less sensitive than suspended coil galvanometer.

CHAPTER TEST

01 Mark Questions (MCQs)

1 In a radial magnetic field

(a) the plane of the coil remains parallel to the lines of forces in every position
(b) it remains perpendicular to the lines of forces
(c) torque experienced by the coil is zero in every position
(d) None of the above

2 Sensitivity of a moving coil galvanometer can be increased by

(a) increasing number of turns
(b) increasing magnetic field intensity
(c) increasing area of the coil
(d) All of the above

3 Phosphor-bronze strip in a suspended coil galvanometer is used as a suspension fibre

(a) as it is good conductor of electricity
(b) as it does not oxidise at working temperature and its torsion couple per unit twist is least
(c) as it has very less elastic after effect
(d) All of the above

4 In an ammeter, 5% of the main current is passing through the galvanometer. If the resistance of the galvanometer is G, then the resistance of the shunt will be

(a) $19\,G$ (b) $20\,G$ (c) $G/20$ (d) $G/19$

01 Mark Questions (VSA)

5 Write two factors by which current sensitivity of a moving coil galvanometer can be increased.

6 When a current carrying loop is placed in a magnetic field **B**, write the expression for the torque acting on it.

7 Why should the spring/suspension wire in a moving coil galvanometer have low torsional constant?

02 Marks Questions

8 A rectangular coil of 100 turns has length 5 cm and width 4 cm. It is placed with its plane parallel to a uniform magnetic field and a current of 2 A is passed through the coil. If the torque acting on the coil is 0.2 Nm, find t`he magnitude of the magnetic field.

9 A circular coil of 200 turns and radius 10 cm is placed in a uniform magnetic field of 0.5 T normal to the plane of the coil. If the current in the coil is 3.0 A, calculate the

(i) total torque on the coil
(ii) total force on the coil
(iii) average force on each electron in the coil due to the magnetic field. Assume the area of cross-section of the wire to be 10^{-5} m^2 and the free electron density is 10^{29} per m^3.

03 Marks Questions

10 Define current sensitivity and voltage sensitivity of galvanometer. Increasing the current sensitivity may not necessarily increase the voltage sensitivity of a galvanometer. Justify your answer.

11 A square coil of side 10 cm has 20 turns and carries a current of 12 A. The coil is suspended vertically and normal to the plane of the coil, makes an angle θ with the direction of a uniform horizontal magnetic field of 0.80 T. If the torque, experienced by the coil equals 0.96 N-m. Find the value of θ.

05 Marks Questions

12 (i) Explain the term cyclotron and discuss about its limitations.
(ii) Derive the expression on torque on a current loop with diagram.

13 What do you mean by ''Moving coil galvanometer? Discuss its construction, working and uses. Also describe the conversion of a galvanometer into voltmeter and ammeter.

Answers

1. (a) **2.** (d) **3.** (d) **4.** (d)

8. $B = 0.5$ T

9. (i) $\tau = 9.42$ N-m (ii) $F_{\text{total}} = 0$ (iii) $F = 1.5 \times 10^{-24}$ N

11. $\theta = \pi/6$

08

Bar Magnet

TREND ANALYSIS 4 YEARS

Average No. of Questions Across all Sets

	Types of Questions	2024	2023	2020	2019
Bar Magnet	1 Mark	–	–	–	–
	2 Marks	–	–	–	–
	3 Marks	–	–	–	–
	5 Marks	–	–	–	–

Magnetism

A naturally occurring ore of iron, magnetite or lodestone attracts small pieces of iron towards it. The phenomenon of attraction of small pieces of iron, steel, nickel, cobalt, etc. towards the ore is called magnetism.

Magnets are of two types such as

(*i*) **Natural magnets** These are generally irregular in shapes and weak in strength.

(*ii*) **Artificial magnets** These magnets have desired shapes and desired strength. A bar magnet, a horse shoe magnet, compass needle etc., all are artificial magnets.

The Bar Magnet (Magnetic Dipole)

The bar magnet has two poles similar to the positive and negative charges of an electric dipole. One pole is designated as **North-pole** and the other as **South-pole**.

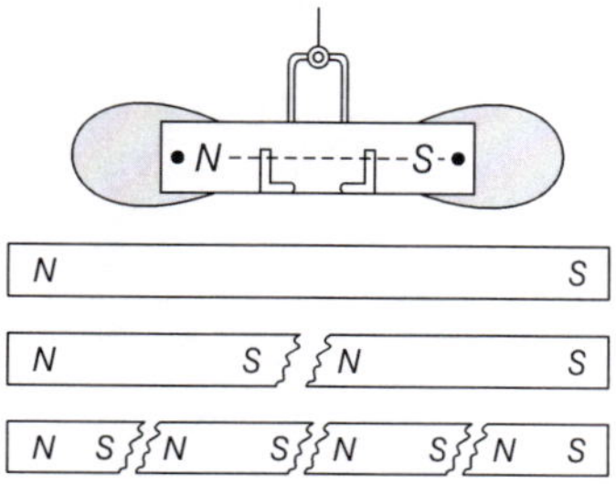

Magnetic poles always exist in pairs

Magnetic Dipole

A magnetic dipole is an arrangement of two magnetic poles of equal and opposite strengths separated by a small distance. e.g. A bar magnet, a compass needle, etc., are magnetic dipoles.

- The **magnetic dipole moment** of a magnetic dipole is given by

$$\boxed{\mathbf{M} = m \times 2l}$$

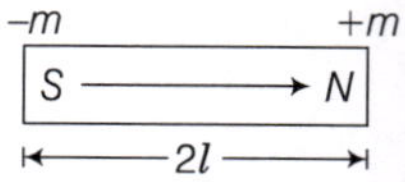

where, m is pole strength and $2l$ is dipole length directed from S to N.

SI unit of magnetic dipole moment is A-m^2 or J/T.

NOTE If we cut a magnet (bar) along its geometrical axis its pole strength does not change.

- Magnitude of force acting between two magnetic poles is given by

$$\boxed{F = \frac{\mu_0}{4\pi} \cdot \frac{m_1 m_2}{r^2}}$$

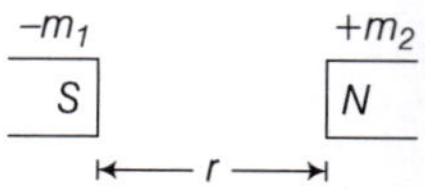

where, m_1 and m_2 are magnetic strengths of the poles belonging to two different magnets, r is distance between the poles and μ_0 is the permeability of vacuum. This is known **Coulomb's law in magnetism.**

Magnetic Field Lines

These are imaginary lines which gives pictorial representation for the magnetic field inside and around the magnet (bar magnet).

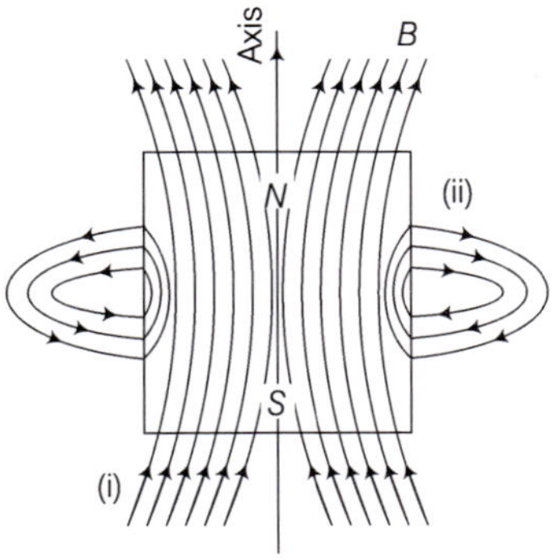

Properties of magnetic field lines are

(*i*) These lines form continuous closed loops.

(*ii*) The tangent to the field line gives direction of the field at that point.

(*iii*) Larger the density of the lines, stronger will be the field.

(*iv*) These lines do not intersect one another.

(*v*) The closed nature of magnetic field lines supports the phenomenon of non-existence of magnetic monopole.

Magnetic Flux

The magnetic flux linked with any surface is equal to the total number of magnetic lines of force passing normally through it. It is a scalar quantity.

Suppose, we consider small area $d\mathbf{A}$ in field $\mathbf{B}$, then

magnetic flux

$$\boxed{\phi = \int \mathbf{B} \cdot d\mathbf{A}}$$

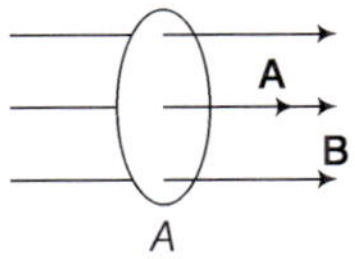

Flux, $\phi = BA =$ Maximum value

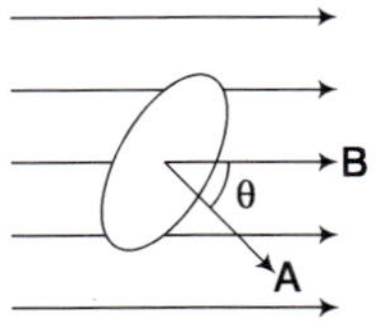

Magnetic flux, $\phi = BA \cos\theta = \mathbf{B} \cdot \mathbf{A}$

The SI unit of magnetic flux is weber (Wb) and CGS unit of magnetic flux is maxwell (Mx).

$$1 \text{ Wb} = 10^8 \text{ Mx} = 1 \text{ Tm}^2$$

The magnetic flux is a scalar quantity and its dimensional formula is $[ML^2T^{-2}A^{-1}]$.

Magnetic Flux Density

The number of magnetic field lines crossing normally through a unit area is called magnetic flux density. It is expressed as

$$\boxed{B = \frac{\phi}{A} = \mu H}$$

Because $\mu = \frac{B}{H}$ where, $B =$ magnetic induction,

$H =$ magnetic intensity

$\mu =$ permeability of the medium

The SI unit of magnetic flux density is Wb/m^2 or tesla (T).

Superposition of Magnetic Fields

The resultant magnetic field at a particular point in a region, where magnetic fields $\mathbf{B}_1, \mathbf{B}_2, \mathbf{B}_3, \ldots, \mathbf{B}_N$ are present and can be calculated by the vector sum of these individual fields. Hence, according to the principle of superposition, $\mathbf{B}_{\text{net}} = \mathbf{B}_1 + \mathbf{B}_2 + \mathbf{B}_3 + \cdots + \mathbf{B}_N$

$$\Rightarrow \qquad \boxed{\mathbf{B} = \sum_{i=1}^{N} \mathbf{B}_i}$$

where, sigma (Σ) represents summation.

Magnetic Field Strength at a Point due to a Bar Magnet

(*i*) **On axial point (End-on-position)**

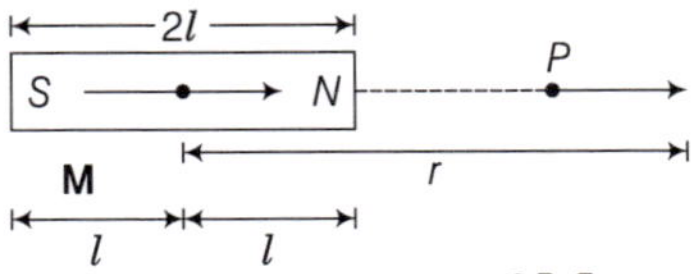

$$B = \frac{\mu_0}{4\pi} \frac{2\mathbf{M}r}{(r^2 - l^2)^2}$$

$$\boxed{B \approx \frac{\mu_0}{4\pi} \cdot \frac{2\mathbf{M}}{r^3}} \qquad [\because r >> l]$$

The direction of magnetic field is along the direction of the magnetic dipole moment (M).

(*ii*) **On equatorial point (broad side-on-position)**

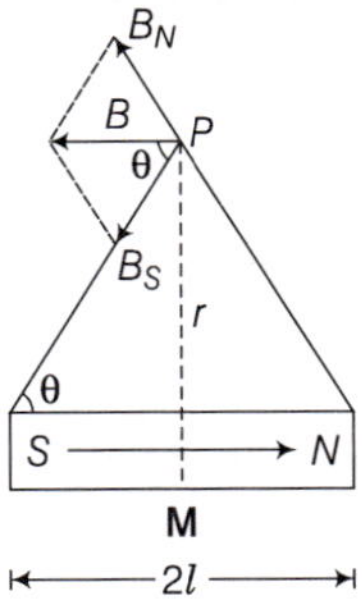

$$B = \frac{\mu_0}{4\pi} \frac{M}{(r^2 + l^2)^{3/2}}$$

$$\boxed{B \approx \frac{\mu_0}{4\pi} \cdot \frac{M}{r^3}} \qquad [\because r >> l]$$

The direction of magnetic field is parallel to the axis of magnetic dipole and opposite to the direction of dipole moment.

NOTE The direction of magnetic field between the poles of the dipole is in the direction opposite to the magnetic moment (South to North) while inside the current loop it is in the same direction to that of the magnetic moment.

Bar Magnet in a Uniform Magnetic Field

In figure, a uniform magnetic field **B** is represented by equidistant parallel lines. *NS* is a bar magnet of length $2l$ and strength of each pole is *m*.

The magnet is held at $\angle\theta$ with the direction of **B**

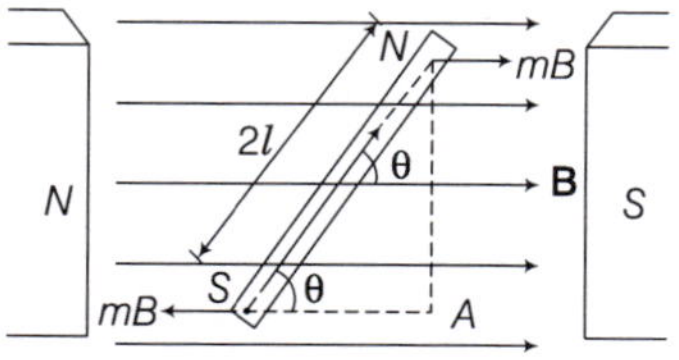

Bar magnet in a uniform magnetic field

Important Formulae

- **Torque** on a bar magnet in uniform magnetic field is

$$\tau = \mathbf{M} \times \mathbf{B} = MB \sin\theta$$

where, θ is the angle between **M** and **B**.

- **Potential energy** of a magnetic dipole in a magnetic field is

$$U = -MB\cos\theta = -\mathbf{M} \cdot \mathbf{B}$$

where, θ is the angle between **M** and **B**.

- **Work done** in rotating the dipole in uniform magnetic field from θ_1 to θ_2 is given by

$$W = MB(\cos\theta_1 - \cos\theta_2).$$

Bar Magnet as an Equivalent Solenoid

The magnetic field lines for a bar magnet and a current carrying solenoid resemble very closely. Therefore, a bar magnet can be thought as a large number of circulating currents in analogy with a solenoid.

To prove mathematically that magnetic field produced by a solenoid on any point on the axial line is same as that of a bar magnet.

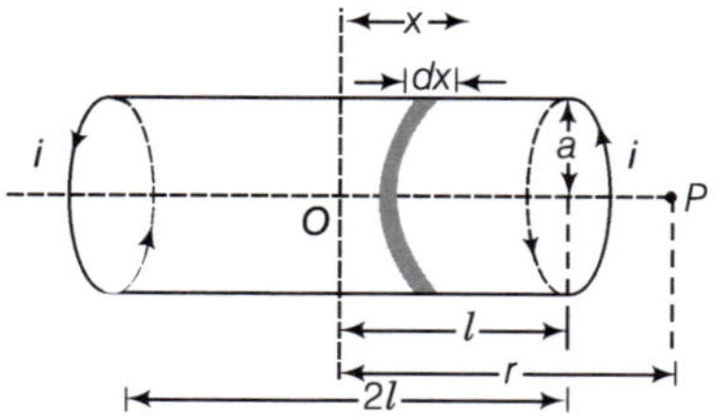

If **M** is the magnetic moment of the solenoid, then, **M** = total number of turns × current × Area of cross-section.

$$\mathbf{M} = n(2l) \times i \times \pi a^2$$

$$\Rightarrow \qquad B = \frac{\mu_0}{4\pi} \cdot \frac{2M}{r^3}$$

The Dipole Analogy

	Electrostatics	**Magnetism**
Dipole moment	**p**	**M**
Equatorial field for a short dipole	$-\mathbf{p}/4\pi\varepsilon_0 r^3$	$-\mu_0\mathbf{M}/4\pi r^3$
Axial field for a short dipole	$2\mathbf{p}/4\pi\varepsilon_0 r^3$	$\mu_0 2\mathbf{M}/4\pi r^3$
External field : Torque	$\mathbf{p} \times \mathbf{E}$	$\mathbf{M} \times \mathbf{B}$
External field : Energy	$-\mathbf{p} \cdot \mathbf{E}$	$-\mathbf{M} \cdot \mathbf{B}$
Formula	$\mathbf{p} = \mathbf{q}(2\mathbf{a})$	$\mathbf{M} = \mathbf{m}(2\mathbf{l})$

PYQs Previous Years Questions

1 Mark Questions

1. SI unit of magnetic dipole moment is **ISC 2022 Sem-I**
   (a) A-m (b) A-m^2 (c) Hm^{-1} (b) Wbm^{-2}
2. State the SI unit of magnetic dipole moment. **ISC 2013**
3. State the SI unit of the magnetic moment of a magnet, indicating its direction. **ISC 2006**

2 Marks Questions

4. Study the diagram given below. **ISC 2022 Sem-I**

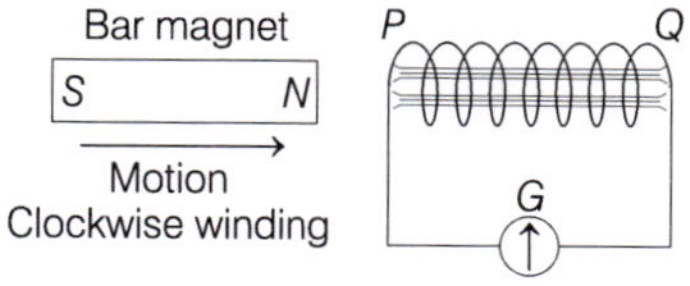

(*i*) The direction of the current at end P will be
   (a) anti-clockwise
   (b) clockwise
   (c) towards the magnet
   (d) away from the magnet

(*ii*) The magnetic poles induced at the end Q of the coil will be
   (a) north pole
   (b) south pole
   (c) anti-clockwise
   (d) no pole

5. A rectangular coil having 60 turns and area of $0.4\ m^2$ is held at right angles to a uniform magnetic field of flux density 5×10^{-2} T. Calculate the magnetic flux passing through it. **ISC 2018**

6. Derive an expression for the magnetic field at a point on the axis located at a distance x from the centre of a magnetic dipole of length $2l$ and magnetic moment M. **ISC 2006**

7. If the bar magnet in Q.4 is turned around by 180°, where will the new null points be located? **ISC 2005**

Explanations

1. (b) In dipole moment, the SI unit si $A\text{-}m^2$.

2. SI unit of magnetic dipole moment is $A\text{-}m^2$.

3. Refer to text on page 110.

It is directed along the axis of dipole from South-pole to North-pole.

4. (*i*) (a) The motion of magnet is towards the coil PQ. The point P will become north pole which opposes the relative motion between coil and magnet. Therefore, anti-clockwise current will flow at P.

(*ii*) (b) South pole.

5. The magnetic flux passing through a coil having N turns and area A is given by

$$\phi = NBA = 60\times5\times10^{-2}\times0.4 = 120\times10^{-2}$$

$$\phi = 1.2 \text{ Wb}$$

6. To find magnetic field at an axial point, we have to apply principle of superposition of magnetic field.

Consider the situation shown in the diagram. We have to find net magnetic field at point P, on axial point. Find magnetic field at P corresponding to each pole.

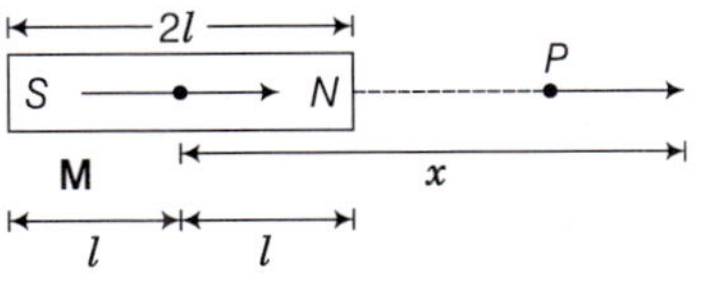

Net magnetic field at P, $B = B_N - B_S$

$$= \frac{\mu_0}{4\pi}\frac{2Mx}{(x^2-l^2)^2}$$

$$\approx \frac{\mu_0}{4\pi}\frac{2M}{x^3} \qquad [\text{for } l << x]$$

7. When a bar magnet is turned by 180°, then the null points are obtained on the equatorial line.

So, magnetic field on the equatorial line at a distance d' is given by

$$B' = \frac{\mu_0}{4\pi}\cdot\frac{m}{d'^3}$$

This magnetic field is equal to the horizontal component of the earth's magnetic field,

$$B' = \frac{\mu_0}{4\pi}\cdot\frac{m}{d'^3} = H \qquad \ldots(i)$$

As we know,

$$\text{Magnetic field, } B_1 = \frac{\mu_0}{4\pi}\cdot\frac{2m}{d^3} = H \qquad \ldots(ii)$$

From Eqs. (i) and (ii), we get

$$\frac{\mu_0}{4\pi}\cdot\frac{m}{d'^3} = \frac{\mu_0}{4\pi}\cdot\frac{2m}{d^3}$$

or $$\frac{1}{d'^3} = \frac{1}{d^3}$$

or $$d'^3 = \frac{d^3}{2} = \frac{(14)^3}{2} \quad (d = 14 \text{ cm})$$

or $$d' = \frac{14}{(2)^{1/3}} = 11.1 \text{ cm}$$

Thus, the null points are located on the equatorial line at a distance of 11.1 cm.

CHAPTER TEST

01 Mark Questions (MCQs)

1 When a magnet is placed in a uniform magnetic field, it experiences

(a) a force but no torque
(b) a torque but no force
(c) a force and also a torque
(d) neither a force nor a torque

2 In a plane perpendicular to magnetic meridian the dip needle will be

(a) vertical
(b) horizontal
(c) inclined equal to the angle of dip at that place
(d) pointing in any direction

01 Mark Questions (VSA)

3 What do you mean by bar magnet?

4 What do you mean by magnetic dipole ?

5 What do you understand from the term "magnetic flux density"?

02 Marks Question

6 A short bar magnet has a magnetic moment of 0.24 JT^{-1}. Calculate the magnitude of the magnetic field produced by the magnet at a distance of 10 cm from the centre of the magnet on the axis of the magnet.

Answers

1. (b) **2.** (a) **6.** 4.8×10^{-5} T

09

Magnetic Classification of Substances

TREND ANALYSIS 4 YEARS

Average No. of Questions Across all Sets

Magnetic Classification of Substances	Types of Questions	2024	2023	2020	2019
	1 Mark	2	–	–	–
	2 Marks	–	–	–	–
	3 Marks	–	–	–	–
	5 Marks	–	–	–	–

Magnetic materials are those materials that can be either attracted or repelled, when placed in an external magnetic field and can be magnetised. The classification of materials on the basis of their magnetic property is known as **magnetic classification**.

Magnetic materials are classified into three classes such as

(*i*) Diamagnetic Substances

Those substances when placed in an external magnetic field acquire a very very feeble magnetism in a direction opposite to the applied field are called diamagnetic substances.

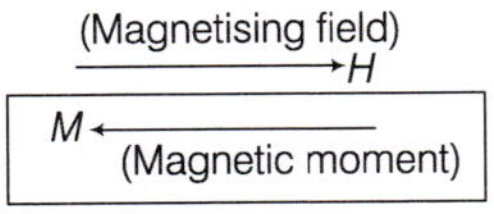

e.g., Copper (Cu), Silver (Ag), Bismuth (Bi), Zinc (Zn), Diamond (C), Salt (NaCl), Water (H_2O), Mercury (Hg), Nitrogen (N_2), Hydrogen (H_2), Magnesium (Mg), Gold (Au), etc.

(*ii*) Paramagnetic Substances

Those substances when placed in an external field, acquire a weak magnetism in the direction of field are called paramagnetic substances.

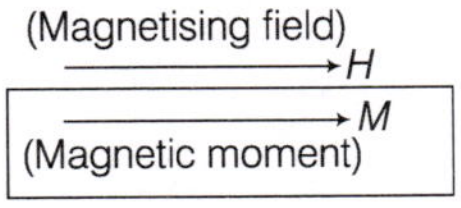

e.g., Aluminium (Al), Sodium (Na), Potassium (K), Platinum (Pt), Manganese (Mn), Copper sulphate ($CuSO_4$), Oxygen (O_2), etc.

(*iii*) Ferromagnetic Substances

Those substances, when placed in a magnetic field, acquire a strong magnetism in the direction of external field are called ferromagnetic substances.

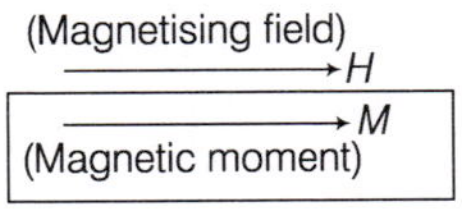

e.g., Iron (Fe), Nickel (Ni), Cobalt (Co), Magnetite (Fe_3O_4) or natural magnet, etc.

Diagrammatic representation of dia, para and ferromagnet with respect to degree of lines of force passing through the material are shown below.

Diamagnetic Rod

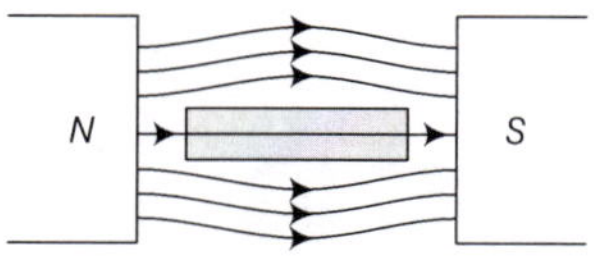

Lines of force gets reduced in diamagnetic materials

Paramagnetic Rod

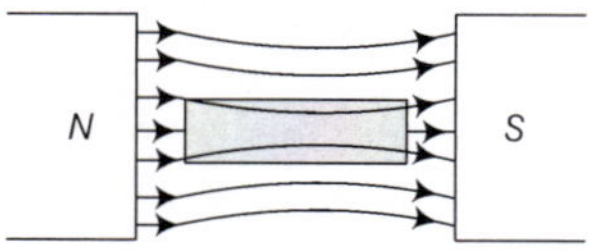

Lines of force start concentrating from weaker to stronger field

Ferromagnetic Rod

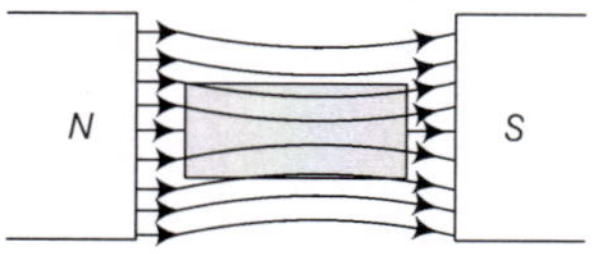

Highly concentrated lines of force passing through ferromagnetic substances

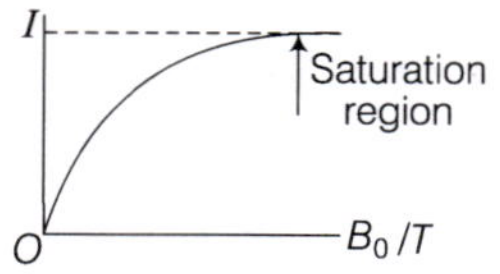

At a particular stage, all the atomic dipoles present in the specimen align in the direction of the external field and this leads to saturation region.

Terms Related to Magnetic Properties of Material

(i) Magnetising Field (H)

The magnetic field which induces magnetic property in magnetic material is known as magnetising field. It is an applied field. It is expressed as

$$\boxed{\mathbf{H} = \frac{\mathbf{B}}{\mu_0} - \mathbf{I}}$$

where, $\mathbf{B}$ = resultant magnetic field, $\mathbf{I}$ = intensity of magnetisation and

μ_0 = permeability of free space $= 4\pi \times 10^{-7}$ T-mA^{-1}

Its SI unit is ampere/metre (A/m) or Am^{-1}. It is a vector quantity. Its dimension is $[L^{-1}A]$.

(ii) Magnetic Induction (B)

If a current I is passed through a toroid (ring) a magnetic field and hence magnetic intensity is introduced due to which ring itself gets magnetised with intensity of magnetisation I. If magnetic intensity is H, then the total magnetic induction or field B,

$$\boxed{B = \mu_0 (H + I)}$$

where, μ_0 = permeability of free space, H = magnetising field and I = intensity of magnetisation.

Its SI unit is tesla (T) or weber per metre square (Wb/m^2). It is a vector quantity.

Its dimensions are $[MT^{-2}A^{-1}]$.

(iii) Intensity of Magnetisation (I)

The net magnetic dipole moment (M) produced per unit volume (V) in specimen of magnetic material in magnetising field is known as intensity of magnetisation. It is expressed as

$$\boxed{|\mathbf{I}| = \frac{|\mathbf{M}|}{V} = \frac{m}{A}}$$

[as $M = ml, V = Al$]

where, M = magnetic dipole moment, m = pole strength,

V = volume of specimen and

A = cross-sectional area.

It SI unit is ampere per metre (A/m). It is a vector quantity. Its dimensions are $[L^{-1}A]$.

NOTE Magnetic intensity is the amount of flux perpendicularly crossing through unit area in the direction of magnetic flow. It is given by $\theta/\mu_0 V$.

(iv) Magnetic Permeability (μ)

It is a measure of conduction of magnetic field lines through a substance. It is equal to the ratio of magnetic induction and magnetising field. It is expressed as

$$\boxed{\mu = \frac{|\mathbf{B}|}{|\mathbf{H}|}}$$

SI unit of $\mu = \dfrac{\text{tesla}}{\text{ampere metre}^{-1}} = \text{TmA}^{-1}$

and dimensions of $\mu = [MLT^{-2}A^{-2}]$

(v) Magnetic Susceptibility (χ_m)

It is equal to the ratio of intensity of magnetisation and magnetising field. It is expressed as

$$\chi_m = \frac{|\mathbf{I}|}{|\mathbf{H}|}$$

As units of H and I are same (Am^{-1}) hence χ_m has no unit. Material with positive value of χ_m are paramagnetic. Material with negative value of χ_m are diamagnetic. It is a scalar quantity. It has no dimensions.

(*vi*) Relative Magnetic Permeability (μ_r)

It is the ratio of magnetic permeability μ of a substance to the permeability of free space μ_0, that is $\mu_r = \frac{\mu}{\mu_0}$ or $\frac{B}{B_0}$, where B and B_0 are initial magnetic field (in vacuum) and increased magnetic field respectively. The value of μ_r is 1 for vacuum.

Relation between Magnetic Permeability (μ_r) and Magnetic Susceptibility (χ_m)

$$\chi_m = \mu_r - 1$$

Curie's Law

According to Curie's law, the magnetic susceptibility of paramagnetic substance is inversely proportional to the absolute temperature i.e.

$$\chi \propto \frac{1}{T}$$

$$\Rightarrow \text{ or } \quad \chi = \frac{C\mu_0}{T}$$

Here, T = absolute temperature,

χ = magnetic susceptibility

and C = Curie's constant.

On increasing temperature, magnetic susceptibility of paramagnetic substances decreases or *vice-versa*. The χ-T graph for diamagnetic, paramagnetic and ferromagnetic substances are shown in the figure.

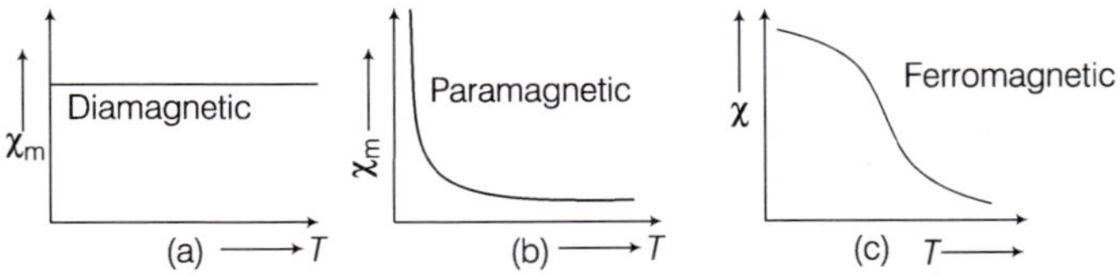

Variations of susceptibility with temperature in different materials

Curie Temperature

The magnetic susceptibility of these substances decreases on increasing the temperature and above a particular temperature, a ferromagnetic substance behaves like a paramagnetic substance. This particular temperature is called the Curie temperature T_C of the substance.

Curie-Weiss Law

At temperature above Curie point, the magnetic susceptibility of ferromagnetic substances is inversely proportional to $(T - T_C)$

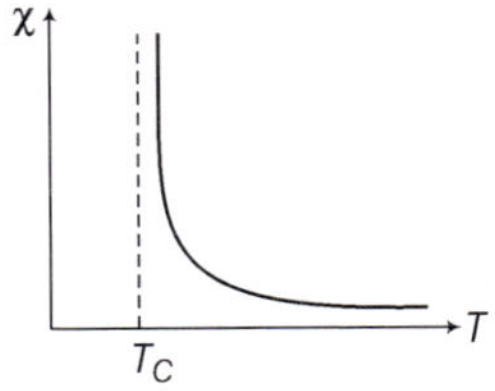

Variations of susceptibility with temperature

i.e. $\quad \chi \propto \frac{1}{T - T_C}$ or $\chi = \frac{C}{T - T_C}$ $\quad (\because T > T_C)$

Here, T_C = Curie temperature,

T = Absolute temperature (in kelvin.)

NOTE In many materials the Curie-Weiss law failed to describe the susceptibility in the immediate vicinity of the Curie point. Since, it is based on a mean field approximation. Instead there is a critical behaviour of the form.

$$\chi \simeq \frac{1}{(T - T_C)^\gamma}$$

where, γ is a critical exponent.

Magnetic Materials on the Basis of their Properties

Property	Diamagnetic Substance	Paramagnetic Substance	Ferromagnetic Substance
Effect of magnets	They are feebly repelled by magnets.	They are feebly attracted by magnets.	They are strongly attracted by magnets.
In external magnetic field	Acquire feeble magnetisation in the opposite direction of the magnetising field.	Acquire feebly magnetisation in the direction of the magnetising field.	Acquire strong magnetisation in the direction of the magnetising field.
In a non-uniform magnetic field	Tend to move slowly from stronger to weaker parts of the field.	Tend to move slowly from weaker to stronger parts of the field.	Tend to move quickly from weaker to stronger parts of the field.
In a uniform magnetic field	A freely suspended diamagnetic rod aligns itself perpendicular to the field.	A freely suspended paramagnetic rod aligns itself parallel to the field.	A freely suspended ferromagnetic rod aligns itself parallel to the field.
Susceptibility value (χ_m)	Susceptibility is small and negative $-1 \leq \chi_m < 0$	Susceptibility is small and positive $0 < \chi_m < \varepsilon_r$, where ε_r is a small number	Susceptibility is very large and positive. $\chi_m > 1000$
Relative permeability value (μ_r)	Slightly less than 1 $0 \leq \mu_r < 1$	Slightly greater than 1 $1 < \mu_r < 1 + \varepsilon$	Of the order of thousands $\mu_r > 1000$
Effect of temperature	Susceptibility is independent of temperature	Susceptibility varies inversely as temperature $\chi_m \propto \frac{1}{T}$.	Susceptibility decreases with temperature in a complex manner. $\chi_m \propto \frac{1}{T - T_C}$ $(T > T_C)$
Variation of I with H	I changes linearly with H.	I changes linearly with H and attains saturation at low temperature and in very strong fields.	I changes with H non-linearly and ultimately attains saturation.
Examples	Bi, Cu, Pb, Si, N_2(at STP), H_2O, NaCl	Al, Na, Ca, O_2(at STP), $CuCl_2$	Fe, Ni, Co, Gd, Fe_2O_3, Alnico

Hysteresis Loop

The lag of intensity of magnetisation (I) behind the magnetising field (H) during the process of magnetisation and demagnetisation of a ferromagnetic material is called **hysteresis**. The loop formed as the plot for hysteresis is known as **hysteresis loop**.

The hysteresis curve represents the relation between the magnetic induction B or intensity of magnetisation I of a ferromagnetic material with magnetic intensity H.

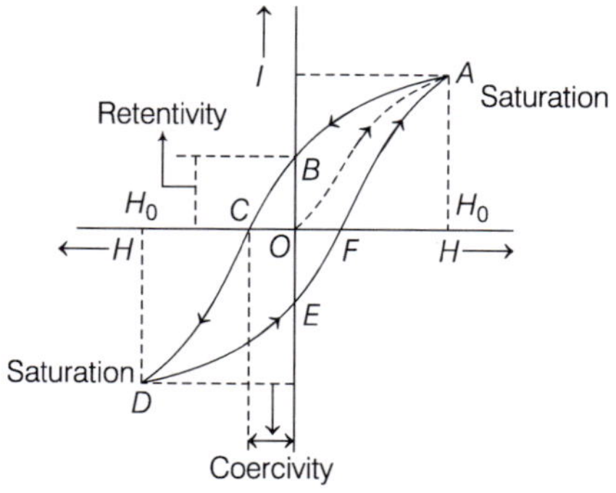

Hysteresis loop

The graph follows that

- Corresponding to point O, the magnetisation (H) is zero and likewise intensity of magnetisation (I) is also zero. The value of B at $H = 0$ is called **retentivity**.
- We again obtain saturation in the reverse direction at d. The value of H at C is called coercivity.
- As magnetising field is increased, intensity of magnetisation I also increases along OA and becomes maximum at A. This maximum value is called **saturation value**.

NOTE The area of hysteresis loop represents the energy loss in magnetisation and demagnetisation of a magnetic material. Retentivity is residual magnetism in the material.

Ferromagnetic materials can be divided into two groups-

(*i*) **Soft ferromagnets** (e.g., soft iron) Magnetism disappears on the removal of the external magnetising field.
Use → solenoid, transformers.

(*ii*) **Hard ferromagnets** (e.g., steel, alnico)
-Retain magnetism even after removal of the external magnetising field. Use for making permanent magnet.

Soft ferromagnets	Hard ferromagnets
Low retentivity	Low retentivity
Low coercivity	High coercivity
Low hysteresis loss	High hysteresis loss

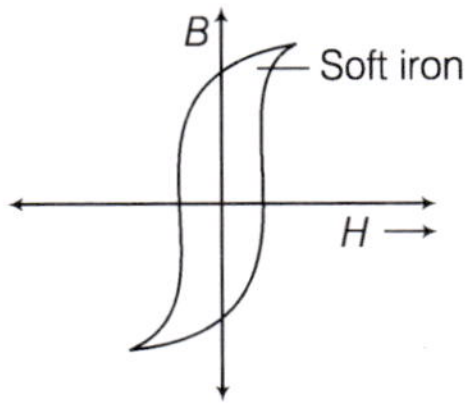

Hysteresis curve for soft iron

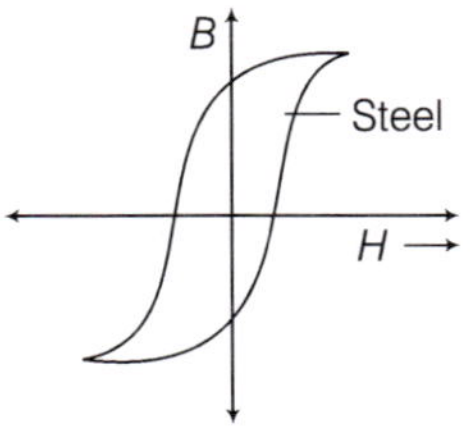

Hysteresis curve for steel

Permanent Magnets and Electromagnets

Permanent Magnets

The substances which at room temperature retain their ferromagnetic property for a long period of time are called permanent magnets.

The material used for making permanent magnets should have high retentivity, so that the magnet is strong and have high coercivity. So, the magnetisation is not erased by stray magnetic fields/temperature fluctuations or minor mechanical damage.

Electromagnets

Electromagnets are usually in the form of iron core solenoids. The core of an electromagnet is made of ferromagnetic materials which have high permeability and low retentivity. Soft iron is suitable material for electromagnets.

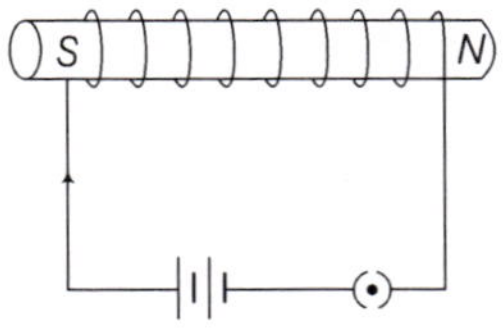

Electromagnets are used in electric bells, loudspeakers and telephone diaphragms. Giant electromagnets are used in cranes to lift machinery and bulk quantities of iron and steel.

Factors on which strength of electromagnet depends are as follows.

(*i*) Number of turns of the coil.

(*ii*) Its value of permeability and retentivity i.e. on the material of the core. Soft iron is suitable for electromagnet because it has low retentivity but high permeability.

(*iii*) Amount of current flowing through the circuit.

PYQs Previous Years Questions

1 Mark Questions

1. Why is the core of a transformer made of soft iron and not of steel? **ISC 2024**
2. Explain the meaning of the following statement Curie temperature for soft iron is 770°C. **ISC 2024**
3. Why is soft iron preferred to steel in making the core of a transformer? **ISC 2018**
4. Explain the term of Curie temperature. **ISC 2018**
5. Magnetic susceptibility of platinum is 0.0001. Its relative permeability is **ISC 2017**

   (a) 1.0000 (b) 0.9999 (c) 1.0001 (d) 0
6. (*i*) Define Curie temperature.

   (*ii*) If magnetic susceptibility of a certain magnetic material is 0.0001, find its relative permeability. **ISC 2016**
7. State how magnetic susceptibility is different for the three types of magnetic materials, i.e. diamagnetic, paramagnetic and ferromagnetic materials. **ISC 2015**
8. Two substances A and B have their relative permeabilities slightly greater and slightly less than 1 respectively. What do you conclude about A and B as far as their magnetic materials are concerned? **ISC 2014**
9. At a certain temperature, a ferromagnetic material becomes paramagnetic. What is the temperature called? **ISC 2014**
10. Arrange the three types of magnetic materials i.e. paramagnetic, diamagnetic and ferromagnetic materials, in decreasing order of their magnetic susceptibility. **ISC 2010, 03**
11. State how the magnetic susceptibility of a ferromagnetic material changes when it is heated. **ISC 2009**

2 Marks Question

12. Distinguish between diamagnetic and paramagnetic substances in terms of its relative permeability (μ_r) and magnetic susceptibility (χ).

ISC 2005

3 Marks Questions

13. (*i*) What is meant by a paramagnetic substance? State Curie's law.

(*ii*) What is the value of magnetic susceptibility of aluminium, if its relative permeability is 1.000022?

ISC 2011

14. Draw a hysteresis loop with axis labelled and showing retentive and coercive force. What does the area of the loop represent? **ISC 2002**

Case Based Question
(For Complete Chapter)

15. Direction *Read the passage given below and answer the questions that follow.*

Hysteresis Loss A ferromagnetic substance consists of local regions called 'domains', each of which is spontaneously magnetised. In an unmagnetised substance the directions of magnetisation in different domains are different so that, on an average, the resultant magnetisation is zero.

When we magnetise the substance by placing it in an external magnetising field, then those domains which are favourably oriented with respect to the external field grow in size and also each domain rotates so that its direction of magnetisation becomes aligned with the field direction. During this process energy is taken by the substance. When the external field is removed, the domain boundaries do not move completely back to their original positions, that is, the substance retains some magnetisation (hysteresis effect). Therefore, the energy supplied to the substance during magnetisation is not fully recovered. The balance of energy left in the substance is lost as heat. This is called 'hysteresis loss'.

(*i*) What do you mean by hysteresis loss? **(1)**

(*ii*) What do you mean by hysteresis effect? **(1)**

(*iii*) Define the term 'Domains'. **(1)**

(*iv*) In which material have smaller hysteresis loss iron or steel? **(1)**

(*v*) How can we reduce the hysteresis loss? **(1)**

Explanations

1. Soft iron loses all its magnetic properties when the current in the coil is switched OFF, whereas steel does not loss its magnetic properties when the current is stopped. Soft iron has high coercivity and low retentivity.

2. Soft iron is a ferromagnetic material. So, above 770°C temperature, it loses its permanent magnetic field and the magnetism completely disappears. Above this temperature, the ferromagnetic material behaves as a paramagnetic substance.

3. Soft iron is used to make core of transformer because hysteresis loop of soft iron is narrow than steel, therefore energy loss is small.

4. Refer to text on page 117. (Curie Temperature)

5. (c) Magnetic susceptibility of platinum

$$\chi_m = 0.0001$$

Relative permeability $\mu_r = 1 + \chi_m = 1 + 0.0001$

$$= 1.0001$$

Common Mistake Generally, there is a confusion for the relation between χ and μ_r. Correct relation is $\mu_r = 1 + \chi$.

6. (*i*) Curie temperature (T_C) is the temperature at which certain materials lose their ferromagnetic property to become paramagnetic.

(*ii*) Given, magnetic susceptibility of material, $\chi_m = 0.0001$

Since, relative magnetic permeability,

$$\mu_r = 1 + \chi_m$$

$$\Rightarrow \quad \mu_r = 1 + 0.0001$$

$$\mu_r = 1.0001$$

7. For diamagnetic material, susceptibility is less than 0.
For paramagnetic material, susceptibility is more than zero but less than 1.
Ferromagnetic material has very high value in positive.

8. For paramagnetic substances $\mu_r > 1$ and for diamagnetic substances $\mu_r < 1$, where μ_r is relative permeability. Thus, A is paramagnetic and B is diamagnetic material.

9. At a temperature known as Curie temperature ferromagnetic material becomes paramagnetic.

10. For ferromagnetic materials, χ_m is very high and positive.

For paramagnetic materials, χ_m is positive and $\chi_m > 1$

For diamagnetic materials, χ_m is negative and $\chi_m < 1$

So, decreasing order of magnetic susceptibility is ferromagnetic, paramagnetic and diamagnetic.

11. The magnetic susceptibility (χ) of a ferromagnetic substance varies with temperature as

$$\chi \propto \frac{1}{T - T_C} \qquad [T > T_C]$$

Concept Enhancer Magnetic susceptibility (χ) of a ferromagnetic substance is in the range of 1000 – 10000.

12.

Property	Diamagnetic	Paramagnetic
Relative permeability (μ_r)	$\mu_r < 1$	$\mu_r > 1$
Magnetic susceptibility (χ)	Low and negative	Low and positive

13. (*i*) These substances (paramagnetic) when placed in a magnetic field, acquire feeble magnetism in the direction of the magnetic field.

Curie's law state that, susceptibility (χ) of a paramagnetic substance varies inversely with absolute temperature of the substance

i.e. $$\chi \propto \frac{1}{T}$$

(*ii*) According to the question, $\mu_r = 1.000022$

$\Rightarrow \quad \chi_m = ?$

We know, $\quad \mu_r = 1 + \chi_m$

$\Rightarrow \quad \chi_m = \mu_r - 1 = 1.000022 - 1$

$= 0.000022$

14. We have to draw curves corresponding to magnetisation and demagnetisation of the ferromagnetic material.

For hysteresis loop with axis labelled and showing retentive and coercive force

Refer to text on page 118 (Hysteresis Loop)

The area of hysteresis loop represents the energy loss in magnetisation and demagnetisation.

15. (*i*) During the cycle of magnetisation and demagnetisation of magnetic substances, energy is spent and this is spent energy appears in the form of heat. This heat loss is known as hysteresis loss.

(*ii*) When the magnetisation of ferromagnetic materials lags behind the magnetic field. This effect can be described as the hysteresis effect.

(*iii*) A ferromagnetic substance consists of local regions called domains.

(*iv*) In soft iron has smaller hysteresis loss than of steel.

(*v*) Hysteresis losses can be reduced by using material that has less area of the hystesesis loop.

CHAPTER TEST

01 Mark Questions (MCQs)

1 Which of the following is repelled by an external magnetic field?

(a) Iron (b) Cobalt
(c) Steel (d) Copper

2 Magnetic susceptibility of platinum is 0.0001. The relative permeability is

(a) 1.0000 (b) 0.9999
(c) 1.0001 (c) 0

3 If a diamagnetic solution is poured into a U-tube and one arm of this U-tube is placed between the poles of a strong magnet with the meniscus in a line with the field, then the level of the solution will

(a) rise (b) fall
(c) oscillate slowly (d) remain as such

4 A uniform magnetic field exists in space in the plane of paper and is initially directed from left to right. When a bar of soft iron is placed in the field parallel to it, the lines of force passing through it will be represented by

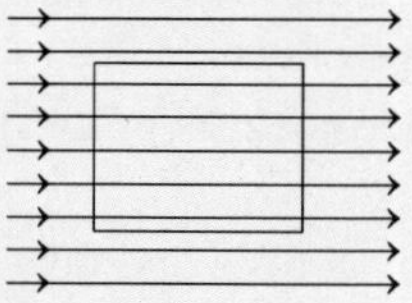

A.

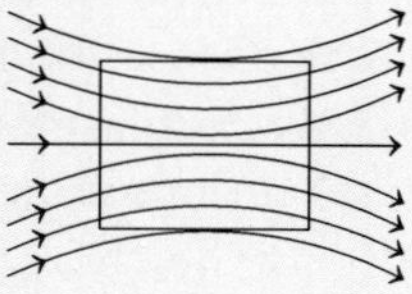

B.

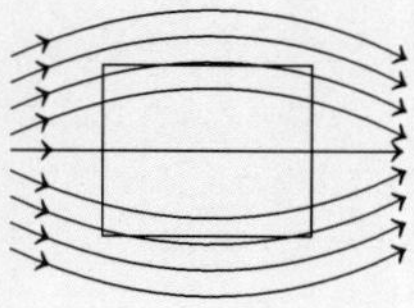

C.

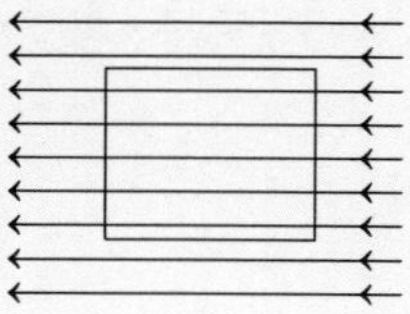

D.

(a) A (b) B
(c) C (d) D

01 Mark Questions (VSA)

5 What do you mean by diamagnetic substances?

6 The permeability of a magnetic material is 0.9983. Name the type of magnetic material it represents.

7 What is the characteristic property of a diamagnetic material?

8 The susceptibility of a magnetic material is -4.2×10^{-6}. Name the type of magnetic material it represents.

02 Marks Questions

9 The relative magnetic permeability of a magnetic material is 800. Identify the nature of magnetic material and state its two properties.

10 Draw a plot showing the variation of intensity of magnetisation with the applied magnetic field intensity for bismuth. Under what condition does a diamagnetic material exhibit perfect conductivity and perfect diamagnetism?

03 Marks Questions

11 (i) How does angle of dip change as line goes from magnetic pole to magnetic equator of the earth?

(ii) A uniform magnetic field gets modified as shown in figure when two specimens X and Y are placed in it. Identify whether the two specimens X and Y are diamagnetic, paramagnetic or ferromagnetic.

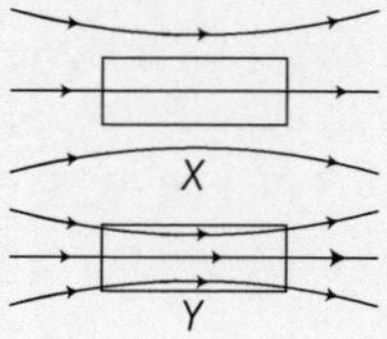

12 What do you mean by curie temperature? State curie's law and also show the graphs susceptibility and temperature.

Answers

1. (d) **2.** (c) **3.** (b) **4.** (b)

6. Diamagnetic

8. Diamagnetic

9. Ferromagnetic

11. (ii) X : paramagnetic, Y : ferromagnetic

10

Electromagnetic Induction

TREND ANALYSIS 4 YEARS

Electromagnetic Induction

Average No. of Questions Across all Sets

Types of Questions	2024	2023	2020	2019
1 Mark	–	2	–	–
2 Marks	1	2	2	1
3 Marks	1	–	–	–
5 Marks	–	1	–	–

Magnetic Flux

The magnetic flux linked with any surface is equal to the total number of magnetic lines of field passing normally through it.

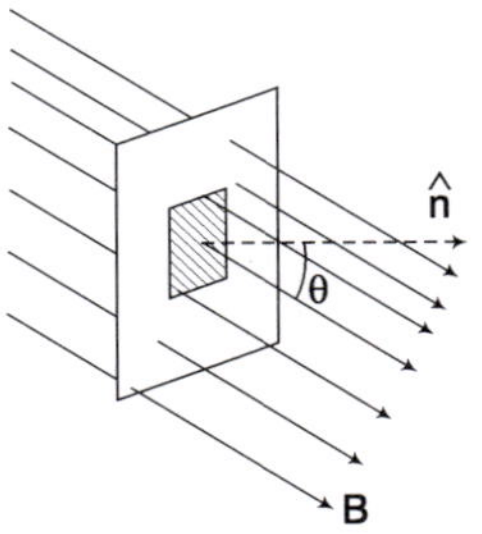

Net flux through surface $\phi = \oint \mathbf{B} \cdot d\mathbf{A} = BA\cos\theta$, where θ is the angle between area vector and magnetic field vector.

If $\theta = 0°$, then $\phi = BA$ (maximum value), if $\theta = 90°$, then $\phi = 0$

Unit and Dimensions Magnetic flux is a scalar quantity. Its SI unit is weber (Wb), CGS unit is Maxwell (Mx) or Gauss $\times \text{cm}^2$, ($1 \text{ Wb} = 10^8$ Mx).

Other Units $1 \text{ Wb} = 1 \text{ T-m}^2$

$$\text{Tesla} \times \text{m}^2 = \frac{\text{N} \times \text{m}}{\text{amp}} = \frac{\text{joule}}{\text{amp}} = \frac{\text{volt} \times \text{coulomb}}{\text{amp}}$$

$$= \text{volt} \times \text{second} = \text{ohm} \times \text{coulomb} = \text{henry} \times \text{amp}$$

Its dimensional formula is $[\phi] = [ML^2T^{-2}A^{-1}]$.

Electromagnetic Induction

The phenomenon of generation of current or emf in a conducting circuit by changing the magnetic flux is known as electromagnetic induction (EMI).

Faraday's Laws of Electromagnetic Induction

First law Whenever the number of magnetic lines of force (magnetic flux) passing through a circuit changes, an emf is produced in the circuit called induced emf. The induced emf persists only as long as there is a change of magnetic flux.

Second law The magnitude of induced emf in a closed loop or circuit, is directly proportional to the rate of change of magnetic flux linked with the closed loop or circuit.

i.e. $e \propto \dfrac{\Delta\phi}{\Delta t} \Rightarrow e = -K\dfrac{\Delta\phi}{\Delta t} = -\Delta\phi / \Delta t$

where, K is constant of proportionality having value 1 in all system of units.

Negative sign indicates that induced emf (e) opposes the change of magnetic flux.

In case of a closely wound coil of N-turns, the change of flux associated with each turn is same. Therefore, the total induced emf is given by, $e = -N\dfrac{\Delta\phi}{\Delta t}$

Other Formulae As, $\phi = BA\cos\theta$, hence, ϕ will change if either, B, A or θ will change.

So, $e = -N\dfrac{\Delta\phi}{\Delta t} = -N\dfrac{(\phi_2 - \phi_1)}{\Delta t} = -\dfrac{NA(B_2 - B_1)\cos\theta}{\Delta t}$

Also, $e = -\dfrac{NBA(\cos\theta_2 - \cos\theta_1)}{\Delta t}$

Expressions for Induced *i*, *q* and *P*

Induced current (i)	**Induced charge** (q)	**Induced power** (P)
$i = \dfrac{e}{R} = -\dfrac{N}{R}\cdot\dfrac{\Delta\phi}{\Delta t}$	$\Delta q = i\,\Delta t = -\dfrac{N}{R}\cdot\Delta\phi$ It is time independent	$P = \dfrac{e^2}{R} = \dfrac{N^2}{R}\left(\dfrac{\Delta\phi}{\Delta t}\right)^2$ It depends on time and resistance.

Lenz's Law

According to this law, the direction of induced emf or induced current in a circuit is such as to oppose the cause that produces it.

Lenz's Law and Energy Conservation

Lenz's law is based upon law of conservation of energy. As the induced emf opposes the change in flux, work has to be done against the opposition offered by induced emf/current in changing the flux. The work done appears as electrical energy in the circuit.

Direction of Induced current at Various Positions of Relative Motion between the Magnet and Coil

Position of magnet			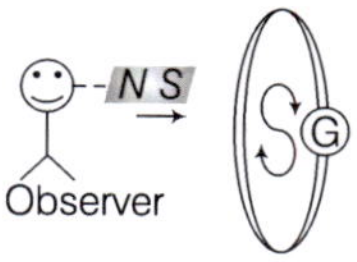	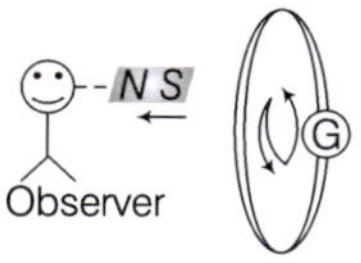
Direction of induced current	Anti-clockwise direction	Clockwise direction	Clockwise direction	Anti-clockwise direction
Behaviour of face of the coil	As a North-pole	As a South-pole	As a South-pole	As a North-pole
Type of magnetic force opposed	Repulsive force	Attractive force`	Repulsive force	Attractive force
Magnetic field linked with the coil and it's progress as viewed from left	Cross (×), Increases	Cross (×), Decreases	Dot (·), Increases	Dot (·), Decreases

Induced Current in a Coil

If N is the number of turns and R is the resistance of a coil. The magnetic flux linked with its each turn changes by $\Delta\phi$ in short time interval Δt, then induced current flowing through the coil is given by

$$i = \frac{|e|}{R} = \frac{1}{R}\left(N\frac{\Delta\phi}{\Delta t}\right) \qquad [\because \phi = NBA\cos\theta \Rightarrow \phi = NBA\cos\omega t]$$

If induced current is produced in a coil rotated in a uniform magnetic field, then

$$i = \frac{NBA\omega\sin\omega t}{R} = i_0\sin\omega t \qquad \left[\because i_0 = \frac{NBA\omega}{R}\right]$$

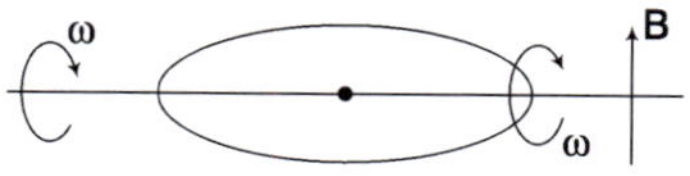

Coil

where, i_0 = peak value of induced current,
N = number of turns in the loop
ω = angular speed of the coil
A = area of cross-section of the coil
and R = resistance of the coil.

Motional EMF

Let conductor PQ slides a distance Δx in time Δt, then the change in magnetic flux in this time

$$\boxed{\Delta\phi = B\Delta A = B(l\Delta x)}$$

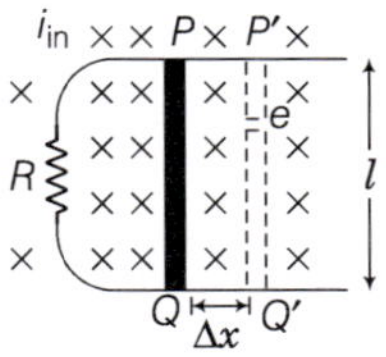

and $$\boxed{|e| = \frac{\Delta\phi}{\Delta t} = Bl\left(\frac{\Delta x}{\Delta t}\right) = Blv}$$

As, this emf ($e = Blv$) is produced due to the motion of a conductor, so it is called as motional emf.

- Induced current, $i_{in} = \frac{e}{R} = \frac{Bvl}{R}$
- Magnetic force on the conductor opposite to the direction of motion,
$$F_m = Bi_{in}l = B\left(\frac{Bvl}{R}\right)l = \frac{B^2vl^2}{R}$$
- Power required by the agent to move the conductor,
$$P_{agent} = \frac{dW}{dt} = \mathbf{F}_{agent}\cdot\mathbf{v} = \frac{B^2vl^2}{R}\times v = \frac{B^2v^2l^2}{R}$$
- Electrical power dissipated through the resistance,
$$P_{thermal} = i^2R = \left(\frac{Bvl}{R}\right)^2 R = \frac{B^2v^2l^2}{R}$$

Clearly, $P_{agent} = P_{thermal}$
This is contrast with the law of conservation of energy.

Fleming's Right Hand Rule to Find the Direction of Induced emf

If the thumb, fore finger and middle finger of right hand are held mutually perpendicular to each other and the forefinger represents the direction of magnetic field, thumb represents the direction of motion of the conductor, then the middle finger will represent the direction of induced current.

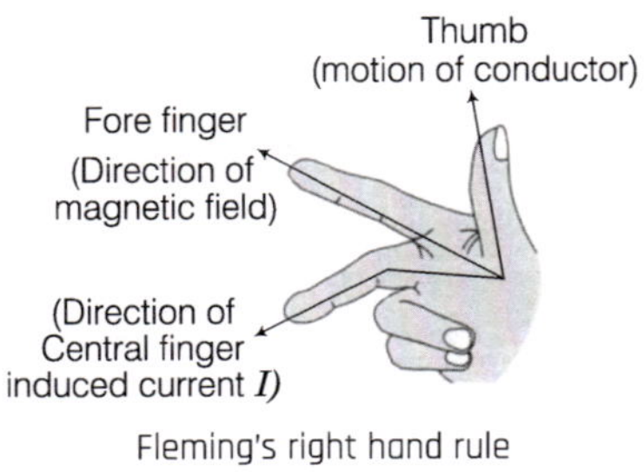

Fleming's right hand rule

Eddy Current

Eddy currents are the currents induced in a bulk pieces of the conductors when the magnetic flux linked with the conductor changes and their flow patterns resemble eddies in water. It causes undesirable heating.

The direction of eddy currents is given by Lenz's law or Fleming's right hand rule.

Applications of Eddy Currents

Inspite of undesirable effect, eddy currents are used in many ways. Some of them are given below.

(*i*) Speedometer (*ii*) Induction furnace
(*iii*) Induction motor (*iv*) Electric brakes

Self-Induction

The phenomenon of production of induced emf in a coil, when a current passes through it, undergoes a change is called self-induction. The induced emf is also called back emf.

$\therefore$ Total flux linked with coil, $N\phi \propto i \Rightarrow N\phi = Li$

where, ϕ = flux linked with each turn,

and L = coefficient of self-induction or self-inductance.

Also, induced emf, $e = -L\frac{di}{dt}$

The SI unit of self-inductance is henry (H).

1 henry (H) = 1 V-s/A or 1 T-m^2/A

Its dimensional formula is $[L] = [ML^2T^{-2}A^{-2}]$.

Self-inductance of a long solenoid is given by

$$L = \frac{\mu_0 N^2 A}{l}$$

where, N = total number of turns, A = area of cross-section solenoid

and l = length of the solenoid.

and μ_0 = permeability in free space.

If the coil is wound over a material of high relative permeability (μ_r), then

$$\boxed{L = \frac{\mu_0\mu_r N^2 A}{l}}$$

Mutual Induction

The phenomenon of generation of induced emf in secondary coil, when current linked with primary coil changes is called mutual induction.

So, magnetic flux linked with the secondary coil ∝ current in primary coil

i.e. $\phi \propto I$

$\Rightarrow \quad \phi = MI$

$N_2\phi_2 = Mi_1$

where, $N_2\phi_2$ = flux linked with secondary coil.

i_1 = current in primary coil

and M = constant of proportionality called the mutual inductance of two coils.

Also, $e_2 = -\frac{Mdi_1}{dt}$

$$\Rightarrow \quad M = \left| -\frac{e_2}{di_1 / dt} \right|$$

If $\frac{di_1}{dt} = 1$, then $M = e_2$. Thus, coefficient of mutual induction of two coils is equal to the emf induced in one coil when time of rate of change of current through other coil is unity.

The SI unit of mutual inductance is henry (H).

1 henry (H) = 1 V-s / A or 1 T-m^2/A

Its dimensional formula is similar to self-inductance (L).

Mutual inductance (M) of closely wound solenoids is given by

$$M = \frac{\mu_0 N_1 N_2 A}{l}$$

where, N_1 and N_2 = number of turns in primary and secondary solenoids, respectively,

A = common cross-sectional area of solenoids

and l = length of longer solenoid (when two solenoids are of different lengths)

Transformer

It is a device which is used for changing the voltage in AC circuits. It is based upon the principle of mutual induction. It works with AC only. It consists of two coils wound on the same core. The alternating current passing through the primary coil creates a continuously changing flux through the core. This changing flux induces an alternating emf in the secondary coil.

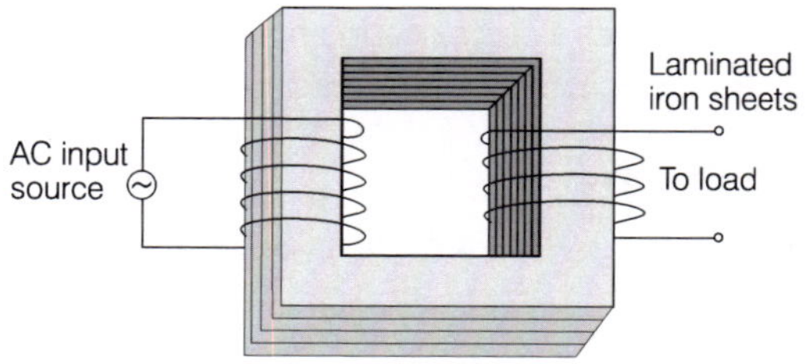

(a) Step-down transformer

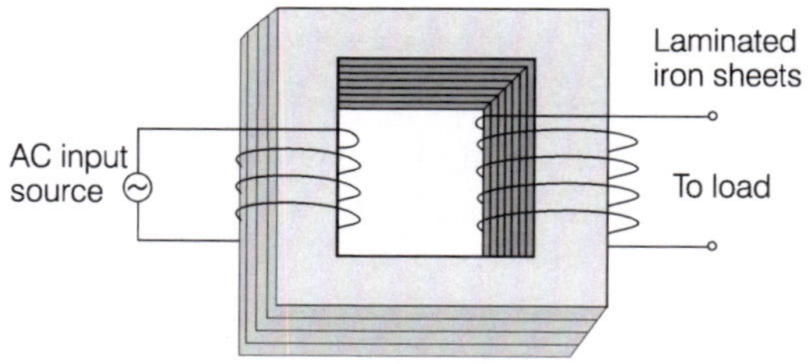

(b) Step-up transformer

For ideal transformer

$$P_{\text{out}} = P_{\text{in}} \quad \text{or} \quad V_s i_s = V_p i_p$$

$$\Rightarrow \quad \frac{V_s}{V_p} = \frac{i_p}{i_s}$$

where, V_s = voltage across secondary coil,

V_p = applied (input) voltage to primary coil,

i_p = current in primary coil

and i_s = current in secondary coil.

Same flux links in both primary and secondary coils, so the induced emf per turn is the same in each coil.

Hence, $$\boxed{\frac{V_s}{V_p} = \frac{e_s}{e_p} = \frac{N_s}{N_p} = \frac{i_p}{i_s} = K}$$

where, K is called **transformer ratio**. If $K > 1$, then it is used for step-up transformer ($N_s > N_p$).

If $K < 1$, then it is used for step-down transformer ($N_s < N_p$).

The symbol of transformer is 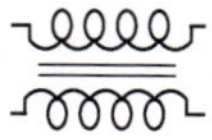.

Difference between Step-up and Step-down Transformer

Step-up transformer	Step-down transformer
It increases voltage and decreases current.	It decreases voltage and increases current.
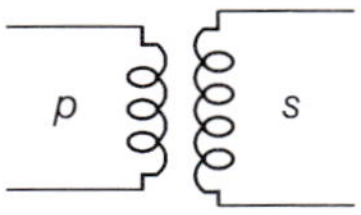	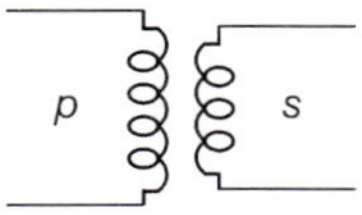
$V_s > V_p$	$V_s < V_p$
$N_s > N_p$	$N_s < N_p$
$i_s < i_p$	$i_s > i_p$
$R_s > R_p$	$R_s < R_p$

Efficiency of Transformer (η)

It is defined as the ratio of output to the input power. It is expressed as,

$$\eta\,(\%) = \frac{P_{\text{out}}}{P_{\text{in}}} \times 100 = \frac{V_s i_s}{V_p i_p} \times 100$$

In practice, η can be achieved from 90% to 99%.

Losses in Transformer

In transformer, some power is always lost due to many reasons, which are given below.

(*i*) **Eddy current loss** Eddy currents in iron core of transformer facilitate the loss of energy in the form of heat. To minimise this loss, transformer cores are laminated and silicon is added to the core material as it increases the resistivity.

(*ii*) **Flux leakage** The leakage of magnetic flux occurs in spite of best insulations.

(*iii*) **Copper loss** Due to heating, energy loss takes place in copper wires of primary and secondary coils. These are minimised using thick wires of low resistance.

(*iv*) **Hysteresis loss** The energy loss takes place in magnetising and demagnetising the iron core over every cycle. Therefore, the core of transformer is made of soft iron.

This loss can be minimised by using a core with a material having the least hysteresis loss.

(*v*) **Humming loss** As the transformer works its core vibrates during each cycle of alternating voltage due to a phenomenon called magnetostriction. This gives rise to humming sound, which is referred as humming loss.

Uses of Transformer

The long distance power transmission takes place at high alternating voltage, so as to minimise losses in the form of heat, therefore step-up transformers are used at power stations and step-down transformers at receiving ends (like radio receivers, telephones, etc).

PYQs Previous Years Questions

1 Mark Questions

1. What is meant by "Motional emf"? **ISC 2023**

2. Give any one reason why efficiency of a transformer is always less than 1. **ISC SQP 2023**

3. Two coils P and S are wound on a common core, their coefficient of mutual inductance does not depend on **ISC 2022 Sem-I**
   (a) number of turns in the coil P
   (b) number of turns in the coil S
   (c) material of the core
   (d) voltage applied to the coil P or Q

4. Why is the core of a transformer laminated? **ISC 2018**

5. A coil has a self-inductance of 0.05 H. Find magnitude of the emf induced in it when the current flowing through it is changing at the rate 100 As^{-1}. **ISC 2016**

6. What is an ideal transformer? **ISC 2016**

7. What is the turns ratio i.e., transformer ratio, $N_s : N_p$, in an ideal transformer which increases AC voltage from 220 V to 33000 V?0 **ISC 2014**

8. An emf of 2V is induced in a coil, when current in it is changed from 0A to 10 A in 0.40s. Find the coefficient of self-inductance of the coil. **ISC 2011**

9. Choose the correct option.

The loss of power in a transformer can be reduced by **ISC 2010**

(a) increasing the number of turns in primary coil.
(b) increasing AC voltage applied to primary coil.
(c) using a solid core made of steel.
(d) using a laminated core of soft iron.

10. The SI unit of coefficient of inductance is henry. Using any defining equation for L or M show that 1 H $=1\,\Omega$-s. **ISC 2007, 03**

11. A rectangular coil of area $50\,\text{cm}^2$ and 100 turns is placed perpendicular to a magnetic field of $10^{-2}\,\text{Wb/m}^2$. If the coil is withdrawn from the field in 40 ms, calculate the emf induced. **ISC 2005**

12. What causes the core of a transformer to get heated up under operation? **ISC 2004**

2 Marks Questions

13. (i) What type of transformer is used in a mobile phone charger?

(ii) Why is the core of a transformer made of soft iron and not of steel? **ISC 2024**

14. When an electric current is passed through a wire or a coil, a magnetic field is produced. Is the reverse phenomenon possible i.e., can a magnetic field produce an electric current? Explain with the help of an appropriate example. **ISC 2023**

15. Explain why a blue coloured spark is often seen in a switch when a circuit containing an electric iron/geyser is switched off. **ISC SQP 2023**

16. Consider a strong bar magent *NS* and a solenoid *AB* as shown in figure below. *G* is a central zero galvanometer. Both the bar magnets and the solenoid are at rest. **ISC 2022 Sem-I**

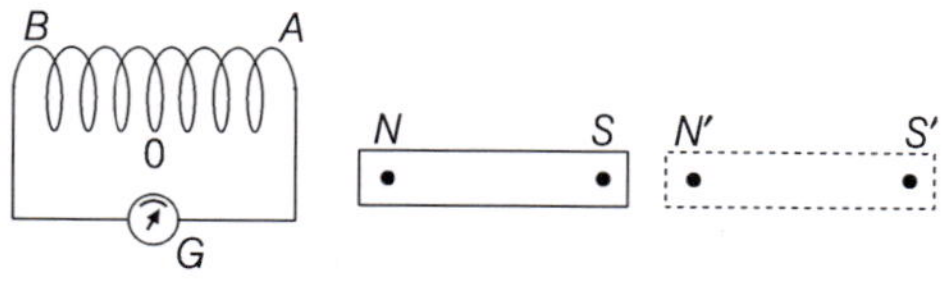

(*i*) The bar magnet is now moved slowly to the new position $N'S'$. The pointer of the galvanometer *G*

(a) remains undeflected at 0 mark
(b) shows a constant deflection
(c) shows a momentary deflection and comes back to zero
(d) vibrates simple harmonically about 0 mark

(*ii*) If the bar magnet be once again taken from its initial position *NS* to the final position $N'S'$ but more rapidly, then the pointer of the galvanometer *G*

(a) remains undeflected at O mark.
(b) shows a constant and greater deflection
(c) shows a momentary and a smaller deflection and comes back to zero
(d) shows a momentary and a greater deflection and comes back to zero

17. A solenoid having self-inductance of 8H is connected to a battery through a switch. When the switch is closed, current through the solenoid increases from 0 A to 5 A in 0.2 s. **ISC 2022 Sem-I**

(*i*) Magnitude of the emf induced in the solenoid is

(a) 2 V (b) 20 V
(c) 200 V (d) 2000 V

(*ii*) If the switch is now opened, magnitude of the emf induced in the solenoid will be

(a) same as in part (i)
(b) more than that in part (i)
(c) less than that in part (i)
(d) zero

18. When current flowing through one coil changes from 0 A to 15 A in 0.2 s, an emf of 750 V is induced in an adjacent coil. Calculate the coefficient of mutual inductance of the two coils. **ISC 2020**

KEY idea

To calculate the mutual inductance. First calculate the current difference then calculate mutual inductance,

$$\left(M = \frac{|\varepsilon|}{\left|\frac{\Delta i}{\Delta t}\right|}\right)$$

19. Figure below shows a metallic rod *MN* of length $l =$ 80 cm, kept in a uniform magnetic field of flux density $B = 0.5$ T, on two parallel metallic rails *P* and *Q*. Calculate the emf that will be induced between its two ends, when it is moved towards right with a constant velocity v of 36 km/h. **ISC 2020**

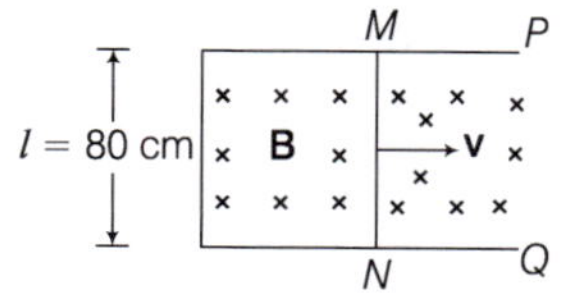

20. A transformer is used to step-up an alternating emf of 200 V to 440 V. If the primary coil has 1000 turns, calculate the number of turns in the secondary coil. **ISC 2019**

21. What is motional emf? State any two factors on which it depends? **ISC 2018**

22. (i) Briefly explain the following term : Self-induction **ISC SQP 2018**

Or

(ii) Name any two types of energy losses in a transformer. State how any one of them can be minimised.

3 Marks Questions

23. When current flowing through a solenoid decreases from 5A to 0 in 20 millisecond, an emf of 500 V is induced in it.

(i) What is this phenomenon called?

(ii) Calculate coefficient of self-inductance of the solenoid. **ISC 2024**

24. With reference to a transformer, choose the correct option. **ISC 2022 Sem-I**

(*i*) The principle of its working is

(a) self-induction
(b) mutual induction
(c) magnetic effect of current
(d) chemical effect of current

(*ii*) In an actual transformer,

(a) output voltage is always equal to the input voltage
(b) output current is always equal to the input current
(c) output power is always equal to the input power
(d) output power is always less than input power

(*iii*) For a step-up transformer,

(a) output voltage is greater than input voltage
(b) output current is greater than input current
(c) output power is greater than input power
(d) number of turns in primary coil is greater than that in secondary coil

25. (*i*) *AB* and *CD* are two parallel conductors kept 1 m apart and connected by a resistance *R* of 6 Ω, as shown in figure below. They are placed in a magnetic field $B = 3 \times 10^{-2}$ T which is perpendicular to the plane of the conductors and directed into the paper. A wire *MN* is placed over *AB* and *CD* and then made to slide with a velocity 2 ms^{-1}. (Neglect the resistance of *AB*, *CD* and *MN*.)

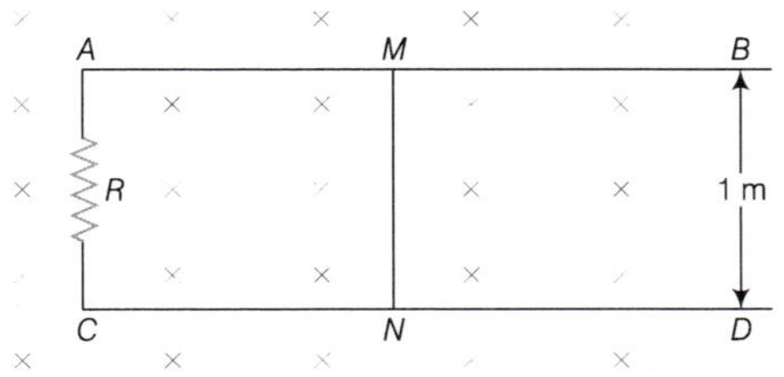

Calculate the induced current flowing through the resistor *R*.

(*ii*) In an ideal transformer, an output of 66 kV is required when an input voltage of 220 V is available. If the primary has 300 turns, how many turns should the secondary have? **ISC 2017**

> **KEY idea**
> To calculate the current, first calculate the emf induced in the coil $\left(e = -\frac{d\phi}{dt}\right)$, then calculate current with the help of $\left(I = \frac{e}{r}\right)$.

26. A metallic rod *CD* rests on a thick metallic wire *PQRS* with arms *PQ* and *RS* parallel to each other, at a distance $l = 40$ cm, as shown in figure. A uniform magnetic field $B = 0.1$ T acts perpendicular to the plane of this paper, pointing inwards (i.e. away from the reader). The rod is now made to slide towards right with a constant velocity of $v = 5.0$ ms^{-1}.

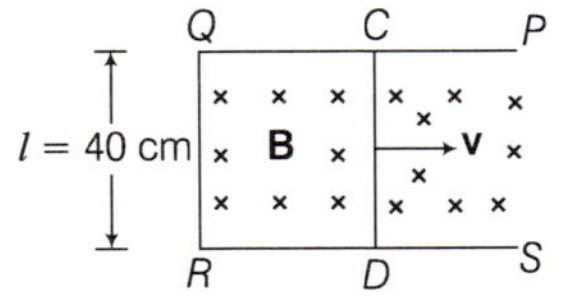

(*i*) How much emf is induced between the two ends of the rod *CD*?

(*ii*) What is the direction in which the induced current flows? **ISC 2013**

27. With the help of a neatly drawn labelled diagram, prove that the magnitude of motional emf *e* is given by $e = Blv$, where *l* is the length of a metallic rod and *v* is the velocity with which it is pulled in a transverse magnetic field *B*. **ISC 2010, 03**

28. (*i*) Mention any two useful applications of eddy currents.

(*ii*) When the current flowing through a coil *P* decreases from 5 A to 0 in 0.2 s, an emf of 60 V is induced across the terminals of an adjacent coil *Q*. Calculate the coefficient of mutual inductance of the two coils *P* and *Q*. **ISC 2009**

29. Define self-inductance. Obtain the expression for the self-inductance of a solenoid, explaining steps with the help of a diagram. **ISC 2000**

5 Marks Questions

30. (*i*) An AC generator generates an emf which is given by $e = 311 \sin(240\pi t)$ V. Calculate: **ISC 2023**

(a) frequency of the emf

(b) rms value of the emf

(*ii*) The primary coil of a transformer has 60 turns, whereas its secondary coil has 3000 turns.

(a) If a 220V AC voltage is applied to the primary coil. How much emf is induced in the secondary coil?

(b) If a current of 5A flows in the primary coil. How much current will flow in a load in the secondary coil? State the assumption you have made regarding the transformer, in this calculation.

31. *PQ* and *MN* are two parallel conductors at a distance l apart and connected by a resistance R as shown in figure. They are placed in a magnetic field B which is perpendicular to the plane of the conductors. A wire *XY* is placed over *PQ* and *MN* and then made to slide over *PQ* and *MN* with a velocity v. Neglecting the resistance of *PQ*, *MN* and wire *XY*, calculate the work done per second to slide the wire *XY*. **ISC 2006**

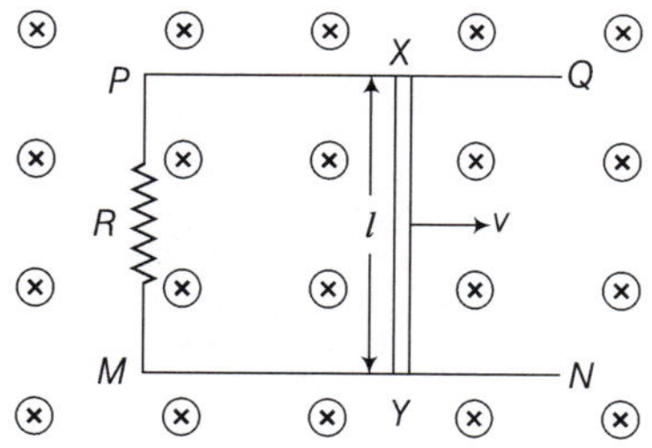

Case Based Question
(For Complete Chapter)

32. Direction *Read the passage given below and answer the questions that follows.*

The teacher of Priti's school took the students on a study trip to a power generating station, located nearly 250 km away from the city. The teacher explained that electrical energy is transmitted over such a long distance to their city, in the form of alternating current (AC) raised to a high voltage. At the receiving end in the city, the voltage is reduced to operate the devices. As a result, the power loss is reduced. Priti listened to the teacher and asked questions about how the AC is converted to a higher or lower voltage. **ISC SQP 2022 [4]**

(i) What is the device used to change the alternating voltage to a higher or lower value?

(a) Transformer (b) Rectifier

(c) Ammeter (d) Voltmeter

(ii) What is the cause for power dissipation in the device referred to above?

(a) Hysteresis

(b) Eddy current

(c) Flux loss

(d) All of the above

(iii) In the device used above, what is the relation between the power output and power input for an ideal case?

(a) Power output is less than power input

(b) Power output is greater than power input

(c) Power output is equal to power input

(d) It depends upon the situation

(iv) What source input should be used in this device?

(a) AC source

(b) DC source

(c) Half-wave rectifier

(d) Full wave rectifier

Explanations

1. Refer to text on page no.125 (Motional EMF).

2. Practically there are numerous factors leading to energy loss in a transformer and hence, the efficiency is always less than one.

3. (d) Voltage applied to the coil P or Q

4. The alternating magnetic flux induces eddy currents in iron core of transformer and because of this, the loss of energy takes place in the form of heat. To minimise this loss, transformer cores are laminated.

5. Given, self-inductance, $L = 0.05\text{ H}$

Rate of change of current, $\frac{di}{dt} = 100\text{ As}^{-1}$

Magnitude of induced emf will be given as

$$e = \left|-L \times \frac{di}{dt}\right| = 0.05 \times 100$$

$$\Rightarrow \quad e = 5\text{ V}$$

6. An ideal transformer is an imaginary transformer which has no copper losses (no winding resistance), no iron loss in core and no leakage flux. In other words, an ideal transformer gives output power exactly equal to the input power.

7. Transformer ratio, K

$$= \frac{\text{Number of turns in secondary coil } (N_s)}{\text{Number of turns in primary coil } (N_p)}$$

$$\Rightarrow \frac{N_s}{N_p} = \frac{V_s}{V_p} = \frac{33000\text{ V}}{220\text{ V}} = 150$$

where, V_s is voltage in secondary coil and V_p is voltage in primary coil.

8. Given, $e = 2\text{ V}$ and change in current, $\frac{di}{dt} = \frac{10}{0.4}$

$\therefore$ Coefficient of self-inductance of coil is given by

$$L = e \times \frac{dt}{di} \Rightarrow L = 2 \times \frac{0.4}{10} = \frac{0.8}{10} = 0.08\text{H}$$

9. (*d*) The loss of power in a transformer can be reduced by using a laminated core of soft iron.

Thus, option (d) is correct.

10. We know that,

$$|\varepsilon| = \frac{-\Delta\phi}{\Delta t} = -M\frac{\Delta i}{\Delta t} = -M\frac{di}{dt}$$

where, $|\varepsilon|$ = magnitude of induced emf

$\Delta\phi$ = change in magnetic flux

Δt = duration of change in flux

M = coefficient of mutual inductance

$$\text{So, } M = \frac{|\varepsilon|}{\frac{di}{dt}} \Rightarrow 1\text{ henry} = \frac{\text{volt}}{\left(\frac{\text{ampere}}{\text{second}}\right)} = 1\,\Omega\text{-s}$$

[by writting units]

[taking all the values as unity]

$$\left[\because \text{ohm} = \frac{\text{volt}}{\text{ampere}}\right]$$

11. When the coil is withdrawn from the magnetic field, flux linked with the coil reduces to zero. The magnetic flux through each turn of a coil of area A placed perpendicular to a magnetic field B is, $\phi_B = BA$

When the coil is withdrawn from the field, the flux with it becomes zero. So, the change in flux is,

$$\Delta\phi_B = 0 - \phi_B = -\phi_B = -BA$$
$$= -(10^{-2} \times 50 \times 10^{-4})$$
$$= -5 \times 10^{-5}\text{ Wb}$$

Time interval for the change of flux,

$$\Delta t = 40\text{ ms} = 40 \times 10^{-3}\text{ s}$$

By Faraday's law, the emf induced in the coil is,

$$\varepsilon = -N\frac{\Delta\phi_B}{\Delta t} = -100 \times \frac{(-5 \times 10^{-5})}{40 \times 10^{-3}} = 0.125\text{ V}$$

12. When a metallic wire moves in a uniform magnetic field, due to change in magnetic flux of the wire, emf is induced between two ends of the wire.

The core of a transformer gets heated up due to eddy current and copper losses.

13. (i) Mobile phone charger contain a step-down transformer to convert the input of 220 V to a working output voltage of around 5 V. Since, it works on the simple principle of conversion of AC (alternating current) to DC (direct current).

(ii) Soft iron loses all its magnetic properties when the current in the coil is switched OFF, whereas steel does not loss its magnetic properties when the current is stopped. Soft iron has high coercivity and low retentivity.

14. If the magnetic flux linked with a coil changes with time, then induced current is produced in the coil. For example, AC generators and electrical transformers work on the principle of electromagnetic induction.

15. While switching off, the terminals come close to each other. It produces very high induced emf. Due to this high emf, charges move from one end to the other end of the switch. This spark appears blue.

16. (*i*) (c) Shows a momentary deflection and comes back to zero.

(*ii*) (d) Shows a momentary and a greater deflection and comes back to zero.

17. Given, $L = 8$ H, $\Delta I = 5 - 0 = 5$ A, $\Delta t = 0.2$ s

(*i*) (c) Magnitude of induced emf $(e) = \left| -L \cdot \dfrac{\Delta I}{\Delta t} \right|$

$$= 8 \times \frac{5}{0.2} = 200 \text{ V}$$

(*ii*) (b) As $e \propto \dfrac{1}{\Delta t}$

$$\frac{e_0}{e_c} = \frac{\Delta t_c}{\Delta t_0} > 1 \Rightarrow e_0 > e_c$$

18. As we know that, $|\varepsilon| = \left| \dfrac{d\phi}{dt} \right| = M \left| \dfrac{\Delta i}{\Delta t} \right|$

$$\Rightarrow \quad M = -\frac{|\varepsilon|}{\left| \dfrac{\Delta i}{\Delta t} \right|}$$

According to the question, $|\varepsilon| = 750$ V

$\Delta i = 0 - 15 = -15$ A

and $\Delta t = 0.2$ s

So, $M = \dfrac{750}{15/02} = \dfrac{750 \times 0.2}{15} = 10$ H

19. We know that, motional emf associated with a moving rod in a magnetic field is $\varepsilon = vBl$

Given, length of the rod, $l = 80$ cm $= 0.8$ m

Velocity, $v = 36$ km/h $= 10$ m/s and magnetic field, $B = 0.5$ T

$\Rightarrow \varepsilon = 10 \times 0.5 \times 0.8 = 4$ V

20. Given, $N_P = 1000, V_P = 200$ V, $V_S = 440$ V

We have, $\dfrac{V_S}{V_P} = \dfrac{N_S}{N_P} \Rightarrow \dfrac{440}{200} = \dfrac{N_S}{1000}$

$$N_S = \frac{440 \times 1000}{200}$$

$$\Rightarrow \quad N_S = 2200$$

21. When a conducting rod is moved through constant magnetic field, then emf is generated by a conducting rod. This emf is called motional electromotive force, because it arises due to motion of charges through a magnetic field. The expression for motional emf is given by $e = Bvl$. Therefore, the motional emf depends upon the magnetic field, speed and length of a conductor.

22. (i) Self-induction is the property of a coil by virtue of which, the coil opposes any change in the current flowing through it by inducing an emf in itself. It is also called inertia of electricity due to this property.

Or

(ii) **Iron loss** It is the energy loss in the form of heat in the iron core of the transformer. This occurs because of the presence of eddy current in iron core.

Hysteresis loss This is the loss of energy due to repeated magnetisation and demagnetisation of the iron core when AC is fed to it. The loss can be minimised by using a magnetic material which has low hysteresis loss.

23. (i) Self-inductance of long solenoid.

(ii) Given, $\Delta I = -5$ A, $\Delta t = 20 \times 10^{-3}$ s

$e = 500$ V, $L = ?$

$\therefore$ Induced emf, $e = -L \dfrac{\Delta I}{\Delta t}$

$$\Rightarrow \quad 500 = -L\left(\frac{-5}{20 \times 10^{-3}}\right) \Rightarrow L = 2 \text{ H}$$

24. (*i*) (b) Mutual induction

(*ii*) (d) Output power is always less than input power

(*iii*) (a) Output voltage is greater than input voltage

25. (*i*) Given, $B = 3 \times 10^{-2}$ T

$MN = BD = 1$ m (according to the figure)

$v = 2 \text{ ms}^{-1}$

The emf induced in the coil, $e = -\dfrac{d\phi}{dt}$

$$e = -\frac{d(BA)}{dt}$$

A = area of the loop $= l \times x$

$$e = -\frac{d(Bl \times x)}{dt} = -Bl\frac{dx}{dt} = -Blv$$

$$= -3 \times 10^{-2} \times 1 \times 2 = -6 \times 10^{-2} \text{ V}$$

Current, $I = \frac{e}{R} = \frac{6 \times 10^{-2}}{6} = 10^{-2} = 0.01\ \text{A}$

(*ii*) According to the question,

$N_P = 300$ turns (turns of primory)

$N_S = ?$ (turns of secondary)

$V_S > V_P$ because $V_S = 66\ \text{kV}$

$V_P = 220\ \text{V}$

Hence, $\frac{V_S}{V_P} = \frac{N_S}{N_P} \Rightarrow \frac{66 \times 1000}{220} = \frac{N_S}{300}$

$$\Rightarrow \quad N_S = \frac{66 \times 1000 \times 300}{220}$$

$$= 9 \times 10^4 \text{ turns} = 90000 \text{ turns}$$

26. (*i*) We know that motional emf associated with a moving rod in a magnetic field is

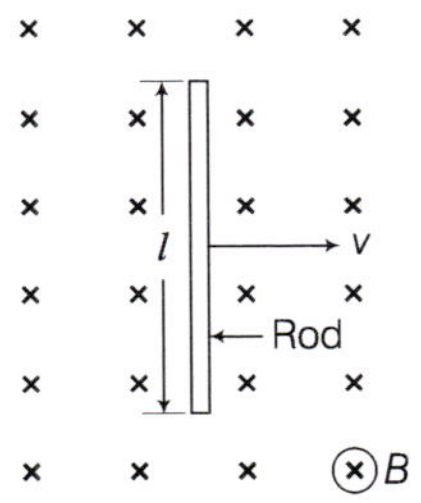

$$\varepsilon = vBl$$

where, ε = emf induced

v = speed of the rod

l = length of the rod.

Given, $v = 5\ \text{m/s}$, $l = 40\ \text{cm}$, $B = 0.1\ \text{T}$

$$\Rightarrow \quad \varepsilon = vBl = 5 \times 0.1 \times 0.4 = 0.2\ \text{V}$$

(*ii*)

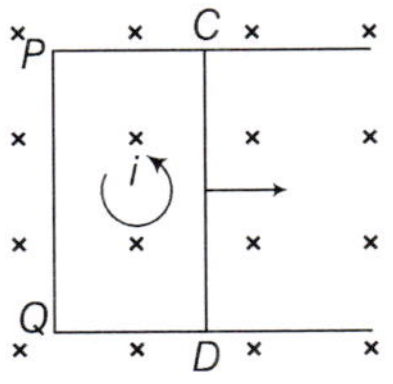

According to Lenz's law, the direction of induced current is from D to C or anti-clockwise.

27. To calculate the induced emf, the rate of change of flux needs to be calculated first. Here magnetic field is uniform, so change in flux takes place due to change in area swept by loop. By calculating the rate of change of area, we can calculate the rate of change of flux, i.e. induced emf.

Let the lengths of horizontal arms of circuit be x_1 and x_2 at instants, t_1 and t_2, respectively.

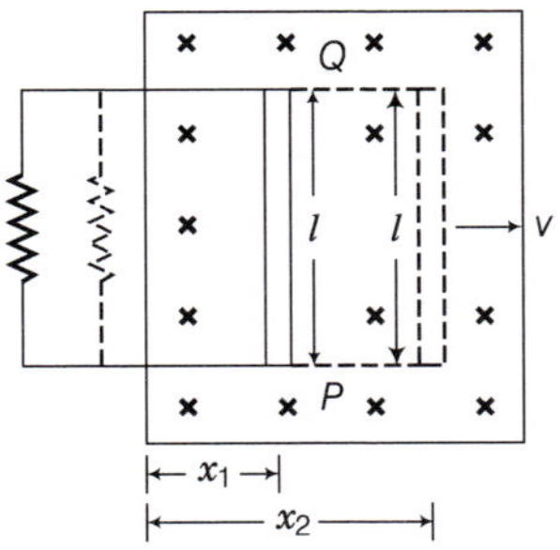

$\therefore$ Area of loop inside the magnetic field,

$$A_1 = lx_1,\ A_2 = lx_2$$

$$\therefore \quad \Delta A = A_2 - A_1 = l(x_2 - x_1) = l\Delta x$$

$$\Delta\phi = B\Delta A = Bl\Delta x$$

$$\therefore \quad \frac{\Delta\phi}{\Delta t} = Bl\frac{\Delta x}{\Delta t} = Blv$$

By Faraday's law, induced emf,

$$e = \frac{\Delta\phi}{\Delta t} = vBl$$

28. (*i*) Refer to text on page no 125. (Eddy Current)

(*ii*) We know that, $|\varepsilon| = \frac{d\phi}{dt} = M\frac{\Delta i}{\Delta t}$

where, M = coefficient of mutual inductance

Δi = change in current

Δt = duration of change of current

$$\Rightarrow \quad M = \frac{|\varepsilon|}{\frac{\Delta i}{\Delta t}}$$

According to the question, $|\varepsilon| = 60\ \text{V}$

$\Delta I = 5 - 0 = 5\ \text{A} \quad \Delta t = 0.2\ \text{s}$

So, $M = \frac{60}{5/0.2} = \frac{60 \times 2}{5 \times 10} = 2.4\ \text{H}$

29. Self-inductance of a solenoid is associated with the geometry of the coil.

Self- inductance of a coil is equal to the total magnetic flux linked with the coil, when unit current passes through it.

Self-inductance of a coil is equal to the emf induced in coil, when rate of change of current in the coil is 1 A/s.

The SI unit of self-inductance is henry (H).

$$1\ \text{H} = 1\ \text{V-s/A}$$

Let the radius and length of air cored solenoid be r and l, respectively such that $r << l$ and having n turns per unit length.

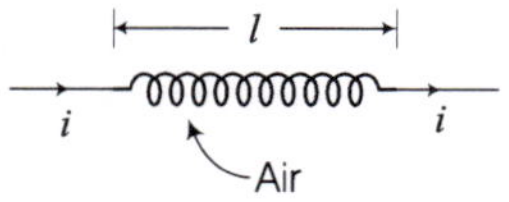

$\therefore \quad n = \dfrac{N}{l}$ ...(i)

where, N = total number of turns.

If i current flows through the coil, then magnetic field is given by

$$B = \mu_0 ni$$

where, n = number of turns per unit length.

$\therefore$ Magnetic flux linked with each turn,

$$\phi = BA = \mu_0 niA$$

$\therefore$ Total magnetic flux linked with the solenoid,

$$N\phi = (\mu_0 niA)N$$

But $\quad N\phi = Li$

where, L is the coefficient of self-induction.

$$\mu_0 niAN = Li$$

$$\Rightarrow \quad L = \mu_0 nAN$$

$$= \mu_0 \left(\frac{N}{l}\right) AN = \frac{\mu_0 AN^2}{l}$$

This is the required expression.

Concept Enhancer The coefficient of self-inductance of a coil numerically equal to the emf induced in the coil when the rate of current in the coil is unity.

30. (*i*) The equation for the emf generated by the AC generator is $e = 311 \sin (240\pi t)$ V.

(a) The frequency of the emf is given by the formula

$$f = \frac{\omega}{2\pi}$$

where, ω is the angular frequency, which is equal to 240π radians per second.

Therefore, the frequency is

$$f = \frac{240\pi}{2\pi} = 120 \text{ Hz}$$

So, the frequency of the emf is 120 Hz.

(b) The rms value of the emf is given by the formula

$$E_{\text{rms}} = \frac{1}{\sqrt{2}} E_m$$

where, E_m is the maximum value of the emf, which is equal to 311 V.

Therefore, the r.m.s value is

$$E_{\text{rms}} = \frac{1}{\sqrt{2}} \times 311 \text{ V}$$

$$= 220 \text{ V}$$

(*ii*) Given, the primary coil of a transformer has 60 turns and the secondary coil has 3000 turns.

(a) The transformer equation is

$$\frac{V_P}{V_S} = \frac{N_P}{N_S}$$

where, V_P and V are the voltage in the primary and secondary coils respectively, and N_P and N_S are the number of turns in the primary and secondary coils, respectively.

If a 220 V AC voltage is applied to the primary coil, then the voltage induced in the secondary coil is,

$$\frac{V_P}{V_S} = \frac{N_P}{N_S}$$

$$\frac{220}{V_S} = \frac{60}{3000}$$

$$\Rightarrow \quad V_S = 110000 \text{ V}$$

Therefore, the emf induced in the secondary coil is 110 kV.

(b) According to the transformer equation, the current in the secondary coil is

$$\frac{I_P}{I_S} = \frac{N_S}{N_P}$$

where, I_P and I_S are the current in the primary and secondary coils, respectively and N_P and N_S are the number of turns in the primary and secondary coil, respectively.

Assuming an ideal transformer, which means that there is no energy loss in the transformer, we can say that the power in the primary coil is equal to the power in the secondary coil. Thus, we use the formula

$$I_p V_p = I_s V_s$$

where, I_P and V_P are the current and voltage in the primary coil and I_S and V_S are the current and voltage in the secondary coil.

Substituting the values, we get

$$5 \text{ A} \times 220 \text{ V} = I_S \times 110000 \text{ V}$$

$$I_S = 1 \times 10^{-2} \text{ A}$$

Therefore, the current flowing in the load in the secondary coil is 1×10^{-2} A.

31. When a wire slides in a magnetic field on two conducting wires, an emf is induced in the wire and current flows through the wire, hence a force acts which is opposite to the motion of the wire.

According to the question, we have figure as shown below

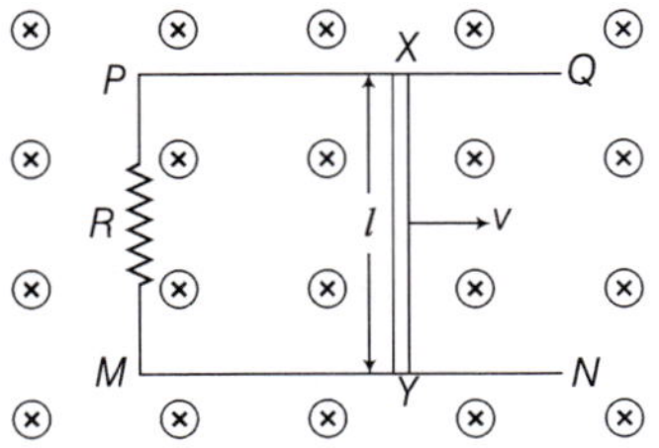

For induced emf refer to solution 10 on Page 131.

By Faraday's law of induced emf,

$$\varepsilon = vBl$$

If resistance of loop is R, then

$$i = \frac{vBl}{R}$$

$\therefore$ Magnetic force $= iBl \sin 90°$

$$= \left(\frac{vBl}{R}\right) Bl = \frac{vB^2l^2}{R}$$

$\therefore$ External force must be equal to magnetic force and in opposite directions.

$\therefore$ External force $= \dfrac{vB^2l^2}{R}$

Now, if under the influence of external force, the rod XY undergoes displacement Δx in the direction of the force in time interval Δt. Then, the work done on the rod will be given by,

$$W = \text{External force} \times \Delta x$$

$$= \frac{vB^2l^2}{R} \cdot \Delta x$$

As, $\Delta x = v \times \Delta t$

$$\Rightarrow \quad = \frac{v^2B^2l^2}{R} \Delta t$$

So, work done per second to slide the wire XY is $\dfrac{v^2B^2l^2}{R}$

32. (*i*) (a)

(*ii*) (d)

(*iii*) (c)

(*iv*) (a)

CHAPTER TEST

01 Mark Questions (MCQs)

1 In a uniform magnetic field of induction B, a wire in the form of semi-circle of radius r rotates about the diameter of the circle with ω. If the total resistance of the circuit is R, then the mean power generated per period of rotation is

(a) $\frac{B\pi r^2\omega}{2R}$ (b) $\frac{(B\pi r^2\omega)^2}{8R}$

(c) $\frac{(B\pi r\omega)^2}{2R}$ (d) $\frac{(B\pi r\omega^2)^2}{8R}$

2 For rails with electromagnets, when electromagnets are activated, ...A... in the rails ...B... the motion of the train. Here, A and B refer to

(a) eddy currents induced, oppose
(b) eddy currents induced, support
(c) springs, cause increase in speed of
(d) springs, increase

3 A current passing through a coil of self-inductance of 2 mH changes at the rate of 20 mAs^{-1}. The emf induced in the coil is

(a) 10 μV (b) 40 μV (c) 10 mV (d) 40 mV

01 Mark Questions (VSA)

4 A closed loop ($PQRS$) of wires is moved into a uniform magnetic field towards right on the plane of the paper as shown in the figure. Predict the direction of the induced current in the loop.

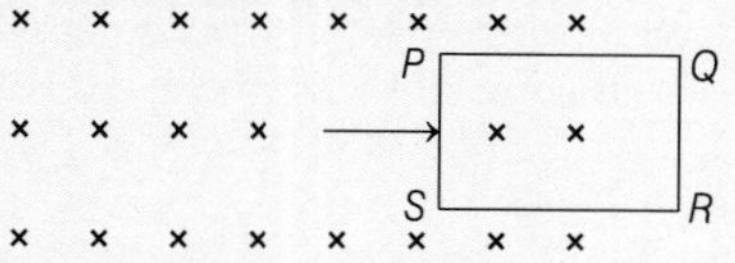

5 Predict the direction of induced current in metal rings 1 and 2, when current I in the wire is steadily decreasing.

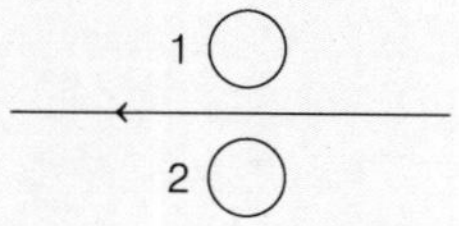

02 Marks Questions

6 Why is the core of a transformer laminated?

7 A current is induced in coil C_1 due to the motion of current carrying coil C_2.

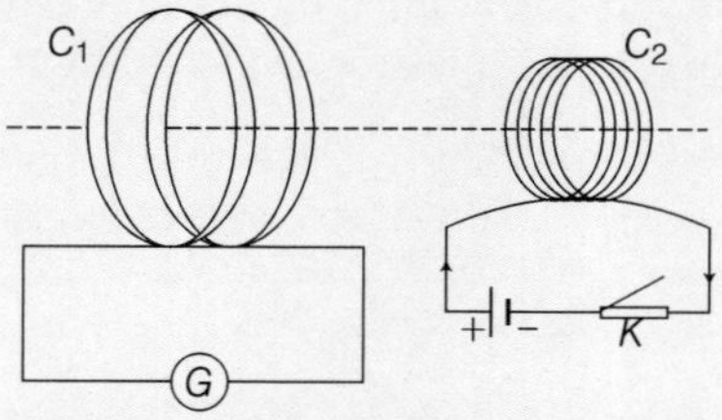

(i) Write any two ways by which a large deflection can be obtained in the galvanometer G.

(ii) Suggest an alternative device to demonstrate the induced current in place of a galvanometer.

03 Marks Questions

8. The figure given below shows an arrangement by which current flows through the bulb X connected with coil B, when AC is passed through coil A.

(i) Name the phenomenon involved.

(ii) If a copper sheet is inserted in the gap between the coils, explain how the brightness of the bulb would change?

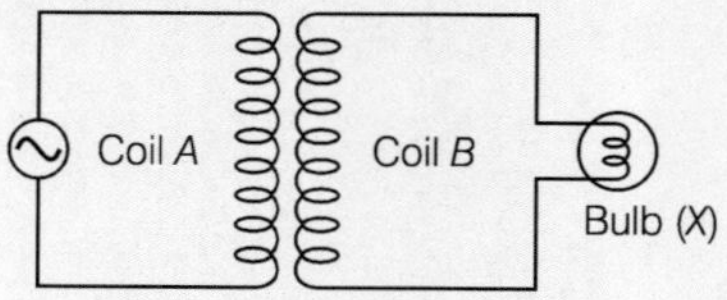

9. State the law that gives the polarity of the induced emf. Give its illustration.

05 Marks Questions

10. State Lenz's law. Give one example to illustrate this law. Lenz's law is a consequence of principle of energy conservation. Justify this statement.

11. How is the mutual inductance of a pair of coils affected, when

(i) separation between the coils is increased?

(ii) the number of turns of each coil is increased?

(iii) a thin iron sheet is placed between the two coils, other factors remaining the same? Explain your answer in each case.

Answers

1. (b) **2.** (a) **3.** (b)

4. Clockwise

5. Ring-1 clockwise, ring-2 anti-clockwise

11

Alternating Current Circuits

TREND ANALYSIS 4 YEARS

Average No. of Questions Across all Sets

Topic	Types of Questions	2024	2023	2020	2019
TOPIC 01 Introduction of Alternating Current	1 Mark	–	–	–	–
	2 Marks	1	1	–	1
	3 Marks	–	–	–	–
	5 Marks	–	–	–	–
TOPIC 02 Basic AC Circuits (*R*, *L* and *C* Circuits)	1 Mark	–	–	–	–
	2 Marks	–	–	–	–
	3 Marks	–	–	–	–
	5 Marks	–	–	–	–
TOPIC 03 *L-C-R*, *R-L* and *R-C* Series Circuits	1 Mark	–	–	–	1
	2 Marks	–	–	–	1
	3 Marks	–	–	–	–
	5 Marks	1	–	2	1

TOPIC 1

Introduction of Alternating Current

Alternating Voltage and Current

An alternating current or voltage is one whose magnitude changes continuously with time between zero and a maximum value and whose sense of flow reverses periodically.

When a battery is connected to a circuit, the current moves steadily in only one direction, from positive terminal to negative terminal. This is called a **direct current** or DC.

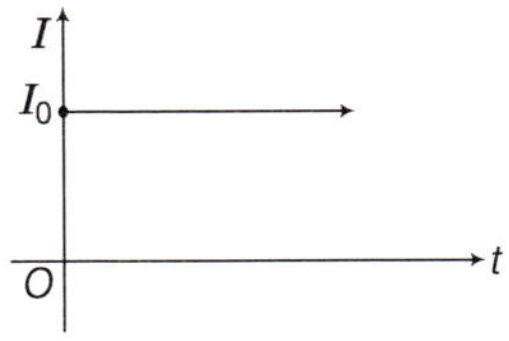

Direct current

An alternating current varies sinusoidally. Electric generator and power plants produce **alternating current** or AC.

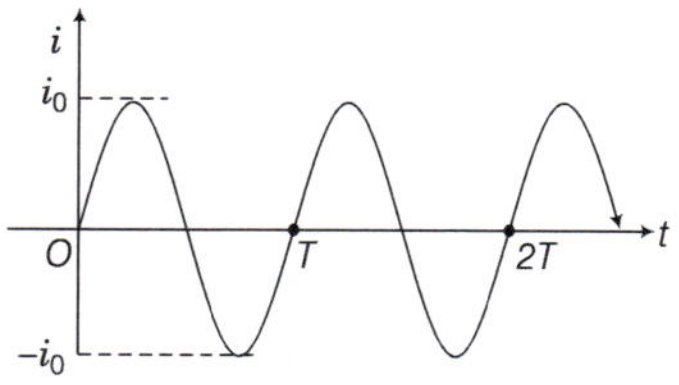

Alternating current

Comparison of AC with DC
(Basic Differences between AC and DC)

Alternating current	Direct current
Safe to transfer over longer distances and can provide more power.	Voltage of DC cannot travel very far until it begins to lose energy.
The frequency of alternating current is 50 Hz or 60 Hz depending upon the country.	The frequency of direct current is zero.
It reverses its direction while flowing in a circuit.	It flows in one direction in the circuit.
It is the current of magnitude varying with time.	It is the current of constant magnitude.
Obtained from AC generator, through mains.	Obtained from cell or battery.

EMF and Current Equations

Alternating current or voltage varying as sine function can be represented as

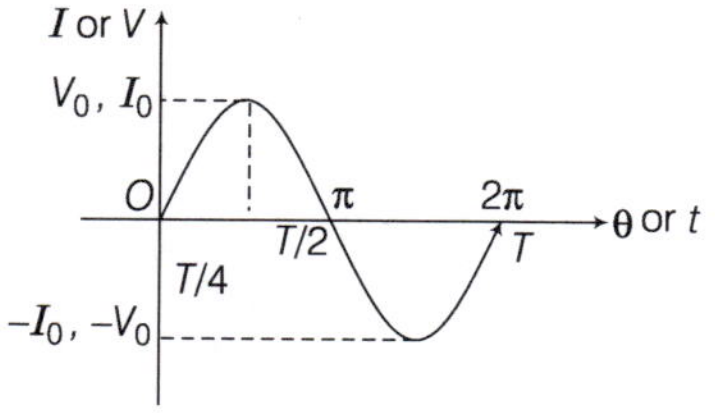

$$i = i_0 \sin \omega t = i_0 \sin 2\pi f t \qquad (\omega = 2\pi f)$$
$$= i_0 \sin \frac{2\pi}{T} t \qquad \left(\omega = \frac{2\pi}{T}\right)$$

Similarly, $V = V_0 \sin \omega t = V_0 \sin 2\pi f t = V_0 \sin \frac{2\pi}{T} t$

where, i and V = instantaneous values of current and voltage respectively,

i_0 and V_0 = peak (maximum) values of current and voltage respectively,

f = frequency in hertz $= \frac{1}{T} = \frac{\omega}{2\pi}$

- Time taken to complete one cycle of variations is called **time period** $(T) = \frac{2\pi}{\omega}$.

T = time period, ω = angular velocity in rad/s $= \frac{2\pi}{T} = 2\pi f$

and t = time at any instant

- i or V reaches to the maximum values at $t = T/4$ sec.

Peak Value (i_0 or V_0)

The maximum value of alternating quantity (i or V) is called its peak value or amplitude.

Mean Square Value (V^2) or $\langle i^2 \rangle$

The average square of instantaneous values in one cycle is called mean square value. It is always positive for one complete cycle.

e.g. $$\langle V^2 \rangle = \frac{1}{T}\int_0^T V^2 dt = \frac{V_0^2}{2} \text{ or } \langle i^2 \rangle = \frac{i_0^2}{2}$$

Root Mean Square (rms) **Value of AC**

It is defined as the value of AC over a complete cycle which would generate same amount of heat in a given resistor that is generated by a steady current in the same resistor and in the same time during a complete cycle.

$$i_{rms} = \sqrt{\frac{i_1^2 + i_2^2 + \cdots + i_n^2}{n}} = \sqrt{\langle i^2 \rangle}$$
$$= \sqrt{\frac{\int_0^T i^2 dt}{\int_0^T dt}} = \frac{i_0}{\sqrt{2}} = 0.707\, i_0$$

Similarly, $$V_{rms} = \frac{V_0}{\sqrt{2}} = 0.707 V_0 = 70.7\% \text{ of } V_0$$

- The rms value of alternating current is also called **virtual value** or **effective value**.

Mean or Average Value (i_{av} or V_{av})

The average value of alternating quantity for one complete cycle is zero, because positive half and negative half cycles cancel each other.

So, we consider average value of AC over half cycle ($t = 0$ to $T/2$).

i.e. $$i_{av} = \frac{\int_0^{T/2} i dt}{\int_0^{T/2} dt} = \frac{2i_0}{\pi} = 0.637 i_0 = 63.7\% \text{ of } i_0$$

Similarly, $$V_{av} = \frac{2V_0}{\pi} = 0.637 V_0 = 63.7\% \text{ of } V_0$$

PYQs Previous Years Questions

1 Mark Questions

1. Figure below shows emf e generated by an AC generator *versus* time t.

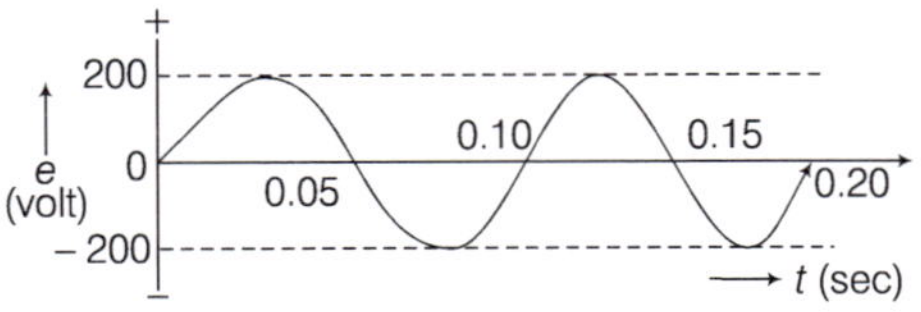

What is the frequency of emf? **ISC 2022 (Sem-I), 10**

2. The graph below shows how emf e generated by an AC generator varies with time t. **ISC 2022 Sem-I**

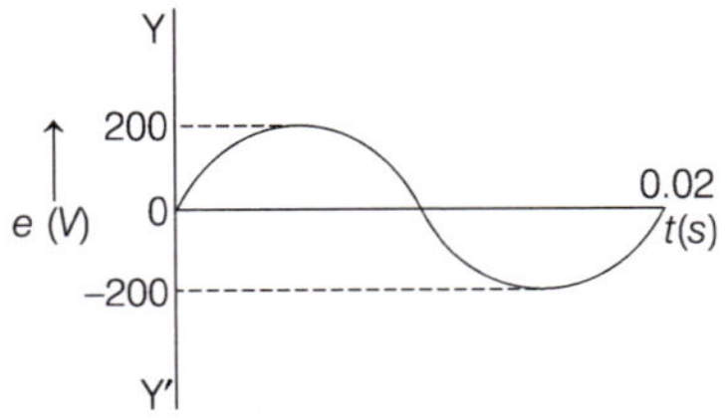

Mean value of the emf for the whole cycle is

(a) zero (b) $(400/\pi)$ V

(c) $(200\sqrt{2})$ V (d) $(200/\sqrt{2})$ V

3. An AC generator generates an emf ε, where $\varepsilon = 314\sin(50\pi t)$ volt. Calculate the frequency of the emf ε. **ISC 2017**

4. An AC generator generates an emf ε given by $\varepsilon = 311\sin(100\pi t)$ volt. Then, find the rms value of the emf generated by the generator. **ISC 2009**

5. The electric main in a house is marked 220 V, 50 Hz. Write down the equation for the instantaneous voltage. The only variable in the equation should be t. **ISC 2005**

2 Marks Questions

6. (*i*) RMS value of an alternating current flowing in a circuit is 5A. Calculate its peak value.

(*ii*) State any one difference between a direct current (DC) and an alternating current. **ISC 2024**

7. An AC generator generates an emf, which is given by $e = 311\sin(240\pi t)$ V. Calculate **ISC 2023**

(*i*) frequency of the emf (*ii*) rms value of the emf

8. An AC source of emf $E = 200\sin\omega t$ is connected to a resistor of 50 Ω. Calculate **ISC 2019**

(*i*) average current (I_{av}) and

(*ii*) root mean square (rms) value of emf.

5 Marks Questions

9. A school organised an educational tour to two places. First one was to a thermal power station and the second one was to a factory manufacturing dry cells. The engineer at the power station explained to the students, how electric power is generated at the power station and how it is transmitted to the city. The manager at the factory took them around the factory and explained to them the importance of dry cells in our daily life. **ISC 2022 Sem-I**

(*i*) Voltages generated by the power station and the dry cell are

(a) DC voltage and AC voltage respectively

(b) AC voltage and DC voltage respectively

(c) Both AC voltages

(d) Neither AC voltages nor DC voltages

(*ii*) AC voltage generated all over the world has a frequency of about

(a) 50 Hz (b) 500 Hz

(c) 1000 Hz (d) 1500 Hz

(*iii*) Which one of the following statements is true?

(a) DC voltage can be stepped up or down.

(b) AC voltage can be stepped up or down.

(c) Both DC and AC voltages can be stepped up or down.

(d) Neither AC nor DC voltage can be stepped up or down.

(*iv*) Refer to graphs G_1 and G_2 shown below and choose the correct option.

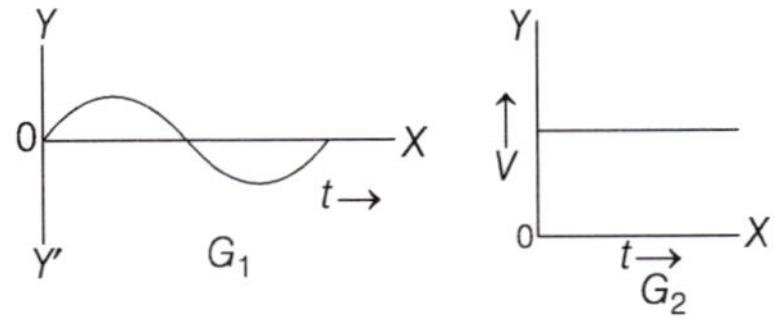

(a) Both represent AC voltage

(b) Both represent DC voltage

(c) G_1 represents AC voltage

(d) G_1 represents DC voltage

10. An AC generator generating an emf E given by $E = 311\sin(10t)$ is connected to a 44 Ω resistor. Calculate

(a) rms value of AC flowing through the resistor

(b) frequency of the current

(c) mean value of emf generated by the generator in time interval 0.06s to 0.08s **ISC SQP 2018**

Explanations

1. From the graph,

Time period $T = 0.10$ s

Frequency, $f = \frac{1}{T} = \frac{1}{0.10} = 10$ Hz

2. (a) $V = V_o \sin \omega t = 200 \sin \omega t$

Mean value of emf for complete cycle ($t = 0$ to T),

$$V_{av} = \frac{\int_0^T V dt}{\int_0^T dt} = \frac{\int_0^T 200 \sin \omega t \, dt}{T}$$

$$= \frac{1}{T} \times 200 \int_0^T \sin \omega t \, dt = \frac{200}{T}\left[\frac{-\cos \omega t}{\omega}\right]_0^T$$

$$= \frac{200}{\omega T}[\cos 0 - \cos \omega T]$$

$$= \frac{200}{2\pi}[1 - \cos 2\pi] = \frac{200}{2\pi}[1 - 1] = 0$$

3. According to the question,

$$\varepsilon = 314 \sin(50\pi t) \text{V}$$

On comparing with,

$$\varepsilon = \varepsilon_0 \sin \omega t$$

Here, ω = angular frequency $= 50\pi$

so, $\omega = 2\pi f$

$\Rightarrow \quad f = \frac{2\pi}{\omega} = \frac{2\pi}{50\pi} = \frac{1}{25} = 0.04$

4. According to the question,

Given, $\varepsilon = 311 \sin(100\pi t)$ volt

On comparing with $\varepsilon = \varepsilon_0 \sin \omega t$

Peak emf, $\varepsilon_0 = 311$ V

So, $\varepsilon_{rms} = \frac{\varepsilon_0}{\sqrt{2}} = \frac{311}{\sqrt{2}} = 219.9 \text{ V} \approx 220 \text{ V}$

5. Given, $V_{rms} = 220$ V, $f = 50$ Hz

The equation of an alternating voltage can be written as

$$V = V_0 \sin \omega t$$

where, V_0 = peak voltage

$$= \sqrt{2} V_{rms} = \sqrt{2} \times 220 = 311 \text{V} \quad \left(V_{rms} = \frac{V_0}{\sqrt{2}}\right)$$

$\therefore \quad V = 311 \sin 2\pi \times 50t \quad [\because \omega = 2\pi f]$

$\Rightarrow \quad V = 311 \sin 100 \pi t$

6. (i) Peak value of current, $I_0 = \sqrt{2} I_{rms}$

$\Rightarrow \quad \sqrt{2} = 5 = 7.07$ A

(ii) Alternating current (AC) is the current of magnitude varying with time and direct current (DC) is the current of constant magnitude.

7. $E = 311 \sin(240\pi t)$ V

(*i*) $\omega t = 240\pi t$

$2\pi f = 240\pi$

$f = 120$ Hz

(*ii*) $E_{rms} = 0.707 \times 311 = 219.87$ V

8. Emf of AC source, $E = 200 \sin \omega t$

$R = 50\Omega$

$E_0 = 200$ V

(*i*) Peak current, $I_0 = \frac{E_0}{R} = \frac{200}{50} = 4$A

Average current, $I_{av} = 0.637 I_0$

$= 0.637 \times 4 = 2.55$A

(*ii*) rms value of emf, $E_{rms} = \frac{E_0}{\sqrt{2}} = \frac{200}{\sqrt{2}} = 141.42$V

9. (i) (b) (ii) (a) (iii) (b) (iv) (c)

10. Given, $E_0 = 311$ V, $R = 44\,\Omega$, $\omega = 10$

(a) $E_{rms} = \frac{E_0}{\sqrt{2}} = \frac{311}{\sqrt{2}} = \frac{311}{1.41} = 220$ V

$I_{rms} = \frac{E_{rms}}{R} = \frac{220}{44} = 5$ A

(b) $\omega = 2\pi\nu$

$\Rightarrow \quad 2\pi\nu = 10$

$\nu = \frac{10}{2\pi} = \frac{10 \times 7}{2 \times 22} = 1.59$ Hz

(c) $T = \frac{2\pi}{\omega} = \frac{2 \times 3.14}{10} = \frac{6.28}{10} = 0.628$

$$E_{avg} = \frac{1}{T}\int_{t_1}^{t_2} E(t) dt = \frac{1}{T}\int_{t_1}^{t_2} 311 \sin(10t)\, dt$$

$$= \frac{1}{0.628}\int_{0.06}^{0.08} 311 \sin(10t)\, dt$$

$$= -\frac{311}{0.628 \times 10}[\cos \omega t_2 - \cos \omega t_1]$$

$$= -\frac{311}{6.28}[\cos 10 \times 0.08 - \cos 10 \times 0.06]$$

$$= 49.5[0.696 - 0.825] = 6.38 \text{ V}$$

TOPIC 2

Basic AC Circuits (R, L and C Circuits)

Phase A physical quantity which represents both the instantaneous value and direction of alternating quantity at any instant is called its phase. It is a dimensionless quantity and its unit is radian.

Phasor A quantity which varies sinusoidally with time and represented as projection of a rotating vector is called a phasor.

Phasor Diagram A diagram representing alternating current and alternating voltage (of same frequency) as rotating vectors (phasors) with the phase angle between them is called as phasor diagram.

If an alternating quantity is expressed as $X = X_0 \sin(\omega t \pm \phi_0)$, then the argument of $\sin(\omega t \pm \phi_0)$ is called its phase.

where, ωt = instantaneous phase (change with time)

and ϕ_0 = initial phase (constant w.r.t. time).

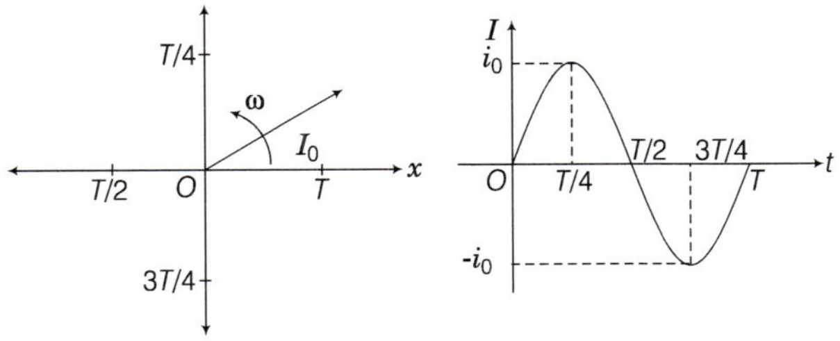

Phase Difference or Phase Constant The difference between the phase of current and voltage is called phase difference.

Time Difference If the phase difference between alternating current and voltage is ϕ, then time difference between them is given as, $\text{TD} = \frac{T}{2\pi} \times \phi$

AC with a Resistive Load (AC Circuit Containing Resistor only)

For a pure resistor connected across an AC source of emf $E = E_0 \sin \omega t$,

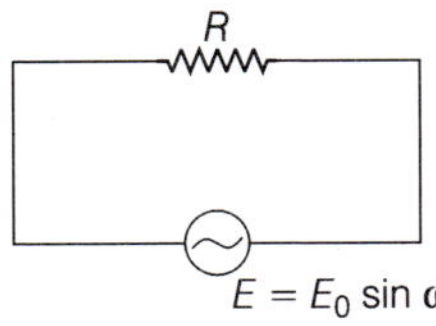

An AC source connected to a resistor

The current in the above circuit is given by Ohm's law (i.e. $E = iR$)

or
$$i = \frac{E}{R} = \frac{E_0}{R} \sin \omega t = i_0 \sin \omega t$$

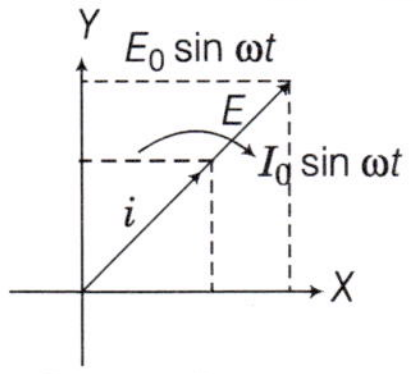

Phasor diagram

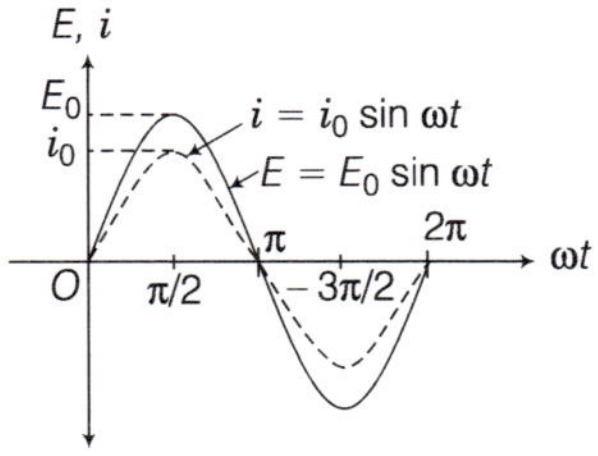

Peak current is given by, $i_0 = \frac{V_0}{R}$ or $\frac{E_0}{R}$

The phase difference between current and voltage is given by $\Delta\phi = 0°$

AC with an Inductive Load (AC Circuit Containing Inductor only)

Let an inductor of inductance L be connected to an alternating emf which is given by $E = E_0 \sin \omega t$

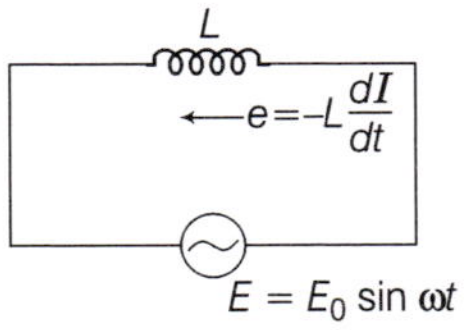

An AC source connected to an inductor

Now according to Kirchhoff's loop law, total voltage across the circuit containing inductor will be zero.

So, $E + e = 0$ $[\because \Sigma V = 0]$

$$\Rightarrow \quad E - \frac{L\,di}{dt} = 0 \Rightarrow \boxed{i = i_0 \sin\left(\omega t - \frac{\pi}{2}\right)}$$

Hence, current lags behind the emf by a phase difference of $\frac{\pi}{2}$ (or $90°$) or a time lag of $\frac{T}{4}$ sec.

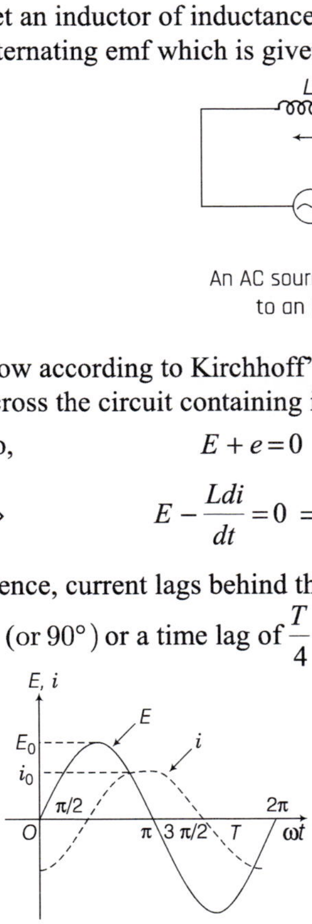

Plot of E and i_0 versus ωt

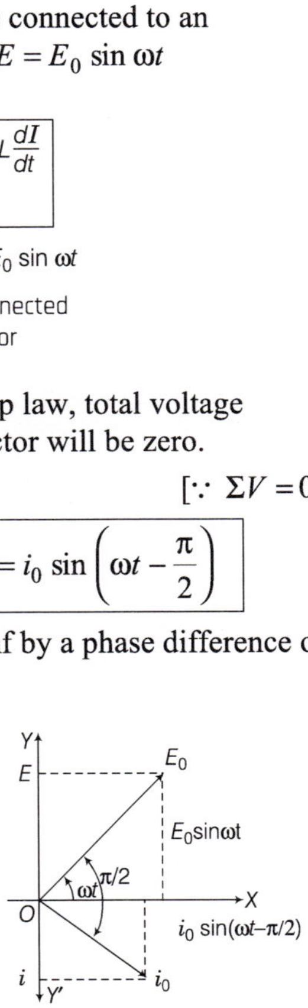

Phasor diagram

(voltage leads the current by $\pi/2$)

Resistance offered to the flow of an AC by an inductor is called **inductive reactance**. It is denoted by X_L.

where, X_L = inductive reactance $= L\omega = 2\pi\nu L$

$\Rightarrow X_L \propto \nu$, inductive reactance increases linearly with increase in frequency.

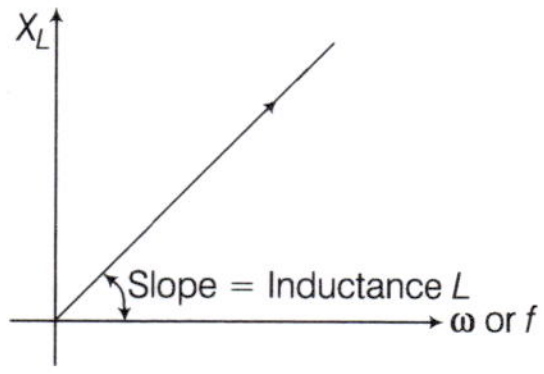

Plot of X_L versus ω

NOTE For DC current, $\omega = 0$. So, inductive reactance for DC current is $L\omega = 0$ and when ω is high for a high frequency AC. The inductive reactance reaches infinity. Hence, an inductor acts like an open switch for DC (i.e. it allows DC) and a closed switch for high frequency AC.

AC with a Capacitive Load

(AC Circuits Containing Capacitor only)

Let a capacitor of capacitance C be connected to an alternating emf.

$$E = E_0 \sin \omega t$$

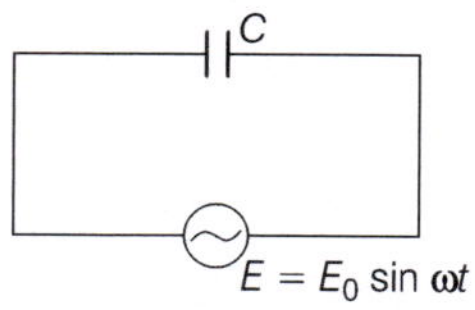

An AC source connected to a capacitor

Now the instantaneous charge stored by the capacitor is given by

$$q = CV$$

or $$q = CE_0 \sin \omega t \qquad [V = E = E_0 \sin \omega t]$$

As, we know that instantaneous current,

$$i = \frac{dq}{dt}$$

$$\Rightarrow \qquad i = i_0 \sin\left(\omega t + \frac{\pi}{2}\right)$$

Phase of current is $\frac{\pi}{2}$ more than that of emf. So the current leads the voltage by phase angle $\frac{\pi}{2}$.

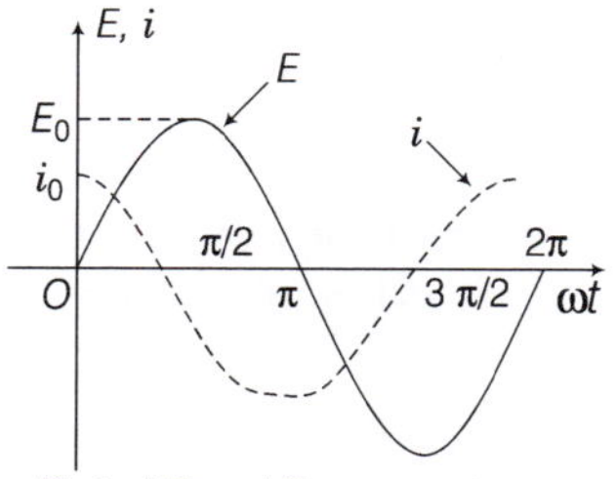

Plot of E and I versus ωt

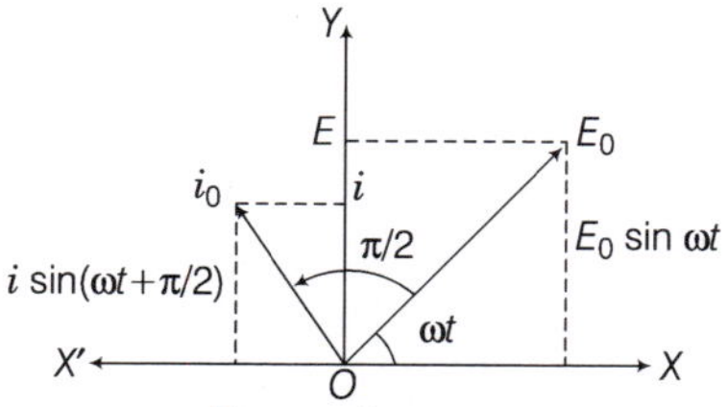

Phasor diagram

Resistance offered to the flow of AC by a capacitor, is called **capacitive reactance**. It is denoted by X_C and $X_C = \frac{1}{\omega C} = \frac{1}{2\pi\nu C}$.

The capacitor opposes low frequency AC source and allows high frequency AC (as $X_C \propto \frac{1}{f}$)

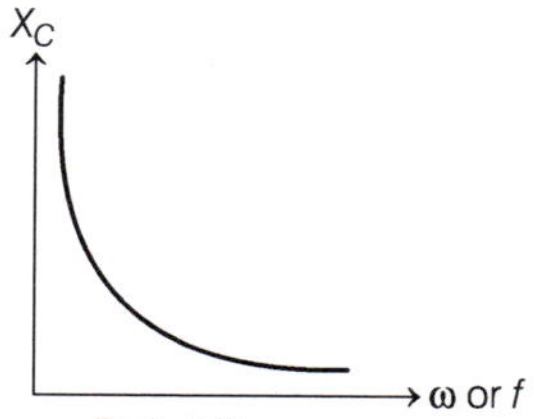

Plot of X_C versus ω or f

NOTE Both X_L and X_C have same dimensions as that of resistance and are measured in ohms.

PYQs Previous Years Questions

1 Mark Questions

1. A graph of reactance of a capacitor X_C *versus* frequency f of an AC source is **ISC 2022 Sem-I, 2012**

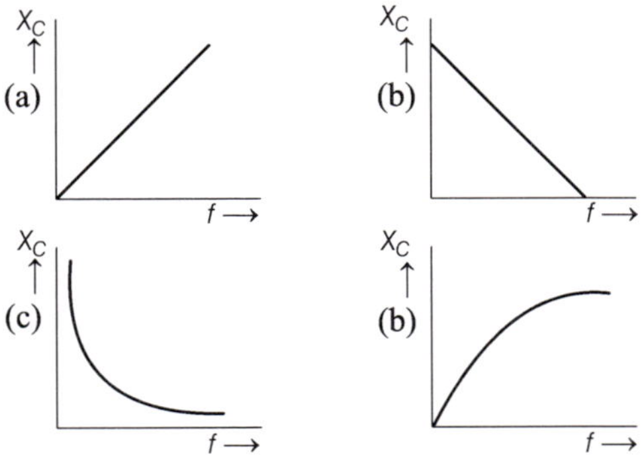

2. Alternating current flowing through a certain electrical device leads over the potential difference across it by 90°. State whether this device is a resistor, capacitor or an inductor. **ISC 2013**

3. Which one of the following graph in figure represents variation of reactance X_C of a capacitor with frequency f of an AC supply? **ISC 2012**

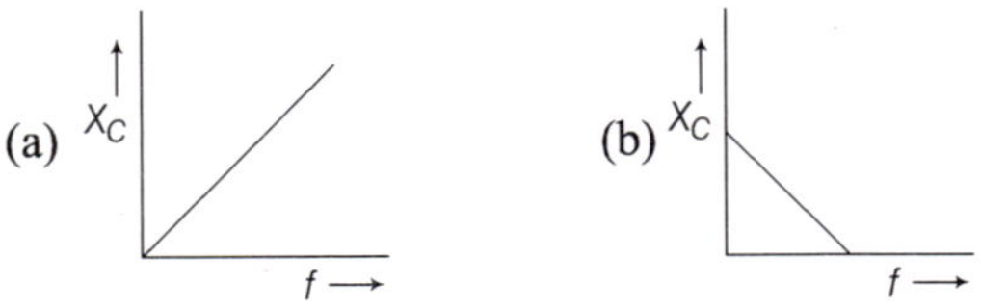

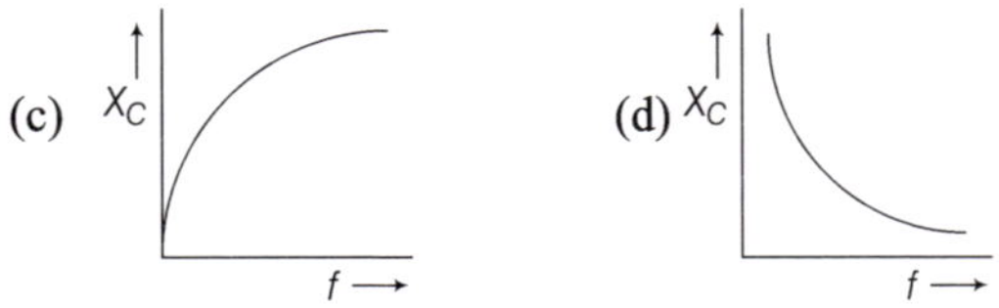

4. When an alternating emf $e = 300 \sin(100\pi t + \pi/6)$ volt is applied to a circuit, the current I through it is $I = 5.0 \sin(100\,\pi t - \pi/6)$ ampere. Then, find the phase difference between the emf and current. **ISC 2009**

3 Marks Questions

5. Obtain the relation for the current $I = I_0 \sin(\omega t - \pi/2)$ for a pure inductor across which an alternating emf $\varepsilon = \varepsilon_0 \sin \omega t$ is applied. **ISC 2007**

6. Obtain the relation $I = I_0 \sin(\omega t + \pi/2)$ and $X_L = 1/\omega C$ for a pure capacitor across which an AC emf of $\varepsilon = \varepsilon_0 \sin \omega t$ is applied as shown in the figure. Draw a phasor diagram showing emf ε, current I and their phase difference ϕ. **ISC 2003**

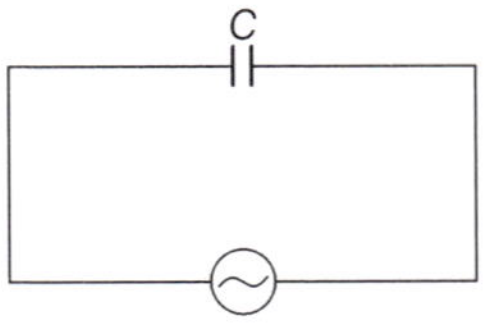

Explanations

1. (c) We know that, reactance (X_C) of a capacitor is given by

$$X_C = \frac{1}{\omega C}$$

$$\Rightarrow \quad X_C = \frac{1}{2\pi f C}$$

where, C is capacitance and f is frequency.

So, $\quad X_C \propto \frac{1}{f} \quad$ [$\because C$ is constant]

The graph will be rectangular hyperbola as shown below.

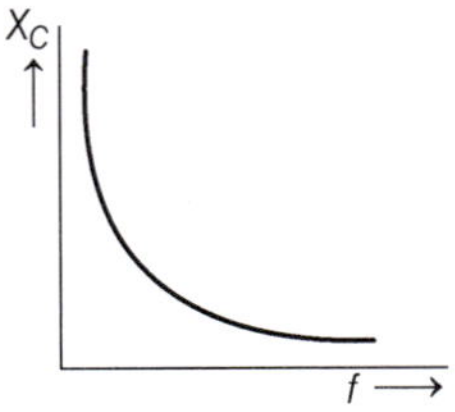

2. As, the current is leading over voltage, hence the device must be capacitor.

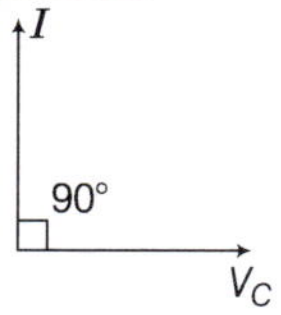

3. (d) We know that, reactance (X_C) of a capacitor is given by $X_C = \frac{1}{\omega C} \Rightarrow X_C = \frac{1}{(2\pi f)C}$

where, C is capacitance and f is frequency.

So, $X_C \propto \frac{1}{f}$ [$\because C$ is constant]

The graph will be rectangular hyperbola as shown below.

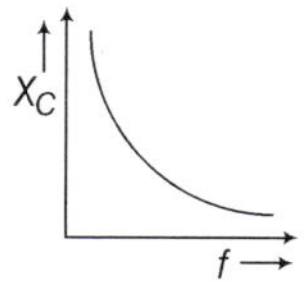

4. Given, $e = 300 \sin(100\pi t + \pi/6)$V ...(i)

and $I = 5 \sin(100\pi t - \pi/6)$ A ...(ii)

Comparing Eqs. (i) and (ii) with standard equation, the phase difference between emf (e) and current (I) is

$$\Delta\phi = \phi_1 - \phi_2 = \frac{\pi}{6} - \left(-\frac{\pi}{6}\right) = \frac{\pi}{3} \text{ rad} = 60°$$

5. Consider the circuit containing inductor.

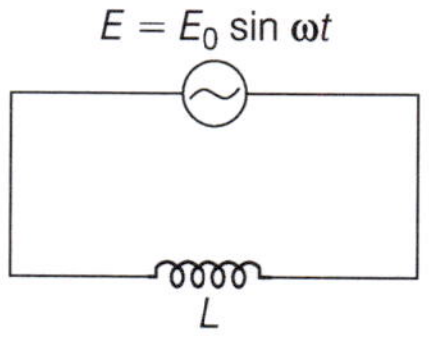

Let the emf $E = E_0 \sin \omega t$ is applied across a pure inductor L.

Since, there is no resistance in the circuit, the net instantaneous emf is zero.

Applying KVL across the circuit, we have

$$E_0 \sin \omega t - L\frac{dI}{dt} = 0 \quad \text{or} \quad dI = \frac{E_0}{L} \sin \omega t \, dt$$

Integrating, we have $\int dI = \frac{E_0}{L} \int \sin \omega t \, dt$

$$I = \frac{E_0}{L}\left(\frac{-\cos \omega t}{\omega}\right) = \frac{E_0}{\omega L} \sin\left(\omega t - \frac{\pi}{2}\right)$$

$$\left[\because -\cos \omega t = \sin\left(\omega t - \frac{\pi}{2}\right)\right]$$

or $I = I_0 \sin(\omega t - \pi/2)$

where, $I_0 = \frac{E_0}{\omega L}$ is the maximum value of the current or peak current.

> **Concept Enhancer** An opposing emf is induced in the inductor due to time varying flux which appears due to a time varying current through it.

6. Let alternating voltage, $E = E_0 \sin \omega t$ is applied across a capacitor C. At any instant, the potential difference across the capacitor is equal to applied voltage.

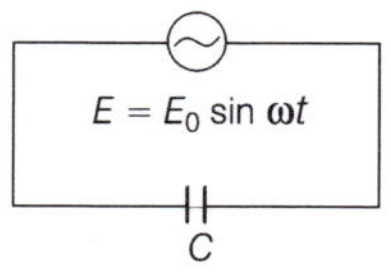

$\therefore$ E = Potential difference across the capacitor $= \frac{q}{C}$

But $E = E_0 \sin \omega t$ ...(i)

$\therefore$ $E_0 \sin \omega t = \frac{q}{C} \Rightarrow q = E_0 C \sin \omega t$

$\therefore$ $\frac{dq}{dt} = \omega C E_0 \cos \omega t$

$\Rightarrow$ $I = \frac{E_0}{1/\omega C} \cos \omega t$

or $I = I_0 \sin\left(\omega t + \frac{\pi}{2}\right)$ ...(ii)

where, $I_0 = \frac{E_0}{\left(\frac{1}{\omega C}\right)} = \frac{E_0}{X_C}$

Capacitive reactance, $X_C = \frac{1}{\omega C}$

From Eqs. (i) and (ii), current leads the voltage by phase $\pi/2$.

The graph between E and I *versus* ωt phasor diagram as shown below.

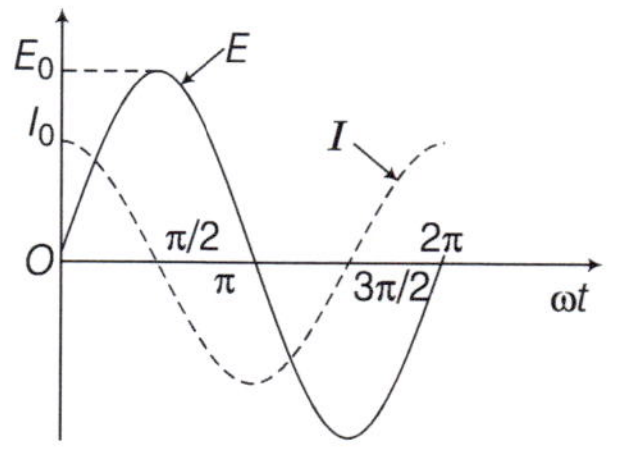

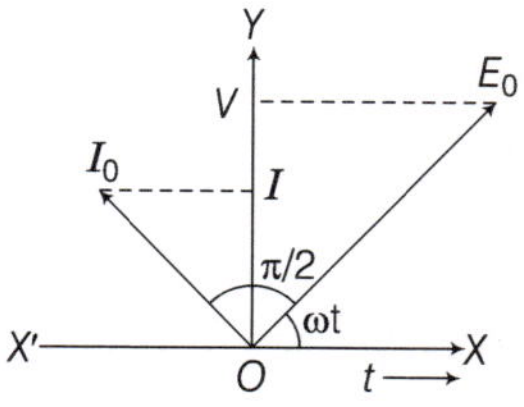

Phasor diagram

TOPIC 3

L-C-R, R-L and R-C Series Circuit

R-L and *R-C* Circuits

R-L and *R-C* circuits are the circuits containing a combination of only two components of a *L-C-R* circuit.

Resistive, Inductive Circuit (*R-L* circuit)

$V_L = X_L I$ across the inductance L is ahead of current I in phase by $\pi/2$ and by parallelogram law of vector addition,

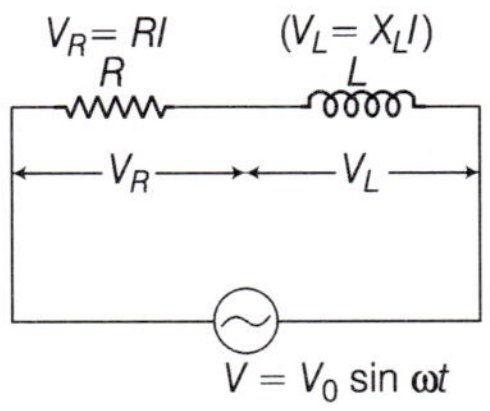

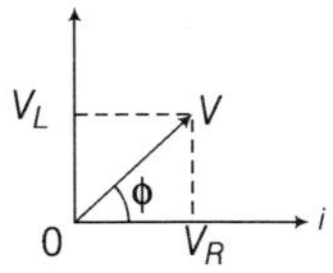

(*i*) Applied voltage, $V = \sqrt{V_R^2 + V_L^2}$

(*ii*) Impedance, $Z = \sqrt{R^2 + X_L^2} = \sqrt{R^2 + \omega^2 L^2}$ $\quad [X_L = \omega L]$

$$= \sqrt{R^2 + 4\pi^2 f^2 L^2}$$

(*iii*) Current, $i = i_0 \sin(\omega t - \phi)$

(*iv*) Peak current, $i_0 = \dfrac{V_0}{Z}$

$$= \frac{V_0}{\sqrt{R^2 + X_L^2}} = \frac{V_0}{\sqrt{R^2 + 4\pi^2 f^2 L^2}}$$

(*v*) Phase difference, $\phi = \tan^{-1}\left(\dfrac{X_L}{R}\right) = \tan^{-1}\left(\dfrac{\omega L}{R}\right)$

(*vi*) Power factor, $\cos\phi = \dfrac{R}{\sqrt{R^2 + X_L^2}}$

(*vii*) Leading quantity is voltage.

(*viii*) Graph of Z *versus* f

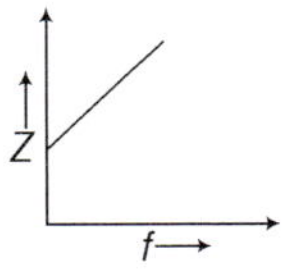

Resistive, Capacitive Circuit (*R-C* Circuit)

(*i*) Applied voltage, $V = \sqrt{V_R^2 + V_C^2}$

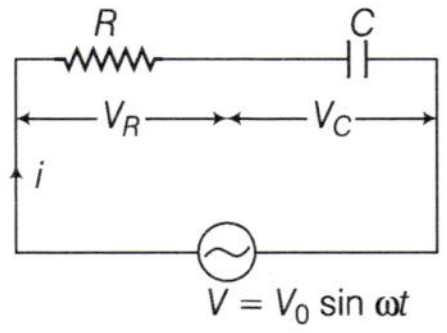

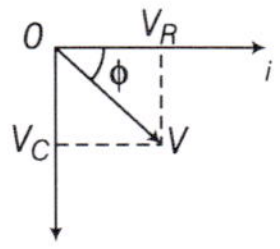

(*ii*) Impedance, $Z = \sqrt{R^2 + X_C^2} = \sqrt{R^2 + \left(\dfrac{1}{\omega C}\right)^2}$

$$\left[X_C = \frac{1}{\omega C}\right]$$

(*iii*) Current, $i = i_0 \sin(\omega t + \phi)$

(*iv*) Peak current, $i_0 = \dfrac{V_0}{Z} = \dfrac{V_0}{\sqrt{R^2 + X_C^2}}$

$$= \frac{V_0}{\sqrt{R^2 + \dfrac{1}{4\pi^2 f^2 C^2}}}$$

(*v*) Phase difference, $\phi = \tan^{-1}\left(\dfrac{X_C}{R}\right) = \tan^{-1}\left(\dfrac{1}{\omega CR}\right)$

(*vi*) Power factor, $\cos\phi = \dfrac{R}{\sqrt{R^2 + X_C^2}}$

(*vii*) Leading quantity is current.

(*viii*) Graph of Z *versus* f

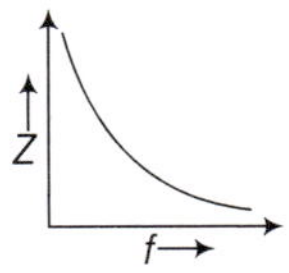

NOTE Reactance (X) The opposition offered by inductor or capacitor (or both) to the flow of AC through it is defined as reactance. It is of the following two types.

(*i*) **Inductive reactance** (X_L) Opposition offered by inductive circuit, $X_L = \omega L = 2\pi f L$, $f_{DC} = 0$, so for DC, $X_L = 0$.

(*ii*) **Capacitive reactance** (X_C) Opposition offered by capacitive circuit, $X_C = \dfrac{1}{\omega C} = \dfrac{1}{2\pi f C}$, so for DC, $X_C = \infty$.

Series *L-C-R* Circuit

It is a circuit which contains an inductor, a capacitor and a resistor in series across an AC source.

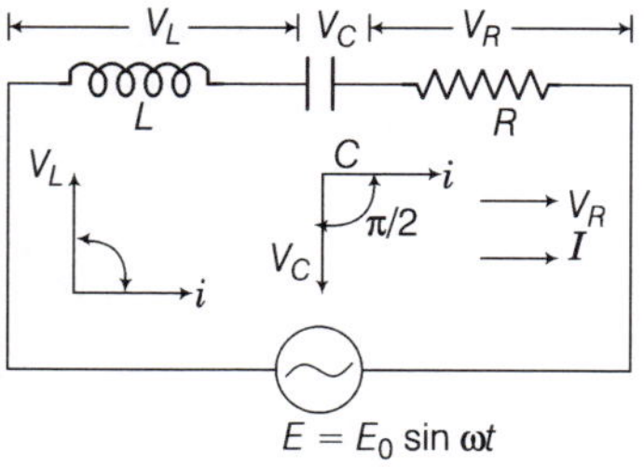

An AC source connected to series *L-C-R* circuit

The current at any instant of time is same for all three components.

The potential across inductor V_L capacitor V_C and resistor V_R are shown in the graph.

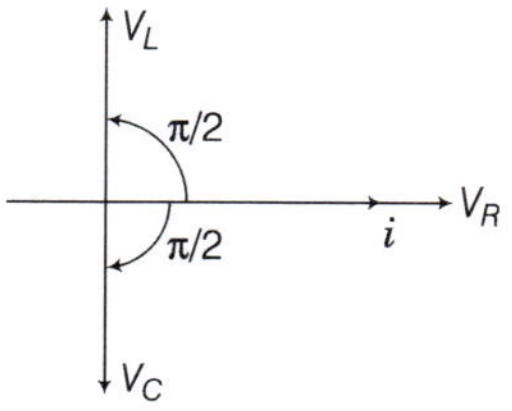

The resultant of V_L and V_C phasors is $V_L - V_C$.

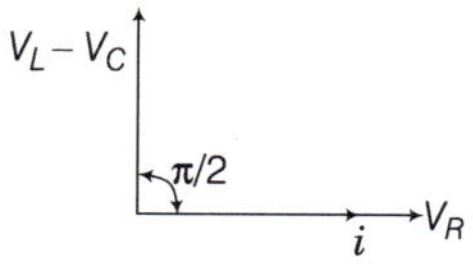

The resultant of $(V_L - V_C)$ and V_R is the total applied emf E.

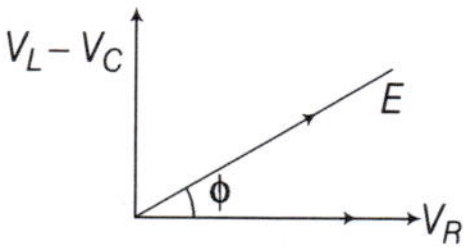

Phasor diagram for *L-C-R* circuit

Clearly, $$E = \sqrt{(V_L - V_C)^2 + V_R^2}$$

Also, $$V_L = iX_L$$

$\Rightarrow$ $$V_C = iX_C \text{ and } V_R = iR$$

$\Rightarrow$ $$E = \sqrt{(iX_L - iX_C)^2 + (iR)^2}$$

$\Rightarrow$ $$E = i\sqrt{(X_L - X_C)^2 + R^2}$$

where, $\sqrt{(X_L - X_C)^2 + R^2}$ is the total opposition of *L-C-R* circuit to the flow of an AC and is called **impedance** of *L-C-R* series circuit (*Z*).

So, $$Z = \sqrt{(X_L - X_C)^2 + R^2} = \sqrt{\left(\omega L - \frac{1}{\omega C}\right)^2 + R^2}$$

Hence, $E = iZ \Rightarrow E_0 = i_0 Z$

and $E_{\text{rms}} = i_{\text{rms}} Z$

The phase difference ϕ between applied emf E and circuit current i is given by

$$\tan\phi = \frac{V_L - V_C}{V_R} = \frac{X_L - X_C}{R}$$

or $$\phi = \tan^{-1}\left(\frac{X_L - X_C}{R}\right)$$

- When $X_L = X_C$, $V_L = V_C$

  $\therefore$ $Z = R$ and $\tan\phi = 0$ $[\because \phi = 90°]$
- Hence, voltage and current are in the same phase. The AC circuit is resistive only. The circuit is in resonance.
- When $X_L > X_C$, then $\tan\phi$ is positive.
  Hence, voltage leads the current by a phase angle ϕ. The AC circuit is inductive dominated circuit. The circuit behaves like *L-R* circuit.
- When $X_C > X_L$, then $\tan\phi$ is negative.
  Hence, voltage lags behind the current by a phase angle ϕ. The AC circuit is capacitive dominated circuit and the circuit behaves like *C-R* circuit.

Resonance in *L-C-R* Series Circuit

The rms current in *L-C-R* series circuit is given by

$$i_{\text{rms}} = \frac{E_{\text{rms}}}{Z} = \frac{E_{\text{rms}}}{\sqrt{(X_L - X_C)^2 + R^2}} = \frac{E_{\text{rms}}}{\sqrt{\left(L\omega - \frac{1}{C\omega}\right)^2 + R^2}}$$

As, reactance of inductors and capacitors depends on frequency $f = \frac{\omega}{2\pi}$ of source, the current in *L-C-R* circuit depends on source frequency f.

At certain frequency $X_L = X_C$

i.e., $$L\omega - \frac{1}{C\omega} = 0 \Rightarrow L\omega = \frac{1}{C\omega}$$

$\Rightarrow$ $$\omega^2 = \frac{1}{LC}$$

$\Rightarrow$ $$\omega = \frac{1}{\sqrt{LC}}$$

At this frequency, the impedance of the *L-C-R* series is minimum and current in the circuit is maximum. This frequency is called **angular resonance frequency** ω_0.

$$\omega_0 = \frac{1}{\sqrt{LC}} \Rightarrow 2\pi f = \frac{1}{\sqrt{LC}}$$

$\Rightarrow$ **Resonance frequency,** $f = \dfrac{1}{2\pi\sqrt{LC}}$, its independent of the resistance of the circuit.

At resonance, $X_L = X_C \Rightarrow Z = R$, the circuit behaves like a resistive circuit.

$V_L = V_C \Rightarrow E = V_R$, the whole applied emf appears across the resistor.

Phase difference

i.e., $\phi = \tan^{-1}\left(\dfrac{X_L - X_C}{R}\right) = \tan^{-1}(0) = 0$

Current $i_0 = \dfrac{V_0}{R} = \dfrac{E}{R}$

The impedance of a *L-C-R* circuit depends on the frequency. The frequency is taken on logarithmic scale because of its wide range.

(a) *i-f* graph (b) *Z-f* graph (c) (X_L, X_C)-f graph

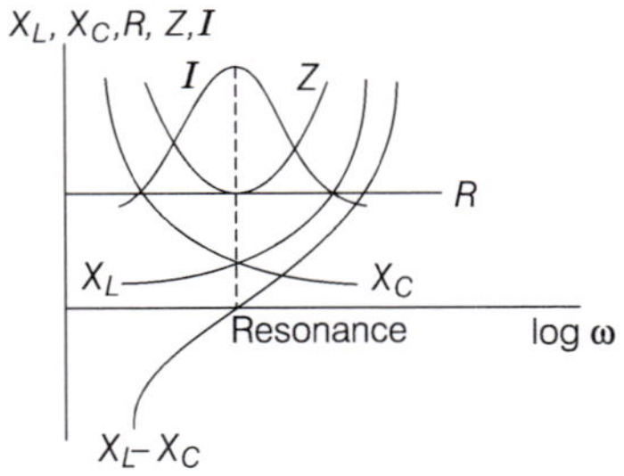

Impedance (Z) versus log ω graph for a series *L-C-R* circuit

Quality Factor (Q-Factor) Or Sharpness of Resonance

It defines the *i-f* curve at resonance.

The characteristic of a series resonant circuit is determined by the quality factor (*Q*-factor).

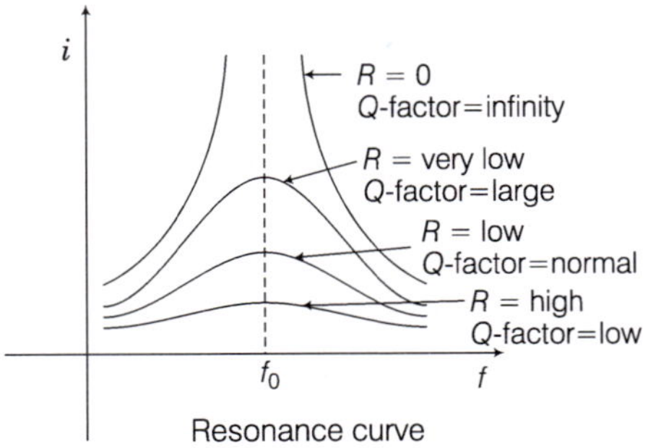

Resonance curve

The ratio of resonant frequency to bandwidth which is responsible for sharpness of resonance is called *Q*-factor or quality factor of the circuit. It is represented as

$$\therefore Q\text{-factor} = \frac{V_L}{V_R} = \frac{V_C}{V_R} = \frac{1}{R}\sqrt{\frac{L}{C}} = \frac{\omega_0}{2\Delta\omega} = \frac{1}{\omega_0 CR} = \frac{\omega_0 L}{R}$$

[ω_0 = resonant frequency]

It defines the sharpness of *i* and *f* curve at resonance. *Q*-factor is higher for a more sharp curve.

It is also defined as, *Q*-factor

$$= 2\pi \times \frac{\text{Maximum energy stored}}{\text{Energy dissipated}}$$

Power in AC Circuit

In DC circuit, power is given by $P = Vi$.

In AC circuit,

Thus, $P = Vi\cos\phi$

where, V and i are the rms value of voltage and current.

Instantaneous Power Suppose in a circuit $V = V_0 \sin \omega t$ and $i = i_0 \sin(\omega t + \phi)$, then

$P_{\text{inst}} = Vi = V_0 i_0 \sin \omega t \sin(\omega t + \phi)$.

Average Power or True Power The average of instantaneous power in an AC circuit over a full cycle is called average power. It's unit is watt. It is expressed as

$$P_{av} = V_{rms}\, i_{rms} \cos\phi = \frac{V_0}{\sqrt{2}} \cdot \frac{i_0}{\sqrt{2}} \cos\phi$$

$$= \frac{1}{2} V_0 i_0 \cos\phi$$

$$= I_{rms}^2 Z \cos\phi$$

[where, $\cos\phi$ = power factor]

Apparent or Virtual Power The product of apparent voltage and apparent current in an electric circuit is called apparent power. This is always positive,

$$P_{app} = V_{rms} i_{rms} = \frac{V_0 i_0}{2}$$

Power Factor

(i) It may be defined as cosine of the angle of lag or lead (i.e. $\cos\phi$).

(ii) It is also defined as, the ratio of resistance and impedance $\left(\text{i.e.} \dfrac{R}{Z}\right)$.

i.e. $$\cos\phi = \frac{R}{\sqrt{R^2 + \left(\omega L - \dfrac{1}{\omega C}\right)^2}}$$

(iii) It is the ratio $= \dfrac{\text{True power}}{\text{Apparent power}} = \dfrac{\text{W}}{\text{VA}} = \dfrac{\text{kW}}{\text{kWA}} = \cos\phi$

(iv) For a purely resistive circuit, $\phi = 0 \Rightarrow \cos\phi = \cos 0 = 1$

$\therefore$ $P_{resistor} = V_{rms}\, i_{rms}$, power factor assumes the maximum value

(v) For a pure inductor or pure capacitor, $\phi = \frac{\pi}{2}$

$$\Rightarrow \quad \cos\phi = \cos\frac{\pi}{2} = 0$$

$$\therefore \; P_{inductor} \text{ or } P_{capacitor} = V_{rms}\, i_{rms} \cos\frac{\pi}{2} = 0$$

In an inductor or capacitor power dissipated is zero and the current is called **wattless current**.

(vi) For an *L-C-R* circuit, $\tan\phi = \frac{(X_L - X_C)}{R}$

$$\Rightarrow \quad \cos\phi = \text{power factor} = \frac{R}{Z}$$

So, $P_{L\text{-}C\text{-}R} = V_{rms} i_{rms} \cos\phi$

(vii) For an *L-C-R* circuit at resonance, $X_L = X_C \Rightarrow \phi = 0°$

Power factor, $\cos\phi = 1$

$$\therefore \quad P_{L\text{-}C\text{-}R\,(\text{resonance})} = V_{rms} i_{rms}$$

Half Power Frequencies and Bandwidth

The frequencies at which the power in the circuit is half of the maximum power i.e. power at resonance, are called half power frequencies.

There are many factors related to half power frequency which are as follows :

(i) The current in the circuit at Half Power Frequencies (HPF) is $\frac{1}{\sqrt{2}}$ or 0.707 or 70.7% of maximum current or current at resonance.

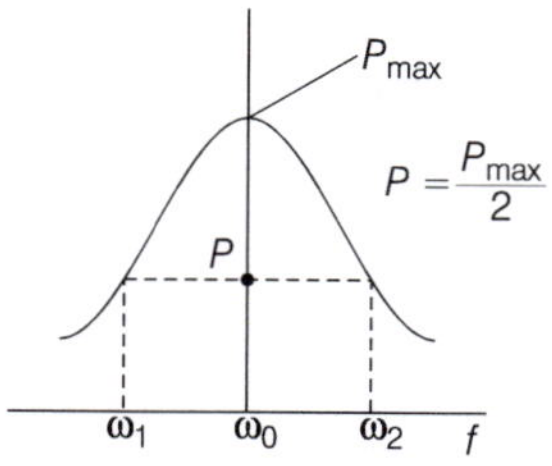

Half power points in series *L-C-R* circuit

(ii) There are two half power frequencies which are as follows

(a) ω_1 is called lower half power frequency. At this frequency the circuit is capacitive.

(b) ω_2 is called upper half power frequency. It is greater than ω_0. At this frequency, the circuit is inductive.

(iii) **Bandwidth** ($\Delta\omega$) The difference of half power frequencies ω_1 and ω_2 is called bandwidth.

It is expressed as $\Delta\omega = \omega_1 - \omega_2$. For series resonant circuit, the bandwidth will be $\Delta\omega = \left(\frac{R}{L}\right)$.

Wattless Current

In an AC circuit, if $R = 0 \Rightarrow \cos\phi = 0$, so $P_{av} = 0$, i.e. in resistance less circuit the power consumed is zero. Phasor diagram given below,

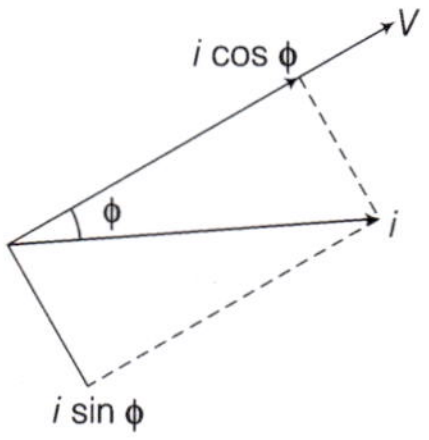

The component of current which does not contribute to the average power dissipation is called wattless current. Also,

(i) the average of wattless component over one cycle is zero.

(ii) the amplitude of wattless current is equal to $i_0 \sin\phi$ and rms value of wattless current $i_{rms} \sin\phi = \frac{i_0}{\sqrt{2}}\sin\phi$ is equal.

Choke Coil

Choke coils (or ballast) is a device having high inductance and negligible resistance. It is used to control current in AC circuits and is used in fluorescent tubes. The power loss in a circuit containing choke coil is least.

Following are the important points about choke coil.

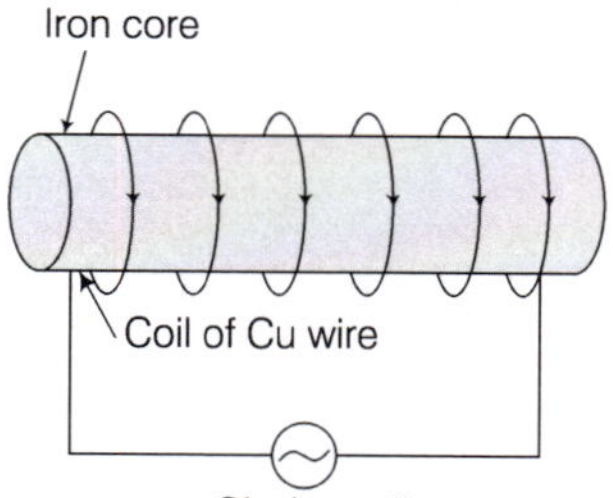

Choke coil

(*i*) The inductive reactance or effective opposition of the choke coil is given by $X_L = \omega L = 2\pi f L$.

(*ii*) For an ideal choke coil $R = 0$, no electric energy is wasted, i.e., average power $P = 0$.

(*iii*) Choke coils for different frequencies are made by using different substances in their core.

For low frequency, L should be large thus iron core choke coil is used. For high frequency AC circuit, L should be small, so air cored choke coil is used.

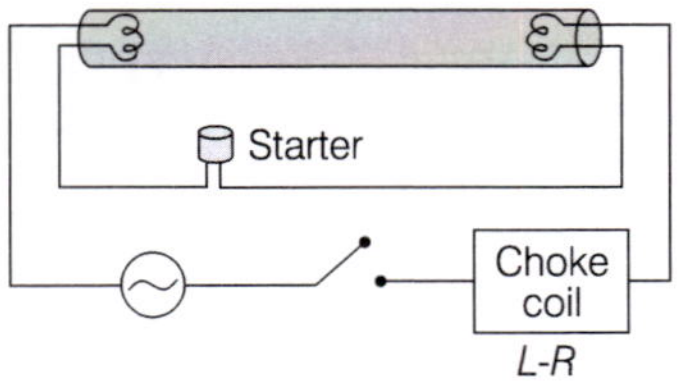

Application of choke coil

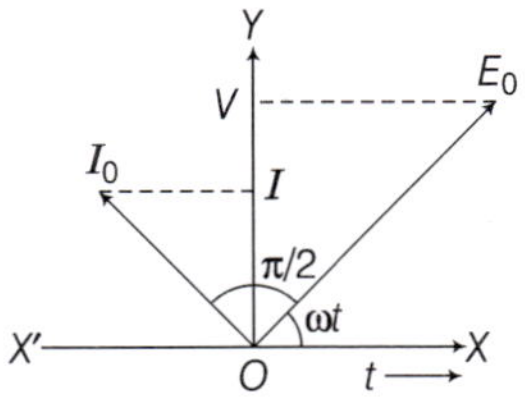

AC Generator

A generator produces electrical energy from mechanical work.

Principle

It works on the principle of electromagnetic induction. Whenever, the amount of magnetic flux linked with a coil changes, an emf is induced in the coil.

Working

When a closed armature coil rotates in a uniform magnetic field with its axis perpendicular to the magnetic field, the magnetic flux linked with the loop changes and emf induces in the coil.

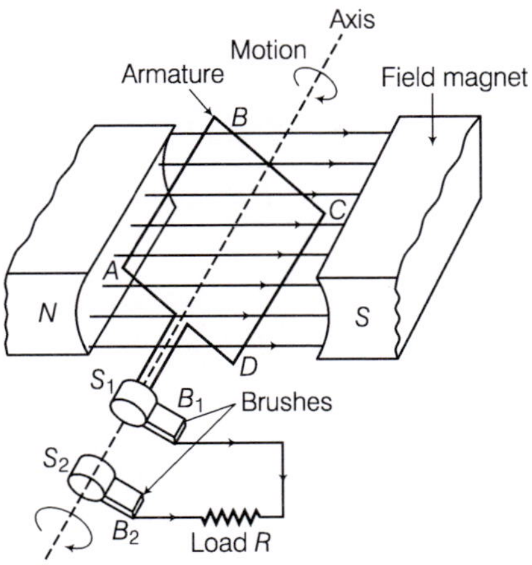

Construction of an AC generator

So, as per the working, the direction of flow of current in resistance R get changed alternatively after every half cycle.

Thus, AC is produced in coil.

- If ε is the emf induced in the coil, then

$$\varepsilon = NBA\omega \sin \omega t = \varepsilon_0 \sin \omega t$$

where, N = number of turns in the coil,
B = strength of magnetic field,
A = area of each turn of the coil,
ω = angular velocity of rotation,
and $\varepsilon_0 = NBA\omega$ = peak value of emf

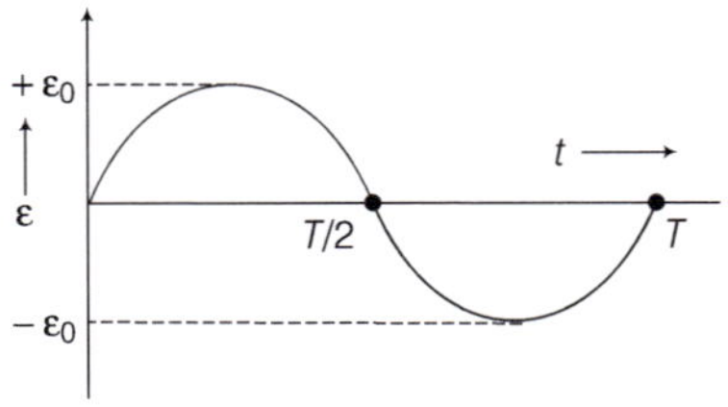

Variation of emf in AC generator

- If resistance of the coil is R, then

Current, $i = \dfrac{\varepsilon_1}{R} = \dfrac{\varepsilon_0}{R} \sin \omega t$

$\Rightarrow \quad i = i_0 \sin \omega t$

where, $si_0 = \dfrac{NBA\omega}{R}$ = peak value of current.

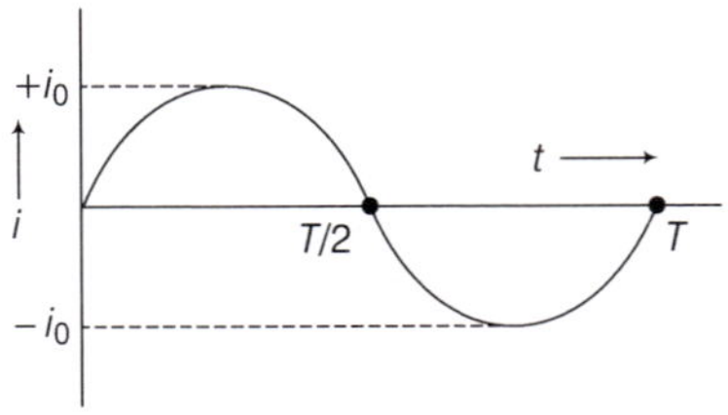

Variation of current in AC generator

Uses

- AC generators are used for efficient transmission of power over long distance and in larger amounts.
- AC power can easily be stepped up or stepped down in voltage by using transformers.
- AC can be reduced by using a choke coil without wasting energy.
- AC can be easily converted into DC by using rectifier.
- AC machines require less maintenance.

PYQs Previous Years Questions

1 Mark Questions

1. A graph showing variation in impedance Z of a series LCR circuit, with frequency f of alternating emf applied to it is shown below. What is the minimum value of this impedance? **ISC 2022 Sem-1**

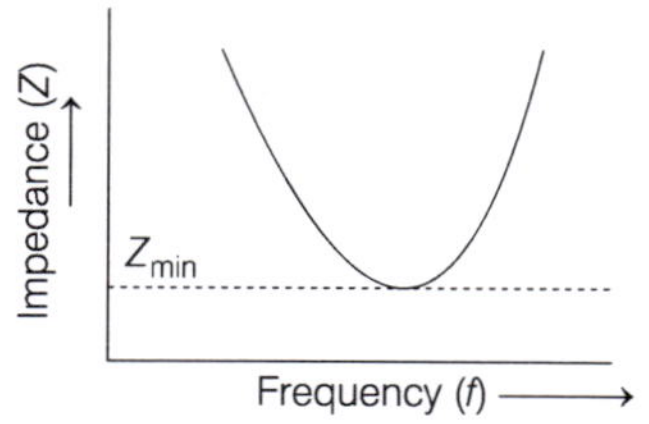

(a) R (b) $Z = \sqrt{R^2 + (X_L - X_C)^2}$
(c) $Z_{\min}$ (d) $X_L = X_C$

2. Which of the following is not the characteristic of resonance in an LCR series circuit? **ISC 2022 Sem-1**

(a) $X_L = X_C$ (b) $\omega L = \dfrac{1}{\omega C}$
(c) $2\pi f L = 2\pi f C$ (d) $f_0 = \dfrac{1}{2\pi}\sqrt{\dfrac{1}{LC}}$

3. An AC generator generating an emf of $\varepsilon = 300 \sin (100\pi)t$ is connected to a series combination of $16\mu F$ capacitor, 1H inductor and 100Ω resistor. What is the frequency of AC? **ISC 2022 Sem-1**

(a) 100 Hz (b) 50 Hz (c) 300 Hz (d) 25 Hz

4. Which one of the following statements is not true at resonance of a series L-C-R circuit? **ISC 2022 Sem-I**

(a) Reactance of the capacitor is equal to the reactance of the inductor.
(b) Impedance of the circuit is minimum.
(c) Current in the circuit is minimum.
(d) Current is in phase with supply voltage.

5. If potential difference across a resistor of 80 Ω varies as shown in the graph below, average power consumed by the resistor is **ISC 2022 Sem-I**

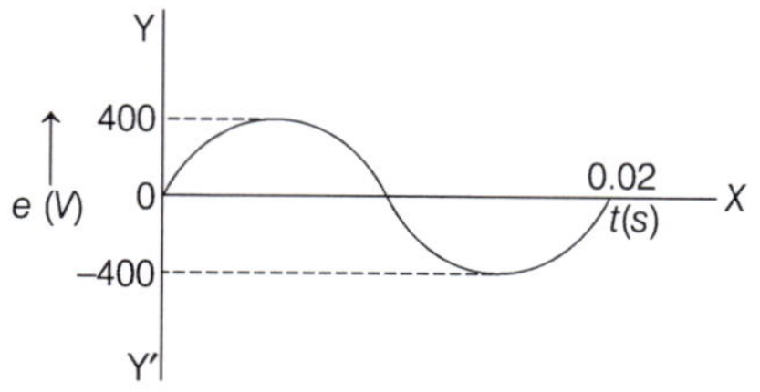

(a) zero (b) 500 W
(c) 1000 W (d) 2000 W

6. What is the value of power factor for a pure resistor connected to an alternating current source? **ISC 2019**

7. What is the value of power factor in a series of L-C-R circuit at resonance? **ISC 2009**

8. An alternating current of frequency f is flowing through an ideal choke coil of self-inductance L. If V_0 and I_0 be the peak values of the voltage and current, then find the average power consumed, if any, by the choke coil. **ISC 2009**

9. What is the power factor of a series L-C-R circuit? **ISC 2008**

10. In a graphical variation of emf induced with time for the output of an AC generator, mark the peak value of emf induced and the time period. **ISC 2007**

11. An ideal inductor does not consume any power even though both V and I are non-zero. Explain in brief. **ISC 2005, 01**

12. In an AC circuit, $R = 4\,\Omega$, $Z = 5\,\Omega$, $V_{rms} = 200$ V and $I_{rms} = 1.5$ A. Calculate the average power consumed over a full cycle. **ISC 2003**

13. Mention any two special properties of an L-C-R circuit at resonance. **ISC 2003**

14. Give the expression for the power factor in an L-R circuit in terms of the resistance R and the inductive reactance X_L. **ISC 2002**

15. What is meant by wattless current? **ISC 2000**

2 Marks Questions

16. State any two characteristics of resonance in an L-C-R series circuit. **ISC 2019**

17. In a series L-C-R circuit, obtain an expression for the resonant frequency. **ISC 2017**

18. When an alternating emf, $e = 300 \sin (100\pi t + \pi/6)$ volt is applied to a circuit, the current I through it is $I = 5.0 \sin (100\pi t - \pi/6)$ ampere. Then, find the average power consumed by the circuit. **ISC 2009**

3 Marks Questions

19. A $2\,\mu F$ capacitor, $100\,\Omega$ resistor and 8 H inductor are connected in series with an AC source. At a certain frequency of about 40 Hz for this AC source, the current drawn in the circuit is maximum.

If the peak value of emf of the source is 200V **ISC 2022 Sem-I**

(*i*) What is the peak value of current in the circuit?
(a) 1.4 A (b) 2.2 A
(c) 2.0 A (d) 1.8 A

(*ii*) What is the phase relation between voltages across inductor and resistor?
(a) $\pi/2$ radian (b) $\pi/3$ radian
(c) $\pi/4$ radian (d) π radian

(*iii*) What is the phase difference between voltages across inductor and capacitor?
(a) $\pi/2$ radian (b) $\pi/3$ radian
(c) $\pi/4$ radian (d) π radian

20. When a capacitor, an inductor and a resistor are connected in series to an AC source, **ISC 2022 Sem-I**

(*i*) Average power consumed by the capacitor is
(a) $I^2 \times X_C$ (b) $I^2 \times C$
(c) $I^2 \times R$ (d) zero

(*ii*) Phase difference between potential difference across a capacitor and that across an inductor is
(a) 90°
(b) 180°
(c) $\tan^{-1}(X_L - X_C)/R$
(d) $\cos^{-1}(X_L - X_C)/R$

(*iii*) Current flowing through the circuit is maximum, when
(a) $X_L = X_C$ (b) $X_L > X_C$
(c) $X_L < X_C$ (d) $Z > R$

21. Plot a labelled graph showing variation in impedance Z of a series L-C-R circuit with frequency f of alternating emf applied to it. What is the minimum value of this impedance? **ISC 2010**

22. Obtain an expression for resonant frequency f_0 of a series L-C-R circuit. **ISC 2009**

23. A resistance of $150\ \Omega$ and a capacitance of $15\ \mu F$ are connected in series with an AC source of 220 V. The peak value of the current is 0.20 A. Calculate the average power consumed in the circuit. If the capacitor is removed but the current is kept the same, what is the average power consumed in the resistor alone? **ISC 2007**

> **KEY idea**
> To calculate the average power first calculate the impedance, then calculate the $P_{av} = V_{rms} I_{rms} \cos\phi$

24. An AC circuit with resistance R, inductance L and capacitance C are connected in series. The value of C is adjusted for resonance. State any three properties of this circuit which hold true for resonance only. (Give the properties in words or equations, relating X_L, X_C, Z, R, ϕ, power, etc.) **ISC 2006**

25. An alternating emf of frequency 50 Hz is applied to a circuit with a resistor of $20\ \Omega$, an inductor of 100 mH and a capacitor of $30\ \mu F$ connected in series.

(*i*) What is the angle by which the current leads or lags the applied emf?

(*ii*) Represent the voltage and the current in a vector diagram showing the phase angle. **ISC 2006**

26. A current of 4 A flows in a coil when connected to a 12 V DC source. If the same coil is connected to a 12 V, 8 Hz AC source, a current 2.4 A flows in the coil. Calculate the coefficient of self-inductance L of the coil. **ISC 2005**

27. In the R-L circuit shown in the given figure, the resistance, $R = 30\ \Omega$, reactance, $X_L = 40\ \Omega$ and peak emf, $\varepsilon_0 = 220$ V.

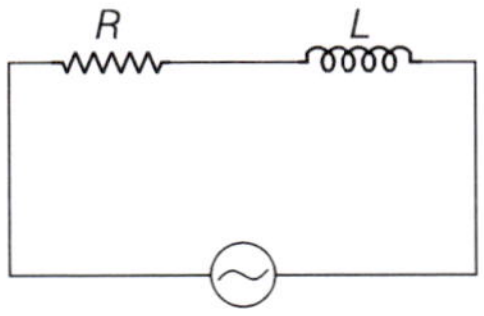

Calculate
(i) the impedance Z.
(ii) phase difference between the emf and current.
(iii) the peak current I_0 in circuit. **ISC 2004**

28. A lamp with a resistance of $8\ \Omega$ is connected to a choke coil as shown in the figure.

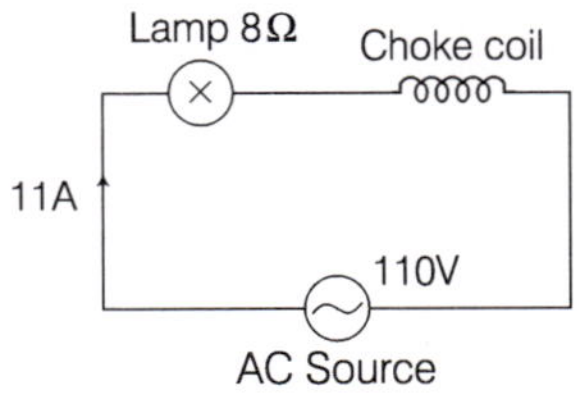

This arrangement is connected to an alternating source 110 V. The current in the circuit is 11 A. The frequency of the AC is 60 Hz. Then, find the
(i) impedance of the circuit.
(ii) value of inductive reactance of the choke coil.
ISC 2000

29. In an *L-C-R* circuit, all components connected in series, the emf and the current flowing in the circuit are given by the following equations.

$$\varepsilon_0 = 200\sin\left(314t + \frac{\pi}{6}\right)\text{V}, \quad I = 5\sin 314t \text{ A}$$

Obtain

(*i*) the peak values of current and emf.

(*ii*) the frequency of the AC source.

(*iii*) the phase difference between current and emf.

ISC 2000

30. A 60Ω resistor, a 10 H inductor and a 4 μF capacitor are connected in series to AC supply generating an emf $e = 300\sin(500t)V$. Calculate **ISC 2000**

(a) impedance of the circuit.

(b) peak value of the current flowing through the circuit.

(c) phase difference between the current and the supply voltage.

4/5 Marks Questions

31. (i) A 220 V, 50 Hz AC source is connected to a coil having coefficient of self-inductance of 1H and a resistance of 400 Ω. Calculate

(a) the reactance of the coil.

(b) the impedance of the coil.

(c) the current flowing through the coil.

(ii) Draw a labelled graph showing variation of impedance (Z) of a series *L-C-R* circuit *versus* frequency (f) of the AC supply. Mark the resonant frequency as f_0. **ISC 2024**

32. A 220 V, 50 Hz AC source is connected to a series combination of a 3.16 μF capacitor, a 0.63 H inductor and a 600 Ω resistor. Then, (approximately)

ISC 2022 Sem-I

(*i*) Reactance of the capacitor is

(a) 1000 Ω (b) 900 Ω

(c) 1 Ω (d) 0.1 Ω

(*ii*) Reactance of the inductor is

(a) 400 Ω (b) 300 Ω

(c) 200 Ω (d) 100 Ω

(*iii*) Impedance of the circuit is

(a) 800 Ω (b) 1000 Ω

(c) 1200 Ω (d) 1400 Ω

(*iv*) Phase difference between the current and the supply voltage is

(a) 53°, with current leading over supply voltage

(b) 53°, with current lagging behind supply voltage

(c) 37°, with current lagging behind supply voltage

(d) 37°, with current leading over supply voltage

KEY idea

To determine the phase difference between the current and the supply voltage first calculate the X_C and X_L, then calculate the phase difference with the help of formula $\left(\tan\phi = \frac{X_L - X_C}{R}\right)$.

33. (*i*) A 400 Ω resistor, a 3H inductor and a 5 μF capacitor are connected in series to a 220V, 50 Hz AC source. Calculate the

(a) impedance of the circuit.

(b) current flowing through the circuit.

(*ii*) Draw a labelled graph showing the variation of impedance (Z) of a series *L-C-R* circuit *versus* frequency (f) of the AC supply. **ISC 2020**

34. (*i*) When an alternating emf $e = 310\sin(100\pi t)$ V is applied to a series *L-C-R* circuit, current flowing through it is $i = 5\sin(100\pi t + \pi/3)$ A.

(a) What is the phase difference between the current and the emf?

(b) Calculate the average power consumed by the circuit.

(*ii*) Obtain an expression for the resonant frequency (f_0) of a series *L-C-R* circuit. **ISC 2020**

35. (i) An alternating emf of 200V, 50Hz is applied to an *L-R* circuit, having a resistance R of 10 Ω and an inductance L of 0.05H connected in series. Calculate

(a) impedance.

(b) current flowing in the circuit.

(ii) Draw a labelled graph showing the variation of inductive reactance X_L *versus* frequency f.

ISC 2019

KEY idea

To calculate the current flowing in the circuit. First calculate the Impedance (Z), then calculate the current with the help of formula $\left(I = \frac{V_{rms}}{Z}\right)$.

36. An alternating emf of 220 V is applied to a circuit containing a resistor R having resistance of 160 Ω and a capacitor C in series. The current is found to lead the supply voltage by an angle $\theta = \tan^{-1}\left(\frac{3}{4}\right)$. **ISC 2018**

(a) Calculate

I. the capacitive reactance

II. impedance of the *R-C* circuit.

III. current flowing in the circuit.

(b) If the frequency of the applied emf is 50 Hz, what is the value of the capacitance of the capacitor C ?

37. An AC generator generating an emf of $\varepsilon = 300\sin(100\pi t)\text{V}$ is connected to a series combination of $16\mu\text{F}$ capacitor, 1H inductor and 100Ω resistor. Calculate **ISC 2018**

(a) impedance of the circuit at the given frequency

(b) resonant frequency f_0.

(c) power factor at resonant frequency f_0.

38. An 8 H inductor, a $2\mu\text{F}$ capacitor and a 100Ω resistor are connected in series to an AC supply of 220 V and 50 Hz. Calculate **ISC SQP 2018**

(a) impedance of the circuit

(b) current flowing through the circuit

(c) phase difference between the current and the supply voltage

(d) average power consumed by the circuit.

39. (*i*) A coil having self-inductance of 0.7 H and resistance of $165\,\Omega$ is connected to an AC source of 275 V, 50 Hz. If $\pi = \frac{22}{7}$, then calculate

(a) reactance of the coil

(b) impedance of the coil

(c) current flowing through the coil.

(*ii*) Draw a labelled graph showing variation of impedance of a series *L-C-R* circuit with frequency of the AC supply. **ISC 2016**

40. (*i*) Figure below shows a capacitor C, an inductor L and a resistor R connected in series to an AC supply of 220 V.

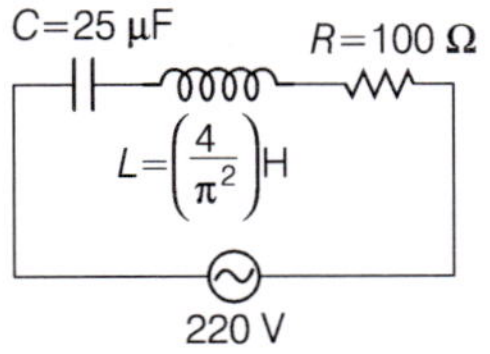

Calculate

(a) the resonant frequency of the given *L-C-R* circuit.

(b) current flowing through the circuit.

(c) average power consumed by the circuit.

(*ii*) In a series *L-C-R* circuit, what is the phase difference between V_L and V_C, where V_L is the potential difference across the inductor and V_C is the potential difference across the capacitor? **ISC 2015**

41. An alternating emf of 110 V is applied to a circuit containing a resistance R of 80 Ω and an inductor L in series. The current is found to lag behind the supply voltage by an angle, $\theta = \tan^{-1}(3/4)$. Then, find the

(*i*) inductive reactance.

(*ii*) impedance of the circuit.

(*iii*) current flowing in the circuit.

(*iv*) if the inductor has coefficient of self-inductance of 0.1 H, what is the frequency of the applied emf? **ISC 2014**

42. (*i*) Figure below shows a series *L-C-R* circuit connected to an AC source which generates an alternating emf of frequency of 50 Hz. The reading of voltmeters V_1 and V_2 are 80 V and 60 V, respectively.

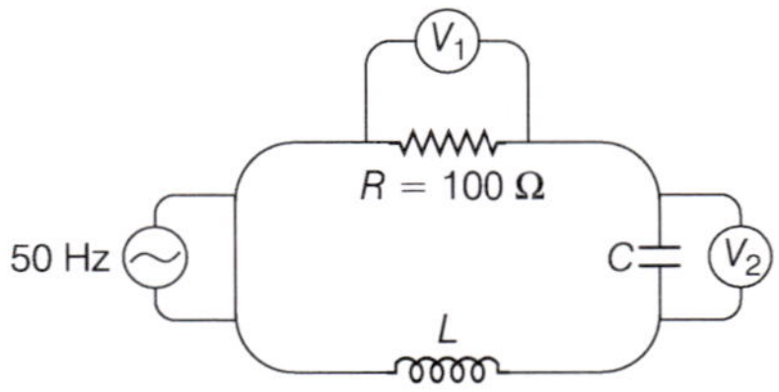

Find

(a) the current in the circuit.

(b) the capacitance C of the capacitor.

(*ii*) At resonance, what is the relation between impedance of a series *L-C-R* circuit and its resistance R? **ISC 2013)**

43. A 50 µF capacitor, a 30 Ω resistor and a 0.7 H inductor are connected in series to an AC supply which generate an emf e given by, $e = 300\sin(200t)$ V. Calculate peak value of the current flowing through the circuit. **ISC 2012**

> **KEY idea**
> To calculate the peak value of current, first calculate the impedance with the help o2f formula $(Z = \sqrt{R^2 + (X_L - X_C)^2}$ then apply the formula $\left(I_o = \frac{e_o}{Z}\right)$.

44. A 30 µF capacitor, 0.2 H inductor and a 50 Ω resistor are connected in series to an AC source whose emf is given by $E = 310\sin(314t)$, where E is in volt and t is in second. Calculate **ISC 2008**

(*i*) the impedance of the circuit.

(*ii*) peak value of current in the circuit.

Case Based question (For complete Chapter)

45. Direction *Read the passage given below and answer the questions that follows.*

Quality Factor

It defines the $i - f$ curve at resonance.

The characteristic of a series resonant circuit is determined by the quality factor (Q–factor).

If resonance in an $L - C - R$ circuit is less sharp (see graph) not only the maximum current in the circuit is less, the circuit is closed to resonance for a larger range of frequency ($\Delta\omega$) and tuning of circuit is difficult. So, if resonance is more sharp, circuit is more selective for a particular frequency and current in the circuit is large.

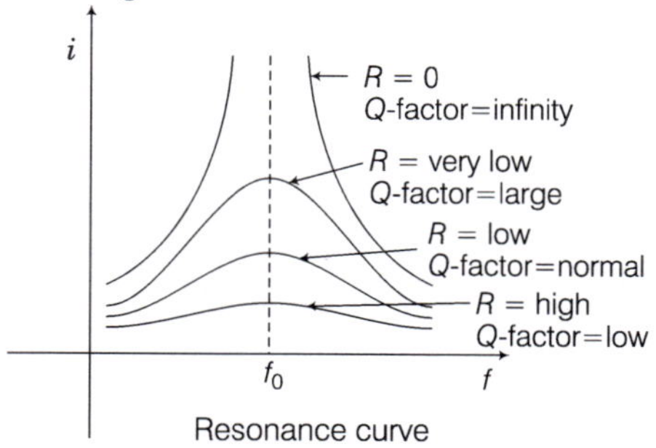

Resonance curve

The ratio of resonant frequency to band width which is responsible for sharpness of resonance is called Q-factor or quality factor of the circuit. It is represented as

$$\therefore\ Q - \text{factor} = \frac{V_L}{V_R} = \frac{V_C}{V_R}$$

$$= \frac{1}{R}\sqrt{\frac{L}{C}}$$

$$= \frac{\omega_0}{2\Delta\omega} = \frac{1}{\omega_0 CR} = \frac{\omega_0 L}{R}$$

[ω_0 = resonant frequency]

(*i*) What is the other name of quality factor? **(1)**

(*ii*) What is the voltage across the capacitor when the source voltage is 100 V and Q-factor is 10. **(1)**

(*iii*) Find the Q-factor when the voltage across the capacitor is 1000 V and the source voltage is 100 V. **(1)**

(*iv*) What happens to the voltage across the capacitor when the Q-factor increases? **(1)**

(*v*) What happens to the voltage across the inductor when the Q-factor decreases? **(1)**

Explanations

1. (a) $Z = \sqrt{\left(L\omega - \frac{1}{C\omega}\right)^2 + R^2}$

Z is minimum, when

$$L\omega = \frac{1}{C\omega}$$

$$\therefore \quad Z = \sqrt{(0)^2 + (2)^2} \Rightarrow Z = R$$

2. (c) $2\pi f L = 2\pi f C$

3. (b) $E = 300 \sin (100\pi t)$

$f = ?$

$\omega = 100\pi$

$2\pi f = 100\pi$

$f = 50$ Hz

4. (c)

5. (c) $V_0 = 400\text{V}, R = 80\Omega$

$\because$ Purely resistive

$$\therefore \quad \phi = 0$$

$$\therefore\ P_{av} = V_{rms} \cdot I_{rms} \cos\phi = \frac{V_0}{\sqrt{2}} \cdot \frac{I_0}{\sqrt{2}} \cos\phi$$

$$= \frac{1}{2} V_0 I_0 \cos\phi = \frac{1}{2} V_0 \cdot \frac{V_0}{R} \cos\phi \qquad [\because V_0 = I_0 R]$$

$$= \frac{1}{2} \times \frac{400 \times 400}{80} \cos 0°$$

$$= 1000 \text{ W}$$

6. For pure resistor, phase difference between alternating current and alternating voltage,

$$\phi = 0°$$

$\therefore$ Power factor $= \cos\phi = \cos 0° = 1$

7. For a L-C-R series circuit, its defined as cosine of the angle of lag or lead or resistance/impedance.

i.e. power factor,

$$\cos\phi = \frac{R}{Z} = \frac{R}{\sqrt{(X_C - X_L)^2 + R^2}}$$

where, $Z = \text{impedance}$

$$= \sqrt{(X_C - X_L)^2 + R^2}$$

At resonance, $X_C = X_L \Rightarrow \cos\phi = 1$

8. We know that average power consumed

$$P_{av} = I_{rms} V_{rms} \cos\phi$$

For ideal choke coil, phase difference between current (I) and voltage (V) is $\frac{\pi}{2}$.

i.e. $\phi = 90°$

$\Rightarrow \cos\phi = 0$

$$P_{av} = V_{rms} I_{rms} \cos 90°$$
$$= (V_{rms} I_{rms})(0) = 0$$

Hence, no power consumed by an ideal choke coil.

9. If ϕ is the angle of lag or lead of emf or current in a series L-C-R circuit, then $\cos\phi$ component in the equation of power average is called power factor.

$$\cos\phi = \frac{R}{Z} = \frac{R}{\sqrt{\left(\omega L - \frac{1}{\omega L}\right)^2 + R^2}}$$

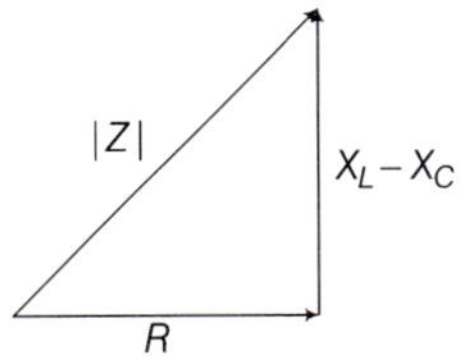

10. The graphical variation of emf induced with time for the output of an AC generator is shown as below.

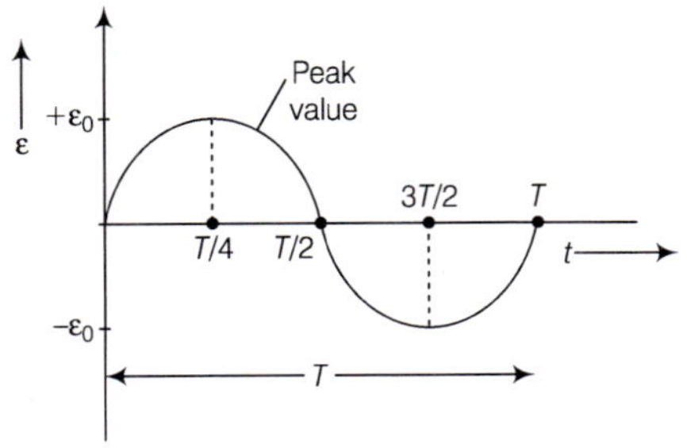

11. We know that power consumed

$$P_{av} = V_{rms} I_{rms} \cos\phi$$

For an ideal inductor, $\phi = 90°$

(i.e. phase difference between V and I is $\frac{\pi}{2}$)

$\Rightarrow \cos\phi = 0$

Power consumed $P = (V_{rms})(I_{rms})(0) = 0$

12. Given,

$R = 4\,\Omega, V_{rms} = 200\text{ V}, Z = 5\,\Omega, I_{rms} = 1.5\text{ A}$

As, we know power of an AC circuit is given by

$$P_{av} = V_{rms} I_{rms} \cos\phi$$

(where, $\cos\phi = \text{power factor} = \frac{R}{Z}$)

$\therefore \quad P = 200 \times 1.5 \times \frac{4}{5} = 240\text{ W}$

13. (i) At resonance, $X_L = X_C$ i.e. $R = Z$, circuit behaves like a purely resistive circuit. Current and voltage are in phase.

(ii) At resonance, $Z = R$ (min), $\cos\phi = 1$

$\therefore \quad P = I_{rms} V_{rms}$

So, power utilisation in the circuit is maximum.

14. Power factor $= \cos\phi = \frac{R}{Z} = \frac{R}{\sqrt{R^2 + X_L^2}}$

$[Z = (R^2 + X_L^2)^{1/2}]$

15. When current flows through inductor or capacitor, there is zero power loss due to $(\pi/2)$ phase difference between current and voltage in two cases. As we know the SI unit of power is watt, so the current through inductor or capacitor is called wattless current.

16. Characteristics of series resonant circuit

(a) The applied alternating voltage and the resulting current are in the same phase.

(b) The impedance Z of the circuit is minimum and is equal to the resistance R in the circuit.

17. Refer to the text on page 146 (Series L-C-R circuit).

18. Given $I = 5\sin\left(100\pi t - \frac{\pi}{6}\right)$

$$e = 300\sin\left(100\pi t + \frac{\pi}{6}\right)$$

We know that, average power consumed

$$P_{av} = E_{rms} I_{rms} \cos\phi = \frac{E_0}{\sqrt{2}} \times \frac{I_0}{\sqrt{2}} \cos\phi$$

where, $E_0 = \text{peak emf} = 300\text{ V}$

$I_0 = \text{peak current} = 5\text{ A}$

$\cos\phi = \text{power factor} = \cos 60° = \frac{1}{2}$ $\left[\because \phi = \phi_1 - \phi_2 = \frac{\pi}{6} + \frac{\pi}{6} = \frac{\pi}{3}\right]$

$\therefore \quad P_{av} = \frac{300}{\sqrt{2}} \times \frac{50}{\sqrt{2}} \times \frac{1}{2} = 3750\text{ W}$

19. $C = 2\mu\text{F} = 2 \times 10^{-6}\text{ F}$

$R = 100\,\Omega, L = 8\text{H}, \varepsilon_o = 200\text{V}, I_0 = ?,$

$X_L = ?, X_C = ?\ Z = ?$

$$\nu = \nu_r = \frac{1}{2\pi\sqrt{LC}}$$

$$= \frac{1}{2\times 3.14\sqrt{8\times 2\times 10^{-6}}}$$

$$= \frac{1000}{8\times 3.14} = 39.8 \text{ Hz}$$

(*i*) (c) Peak value of current

$$I_0 = \frac{E_o}{K} = \frac{200}{100} = 2\text{A}$$

(*ii*) (a) The voltage across inductor is ahead of voltage across resistor by a phase angle of 90°.

(*iii*) (d) The voltages across inductor and capacitor differ in phase by 180°.

20. (*i*) (d) P_{av} by capacitor $= VI\cos\frac{\pi}{2} = 0$

(*ii*) (b) For *L-C-R* circuit,

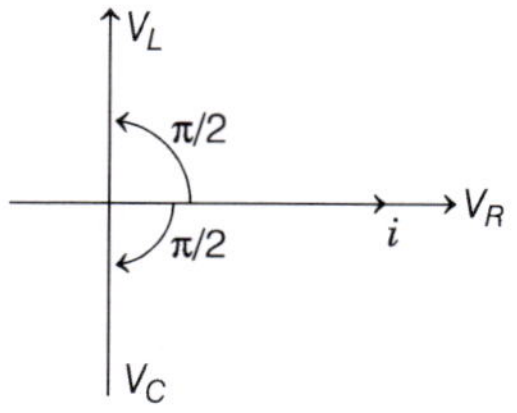

∴ Phase difference between V_L and

$$V_C = \frac{\pi}{2} + \frac{\pi}{2} = \pi = 180°$$

(*iii*) (a) At resonance i.e., $X_L = X_C$ maximum current flows in a circuit.

21. At $f = f_0, Z = R$. This is the minimum value of impedance.

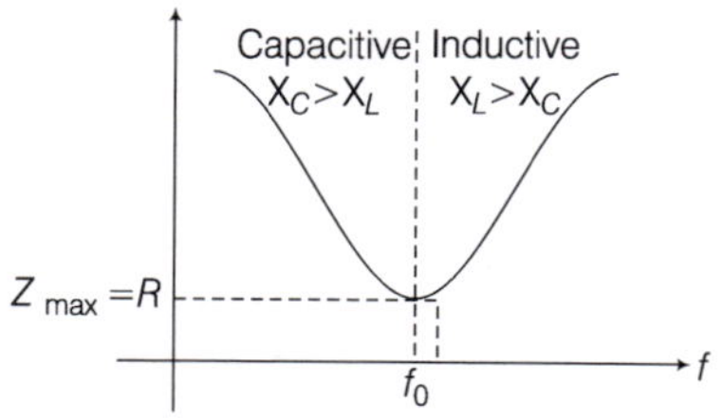

22. For a series *L-C-R* circuit at resonance $X_C = X_L$, i.e. reactance of capacitor and inductor must be equal.

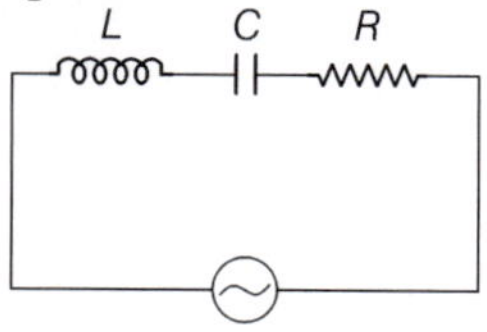

Now according to question

$$\Rightarrow \quad \omega_0 L = \frac{1}{\omega_0 C} \Rightarrow \omega_0^2 = \frac{1}{LC}$$

$$\Rightarrow \quad \omega_0 = \frac{1}{\sqrt{LC}}$$

$$\Rightarrow \quad 2\pi f_0 = \frac{1}{\sqrt{LC}}$$

∴ Resonant frequency

$$f_0 = \frac{1}{2\pi}\sqrt{\frac{1}{LC}}$$

23. Initially, $R = 150\ \Omega$

$C = 15\ \mu\text{F}$, peak current, $I_0 = 0.2$ A

Impedance of circuit

$$Z = \frac{V_0}{I_0} = \frac{V_{rms}\times\sqrt{2}}{I_0}$$

$$= \frac{220\times\sqrt{2}}{0.20} = \frac{220\times 100}{20}\times\sqrt{2}$$

$$= 220\times 5\times\sqrt{2} = 1100\sqrt{2}\ \Omega$$

∴ Average power consumed

$$P_{av} = V_{rms} I_{rms}\cos\phi \qquad \left[\because \cos\phi = \frac{R}{Z}\right]$$

$$P_{av} = 220\times\frac{0.2}{\sqrt{2}}\times\frac{150}{1100\sqrt{2}}$$

$$P_{av} = 3\text{ W}$$

When there is only resistor in the circuit, power consumed is

$$P_{av} = I_{rms}^2 R = \left(\frac{I_0}{\sqrt{2}}\right)^2 R$$

$$= \left(\frac{0.2}{\sqrt{2}}\right)^2 \times 150 = 3\text{ W}$$

24. At resonance, $X_L = X_C \Rightarrow \omega = \frac{1}{\sqrt{LC}}$

So, the circuit has following characteristics at resonance.

(*i*) Current in the circuit is maximum $\frac{\varepsilon_0}{R}$ or circuit impedance is minimum and purely resistive.

(*ii*) There is no phase difference between current and the applied voltage.

(*iii*) Power utilisation by the circuit is maximum. i.e. $\frac{\varepsilon_{rms}^2}{R}$.

25. According to the question,

Given, $f = 50\text{ Hz}, R = 20\,\Omega, L = 100\text{ mH}$

$= 100 \times 10^{-3}\text{ H}$

$C = 30\,\mu\text{F} = 30 \times 10^{-6}\text{ F}$

(*i*) $X_L = 2\pi fL$

$= 2 \times 3.14 \times 50 \times 100 \times 10^{-3}$

$= 31.4\,\Omega$

$$X_C = \frac{1}{2\pi fC} = \frac{1}{2 \times 3.14 \times 50 \times 30 \times 10^{-6}}$$

$= 106.16\,\Omega$

As we know that, $\tan\phi = \dfrac{X_C - X_L}{R}$

[ϕ = phase difference between current and voltage]

$$= \frac{106.16 - 31.4}{20} = 3.73$$

$\Rightarrow \quad \phi = 75°$

(*ii*) As $X_C > X_L$

$\Rightarrow V_C > V_L$

Hence, current leads the voltage by angle $\phi = 75°$ as shown.

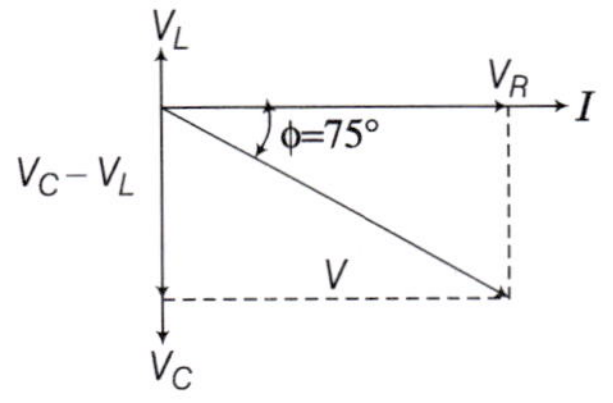

Common Mistake The values of X_L, X_C and R to be with proper units.

26. For DC source, the inductor will act as short circuit and only resistor has to be taken for calculation of current.

Now for DC source connected to the circuit

$X_L = \omega L = 0 \qquad [\because \omega = 0]$

So, resistance, $R = \dfrac{E}{I} = \dfrac{12\text{ V}}{4\text{ A}} = 3\,\Omega$

When the coil is connected to AC source, then

$$i = \frac{E}{\sqrt{R^2 + (\omega L)^2}} \qquad [\because Z = \sqrt{R^2 + (\omega L)^2}]$$

$$2.4 = \frac{12}{\sqrt{3^2 + (2\pi fL)^2}}$$

$$\Rightarrow 9 + (2\pi fL)^2 = \left(\frac{12}{2.4}\right)^2 = 25$$

$(2\pi fL)^2 = 25 - 9 = 16$

$\Rightarrow \quad 2\pi fL = 4$

$$\Rightarrow \quad L = \frac{1}{2\pi f} \times 4 = \frac{1}{2\pi \times 8} \times 4 \qquad [\because f = 8\text{ Hz}]$$

$\therefore \quad L = \dfrac{1}{4\pi}\text{ H}$

$= 0.0795\text{ H}$

27. (*i*) For an *R-L* circuit, we have to use

Impedance, $Z = \sqrt{R^2 + X_L^2}$ ...(i)

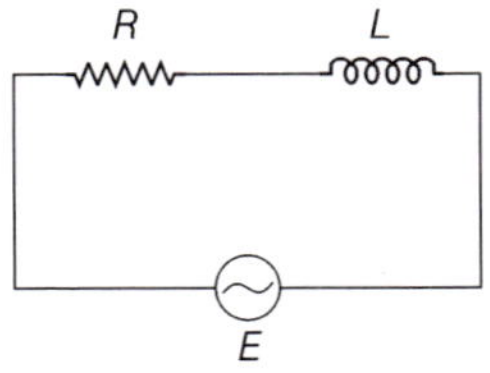

According to the question,

$R = 30\,\Omega, X_L = 40\,\Omega$

$\Rightarrow Z = \sqrt{(30)^2 + (40)^2} = 50\,\Omega \qquad$ [from Eq.(i)]

(*ii*) ϕ = phase difference

$$= \tan^{-1}\left(\frac{X_L}{R}\right)$$

$$= \tan^{-1}\left(\frac{40}{30}\right) = 53°$$

(*iii*) Peak value of current,

$$I_0 = \frac{V_0}{Z} = \frac{220}{50} = 4.4\text{ A}$$

28. (*i*) According to the question,

Applied emf = 110 V, current, $I = 11$ A

Impedance of the circuit, $Z = \dfrac{E}{I} = \dfrac{110}{11} = 10\,\Omega$

(*ii*) As we know

Impedance, $Z = \sqrt{R^2 + X_L^2}$

$\Rightarrow \quad X_L = \sqrt{Z^2 - R^2}$

$= \sqrt{10^2 - 8^2} = \sqrt{100 - 64}$

$= \sqrt{36} = 6\,\Omega$

The inductive reactance of the chock coil is

$X_L = 6\,\Omega$

29. According to the given equations in the question,

$$E_0 = 200\sin\left(314t + \frac{\pi}{6}\right) \text{ and } I = 5\sin(314t)\text{A}$$

Comparing above two equations with standard equation.

(*i*) Peak value of the current,

$$I_0 = 5 \text{ A and emf, } \varepsilon_0 = 200 \text{ V}$$

(*ii*) $\omega = 2\pi f = 314 \Rightarrow f = \frac{314}{2\times 3.14} = 50 \text{ Hz}$

(*iii*) The phase difference between the current and emf,

$$\phi = \frac{\pi}{6} = 30°$$

30. $\varepsilon = 300\sin(500t)$V

Total reactance of the circuit is combination of capacitance and inductive reactances.

$$(X_C - X_L) = \left|\frac{1}{\omega_C} - \omega_L\right|$$

$$= \left|\frac{1}{500\times 4\times 10^{-6}} - 500\times 1\right|$$

$$= \left|5\times 10^2 - 500\right|$$

$\therefore$ $(X_C - X_L) = 0$

(a) $Z = \sqrt{R^2 + (X_C - X_L)^2}$

$$= \sqrt{(60)^2 + 0}$$

$$= 60\ \Omega$$

(b) $I_0 = \frac{E_0}{Z} = \frac{300}{60} = 5\text{ A}$

(c) $\tan\phi = \left|\frac{X_C - X_L}{R}\right| = \frac{0}{60} = 0°$

31. (i) According to the question,

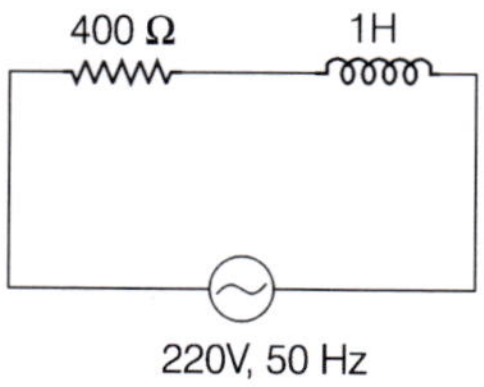

(a) The reactance of the coil is $\omega L = X_L = 2\pi f L$

$$= 2\times\frac{22}{7}\times 50\times 1 = 314.28\ \Omega$$

(b) Impedance of the coil, $= \sqrt{X_L^2 + R^2}$

$$= \sqrt{(\omega L)^2 + (R)^2}$$

$$= \sqrt{(2\pi\times 50\times (1)^2 + (400)^2}$$

$$= \sqrt{258596} = 508.52\ \Omega$$

(c) Current flowing through the coil,

$$V = IR$$

$$I = \frac{220}{508.52} = 0.43$$

(ii) The variation of impedance of a series *LCR* circuit with frequency of AC supply is given below

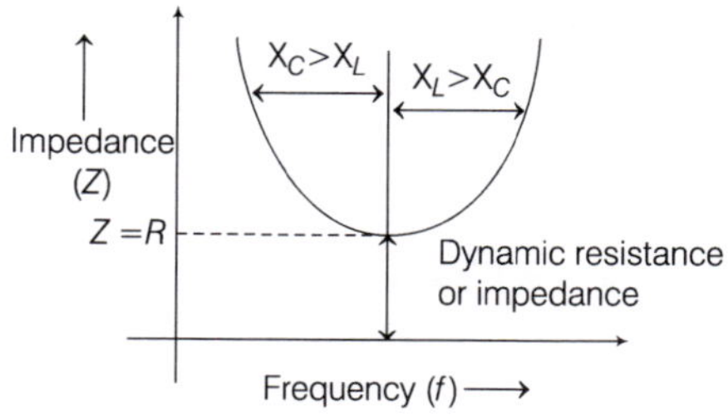

32. Given, $f = 50$ Hz, $R = 600\ \Omega$,

$C = 3.16\ \mu\text{F} = 3.16\times 10^{-6}$ F, $L = 0.63$ H

(*i*) (a) $X_C = \frac{1}{\omega C} = \frac{1}{2\pi f C}$

$$= \frac{1}{2\pi\times 50\times 3.16\times 10^{-6}}$$

$$= 1000\ \Omega$$

(*ii*) (c) $X_L = \omega L = 2\pi f L = 2\pi\times 50\times 0.63$

$$= 2\pi\times 50\times\frac{2}{\pi} = 200\ \Omega$$

(*iii*) (b) $Z = \sqrt{R^2 + (X_L - X_C)^2}$

$$= \sqrt{600^2 + (200 - 1000)^2} = 1000\ \Omega$$

(*iv*) (a) $\tan\phi = \left|\frac{X_L - X_C}{R}\right|$

$$= \left|\frac{200 - 1000}{600}\right|$$

$$= \left|\frac{-800}{600}\right| = \left|-\frac{4}{3}\right|$$

$\therefore$ $\tan\phi = \frac{4}{3}$

$\Rightarrow$ $\phi = \tan^{-1}\left(\frac{4}{3}\right) = 53°$

$\therefore$ Current leads the voltage by 53° $(\because X_C > X_L)$

33. (*i*) Given, capacitance, $C = 5\ \mu\text{F} = 5\times 10^{-6}$ F

Resistance, $R = 400\Omega$

Inductance, $L = 3$ H

V_{rms} value of voltage, $E_V = 220$ V

Frequency, $\nu = 50$ Hz

(a) Since, capacitive reactance,

$$X_C = \frac{1}{\omega C} = \frac{1}{2\pi\nu C}$$

$$= \frac{1}{2 \times 3.14 \times 50 \times 5 \times 10^{-6}}$$

$$X_C = 636.9\,\Omega$$

and inductive reactance

$$X_L = \omega L = 2\pi\nu L$$

$$= 2 \times 3.14 \times 50 \times 3$$

$$= 942\,\Omega$$

$\because$ Impedance,

$$Z = \sqrt{R^2 + (X_L - X_C)^2}$$

$$= \sqrt{(400)^2 + (942 - 636.9)^2}$$

$$= \sqrt{(400)^2 + (305.1)^2} = 503.1\,\Omega$$

(b) Current flowing through the circuit,

$$I = \frac{E}{Z} = \frac{220}{503.1} = 0.437\text{ A}$$

(*ii*) Refer to text on page 146 (Series *L-C-R* circuit).

34. (*i*) Given, $e = 310\sin(100\pi t)$V ...(i)

and $I = 5\sin\left(100\pi t + \dfrac{\pi}{3}\right)$A ...(ii)

(a) Comparing Eqs. (i) and (ii) with standard equation, the phase difference between emf (e) and current (I) is

$$\Delta\phi = |\phi_1 - \phi_2|$$

$$= \left|0 - \frac{\pi}{3}\right| = \left|-\frac{\pi}{3}\right| = 60°$$

(b) We know that, average power consumed,

$$P_{av} = E_{rms} I_{rms} \cos\theta$$

$$= \frac{E_o}{\sqrt{2}} \times \frac{I_o}{\sqrt{2}} \times \cos\phi$$

$E_0 =$ peak emf $= 310$ V

$I_0 =$ peak current $= 5$ A

$\cos\phi =$ power factor $= \cos 60° = \dfrac{1}{2}$

$$\therefore \quad P_{av} = \frac{310}{\sqrt{2}} \times \frac{5}{\sqrt{2}} \times \frac{1}{2}$$

$$= \frac{1550}{4} = 387.5\text{ W}$$

(*ii*) Refer to text on page 146 (Resonance in *L-C-R* Series Circuit).

35. (*i*) Given, $V_{rms} = 200$ V, $L = 0.05$ H, $R = 10\,\Omega$, $f = 50$ Hz

Angular frequency, $\omega = 2\pi f$

$$= 2\pi \times 50$$

$$= 100\pi\text{ rad/s}$$

Inductive reactance, $X_L = \omega L$

$$= 100\pi \times 0.05$$

$$= 5\pi\,\Omega$$

(a) Impedance, $Z = \sqrt{R^2 + X_L^2}$

$$= \sqrt{(10)^2 + (5\pi)^2}$$

$$= \sqrt{100 + 25\pi^2} = \sqrt{346.74}$$

$$= 18.620\,\Omega$$

(b) Current flowing in the circuit,

$$I = \frac{V_{rms}}{Z} = \frac{200}{18.614} = 10.744\text{A}$$

(*ii*) Graph showing the radiation of inductive reactance X_L *versus* frequency f.

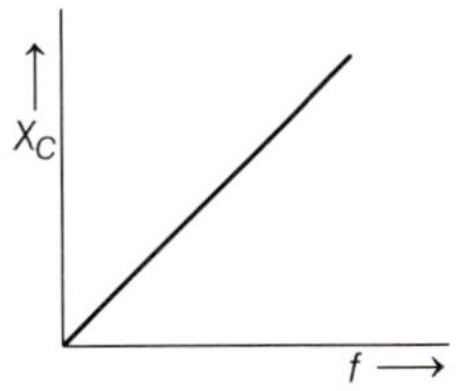

36. We have, $\tan\theta = \dfrac{X_C}{R}$

$\because \quad \theta = \tan^{-1}\left(\dfrac{3}{4}\right)$

$\Rightarrow \quad \tan\theta = \dfrac{3}{4}$

$\therefore \quad \dfrac{3}{4} = \dfrac{X_C}{160}$

(a) I. Capacitive reactance,

$$X_C = 160 \times \frac{3}{4} = 120\,\Omega$$

II. Impedance of the *R-C* circuit,

$$Z = \sqrt{R^2 + (X_C)^2}$$

$$= \sqrt{(160)^2 + (120)^2}$$

$$= \sqrt{40000} = 200\,\Omega$$

III. We have, $\quad Z = \dfrac{V}{i}$

Current flowing in the circuit,

$$i = \frac{V}{Z} = \frac{220}{200} = 1.1\text{A}$$

(b) $X_C = \dfrac{1}{2\pi fC}$

$$\Rightarrow 120 = \frac{1}{2\pi \times 50 \times C} \Rightarrow C = \frac{1}{2\pi \times 50 \times 120}$$

$\therefore$ Capacitance, $C = 2.65 \times 10^{-5}$ F

37. The equation of emf is given by

$\varepsilon = 300 \sin(100\pi t)$ V

The standard equation of emf,

$$\varepsilon = \varepsilon_0 \sin \omega t$$

$\therefore \quad \omega = 100\pi$

$\Rightarrow \quad 2\pi f = 100\pi \quad [\because \omega = 2\pi f]$

(a) Impedance of the circuit $(L - C - R)$,

$$Z = \sqrt{R^2 + (X_L - X_C)^2}$$

$$= \sqrt{R^2 + \left(2\pi fL - \frac{1}{2\pi fC}\right)^2}$$

$$= \sqrt{100^2 + \left(100\pi \times 1 - \frac{1}{100\pi \times 16 \times 10^{-6}}\right)^2}$$

$$= \sqrt{100^2 + (314 - 199)^2}$$

$$= \sqrt{100^2 + 115^2} = 152.39\ \Omega$$

(b) Resonant frequency,

$$f_0 = \frac{1}{2\pi\sqrt{LC}} = \frac{1}{2\pi\sqrt{1 \times 16 \times 10^{-6}}}$$

$$= \frac{1}{2\pi \times 4 \times 10^{-3}} = 39.8\ \text{Hz}$$

(c) Power factor, $\cos\phi = \dfrac{R}{Z}$

At resonant frequency, $R = Z$

$\therefore \quad \cos\phi = 1$

Concept Enhancer At resonance, the inductive reactance is equal to capacitive reactance. So, the impedence of the circuit is equal to its resistance and hence power factor becomes unity.

38. Given, $L = 8\text{H}$, $C = 2\mu\text{F} = 2 \times 10^{-6}$ F.

$R = 100\Omega$, $\nu = 50$ Hz, $E_{rms} = 220$V

(a) $X_L = \omega L = 2\pi\nu \times L$

$$2 \times 314 \times 50 \times 8 = 2512\ \Omega$$

$$X_C = \frac{1}{\omega C}$$

$$= \frac{1}{2 \times 3.14 \times 50 \times 2 \times 10^{-6}} = 1592\ \Omega$$

Impedance, $Z = \sqrt{R^2 + (X_L - X_C)^2}$

$$= \sqrt{(100)^2 + (2512 - 1592)^2}$$

$$= 925.41\ \Omega = 925\Omega$$

(b) $I_{\text{rms}} = \dfrac{E_{\text{rms}}}{Z} = \dfrac{220}{925} = 0.238\text{A}$

(c) Phase difference

$$\phi = \tan^{-1}\frac{(X_L - X_C)}{R}$$

$$= \tan^{-1}\frac{(2512 - 1529)}{100}$$

$$= \tan^{-1}(9.2) = 83°7$$

(d) Average power $(P) = I_{\text{rms}} E_{\text{rms}} \cos\theta$

$$= 0.238 \times 220 \times \cos 83°7'$$

$$= 0.23 \times 220 \times 0.119 = 6.02\ \text{W}$$

39. (i) According to the question,

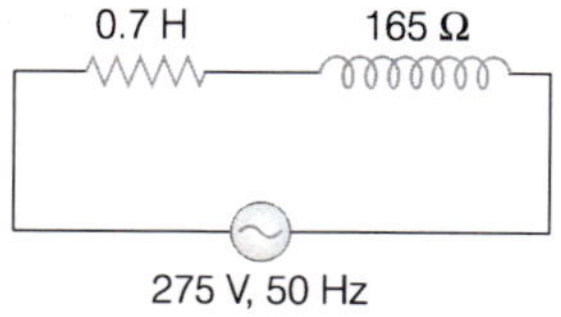

(a) Reactance of the coil is

$$X_L = \omega L$$

$$= 2\pi fL = 2 \times \frac{22}{7} \times 50 \times 0.7$$

$$= 220\ \Omega$$

(b) Impedance of the coil, Z

$$= \sqrt{X_L^2 + R^2}$$

$$= \sqrt{(\omega L)^2 + R^2}$$

$$= \sqrt{(2\pi \times 50 \times 0.7)^2 + (165)^2}$$

$$= \sqrt{48400 + 27225}$$

$$= \sqrt{75625} = 275$$

(c) Current flowing through the coil, $V = IR$

$\Rightarrow \quad I = \dfrac{V}{R}$ (R = resistance of circuit and V = voltage applied)

$\Rightarrow \quad I = \dfrac{275}{275} \quad \Rightarrow \quad I = 1$ A

(ii) The variation of impedance of a series L-C-R circuit with frequency of AC supply is given below:

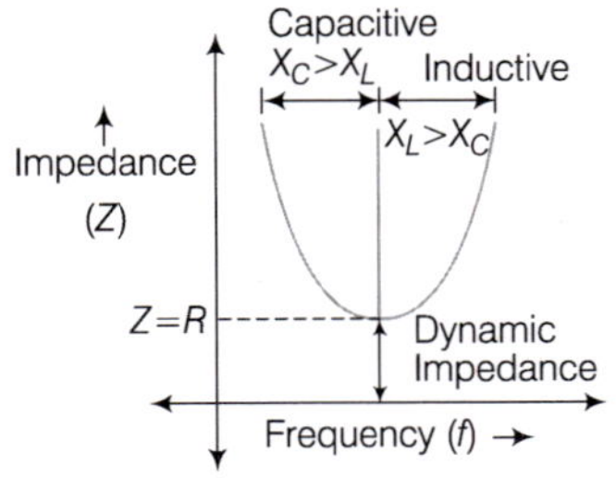

40. (i) Given, $E_{rms} = 220\text{ V}, C = 25\mu\text{F} = 25\times10^{-6}$ F,

$L = \frac{4}{\pi^2}$ H, $R = 100\,\Omega$

(a) Resonant frequency is given by

$$f_r = \frac{1}{2\pi\sqrt{LC}}$$

$$= \frac{1}{2\times3.14\times\sqrt{\frac{4}{\pi^2}\times25\times10^{-6}}}$$

$$= \frac{1}{2\times3.14\times\frac{2}{3.14}\times5\times10^{-3}} = 50\text{ Hz}$$

(b) Impedance of the circuit is given by

$$Z = \sqrt{R^2 + (X_L - X_C)^2} \quad \ldots\text{(i)}$$

We know that $X_C = \frac{1}{\omega C} = \frac{1}{2\pi fC}$

$$= \frac{1}{2\times3.14\times50\times25\times10^{-6}} = 127.3\,\Omega$$

$$X_L = \omega L = 2\pi fL = 2\times3.14\times\frac{4}{\pi^2}\times50 = 127.3\,\Omega$$

Substituting the all values in Eq. (i), we get

$$Z = \sqrt{(100)^2 + (127.3 - 127.3)^2}$$

$$= \sqrt{(100)^2} = 100\,\Omega$$

We know that $I_{rms} = \frac{E_{rms}}{Z} = \frac{220}{100} = 2.2\text{A}$

(c) Average power consumed by the circuit

$$= E_{rms}\times I_{rms}\times\frac{R}{\sqrt{R^2 + \left(L\omega - \frac{1}{C\omega}\right)^2}}$$

$\because \quad Z = R = 100\,\Omega$

So, power $= E_{rms}\times I_{rms}$

$= 220\times2.2 = 484$ W

(ii) Phasor diagram of L-C-R circuit is shown below:

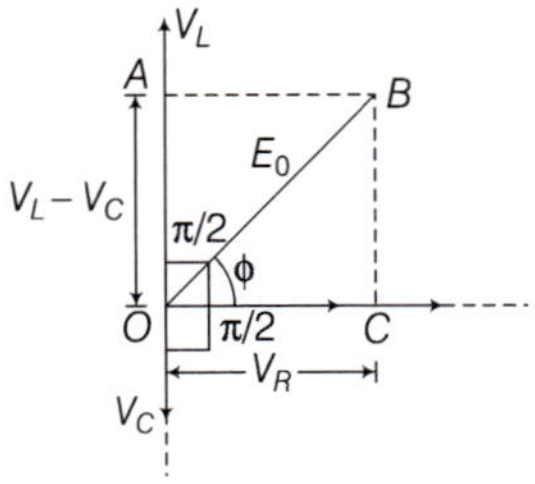

The phase difference across the inductor and phase difference across the capacitor is 180°.

41. We have to apply formula to

$$\tan\phi = \frac{X_L}{R}.$$

Net impedance can be calculated by

$$Z = \sqrt{X_L^2 + R^2}$$

(*i*) We can write

$$\tan\phi = \frac{X_L}{R} = \frac{3}{4} \qquad \text{[given in the question]}$$

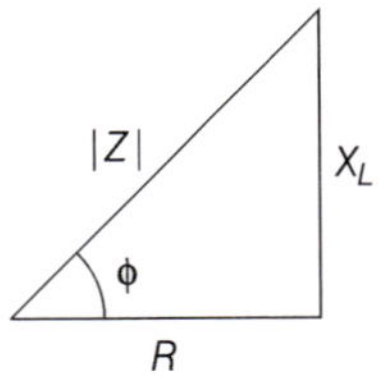

$\Rightarrow \quad \frac{X_L}{R} = \frac{3}{4}$

$\therefore \quad R = 80\,\Omega$

$\Rightarrow \quad X_L = \frac{3}{4}\times R = \frac{3}{4}\times80\,\Omega = 60\,\Omega$

(*ii*) Impedance, $Z = \sqrt{X_L^2 + R^2}$

$= \sqrt{(60)^2 + (80)^2} = 100\,\Omega$

(*iii*) Current, $I_{rms} = \frac{V_{rms}}{Z} = \frac{110}{100} = 1.1$ A

(*iv*) We know that,

$X_L = \omega L$

$\Rightarrow \quad 60 = (0.1)\times\omega \qquad [\because L = 0.1\text{ H}]$

$\Rightarrow \quad \omega = 600$ rad/s

$\Rightarrow \quad 2\pi f = 600$ rad/s

$\Rightarrow \quad f = 95.5\text{ Hz} = 96\text{ Hz}$

42. (*i*) Apply $I = V / R$ to obtain current through the resistor. At resonance, impedance of capacitor and inductor can be equated and cancelled.

Now according to the question,

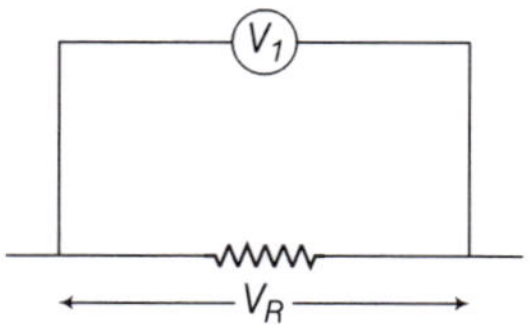

(a) Electric current in the circuit

$$I = \frac{V_R}{R} = \frac{V_1}{R} = \frac{80}{100} = 0.8 \text{ A}$$

(b) Current through the capacitor, I_C is equal to the current through resistor as they are in series

$$I_R = I_C \Rightarrow 0.8 = \frac{V_C}{X_C}$$

$$\Rightarrow \quad V_C = V_L \Rightarrow (0.8) \times X_C = (0.8)\left(\frac{1}{\omega C}\right)$$

$$\Rightarrow \quad \frac{1}{C} = \frac{V_2 \times \omega}{0.8} = \frac{60 \times 2\pi f}{0.8} \quad [\because V_L = V_C]$$

$$= \frac{600 \times 2\pi \times 50}{8}$$

$$\Rightarrow \quad C = \frac{8}{6 \times 5 \times 2\pi \times 10^3}$$

$$\Rightarrow \quad C = 42.46 \text{ μF}$$

(*ii*) At resonance, $X_L = X_C$

$$Z = \sqrt{R^2 + (X_L - X_C)^2}$$

$$= \sqrt{R^2 + 0} = R$$

At resonance, net impedance is equal to resistance (R).

43. According to the question,

$$C = 50\mu\text{F}, R = 30\,\Omega, L = 0.7\text{ H},$$

$$e = 300 \sin(200\,t),$$

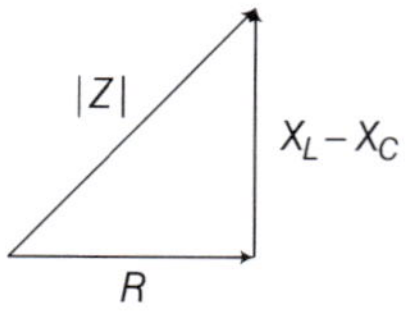

By comparing with $e = e_0 \sin \omega t$

$$\omega = 200 \text{ rad/s}, e_0 = 300 \text{ V}$$

Impedance

$$Z = \sqrt{R^2 + (X_L - X_C)^2}$$

$$= \sqrt{(30)^2 + \left(\omega L - \frac{1}{\omega C}\right)^2}$$

$$= \sqrt{(30)^2 + \left(200 \times 0.7 - \frac{10^6}{200 \times 50}\right)^2}$$

$$= \sqrt{900 + (140 - 100)^2} \Rightarrow Z = 50\,\Omega$$

I_0 = Peak value of current

$$= \frac{\text{Peak value of voltage}}{\text{Impedance}}$$

$$= \frac{e_0}{Z} = \frac{300}{50} = 6 \text{ A}$$

44. This is a similar question as that of the previous one hence, follow the similar method to calculate impedance and peak current.

(*i*) $Z = 66.2\,\Omega$ (*ii*) $I_0 = 4.68$ A

45. (i) Quality factor is also known as voltage magnification because the voltage across the capacitor or inductor in resonance condition is Equal to Q-times the source voltage.

(ii) Voltage across the capacitor in resonance condition is equal to Q-times the source voltage.

$$Q = V_C / V_S$$

$$10 = \frac{V_C}{100}$$

$$V_C = 1000 \text{ V}$$

(iii) $Q = \frac{V_C}{V_S} = \frac{1000}{100} = 10 \text{ V}$

(iv) As, we know the voltage across the capacitor in resonance condition is Equal to Q-times the source voltage. Hence, as the Q-factor increases, the voltage across the capacitor also increases.

(v) When the Q-factor decrease, the voltage across the inductor also decreases because the voltage across the inductor in resonance condition is equal to Q times the source voltage.

CHAPTER TEST

01 Mark Questions (MCQs)

1 An alternating emf is given by $V = 200\sin(50\pi t)$V. The rms value of the emf is

(a) $100\sqrt{2}$V (b) $200\sqrt{2}$ V
(c) 100V (d) 200V

2 The peak voltage in an AC circuit is 707 V. The virtual voltage is

(a) 70.7 V (b) 1000 V (c) 500 V (d) 707 V

3 An ammeter in an AC circuit reads 4A. The maximum instantaneous magnitude of the current in the circuit is

(a) 4 A (b) $4\sqrt{2}$ A (c) 8 A (d) $8\sqrt{2}$ A

4 An AC having a peak value 1.41 is used to heat a wire. A DC producing the same heating rate will be of

(a) 1.41 A (b) 2.0 A
(c) 0.705 A (d) 1.0 A

01 Mark Questions (VSA)

5 The current flowing through a pure inductance of 2 mH is $I = (15\cos 300t)$ A. What is the (i) rms and (ii) average value of current for a complete cycle?

6 Define the term rms value of the current. How it is related to the peak value?

7 The electric main in a house is marked as 110 V and 50 Hz. Write down the equation for instantaneous voltage.

8 The equation of an alternating current is $i = 5\cos(100\pi t - \phi)$ A. Calculate the peak value and frequency of AC.

02 Marks Questions

9 A sinusoidal voltage $V = 200\sin 314t$ is applied to a resistor of $10\ \Omega$.

Calculate

(i) rms value of voltage
(ii) rms value of current.

10 The electric current in a circuit is given by $I = I_0(t/K)$ for some time. Find the rms value of current for the period $t = 0$ to $t = K$.

03 Marks Questions

11 An AC voltage $V = V_0 \sin \omega t$ is applied across a pure capacitor C. Obtain an expression for the current I in the circuit and hence, obtain

(i) the capacitive capacitance of the circuit.
(ii) the phase of the current flowing with respect to the applied voltage.

12 An AC voltage $V = V_0 \sin \omega t$ is applied across a pure inductor L. Obtain an expression for the current I in the circuit and hence, obtain

(i) the inductive reactance of the circuit.
(ii) the phase of the current flowing with respect to voltage.

05 Marks Questions

13 An AC source of voltage $V = V_m \sin \omega t$ is connected one-by-one to three circuit elements, X, Y and Z. It is observed that the current flowing in them

(i) is in phase with applied voltage for element X.
(ii) leads the voltage in phase by $\pi/2$ for element Y.
(iii) lags the applied voltage in phase by $\pi/2$ for element Z. Identify the three circuit elements.

14 The figure given below shows a series $L-C-R$ circuit with $L = 10.0$ H, $C = 40\mu$F, $R = 60\Omega$ connected to a variable frequency 240 V source. Calculate

(i) the angular frequency of the source which drives the circuit at resonance.
(ii) the current at the resonating frequency.
(iii) the rms potential drop across the inductor at resonance.

Answers

1. (a) **2.** (c) **3.** (b) **4.** (d)

5. (i) $I_{rms} = \frac{15}{\sqrt{2}}$ A (ii) $I_{av} = 0$

8. 5A, 502Hz **9.** (i) 141.1 V (ii) 14.14 A

10. $\frac{I_0}{\sqrt{3}}$ **11.** (i) $X_C = \frac{1}{\omega C}$ (ii) $\phi = \frac{\pi}{2}$ lead

12. (i) $X_L = \omega L$ (ii) Lags behind by $\phi = \frac{\pi}{2}$

13. (i) $X \rightarrow$ Resistor (ii) $Y \rightarrow$ Capacitor (iii) $Z \rightarrow$ Inductor

14. (i) $\omega_0 = 50$ rad/s (ii) $I_{rms} = 4$A (iii) $V_{rms} = 2000$ V

12

Electromagnetic Waves

TREND ANALYSIS 4 YEARS

Average No. of Questions Across all Sets

	Types of Questions	2024	2023	2020	2019
Electromagnetic Waves	1 Mark	–	–	–	–
	2 Marks	1	2	1	1
	3 Marks	–	–	–	–
	5 Marks	–	–	–	–

Electric current produces magnetic field and a magnetic field changing with time gives rise to an electric field. This brought together the phenomena of electricity and magnetism into a coherent and unified theory.

After this discovery, Maxwell predicted the transmission of energy by electromagnetic waves, which could travel with the speed of light. This led him to conclude that the light itself is an electromagnetic wave.

Its electric and magnetic fields are perpendicular to each other and the direction of propagation of wave is perpendicular to both E and B.

Displacement Current

It is defined as that current which comes into play in the region in which the electric field and electric flux is changing with time. It is denoted by I_D and expressed as

$$\boxed{I_D = \varepsilon_0 \frac{d\phi_E}{dt}}$$

where, ε_0 = permittivity of free space

and $\frac{d\phi_E}{dt}$ = rate of change of electric flux through the area between the plates of capacitor.

Need for Displacement Current

Ampere's circuital law for conduction current during charging a capacitor was found inconsistent. Therefore, Maxwell modified Ampere's circuital law by introducing displacement current.

Ampere's circuital law ($\oint \mathbf{B} \cdot d\mathbf{l} = \mu_0 I$) was modified to $\oint \mathbf{B} \cdot d\mathbf{l} = \mu_0 (I_C + I_D)$.

where, I_C is conduction current and I_D is displacement current.

It is called **modified Ampere's circuital law** or **Ampere-Maxwell's circuital law.**

Following inferences can be drawn from the above discussion

(*i*) The conduction and displacement currents are individually discontinuous but the currents together possess the property of continuity through any closed electric circuit.

(*ii*) The displacement current is precisely equal to the conduction current, when these two are present in different parts of the circuit.

(*iii*) This displacement current arises due to the rate of change of electric flux between the two plates of the capacitor.

(*iv*) Just as the conduction current, the displacement current is also the source of magnetic field.

Electromagnetic Waves

An electromagnetic wave is a wave radiated by an accelerated or oscillatory charge in which varying magnetic field is the source of electric field and varying electric field is the source of magnetic field. Thus, two fields becomes source of each other and the wave propagates in a direction perpendicular to both the fields.

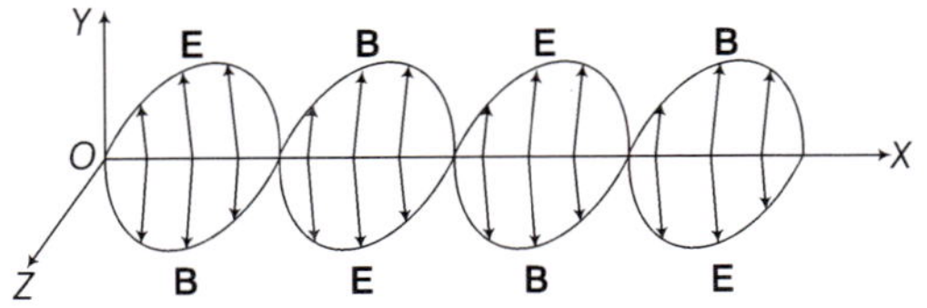

Direction of propagation ⟶

Important Characteristics of Electromagnetic Waves

- These waves do not require any material medium for propagation.
- These waves travel in free space with the speed of light ($c = 3.0 \times 10^8 \text{ ms}^{-1}$) given by the relation

$$\boxed{c = 1/\sqrt{\mu_0 \varepsilon_0}}$$

where, μ_0 = permeability of free space or vacuum

and ε_0 = permittivity of free space or vacuum

- The variations in electric and magnetic fields occur simultaneously and the field acquire their maximum values E_0 and B_0 at the same place and at the same time.
- In free space, the magnitude of electric and magnetic fields in electromagnetic waves are related by $\mathbf{E}_0 / \mathbf{B}_0$.
- The energy in electromagnetic waves is divided, on average, equally between electric and magnetic fields.

  i.e., $U_E = U_B$

where, U_E and U_B are energy of electric and magnetic fields.

- The average of energy density (energy per unit volume) in an electric field **E** in vacuum is $\frac{1}{2}\varepsilon_0 E^2$ and that in magnetic field **B** is $\frac{B^2}{2\mu_0}$.
- Average energy associated with an electromagnetic wave is given by

$$U_{av} = \frac{1}{2}\varepsilon_0 E^2 + \frac{1}{2}\frac{B^2}{\mu_0}$$

- Electromagnetic waves are transverse in nature i.e., electric and magnetic fields are perpendicular to each other and to direction of wave propagation.
- Electromagnetic waves being uncharged, are not deflected by electric and magnetic fields.
- The electromagnetic wave like other waves carries energy and momentum. Since, it carries momentum, an electromagnetic wave also exerts pressure called **radiation pressure (p)**.

$$\boxed{p = \frac{U}{c}}$$

where, U = energy delivered to material surface on which electromagnetic wave is incident

and c = velocity of light.

Electromagnetic Spectrum

The orderly arrangement of EM wave in increasing or decreasing order of wavelength (λ) or frequency (ν) is called electromagnetic spectrum. The range varies from 10^{-12} m to 10^4 m i.e., from γ-rays to radiowaves.

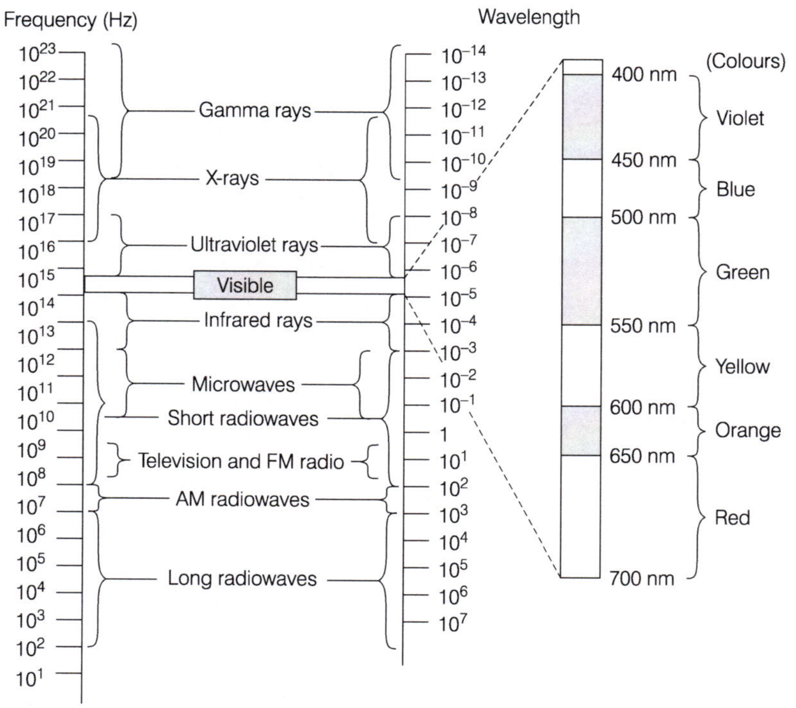

Electromagnetic Spectrum

Different Types of Electromagnetic Waves, their Production and Detection

Types of waves	Wavelength range	Frequency range (in Hz or cycle/second)	Production	Detection
Radiowave	> 0.1 m	3×10^3 to 3×10^8	Rapid acceleration and deceleration of electrons in aerials.	Receiver's aerials
Microwave	0.1 m to 1 mm	3×10^8 to 3×10^{11}	Klystron valve or magnetron valve.	Point contact diodes
Infrared wave	1 mm to 700 mm	3×10^{11} to 4×10^{14}	Vibration of atoms and molecules.	Thermopiles Bolometer, Infrared photographic film.
Light	700 nm to 400 nm	4×10^{14} to 8×10^{14}	Electrons in atoms emit light when they move from one energy level to a lower energy level.	The eye, photocells, photographic film.
Ultraviolet rays	400 nm to 1 nm	8×10^{14} to 8×10^{16}	Inner shell electrons in atoms moving from one energy level to a lower level.	Photocells, photographic film.
X-rays	1 nm to 10^{-3} nm	3×10^{16} to 1×10^{21}	X-ray tubes or inner shell electrons.	Photographic film, Geiger tubes, ionisation chamber.
γ-rays	< 10^{-3} nm	5×10^{18} to 5×10^{22}	Radioactive decay of the nucleus.	Photographic film, ionisation chamber

Uses of Some Electromagnetic Waves

Radiowaves

(a) In radio and TV communication.

(b) In astronomical field.

Microwaves

(a) In radar communication.

(b) In analysis of molecular and atomic structure.

(c) For cooking purpose.

Infrared Waves

(a) In knowing molecular structure.

(b) In remote control of TV, VCR, etc.

Ultraviolet Rays

(a) Used in burglar alarm.

(b) To kill germs in minerals.

X-Rays

(a) In medical diagnosis as they pass through the muscles not through the bones.

(b) In detecting faults, cracks, etc., in metal products.

γ-Rays

(a) As food preservation.

(b) In radiotherapy.

PYQs Previous Years Questions

1 Mark Questions

1. Which is the most harmful radiation entering the atmosphere of earth from outer space? **ISC 2022 Sem-I**

(a) X-rays (b) Visible rays
(c) Gamma radiations (d) Radio waves

2. Radiowaves and gamma waves are both transverse in nature and electromagnetic in character and have the same speed in vacuum. In what respects, are they different? **ISC 2022 Sem-I**

(a) Frequency (b) Wavelength
(c) Both (a) and (b) (d) None of these

3. Which of the following groups belongs only to the electromagnetic spectrum? **ISC 2022 Sem-I**

(a) Alpha rays, beta rays, gamma rays
(b) Ultrasonic rays, radio waves, infrared rays
(c) Gamma rays, cathode rays, X-rays
(d) X-rays, radio waves, infrared rays

4. Which electromagnetic radiation has wavelength greater than that of X-rays and smaller than that of visible light? **ISC 2022 Sem-I**

(a) Radio waves (b) Microwaves
(c) Infrared rays (d) Ultraviolet rays

5. Which one of the following travels with the speed of light in vacuum? **ISC 2022 Sem-I**

(a) Alpha rays (b) Beta rays
(c) Gamma rays (d) Ions

6. Consider four electromagnetic radiations namely infrared radiations, ultraviolet radiations, microwaves and light. Which one of these has maximum frequency? **ISC 2022 Sem-I**

(a) Infrared radiations (b) Ultraviolet radiations
(c) Microwaves (d) Light

7. Which one of the following is used to detect infrared radiations? **ISC 2022 Sem-I**

(a) Photocell
(b) Fluorescent screen
(c) Ionisation chamber
(d) Thermopile

8. Which one of the following is used to study crystal structure of a crystalline salt? **ISC 2022 Sem-I**

(a) UV-rays (b) X-rays
(c) Microwaves (d) Radiowaves

9. To which regions of the electromagnetic spectrum do the following wavelength belong: **ISC 2016**

(a) 250 nm (b) 1500 nm

10. Which electromagnetic radiation has wavelength greater than that of X-rays and smaller than that of visible light? **ISC 2012**

11. In which part of electromagnetic spectrum, do the following radiations lie **ISC 2009**

(*i*) having wavelength of 20 nm
(*ii*) having frequency of 10 MHz

2 Marks Questions

12. (*i*) Name the electromagnetic radiation whose frequency is 10^{11} Hz. **ISC 2024**

(*ii*) What is the speed of radio waves in vaccum?

13. (*i*) State how vector **E**, **B** and **c** are oriented in an electromagnetic wave.

(*ii*) Name the electromagnetic wave / radiation which is used to study crystal structure. **ISC 2023**

14. Name the electromagnetic radiation

(*i*) used for viewing through haze and fog.

(*ii*) which has the wavelength of 0.1 nm. **ISC SQP 2023**

15. (*i*) State any one use of infrared radiations.

(*ii*) State any one source of ultraviolet radiations. **ISC 2020**

16. State any two properties of microwaves. **ISC 2019**

17. (*i*) What is the ratio of the speed of gamma rays to that of radio waves in vacuum?

(*ii*) Name an electromagnetic wave which is used in the RADAR system for aircraft navigation. **ISC 2018**

18. (*i*) What is displacement current?

(*ii*) Which electromagnetic radiation is used to study the crystal structure **ISC SQP 2018**

19. (*i*) State any one property which is common to all electromagnetic waves.

(*ii*) Arrange the following electromagnetic waves in increasing order of their frequencies (i.e. begin with the lowest frequency):

Visible light, γ-rays, X-rays, microwaves, radio waves, infrared radiations and ultraviolet radiations. **ISC 2017**

20. Name the part of the electromagnetic spectrum which is

(*i*) suitable for radar systems used in aircraft navigation.

(*ii*) produced by bombarding a metal target with high speed electrons. **ISC 2014**

21. (*i*) In an electromagnetic wave, how are electric vector (**E**), magnetic vector (**B**) and velocity of propagation of the wave (**c**) oriented?

(*ii*) How long would gamma radiation take to travel from the Sun to the Earth, a distance of 1.5×10^{11} m? **ISC 2013**

3 Marks Questions

22. (*i*) Arrange all the seven types of electromagnetic radiations in increasing order of their frequencies. You must begin with a radiation with lowest frequency and end with the one having the highest frequency. **ISC 2014, 11**

(*ii*) State how electric vector **E**, magnetic vector **B** and velocity vector **c** are oriented in an electromagnetic wave? **ISC 2015, 08**

23. Name any two electromagnetic waves. State any one similarity and one difference between them. **ISC 2007, 03**

4/5 Marks Question

24. Describe very briefly and four regions of electromagnetic spectrum mentioning their special properties/features. **ISC 2002**

Case Based Question
(For Complete Chapter)

25. Direction *Read the passage given below and answer the questions that follow.*

The sunlight visible spectrum, discovered by Newton, extends in wavelength roughly from 4×10^{-7}m in the violet region to 8×10^{-7} m in the red region. After Newton, it was found that sun's spectrum is not limited from violet to red region, but is considerably spread below the violet region and also above the red region. These parts of the spectrum are not visible by our eye; so they are called 'invisible,spectra' of sun. The part of smaller wavelengths below violet is called the ultraviolet spectrum and that of longer wavelengths above red is called the infrared spectrum.

(*i*) Who discovered the visible spectrum? **(1)**

(*ii*) Wavelength range of visible spectrum is .... **(1)**

(*iii*) In the electromagnetic spectrum, which radiation has maximum wavelength? **(1)**

(*iv*) In the electromagnetic spectrum which radiation has maximum wavelength and maximum frequency? **(1)**

(*v*) Which parts of the electromagnetic spectrum is not visible by our eye?

Explanations

1. (c)
2. (c)
3. (d)
4. (d)
5. (c)
6. (b)
7. (d)
8. (b)
9. (a) Wavelength 250 nm corresponds to the visible region of electromagnetic spectrum.
   (b) Wavelength 1500 nm corresponds to the infrared region of electromagnetic spectrum.
10. Wavelength of ultraviolet radiation $(1\times10^{-8}\text{ m to }4\times 10^{-7}\text{ m})$ lies in between X-ray and visible light. It is shorter than light wave $(4\times 10^{-7}\text{ to }8\times 10^{-7}\text{ m})$ and longer than X-ray $(1\times 10^{-11}\text{ to }3\times 10^{-8}\text{ m})$.
11. Electromagnetic waves lies in the region of
   (*i*) X-rays [wavelength, $\lambda = 20$ nm]
   (*ii*) radiowaves [frequency, $\nu = 10$ MHz]
12. (*i*) Infrared radiation has frequency range 3×10^{11} Hz to 4×10^{14} Hz.
   (*ii*) Radio wave is an electromagnetic wave. These waves do not require any material medium for propagation and travel in vacuum with the speed of light. i.e. 3×10^{8} m/s.
13. (*i*) Refer to sol. 21 (i) on page 170.
   (*ii*) To study the structure of crystals, we use X-rays as the distance between 2 atoms in a crystal is very similar to wavelength of X-rays.

Concept Enhancer X-rays have wavelengths similar to the size of atoms, they are useful to study the crystal structures of atoms.

14. (*i*) Infrared rays are used for viewing objects through haze and fog.
   (*ii*) X-rays have a wavelength of nearly 0.1 nm.
15. (*i*) Infrared radiations are used in thermal imaging cameras, which allow a fire fighter to see areas of heat through smoke, darkness or heat permeable barriers.
   (*ii*) The Sun is our primary natural source of ultraviolet radiation.
16. (*i*) Microwaves have wavelength such that they induces vibration in liquid contained in the foods. Thus, they are used to cook food.
   (*ii*) Microwaves can reflect and focused at any point after reflection from a particular substance (usually metal).
17. (*i*) The speed of gamma rays and radio waves in vacuum are same. So, the ratio of speed of gamma rays to that of radio waves will be 1 : 1.
   (*ii*) Microwaves are used in the RADAR system for aircraft navigation.
18. (*i*) **Displacement current** It is a current which is produced due to the rate of change of electric flux with respect to time. It is given by

$$I_d = \varepsilon_0 \frac{d}{dt}(\phi_E)$$

   (*ii*) X-rays can be reflected and diffracted by the crystals. Hence, it is used to study the crystal structure.
19. (*i*) One property which is common to all electromagnetic waves is as follows.
   The energy associated with the EM waves is equally divided between electric and magnetic field.
   Energy density of electric field,

$$u_e = \frac{1}{2}\varepsilon_0 E^2$$

   Energy density of magnetic field,

$$u_B = \frac{1}{2}\frac{B^2}{\mu_0}$$

   So, the total energy per unit volume is given as,

$$U = U_e + U_B$$
$$= \frac{1}{2}\varepsilon_0 E^2 + \frac{1}{2}\frac{B^2}{\mu_0}$$

   Also, the average energy density is,

$$u_{\text{av}} = \frac{1}{2}\varepsilon_0 E_0^2$$
$$= \frac{B_0^2}{2\mu_0}$$

   (*ii*) Electromagnetic waves in increasing order of their frequencies are as follows.
   Radio waves < Microwaves < Infrared radiations < Visible light < Ultraviolet radiations < *X*-rays < Gamma rays

20. (*i*) Microwaves are suitable for radar systems used in aircraft navigation.

(*ii*) When a metal target is bombarded with high speed electrons, X-rays are produced.

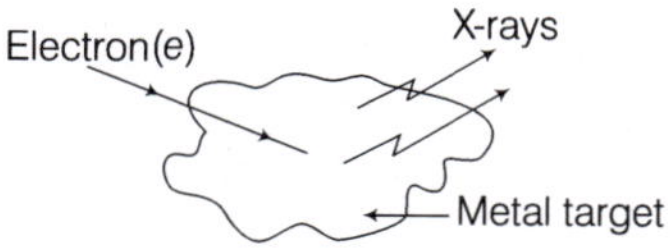

21. (*i*) In an electromagnetic waves, **E** and **B** are perpendicular to each other and **c** (i.e., velocity of propagation of electromagnetic wave) is perpendicular to both **E** and **B**.

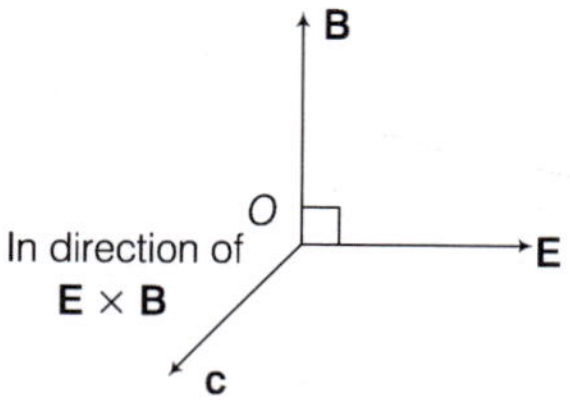

(*ii*) Speed of γ-radiation is $c = 3 \times 10^8$ m/s.

Given, distance $= 1.5 \times 10^{11}$ m

Time taken by γ-radiation to travel from the Sun to the Earth is given by

$$\therefore \quad \text{Time} = \frac{\text{Distance}}{\text{Velocity}} = \frac{1.5 \times 10^{11}}{3 \times 10^8} = 5 \times 10^2 \text{s}$$

22. (*i*) Electromagnetic radiations in increasing order of their frequencies are

radiowaves < microwaves < infrared radiation < visible light < ultraviolet radiation < X-rays < gamma rays.

(*ii*) Refer to sol. 21 (i) on page 170.

23. Example of two electromagnetic waves are microwaves and radiowaves.

Similarity Both the waves travel with the same speed in vacuum as the speed of light (3×10^8 m/s).

Difference Radiowaves are having frequency range 3×10^9 to 3×10^4 Hz while microwaves are having frequency range 3×10^{11} to 1×10^9 Hz.

24. The distribution of electromagnetic radiations according to their wavelength or frequency is called the electromagnetic spectrum.

Four regions of electromagnetic spectrum are

(*i*) X-rays

(*ii*) Infrared rays

(*iii*) Ultraviolet rays

(*iv*) γ-rays

Name	Wavelength (in m)	Frequency (in Hz)	Source
γ-rays	6×10^{-14} to 1×10^{-10}	5×10^{20} to 3×10^{19}	Radioactive decay of the nucleus
X-rays	1×10^{-10} to 3×10^{-8}	3×10^{19} to 1×10^{16}	X-ray tubes or inner shell electrons
Ultraviolet rays	3×10^{-8} to 4×10^{-7}	10^{16} to 8×10^{14}	Excitation of atom, spark and arc lamp
Infrared rays	8×10^{-7} to 3×10^{-5}	4×10^{14} to 1×10^{13}	Excitation of atoms and molecules

25. (*i*) The visible spectrum was discovered by Newton.

(*ii*) 4×10^{-7}m in the violet region to 8×10^{-7}m in the red region.

(*iii*) Radiowave has the maximum wavelength from the electromagnetic spectrum.

(*iv*) Radiowave has the maximum wavelength from the electromagnetic spectrum and gamma rays has the maximum frequency.

(*v*) Except the visible spectrum all the radiation from the electromagnetic spectrum is not visible by our eye.

CHAPTER TEST

01 Mark Questions (MCQs)

1 Point out the wrong statement : electromagnetic waves
(a) are transverse
(b) are produced by accelerating charges
(c) travel with same speed in all media
(d) travel with speed of light in free space

2 Heat radiations are
(a) γ-rays (b) microwaves
(c) Infrared radiations (d) radiowaves

3 Which of the following are not electromagnetic waves?
(a) Cosmic rays (b) Gamma rays
(c) β-rays (d) X-rays

4 The decreasing order of wavelength of infrared, microwaves, ultraviolet and gamma rays is
(a) infrared, microwaves, ultraviolet, gamma rays
(b) microwaves, infrared, ultraviolet, gamma rays
(c) gamma rays, ultraviolet, infrared, microwaves
(d) microwaves, gamma rays, infrared, ultraviolet.

5 Which of the following waves have a maximum frequency?
(a) Infrared waves (b) Gamma rays
(c) Microwaves (d) Radiowaves

02 Marks Questions (VSA)

6 What do you understand by the term ''electromagnetic waves''?

7 Name the constituent radiation of electromagnetic spectrum which is used for
(i) aircraft navigation
(ii) studying the crystal structure

8 Write the wavelength and frequency of the following electromagnetic waves.
(i) Infrared waves
(ii) γ-rays

9 Name the wave used in RADAR. Justify your answer.

03 Marks Questions

10 Give the name of the electromagnetic waves which have one similarity and one differences between them.

11 Give one use of the following electromagnetic waves.
(i) Microwaves
(ii) Ultraviolet rays
(iii) Infrared rays
(iv) X-rays

12 Describe in briefly and four regions of electromagnetic spectrum and mention about their wavelength and frequency as well as their uses.

05 Marks Questions

13 Define the term ''Electromagnetic waves''. Show in diagram that electric field, magnetic field and direction of propagation of the wave, are mutually perpendicular.

14 List the electromagnetic waves in ascending order of wavelength. Write the properties and source of emission of X-rays, γ-rays and UV rays.

Answers

1. (c) **2.** (c) **3.** (c) **4.** (b) **5.** (b)

13

Ray Optics

TREND ANALYSIS 4 YEARS

Topic	Types of Questions	2024	2023	2020	2019
		Average No. of Questions Across all Sets			
TOPIC 01 Reflection and Refraction of Light	1 Mark	–	1	1	1
	2 Marks	–	–	–	1
	3 Marks	–	–	–	–
	5 Marks	–	–	–	–
TOPIC 02 Refraction Through a Prism	1 Mark	–	–	–	–
	2 Marks	–	–	1	–
	3 Marks	1	2	–	1
	5 Marks	–	–	–	–
TOPIC 03 Refraction at a Spherical Surface	1 Mark	–	1	–	–
	2 Marks	–	–	1	–
	3 Marks	1	–	1	1
	5 Marks	–	–	–	–
TOPIC 04 Dispersion	1 Mark	1	–	–	–
	2 Marks	–	2	–	1
	3 Marks	–	–	–	–
	5 Marks	–	–	–	–

TOPIC 1

Reflection and Refraction of Light

Reflection of Light

Reflection is the phenomenon of change in the path of light without any change in the medium.

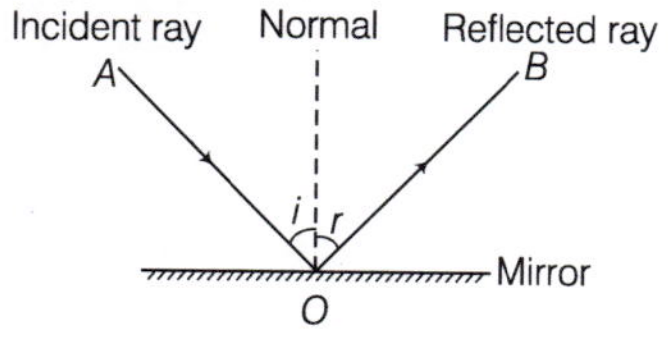

The returning back of light in the same medium from which it has come after striking a surface is called **reflection of light**.

Laws of Reflection

The laws of reflection are as given below:

(*i*) The incident ray, the reflected ray and the normal to the reflecting surface at the point of incidence, all lie in the same plane.

(*ii*) The angle of reflection (r) is equal to the angle of incidence (i), i.e. $\angle i = \angle r$.

For normal incidence, $\angle i = 0°$. Therefore, $\angle r = 0°$.

Hence, a ray of light falling normally on a mirror, retraces its path on reflection.

Reflection of Light by Spherical Mirrors

Spherical mirror is a mirror whose reflecting surface is a part of a hollow sphere. Spherical mirrors are of two types:

(*i*) **Concave Spherical Mirror** A spherical mirror whose reflecting surface is towards the centre of the sphere is called concave spherical mirror.

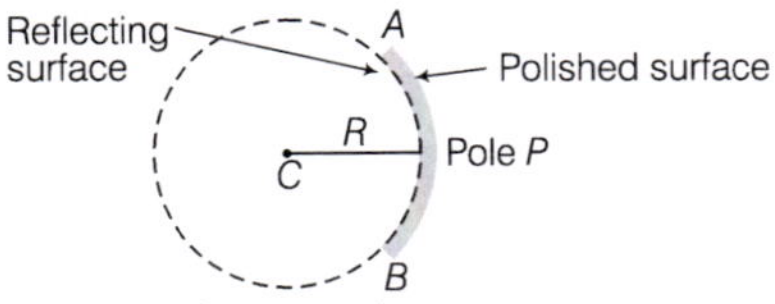

Concave mirror

(*ii*) **Convex Spherical Mirror** A spherical mirror whose reflecting surface is away from the centre of the sphere is called convex spherical mirror.

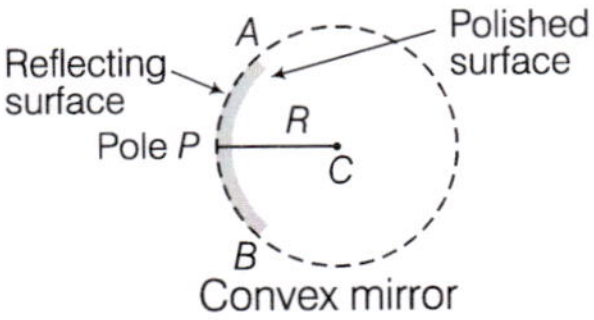

Convex mirror

Focal Length of Spherical Mirrors

When a parallel beam of light is incident on a concave or convex mirror, the reflected rays converge or appear to diverge from a point F on principal axis called principal focus of the mirror.

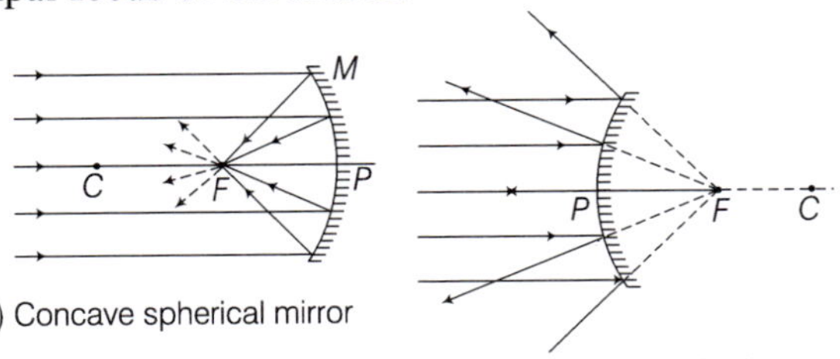

(a) Concave spherical mirror

(b) Convex spherical mirror

Paraxial rays meeting/appear to meet at focus.

Mirror Formula

Mirror formula is a relation between focal length of the mirror, distance of object and image from the mirror.

$$\frac{1}{v}+\frac{1}{u}=\frac{1}{f}$$

where, f = Focal length,

u = Distance of the object from mirror,

v = Distance of the image from mirror.

$$\text{Focal length of mirror }(f)=\frac{\text{Radius of curvature }(R)}{2}$$

$$\Rightarrow \quad f=\frac{R}{2}$$

Refraction of Light at Plane Surface

Light is a form of energy which is an electromagnetic radiation belonging to the region of visible spectrum of wavelength of about 400 nm to 700 nm.

When a beam of light encounters another transparent medium, a part of light gets reflected back into the first medium while the rest enters the other. The direction of propagation of an obliquely incident ray of light, that enters the same medium, changes at the interface of two media. This phenomenon is called reflection of light.

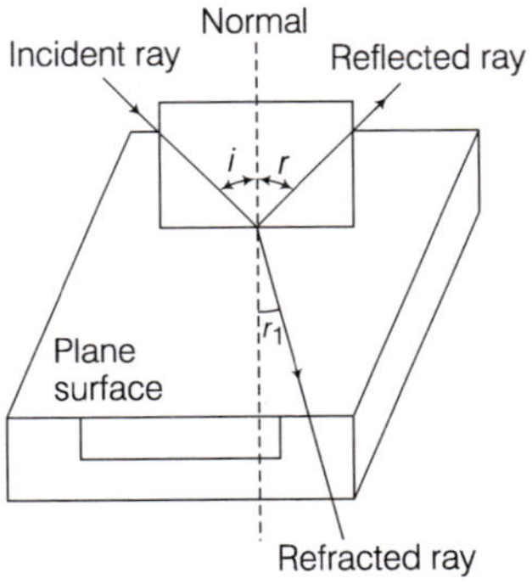

Refraction of Light

Reflection is a phenomena that involves change in the path of light without any change in the medium, whereas refraction involves change in the path of light due to change in the medium. The phenomenon of change in the path of light as it goes from one medium to another is called **refraction of light.**

Laws of Refraction

- The incident ray, refracted ray and normal to the refracting surface (or interface) at the point of incidence, all lie in the same plane.

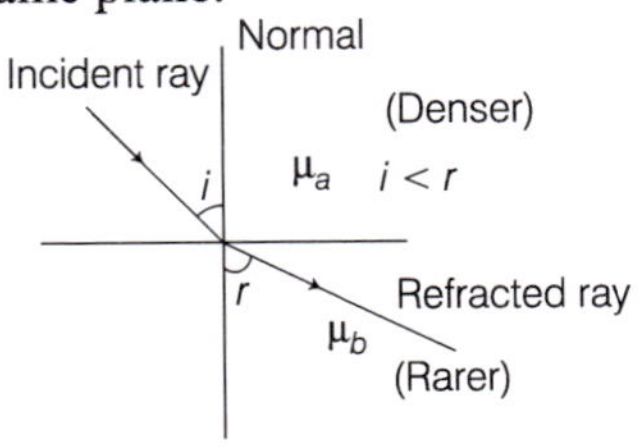

Refraction from denser to rarer medium

- The ratio of the sine of the angle of incidence to the sine of the angle of refraction is constant for the two given media. This constant is denoted by ${}^a\mu_b$ and is called the **relative refractive index** of medium b with respect to the medium a.

$$\boxed{\frac{\sin i}{\sin r} = {}^a\mu_b} \quad [\text{where, } \mu_a > \mu_b]$$

This law is also called **Snell's law** of refraction. This relative refractive index is a measure of how much light bends when it travels from one medium to other.

Refractive Index

Mathematically, refractive index is given by the relation as below

$$\mu = \frac{\text{Speed of light in the vacuum}}{\text{Speed of light in the material}} = \frac{c}{v} \quad [c = 3 \times 10^8 \text{ m/s}]$$

It is also referred as absolute refractive index of the substance.

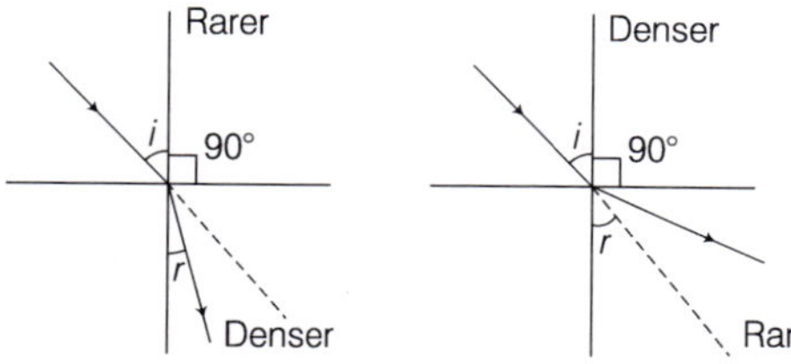

The medium in which speed of light lower w.r.t. other medium is called optically **denser** medium and the medium in which speed of light is higher w.r.t. other medium is called optically **rarer** medium. The optical density is the ratio of the speed of light in two media. i.e.

$$\boxed{{}^1\mu_2 = \frac{v_1}{v_2}}$$

Principle of Reversibility of Light

When a light ray after suffering many number of reflection and refractions, has its final path reversed or it travels back (reflects) along its entire initial path. This is called principle of reversibility of light.

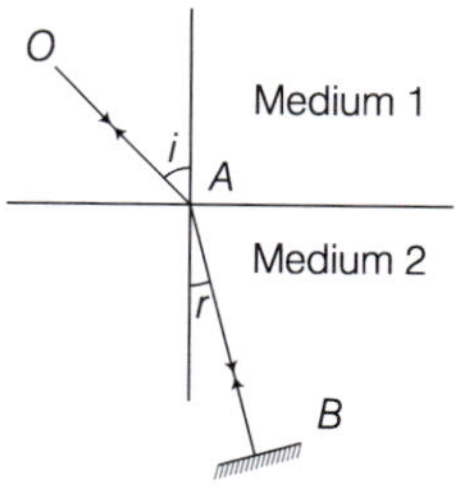

By Snell's law, the refractive index of medium 2 relative to medium 1 is given by

$${}^1\mu_2 = \frac{\sin i}{\sin r} \quad \ldots\text{(i)}$$

Correspondingly, r is angle of incidence and i is angle of refraction. Again, by Snell's law, the refractive index of medium 1 relative to medium 2 is given by

$${}^2\mu_1 = \frac{\sin r}{\sin i} \quad \ldots\text{(ii)}$$

After multiplying Eqs. (i) and (ii), we obtain

$$\boxed{{}^1\mu_2 = \frac{1}{{}^2\mu_1}}$$

Thus, the refractive index of medium 2 relative to medium 1 is equal to the reciprocal of the refractive index of medium 1 relative to medium 2.

Refraction Through Parallel Multiple Media

Let a light ray OA travelling in a medium 1 is first refracted along AB in medium 2 then along BC is parallel in medium 3 and finally emerges along CD in its initial medium 1.

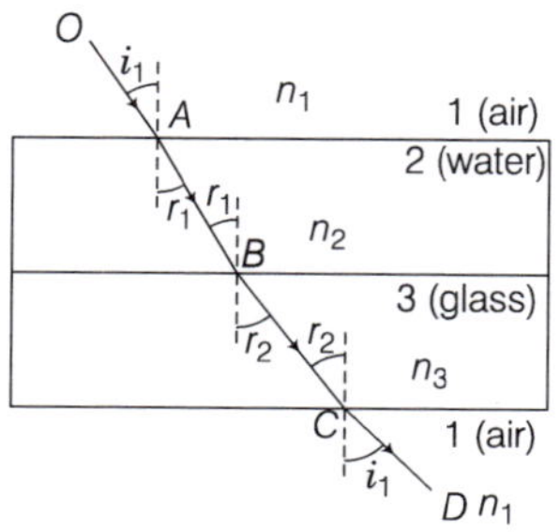

At A, i_1 an r_1 are angles of incidence and refraction at media 1 and 2, then

$${}_1n_2 = \frac{\sin i_1}{\sin r_1} \quad \ldots\text{(i)}$$

At B, r_1 is the angle of incidence and r_2 be the angle of refraction at media 2 and 3, then

$${}_2n_3 = \frac{\sin r_1}{\sin r_2} \quad \ldots\text{(ii)}$$

At C, r_2 is the angle of incidence and i_1 be the angle of emergent at media 3 and 1. So,

$${}_3n_1 = \frac{\sin r_2}{\sin i_1} \quad \ldots\text{(iii)}$$

On multiplying Eqs. (i), (ii) and (iii), we get

$${}_1n_2 \times {}_2n_3 \times {}_3n_1 = \frac{\sin i_1}{\sin r_1} \times \frac{\sin r_1}{\sin r_2} \times \frac{\sin r_2}{\sin i_1}$$

$$\boxed{{}_1n_2 \times {}_2n_3 \times {}_3n_1 = 1}$$

or $${}_1n_2 \times {}_2n_3 = \frac{1}{{}_3n_1}$$

$$\Rightarrow \quad \boxed{{}_1n_3 = {}_1n_2 \times {}_2n_3}$$

Lateral Displacement

When a ray of light passes from one medium to other medium, the shift in the path of light on emerging from a refracting medium with parallel faces is called lateral displacement. It is actually the perpendicular distance between the incident and emergent rays.

Apparent Depth & Real Depth

The depth of an object immersed in water appears to be lesser than its actual depth. Hence, they are related by the following relation:

$$\text{Refractive index} = \frac{\text{Real depth}}{\text{Apparent depth}}$$

When light ray travels from denser to rarer medium

$$H_{\text{apparent}} = \frac{H_{\text{real}}}{\mu_w}$$

Apparent shift,

$$x = H_{\text{real}} - H_{\text{apparent}}$$
$$= H_{\text{real}} - \frac{H_{\text{real}}}{\mu_w}$$
$$= H_{\text{real}}\left(1 - \frac{1}{\mu_w}\right)$$

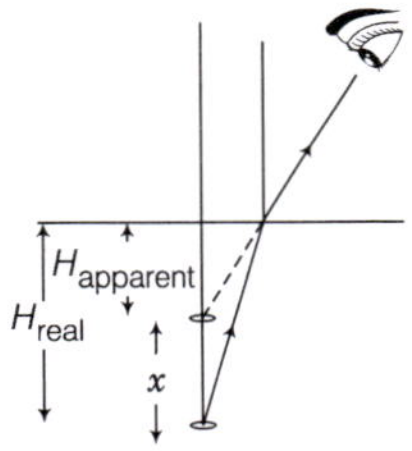

e.g. The depth of an bucket full of water appears to be lesser.

When light ray travels from rarer to denser medium

$$H_{\text{apparent}} = H_{\text{real}} \times \mu$$

Apparent shift, $x = H_{\text{apparent}} - H_{\text{real}}$
$$= H_{\text{real}} \times \mu - H_{\text{real}}$$
$$= H_{\text{real}}(\mu - 1)$$

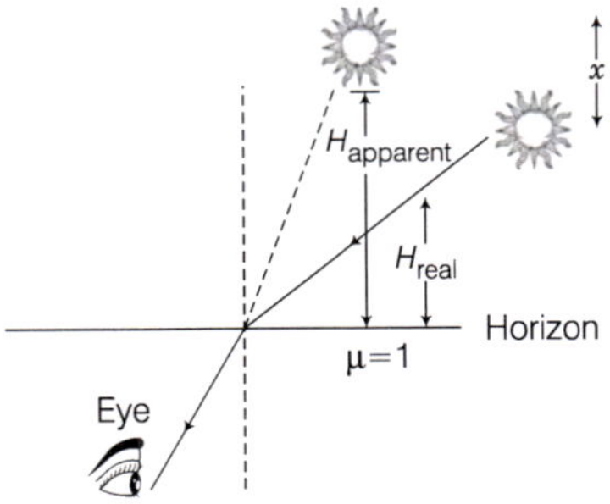

e.g. The Stars look above than they actually are, the sun is visible before actual sunrise and after actual sunset due to apparent shift.

Critical Angle (i_C)

The angle of incidence in denser medium for which angle of refraction in rarer medium is 90°, is called critical angle of denser medium and is denoted by i_C. The value of critical angle depends on the **nature of two media** and **colour of the light.**

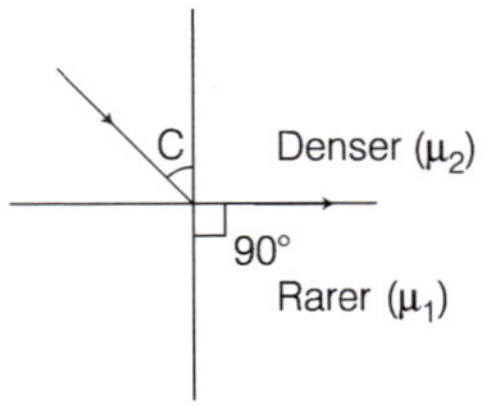

Then by Snell's law, $\sin i_c \times \mu_2 = \sin 90° \times \mu_1$

$$\sin i_c = \frac{1}{\mu_2} \qquad \begin{bmatrix} \sin 90° = 1 \\ \mu_1(\text{air}) = 1 \end{bmatrix}$$

So, $$\boxed{\mu_2 = \frac{1}{\sin i_c}}$$

where, μ_2 = refractive index of denser medium.

Total Internal Reflection

When a ray of light travelling from denser medium to rarer medium is incident at the interface of two media at an angle greater than the critical angle, the ray is totally reflected back to denser medium. This phenomenon is called **Total Internal Reflection (TIR).**

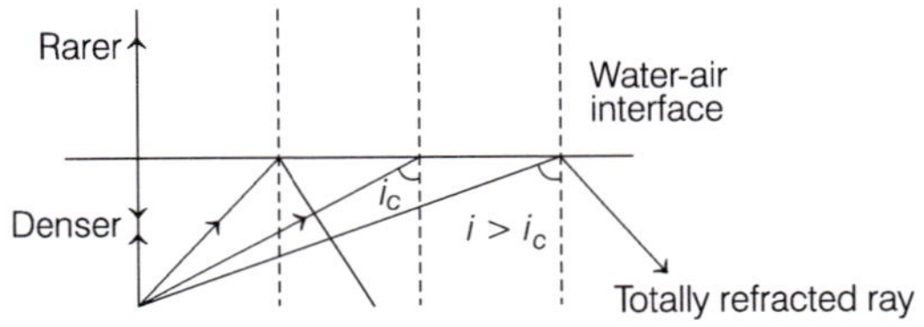

Necessary conditions for total internal reflection to take place are as follow.

(*i*) The incident ray on the interface of two media should travel from denser medium to rarer medium.

(*ii*) The angle of incidence in the denser medium should be greater than critical angle for the two media.

Technological Applications of Total Internal Reflection

Total Reflecting Prisms

These prisms are right angled isosceles prism which turn the light through 90° or 180°. They are based on the phenomenon of total internal reflection of light.

Refractive index (μ) for glass is 1.5, so that critical angle for glass air interface is 42°. For total internal reflection in glass prisms. The angle of incidence is made of 45° ($> i_c$).

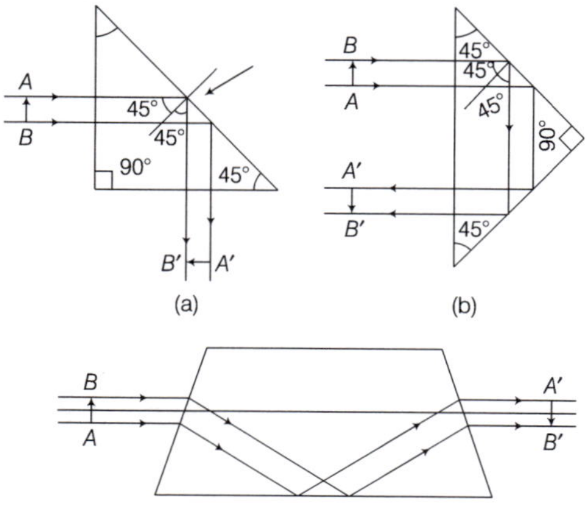

(a) (b) (c)

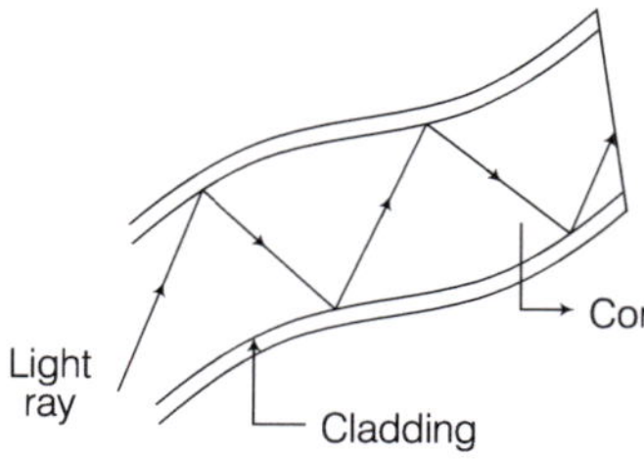

Structure of optical fibre

Optical Fibre

An optical fibre is a thin tube of transparent material that allows light to pass through it without being refracted into the air of external medium. It is based on the phenomenon of total internal reflection. Optical fibres are fabricated with high quality composite glass or quartz fibres.

The refractive index of core is higher than that of the cladding. When a signal in the form of light is directed at one end of the fibre at a suitable angle, it undergoes repeated total internal reflection along the length of the fibre and finally comes out from other end.

Due to total internal reflection at each stage, no absorption of light take place i.e. there is no appreciable loss in the intensity of light.

Uses

(*i*) In transmitting electrical and optical signal.

(*ii*) In visual examination of internal organs like oesophagus, stomach and intestine.

(*iii*) In decorative lamps.

PYQs Previous Years Questions

1 Mark Questions

1. If an object is placed at a distance of 10 cm in front of a concave mirror of focal length 20 cm, the image formed will be **ISC 2023**

(a) real and 20 cm in front of the mirror
(b) real and 6.67 cm in front of the mirror
(c) virtual and 20 cm behind the mirror
(d) virtual and 6.67 cm behind the mirror

2. Name the physical principle on the basis of which optical fibres work. **ISC 2020, 16, 14**

3. Define critical angle for a given medium. **ISC 2019**

4. An object is kept on the principal axis of a concave mirror of focal length 10 cm, at a distance of 15 cm from its pole. The image formed by the mirror is **ISC 2018**

(a) virtual and magnified (b) virtual and diminished
(c) real and magnified (d) real and diminished

5. Complete the ray diagram shown in figure, given that the critical angle for air-glass pair is $i_c = 42°$. **ISC SQP 2018**

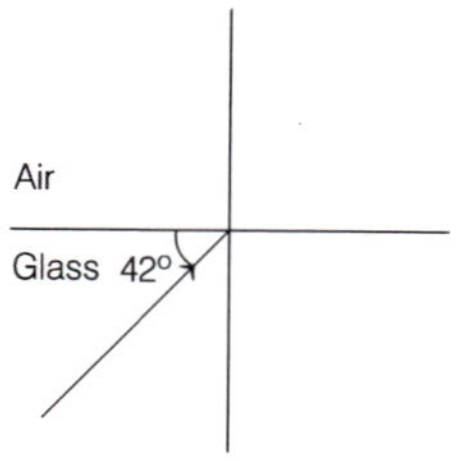

6. When a light wave travels from air to glass

(a) its wavelength decreases.
(b) its wavelength increases.
(c) there is no change in wavelength
(d) its frequency decreases. **ISC 2017**

7. Name the physical principle on which the working of optical fibre is based. **ISC 2016, 2014**

8. A fish which is at a depth of 12 cm in water ($\mu = 4/3$) is viewed by an observer on the bank of a lake. Its apparent depth as observed by the observer is **ISC 2015**

(a) 3 cm (b) 9 cm
(c) 12 cm (d) 16 cm

9. Calculate the critical angle for glass and water pair. (Take, refractive index for glass is 1.50 and the refractive index for water is 1.33.) **ISC 2010**

10. Draw a diagram to show how an image is produced by a pair of two reflecting plane mirrors arranged as in a periscope. **ISC 2001**

11. Name the physical principle and one advantage in the use of optical fibres. **ISC 2000**

2 Marks Questions

12. Write any one use for each of the following mirrors. **ISC 2019**

(*i*) Convex (*ii*) Concave

13. Find critical angle for glass and water pair, given refractive index of glass is 1.62 and that of water is 1.33. **ISC 2016**

14. A point source of monochromatic light S is kept at the centre C of the bottom of a cylinder. The radius of the circular base of the cylinder is 15.0 cm.

The cylinder contains water $\left(\text{refractive index } = \frac{4}{3}\right)$ to a height of 7.0 cm as shown in the figure. Find the area surface through which light emerges in air. (Take, $\pi = 22/7$) **ISC 2009**

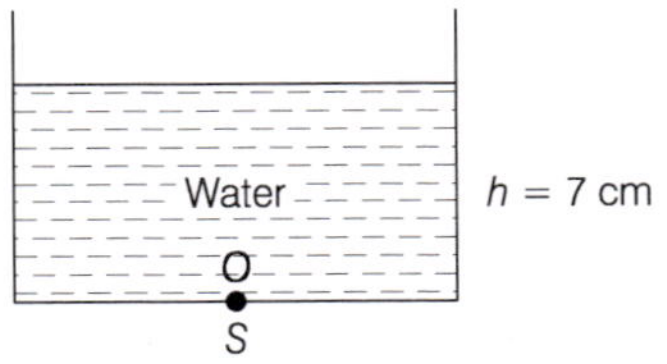

15. A fish is located at a distance of 10 cm from the wall of fish pond. The thickness of the glass wall is 2 cm. Find the apparent position of the fish. (Given, ${}_a\mu_g = 3/2$ and ${}_a\mu_w = 4/3$) **ISC 2004**

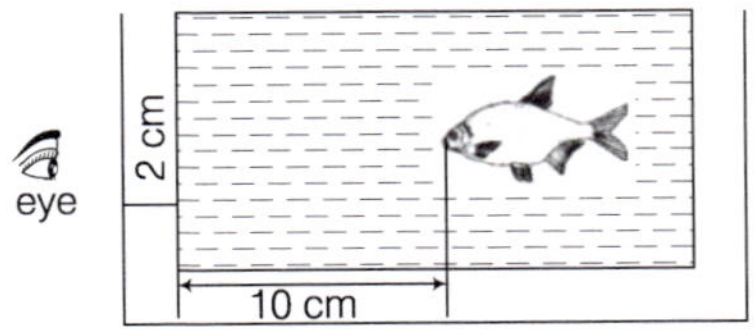

KEY idea

Apparent position of fish can be calculated by adding apparent positions of glass and water indivisually.

Explanations

1. (c) Virtual and 20 cm behind the mirror.

By using mirror formula , $\frac{1}{f} = \frac{1}{u} + \frac{1}{v}$

$$\Rightarrow \quad \frac{1}{-20} = \frac{1}{v} + \frac{1}{-10}$$

$$\Rightarrow \quad \frac{1}{v} = \frac{1}{-20} + \frac{1}{10}$$

$$\Rightarrow \quad \frac{1}{v} = \frac{-1+2}{20} = \frac{1}{20}$$

$$\Rightarrow \quad v = 20 \text{ cm}$$

2. Total internal reflection.

3. The critical angle for two given media is the angle of incidence in the denser medium for which the angle of refraction in the rarer medium is 90°.

4. (c) $\because \quad u > f$ (but less than $2f$)

$$\therefore \quad v > 2f \text{ and } |m| > 1$$

Thus, when the object lies between the focus and centre of curvature, a real, inverted and magnified image is formed beyond the centre of curvature of the concave mirror.

5. When incident angle is greater than or equal to the critical angle, only then total internal reflection takes place.

Here, $\angle i = \angle C$, $\angle r = 90°$

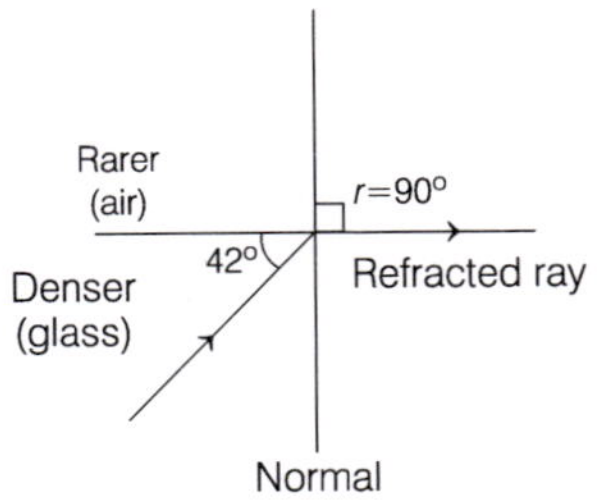

6. (a) Its wavelength decreases because they are related by the formula, $\mu = \frac{\lambda_{vac}}{\lambda_{med}}$

Here, $\mu = \frac{\lambda_{air}}{\lambda_{glass}}$

as velocity in medium decreases hence its wavelength decreases,

$\therefore \quad v = \nu\lambda$

7. Optical fibre works on the principle of total internal reflection. Total internal reflection of light (TIR) is the phenomena, when a ray of light travelling from denser medium to rarer medium is incident at the interface of two media at angle greater than the critical angle for the two media, the ray is totally reflected back to denser medium.

8. (b) We know that refractive index

$$= \frac{\text{Real depth}}{\text{Apparent depth}}$$

Now, Apparent depth $= \frac{\text{Real depth}}{\text{Refractive index}}$

Here, real depth $= 12$ cm,

refractive index $= 4/3$

$\therefore$ Apparent depth $= 12 \times \frac{3}{4} = 9$ cm

9. Given, refractive index of glass $\mu_g = 1.50$

Refractive index of water $\mu_w = 1.33$

Let C be critical angle, then from Snell's law

$$\sin C = \frac{1}{{}_w\mu_g} = \frac{\mu_w}{\mu_g} = \frac{1.33}{1.50}$$

$$\Rightarrow \quad C = \sin^{-1}\left(\frac{1.33}{1.50}\right) = 62.5°$$

10. The ray diagram of the periscope is shown as below (It uses right angled isosceles prism).

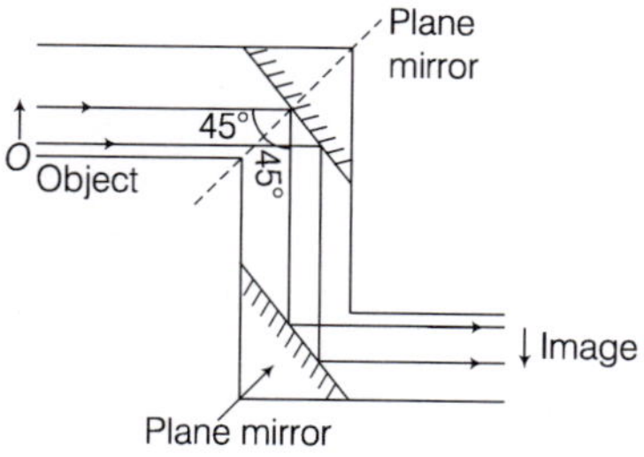

11. The working of optical fibres is based on the principle of total internal reflection of light i.e. when a ray of light travels from a denser medium to a rarer medium such that the angle of incidence is greater than the critical angle for two pairs of media, then the light is reflected back in the same denser medium.

Refer to text on page 176 (Optical fibre).

12. (*i*) A convex mirror is used as a reflector in street lamps.

(*ii*) Concave mirrors are used by ENT doctors to examine ear, nose and throat.

13. Given,

refractive index of glass is $\mu_g = 1.62$

refractive index of water is, $\mu_w = 1.33$

From Snell's law of refraction,

$${}^a\mu_g = \frac{\sin i}{\sin r} = \frac{\mu_w}{\mu_g}$$

$\Rightarrow$ For the critical for glass-water pair, $r = 90°$

$$\Rightarrow \quad \frac{\sin i_C}{\sin 90°} = \frac{1.33}{1.62}$$

$$\Rightarrow \quad \sin i_C = 0.820$$

$$\Rightarrow \quad i_C = \sin^{-1}(0.820) = 55.08°$$

14. We have to use the concept of critical angle and the area of the circle will be confined within the two totally reflecting points.

According to the question,

Given, $h = 7$ cm,

$$\frac{\mu_w}{\mu_a} = {}_a\mu_w = \frac{4}{3}$$

We can write

$$\sin\theta_c = \frac{1}{{}_a\mu_w} = \frac{3}{4} = 0.75$$

$$\theta_c = \sin^{-1} 0.75 = 48.6°$$

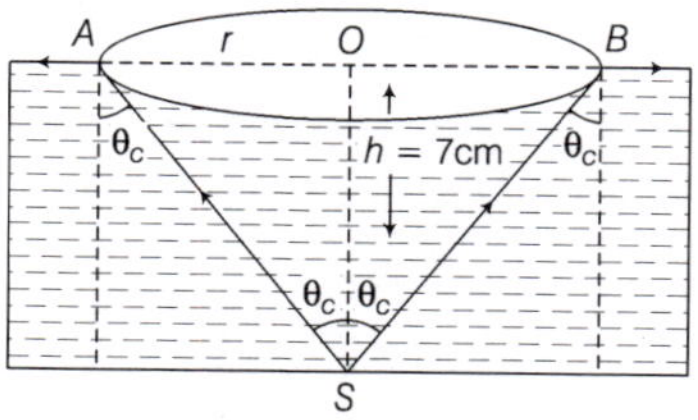

Now, $\tan\theta_c = \frac{\text{Perpendicular}}{\text{Base}} = \frac{r}{h}$

$$\Rightarrow \quad r = h\tan\theta_c = 7 \times \tan 48.6°$$

$$\therefore \quad r = 7.94 \text{ cm (approx)}$$

$$\text{Area} = \pi r^2 = \frac{22}{7} \times (7.94)^2 = 198 \text{ cm}^2$$

15. $\because$ Apparent position $= 2 \times \dfrac{\mu_g}{\mu_a} + 10 \times \dfrac{\mu_w}{\mu_a}$

$$= 2 \times \frac{2}{3} + 10 \times \frac{3}{4} = \frac{4}{3} + \frac{30}{4} = \frac{16+90}{12}$$

$$= \frac{106}{12} = \frac{53}{6} = 8.8 \text{ cm}$$

TOPIC 2

Refraction Through a Prism

A prism is an optical device which splits white light into 7 colours. It has got the property of bending the incident light towards its base.

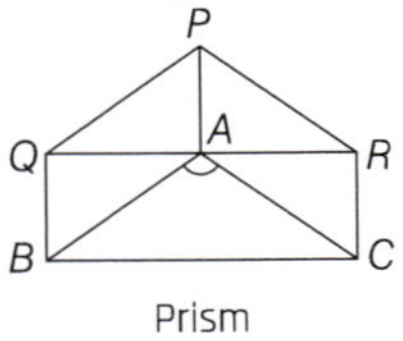

Prism

A prism is a portion of a transparent medium bounded by two plane faces inclined to each other at a suitable angle. In the given figure, $ABQP$ and $ACRP$ are the two refracting faces and $\angle A$ is the angle of prism.

Refraction of Light Through a Prism

The figure below shows the passage of light through a triangular prism ABC.

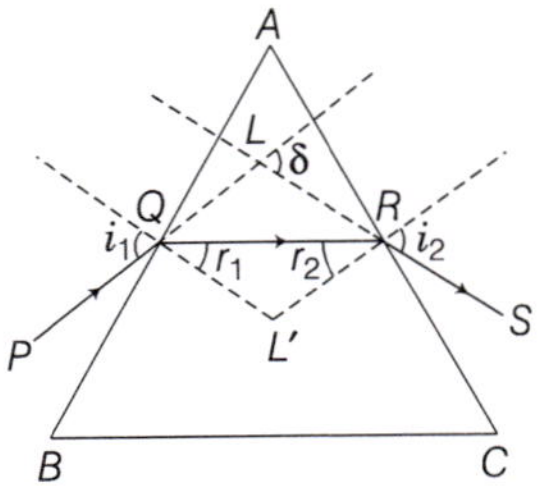

In triangle QLR, the exterior angle δ is given by

$$\delta = \angle LQR + \angle LRQ$$

$\delta =$ angle of deviation

$$\delta = (i_1 - r_1) + (i_2 - r_2)$$

At, $\angle LQR = i_1 - r_1$

$$\angle LRQ = i_2 - r_2 = (i_1 + i_2) - (r_1 + r_2) \quad \ldots\text{(i)}$$

In quadrilateral $AQL'R$, we have

$$\left.\begin{aligned} \angle A + \angle L' &= 180^\circ \\ \text{In } \Delta QL'R, r_1 + r_2 + L' &= 180^\circ \end{aligned}\right\} \quad \ldots\text{(ii)}$$

From Eq. (ii), we get

$$r_1 + r_2 = A \quad \ldots\text{(iii)}$$

Putting the value of $(r_1 + r_2)$ in Eq. (i), we have

$$\delta = i_1 + i_2 - A \quad \ldots\text{(iv)}$$

A prism is an optical device which splits white light into 7 colours. It has got the property of bending the incident light towards its base.

A prism is a portion of a transparent medium bounded by two plane faces inclined to each other at a suitable angle. In the given figure, $ABQP$ and $ACRP$ are the two refracting faces and $\angle A$ is the angle of prism.

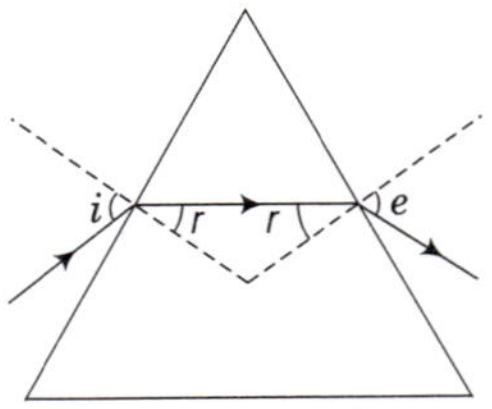

Condition for minimum deviation

For minimum deviation, $i_1 = i_2 = i$

and $r_1 = r_2 = r, \delta = \delta_m$

Then, from Eqs. (iii) and (iv), we have

$$\delta_m + A = 2i$$

$$\Rightarrow \quad i = \frac{\delta_m + A}{2}$$

$$2r = A \quad \Rightarrow \quad r = \frac{A}{2}$$

By Snell's law,

Refractive index of glass,

$$\mu = \frac{\sin i}{\sin r}$$

$$\Rightarrow \quad \boxed{\mu = \frac{\sin\left(\dfrac{\delta_m + A}{2}\right)}{\sin \dfrac{A}{2}}}$$

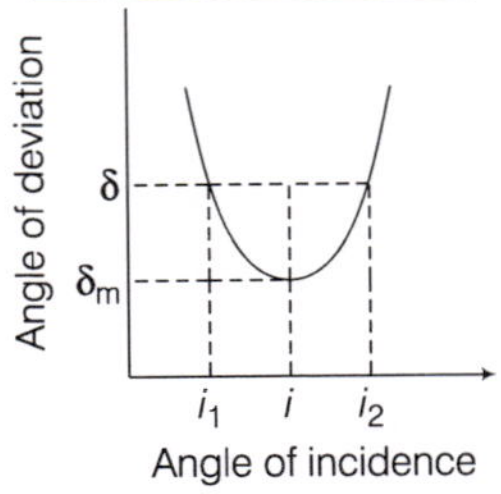

NOTE When a ray suffers minimum deviation through a prism, the ray inside the prism will be parallel to the base.

PYQs Previous Years Questions

1 Mark Questions

1. In case of a regular prism, in minimum deviation position, angle made by the refracted ray (inside the prism) with the normal drawn to the refracting surface is **ISC 2022 Sem-II**

(a) 90° (b) 60° (c) 45° (d) 30°

2. In a regular prism, what is the relation between angle of incidence and angle of emergence when it is in the minimum deviation position? **ISC 2017**

3. A narrow beam of monochromatic light *PQ* is incident normally on one face of an equiangular glass prism of refractive index 1.45. When the prism is immersed in a certain 'liquid, the ray makes a grazing emergence along the other face as shown in the figure. Find the refractive index of this liquid. **ISC 2014**

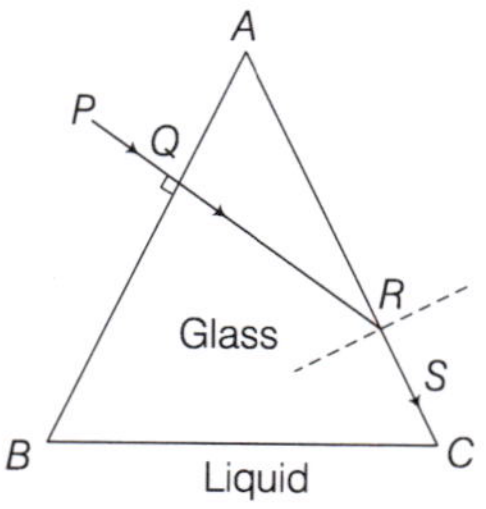

4. A ray of light *LM* incident normally on the surface *AC* of an isosceles right angled prism *ABC* (where, $AB = BC$) emerges along *PQ*, parallel to *LM*, as shown in the figure below. What can you say about refractive index μ of the material of the prism? **ISC 2011**

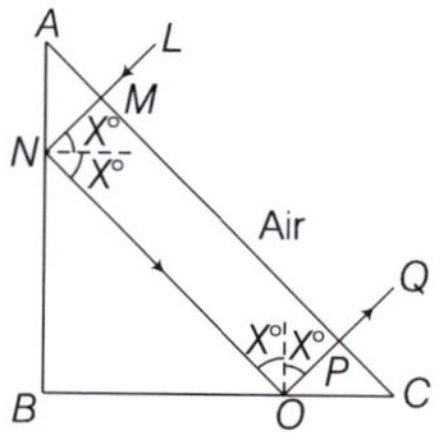

5. Calculate angle of minimum deviation (δ_m) for a regular glass prism.
(Take refractive index of glass $= 1.6$). **ISC 2011**

6. A ray *LM* of monochromatic light incident normally on one refracting surface *AB* of a regular glass prism *ABC* emerges in air from the adjacent surface *AC* as shown in the figure. Calculate the refractive index of the material of the prism. **ISC 2009**

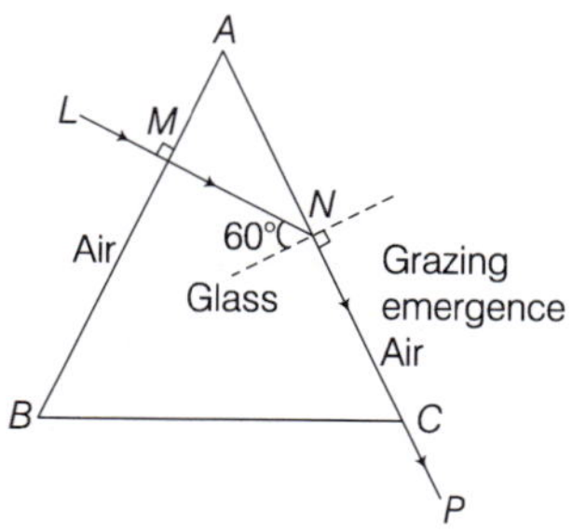

7. What is the angle of refraction made by a ray of light inside a regular i.e. an equilateral glass prism in the minimum deviation? **ISC 2007**

8. The angle of an equilateral glass prism is 59.5°. The angle of minimum deviation is 38.5°. Without using the value of refractive index of the glass. Calculate the angle of incidence for a ray of light suffering minimum deviation. **ISC 2007**

9. A ray of light falls on a right angled prism *ABC* ($AB = BC$) and travels as shown in the figure. What is the refractive index of the material of the prism? **ISC 2006**

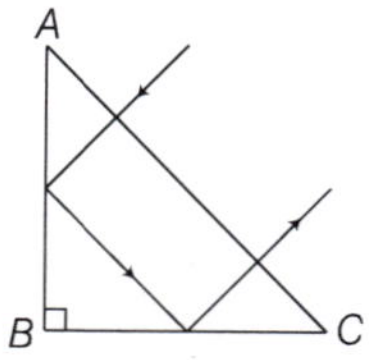

10. Find the refractive index of the liquid if a ray of light strikes surface *AB* normally and then comes out from face *AC* at grazing emergence. ($^a\mu_g = 3/2$) **ISC 2004**

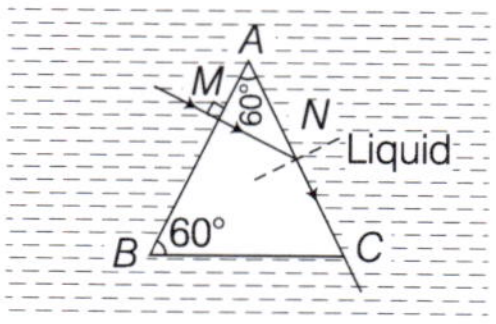

2 Marks Questions

11. Calculate refractive index of the material of an equilateral prism if its angle of minimum deviation is 30°. **ISC 2022 Sem-II**

12. Draw a labelled graph of angle of deviation (δ) *versus* angle of incidence (i) of a prism. **ISC 2020**

13. Find the angle of incidence at which a ray of monochromatic light should be incident on the first surface *AB* of a regular glass prism *ABC* so that the emergent ray grazes the adjacent surface *AC*.
(Refractive index of glass $= 1.56$) **ISC 2016**

14. At what angle, a ray of light should be incident on the first face *AB* of a regular glass prism *ABC*, so that the emergent ray grazes the adjacent face *AB*?
(Refractive index of glass $= 1.6$) **ISC 2013**

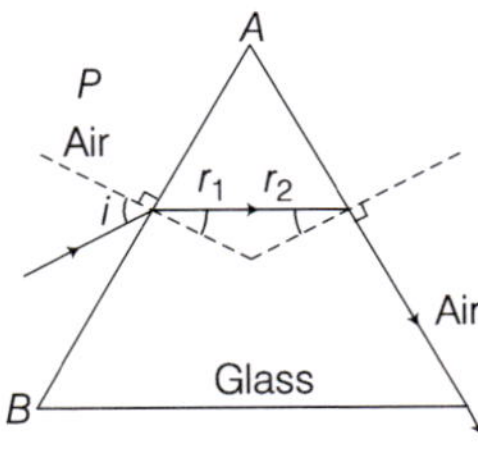

> **KEY idea**
> To calculate the angle of incidence, first calculate the angle of refraction, then apply the formula $\left(\frac{\sin i}{\sin r} = {}_a\mu_g\right)$ to know the angle of incidence.

3 Marks Questions

15. Figure below shows a ray of monochromatic light *LM* incident on the first surface *AB* of a regular (equilateral) glass prism *ABC*. The emergent ray grazes the adjacent surface *AC*. Calculate the angle of incidence. (Refractive index of glass = 1.5) **ISC 2024**

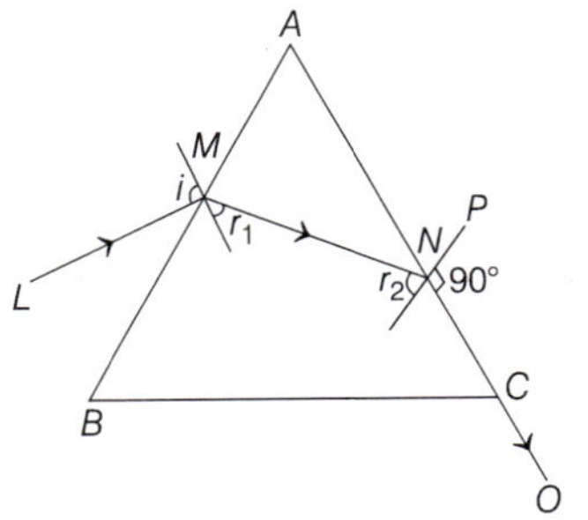

16. (*i*) For any prism, obtain a relation between angle of the prism (*A*), angle of minimum deviation (δ_m) and refractive index of its material (μ or *n*).

Or

(*ii*) Obtain an expression for refraction at a single convex spherical surface i.e., the relation between μ_1(rarer medium), μ_2 (denser medium), object distance *u* image distance *v* and the radius of curvature *R*. **ISC 2023**

17. Obtain prism formula i.e. prove that

$$n = \frac{\sin\{A + \delta_m / 2\}}{\sin\left(\frac{A}{2}\right)}$$

Where the terms have their usual meaning. **ISC SQP 2023**

18. A ray of light is incident on a prism whose refractive index is 1.52 at an angle of 40°. If the angle of emergence is 60°, calculate the angle of the prism. **ISC 2019**

> **KEY idea**
> To calculate the angle of prism first calculate the refracted angles, then apply $A = r_1 + r_2$ to calculate the angle of prism.

19. For any prism, show that refractive index of its material is given by

$$n \text{ or } \mu = \sin\left(\frac{A + \delta_{\min}}{2}\right) \Big/ \sin\left(\frac{A}{2}\right)$$

where, the terms have their usual meanings. **ISC 2018, 10**

20. A ray *EF* of monochromatic light is incident on the refracting surface *AB* of a regular glass prism (refractive index = 1.5) at an angle of incidence of $i = 55°$. If it emerges through the adjacent face *AC*, calculate the angle of emergence '*e*'. **ISC 2010**

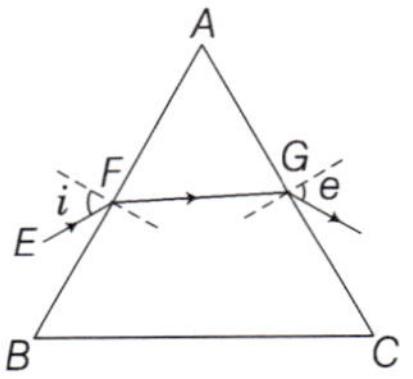

21. In the figure, *ABC* is the cross-section of a right angled prism with angle $B = 60°$ and angle $A = 30°$. *PQ* is a ray incident normally at *Q*. Copy the diagram and complete the passage of the ray through the prism. Explain briefly what happens at the interfaces between glass and air? Calculate sin i_2, where i_2 is the angle of emergence in air. Take critical angle for glass as 42° and refractive index of glass is 1.5. **ISC 2007**

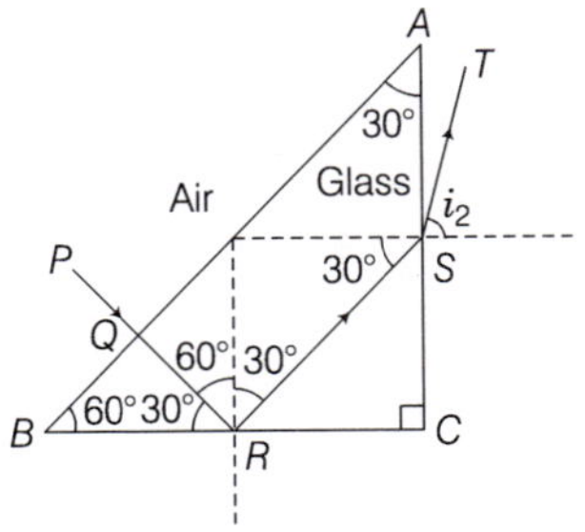

22. A ray of light which is incident in air on the surface of a glass block is deviated through 15°. The angle of incidence in air is 60°. What is the angle of refraction in glass? Also, calculate the critical angle for a glass-air interface. **ISC 2005**

> **KEY idea**
> To calculate the critical angle (I_c), first calculate the angle of refraction, then calculate the refractive index and after that critical angle.

Explanations

1. (d) 30°

2. Refer to text on page 179 (Refraction of light through a prism).

3. Light ray incident normally on face AB passes without deviation and strikes the face AC at point R at an angle of incidence 60°. This angle will be critical angle for glass-air interface, Now by applying Snell's law .

$$\mu_{\text{glass}} \sin 60° = \mu_{\text{liquid}} \sin 90°$$

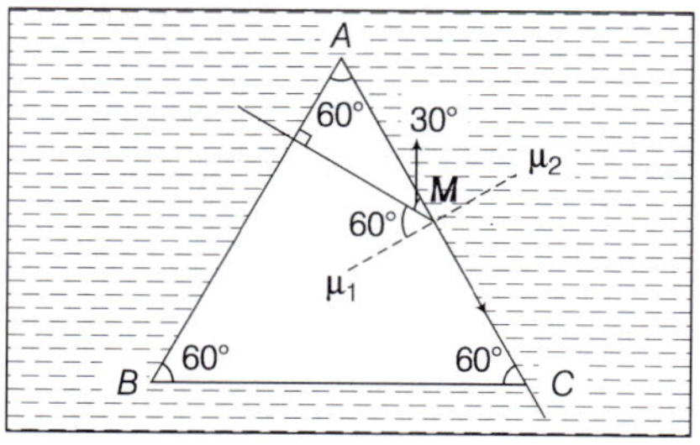

$$1.45 \times \sin 60° = \mu_{\text{liquid}} \sin 90°$$

$\Rightarrow \quad 1.45 \times 0.866 = \mu_{\text{liquid}}$

$\therefore \quad \mu_{\text{liquid}} = 1.256$

4. Since, ΔABC is an isosceles right angled prism.

$\therefore \quad \angle A = \angle C = 45°$

$\Rightarrow \quad \angle x = 45°$

For total internal reflection to take place at faces AB and BC, $\sin x > \frac{1}{\mu}$

where, μ is the refractive index of prism w.r.t. air.

$$\sin 45° > \frac{1}{\mu} \Rightarrow \mu > \frac{1}{\sin 45°}$$

$\Rightarrow \quad \mu > \sqrt{2}$

5. Given, $\mu = 1.6, \delta_{\text{min}} = ?$

For minimum deviation, we know that

$$\mu = \frac{\sin\left(\frac{A + \delta_{\text{min}}}{2}\right)}{\sin\left(\frac{A}{2}\right)}$$

Symbols have their usual meaning.

$$1.6 = \frac{\sin\left(\frac{60° + \delta_{\text{min}}}{2}\right)}{\sin\left(\frac{60°}{2}\right)}$$

$\Rightarrow \quad 0.8 = \sin\left(\frac{60° + \delta_{\text{min}}}{2}\right)$

$\Rightarrow \quad \frac{60° + \delta_{\text{min}}}{2} = 53.13°$

$\therefore \quad \delta_{\text{min}} = 46.26°$

6. By applying Snell's law at point N, we have

$$\mu_{\text{glass}} \sin 60° = \mu_{\text{air}} \sin 90°$$

Symbols have their usual meaning

$\Rightarrow \quad \mu_{\text{glass}} = \frac{2}{\sqrt{3}} = 1.15$

7. When refraction takes place through a prism

$\angle A = r_1 + r_2$

$\angle A$ = Angle of prism, $\angle r_1$ and $\angle r_2$ are refracting angle.

For minimum deviation, $r_1 = r_2 = r$

$\Rightarrow \quad \angle A = 2r$

$\Rightarrow \quad 60° = 2r \Rightarrow r = 30°$

8. As, we know for the case of minimum deviation,

$$i = \frac{A + \delta_{\text{min}}}{2}$$

where, δ_{min} = minimum deviation angle,
i = angle of incidence.

Given, $\angle A = 59.5°, \delta_{\text{min}} = 38.5°$

$$i = \frac{59.5 + 38.5}{2} \Rightarrow i = 49°$$

9. For the ray incident on the face,

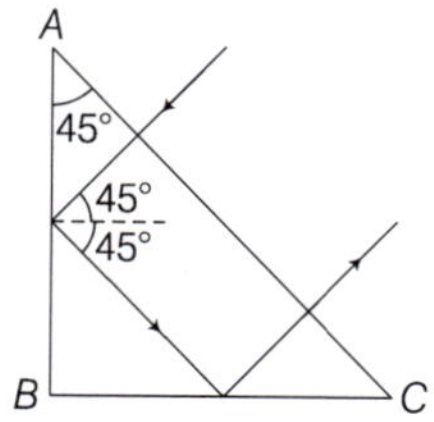

As there is total internal reflection takes place at AB.
Angle of incidence $i >$ Critical angle i_c
In this case $i > i_c$, $\mu = \operatorname{cosec} i_c$
where, μ = refractive index of prism

$\therefore \quad \mu > \operatorname{cosec} 45°$

$\Rightarrow \quad \mu > \sqrt{2}$

10. Applying Snell's law at N.

$$^{a}\mu_g \sin 60° = \mu_2 \sin r$$

$$\frac{3}{2} \times \frac{\sqrt{3}}{2} = \mu_2 \sin 90°$$

$$\Rightarrow \qquad \mu_2 = \frac{3\sqrt{3}}{4}$$

11. Given, $\delta_m = 30°$

For equilateral prism, $A = 60°$

$$\therefore \text{Refractive index, } \mu = \frac{\sin\left(\frac{\delta_m + A}{2}\right)}{\sin\frac{A}{2}}$$

$$= \frac{\sin\left(\frac{30° + 60°}{2}\right)}{\sin\left(\frac{60°}{2}\right)} = \frac{\sin 45°}{\sin 30°} = \sqrt{2} = 1.414$$

12. Graph between angle of deviation (δ) *versus* angle of incidence (i) of a prism.

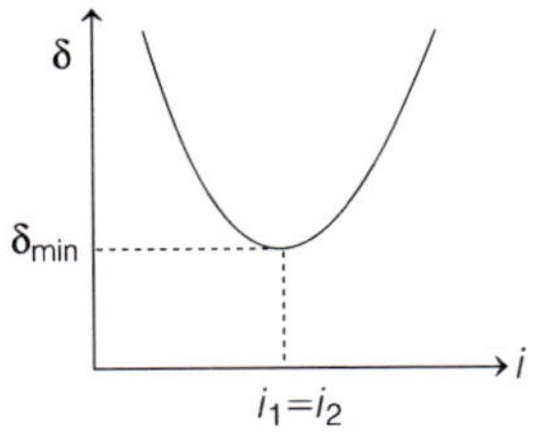

13. According to the question,

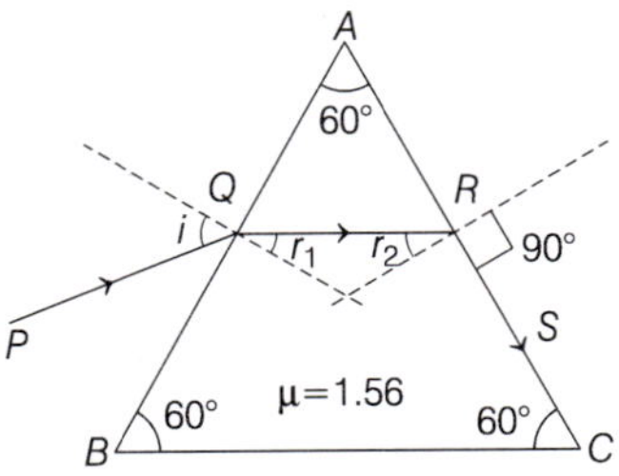

The refracted ray RS will just suffer total internal reflection or grazes the surface AC. If it is incident at the critical angle i_c.

i.e. $\qquad r_2 = i_c$

Now, for face AC

$$\sin i_c = \frac{1}{\mu} = \frac{1}{1.56}$$

$$\Rightarrow \qquad i_c = r_2 = 41°$$

But $\qquad r_2 + r_1 = A$

$$\Rightarrow \qquad r_1 = A - r_2 = A - i_c = 60° - 41° = 19°$$

From Snell's law, $\mu = \dfrac{\sin i}{\sin r_1}$

$$\Rightarrow \qquad \sin i = \mu \sin 190° = 1.56 \times 0.325 = 0.507$$

$$\Rightarrow \qquad i = \sin^{-1} 0.507 \approx 30°$$

Thus, angle of incidence, $i \approx 30°$

14. At face AC, by Snell's law

$$\sin r_2 = \frac{1}{_a\mu_g} \Rightarrow \sin r_2 = \frac{1}{1.6}$$

$$\Rightarrow \qquad r_2 = \sin^{-1}\left(\frac{1}{1.6}\right)$$

$$\therefore \qquad r_2 = 38.68°$$

and $\qquad r_1 + r_2 = A \qquad$ [A = Angle of prism]

$$r_1 = 60° - 38.68° = 21.32°$$

At face AB, by Snell's law, we have

$$\frac{\sin i}{\sin r} = {_a\mu_g}$$

$$\Rightarrow \qquad \sin i = \sin r_1 \times {_a\mu_g} = \sin 21.32° \times 1.6$$

$$\Rightarrow \qquad \sin i = 0.5817$$

$$\Rightarrow \qquad i = \sin^{-1}(0.5817)$$

$$\therefore \qquad i = 35.57°$$

15.

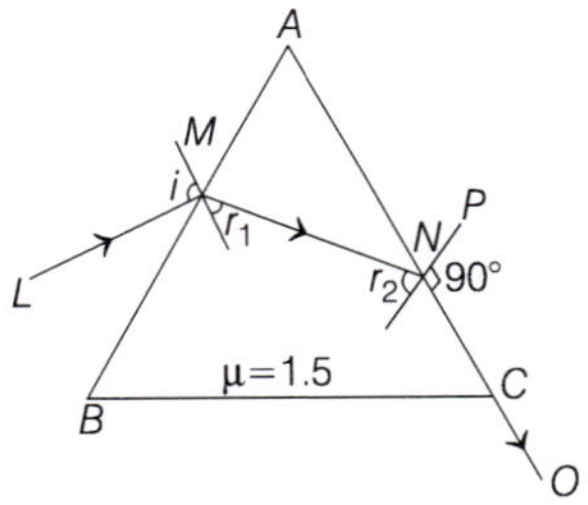

The refracted ray NO will just suffer total internal reflection or grazes the surface AC, if it is incident at the critical angle i_c. i.e. $r_2 = i_c$

Now, for face AC,

$$\sin i_c = \frac{1}{\mu} = \frac{1}{1.50} = 0.66$$

$$i_c = r_2 = 41.29°$$

But $r_2 + r_1 = A$ = Angle of prism

$$\Rightarrow \qquad r_1 = A - r_2 = A - i_c$$

$$= 60° - 41.29° = 18.70°$$

From Snell's law, $\mu = \dfrac{\sin i}{\sin r_1}$

$$\Rightarrow \qquad \sin i = \mu \sin(18.70°)$$

$$= 1.5 \times 0.320 = 0.480$$

$$\Rightarrow \qquad i = \sin^{-1}(0.480) = 28.68°$$

Thus, angle of incidence, $i \approx 29°$

16. (i) Refer to text on page 179 (Refraction of light Through a Prism).

Or

(ii) Refer to text on page 185 (Refraction Formula at Convex Surface)

17. Refer to text on page 179 (Refraction of light Through a Prism).

18. Given, refractive index, $n = 1.52$

Angle of incidence, $i = 40°$

Angle of emergence, $e = 60°$

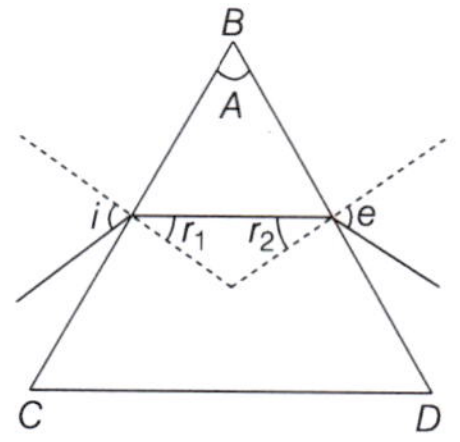

For face BC, $n = \dfrac{\sin i}{\sin r_1}$

$$1.52 = \frac{\sin 40°}{\sin r_1}$$

$$\sin r_1 = \frac{\sin 40°}{1.52} = \frac{0.642}{1.52}$$

$$\sin r_1 = 0.4223$$

$$r_1 = \sin^{-1}(0.4223) = 24.98$$

Again, for face BD,

$$\frac{\sin r_2}{\sin e} = \frac{1}{n}$$

$$\frac{\sin r_2}{\sin 60°} = \frac{1}{1.52}$$

$$\sin r_2 = \frac{\frac{\sqrt{3}}{2}}{1.52} = \frac{0.8660}{1.52}$$

$$r_2 = \sin^{-1}(0.569) = 34.68$$

Angle of prism, $A = r_1 + r_2 = 24.98° + 34.68°$

$$= 59.66° \simeq 60°$$

19. Refer to text on page 179 (Refraction of light Through a Prism).

20. At F, applying Snell's law, $\dfrac{\sin i}{\sin r_1} = \mu = 1.5$

$$i = 55° \quad \text{[given]}$$

$$\sin r_1 = \frac{\sin 55°}{1.5} = 0.5461$$

Now, $r_1 = \sin^{-1}(0.5461) = 33.1°$

$$r_1 + r_2 = A$$

$\therefore$ $r_2 = 60° - 33.1° = 26.9°$

At G, $\dfrac{\sin e}{\sin r_2} = \mu = 1.5$

$\Rightarrow$ $\sin e = 1.5 \times \sin 26.9° = 1.5 \times 0.453 = 0.68$

$\therefore$ $e = 42.7°$

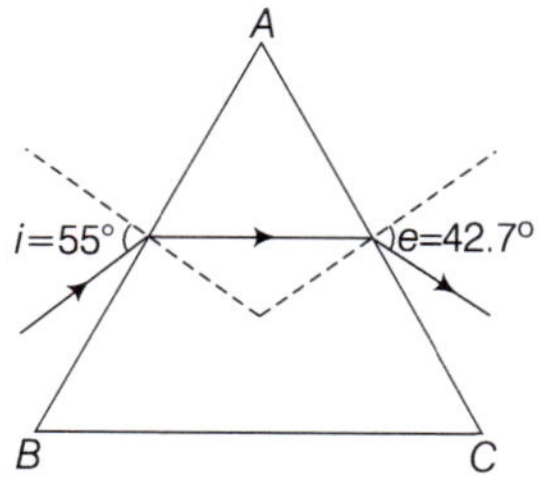

21. Consider the diagram in which ray of light P, strikes at 90°, it goes undeviated and then it strikes on the face BC at an angle of incidence 60°, which is greater than the critical angle for the glass-air surface.

Hence, on the surface BC, total internal reflection of light will take place. Totally, internally reflected ray, then strikes on the face AC at S, at the angle of incidence 30°, where the refraction of light will take place such that i_2 will be final angle of emergence.

Using Snell's law, $\dfrac{\sin 30°}{\sin i_2} = {}_g\mu_a = \dfrac{1}{{}_a\mu_g}$

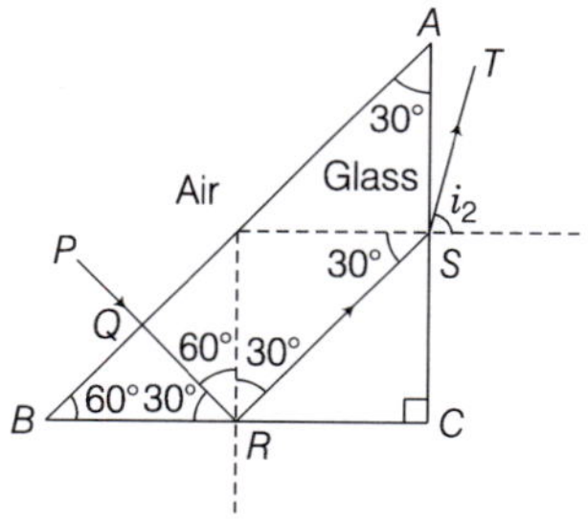

Hence, $\sin i_2 = \sin 30° \times {}_a\mu_g$

$\Rightarrow$ $\sin i_2 = \dfrac{1}{2} \times 1.5 = 0.75 = \dfrac{3}{4}$

22. We will apply Snell's law at each face.

As $${}_a\mu_g = \frac{\sin\left(\dfrac{\delta_m + A}{2}\right)}{\sin \dfrac{A}{2}}$$

$${}_a\mu_g = \frac{\sin (60° + 15°)/2}{\sin 60°/2} = \frac{\sin 37.5°}{\sin 30°}$$

$${}_a\mu_g = \frac{\sin i}{\sin r}$$

So, $\dfrac{\sin i}{\sin r} = \dfrac{\sin 37.5°}{\sin 30°}$

Angle of refraction $= 30°$

For refractive index $_a\mu_g = \dfrac{\sin\left(\dfrac{\delta_{min} + A}{2}\right)}{\sin\left(\dfrac{A}{2}\right)}$

$\delta_{min} = 15°, \angle i = 60°$

$_a\mu_g = \dfrac{\sin(60° + 15°)/2}{\sin 60/2°}$

$= \dfrac{\sin 37.5°}{\sin 30°} = 1.217$

$\sin i_c = \dfrac{1}{_a\mu_g}$ [i_c = critical angle]

$\Rightarrow \sin i_c = \dfrac{1}{1.217}$

$= \sin^{-1} 0.821° = 55.2$

TOPIC 3

Refraction at a Spherical Surface

Refraction Formula at Convex Surface

A refracting surface which is a part of a sphere of transparent refracting material is called spherical refracting surface.

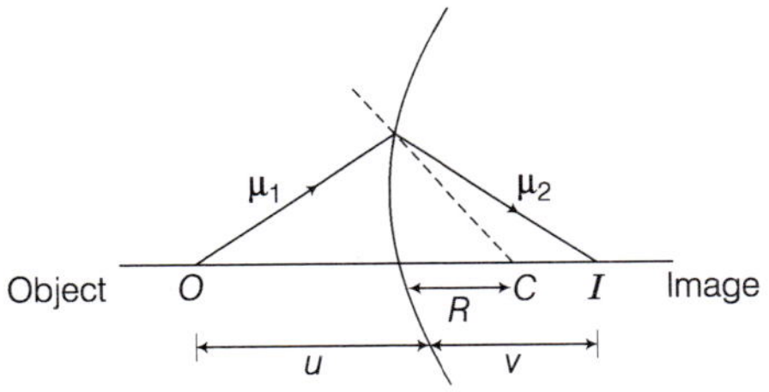

Let O be the point object placed on the principal axis and I be its real image formed due to refraction by the surface.

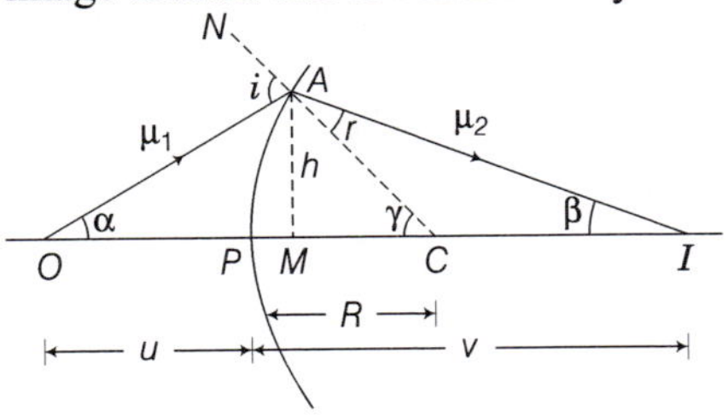

From ΔCOA, $\quad i = \alpha + \gamma$ ...(i)

Again, in ΔCIA, $\quad \gamma = r + \beta$

because, the exterior angle is equal to the sum of two opposite interior angles

So, $\quad r = \gamma - \beta$

By Snell's law, $\quad \dfrac{\sin i}{\sin r} = \dfrac{\mu_2}{\mu_1}$

As aperture is very small, so $\sin i = i$, $\sin r = r$, So, we have $\mu_1 i = \mu_2 r$

Putting the values of i and r in the above equation, we get

$\Rightarrow \quad \mu_1(\alpha + \gamma) = \mu_2(\gamma - \beta)$

$\mu_2\beta + \mu_1\alpha = (\mu_2 - \mu_1)\gamma$ ...(ii)

Now, $\quad \alpha = \tan\alpha = \dfrac{h}{-u}$,

$\beta = \tan\beta = \dfrac{h}{v}$

[as it is very small $\tan\theta = \theta$]

and $\quad \gamma = \tan\gamma = \dfrac{h}{R}$

On putting these values in Eq. (ii), we get

$$\mu_2 \frac{h}{v} + \mu_1\left(\frac{h}{-u}\right) = (\mu_2 - \mu_1)\frac{h}{R}$$

$$\Rightarrow \boxed{\frac{\mu_2}{v} - \frac{\mu_1}{u} = \frac{\mu_2 - \mu_1}{R}}$$

Cartesian Sign Convention for Spherical Surfaces

(*i*) The principal axis of the spherical surface is taken as X-axis and the optical centre as origin.

(*ii*) The direction of the incident light is taken as the positive direction of X-axis and opposite to it as negative.

(*iii*) The upward direction is taken as positive and the downward direction as negative.

Lens

Lens is a transparent medium bounded by two refracting surfaces of which one or both surfaces are spherical. Lenses are of two types such as,

Convex or Converging Lens

A lens which is thicker at the centre and thinner at its end is called convex lens.
Convex lenses is of three types as shown below.

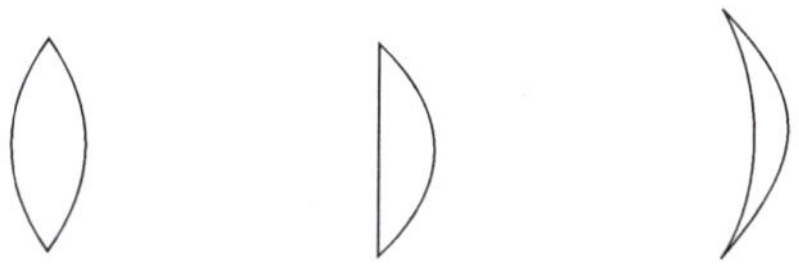

(a) Double-convex lens (b) Plano-convex lens (c) Concavo-convex lens

A convex lens is also known as converging lens because it converges a parallel beam of light towards principal axis as rays pass through it.

Concave or Diverging Lens

A lens which is thinner at the centre and thicker at its end is called a concave lens.
Concave lenses are of three types as shown below.

(a) Double-concave lens (b) Plano-concave lens (c) Concavo-concave lens

A concave lens is also known as diverging lens because it diverges a parallel beam of light away from principal axis as rays pass through it.

Image Formation in Lenses

For drawing ray diagrams in lenses alike spherical mirrors, we consider any two of the following rays.

(*i*) Rays which are parallel to the principal axis after refraction will pass through principal focus in case of convex lens and will appear to be coming from principal focus in case of concave lens, O being the optical centre of the lens.

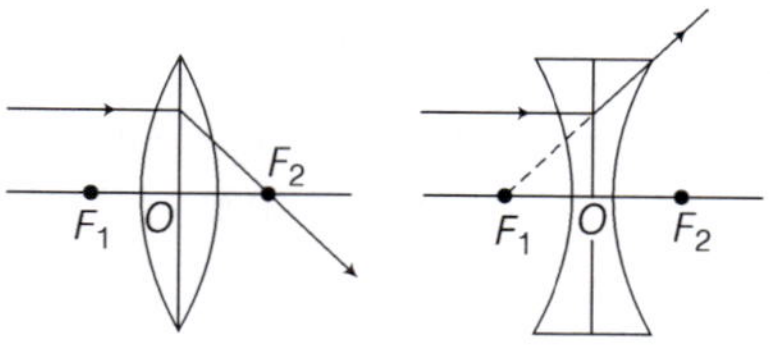

(*ii*) Ray passing through or directed to the focus will emerge parallel to the principal axis for both the lenses.

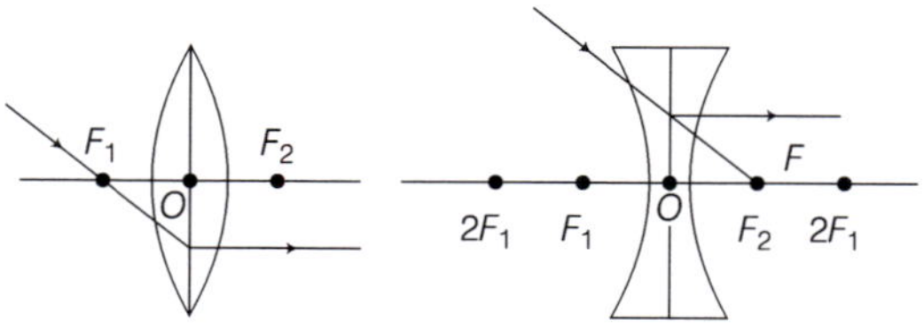

(*iii*) Ray directed to optical centre will emerge out undeviated.

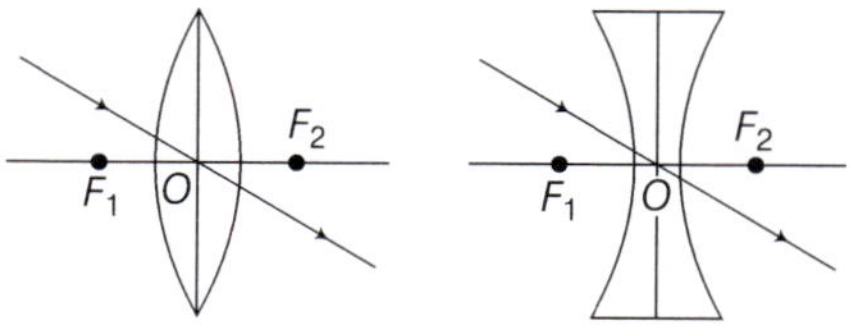

Lens Maker's Formula

The lens maker's formula relates to the focal length of a lens to the refractive index of the material of the lens and the radii of curvature of the two surfaces of the lens. It is expressed as

$$\frac{1}{f} = (\mu - 1)\left(\frac{1}{R_1} - \frac{1}{R_2}\right)$$

where, μ is refractive index of material of lens w.r.t. surrounding media and R_1, R_2 are the radii of curvature of two surfaces.

For plano-convex or plano-concave lens,

$$R_1 = R \text{ and } R_2 = \infty \text{ (for plane surface).}$$

Focal length of lens depends on

(*i*) Radii of curvature of lens

(*ii*) Refractive index of material of lens.

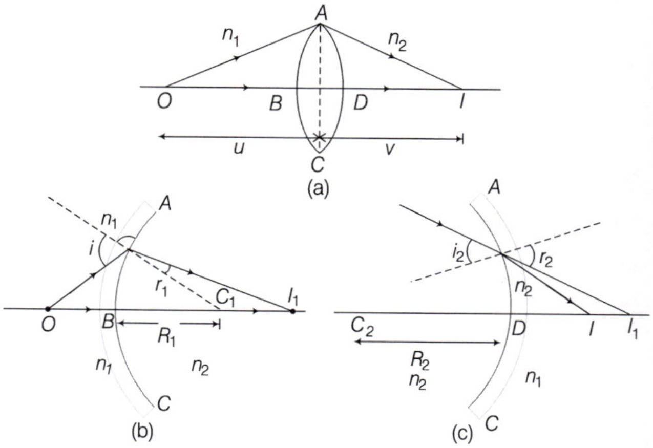

The above figures show the image formation by a convex lens.

Assumptions Made in the Lens Maker Formula

(*i*) The lens is thin, so that distances measured from the poles of its surfaces can be taken as equal to the distance from the optical centre of the lens.
(*ii*) The aperture of the lens is small.
(*iii*) The object considered as a point lying on the principal axis of the lens.
(*iv*) The incident ray and refracted ray make small angles with the principal axis of the lens.
(*v*) A convex lens is made up of two convex spherical refracting surfaces.
(*vi*) The first refracting surface forms image I_1 of the object O [Fig. (b)].
(*vii*) Image I_1 acts as virtual object for the second surface that forms the image at I [Fig. (c)].

When lens of refractive index μ is immersed in a medium of refractive index μ'

Then, focal length changes to f_m, which is given by

$$\frac{1}{f_m} = \left(\frac{\mu}{\mu'} - 1\right)\left(\frac{1}{R_1} - \frac{1}{R_2}\right) \quad ...(i)$$

If $\mu' = 1$ i.e. medium is air then the focal length of lens (i.e. f_a) is given by

$$\frac{1}{f_a} = (\mu - 1)\left(\frac{1}{R_1} - \frac{1}{R_2}\right) \quad ...(ii)$$

On dividing Eq. (ii) by Eq. (i), we get

$$\frac{f_m}{f_a} = \frac{(\mu - 1)}{\left(\frac{\mu}{\mu'} - 1\right)}$$

(*i*) If $\mu = \mu' \Rightarrow f_m = \infty \Rightarrow$ lens behaves like a glass slab.The ray passes undeviated.
(*ii*) If $\mu < \mu' \Rightarrow f_m > f_a$ and nature of lens reversed. i.e. convex lens will behave like convex and concave lens will behave like convex.
(*iii*) If $\mu > \mu' \Rightarrow f_m < f_a$ and nature of lens remains same, but its focal length increases and hence its power of lens decrease.

Thin Lens Formula

It is a relation among the focal length of a lens (f), distance of object (u) and image (v) from optical centre of the lens.

The lens formula is given by

$$\frac{1}{v} - \frac{1}{u} = \frac{1}{f}$$

Power of a Lens

The ability of a lens to converge or diverge the ray of light incident on it is called the power of the lens.

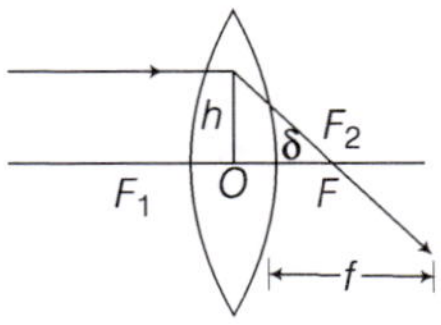

The power of a lens is defined as the tangent of the angle by which it converges or diverges a beam of light falling at unit distance from the optical centre. It is given by

$$P = \frac{1}{f\,(\text{m})}$$

where, f is focal length in metre.

The SI unit of power of lens is dioptre (D).

$$\left\{\tan\delta = \frac{h}{f} \text{ if } h = 1,\ \tan\delta = \frac{1}{f} \text{ for small values of } \delta,\ \tan\delta \approx \delta,\ \delta = \frac{1}{f}\right\}$$

We have $$P = (\mu - 1)\left(\frac{1}{R_1} - \frac{1}{R_2}\right)$$

Here, R_1 and R_2 are to be measured in metre.

For converging (convex) lens, power is positive and for diverging (concave) lens, power is negative.

Linear Magnification Produced by a Lens

The linear magnification of a lens is defined as the ratio of height of the image formed by the lens with height of the object. It is expressed as

$$m = \frac{\text{Height of image } (I)}{\text{Height of object } (O)}$$

The linear magnification (m) is also given by the ratio of image distance with object and expressed as distance

$$m = \frac{v}{u}$$

The other magnification formula is

$$m = \frac{v}{u} = \frac{f - v}{f} = \frac{f}{f + u}$$

A negative magnification corresponds to a real, inverted image while a positive magnification corresponds to a virtual, erect image.

Combination of Thin Lenses in Contact

Consider two lenses A and B of focal length f_1 and f_2 placed in contact with each other. An object is placed at a point O beyond the focus of the first lens A. The first lens produces an image at I_1 which serves as a virtual object for the second lens B producing the final image at I.

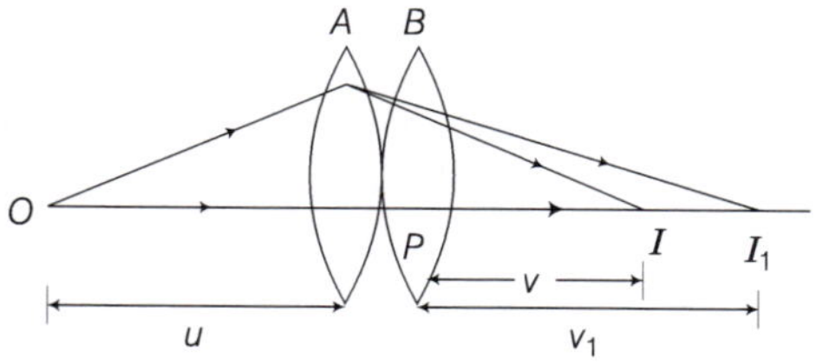

Equivalent power of the system

$$\boxed{P = P_1 + P_2}$$

where, $\quad P_1 = \dfrac{1}{f_1}$

$\Rightarrow \quad P_2 = \dfrac{1}{f_2}$

(symbols have their usual meanings.)

So, combined focal length is given by

$$\boxed{\frac{1}{f} = \frac{1}{f_1} + \frac{1}{f_2}}$$

Magnification by Combination of Lenses

When lenses are used in combination, each lens magnifies the image formed by the preceding lens. Thus, the magnification m of the final image is given by

$$\boxed{m = m_1 \times m_2}$$

Combination of Lens and Mirror

Let an object be placed in front of a co-axial arrangement of a lens and a mirror held at a suitable distance apart and object is placed in front of the lens. The following cases arises in the combination of lens and mirror.

(*i*) Combination of concave lens and concave mirror

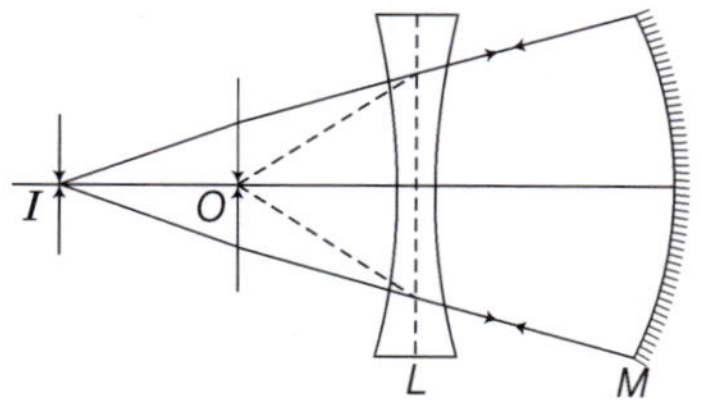

(*ii*) Combination of concave lens and plane mirror

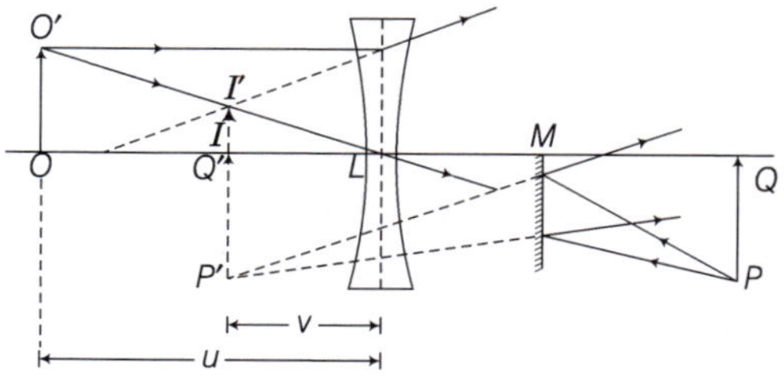

(*iii*) Combination of convex lens and convex mirror

(a)

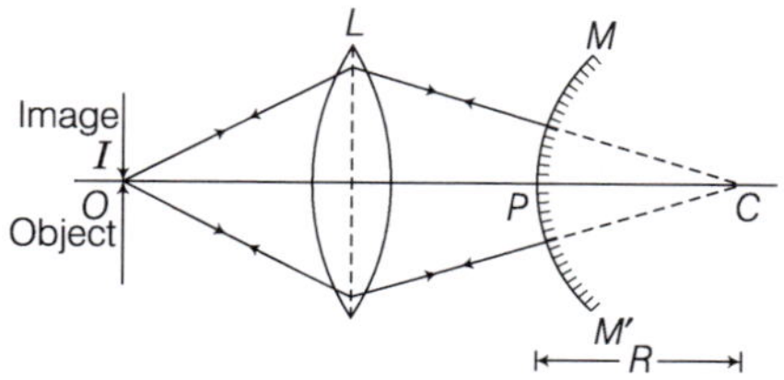

(b) **Combination of convex lens and concave mirror**

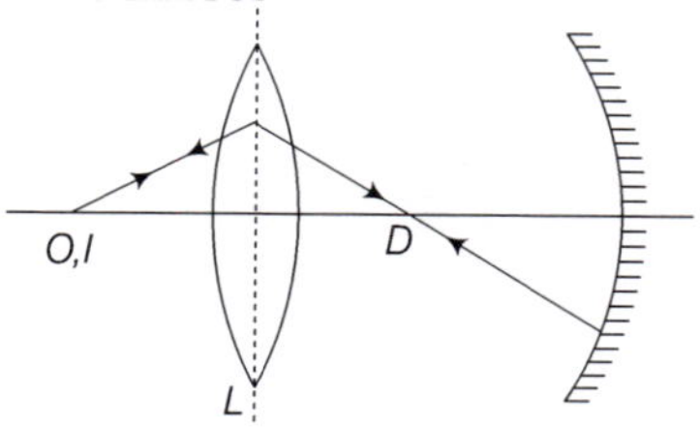

The nature and size of the image will be studied as follow.

- First calculate the position, size and nature of image formed by the lens alone considering that mirror is not there.
- The image formed by the lens acts as real or virtual object for mirror. Using mirror formula, we can calculate the position, size and nature of image formed by mirror.

This calculation will give us the final position, size and nature of image of the given object formed by the combination of lens and mirror.

PYQs Previous Years Questions

1 Mark Questions

1. Two thin lenses having optical powers of -8D and +12D are placed in contact with each other. The focal length of this combination is **ISC SQP 2023**

(a) + 0.25 m (b) – 0.25 m
(c) + 0.25 cm (d) – 0.25 cm

2. Where should an object be kept infront of a convex lens in order to get an image of the same size as the object? **ISC 2022 Sem-II**

3. A convex lens, made of glass, is immersed in water. As a result, its focal length will **ISC SQP 2018**

(a) increase (b) decrease
(c) double (d) remain same

4. A converging lens of focal length 40 cm is kept in contact with a diverging lens of focal length 30 cm. Find the focal length of the combination **ISC 2017**

5. How can the spherical aberration produced by a lens be minimised? **ISC 2017**

6. Two thin lenses having optical power of – 10 D and +6D are placed in contact with each other. The focal length of the combination is

(a) + 0.25 cm (b) – 0.25 cm (c) + 0.25 m (d) – 0.25 m

7. How does focal length of a convex lens change with increase in wavelength of incident light? **ISC 2014**

8. Find the focal length and nature of a lens whose optical power is –5 D. **ISC 2013**

9. A thin convex lens (L_1) of focal length 80 cm and a thin concave lens (L_2) of focal length f are kept co-axially, 20 cm apart as shown in figure below. When a narrow and parallel beam of light is incident on the convex lens, beam emerging from the concave lens is also a parallel beam. Find the value of f. **ISC 2012**

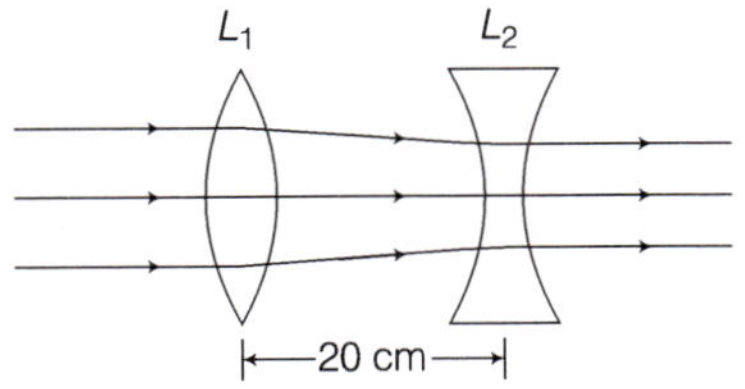

10. A thin converging lens of focal length 15 cm is kept in contact with a thin diverging lens of focal length 20 cm. Find the focal length of this combination. **ISC 2009**

11. A biconvex spherical lens has focal length 20 cm. If it is split into two halves to form two plano-convex lenses, what is the focal length of each plano-convex lens? **ISC 2007**

12. Refractive index of the material of a concave lens is μ. The lens is immersed in a medium of refractive index μ_1 ($\mu_1 > \mu$). A parallel beam of light is incident on the lens. Draw a diagram to show the path of emergent rays. **ISC 2005**

13. State one assumption made in deriving the formula $\frac{n_2}{v} - \frac{n_1}{u} = \frac{n_2 - n_1}{R}$ for refraction at a spherical interface. **ISC 2003**

14. In the figure shown, O is a point object placed in air on the axis of a spherical surface APB of a glass block. OA is an incident ray. The direction of the refracted ray AD in the glass block is parallel to the principal axis PC, $CP = CA = R$ is the radius of the spherical surface. Use the formula given in Q. No. 5 and show that the object distance $PO = u = R/(n-1)$, where $n_2 = n$ and $n_1 = 1$. **ISC 2003**

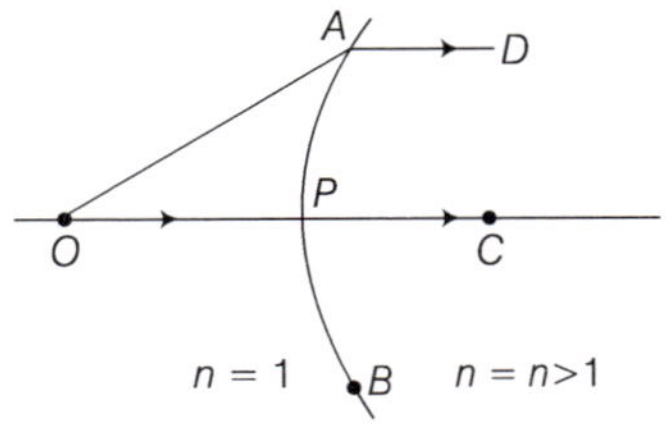

15. Write down the lens maker's formula using standard symbols. **ISC 2002**

16. The lens shown in figure is made of two different materials of refractive indices μ_1 and μ_2, respectively. A point object is placed on the principal axis. How many images of the object will be formed by the lens (neglecting spherical and chromatic aberration)? **ISC 2001**

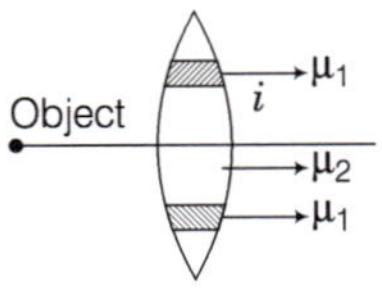

17. Draw a diagram to illustrate spherical aberration of a convex lens. **ISC 2001**

18. Two thin lenses—one convex and the other concave of focal lengths 15 cm and 20 cm respectively, are put in contact. Find the focal length of the doublet lens. **ISC 2000**

19. What is the relation between the refractive indices n_1 and n_2, if the behaviour of light rays is as shown in the given figure? Here, n_1 and n_2 are the refractive indices of the surrounding medium and the lens, respectively. **ISC 2000**

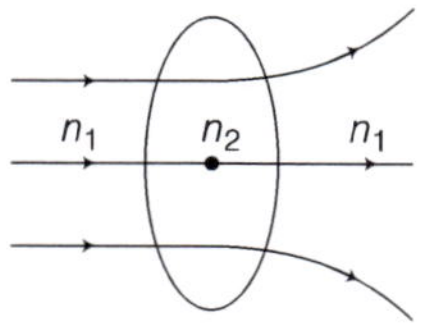

2 Marks Questions

20. A biconvex lens made of glass (refractive index 1.5) has two spherical surfaces having radii 10 cm and 20 cm. Calculate its focal length. **ISC 2022 Sem-II**

21. Where will you keep an object in front of a **ISC 2020**

(i) convex lens in order to get a virtual and magnified image?

(ii) concave mirror to get a real and diminished image?

22. A biconvex lens made of glass (refractive index 1.5) has two spherical surfaces having radii 20 cm and 30 cm. Calculate its focal length. **ISC 2018**

23. A thin convex lens of focal length 20 cm is kept in contact with a thin concave lens of focal length 15 cm. Find the focal length and the nature of the combination. **ISC SQP 2018**

24. State how focal length of a glass lens (refractive index 1.56) changes when it is completely immersed in

(i) water (refractive index =1.33)

(ii) a liquid (refractive index =1.65). **ISC 2016**

25. When two thin lenses of focal lengths f_1 and f_2 are kept co-axially and in contact , prove that their combined focal length f is given by

$$\frac{1}{f}=\frac{1}{f_1}+\frac{1}{f_2}$$ **ISC 2014, 08**

26. The figure below shows the positions of a point object O, two lenses, a plane mirror and the final image I which coincides with the object. The focal length of the convex lens is 20 cm. Calculate the focal length of the concave lens. **ISC 2014**

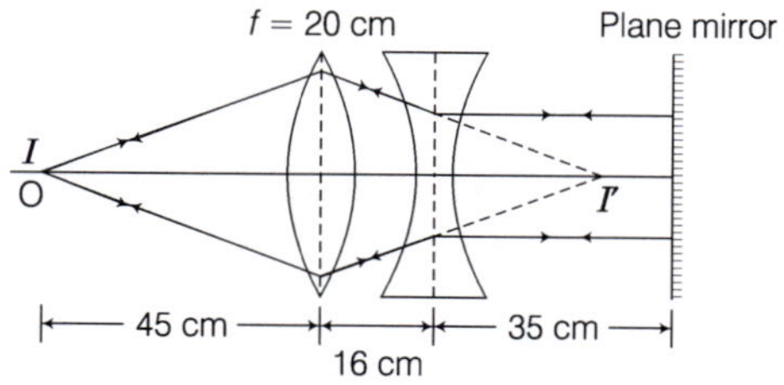

KEY idea

To calculate the focal length first calculate the v with help of lens formula and then calculate the focal length (f)

27. A convex lens L and a plane mirror M are arranged as shown in the figure alongside.

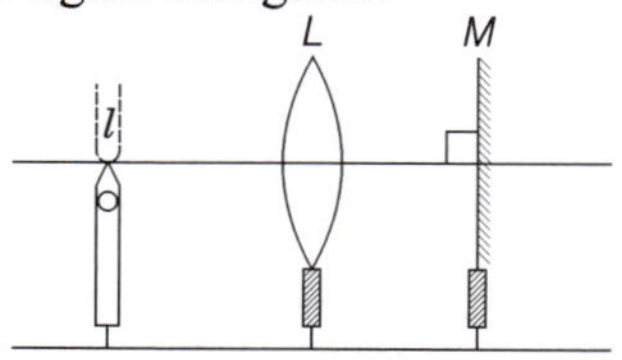

Position of object pin O is adjusted in such a way that the inverted image I formed by the lens mirror combination coincides with the object pin O. Explain how and when this happens. **ISC 2013**

28. Figure below shows a parallel beam of monochromatic light incident on a convex spherical surface, radius of curvature $R = 30$ cm, which separates glass (refractive index = 1.6) from air. Find the position of the image formed due to refraction of light at this single spherical surface. **ISC 2012**

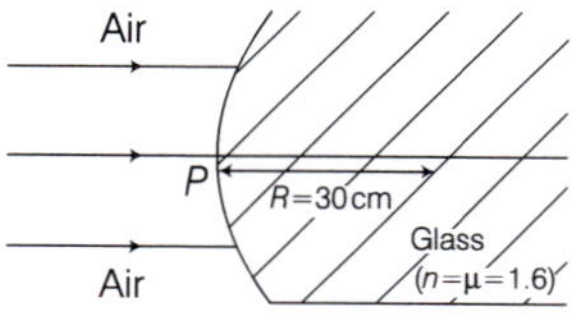

29. Where should an object be kept on the principal axis of a convex lens of focal length 20 cm in order to get an image, which is double of the size of the object? **ISC 2011**

30. Obtain an expression for refraction at a single convex spherical surface, i.e. the relation between μ_1 (rarer medium), μ_2 (denser medium), the object distance u, image distance v and radius of curvature R. **ISC 2011**

31. An equi-convex lens of glass having focal length of 10 cm is split into two identical plano-convex lenses each having focal length f_1 as shown below. Find the value of f_1. **ISC 2010**

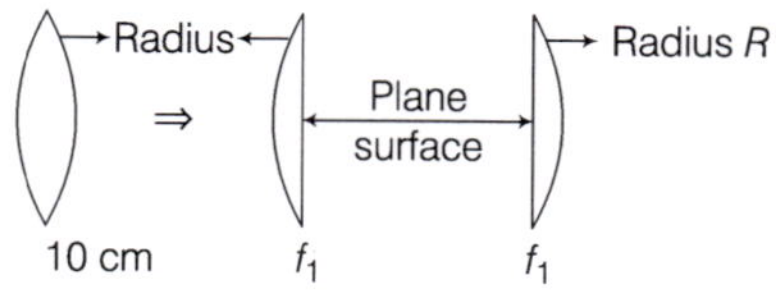

32. An illuminated point object O is kept 20 cm from a thin convex lens L_1 of focal length 15 cm as shown below. A thin diverging lens L_2 of focal length 25 cm is kept co-axial with the first lens and 35 cm from it as shown in the figure.

Find the position of the final image formed by this combination of lenses. **ISC 2010**

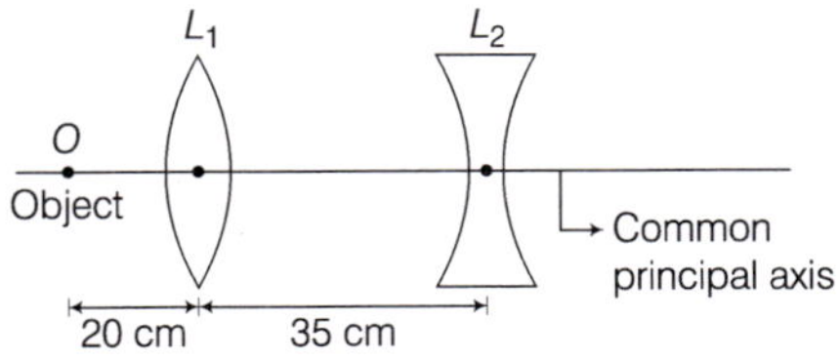

33. A thin convex lens which is made of glass (refractive index 1.5) has a focal length of 20 cm. It is now completely immersed in a transparent liquid having refractive index 1.75. Find the new focal length of the lens. **ISC 2009**

34. A plano-convex lens made of glass ($n = 1.5$) has a focal length 10 cm.

(*i*) Calculate the radius of curvature of its curved surface.

(*ii*) If an identical plano-convex lens is placed in contact with the first (plane surfaces facing each other), what will be the power (in dioptres) of the combination? **ISC 2007**

35. What is the cause of spherical aberration in lenses? State a method to minimise the defect. **ISC 2006**

36. A convex lens and a plane mirror are kept at a distance of 10 cm as shown in the diagram below. Parallel rays incident on the convex lens after reflection from the mirror form an image at the optical centre. Complete the ray diagram and find out the focal length of the lens. **ISC 2005**

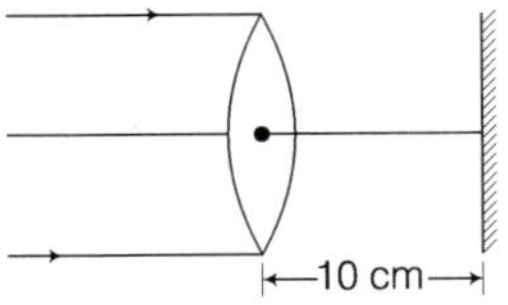

37. See below the diagram.

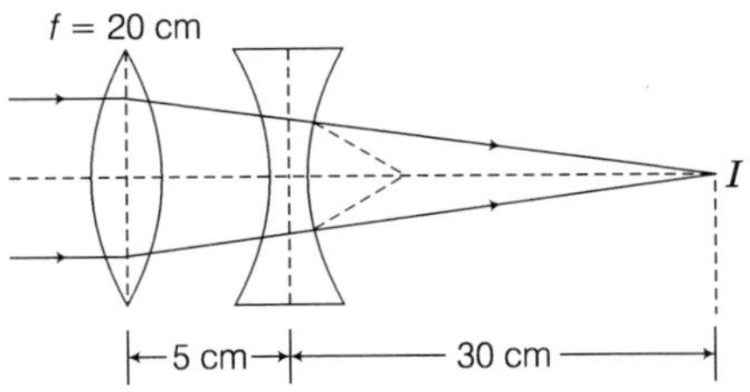

Calculate the focal length of concave lens with the help of above ray diagram. The focal length of convex lens is 20 cm. **ISC 2004**

38. A convex lens of focal length $f = 20$ cm is combined with a diverging lens of power 6.5 D. What are the power and focal length of the combination? **ISC 2003**

39. A plano-convex lens has radius of curvature 10 cm. Its focal length is 80 cm under water. Calculate the refractive index of the material of the lens, given refractive index of water is 4/3. **ISC 2002**

3 Marks Questions

40. A student is performing an experiment to determine focal length of a convex lens by using lens formula, i.e. by no parallax method. The examiner gives some instructions to the student. The student responds to each instruction as per her understanding of the experiment.

State whether the student's response is correct or incorrect. Give a reason for your answer. **ISC 2024**

(i) **EXAMINER** Image formed by the lens is magnified. Reduce the size of the image.

STUDENT moves the lens towards the object pin.

(ii) **EXAMINER** Plot a graph of $(1/v)$ against $(1/u)$.

STUDENT takes $(1/v)$ on Y-axis and $(1/u)$ on X-axis.

(iii) **EXAMINER** Write the relation between the optical power (P) and the focal length (f) of the convex lens.

STUDENT writes $P = 2f$.

41. A thin converging lens of focal length 12 cm is kept in contact with a thin diverging lens of focal length 18 cm. Calculate the effective/equivalent focal length of the combination. **ISC 2022 Sem-II**

42. Radius of curvature of an equi-convex lens of glass ($n = 1.5$) is 30 cm. Find its focal length. An object of height 5.0 cm is placed at a distance of 60 cm from the optical centre of the lens. Find the position and the height of the image formed. **ISC 2022 Sem-II**

43. When two thin lenses are kept in contact, show that the effective focal length or equivalent focal length f is given by **ISC 2022 Sem-II, 18**

$$\frac{1}{f} = \frac{1}{f_1} + \frac{1}{f_2}$$

where the terms have their usual meaning.

44. Derive an expression for refraction at a single (convex) spherical surface, i.e. a relation between u, v, R, n_1 (rarer medium) and n_2 (denser medium), where the terms have their usual meaning. **ISC 2020**

45. Calculate the focal length of a convex lens whose radii of curvature of two surfaces is 10 cm and 15 cm, respectively and its refractive index is 1.5. **ISC 2019**

46. (i) Obtain an expression for refraction at a single convex spherical surface separating the two media having refractive indices n_1 (rarer medium) and n_2 (denser medium) i.e. a relation between u, v, n_1, n_2 and R.

Or

(ii) Derive $R = 2f$ for a spherical mirror, where the symbols have their usual meaning. **ISC SQP 2018**

47. Starting with an expression for refraction at a single spherical surface, obtain lens maker's formula. **ISC 2017**

48. A point object O is placed at a distance of 15 cm from a convex lens L of focal length 10 cm as shown in the figure below. On the other side of the lens, a convex mirror M is placed such that its distance from the lens is equal to the focal length of the lens. The final image formed by this combination is observed to coincide with the object O. Find the focal length of the convex mirror. **ISC 2015**

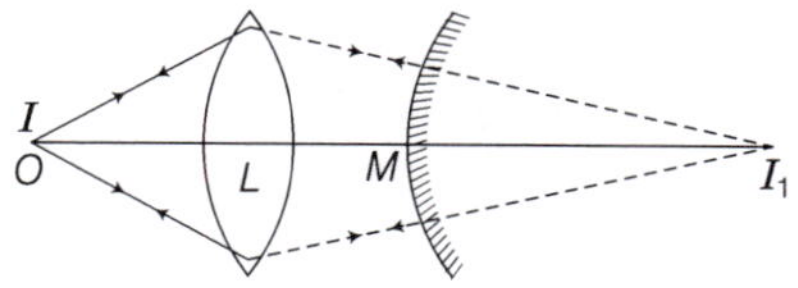

Explanations

1. (a) Given, $P_1 = -8\text{D}$, $P_2 = 12\text{D}$

$\Rightarrow$ $P = P_1 + P_2 = -8 + 12 \Rightarrow P = 4$

$$F = \frac{1}{P} = \frac{1}{4} = 0.25 \text{ m}$$

2. To get an image of the same size as the object in a convex lens, the object should be placed at a distance of twice the focal length or at the centre of curvature of the lens.

3. (a) When a convex lens made up of glass is immersed in water, then due to change in refractive index, focal length of the lens changes. Since water is less denser than glass i.e., refractive index of liquid is less than the refractive index of material of lens, so the focal length increases.

4. The focal length of the combination will be

$$\frac{1}{f} = \frac{1}{f_1} + \frac{1}{f_2} = \frac{1}{40} + \frac{1}{-30}$$

$$= \frac{1}{40} - \frac{1}{30}$$

$$= \frac{3-4}{120} = -\frac{1}{120}$$

$$f = -120 \text{ cm}$$

$$= -\frac{120}{100} = -1.2 \text{ m}$$

5. The inability of a spherical mirror or a lens of large aperture to bring the marginal as will as paraxial rays of a wide beam of right to focus at a single point is called spherical aberration.

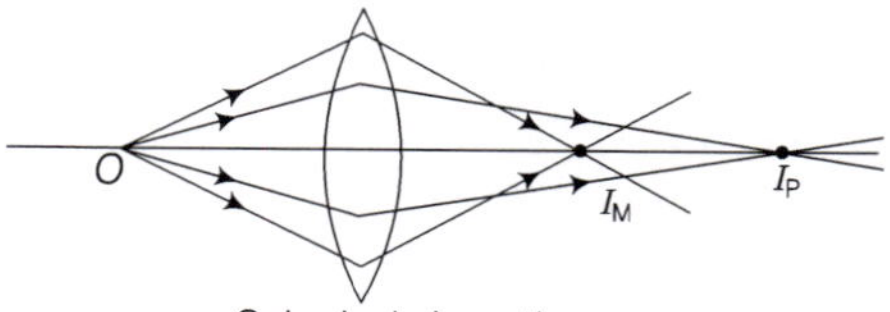

Spherical aberration

6. (d) According to the question,

$P_1 = -10\text{ D}$, $P_2 = +6\text{ D}$

Let power, $P_3 = P_1 + P_2$

$P_3 = -10 + 6 = -4\text{ D}$

As we know power $= \dfrac{1}{f\,(\text{m})} \Rightarrow -4 = \dfrac{1}{f}$

$\Rightarrow$ $f = -\dfrac{1}{4} = -0.25 \text{ m}$

7. Refractive index (μ) varies inversely with the wavelength (λ) of light used and for convex lens focal length (f) is given by

$$\frac{1}{f} = (\mu - 1)\left(\frac{1}{R_1} - \frac{1}{R_2}\right)$$

where, R_1 and R_2 are radius of curvature of two surfaces. So, on increasing wavelength, refractive index decreases and focal length increases.

8. According to the question,

Power of a lens $= -5\text{ D}$

Focal length (metre) $= \dfrac{1}{\text{Power of lens}}$

$$= \frac{1}{-5/100} = -20 \text{ cm}$$

Since, focal length of lens is negative so, it is concave lens.

9. In lens L_2, $v = \infty$, $u = 80 - 20 = 60$ cm

As, $$\frac{1}{v} - \frac{1}{u} = \frac{1}{f_2}$$

$$\Rightarrow \quad \frac{1}{\infty} - \frac{1}{60} = \frac{1}{f_2}$$

$$\Rightarrow \quad f_2 = -60 \text{ cm}$$

Hence, focal length of L_2 is -60 cm.

10. Given,

Focal length of converging lens $f_1 = 15$ cm

Focal length of diverging lens $f_2 = -20$ cm

Since, $$\frac{1}{f_{\text{equivalent}}} = \frac{1}{f_1} + \frac{1}{f_2}$$

$$\Rightarrow \quad \frac{1}{f_{\text{equivalent}}} = \frac{1}{15} + \left(-\frac{1}{20}\right) = \frac{4-3}{60} = \frac{1}{60}$$

$$\therefore \quad f_{\text{equivalent}} = 60 \text{ cm}$$

11. We know that, $\frac{1}{f} = (\mu - 1)\left(\frac{2}{R}\right)$

$$\Rightarrow \quad R = 2f\,(\mu - 1)$$

Biconvex

Plano-convex

When lens splits

$$\frac{1}{f_1} = (\mu - 1)\left(\frac{1}{R}\right)$$

$$\Rightarrow \quad f_1 = \frac{R}{(\mu - 1)} = 2f$$

$$= 2 \times 20 = 40 \text{ cm}$$

Hence, focal length gets doubled.

12. The behaviour is reversed in accordance with Lens Maker's formula.

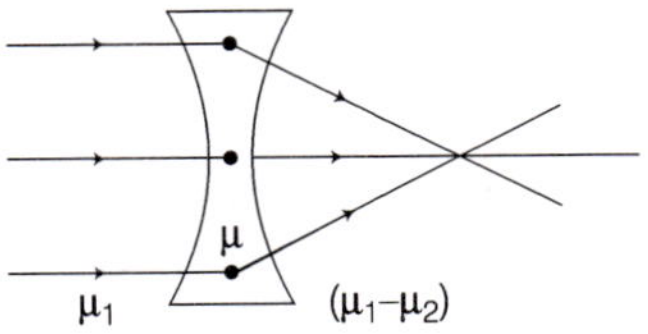

$$\frac{1}{f} = \left(\frac{\mu_2}{\mu_1} - 1\right)\left(\frac{1}{R_1} - \frac{1}{R_2}\right)$$

where, symbols have their usual meaning.

$$\frac{1}{f} = \left(\frac{\mu}{\mu_1} - 1\right)\left(\frac{1}{R_1} - \frac{1}{R_2}\right) = +\text{ve}$$

$\Rightarrow f =$ focal length is positive hence, it will behave as convex lens.

13. The assumption is that we concerned the rays to be paraxial (rays close to principal axis) only.

14. We know that for refraction through a curved boundary.

$$\frac{\mu_2}{v} - \frac{\mu_1}{u} = \frac{\mu_2 - \mu_1}{R}$$

where, v is image distance.

u is object distance.

μ_1 and μ_2 are refractive indices of the media 1 and 2,

R is curvature radius.

As given in question, $\mu_2 = n$ and $\mu_1 = 1$

$$v = \infty, u = -u$$

$$\Rightarrow \quad \frac{n}{\infty} - \frac{1}{-u} = \frac{n-1}{R}$$

$$\Rightarrow \quad 0 + \frac{1}{u} = \frac{n-1}{R}$$

$$\Rightarrow \quad \frac{1}{u} = \frac{n-1}{R} \quad \text{or} \quad u = \frac{R}{n-1}$$

15. Lens maker's formula is

$$\frac{1}{f} = (\mu - 1)\left(\frac{1}{R_1} - \frac{1}{R_2}\right)$$

where, f is focal length of lens

μ is refractive index of material of lens

R_1 is radius of curvature of first surface.

R_2 is radius of curvature of second surface.

16. Two images of the point object will formed by lens because lens is formed from two different materials of different refractive indices μ_1 and μ_2.

17. Spherical aberration in the lens is the defect in the quality of the image because of which, the paraxial and marginal rays are focussed at different points on the principal axis of the lens. This arises due to different focal lengths (or different curvature) of the lens.

The following figure ilustrates it.

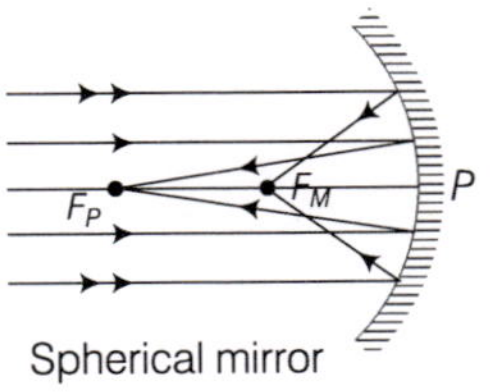

Spherical mirror

Concept Enhancer The focal length of paraxial rays is more than the focal length of the marginal rays.

18. Given, f of convex lens $= +15$ cm

f of concave lens $= -20$ cm

Since, $$\frac{1}{f_{\text{equivalent}}} = \frac{1}{f_1} + \frac{1}{f_2}$$

$$f_{\text{equivalent}} = 60 \text{ cm}$$

19. From figure, it is clear that the convex lens is behaving as a concave lens. It happens only when the refractive index of the lens material is less than the medium in which lens is placed. Therefore, $n_1 > n_2$.

20. Given, $\mu = 1.5$

$$R_1 = 10 \text{ cm}, R_2 = -20 \text{ cm}$$

Using lens Maker's formula

$$\frac{1}{f} = (\mu - 1)\left(\frac{1}{R_1} - \frac{1}{R_2}\right)$$

$$= (1.5 - 1)\left(\frac{1}{10} + \frac{1}{20}\right)$$

$$= 0.5 \times \left(\frac{2+1}{20}\right) = 0.5 \times \frac{3}{20} = \frac{3}{40}$$

$$\Rightarrow \quad f = \frac{40}{3} = 13.3 \text{ cm}$$

21. (*i*) To get a virtual, magnified image of an object from convex lens, we have to keep the object between optical centre and focus of the lens.

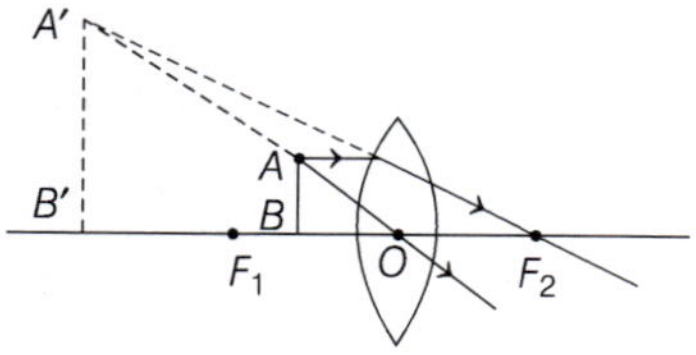

(*ii*) To get a real, diminished image of an object from a concave mirror, the object has to be kept beyond centre of curvature C.

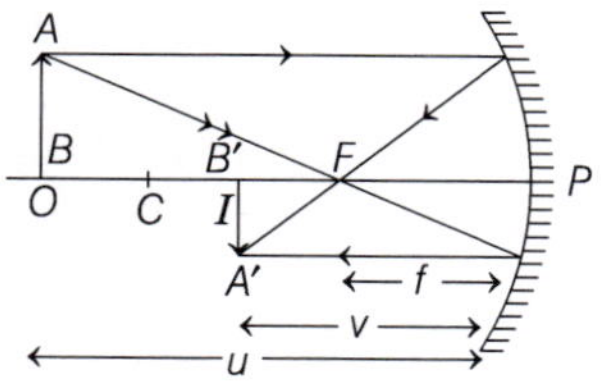

22. Given, $R_1 = 20$ cm and $R_2 = -30$ cm and $n = 1.5$

The focal length of a lens is given by

$$\frac{1}{f} = (n-1)\left[\frac{1}{R_1} - \frac{1}{R_2}\right]$$

$$= (1.5 - 1)\left[\frac{1}{20} + \frac{1}{30}\right] = (0.5)\left[\frac{5}{60}\right]$$

$$\therefore \quad f = \frac{600}{25} = 24 \text{ cm}$$

23. Let f_1 and $-f_2$ be the focal lengths of convex lens and concave lens, respectively. Then total focal length of the combination is

$$\frac{1}{f} = \frac{1}{f_1} + \frac{1}{(-f_2)}$$

Here, $$f_1 = 20 \text{ cm}$$

$$f_2 = -15 \text{ cm}$$

$$\Rightarrow \quad \frac{1}{f} = \frac{1}{20} - \frac{1}{15}$$

$$= \frac{3-4}{60} = -\frac{1}{60}$$

Total focal length, $f = -60$ cm

24. According to the question,

$$\mu_{\text{glass}} = 1.56$$

$$\mu_{\text{water}} = 1.33$$

$$\mu_{\text{liquid}} = 1.65$$

From lens maker formula,

$$\frac{1}{f} = \left(\frac{\mu_2}{\mu_1} - 1\right)\left(\frac{1}{R_1} - \frac{1}{R_2}\right)$$

For air, $$\frac{1}{f} = (\mu_2 - 1)\left(\frac{1}{R_1} - \frac{1}{R_2}\right) \quad \text{...(i)}$$

(i) For water,

$$\frac{1}{f_w} = \left(\frac{\mu_2}{1.33} - 1\right)\left(\frac{1}{R_1} - \frac{1}{R_2}\right) \quad \text{...(ii)}$$

On dividing Eq. (i) by Eq. (ii), we get

$$\frac{f_w}{f} = \frac{(\mu_2 - 1)}{\left(\frac{\mu_2}{1.33} - 1\right)}, \; f_w = f\left(\frac{(\mu_2 - 1)}{\frac{\mu_2}{1.33} - 1}\right)$$

$$= \frac{f(1.56 - 1)}{\frac{1.5}{1.3} - 1} = 3.33f$$

Focal length is positive and it becomes 3.33 times, so the nature of lens remains same.

(ii) For liquid,

$$\frac{1}{f_l} = \left(\frac{\mu_2}{1.65} - 1\right)\left(\frac{1}{R_1} - \frac{1}{R_2}\right) \quad \text{...(iii)}$$

On dividing of Eq. (i) by Eq. (iii), we get

$$\frac{f_l}{f}=\frac{(\mu_2-1)}{\left(\frac{\mu_2}{1.65}-1\right)}$$

$$=f\left(\frac{1.5-1}{\frac{1.5}{1.65}-1}\right)=-\frac{0.5f}{0.09}=5.55f \text{ (approx.)}$$

Focal length becomes 5.55 times and is negative i.e. nature of lens get reversed.

25. Suppose C_1, C_2 be the optical centres of two thin convex lenses L_1 and L_2 held co-axially in contact with each other in air.

Suppose f_1 and f_2 are their respective focal lengths as shown in the figure.

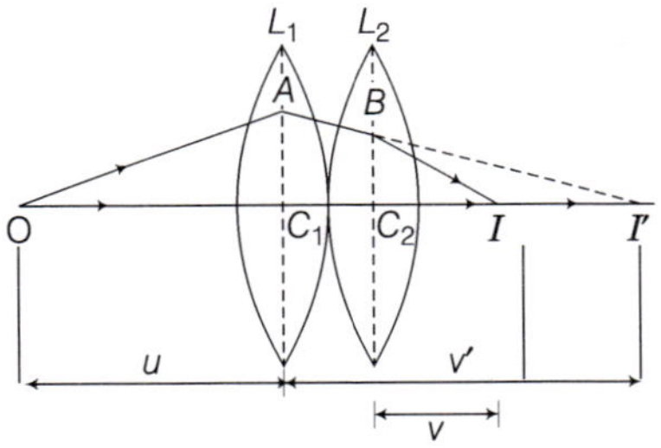

Let a point object O be placed on the common principal axis at a distance $OC_1=u$. The lens L_1 alone would form its image at I, where $C_1I'=v'$. From the lens formula,

$$\frac{1}{v'}-\frac{1}{u}=\frac{1}{f_1} \quad \text{...(i)}$$

I' would serve as a virtual object for lens L_2, which forms a final image I at distance $C_2I=v$.

Since, the lenses are thin, therefore, for the lens

$$L_2, u=C_2I'\approx C_1I'=v'$$

From the lens formula for L_2,

$$\frac{1}{v}-\frac{1}{v'}=\frac{1}{f_2} \quad \text{...(ii)}$$

On adding Eqs. (i) and (ii), we get

$$\frac{1}{v}-\frac{1}{u}=\frac{1}{f_1}+\frac{1}{f_2} \quad \text{...(iii)}$$

Let the two lenses be replaced by a single lens of focal length f, which forms image I at distance v, of an object at distance u from the lens. For this lens,

$$\frac{1}{v}-\frac{1}{u}=\frac{1}{f} \quad \text{...(iv)}$$

From Eqs. (iii) and (iv), we get

$$\frac{1}{f}=\frac{1}{f_1}+\frac{1}{f_2}$$

26. The image formed by the lens will act as object and by applying lens formula for the different lens, we will get the focal length of concave lens.

For convex lens,

$$f=20\text{ cm},\quad u=-45\text{ cm and } v=?$$

By lens formula, $\frac{1}{v}-\frac{1}{u}=\frac{1}{f}$

Symbols have their usual meaning

$$\Rightarrow \quad \frac{1}{v}-\frac{1}{(-45)}=\frac{1}{20} \quad\Rightarrow\quad v=36\text{ cm}$$

For concave lens,

$$u=36-16=20\text{ cm}, v=\infty \text{ and } f=?$$

$$\frac{1}{v}-\frac{1}{u}=\frac{1}{f}$$

$$\Rightarrow \quad \frac{1}{\infty}-\frac{1}{20}=\frac{1}{f}$$

$$\Rightarrow \quad f=-20\text{ cm}$$

Negative sign shows that lens is concave.

27. Consider the ray diagram shown in the figure. It is clear from the figure that, when the object pin O lies in the focal plane of the lens L, the rays of light starting from O after refraction from the lens become parallel to the principal axis of the lens and therefore they strike normally on the plane mirror M kept behind the lens at a small distance.

Due to normal incidence ($i=0$), angle of reflection $r=0°$, i.e. the rays are reflected back by the plane mirror on the same path and then they enter the lens as a parallel beam. The lens converges these rays in its focal plane, hence image I is formed just above the object pin O. The image I is inverted, real and of same size as that of the object O as shown in figure.

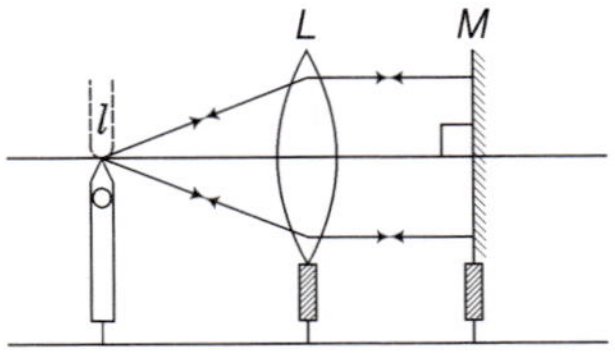

28. According to the question,

$R=30$ cm, $n_2=1.6, n_1=1$ [for air]

We know that, $\frac{n_2}{v}-\frac{n_1}{u}=\frac{n_2-n_1}{R}$

Now by putting the values

(symbols have their usual meaning.)

$$\frac{1.6}{v}+\frac{1}{\infty}=\frac{1.6-1}{30}$$

$$\Rightarrow \quad \frac{1.6}{v}=\frac{0.6}{30} \Rightarrow \frac{1}{v}=\frac{1}{5\times 16}$$

$$\Rightarrow \quad \frac{1}{v}=\frac{1}{80} \quad \Rightarrow v=80\text{ cm}$$

This position of image is 80 cm from the point P.

29. Given, focal length $f=20\text{ cm}$,

magnification, $m=2$

We know that, magnification $m=v/u$

So, $\quad 2=\frac{v}{u}$ [by question, $m=2$]

or $\quad v=2u$

We know that, $\frac{1}{v}+\frac{1}{u}=\frac{1}{f}$ [For convex lens]

where, symbols have their usual meaning.

$$\frac{1}{2u}+\frac{1}{u}=\frac{1}{20} \Rightarrow u=30\text{ cm}$$

Hence, object should be placed at 30 cm.

30. Refer to text on page 185 (Refractive Formula at Convex Surface).

31. As, we know from lens maker's formula that,

$$\frac{1}{f}=(\mu-1)\left(\frac{1}{R_1}-\frac{1}{R_2}\right)$$

Now, for biconvex lens,

$$\frac{1}{10}=(\mu-1)\left(\frac{1}{R}+\frac{1}{R}\right)=\frac{2(\mu-1)}{R}$$

$$\Rightarrow \quad R=20(\mu-1)$$

For plano-convex lens

$$\frac{1}{f_1}=(\mu-1)\left(\frac{1}{R}-\frac{1}{\infty}\right)$$

$$\Rightarrow f_1=\frac{1}{\mu-1}\times R=\frac{1}{\mu-1}\times 20(\mu-1) \Rightarrow f_1=20\text{ cm}$$

32. For convex lens, $\frac{1}{f_1}=\frac{1}{v_1}-\frac{1}{u_1}$

Now by putting the values given in question (symbols have their usual meaning.)

$$\Rightarrow \quad \frac{1}{15}=\frac{1}{v_1}-\left(-\frac{1}{20}\right)=\frac{1}{v_1}+\frac{1}{20}$$

$$\Rightarrow \quad \frac{1}{v_1}=\frac{1}{15}-\frac{1}{20}=\frac{4-3}{60}=\frac{1}{60}$$

$$\Rightarrow \quad v_1=60\text{ cm}$$

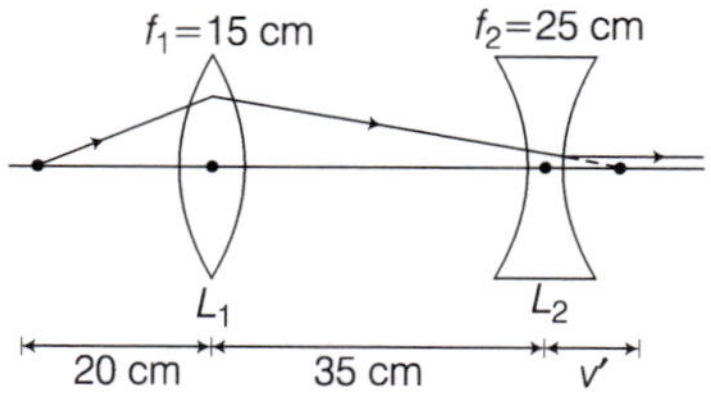

For concave lens, $v_1=u_2=25\text{ cm}$
$=(60\text{ cm}-35\text{ cm})$

$$\frac{1}{f_2}=\frac{1}{v_2}-\frac{1}{u_2}$$

$$\frac{1}{-25}=\frac{1}{v_2}-\frac{1}{25} \Rightarrow \frac{1}{v_2}=0$$

$$\therefore \quad v_2=\infty$$

The final image is at infinity.

33. We have to apply lens maker's formula separately for each case.

According to the question,

Given, refractive index of glass w.r.t. air

$${}_a\mu_g=1.5,$$

Focal length for initial case $f=20\text{ cm}$,

Refractive index of liquid w.r.t. air ${}_a\mu_l=1.75$

So, from lens marker's formula

$$\frac{1}{f}=(\mu-1)\left(\frac{1}{R_1}-\frac{1}{R_2}\right)$$

$$\Rightarrow \quad \frac{1}{R_1}-\frac{1}{R_2}=C\text{ [say]}$$

where, μ = relative refractive index, R_1 and R_2 are radii of curvatures.

$$\frac{1}{f}=(\mu-1)C$$

In air, $\quad \frac{1}{f}=({}_a\mu_g-1)C \quad$ ...(i)

In liquid, $\quad \frac{1}{f_1}=({}_l\mu_g-1)C$

$$\frac{1}{f_1}=\left(\frac{{}_a\mu_g}{{}_a\mu_l}-1\right)C \quad \text{...(ii)}$$

On dividing Eq. (i) by Eq. (ii), we get

$$\frac{1/f}{1/f_1}=\frac{{}_a\mu_g-1}{\frac{{}_a\mu_g}{{}_a\mu_l}-1}=\frac{1.5-1}{\frac{1.5}{1.75}-1}$$

$$\Rightarrow \quad \frac{f_l}{f}=\frac{0.5\times 1.75}{1.5-1.75}$$

$\Rightarrow \quad f_l = \frac{0.5 \times 1.75}{-0.25} \times 20$

$\Rightarrow \quad f_l = -70$ cm [concave]

34. (i) Given, refractive index $n = 1.5$,

focal length, $f = 10\text{cm}$

Applying lens maker's formula,

$$\frac{1}{f} = (n-1)\left(\frac{1}{R_1} - \frac{1}{R_2}\right) \Rightarrow \frac{1}{10} = (1.5-1)\left(\frac{1}{R_1}\right)$$

[for plano-convex lens, $R_2 = \infty$]

Because 2nd surface is plane.

$$\Rightarrow \quad \frac{1}{10} = \frac{0.5}{R_1} \Rightarrow R_1 = 5\text{ cm}$$

(ii) When two plano-convex lenses are placed side by side, this combination acts as biconvex lens. Now, by lens maker's formula,

$$\frac{1}{f} = (n-1)\left(\frac{1}{R_1} - \frac{1}{R_2}\right)$$

$$\Rightarrow \quad \frac{1}{f} = (n-1)\frac{2}{R_1} = \frac{0.5 \times 2}{5} = \frac{1}{5}$$

[$\because R_1 = R = R_2 = 5$ cm]

$$\Rightarrow \quad f = 5\text{ cm} = 0.05\text{ m}$$

$$\therefore \quad \text{Power, } P = \frac{1}{f(\text{m})} = \frac{100}{5} = +20\text{ D}$$

35. The cause of the spherical aberration in lens is that the focal lengths of different zones of the lens are different.

The focal length of the middle portion of the lens is more as compared with the near edge of the lens.

Due to this all the rays passing through the lens are not focussed at a single point, so the image formed is blurred.

Hence, the inability of the lens to form a point image of an axial point object is called spherical aberration.

The spherical aberration can be minimise by using stops in the way of marginal or the paraxial rays or by cutting-off.

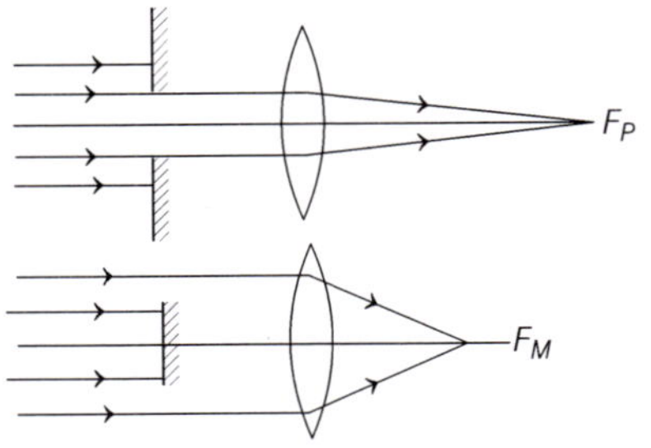

Minimising spherical aberrations using stops

36. Consider the ray diagram shown, parallel rays after refraction through the lens converge towards the point F, which is the focus of the lens.

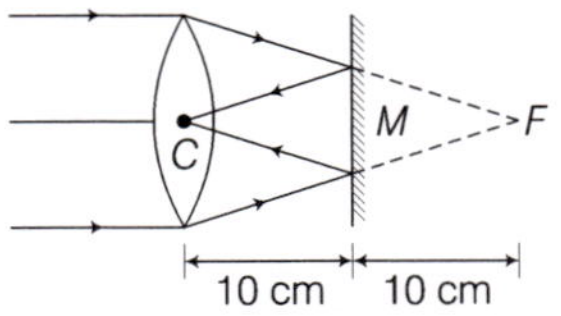

The refracted rays after reflection from the plane mirror placed in the path meet at the optical centre C of lens.

Thus, C is the image of the virtual point object F formed by the plane mirror.

Hence, $MF = MC = 10\text{cm}$

The focal length of the lens is given by

$$f = CF = MC + MF$$
$$= 10 + 10 = 20\text{ cm}$$

37. From the ray diagram, it is clear that

object distance $u = (20-5) = +15\text{ cm}$,

Image distance $v = 30\text{ cm}$

Now, by lens formula $\frac{1}{f} = \frac{1}{v} - \frac{1}{u}$ [f = focal length]

$$\Rightarrow \quad \frac{1}{f} = \frac{1}{30} - \frac{1}{15} \Rightarrow \frac{1}{f} = \frac{1-2}{30}$$

$$f = -30\text{ cm}$$

38. Given, focal length $f = 20\text{ cm} = 20 \times 10^{-2}$ m

and power $P_2 = 6.5$ D

We know power, $P_1 = \frac{1}{f_1} = \frac{1}{20 \times 10^{-2}} = 5$ D

Power of the combination

$$P_{\text{equivalent}} = P_1 + P_2 = 5 + 6.5 = 11.5\text{ D}$$

Focal length of the combination

$$f_{eq} = \frac{1}{P} = \frac{1}{11.5} = 8.7\text{ cm}$$

39. According to lens Maker's formula,

$$\frac{1}{f} = (\mu - 1)\left(\frac{1}{R_1} - \frac{1}{R_2}\right)$$

But for plano-convex lens, $R_2 = \infty$ and thus

$$\frac{1}{f} = (\mu - 1)\left(\frac{1}{R_1}\right)$$

When the lens is placed in water, then

$$\frac{1}{f_\omega} = (\mu_0 - 1)\left(\frac{1}{R_1}\right) = \left(\frac{{}_a\mu_l}{{}_a\mu_w} - 1\right)\left(\frac{1}{R_1}\right)$$

On substituting the values, we get

$$\frac{1}{80} = \left(\frac{{}_a\mu_l}{4/3} - 1\right)\left(\frac{1}{10}\right)$$

$$\Rightarrow \quad \left(\frac{{}_a\mu_l}{4/3} - 1\right) = \frac{10}{80} = \frac{1}{8}$$

$$\Rightarrow \quad \frac{{}_a\mu_l}{4/3} = 1 + \frac{1}{8} = \frac{9}{8}$$

$$\Rightarrow \quad {}_a\mu_l = \frac{9}{8} \times \frac{4}{3}$$

$$\Rightarrow \quad {}_a\mu_l = \frac{3}{2}$$

40. (i) Student's response is incorrect. On decreasing the distance between lens and object image formed by lens is magnified but increasing the distance between lens and objects, forms a small size image.

(ii) Student's response is correct. The graph between $\frac{1}{u}$ and $\frac{1}{v}$ for a thin convex lens in order to determine its focal length is plotted as shown in the figure.

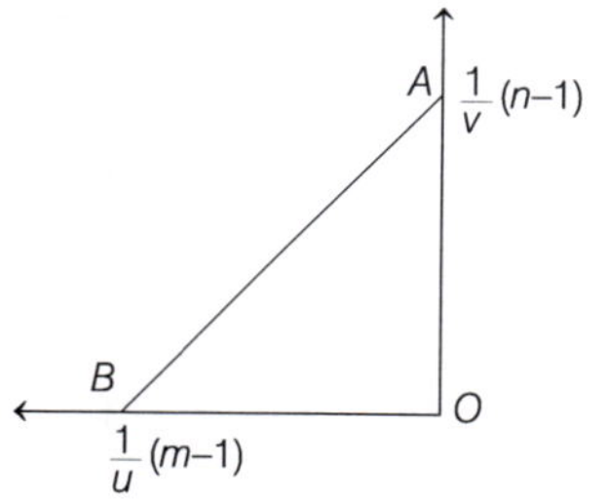

(iii) Student's response is incorrect. The correct relation between the optical power and focal length is

$$\text{Power, } P = \frac{1}{f \text{ (in m)}}$$

Thus, the power of lens or mirror is inversely proportional to the focal length.

41. Focal length of converging lens is positive.

$$\therefore \quad f_1 = +12 \text{ cm}$$

Focal length of diverging lens is negative.

$$\therefore \quad f_2 = -18 \text{ cm}$$

Equivalent focal length of the combination is given by

$$\frac{1}{f} = \frac{1}{f_1} + \frac{1}{f_2}$$

$$\Rightarrow \quad \frac{1}{f} = \frac{1}{12} - \frac{1}{18}$$

$$\Rightarrow \quad \frac{1}{f} = \frac{1}{36}$$

$$\Rightarrow \quad f = 36 \text{ cm}$$

42. Given,

$n = 1.5$, $R_1 = +30$ cm, $R_2 = -30$ cm

$u = -60$ cm

Using lens maker's formula,

$$\frac{1}{f} = (n-1)\left[\frac{1}{R_1} - \frac{1}{R_2}\right]$$

$$\Rightarrow \quad \frac{1}{f} = (1.5 - 1)\left[\frac{1}{30} + \frac{1}{30}\right]$$

$$\Rightarrow \quad \frac{1}{f} = \frac{0.5 \times 2}{30}$$

$$\Rightarrow \quad \frac{1}{f} = \frac{1}{30}$$

$$\therefore \quad f = 30 \text{ cm}$$

Linear magnification, $m = \frac{f}{f+u}$

$$m = \frac{30}{30 - 60}$$

$$m = -1$$

and $\quad m = \frac{v}{u} \Rightarrow -1 = \frac{v}{-60}$

$$\Rightarrow \quad v = 60 \text{ cm}$$

Image will be formed at 60 cm from lens.

Also, $\quad m = \frac{\text{height of image}}{\text{height of object}}$

$$-1 = \frac{\text{height of image}}{5}$$

$$\therefore \quad \text{height of image} = -5 \text{ cm}$$

Negative sign indicate that the image is inverted.

43. Refer to text on page 188 (Combination of Thin Lenses in Contact).

44. Refer to text on pages 185 and 186.

(Refraction Formula at a Spherical Surface).

45. We have, $\frac{1}{f} = (n-1)\left[\frac{1}{R_1} - \frac{1}{R_2}\right]$

Here, $R_1 = +10$ cm, $R_2 = -15$ cm and $n = 1.5$

$$\frac{1}{f} = (1.5-1)\left[\frac{1}{10} - \frac{1}{-15}\right]$$

$$= (0.5)\left[\frac{1}{10} + \frac{1}{15}\right]$$

$$\Rightarrow \quad \frac{1}{f} = (0.5)\left[\frac{3+2}{30}\right]$$

$$\Rightarrow \quad \frac{1}{f} = 0.5\left[\frac{5}{30}\right] = \frac{0.5}{6} = \frac{1}{12}$$

$$\Rightarrow \quad f = 12$$

$\therefore$ Focal length of convex lens, $f = 12$ cm

46. Let APB is a convex refracting surface which separates a rarer and a denser medium having refractive indices n_1 and n_2

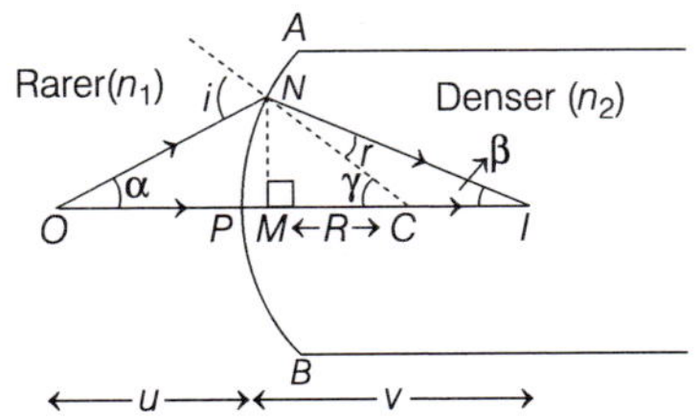

where, i = angle of incidence

and r = angle of refraction

Now in ΔNOC

$$i = \alpha + \gamma$$

Similarly in ΔNIC

$$\gamma = r + \beta \text{ or } r = \gamma - \beta$$

Suppose all rays are paraxial, then the angles i, r, α, β and γ are small.

$$\Rightarrow \quad \alpha \approx \tan\alpha = \frac{NM}{OM} \approx \frac{NP}{OP} \quad [\because P \text{ is close to } M]$$

$$\beta \approx \tan\beta = \frac{NM}{MI} \approx \frac{NM}{PI}$$

$$\gamma = \tan\gamma = \frac{NM}{MC} \approx \frac{NM}{PC}$$

From Snell's law, $\dfrac{\sin i}{\sin r} = \dfrac{n_2}{n_1}$

If i and r are small, then

$$\frac{i}{r} \approx \frac{n_2}{n_1} \text{ or } n_1 i = n_2 r$$

or $\quad n_1(\alpha + \gamma) = n_2(\gamma - \beta)$

$$n_1\left[\frac{NM}{OP} + \frac{NM}{PC}\right] = n_2\left[\frac{NM}{PC} - \frac{NM}{PI}\right]$$

$$n_1\left[\frac{1}{OP} + \frac{1}{PC}\right] = n_2\left[\frac{1}{PC} - \frac{1}{PI}\right]$$

$$\frac{n_1}{OP} + \frac{n_2}{PI} = \frac{n_2 - n_1}{PC}$$

Using sign convention

$$-\frac{n_1}{u} + \frac{n_2}{v} = \frac{n_2 - n_1}{R}$$

or $$\frac{n_2}{v} - \frac{n_1}{u} = \frac{n_2 - n_1}{R}$$

Or

Consider a ray parallel to the principal axis striking the mirror at point M. Then CM will be perpendicular to the mirror at point M. Let θ be the angle of incidence and MD be perpendicular to the principal axis. Then,

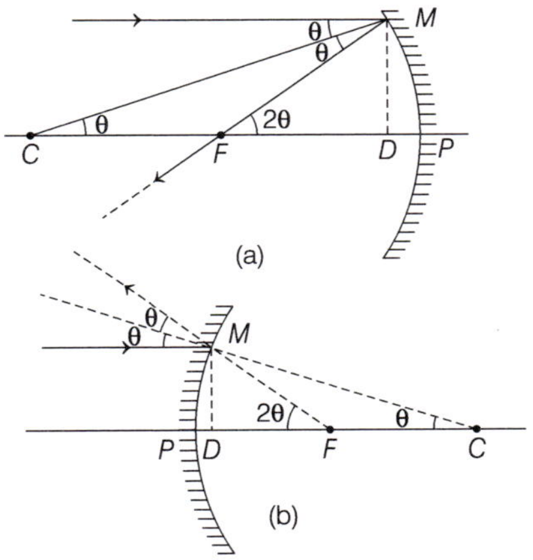

Geometry of reflection of an incident ray on
(a) concave spherical mirror and
(b) convex spherical mirror

$$\angle MCP = \theta \text{ and } \angle MFP = 2\theta$$

Now, $\quad \tan\theta = \dfrac{MD}{CD}$

and $\quad \tan 2\theta = \dfrac{MD}{FD} \quad$ ...(i)

For small θ (condition true for paraxial rays), $\tan\theta \approx \theta$ and $\tan 2\theta \approx 2\theta$

Therefore, from Eq.(i), we get

$$\frac{MD}{FD} = 2\frac{MD}{CD}$$

or $\quad FD = \dfrac{CD}{2} \quad$ ...(ii)

Again, for small θ, we can observe that the point D is very close to the point P. Therefore, $FD = f$ and $CD = R$.

From Eq.(ii), we have

$$f = \frac{R}{2}$$

47. Lens maker's formula

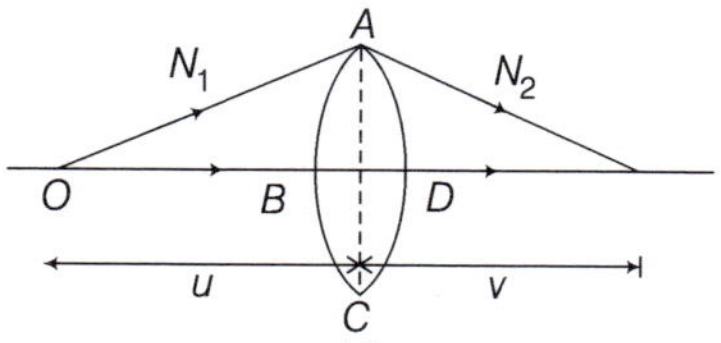

(a)

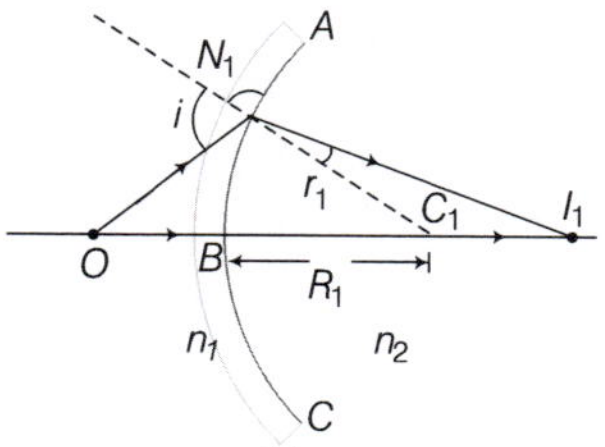

(b)

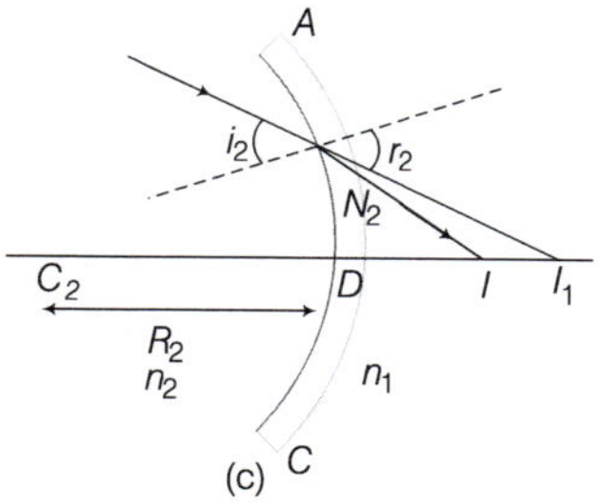

(c)

The above figure shows the image formation by a convex lens.

Applying the equation for spherical refracting surface to the first interface ABC, we obtain

$$\frac{n_1}{OB}+\frac{n_2}{BI_1}=\frac{n_2-n_1}{BC_1} \quad \ldots\text{(i)}$$

A similar procedure applied to the second interface ADC gives,

$$-\frac{n_2}{DI_1}+\frac{n_1}{DI}=\frac{n_2-n_1}{DC_2} \quad \ldots\text{(ii)}$$

For a thin lens, $BI_1 = DI_1$

On adding Eqs. (i) and (ii), we obtain

$$\frac{n_1}{OB}+\frac{n_1}{DI}=(n_2-n_1)\left(\frac{1}{BC_1}+\frac{1}{DC_2}\right) \quad \ldots\text{(iii)}$$

Suppose the object is at infinity i.e.

$$OB \to \infty \text{ and } DI \to f$$

Eq. (iii) can be written as

$$\frac{n_1}{f}=(n_2-n_1)\left(\frac{1}{BC_1}+\frac{1}{DC_2}\right) \quad \ldots\text{(iv)}$$

The point where image of an object placed at infinity is formed is called the focus (f) of the lens and the distance f gives its focal length. A lens has two foci, F and F' on either side of it by sign convention.

$$BC_1 = R_1$$

or

$$DC_2 = -R_2$$

Therefore, Eq. (iv) can be written as

$$\frac{1}{f}=({}_1n_2-1)\left(\frac{1}{R_1}-\frac{1}{R_2}\right) \quad \left[\because {}_1n_2=\frac{n_2}{n_1}\right] \quad \ldots\text{(v)}$$

Eq. (v) is known as the lens maker' formula.

48. Given, $u = -15$ cm,

$f = 10$ cm, $d = f = 10$ cm (Convex lens)

For lens, $\frac{1}{v}-\frac{1}{u}=\frac{1}{f}$

Substituting the all values,

$$\frac{1}{v}-\frac{1}{(-15)}=\frac{1}{10} \quad (\because u=-15\text{ cm})$$

$$\frac{1}{v}=\frac{1}{10}-\frac{1}{15}=\frac{3-2}{30}=\frac{1}{30}$$

$\Rightarrow$ $v = 30$ cm

$\therefore$ $MI = LI - LM = 30 - 10 = 20$ cm

Now, the focal length, $f=\frac{20}{2}=10$ cm

TOPIC 4

Dispersion

Dispersion by a Prism

The phenomenon of splitting of light into its component colours is known as **dispersion**. The pattern of component colour of light is called the spectrum of the sunlight, which is shown in the below figure.

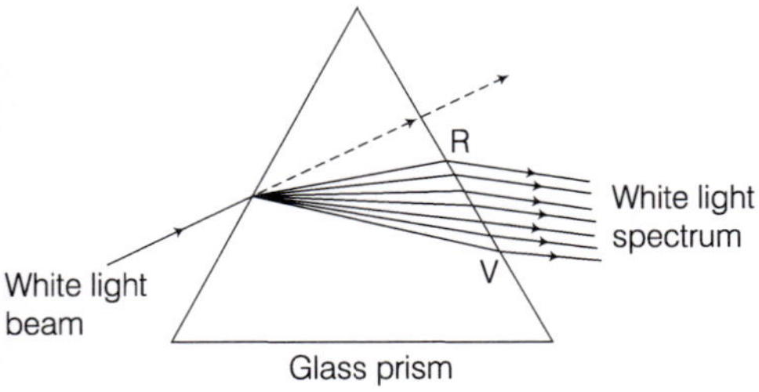

$R \to$ Red
$O \to$ Orange
$Y \to$ Yellow
$G \to$ Green
$B \to$ Blue
$I \to$ Indigo
$V \to$ Violet

Cause of Dispersion

The different colours of the white light have different wavelengths. The wavelength of the violet light is smaller than that of red light. The refractive index of a material in terms of the wavelength of the light is given by Cauchy's expression.

$$\mu = a + \frac{b}{\lambda^2} + \frac{c}{\lambda^4}$$

where, a, b, c are constants for the material.

The refractive index of material of prism is maximum for violet colour (minimum wavelength) and minimum for red colour (maximum wavelength).

$\therefore$ Refractive index for violet colour > Refractive index for red colour i.e. $\mu_v > \mu_r$

For a small angle prism, we have

$$\delta = A(\mu - 1)$$

Since, $\mu_v > \mu_r$, the violet light will suffer greater deviation than red light i.e. $\delta_v > \delta_r$.

Terms Related to Dispersion of Light by Prism

Angular Dispersion

The angular dispersion produced by a prism for white light is the difference in the angle of deviation for two extreme colours, violet and red.

According to given figure, angular dispersion

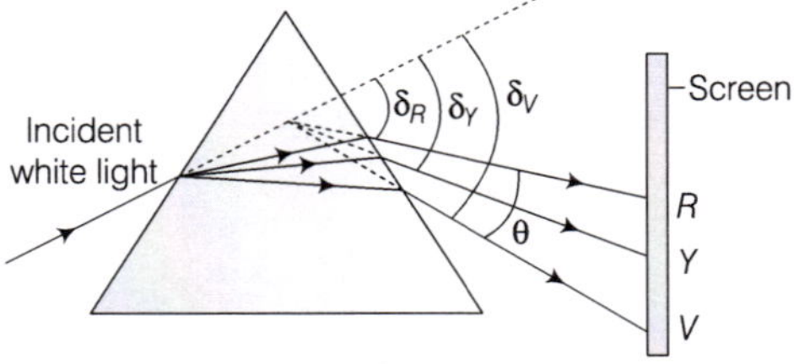

$$\theta = \delta_v - \delta_r = (\mu_v - \mu_r)A$$

where, δ_μ = deviation angle of violet light,
δ_r = deviation angle of red light,
μ_v = refractive index for violet light,
μ_r = refractive index for red light,
A = angle of prism.

Dispersive Power (ω)

Dispersive power of a prism is defined as the ratio of angular dispersion to the mean deviation produced by the prism. It is represented by ω.

$$\text{Dispersive power, } \omega = \frac{\text{Angular dispersion}}{\text{Mean deviation}} = \frac{\delta_V - \delta_R}{\delta} = \frac{(\mu_V - \mu_R)A}{(\mu - 1)A}$$

$$\omega = \frac{\mu_V - \mu_R}{(\mu - 1)}$$

Rainbow Real Life

Rainbow is an real life example of the dispersion of sunlight by the water drops in the atmosphere. It is a spectrum of sunlight in the nature. It occurs in the form of concentric coloured circular arcs in the sky, when the sun shines on rain drops during or after the shower.

This phenomenon occurs due to combined effect of dispersion, refraction and total internal reflection of sunlight by spherical drop of water.

Necessary conditions for the rainbow to take place are as follow:

(*i*) The sun should be shining in part of the sky while it is raining in the opposite part of the sky.

(*ii*) The observer must stand with his back towards the sun.

The ray diagram for the formation of rainbow is shown below

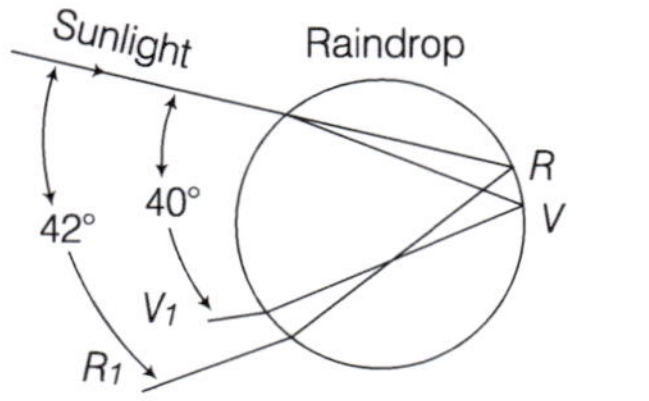

Dispersion of sunlight of a single rainbow

Types of Rainbow

Generally, there are two kinds of rainbow

(*i*) **Primary rainbow** The primary rainbow is a result of three step process. It is formed by the rays which undergo **one internal reflection (total internal reflection**) and two reflections before emerging finally from the water droplets. In primary rainbow, red colour is on the top and violet on the bottom.

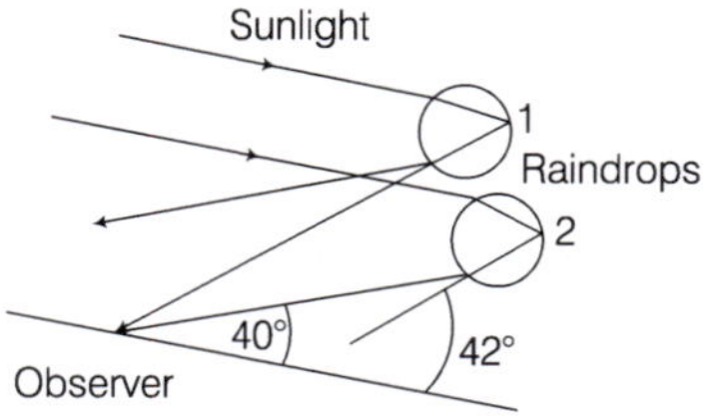

Primary rainbow

(*ii*) **Secondary rainbow** The secondary rainbow is a result of four step process. It is formed by the rays which have undergone **two internal reflections** and **two refractions** before emerging finally from the water droplets. Thus, the sequence of colour in secondary rainbow is oppusite to that of primary rainbow.

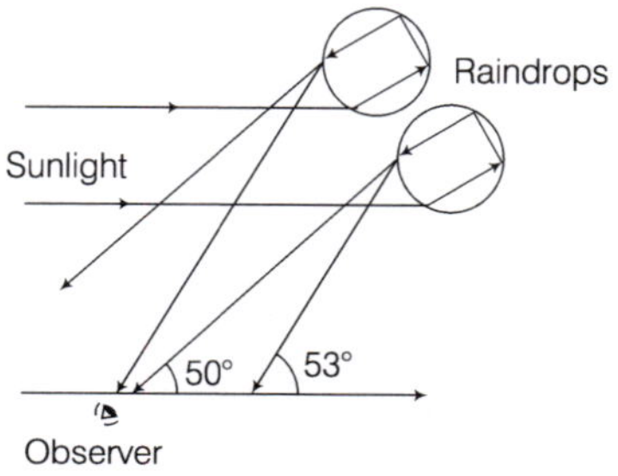

Secondary rainbow

PYQs Previous Years Questions

1 Mark Questions

1. When a ray of white light is incident obliquely on the first surface of a prism, then **ISC 2024**

(a) red colour is deviated most
(b) green colour is deviated most
(c) yellow colour is deviated most
(d) violet colour is deviated most

2. Dispersive power of a prism depends upon **ISC 2022 Sem-II**

(a) shape of the prism
(b) height of the prism
(c) material of the prism
(d) angle of the prism

3. Calculate dispersive power of a transparent material given, $n_v = 1.56, n_r = 1.54, n_y = 1.55$.

4. What are the dark lines seen in the solar spectrum called? **ISC 2013**

5. Name an optical device, which when used with a spectrometer, can determine the wavelength of the given monochromatic light. **ISC 2010**

6. Calculate dispersive power of glass, accurately upto three decimal places from following data.

(*i*) Refractive index of glass for red colour = 1.60
(*ii*) Refractive index of glass for yellow colour = 1.61
(*iii*) Refractive index of glass for violet colour = 1.62

ISC 2010

7. State two basic differences between primary and secondary rainbows. **ISC 2006**

8. Draw ray diagram to illustrate the formation of primary rainbow by refraction and total internal reflection of sunlight in water drops. **ISC 2005, 03**

9. Define dispersive power (for light) of a medium. **ISC 2003**

10. Draw a labelled ray diagram for the production of pure spectrum. **ISC 2002**

2 Marks Questions

11. Name any two phenomena which take place in the formation of a rainbow. **ISC 2023**

12. Draw a neat and labelled ray diagram to show the formation of primary rainbow. **ISC SQP 2023**

13. (i) Define angular dispersion. **ISC 2022 Sem-II**

 (ii) State any one difference between a primary rainbow and a secondary rainbow.

14. The deviation produced for violet, yellow and red lights for crown glass are 3.75°, 3.25° and 2.86° respectively. Calculate the dispersive power of the crown glass. **ISC 2019**

15. State any two differences between primary rainbow and secondary rainbow. **ISC 2018**

16. What is meant by dispersive power? Write an expression of dispersive power in terms of refractive indices. **ISC SQP 2018**

17. The refractive indices of a material for red, violet and yellow colour lights are 1.52, 1.62 and 1.59 respectively. Calculate the dispersive power of the material. If the mean deviation is 40°, what will be the angular dispersion produced by a prism of this material? **ISC 2006**

KEY idea

To calculate the angular dispersion, first calculate the dispersive power $\left(\omega = \frac{n_v - n_R}{n_y - 1}\right)$ and then angular dispersion with the help of formula $\delta_v - \delta_R = \omega \times \delta_y$.

3 Marks Questions

18. (*i*) State three conditions for formation of pure spectrum.

 (*ii*) Draw a ray diagram illustrating the measurement of the angle of a prism using a spectrometer. **ISC 2007**

19. Define dispersive power of the material of prism. The refractive indices of a prism for prism for violet, yellow and red colours are 1.632, 1.620 and 1.613 respectively. Calculate the dispersive power of the material of the prism. **2005**

4/5 Marks Question

20. What is meant by pure and impure spectrum? Explain briefly how you will set up a spectrometer to obtain pure spectrum? Draw a diagram of a spectrometer and describe its parts. **ISC 2000**

Case Based Question
(For Complete Chapter)

21. **Direction** *Read the passage given below and answer the questions that follows.*

Refraction of Light

Refraction involves change in the path of light due to change in the medium.

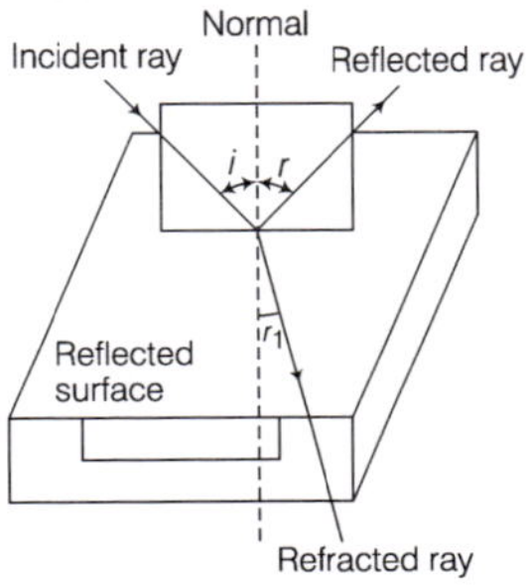

When a beam of light encounters another transparent medium, a part of light gets reflected back into the first medium, while the rest enters the other. The direction of propagation of an obliquely incident ray of light, that enters the other medium, changes at the interface of two media. This phenomenon is called refraction of light.

(*i*) For the same value of angle of incidence, the angles of refraction in three media *A*, *B* and *C* are 15°, 25° and 35°, respectively. In which medium, would the velocity of light be minimum?

(*ii*) Why does a crack in a glass window pane appear silvery?

(*iii*) The refractive index of diamond is much higher than that of glass. How does a diamond cutter make use of this fact?

(*iv*) What is the apparent position of an object below a rectangular block of glass 6 cm thick, if a layer of water 4 cm thick is on the top of the glass?

(Take, $\mu_{ga} = \frac{3}{2}$ and $\mu_{wa} = \frac{4}{3}$)

Explanations

1. (d) The violet colour has the shortest wavelength and less speed and the red colour has lowest wavelength and more speed, due to which violet colour has most deviate.

2. (c) The dispersive power of a prism depends on the nature of material of prism.

3. Given, refractive index of violet colour, $n_v = 1.56$

   Refractive index of red colour, $n_r = 1.54$

   Refractive index of yellow colour, $n_y = 1.55$

   ∴ Dispersive power can be calculated as

$$\omega = \frac{n_v - n_r}{n_y - 1} = \frac{1.56 - 1.54}{1.55 - 1} = \frac{0.02}{0.55} = 0.036$$

4. The dark lines seen in the solar spectrum are called Fraunhoffer's lines.

5. Prism and telescope.

6. Given, Refractive index for violet $\mu_V = 1.62$

   Refractive index for yellow, $\mu_Y = 1.61$

   Refractive index for red, $\mu_R = 1.60$

   Dispersive power, $\omega = \frac{\mu_V - \mu_R}{\mu_Y - 1}$

$$= \frac{1.62 - 1.60}{1.61 - 1.00} = \frac{0.02}{0.61} = 0.032$$

7. Differences between Primary and Secondary Rainbows

Primary Rainbow	Secondary Rainbow
Light rays suffer single total internal reflection.	Light rays suffer two total internal reflections.
Outer edge is red and inner edge is violet.	Outer edge is violet and inner edge is red.

8. Refer to text on page 202 (Primary Rainbow).

9. Refer to text on page 201 (Dispersive Power).

10. Refer to text on pages 201 and 202 (Rainbow Real Life).

11. Refer to text on pages 201 and 202 (Rainbow Real Life).

12. Refer to text on page 202 (Primary Rainbow).

13. (i) Refer to text on page 201 (Angular Dispersion).

    (ii) Refer to text on page 202 (Types of Rainbow).

14. The dispersive power of the prism material,

$$\omega = \frac{\delta_V - \delta_R}{\delta_Y} = \frac{3.75° - 2.86°}{3.25°} = \frac{0.89°}{3.25°} = 0.274°$$

15. Refer to text on page 202 (Types of Rainbow).

16. **Dispersive power** It is the ability of the prism material to cause dispersion. It is defined as the ratio of angular dispersion to the mean deviation when a white light of beam is passed through prism.

    So, dispersive power $(\omega) = \frac{\mu_V - \mu_R}{(\mu - 1)}$

    where, μ_V = refractive index for violet colour

    μ_R = refractive index for red colour.

17. Given, refractive index of red light $n_R = 1.52$,

    Refractive index of violet light, $n_V = 1.62$,

    Refractive index of yellow light, $n_Y = 1.59$

    So, dispersive power,

$$\omega = \frac{n_V - n_R}{n_Y - 1} = \frac{1.62 - 1.52}{1.59 - 1} = \frac{0.1}{0.59} = 0.17$$

    Angular dispersion, $\delta_V - \delta_R = \omega \times \delta_Y$

18. (*i*) Three conditions for the formation of pure spectrum are

    (a) The slit should be narrow.

    (b) The rays falling on the prism should be parallel.

    (c) The prism should be placed in minimum deviation position.

    (*ii*) **Measuring the angle of a prism** The spectrum can be used to measure angle of a prism. The spectrometer is levelled and adjusted for parallel rays. The telescope is rotated for different positions T_1 and T_2. The images of the slit is coincided with vertical cross wire.

    The difference of angular position for two positions T_1 and T_2 is calculated as $2A$, where A is the angle of prism.

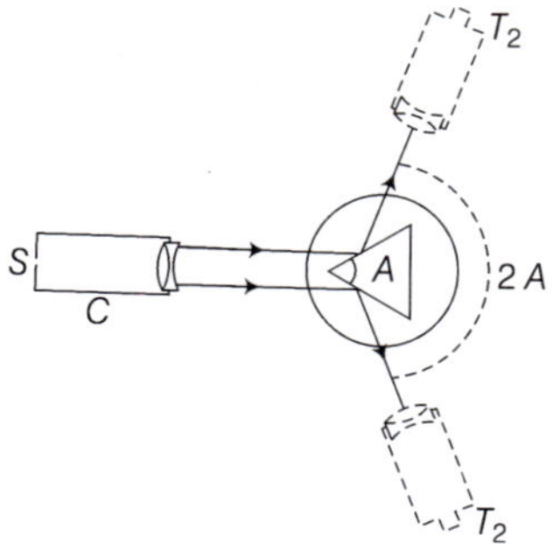

19. Refer to text on page 201 (Dispersive power)

Dispersive power,

$$\omega = \frac{\delta}{\delta_Y} = \frac{\delta_V - \delta_R}{\delta_Y} = \frac{\mu_r - \mu_R}{\mu_Y - 1} \qquad [\because \delta = \mu - 1]$$

Given, $\mu_V = 1.632$ (refractive index for violet)

$\mu_Y = 1.620$ (refractive index for yellow)

$\mu_R = 1.613$ (refractive index for red)

Thus, $\omega = \frac{1.632 - 1.613}{1.620 - 1} = \frac{0.019}{0.62} = 0.03$

Concept Enhancer The dispersive power of a prism depends on the nature of material used, it does not depend upon angle of prism.

20. Impure spectrum Spectrum is said to be impure in which there is a over lapping of different colours.

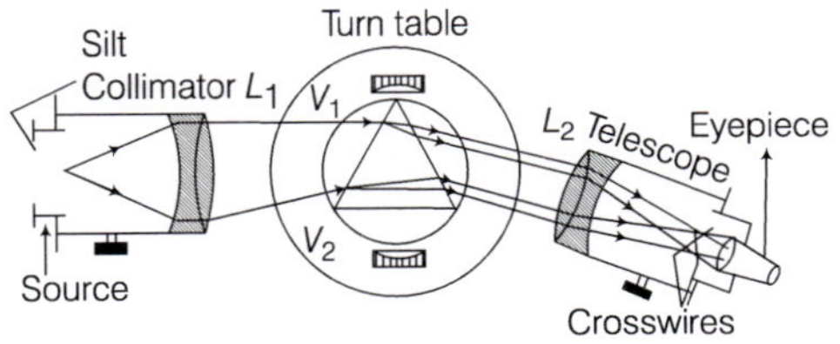

Pure spectrum Pure spectrum is one in which there is no over lapping of different colours take place.

Spectrometer It is an instrument used to study the spectra of luminous objects and also to find out the refractive index of any refracting material say, glass in the form of a prism.

The main parts of a spectrometer are

(*i*) **Collimator** It is a tube provided with a narrow slit S at one end and a converging lens at the other end. The narrow slit S is located at the focus of the lens.

When a source of light is placed in front of S a parallel beam of light emerges from the collimator. These rays are incident on the refractive surface of a prism.

(*ii*) **Prism table** It has a flat circular top, capable of rotating about its vertical axis. The prism is placed on the table with its refracting edge parallel to the slit.

(*iii*) **Telescope** It is an astronomical telescope filled with an eyepiece and crosswires. The spectrum is formed on the focal plane of the telescope and is viewed with an eyepiece having both of its lenses achromatic.

For the production of a pure spectrum, it is necessary that the slit should be very narrow and the incident beam of light should be parallel. Before using, the length of the telescopic tube is so adjusted that the image of the spectrum is well focussed. In this position, rays of different wavelengths (or colours) will be focussed at different points, thus producing a pure spectrum.

21. (*i*) As refractive index of medium

$$\frac{\text{Velocity of light in vacuum}}{\text{Velocity of light in a medium}} = \frac{\sin i}{\sin r}$$

The medium with angle 15° will have the highest refractive index and hence the velocity of light will be minimum.

(*ii*) Because of the presence of air in the crack, which results in total internal reflection.

(*iii*) The refractive index of diamond is more than that of ordinary glass. The critical angle for diamond is less than that for glass. A diamond is cutter uses a large angle of incidence to ensure that the light entering the diamond is totally reflected from its faces, so that the diamond sparkles.

(*iv*) Real depth of glass, $x_1 = 6$ cm

real depth of water, $x_2 = 4$ cm

$$\mu_{ga} = \frac{3}{2},\ \mu_{wa} = \frac{4}{3}$$

if y_1, y_2 are corresponding depths,

then $\frac{x_1}{y_1} = \mu_{ga} = \frac{3}{2}$

$\therefore \quad y_1 = \frac{2}{3} x_1 = \frac{2}{3} \times 6 = 4$ cm

$\frac{x_2}{y_2} = \mu_{wa} = \frac{4}{3}$

$\therefore \quad y_2 = \frac{3}{4} x_2 = \frac{3}{4} \times 4 = 3$ cm

Apparent position of the object

$= (y + y_2) = (4 + 3)$ cm $= 7$cm

$\therefore$ Rise in position of the object.

$= (x_1 + x_2) - (y_1 + y_2)$

$= (6 + 4) - (4 + 3)$

$= 10 - 7 = 3$ cm

CHAPTER TEST

01 Mark Questions (MCQs)

1 If lower half of a concave mirror is blackened, then
(a) image distance increases
(b) image distance decreases
(c) image intensity increases
(d) image intensity decreases

2 For a given lens, the magnification was found to be twice as large as when the object was 0.15 m distant from it as when the distance was 0.2 m. The focal length of the lens is
(a)1.5 m (b) 0.20 m (c) 0.10 m (d) 0.05 m

3 A convex mirror has focal length 20 cm. If an object is placed 20 cm away from the pole of mirror, then what is the distance between image formed and pole?
(a)40 cm (b) 10 cm (c) 20 cm (d) At infinity

01 Mark Questions (VSA)

4 Can refractive index of a medium relative to another medium be less than 1?

5 Calculate the critical angle for glass-water pair.

6 What are the focal length and power of a plane glass plate?

02 Marks Questions

7 Draw a ray diagram to illustrate linear chromatic aberration produced by a convex lens, with red and blue coloured rays labelled.

8 A right angled prism is to be made by selecting a proper material and the angles A and B $(B \leq A)$ as shown in the figure. It is desired that a ray of light incident on the face AB emerges parallel to the incident direction after two internal reflections.

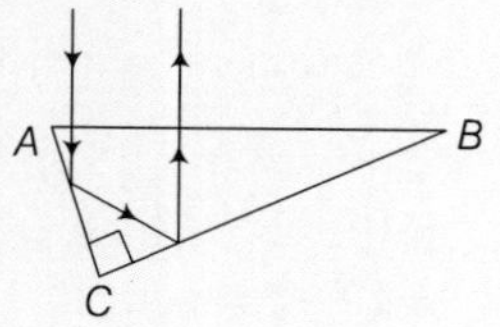

(i) What should be the minimum refractive index n for this to be possible?
(ii) For $n = 5/3$, is it possible to achieve this with the angle B equal to 30°?

03 Marks Questions

9 Minimum deviation suffered by violet, yellow and red beams passing through an equilateral transparent prism are 39.2°, 38.7° and 38.4°, respectively. Calculate the dispersive power in the medium.

10 A beam of light strikes a glass sphere of diameter 15 cm converging towards a point 30 cm behind the pole of the spherical surface.

Find the position of the image, if μ of glass is 1.5.

05 Marks Questions

11 (i) Explain with reason, how the power of a diverging lens changes when
(a) it is kept in a medium of refractive index greater than that of the lens.
(b) incident red light is replaced by violet light.

(ii) Three lenses L_1, L_2 and L_3 each of focal length 30 cm are placed coaxially as shown in the figure. An object is held at 60 cm from the optic centre of lens L_1. The final real image is formed at the focus of L_3. Calculate the separation between (a) (L_1 and L_2) and (b) (L_2 and L_3).

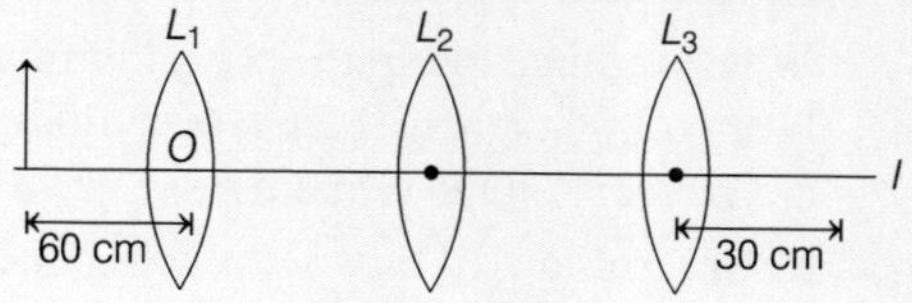

Answers

1. (d) **2.** (c) **3.** (b) **5.** 60°
8. (i) 1.414 (ii) No **9.** 0.0204
10. $v = 22.5$ cm
11. (ii) (a) 90 cm (b) It may take any value.

14

Optical Instruments

TREND ANALYSIS 4 YEARS

Average No. of Questions Across all Sets

Topic	Types of Questions	2024	2023	2020	2019
TOPIC 01 Simple Microscope and Compound Microscope	1 Mark	–	1	–	–
	2 Marks	–	1	–	–
	3 Marks	–	–	1	–
	5 Marks	1	–	–	1
TOPIC 02 Astronomical Telescope	1 Mark	–	–	–	–
	2 Marks	–	–	–	–
	3 Marks	–	–	1	–
	5 Marks	–	2	–	–

TOPIC 1

Simple Microscope and Compound Microscope

Simple Microscope (Magnifying glass)

Microscope is an optical instrument which forms a large image of close and minute objects. A simple microscope is a converging lens (convex lens) of small focal length. Simple microscope is based on the principle that, when an object is placed at a distance less than the focal length of the lens, the image obtained is virtual, erect and magnified.

Consider the diagram shown below. The final image i is formed at $D(A'B')$ for the object AB.

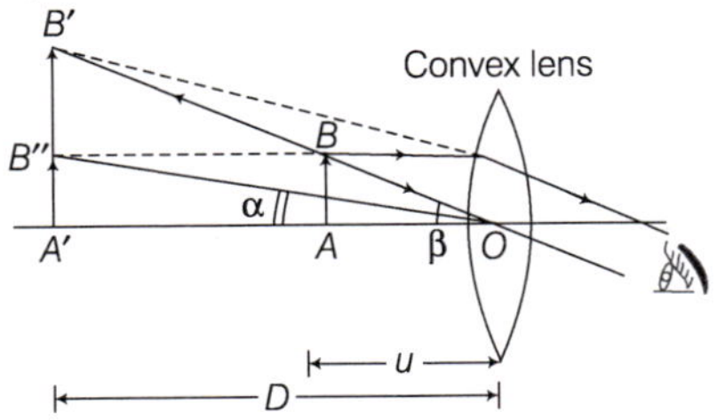

Magnifying power, $m = \dfrac{\beta}{\alpha}$

Using lens formula, $\dfrac{1}{v} - \dfrac{1}{u} = \dfrac{1}{f}$

On multiplying both sides by v, we have

$$\frac{v}{v} - \frac{v}{u} = \frac{v}{f} \Rightarrow 1 - M = \frac{v}{f}$$

$$\Rightarrow \quad \boxed{M = 1 - \frac{v}{f} = 1 + \frac{D}{f}}$$

***Case* I** When image is formed at the near point,

Magnification is given by,

$$\boxed{M = 1 + \frac{D}{f}}$$

In case the eye is placed behind the lens at a distance a,

then $$M = 1 + \frac{(D-a)}{f}$$

***Case* II** When the image is formed at infinity also called, normal adjustment, i.e. $v = \infty$

Magnification, $M = \frac{D}{f}$

where, D is least distance of distinct vision and f is focal length of the lens.

Compound Microscope

A compound microscope consists of two convex lenses, coaxially separated by some distance. The lens nearer to the object is called the objective. The lens through which the final image is viewed is called the eyepiece/ eyelens /ocular.

The objective of compound microscope forms the real, inverted and magnified image of the object. This image serves as the object for the second lens, eyepiece, which produce the final image, virtual highly magnified.

Angular magnification or magnifying power of a compound microscope is defined as the ratio of the angle β subtended by the final image at the eye to the angle α subtended by the object seen directly, when both are placed at the least distance of distinct vision.

$\therefore$ $$\text{Angular magnification, } M = \frac{\beta}{\alpha}$$

$$\text{Magnifying power, } M = m_e \times m_o$$

Consider the image formation by the compound microscope

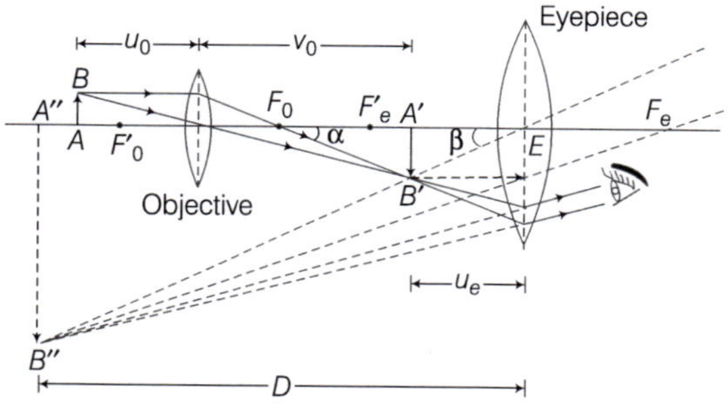

In the above diagram, AB = object

$A''B''$ = final image

Angular magnification of a compound microscope,

$$M = \frac{\beta}{\alpha}$$

Thus, $$M = -\frac{v_0}{u_0}\left(1 + \frac{D}{f_e}\right)$$

This is the required expression for magnifying power.

When the final image is at infinity

If u_o is the distance of the object from the objective and v_o is the distance of the image from the objective, then the magnifying power of the objective is

$$m_o = \frac{v_o}{u_o}$$

When the final image is at infinity, then angular magnification is given by,

$$m_e = \frac{D}{f_e}$$

The total magnification when image is at infinity is given by

$$m = m_o \times m_e = \left(\frac{v_o}{u_o} \times \frac{D}{f_e}\right)$$

If the object is very close to the principal focus of the objective and the image formed by the objective is very close to the eyepiece, then

$$m = \frac{-L}{f_o} \cdot \frac{D}{f_e}$$

where, L = length of the tube of microscope

In this case, the microscope is said to be in normal adjustment.

PYQs Previous Years Questions

1 Mark Questions

1. What is meant by a microscope in normal use? **ISC 2023**

2. A simple microscope or a magnifying glass with a focal length 5 cm forms an image at the near point of the eye. Find its magnification. **ISC 2006**

3. Define the angular magnification of an optical instrument. **ISC 2004**

4. What are the two possible values of the magnifying powers of a simple microscope made of convex lens of focal length $f = 5.0$ cm. **ISC 2003**

2 Marks Questions

5. A thin converging lens of focal length 5cm is used as a simple microscope. Calculate its magnifying power when image formed lies at
   (a) Infinity
   (b) Least distance of distinct vision ($D = 25$cm)
   ISC SQP 2023

6. A convex lens of a focal length 5 cm is used as a simple microscope. Where should an object be placed so that the image formed by it lies at the least distance of distinct vision ($D = 25$ cm)? **ISC 2015**

7. Explain the statement: "Angular magnification of a compound microscope in normal use is 30". **ISC 2010**

8. (*i*) Define the magnifying power of a microscope in terms of visual angles.
   (*ii*) What is the advantage of a compound microscope over a simple microscope? **ISC 2004**

9. Draw a schematic ray diagram of a compound microscope with the final image formed at infinity. **ISC 2000**

3 Marks Questions

10. Draw a neat labelled ray diagram of a simple microscope when the image is formed at the least distance of distinct vision D. Write the expression for its angular magnification (magnifying power) in this set-up. [Derivation of formula is not required.] **ISC 2022 Sem-II**

11. A compound microscope consists of two convex lenses having focal length of 1.5 cm and 5 cm. When an object is kept at a distance of 1.6 cm from the objective, the final image is virtual and lies at a distance of 25cm from the eyepiece. Calculate magnifying power of the compound microscope in this set-up. **ISC 2020**

12. A compound microscope consists of two convex lenses of focal lengths 2 cm and 5 cm. When an object is kept at a distance of 2.1 cm from the objective, a virtual and magnified image is formed 25 cm from the eyepiece. Calculate the magnifying power of the microscope. **ISC 2016**

> **KEY idea**
> To determine the magnifying power of the microscope. First calculate v_o than calculate the magnifying power with the help of formula, $M = \frac{v_o}{u_o}\left(1 + \frac{D}{F_e}\right)$

13. Draw a labelled diagram of an image formed by a compound microscope with image at least distance of a distinct vision. **ISC 2015, 13, 11**

14. Derive the formula for angular magnification of a compound microscope, when the final image is formed at the least distance of distinct vision. Draw the required ray diagram. **ISC 2015**

15. A compound microscope consists of an objective of focal length 2 cm and an eyepiece of focal length 5 cm. When an object is kept 2.4 cm from the objective, final image formed is virtual and 25 cm from the eyepiece. Determine magnifying power of this compound microscope in this set-up i.e. in normal use. **ISC 2012**

16. A convex lens of focal length 5 cm is to be used as a simple microscope. Where should an object be kept, so that image formed by the lens lies at least distance D of distinct vision ($D = 25$ cm)? Also, calculate the magnifying power of this instrument in this set-up. **ISC 2009**

17. In a compound microscope, it consists of two convex lenses of focal length 1.5 cm and 10 cm, the object is 2 cm from the objective and the final image is formed at the least distance of distinct vision ($D = 25$ cm). Find the distance of separation of the two lenses. **ISC 2008**

18. Draw neat ray diagram of a simple microscope. Deduce the formula for angular magnification, when the image is formed at the least distance of distinct vision. **ISC 2002**

5 Marks Questions

19. *Read the passage given below and answer the questions that follow.*

There are two types of optical instruments : Microscopes and Telescopes.

Microscopes are used to magnify very tiny objects whereas telescopes are used to study distant objects. Both of them deploy convex lenses. In his telescope, Newton used a large parabolic mirror to collect light from the stars and reduce aberrations. **ISC 2024**

(i) Rohit observed the launch of Chandrayan 3 with the help of an optical instrument. Name the instrument used by him.

(ii) State any one advantage of a reflecting telescope over a refracting telescope.

(iii) Which instrument is used to study the structure of a virus?

(iv) What is the ability of an optical instrument to form enlarged images called?

(v) What is the difference between a compound microscope and an astronomical telescope (refracting type), as far as their lenses are concerned?

20. Draw a neat labelled ray diagram showing the formation of an image at the least distance of distinct vision D by a simple microscope. When the final image is at D, derive an expression for its magnifying power at D. **ISC 2019**

21. Draw a labelled ray diagram of an image formed by a compound microscope with final image formed at the least distance of distinct vision (D). Derive an expression for its magnifying power (in terms of v_o, u_o, f_e and D). **ISC SQP 2018**

Explanations

1. A microscope is a device that allows you to see items that are too small for the naked eye to see.

2. For a simple microscope, we know that for near point, magnifying power,

$$M = 1 + \frac{D}{f} = 1 + \frac{25}{5} = 6$$

[D = least distance of distinct vision and f = focal length of lens]

3. Angular magnification of an optical instrument is defined as the ratio of the visual angle subtended by the image formed by the instrument at the eye to the visual angle subtended by the object at an unaided eye. i.e. $M = \frac{\beta}{\alpha}$

4. ***Case* I** When image is formed at near point. Magnifying power of lens will be

$$M = 1 + \frac{D}{f}$$

It depends upon the focal length. For normal eye, the least distance of distinct vision,

$$D = 25\text{cm}$$

$$\therefore \quad M = 1 + \frac{25}{5} = 6$$

***Case* II** When image is formed at infinity.

Magnifying power, $M = \frac{D}{f} = \frac{25}{5} = 5$

5. (a) At infinity, $M = \frac{D}{f}$

$$M = \frac{25\text{cm}}{5\text{cm}}$$

$$M = 5$$

(b) At least distance of distinct vision.

$$M = 1 + \frac{D}{f}$$

$$M = 1 + 5$$

$$M = 6$$

6. According to the question, focal length of convex lens $(f) = 5$ cm

i.e. $f = +5$ cm

Image distance $(v) = -D = -25$ cm

Now, from thin lens formula,

$$\frac{1}{v} - \frac{1}{u} = \frac{1}{f}$$

So, $$\frac{1}{u} = \frac{1}{v} - \frac{1}{f}$$

$$\Rightarrow \quad u = \frac{vf}{f-v} = \frac{-25\times 5}{5-(-25)}$$

$$= \frac{-25\times 5}{30} = -4.2 \text{ cm}$$

7. The statement can be explained as the visual angle subtended on eye with telescope is 30 times more than the angle without telescope, when the object is at the least distance of distinct vision.

8. (*i*) Refer to sol. 3 on page 210.

(*ii*) In a simple microscope, there is only one lens, whereas in a compound microscope there are two lenses. Therefore, the magnifying power of a compound microscope is more than that of a simple microscope.

9. The diagram of a compound microscope, when the final image is formed at infinity is shown below.

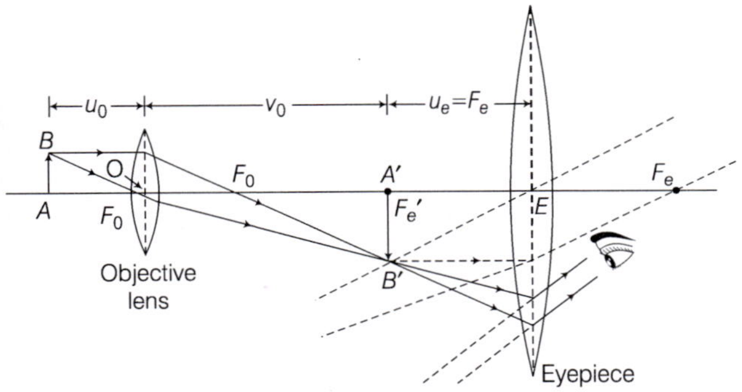

10. Refer to text on pages 207 and 208 (Simple Microscope).

11. Given, $f_o = 1.5$ cm, $f_e = 5$ cm

$u_o = -1.6$ cm and $v_e = -25$ cm

For the objective lens, $\frac{1}{f_o} = \frac{1}{v_o} - \frac{1}{u_o}$

$$\frac{1}{v_o} = \frac{1}{f_o} + \frac{1}{u_o} = \frac{1}{1.5} - \frac{1}{1.6}$$

$$\frac{1}{v_o} = \frac{10}{16\times 15}$$

$$\Rightarrow \quad v_o = \frac{16\times 15}{10} = \frac{240}{10} = 24 \text{ cm}$$

Now, magnification, i.e. magnifying power of the microscope,

$$m = -\frac{v_o}{u_o}\left(1+\frac{D}{f_e}\right) = \frac{-24}{-1.6}\left(1+\frac{25}{5}\right) = 90$$

Common Mistake The value of 'F', 'v', 'u' and 'D' must be with proper sign.

12. Here, $f_0 = 2$ cm, $f_e = 5$ cm, $u_0 = 2.1$ cm, $v_e = 25$ cm, $v_0 = ?$

For the objective lens, $\frac{1}{f_0} = \frac{1}{v_0} - \frac{1}{u_0}$

$$\Rightarrow \quad \frac{1}{v_0} = \frac{1}{f_0} + \frac{1}{u_0} = \frac{1}{2} + \left(\frac{1}{-2.1}\right)$$

$$\Rightarrow \quad \frac{1}{v_0} = \frac{0.1}{4.2}$$

$$\Rightarrow \quad v_0 = 42 \text{ cm}$$

Now, magnification i.e. magnifying power of the microscope,

$$M = \frac{v_0}{u_0}\left(1+\frac{D}{f_e}\right) = \frac{42}{2.1}\left(1+\frac{25}{5}\right)$$

$$= 20(6) = 120$$

13. While drawing the labelled diagram of the compound microscope, we must form final image at the least distance of distinct vision (D).

Consider the image formation by the compound microscope.

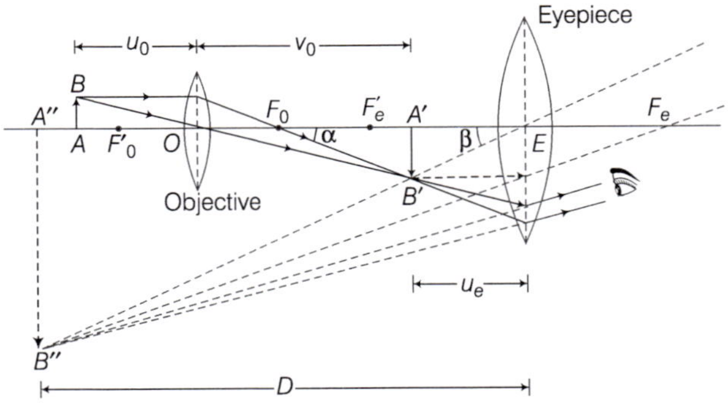

In the above diagram, AB = object and $A''B''$ = final image

14. Refer to text on page 208 (Compound Microscope).

15. According to the question,

Given, object distance of objective lens

$u_0 = -2.4$ cm, $D = 25$ cm,

Focal length of eyepiece, $f_e = 5$ cm,

Focal length of objective, $f_0 = 2$ cm,

Image distance of objective lens, $v_0 = ?$

Applying lens formula, for objective $\frac{1}{v_0} - \frac{1}{u_0} = \frac{1}{f_0}$

$$\Rightarrow \quad \frac{1}{v_0} = \frac{1}{f_0} + \frac{1}{u_0} = \frac{1}{2} - \frac{1}{2.4} = \frac{1.2 - 1}{2.4}$$

$$\Rightarrow \quad \frac{1}{v_0} = \frac{0.2}{2.4} = \frac{2}{24} = \frac{1}{12}$$

$$\Rightarrow \quad v_0 = 12 \text{ cm}$$

Magnifying power, $M = \frac{-v_0}{u_0}\left(1 + \frac{D}{f_e}\right)$

$$= \frac{-12}{-2.4}\left(1 + \frac{25}{5}\right)$$

$$= 5 \times (6) = 30$$

$$\Rightarrow \quad M = 30$$

16. When final image formed by a simple microscope, is at the least distance of distinct vision (D), the magnifying

power is $M = 1 + \frac{D}{f}$.

Given, $f = 5$ cm, $D = -25$ cm $= v$

By lens formula, $\frac{1}{f} = \frac{1}{v} - \frac{1}{u}$

$$\Rightarrow \quad \frac{1}{u} = \frac{1}{v} - \frac{1}{f} = -\frac{1}{25} - \frac{1}{5} = \frac{-1-5}{25} = \frac{-6}{25}$$

$$\therefore \quad u = \frac{-25}{6} = -4.166 \text{ cm} = -4.17 \text{ cm}$$

Magnifying power of a simple microscope

$$M = 1 + \frac{D}{f} = 1 + \frac{25}{5} = 6$$

17. The separation between two lenses can be calculated by the sum of the object distance of eyepiece (u_e) and image distance of objective (v_0).

Given, $f_0 = 15$ cm, $f_e = 10$ cm,

$u_0 = 2$ cm, $v_e = -25$ cm $= D$

For eyepiece, $\frac{1}{f_e} = \frac{1}{v_e} - \frac{1}{u_e}$

$$\frac{1}{u_e} = \frac{1}{v_e} - \frac{1}{f_e} = -\frac{1}{25} - \frac{1}{10} = -\frac{7}{50}$$

$$u_e = -7.14 \text{ cm}$$

For objective, $\frac{1}{v_0} = \frac{1}{u_0} + \frac{1}{f_0}$

$$= -\frac{1}{2} + \frac{1}{1.5} = \frac{-3+4}{6} = \frac{1}{6} \Rightarrow v_0 = 6 \text{ cm}$$

Distance of separation

$$= v_0 + u_e = (6 + 7.14) = 13.14 \text{ cm}$$

18. The ray diagram of a simple microscope is shown below.

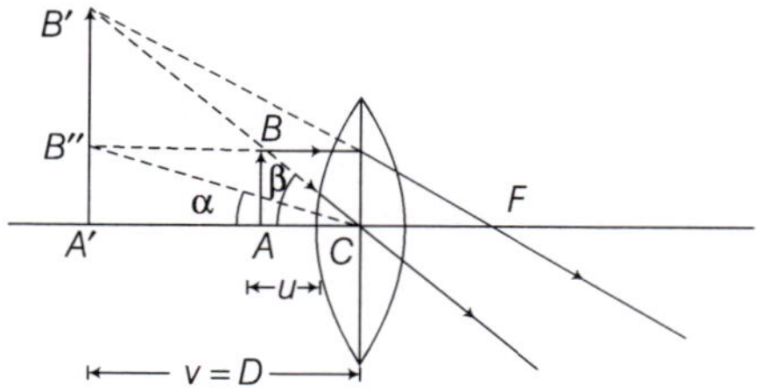

Angular magnification, $M = \frac{\beta}{\alpha}$

If angle are small, $\beta \simeq \tan\beta, \alpha \simeq \tan\alpha$

Hence, $M = \frac{\tan\beta}{\tan\alpha} = \frac{AB/AC}{A'B''/A'C}$

$$A'B'' = AB \quad \therefore \quad M = \frac{A'C}{AC} = \frac{v}{u}$$

We know that, $\frac{v}{u} = 1 - \frac{v}{f}$ [but $v = -D$]

$$\therefore \quad M = 1 - \left(-\frac{D}{f}\right) = 1 + \frac{D}{f}$$

> **Concept Enhancer** Magnifying power depends upon the focal length of the lens. Smaller the focal length greater will be the magnifying power of the lens.

19. (i) Telescope is the instrument used by him.

(ii) The mirror can be made parabolic to reduce spherical aberration. Aberration is further reduced because passage through one layer of glass is eliminated.

(iii) Microscopes are used to magnify very tiny structure of a virus.

(iv) Resolving power of a microscope.

(v) In compound microscope, objective lens has smaller aperture and smaller focal length than the eyepiece, while in telescope, the objective has a larger aperture and larger focal length than the eyepiece.

20. **Simple Microscope** Microscope is an optical instrument which forms large image of close and minute objects. A simple microscope is a converging lens of small focal length. When an object is at a distance less than the focal length of the lens, the image obtained is virtual, erect and magnified.

When the object is at a distance equal to the focal length of the lens, the image is formed at infinity.

When the image is formed at the near point

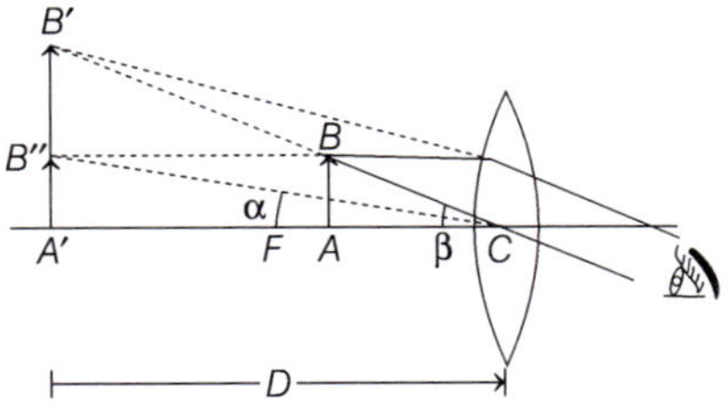

The angular magnification or magnifying power of a simple microscope is defined as the ratio of the visual angle β subtended at the eye by image at the near point to the visual angle α subtended at the unaided eye by the object at the near point.

$\therefore$ Magnifying power, $m = \dfrac{\beta}{\alpha}$ ...(i)

In $\Delta A'B'C$, $\tan\beta = \dfrac{A'B'}{D}$

In $\Delta A'B''C$, $\tan\alpha = \dfrac{A'B''}{D} = \dfrac{AB}{D}$

Since, the angles are small, then $\tan\alpha \approx \alpha$ and $\tan\beta \approx \beta$

$\therefore \quad \beta = \dfrac{A'B'}{D}$ and $\alpha = \dfrac{AB}{D}$

From Eq. (i), we have

$$m = \frac{A'B'}{D} \times \frac{D}{AB} = \frac{A'B'}{AB}$$

This gives the linear magnification produced by the lens.

It can be proved that, $\dfrac{A'B'}{AB} = \dfrac{v}{u}$

We know that, $\dfrac{1}{v} - \dfrac{1}{u} = \dfrac{1}{f}$

Multiplying both sides by v, we have

$$\frac{v}{v} - \frac{v}{u} = \frac{v}{f}$$

$$\Rightarrow \quad 1 - m = \frac{v}{f}$$

$$\Rightarrow \quad m = 1 - \frac{v}{f}$$

$$\therefore \quad m = 1 + \frac{D}{f} \qquad [\because v = -D]$$

21. A compound microscope consists of two convex lenses coaxially separated by some distance. The lens nearer to the object is called the objective. The lens through which the final image is viewed is called the eyepiece.

Ray diagram of an image formed by compound microscope is shown below.

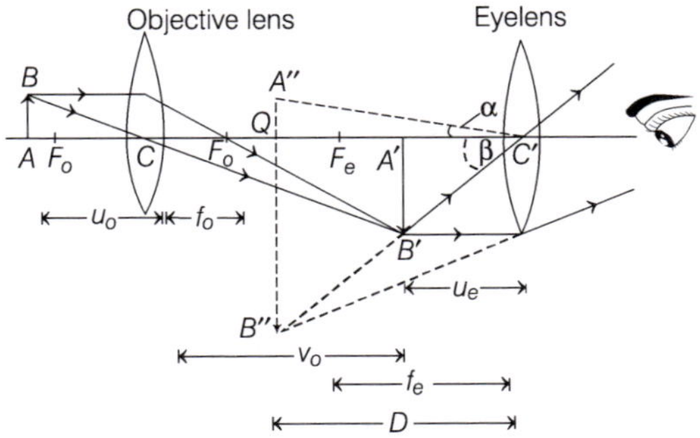

Angular magnification or magnifying power of a compound microscope is defined as the ratio of the angle β subtended by the final image at the eye to the angle α subtended by the object seen directly, when both are placed at least distance of distinct vision.

Angular magnification, $m = \dfrac{\beta}{\alpha}$

Since, the angles are small, then

$$\alpha \approx \tan\alpha \text{ or } \beta \approx \tan\beta$$

$$m = \frac{\tan\beta}{\tan\alpha} \qquad \text{... (i)}$$

From right angled $\Delta C'QB''$, we have

$$\tan\beta = \frac{B''Q}{C'Q} = \frac{B''Q}{D} = \frac{A''B''}{D}$$

Also, from right angle $\Delta C'A''Q$, we have

$$\tan\alpha = \frac{A''Q}{C'Q} = \frac{AB}{D} \qquad [A''Q = AB]$$

$$m = \frac{B''Q}{D} \times \frac{D}{AB}$$

Thus, the magnification produced by the compound microscope is the product of the magnification produced by the eyepiece and objective.

$$m = m_e \times m_o \qquad \text{... (ii)}$$

where, m_e and m_o are the magnifying powers of the eyepiece and objective, respectively.

When the final image is formed at near point.

Linear magnification is given by

$$m_e = 1 + \frac{D}{f_e} \qquad \text{... (iii)}$$

where, f_e is focal length of the eyepiece $\frac{A'B'}{AB}$ is the linear magnification of the object produced by the objective

$$m_o = \frac{v_o}{u_o} \quad \text{... (iv)}$$

From Eqs. (ii), (iii) and (iv), we have

$$m = \frac{v_o}{u_o}\left(1 + \frac{D}{f_e}\right) \quad \text{...(v)}$$

We know that, $\frac{1}{v_o} - \frac{1}{u_o} = \frac{1}{f_o}$

Multiplying both sides by v_o, we have

$$\frac{v_o}{v_o} - \frac{v_o}{u_o} = \frac{v_o}{f_o}$$

$$\Rightarrow \quad -\frac{v_o}{u_o} = -1 + \frac{v_o}{f_o}$$

$$\Rightarrow \quad \frac{v_o}{u_o} = 1 - \frac{v_o}{f_o}$$

Substituting the value of $\frac{v_o}{u_o}$ in Eq. (v), we have

$$m = \left(1 - \frac{v_o}{f_o}\right)\left(1 + \frac{D}{f_e}\right)$$

TOPIC 2

Astronomical Telescope

An astronomical telescope is an optical instrument which is used for observing distinct images of heavenly bodies like stars, planets, etc. The final image is formed at infinity. It is of two types, one of them is refracting type and another is reflecting type.

Refracting Astronomical Telescope

Refracting astronomical telescope has two convex lenses, coaxially separated by some distance. The lens towards the object is called **objective** and has much larger aperture than the eyepiece.

***Case* I** When the final image is formed at infinity.

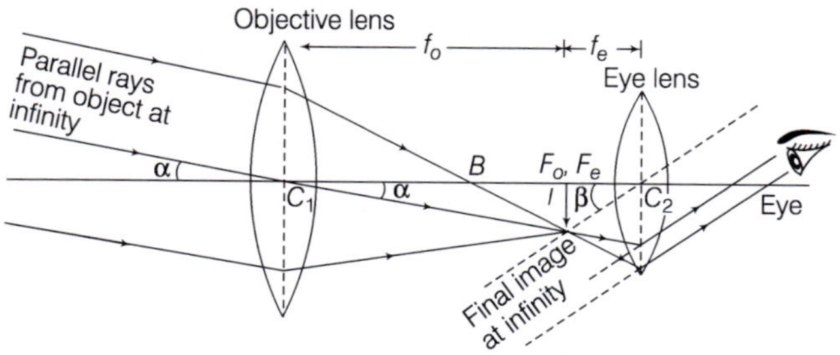

Angular magnification is given by

$$m = \frac{\beta}{\alpha}$$

or

$$\boxed{m = -\frac{f_o}{f_e}}$$

The length of the telescope is

$$\boxed{L = |f_o| + |f_e|}$$

***Case* II** When the final image is formed at near point.

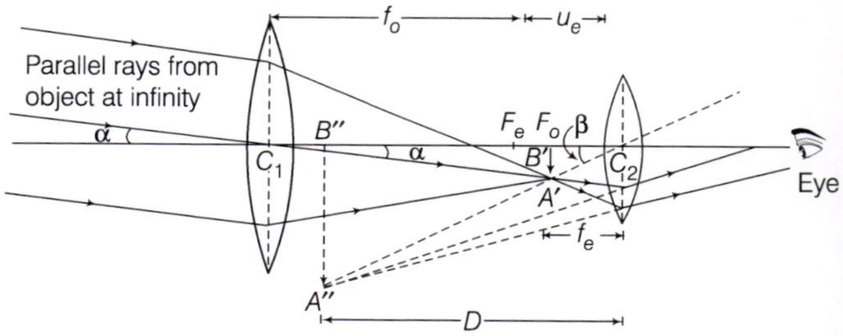

Angular magnification, $m = \frac{\beta}{\alpha}$

$$\boxed{m = -\frac{f_o}{f_e}\left(1 + \frac{f_e}{D}\right)}$$

Reflecting Astronomical Telescope

Reflecting telescope consists of a concave mirror of large aperture and large focal length (objective). A plane mirror is placed between the concave mirror and its focus. A small convex lens works as eyepiece. Its based upon the same principle except that the formation of image take place by reflection instead of by refraction.

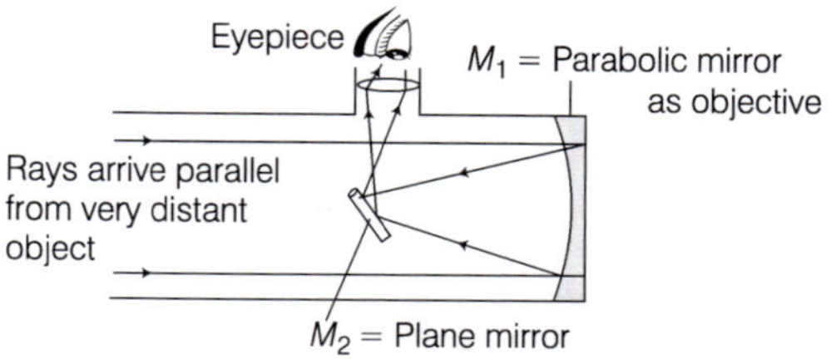

Reflecting telescope

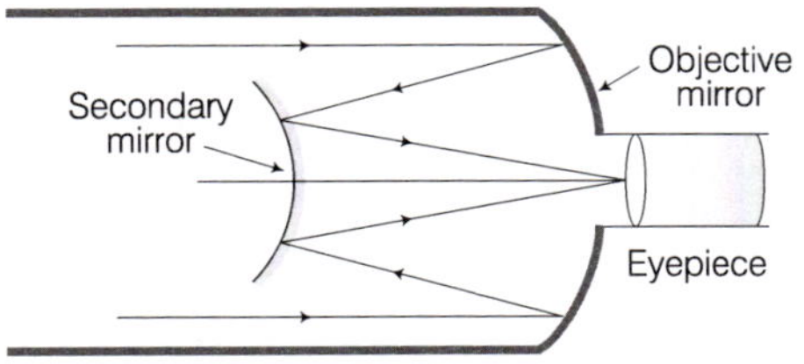

Working of reflecting telescope

In the reflecting telescope, parallel rays from a distant object are intercepted and focused by a reflecting concave mirror rather than a refracting lens. One popular configuration of mirror and eyepiece called the Newtonian reflecting type telescope named after its designer Newton.

$$\text{Magnification} \quad \boxed{M = \frac{\beta}{\alpha} \text{ or } M = \frac{f_o}{f_e}}$$

$$\because \quad \boxed{f_o = \frac{R}{2}}$$

where, R is the radius of curvature of objective mirror.

f_o and f_e are the focal lengths corresponding to objective and eyepiece.

Resolving Power of a Telescope

The resolving power of a telescope is defined as the reciprocal of the smallest angular separation between two distant objects whose images are seen separately.

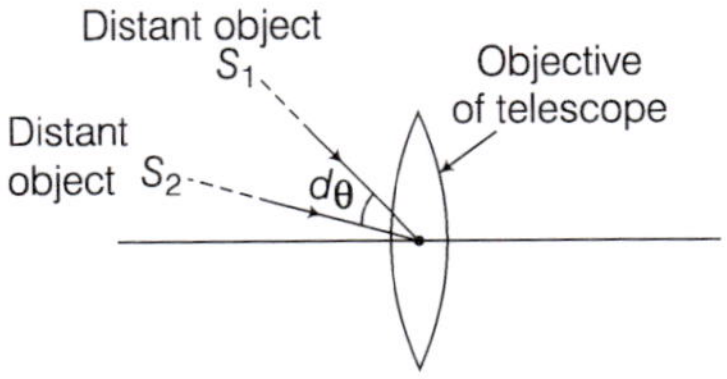

$$\text{Resolving power R.P} = \frac{1}{d\theta} = \frac{D}{1.22\,\lambda}$$

where, D = diameter/aperture of objective lens

λ = wavelength of light used

Resolving power depends on (*i*) wavelength λ and (*ii*) diameter or aperture of the objective D. Thats why, telescope with larger objective aperture are used.

Advantages

- Superior resolving power per inch of aperture, image formed is brighter.
- A mirror is easier to produce with a large diameter, so that it can intercept rays crossing a larger area and direct them to the eyepiece.
- The mirror, can be made parabolic to reduce spherical aberration. Its further reduced because passage through one layer of glass (the objective lens is eliminated).
- Free from chromatic aberration.

Disadvantages

- Very high initial cost relative to reflector.
- A certain amout of secondary spectrum (chromatic aberration) unavoidable (reflector completely free of this)
- The colours cannot focus at one point.
- Long focal ratio means that the instrument is cumbersome.

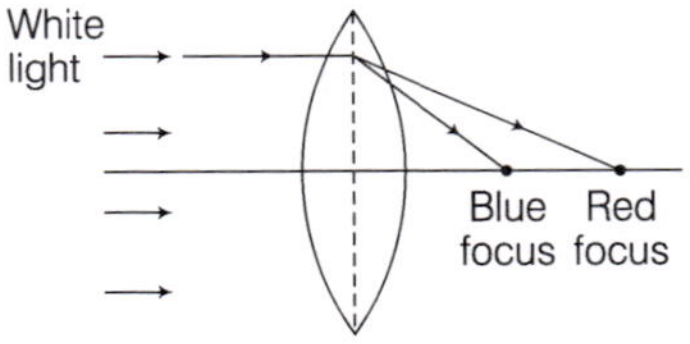

Chromatic aberration

Types of Telescopes

Telescopes may be classified by the wavelengths of light they detect.

- **X-ray telescopes,** using shorter wavelengths than ultraviolet light.
- **Ultraviolet telescopes,** using shorter wavelengths than visible light.
- **Optical telescopes,** using visible light.
- **Infrared telescopes,** using longer wavelengths than visible light.
- **Submillimeter telescopes,** using longer wavelengths than infrared light.

PYQs Previous Years Questions

1 Mark Questions

1. State any one advantage of using a reflecting telescope in place of a refracting telescope. **ISC 2015, 22 Sem-II**

2. Choose the correct option. In an astronomical telescope of refracting type **ISC 2013**
   (a) eyepiece has greater focal length
   (b) objective has greater focal length
   (c) objective and eyepiece have equal focal length
   (d) eyepiece has greater aperture than the objective

3. State how the resolving power of an astronomical telescope can be increased. **ISC 2010**

4. Why all over the world, giant telescopes are of reflecting type? State any one reason. **ISC 2009**

5. Draw ray diagram to illustrate the formation of image at infinity in a refracting telescope. **ISC 2003**

6. An astronomical telescope set for normal adjustment has a magnifying power 10. If the focal length of the objective is 1.20 m, what is the focal length of the eyepiece ? **ISC 2001**

2 Marks Questions

7. With regard to an astronomical telescope of refraction type, state how you will increase its
   (*i*) magnifying power (*ii*) resolving power **ISC 2015**

8. An astronomical telescope uses two lenses of powers 10 D and 1 D. If the final image of a distant object is formed at infinity, calculate the length of the telescope. **ISC 2014**

> **KEY idea**
>
> To calculate the length of telescope. First calculate f_1 and f_2 with the help of $F = \frac{100}{P}$ and then length of telescope $= f_1 + f_2$.

9. (*i*) Define resolving power of a simple astronomical telescope.
   (*ii*) State one advantage of a reflecting telescope over refracting telescope. **ISC 2012**

10. An astronomical telescope consists of two thin convex lenses having focal lengths of 140 cm and 5 cm. The telescope is adjusted to be in normal adjustment.
    (*i*) What is the angular magnification, i.e. magnifying power of the telescope in this set up?
    (*ii*) What is the distance between the two lenses equal to? **ISC 2011**

11. An astronomical telescope consists of two convex lenses having focal lengths 80 cm and 4 cm. When it is in normal adjustment, what is its
    (*i*) length? (*ii*) magnifying power? **ISC 2009**

3 Marks Questions

12. (*i*) What is meant by resolving power of a telescope?
    (*ii*) State any method of increasing the resolving power of an astronomical telescope. **ISC 2017**

13. Draw a labelled ray diagram showing the formation of an image by a refracting telescope when the final image lies at infinity. **ISC 2015**

14. Draw a labelled ray diagram of an image of a distant object formed by a refracting astronomical telescope in normal adjustment. Write (do not derive) an expression for its magnifying power. **ISC 2008**

15. An astronomical telescope is adjusted to form the final image at infinity. The separation between the lenses is 80 cm. The angular magnification is 15. Calculate the focal lengths of the objective lens and the eyepiece. **ISC 2007**

16. (*i*) Draw a ray diagram to show how the image of a distant object is formed by a refracting astronomical telescope, when in normal use.
    (*ii*) State one advantage of a reflecting astronomical telescope over a refracting astronomical telescope. **ISC 2006**

17. Define magnifying power of an optical instrument. An astronomical refracting telescope consists of two lenses of focal lengths 75 cm and 5 cm. Calculate the magnifying power of the telescope, when the final image is formed at a distance of 25 cm from the eye. **ISC 2005**

5 Marks Question

18. (*i*) Draw the ray diagram for the formation of image by a refracting telescope having the final image formed at infinity.
    (*ii*) For refracting telescope, define the angular magnification and derive the formula for the same for image formed at infinity. **ISC SQP 2022 Sem-II, 02**

Case Based Questions
(For Complete Chapter)

19. Direction *Read the passage given below and answer the questions that follows.*

There are two types of lenses: Converging lenses and Diverging lenses, depending on whether they converge or diverge an incident beam of light. They are also called convex or concave lenses. Lenses are usually made of glass. Convex lenses are more popular as they form a real image of an object. They are widely used in our daily life, for instance, in microscopes, telescopes, projectors, cameras, spectacles, etc. Microscopes are used to view small and nearby objects whereas telescopes are used to see distant objects. **ISC 2023**

(*i*) State any one factor on which focal length of a lens depends. **(1)**

(*ii*) Give an example where a convex lens behaves like a diverging lens. **(1)**

(*iii*) What type of lens is used in a camera? **(1)**

(*iv*) Write an expression for magnifying power of a compound microscope when its final image lies at the least distance of distinct vision (D). **(1)**

(*v*) State any one difference between a reflecting telescope and a refracting telescope. **(1)**

20. Direction *Read the passage given below and answer the questions that follows.*

Optical instruments are of great utility. They help us in studying very tiny objects as well as very large heavenly bodies. Scientists have developed microscopes like electron microscopes which aid in studying tiny molecules of matter. They have also devised giant telescopes like Hubble telescope and James Web Space telescope which have enabled us to view distant galaxies hitherto unknown. **ISC SQP 2023**

(*i*) Which optical instrument is used to study detailed structure of a virus? **(1)**

(*ii*) What is the ability of an instrument to form an enlarged image of an object called? **(1)**

(*iii*) Hubble telescope orbits around the earth like a satellite. What is the advantage of such a telescope over a similar one on earth's surface? **(1)**

(*iv*) An astronomical telescope consists of two convex lenses having focal length of 200 cm and 4 cm. When it forms final image at infinity, calculate its (a) magnifying power (b) length. **(1+1)**

Explanations

1. Reflecting telescope removes chromatic and spherical aberration, high resolving power.

2. (b) In an astronomical telescope of refracting type, objective has greater focal length than eyepiece. Thus, option (ii) is correct.

3. By increasing the diameter of objective lens, or by decreasing wavelength of light, we can increase the resolving power of a telescope, because $R = D/1.22\lambda$

4. It has a large aperture due to which it gathers more light and brighter image is obtained.

5. Refer to text on page 214 (Refracting Astronomical Telescope).

6. The magnitude of the magnifying power of the astronomical telescope is given by, $|M| = f_o/f_e$

where, f_o is the focal length of objective and f_e is the focal length of eyepiece.

$$\Rightarrow 10 = \frac{1.20}{f_e} \quad \Rightarrow f_e = \frac{1.20}{10} = 0.12 \text{ m} = 12 \text{ cm}$$

Thus, the eyepiece of the telescope will be of focal length 12 cm.

7. (*i*) Magnifying power can be increased by increasing focal length of objective or by decreasing focal length of eyepiece.

(*ii*) Resolving power of telescope is given by

$$\text{RP} = \frac{1}{d\theta} = \frac{D}{1.22\lambda}$$

So, the resolving power can be increased by increasing diameter of objective lens or by decreasing the wavelength of light.

8. We can write power, $P = \frac{100}{f \text{ (in cm)}} \Rightarrow f = \frac{100}{P}$

$$\therefore \quad f_1 = \frac{100}{10} = 10 \text{ cm} \Rightarrow f_2 = \frac{100}{1} = 100 \text{ cm}$$

Length of telescope $= f_1 + f_2 = 110$ cm

9. Refer to text on pages 214 and 215 (Astronomical Telescope).

10. According to the question,

Given, $f_o = 140$ cm, $f_e = 5$ cm

(i) Angular magnification, $M = \frac{-f_o}{f_e} = \frac{-140}{5} = -28$

(ii) Distance between the lenses $L = f_o + f_e = 140 + 5 = 145\,\text{cm}$

11. Given, $f_o = 80\,\text{cm}, f_e = 4\,\text{cm}$

(i) Length of the telescope $= f_o + f_e = 84\,\text{cm}$

(ii) Magnifying power, $M = \frac{-f_o}{f_e} = \frac{-80}{4} = -20$

12. (i) The resolving power of a telescope is defined as the reciprocal of the smallest angular separation between two distant objects whose images are seen separately.

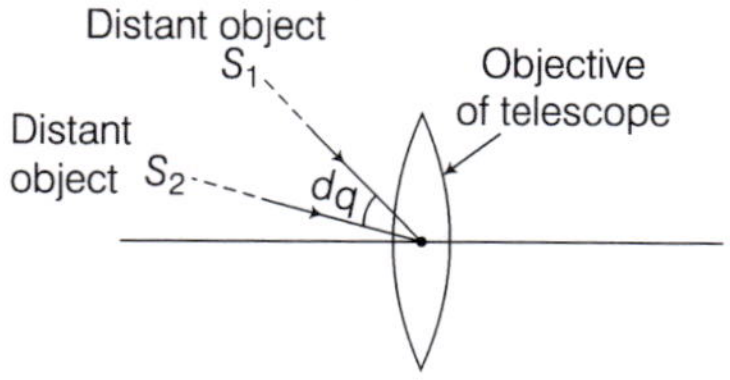

$$\text{Resolving power} = \frac{1}{d\theta} = \frac{D}{1.22\,\lambda} \quad \text{(aperture)}$$

Resolving power depends on (a) wavelength λ and (b) diameter (aperture) of the objective D.

(ii) to increase the resolving power of an astronomical telescope, we need to increase the numerical aperture of the objective.

13. Refer to the text on page 214 (Refracting Astronomical Telescope).

14. Refer to the text on page 214 (Refracting Astronomical Telescope).

15. Let f_o and f_e are the focal lengths of the objective and the eyepiece respectively. When final image is at infinity,

Given, $L = f_o + f_e = 80\,\text{cm}$, $M = 15$, $M = f_o / f_e$

$\Rightarrow \quad f_o = 15 f_e, L = f_o + f_e \quad$ ...(i)

Putting the values of f_o and L in Eq. (i), we get

$$80 = 15 f_e + f_e, \quad f_e = 5\,\text{cm}$$

So, $\quad f_o = 15 f_e = 15 \times 5, \quad f_o = 75\,\text{cm}$

16. (i) Refer to the text on page 214 (Refracting Astronomical Telescope).

(ii) In reflecting telescope, image formed is brighter whereas in refracting telescope, due to absorption and refraction by objective lens some loss of light (intensity of light is lost) occurs, so image is not so bright.

17. **Magnifying power of the optical instrument** The magnifying power or the angular magnification of an optical instrument is defined as the ratio of the angle subtended by the image at the eye to the angle subtended by the object at the unaided eye.

Magnifying power of the telescope

$$M = \frac{f_o}{f_e}\left(1 + \frac{f_e}{D}\right) = \frac{75}{5}\left(1 + \frac{5}{25}\right) = 18$$

18. (i) Refer to the text on page 214 (Refracting Astronomical Telescope).

(ii) Magnifying power of an astronomical telescope in normal adjustment can be defined as the ratio of the angle subtended at the eye by the final image to the angle subtended at the eye by the object directly, when the final image and the object both lie at infinite distance from the eye.

$$M = -\frac{f_o}{f_e} \text{ and } L = f_o + f_e$$

L = length of the telescope

19. (i) One factor on which the focal length of a lens depends is its refractive index. The higher the refractive index, the shorter the focal length for a given curvature of the lens surfaces.

(ii) The convex lens can behave like a diverging lens when it immersed in a medium with a refractive index greater than that of lens material. This can cause the light rays passing through the lens to bend away from the optical axis, resulting in a virtual image that is smaller than the object.

(iii) A camera typically uses a converging lens, such as a double-convex or plano-convex lens, to focus light from the scene onto the image sensor or flim. This allows the camera to form a clear and sharp image of the scene being photographed.

(iv) Refer to text on page 208 (Compound Microscope).

(v) Refer to text on pages 214 and 215 Reflecting Telescope and Refracting Telescope).

20. (i) Electron microscopes (move specifically scanning electrode and transmitting electron microscope) are used to study detailed structure of a virus.

(ii) Magnification is the ability of an instrument to form an enlarged image of an object.

(iii) Hubble telescope (space telescopes) have the advantage of being above the blurring effects of the earth's atmosphere. In addition, there are many wavelengths from the electromagnetic spectrum do not reach earth because they are absorbed or reflected by the earth's atmosphere.

(iv) (a) Magnifying power $(m) = \frac{-f_o}{f_e} = -\frac{200\text{ cm}}{4\text{ cm}} = -50$

(b) Length of telescope $(L) = f_o + f_e = 200 + 4 = 204\,\text{cm}$

CHAPTER TEST

01 Mark Questions (MCQs)

1 The image formed by an objective of a compound microscope is

(a) virtual and diminished (b) real and diminished
(c) real and enlarged (d) virtual and enlarged

2 In order to increase the angular magnification of a simple microscope, one should increase

(a) the object size
(b) the aperture of the lens
(c) the focal length of the lens
(d) the power of the lens

3 F_1 and F_2 are focal lengths of objective and eyepiece respectively, of the telescope. The angular magnification of the given telescope is equal to

(a) $\frac{F_1}{F_2}$ (b) $\frac{F_2}{F_1}$
(c) $\frac{F_1F_2}{F_1+F_2}$ (d) $\frac{F_1+F_2}{F_1F_2}$

4 An astronomical telescope has an angular magnification of magnitude 5 for distant objects. The separation between the objective and the eyepiece is 36 cm and the final image is formed at infinity. The focal length f_o of the objective and the focal length f_e of the eyepiece are

(a) $f_o = 45$ cm and $f_e = -9$ cm
(b) $f_o = -7.2$ cm and $f_e = 5$ cm
(c) $f_o = 50$ cm and $f_e = 10$ cm
(d) $f_o = 30$ cm and $f_e = 6$ cm

01 Mark Questions (VSA)

5 What is simple microscope?

6 What is meant by a compound microscope?

7 What is telescope?

8 Define the angular magnification of an optical instrument.

02 Marks Questions

9 Two convex lenses of same focal length but of aperture A_1 and A_2 ($A_2 < A_1$), are used as the objective lenses in two astronomical telescopes having identical eyepieces. What is the ratio of their resolving power? Which telescope will you prefer and why? Give reason.

10 A convex lens of focal length 25 cm is placed coaxially in contact with a concave lens of focal length 20 cm. Determine the power of the combination. Will the system be converging or diverging in nature?

03 Marks Questions

11 Two convex lenses of focal lengths 20 cm and 1 cm constitute a telescope. The telescope is focused on a point which is 1 m away from the objective. Calculate the magnification produced and the length of the tube, if the final image is formed at a distance 25 cm from the eyepiece.

12 The objective of an astronomical telescope has a diameter of 150 mm and a focal length of 4.00 m. The eyepiece has a focal length of 25.00 mm. Calculate the magnifying and resolving power of telescope ($\lambda = 6000$Å for yellow colour).

05 Marks Questions

13 How is the working of a telescope different from that of a microscope? The focal lengths of the objective and eyepiece of a microscope are 1.25 cm and 5 cm, respectively. Find the position of the object relative to the objective in order to obtain an angular magnification of 30 in normal adjustment.

14 Explain simple microscope on the basis of the following points.

(i) Ray diagram for the formation of image
(ii) Expression for magnifying power when the final image is formed at the least distance of distinct vision and at infinity

Answers

1. (c) **2.** (d) **3.** (a) **4.** (d)

9. $\frac{A_1}{A_2}$, A_1 **10.** – 1 D (diverging)

11. – 20.8 21 cm **12.** 2.05×10^5

13. 2.5 cm

15

Huygens' Principle

TREND ANALYSIS 4 YEARS

Average No. of Questions Across all Sets

	Types of Questions	2024	2023	2020	2019
Huygens' Principle	1 Mark	1	2	1	–
	2 Marks	–	–	–	–
	3 Marks	1	1	–	1
	5 Marks	–	1	–	–

Wave Optics

It is the branch of optics which deals with the studies of diffraction, interference polarisation, etc i.e. wave nature of light for which the ray approximation of geometrical optics is not valid.

In wave optics, we study the properties based on wave nature of light.

Wavefront

The locus of all those particles which are vibrating in the same phase at any instant is called wavefront. Thus, wavefront is a surface having particles vibrating in same phase at any instant at every point on the surface.

Types of Wavefront

Depending on the shape of source of light, wavefronts can be classified as follows:

(*i*) **Spherical Wavefront** When the source of light is a point source, the wavefront is a sphere with source at the centre of the sphere.

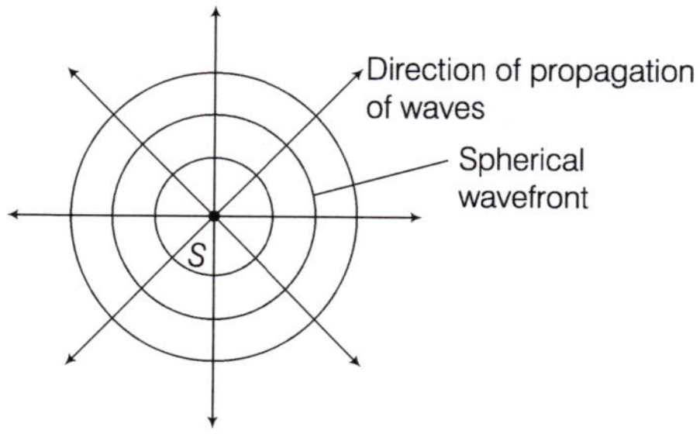

(*ii*) **Cylindrical Wavefront** When the source of light is linear as given in the figure below, all the points equidistant from the source lie on a cylindrical surface. Therefore, the wavefront is cylindrical.

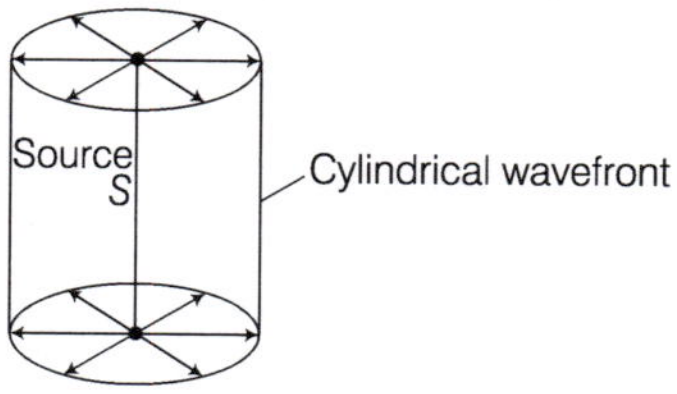

(iii) **Plane Wavefront** When the point source or linear source of light is at a very large distance, a small portion of spherical or cylindrical wavefront appears to be plane. Such a wavefront is called a plane wavefront.

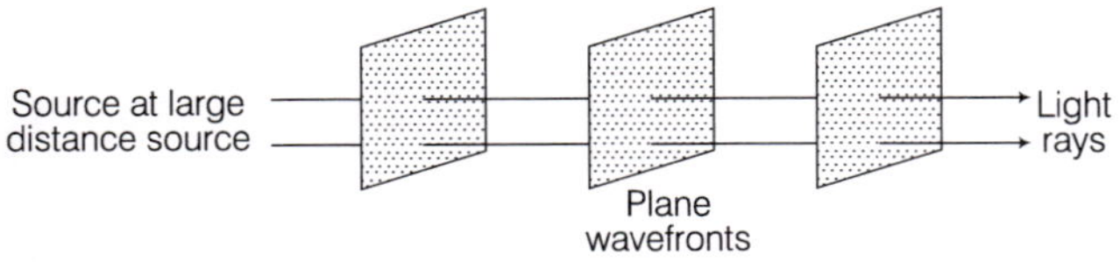

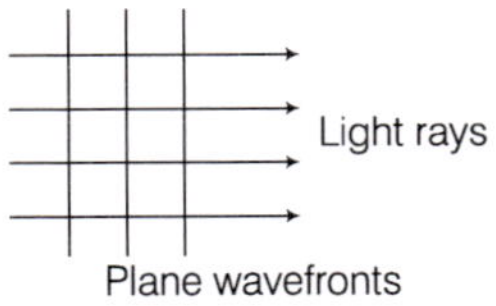

Huygens' Principle

Huygens' principle is essentially a geometrical construction which gives the shape of the wavefront at any time and allows us to determine the shape of the wavefront at a later time.

According to Huygens' principle,

(*i*) Each point on the given wavefront (called primary wavefront) is the source of a secondary disturbance (called secondary wavelets) and the wavelets emanating from these points spread out in all directions with the same speed as that of the wave.

(*ii*) A surface touching these secondary wavelets, tangentially in the forward direction at any instant gives the new wavefront at that instant. This is called **secondary wavefront**.

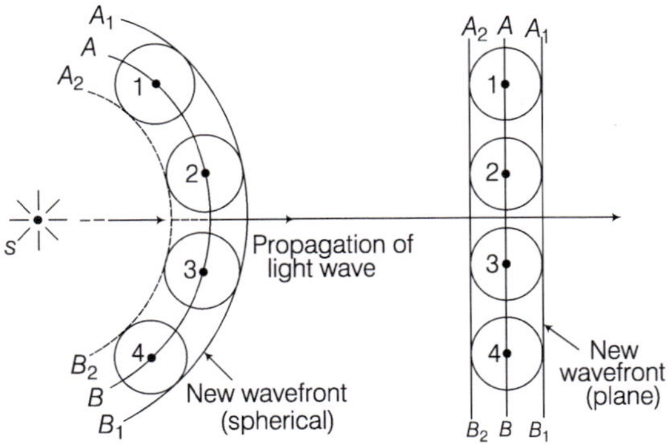

(i) (ii)

The laws of reflection and refraction can be verified by using Huygens' wave theory.

Huygens' wave theory successfully explains the phenomenon of interference, diffraction and polarisation.

As frequency ν is the characteristic of the source, therefore $\nu = \frac{1}{T}$ remains the same as light travels from one medium to another.

Wavelength of the light in a particular medium is inversely proportional to the refractive index μ of the medium.

i.e.,
$$\lambda' = \frac{\lambda}{\mu}$$

where, λ = wavelength of light in free space or air.

Hence, the speed of light wave in a medium of refractive index μ is

$$\boxed{c' = \frac{c}{\mu}}$$

where, c is the speed of light in vacuum (3×10^8 m/s).

Laws of Reflection at a Plane Surface (Huygens' Principle)

Let 1, 2 and 3 be the incident rays and $1', 2'$ and $3'$ be the corresponding reflected rays in the given figure.

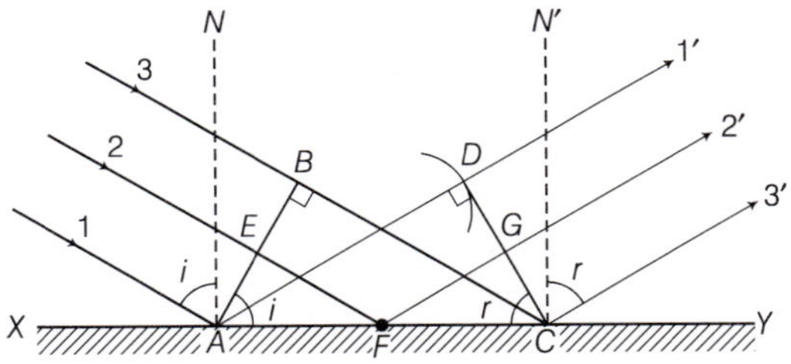

If c is the speed of light, t is the time taken by light to go from B to C or A to D or E to G through F, then

$$t = \frac{EF}{c} + \frac{FG}{c} \qquad \text{... (i)}$$

In ΔAEF, $\sin i = \frac{EF}{AF}$

$\Rightarrow$ $EF = AF \sin i$

In ΔFGC, $\sin r = \frac{FG}{FC}$

$\Rightarrow$ $FG = FC \sin r$

Now, putting the values of EF and FG in Eq. (i), we get

or
$$t = \frac{AF \sin i}{c} + \frac{FC \sin r}{c}$$

or
$$t = \frac{AC \sin r + AF (\sin i - \sin r)}{c}$$

$[\because FC = AC - AF]$

So, t should not depend upon AF. This is possible only, if $\sin i - \sin r = 0$

i.e., $\sin i = \sin r$ or $\angle i = \angle r$

which is the first law of reflection.

Laws of Refraction at a Plane Surface (Based on Huygens' Principle)

Let 1, 2 and 3 be the incident rays and $1'$, $2'$ and $3'$ be the corresponding refracted rays.

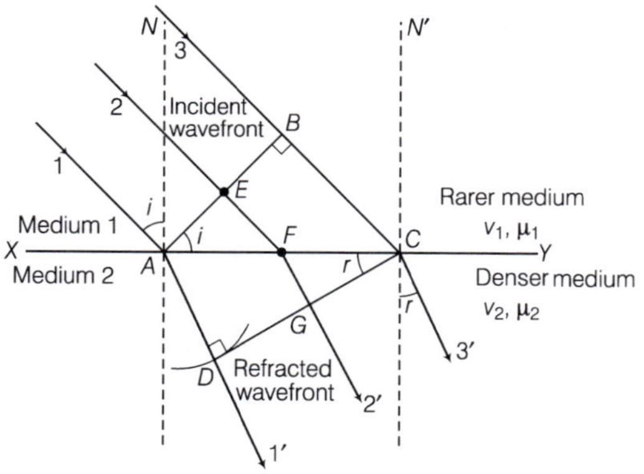

If v_1, v_2 are the speed of light in the two mediums and t is the time taken by light to go from B to C or A to D or E to G through F, then

$$t = \frac{EF}{v_1} + \frac{FG}{v_2} \quad \text{... (i)}$$

In ΔAFE, $\sin i = \frac{EF}{AF} \Rightarrow EF = AF \sin i$

In ΔFGC, $\sin r = \frac{FG}{FC} \Rightarrow FG = FC \sin r$

Now, putting the value of EF and FG in Eq. (i), we get

or $$t = \frac{AF \sin i}{v_1} + \frac{FC \sin r}{v_2}$$

or $$t = \frac{AC \sin r}{v_2} + AF\left(\frac{\sin i}{v_1} - \frac{\sin r}{v_2}\right) \quad [\because AC - AF = FC]$$

This is possible only, if

$$\frac{\sin i}{v_1} - \frac{\sin r}{v_2} = 0 \quad \text{or} \quad \frac{\sin i}{\sin r} = \frac{v_1}{v_2} = \mu \quad \text{(Refractive index)}$$

Now, if c represents the speed of light in vacuum, then $\mu_1 = \frac{c}{v_1}$ and $\mu_2 = \frac{c}{v_2}$ are known as the **refractive indices** of medium 1 and medium 2, respectively.

Then $$\mu_1 \sin i = \mu_2 \sin r$$

$\Rightarrow$ $$\mu = \frac{\sin i}{\sin r}$$

This is known as **Snell's law** of refraction.

Thus, this is the second law of refraction.

PYQs Previous Years Questions

1 Mark Questions

1. What type of wavefronts are associated with a point source of light? **ISC 2024**

2. What type of wavefronts are associated with a source at infinity? **ISC 2023**
   (a) Cylindrical wavefronts
   (b) Plane wavefronts
   (c) Spherical wavefronts
   (d) All types of wavefronts

3. Cylindrical wavefronts are produced by **ISC SQP 2023**
   (a) a point source of light
   (b) a line source of light
   (c) a source at infinity
   (d) all types of sources of light

4. What is the phase difference between any two points lying on the same wavefront? **ISC 2020**

5. What type of wavefront is generated from a line source of light? **ISC 2017, 08, 04**

6. Light of wavelength 4500 Å in vacuum enters into a glass block of refractive index 1.5. What is the wavelength of light in the glass block? **ISC 2005**

2 Marks Question

7. If d is the distance covered by a light wave in the air in t seconds and D is the distance covered in a medium of refractive index μ in the same time, then prove that $d = \mu D$. **ISC 2006**

3 Marks Questions

8. Using Huygens' wave theory, show that (for refraction of light)

$$\frac{\sin i}{\sin r} = \text{constant}$$

where, terms have their usual meanings. You must draw a neat and labelled diagram. **ISC 2024**

9. Derive Snell's law of refraction using Huygens' wave theory. **ISC SQP 2023, 22 Sem-II, 16**

10. Using Huygen's wave theory, prove the law of reflection of light. **ISC 2022, Sem-II, 19**

11. On the basis of Huygens' wave theory, show that when light is incident on a plane mirror obliquely, angle of reflection is equal to the angle of incidence. **ISC 2010, 2006**

4/5 Marks Questions

12. On the basis of Huygens' wave theory of light, show that the angle of reflection is equal to angle of incidence. You must draw a labelled diagram for this derivation. **ISC 2023, 15**

13. On the basis of Huygens' wave theory, prove Snell's law of refraction of light. Draw a neat and labelled diagram. [postulates of Huygens' wave theory not required.] **ISC 2012, 05, 02, 00**

Case Based Question
(For Complete Chapter)

14. **Direction** *Read the passage given below and answer the questions that follows.*

In 1678, Huygen's proposed the wave theory of light. According to Huygen's, light travels in the form of waves. These waves after emerging from the light-source travel in all directions with the velocity of light. Since, waves require a medium to travel, Huygen's imagined an all-pervading medium called 'Luminferous Ether'. It was assumed that this hypothetical medium is weightless and can penetrate through matter. It has all properties necessary for the propagation of light-waves. For example, light travels with a very high speed ($3 \times 10^8 \text{ ms}^{-1}$). Hence, it was assumed that the density of ether is very small and the elasticity is very large

(wave speed $= \sqrt{(\text{Electricity / density})}$). Light waves travel in such a hypothetical medium.

(*i*) Why does light appear to travel in straight lines in spite of its wave nature? **(1)**

(*ii*) Is Huygen's theory, light waves are longitudinal and do not require a material medium for their propagation? **(1)**

(*iii*) Which property of light conclusively support wave nature of light? **(1)**

(*iv*) What is the fault of Huygen's wave theory? **(1)**

(*v*) State any one postulate of Huygen's wave theory? **(1)**

Explanations

1. When the source of light is a point source, the wavefront is a sphere with source at the centre of the sphere.

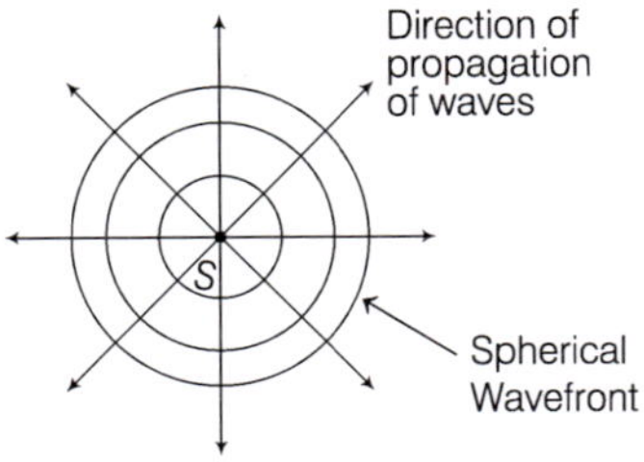

2. (b) 3. (b)

4. The phase difference between any two points lying on the same wavefront is zero.

5. A line source of light produces cylindrical wavelength.

6. Given, wavelength of light in vacuum, $\lambda_v = 4500$ Å and refractive index,

$$\mu = 1.5$$

$\because$ Refractive index, $\mu = \dfrac{\lambda_v}{\lambda_m}$

Thus, wavelength in the medium of refractive index (1.5).

$$\lambda_m = \frac{\lambda_v}{\mu}$$

$$= \frac{4500}{1.5} = 3000 \text{ Å}$$

7. We know that,

Refractive index of medium (μ)

$$= \frac{\text{Speed of light in air } (c)}{\text{Speed of light in medium } (v)}$$

Let c_1 be the velocity of light in the air, then time t taken by it to cover a distance d is

$$t = \frac{d}{c_1} \text{ or } c_1 = \frac{d}{t} \quad \text{...(i)}$$

If c_2 is the velocity of light in the medium and during the same time t, a light cover a distance D is

$$t = \frac{D}{c_2} \text{ or } c_2 = \frac{D}{t} \quad \text{...(ii)}$$

From Eqs. (i) and (ii), we get

$$\frac{c_1}{c_2} = \frac{d/t}{D/t}$$

$$\therefore \quad \mu = \frac{d}{t} \times \frac{t}{D} = \frac{d}{D} \Rightarrow d = \mu D \quad \left[\because \frac{c_1}{c_2} = \mu\right]$$

8. Laws of Refraction at a Plane Surface (Based on Huygens' Principle)

Let 1, 2 and 3 be the incident rays and 1′, 2′ and 3′ be the corresponding refracted rays.

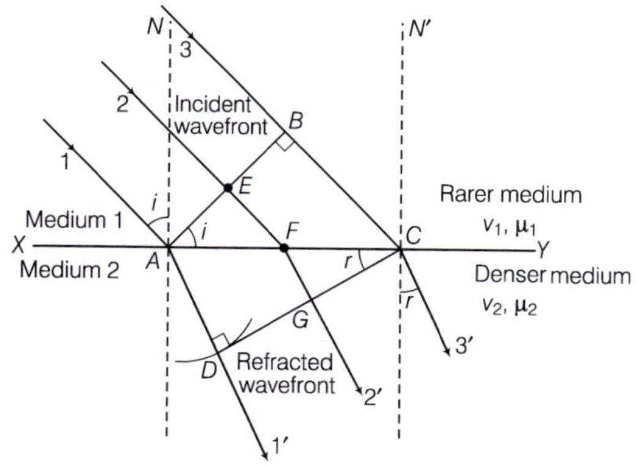

If v_1, v_2 are the speed of light in the two mediums and t is the time taken by light to go from B to C or A to D or E to G through F, then

$$t = \frac{EF}{v_1} + \frac{FG}{v_2} \quad \text{... (i)}$$

In ΔAFE, $\sin i = \frac{EF}{AF} \Rightarrow EF = AF \sin i$

In ΔFGC, $\sin r = \frac{FG}{FC} \Rightarrow FG = FC \sin r$

Now, putting the value of EF and FG in Eq. (i), we get

or $$t = \frac{AF \sin i}{v_1} + \frac{FC \sin r}{v_2}$$

or $$t = \frac{AC \sin r}{v_2} + AF\left(\frac{\sin i}{v_1} - \frac{\sin r}{v_2}\right)$$

$[\because AC - AF = FC]$

This is possible only, if

$$\frac{\sin i}{v_1} - \frac{\sin r}{v_2} = 0$$

or $$\frac{\sin i}{\sin r} = \frac{v_1}{v_2} = \mu \quad \text{(Refractive index)}$$

Now, if c represents the speed of light in vacuum, then $\mu_1 = \frac{c}{v_1}$ and $\mu_2 = \frac{c}{v_2}$ are known as the **refractive indices** of medium 1 and medium 2, respectively.

Then $\quad \mu_1 \sin i = \mu_2 \sin r \Rightarrow \mu = \frac{\sin i}{\sin r}$

This is known as **Snell's law** of refraction.

Thus, this is the second law of refraction.

9. Consider a plane wavefront AB incident on a plane surface XY, separating two media 1 and 2, as shown below.

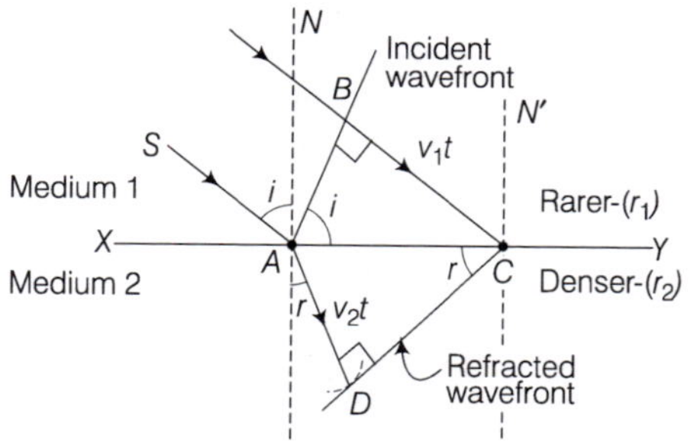

Let v_1 and v_2 be the speeds of light in two media such that $v_2 < v_1$. The wavefront first strikes at point A and then at the successive points towards C. According to Huygens' principle, from each point on AC, the secondary wavelets start growing in the second medium with speed v_2. Let the disturbance takes time t to travel from B to C, then $BC = v_1 t$. During the times the disturbance from B reaches the point C, the secondary wavelets from point A must have spread over a hemisphere of radius $AD = v_2 t$ in the second medium. The tangent plane CD drawn from point C over this hemisphere of radius $v_2 t$ will be the new refracted wavefront. Let the angles of incidence and refraction be i and r respectively from right ΔBAC, $\sin i = \frac{BC}{AC}$, From right ΔADC, we have,

$$\sin r = \frac{AD}{AC} \Rightarrow \frac{\sin i}{\sin r} = \frac{BC}{AD} = \frac{v_1 t}{v_2 t}$$

or $$\frac{\sin i}{\sin r} = \frac{v_1}{v_2} = {}^1\mu_2$$

This proves Snell's law of refraction.

10. Laws of reflection at a plane surface

Let 1, 2, 3 be the incident rays and 1′, 2′, 3′ be the corresponding reflected rays.

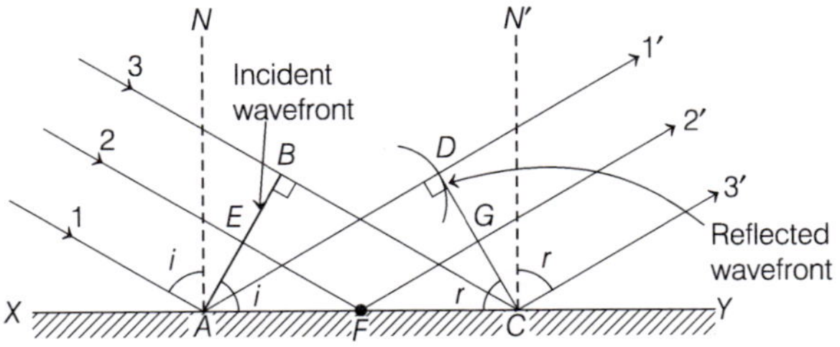

If c is the speed of the light, t is the time taken by light to go from B to C or A to D or E to G through F, then

$$t = \frac{EF}{c} + \frac{FG}{c}$$

In ΔAEF, $\sin i = \frac{EF}{AF}$

In ΔFGC, $\sin r = \frac{FG}{FC}$

or $$t = \frac{AF \sin i}{c} + \frac{FC \sin r}{c}$$

$\Rightarrow$ $$t = \frac{AC \sin r + AF(\sin i - \sin r)}{c}$$

$[\because FC = AC - AF]$

For rays of light from different parts on the incident wavefront, the values of AF are different. But light from different points of the incident wavefront should take the same time to reach the corresponding points on the reflected wavefront.

So, t should not depend upon AF. This is possible only, if

$$\sin i - \sin r = 0$$

i.e. $\sin i = \sin r$ or $\angle i = \angle r$

which is the first law of reflection.

Further, the incident wavefront AB, the reflecting surface XY and the reflected wavefront CD are all perpendicular to the plane of the paper. Therefore, incident ray, normal to the mirror XY and reflected ray all lie in the plane of the paper. This proves the second law of reflection.

11. Refer to text on pages 221 and 222 (Laws of Reflection at a Plane Surface).

12. Let 1, 2, 3 be the incident rays and 1′, 2′, 3′ be the corresponding reflected rays.

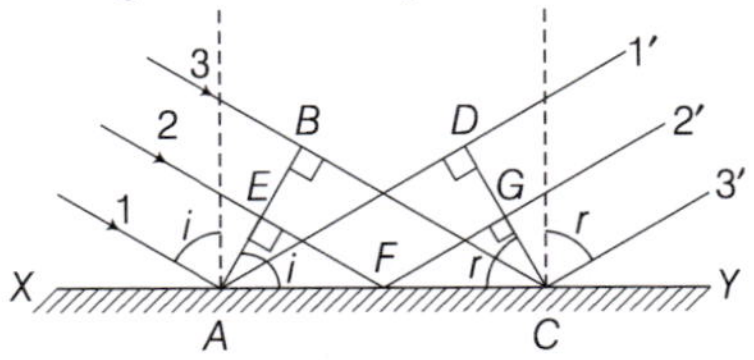

If c is the speed of the light, t is the time taken by light to go B to C or A to D or E to G through F, then

$$t = \frac{EF}{c} = \frac{FG}{c}$$

In ΔAEF, $\sin i = \frac{EF}{AF}$

In ΔFGC, $\sin r = \frac{FG}{FC}$

or $$t = \frac{AF \sin i}{c} + \frac{FC \sin r}{c}$$

$$\Rightarrow t = \frac{AC \sin r + AF(\sin i - \sin r)}{c} \quad [\because FC = AC - AF]$$

For the rays of light from different parts on the incident wavefront, the values of AF are different. But light from different points of the incident wavefront should take the same time to reach the corresponding points on the reflected wavefront. So, t should not depend upon AF. This is possible only if

$$\sin i - \sin r = 0$$

i.e. $\sin i = \sin r$ or $\angle i = \angle r$

which is the first law of reflection.

13. Refer to text on page 222 (Laws of Refraction of Light).

14. (i) Light appears to travel in straight lines in spite of its wave nature because of very small wavelength of light.

(ii) In Huygen's theory, light waves are longitudinal and require a material medium for their propagation. That's why Huygen's assumed the existence of all-pervading hypothetical medium, called ether.

(iii) Interference of light is the property which supports the wave nature of light.

(iv) Huygen's principle failed to explain the photoelectric effect.

(v) The new position of the wavefront at any instant is envelope of the secondary wavelets at that instant.

CHAPTER TEST

01 Mark Questions (MCQs)

1 Which of the following does not support the wave nature of light?
(a) Interference
(b) Diffraction
(c) Polarisation
(d) Photoelectric effect

2 Which of the following properties of light conclusively support wave nature of light?
(a) Light obeys laws of reflection
(b) Light shows interference
(c) Light shows photoelectric effect
(d) Speed of light in water is greater than that in vacuum

3 A plane wavefront is generated by
(a) point source (b) line source
(c) extended source (d) distant source

4 Two points are situated at the same distance from a light source but in opposite directions. The phase difference between the light waves from the two points will be
(a) zero (b) $\pi / 2$
(c) π (d) None of these

01 Mark Questions (VSA)

5 What type of wavefront will emerge from a
(i) point source?
(ii) distant light source?

6 Draw the wavefront coming out from a convex lens when a point source of light is placed at its focus.

7 Sketch the shape of wavefront emerging from a point source of light and also mark the rays.

02 Marks Questions

8 Define wavefront. How is it related to the direction of the corresponding rays?

9 Define the following terms
(i) Cylinderical wavefront
(ii) Plane wavefront

03 Marks Questions

10 Use Huygen's principle to verify the laws of refraction.

11 How is a wavefront defined? Using Huygen's construction, draw a figure showing the propagation of a plane wave refracting at a plane surface separating two media. Hence, verify Snell's law of refraction.

12 Define a wavefront. Use Huygen's geometrical construction to show the propagation of plane wavefront from a rarer medium (i) to a denser medium (ii) undergoing refraction, hence derive Snell's law of refraction.

05 Marks Questions

12 (i) A plane wavefront approaches a plane surface separating two media. If medium one is optically denser and medium two is optically rarer, using. Huygen's principle, explain and show how a refracted wavefront is constructed.
(ii) When a light wave travels from a rarer to a denser medium, the speed decreases. Does it imply reduction in its energy? Explain.

14 (i) Use Huygen's geometrical construction to show the behaviour of a plane wavefront,
(a) passing through a biconvex lens
(b) reflected by a concave mirror
(ii) When monochromatic light is incident on a surface separating two media, why does the refracted light have the same frequency as that of the incident light?

Answers

1. (d) **2.** (b) **3.** (d) **4.** (a)

16

Interference of Light

TREND ANALYSIS 4 YEARS

Average No. of Questions Across all Sets

	Types of Questions	2024	2023	2020	2019
Interference of Light	1 Mark	–	2	–	1
	2 Marks	–	–	–	–
	3 Marks	1	1	1	–
	5 Marks	–	–	–	1

Phase of Wave Motion

During the propagation of wave each particle copies the motion of another particle at its left with a time delay of x/v, where x is the separation between the two particles.

For the particles P and W, shown in figure, the separation is $\Delta x = vT$ and the particle W copies the motion of P after a time delay of $\Delta x/v = T$.

Hence, the particles P and W are vibrating in phase.

Their displacements are identical and their velocities are identical at any instant. Same phase is true for any pair of pasrticles separated by a distance vT. This separation is called the **wavelength** of the wave and is denoted by the Greek letter λ.

Thus, $\lambda = vT$.

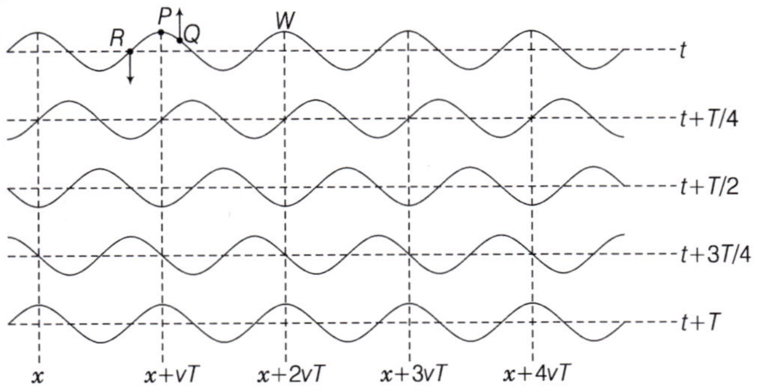

Superposition Principle

According to superposition principle, at a particular point in the medium, the resultant displacement y produced by a number of waves is the vector sum of the displacements produced by each of the waves $(\mathbf{y}_1, \mathbf{y}_2, \ldots)$.

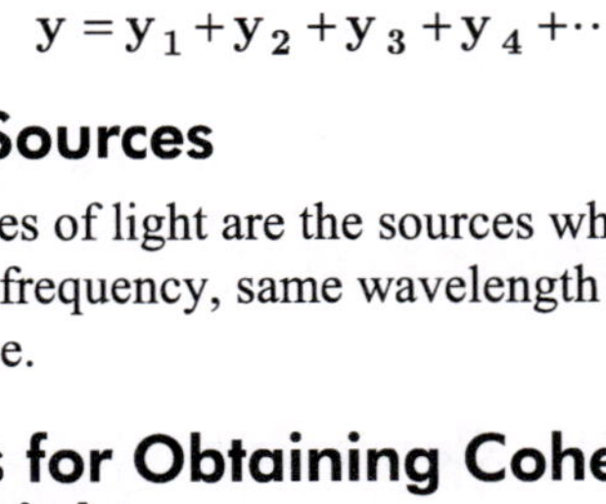

i.e. $$\mathbf{y} = \mathbf{y}_1 + \mathbf{y}_2 + \mathbf{y}_3 + \mathbf{y}_4 + \cdots$$

Coherent Sources

Coherent sources of light are the sources which emit light waves of same frequency, same wavelength and have zero phase difference.

Conditions for Obtaining Coherent Source of Light

(*i*) Coherent sources of light should be obtained from a single source by some device.

Two coherent sources can be obtained by

(a) the source and its virtual image.

(b) the two virtual images of the same source.

(c) two real images of the same source.

(*ii*) The two sources should give monochromatic light.

(*iii*) The path difference between light waves from two sources should be small.

Coherent source of light can also be obtained by deriving two sources from a primary (or initial) source by

(a) division of wavefront

(b) division of amplitude

Incoherent Sources

Two such sources of light, which do not emit light waves with a constant phase difference are called incoherent sources. The superposition of light waves from two incoherent sources does not produces interference. The total intensity at any point is simply the sum of time average intensities of the two sources.

The phase difference ϕ between light waves at a given time and at a given position is the sum of

(*i*) the initial phase difference of two sources A and B.

(*ii*) the phase difference on account of difference in paths.

The later does not change with time (for a given point P).

Hence, initial phase difference between two sources must be constant.

Conditions for Sustained Interference

(*i*) The two sources of light must be coherent.

(*ii*) The amplitude of electric field vector of interfering wave should be equal to have greater contrast.

Interference of Light Waves

The interference of light is the phenomenon of redistribution of light energy in a medium on account of superposition of light waves from two coherent sources.

At the point, where the resultant intensity of light is maximum, the interference is said to be **constructive**. At the point, where the resultant intensity of light is minimum, the interference is said to be **destructive**.

Conditions for Constructive Interference

Phase difference $= 2n\pi$, where $n = 0, 1, 2, 3, \ldots$

Path difference $= n\lambda$, where $n = 0, 1, 2, 3, \ldots$

Conditions for Destructive Interference

Phase difference $= (2n-1)\pi$, where $n = 1, 2, 3, \ldots$

Path difference $= (2n-1)\dfrac{\lambda}{2}$, where $n = 1, 2, 3, \ldots$

Young's Double Slit Experiment

Let two coherent sources of light S_1 and S_2 (narrow slits) be derived from a source S.

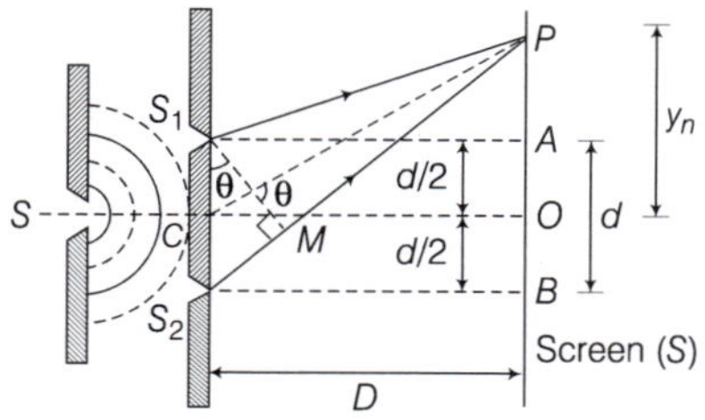

$$\text{Path difference} = S_2P - S_1P = d\left(\frac{y_n}{D}\right)$$

A series of dark or bright strips are observed on the screen is called **fringe**.

The bright fringe formed at middle point (O) on the screen is called **central bright fringe**.

The separation of nth order of bright fringe from central fringe is given by

$$y_n = \frac{n\lambda D}{d}, \text{ where } n = 0, 1, 2, 3, \ldots$$

The separation of nth order of dark fringe from central fringe is given by

$$y_n = (2n-1)\frac{D\lambda}{2d}, \text{ where } n = 1, 2, 3, \ldots$$

Angular position of nth order

The angular position of nth order of bright and dark fringes are given as below

(a) Bright fringe $= \dfrac{y_n}{D} = \dfrac{n\lambda}{d}$

(b) Dark fringe $= \dfrac{y_n}{D} = (2n-1)\dfrac{\lambda}{d}$, where $n = 1, 2, 3, \ldots$

Fringe Width

It is the separation between two consecutive bright fringes or dark fringes.

The fringe width of bright and dark fringes is given by

$$\beta = \frac{D\lambda}{d}$$

and angular fringe width is given by $$\theta = \frac{\beta}{D} = \frac{\lambda}{d}$$

NOTE A coloured fringe pattern is obtained with central white fringe when monochromatic light is replaced by white light (having a range of wavelengths).

Intensity Distribution among the Young's Double Slit Fringes

In Young's double-slit interference pattern, among all fringes, each fringe is of equal widths. All the bright fringes are equal intensities (i.e. $I_{max} = 4Ka^2$ = constant) while all the dark fringes are totally dark (zero intensity).

The distribution of intensity in Young's double-slit experiment is shown below.

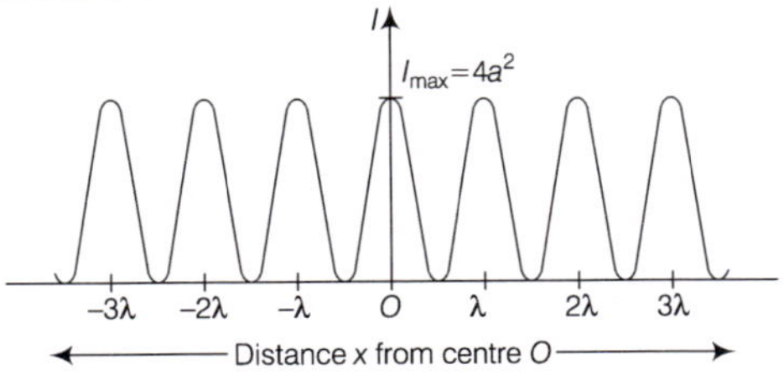

Fresnel Biprism

The figure shows a schematic diagram of a Fresnel biprism and interference of light using it. The biprism is constructed using two prisms. The angle of each prism is $\alpha \approx \frac{1}{2}^\circ$.

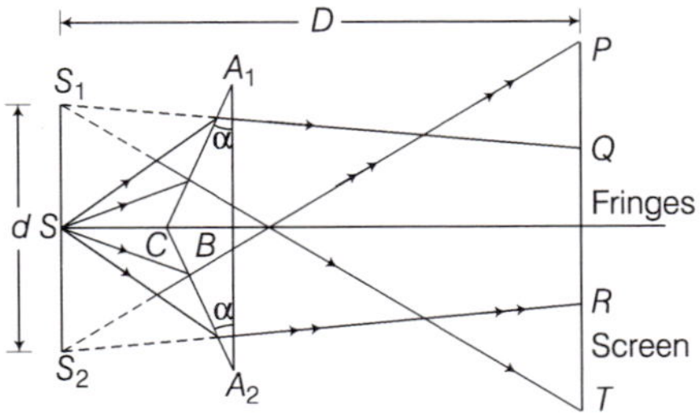

The fringe width (β) obtained on the screen is given by

$$\beta = \frac{D}{d}\lambda$$

where, D = distance of the screen

d = separation between S_1 and S_2 and

λ = wavelength of light used.

PYQs Previous Years Questions

1 Mark Questions

1. Give an example of coherent sources of light. **ISC SQP 2023**
2. In Young's double slit experiment, what is the path difference between the two light waves forming 5th bright fringe on the screen? **ISC SQP 2023**
3. Define coherent sources of light. **ISC 2022 Sem-II, 18, 14**
4. If in Young's double slit interference experiment, the distance between the two slits is made three times, keeping all other conditions same, then the fringe width becomes **ISC 2022 Sem-II**
   (a) one third (b) one ninth
   (c) nine times (d) three times
5. In Young's double slit experiment, what is the effect on fringe pattern, if the slits are brought closer to each other? **ISC 2022 Sem-II**
   (a) Fringes disappear
   (b) Fringe width increases
   (c) Fringe width decreases
   (d) Fringe width remains unaltered
6. What should be the path difference between two waves reaching a point for obtaining constructive interference in Young's double slit experiment? **ISC 2019**
7. How is fringe width of an interference pattern in Young's double slit experiment affected if the two slits are brought closer to each other? **ISC 2017**
8. What is meant by coherent sources of light? **ISC 2014**
9. State one condition for obtaining sustained interference of light. **ISC 2014, 11**
10. How did Fresnel constructed a biprism in order to study interference of light? **ISC 2012**
11. Young's double slit experiment was performed with monochromatic light of blue colour. The experiment was then repeated, first with light of red colour and then with light of yellow colour. Which colour pattern will have maximum separation (i.e., fringe width)? **ISC 2010, 08, 06**

12. Can two sodium vapour lamps act as coherent sources? Explain in brief. **ISC 2009**

13. In Young's double slit experiment, if white light is used in place of monochromatic light, what changes are observed in the interference pattern? **ISC 2004**

14. Obtain the ratio of the interference fringe widths β_1 and β_2 obtained with monochromatic red light of $\lambda_1 = 660$ nm and ultraviolet light of $\lambda_2 = 330$ nm. **ISC 2003**

2 Marks Questions

15. (*i*) What is meant by constructive interference?

(*ii*) In Youngs double slit experiment, what should be the phase difference between the two overlapping waves to obtain 5th dark band/fringe on the screen? **ISC 2022 Sem-II**

16. In Young's double slit experiment, using monochromatic light of wavelength 600 nm, the interference pattern was obtained on a screen kept 1.5 m away from the plane of the two slits. Calculate the distance between the two slits, if fringe separation/fringe width was found to be 1.0 mm. **ISC 2012**

3 Marks Questions

17. In Young's double slit experiment, show that

$$\beta = \frac{\lambda D}{d}$$

where, the terms have their usual meanings. **ISC 2024**

18. (*i*) What is the essential condition for obtaining a sustained interference?

(*ii*) In Young's double slit experiment, the distance of the 4th bright fringe from the centre of the interference pattern is 1.5mm. The distance between the slits and the screen is 1.5m and the wavelength of light used is 500nm. Calculate the distance between the two slits. **ISC 2023**

19. Monochromatic light of wavelength 620 nm is meident on a part of slits which are separated by 1.5 mm. If the screen is kept 60 cm away from the plane of the two slits. **ISC 2022 Sem-II**

Calculate

(*i*) fringe separation i.e. fringe width and

(*ii*) distance of the 10th bright fringe from centre of the interference pattern.

20. In Young's double slit experiment, the screen is kept at a distance of 1.2 m from the plane of the slits. The two slits are separated by 5 mm and illuminated with monochromatic light having wavelength 600 nm. **2020**

Calculate

(*i*) fringe width, i.e. fringe separation of the interference pattern.

(*ii*) distance of 10th bright fringe from the centre of the pattern.

21. In Young's double slit experiment using monochromatic light of wavelength 600nm, 5th bright fringe is at a distance of 0.48 mm from the centre of the pattern. If the screen is at a distance of 80 cm from the plane of the two slits, calculate **ISC 2017**

(*i*) distance between the two slits.

(*ii*) fringe width, i.e. fringe separation.

KEY idea

To calculate the fringe width first calculate the distance between the slits, then calculate the fringe width by the formula ($\beta = D\lambda / d$).

22. Laser light of wavelength 630 nm is incident on a pair of slits which are separated by 1.8 mm. If the screen is kept 80 cm away from the two slits, calculate

(*i*) fringe separation, i.e. fringe width.

(*ii*) distance of 10th bright fringe from the centre of interference pattern. **ISC 2015**

23. In Young's double slit experiment, using monochromatic light, the fringes are obtained on a screen placed at some distance from the slits. If the screen is moved by 5×10^{-2} m towards the slits, the change in the fringe width is 3×10^{-5} m. If the distance between the two slits is 10^{-3} m. Calculate the wavelength of the light used. **ISC 2014, 05, 04**

24. In Young's double slit experiment using monochromatic light L_1 of wavelength 700 nm, 10th bright fringe was obtained at a certain point P on a screen.

Which bright fringe will be obtained at the same point P, if monochromatic light of wavelength 500 nm is used in place of L_1. (No other alterations were made in the experimental set up.) **ISC 2011**

25. In Young's double slit experiment, what is meant by 'fringe width' or 'fringe separation'? State two ways of increasing the fringe width without changing the source of light. **ISC 2009, 01**

26. The distance between the first and the sixth bright fringes formed in Young's double slit experiment (measured by a spectrometer) is found to be 12.5 mm. The separation between the slits 0.12 mm and the distance of the screen from the slits is 60 cm. Calculate

(*i*) the fringe width.

(*ii*) the wavelength of the light used (in nm).

ISC 2007, 2000

4/5 Marks Questions

27. Draw a neat labelled diagram of Young's double slit experiment. Show that $\beta = \frac{\lambda D}{d}$, where the terms have their usual meaning (either for bright or dark fringe). **ISC 2019**

28. Draw a neat and labelled diagram of an experimental set-up of Young's double slit experiment to study the interference of light and show that $\beta = \frac{\lambda D}{d}$ where, the terms have their usual meaning. Show intensity variation in the interference. **ISC SQP 2018**

29. With the help of a labelled diagram, show that fringe separation β in Young's double slit experiment is given by $\beta = \frac{\lambda D}{d}$ where, the terms have their usual meaning. **ISC 2015, 13, 06**

Case Based Question
(For Complete Chapter)

30. **Direction** *Read the passage given below and answer the questions that follow.*

When two or more, waves travel simultaneously in a medium, the resultant displacement at each point of the medium at any instant is equal to the vector sum of the displacements produced by the two waves separately. This principle is called 'principle of superposition'. It holds for all types of waves, except for the waves of very large amplitude, such as laser waves.

The principle of superposition means that if a number of waves are travelling in a medium, then each one travels independently as if the other waves were not present at all; the the shape and other characteristics of any wave are not changed due to the presence of other waves. This is seen in practice. When we listen to an orchestra, we receive a complex sound due to the superposition of sound waves of different characteristics produced by different musical instruments. Still we can recognize separately the sounds of different instruments. Similarly, our radio antenna is open to the waves of different frequencies transmitted simultaneously by different radio stations. But when we tune the radio to a particular station, we receive the programmes of that station only as if the other stations were silent. Thus, the principle of superposition holds not only for mechanical waves but also for electromagnetic waves. Obviously, it holds for light waves also.

(*i*) What do you mean by the term principle of superposition? **(1)**

(*ii*) Which wave is not holds by the principle of superposition? **(1)**

(*iii*) When we listen to an orchestra, the sound waves of different instruments are produces with different characteristics but we feel pleasure why? **(1)**

(*iv*) The principle of superposition holds not only for ________ waves but also for ______ waves. **(1)**

Fill in the blanks to find the appropriate word from the passage.

(*v*) What is the use of principle of superposition in daily life? **(1)**

Explanations

1. Laser light is an example of coherent sources of light.
2. Path difference for the nth bright band,

$$\delta = 2n \cdot \lambda / 2 = n\lambda$$

$$n = 5$$

So, $\delta = 5\lambda$

3. Refer to text on page 227 (Coherent Sources)
4. (a) As, fringe width in YDSE is given by, $\beta = \dfrac{D\lambda}{d}$

Since, D and λ are constants, so $\beta \propto 1/d$

Hence, if distance between two slits (d) is made three times, then fringe width will become one-third.

5. (b) Fringe width, $\beta = \dfrac{D\lambda}{d}$

If two slits are brought closer to each other, d decreases, i.e. $\beta \propto 1/d$. So, fringe width β increases.

6. Path difference x between the interfering waves,

$$x = \frac{\lambda}{2\pi}\phi$$

For maximum intensity, $\phi = 2m\pi$

$$\Rightarrow \quad x = \frac{\lambda}{2\pi}(2m\pi) \Rightarrow x = m\lambda$$

7. According to Young's double slit experiment, fringe width $\beta = \dfrac{D\lambda}{d}$

where, D = distance between slit and screen
d = distance between two slits

If d decreases, i.e. distance between two slits decreases, β will increase.

8. Two sources of light having same frequency and constant phase difference with time are known as coherent sources of light.
9. The sources must be coherent for obtaining sustained interference of light.
10. Consider the diagram. Fresnel constructed the biprism by joining two thin biprisms A_1BC and A_2BC.

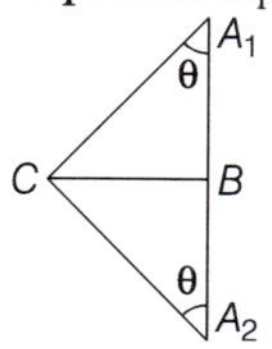

$$A_1 = A_2 \approx \frac{1}{2}^\circ$$

11. In YDSE, we know the fringe width,

$$\beta = \frac{D\lambda}{d}$$

where, D distance between source and screen and d is distance between sources (i.e. slits). As D and d are fixed,

i.e. $\beta \propto \lambda$

And we know that λ for red is more than λ for blue. So, β is more for red colour.

12. The light waves emitted by two sodium vapour lamps cannot be coherent.

The conditions of maxima and minima will change rapidly on the screen producing a uniform illumination.

13. The interference pattern due to different component colours of white light overlap (incoherently).
The central bright fringes for different colours are at the same position and therefore the central bright fringe is white. And offer few fringe no clear fringe pattern is seen.

14. We know that, fringe width, $\beta = \dfrac{\lambda D}{d}$

According to question, by taking the ratio of two different situation.

$$\Rightarrow \quad \frac{\beta_1}{\beta_2} = \frac{\lambda_1 D/d}{\lambda_2 D/d} = \frac{\lambda_1}{\lambda_2} = \frac{660}{330} = 2:1$$

15. (*i*) Refer to text on page 228. (Interference of light waves)
(*ii*) For dark band path difference

$$\Delta x = (2m-1)\frac{\lambda}{2}$$

Here $m = 5$

$$\Delta x = (2 \times 5 - 1)\frac{\lambda}{2} = 9\lambda / 2$$

$\therefore$ Phase difference,

$$\Delta\phi = 2\pi / \lambda \times \Delta x$$

$$= 2\pi/\lambda \times 9\lambda / 2 = 9\pi$$

16. Given, fringe width,

$$\beta = 1\,\text{mm} = 10^{-3}\,\text{m}$$

Wavelength, $\lambda = 600\,\text{nm}$, $D = 1.5\,\text{m}$, $d = ?$

We know that,

$$\beta = \frac{D}{d}\lambda \qquad \text{[from YDSE]}$$

Distance between two slits

$$d = \frac{D\lambda}{\beta} = \frac{(1.5)(600\times 10^{-9})}{10^{-3}} = 9\times 10^{-4}\ \text{m}$$

17. **Young's Double Slit Experiment** Suppose S_1 and S_2 are two fine slits, a small distance d apart. They are illuminated by a strong source S of monochromatic light of wavelength λ. MN is a screen at a distance D from the slits.

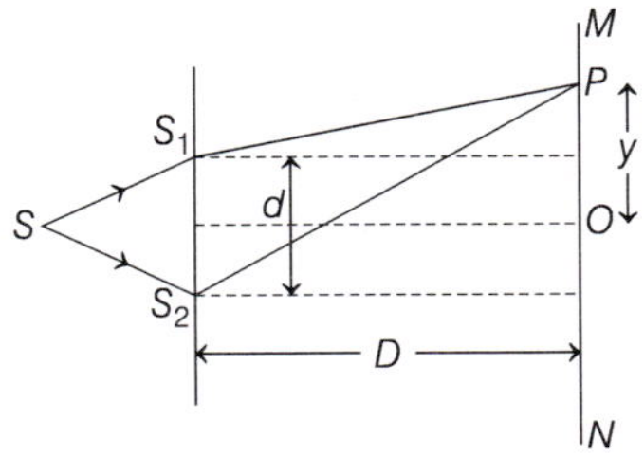

Consider a point P at a distance y from O, the centre of screen.

The path difference between two waves arriving at point P is equal to $S_2P - S_1P$.

Now, $S_2P - S_1P$

$$= \left[D^2 + \left(y + \frac{d}{2}\right)^2\right]^{1/2} - \left[D^2 + \left(y - \frac{d}{2}\right)^2\right]^{1/2}$$

$$= D\left[1 + \frac{(y + d/2)^2}{D^2}\right]^{1/2} - D\left[1 + \frac{(y - d/2)^2}{D^2}\right]^{1/2}$$

$$= D\left[1 + \frac{(y + d/2)^2}{2D^2}\right] - D\left[1 + \frac{(y - d/2)^2}{2D^2}\right]$$

$$= D\left[1 + \frac{(y + d/2)^2}{2D^2} - 1 - \frac{(y - d/2)^2}{2D^2}\right]$$

$$= \frac{D}{2D^2}\left[y^2 + \frac{d^2}{4} + \frac{2yd}{2} - y^2 - \frac{d^2}{4} + \frac{2yd}{2}\right]$$

$$= \frac{1}{2D}[2yd] = \frac{dy}{D}$$

$$\therefore \quad S_2P - S_1P \approx \frac{dy}{D}$$

For constructive interference (Bright fringes)

Path difference $= \dfrac{dy}{D} = n\lambda,$

where, $n = 0, 1, 2, 3, \ldots$

$$\therefore \qquad y = \frac{nD\lambda}{d}$$

Hence, for $n = 0$, $y_0 = 0$ at O (central bright fringe)

For $n = 1$, $\quad y_1 = \dfrac{D\lambda}{d}$ (for 1st bright fringe)

For $n = 2$, $\quad y_2 = \dfrac{2D\lambda}{d}$ (for 2nd bright fringe)

For $n = n$, $\quad y_n = \dfrac{nD\lambda}{d}$ (for nth bright fringe)

The separation between two consecutive bright fringes is equal to fringe width given as

$$\beta = y_n - y_{n-1} = \frac{nD\lambda}{d} - \frac{(n-1)D\lambda}{d} = \frac{D\lambda}{d}$$

> **Concept Enhancer** All the bright and dark fringes are of the same width, the angular width of a fringe is $\theta = \dfrac{\beta}{D} = \dfrac{D\lambda/d}{D} = \dfrac{\lambda}{d}$

18. (*i*) Refer to text on page 228 (Conditions for Sustained Interference).

(*ii*) Distance between two slits is d.

Distance from the slits to the screen is 'D'.

Distance from the central bright fringe to the nth bright fringe is y_n.

The distance from the central bright fringe to the 4th bright fringe $= y_4 = 1.5\text{mm} = 0.0015$ m.

The distance between the slits can be

$$d = \frac{n\times\lambda\times D}{y_n} = \frac{4\times 500\times 10^{-7}\times 1.5}{0.0015}$$

$$= \frac{4\times 500\times 10^{-7}\times 1.5\times 10^4}{15}$$

$$= \frac{4\times 50\times 10^{-3}\times 15}{15}$$

$$= 200\times 10^{-3} = 2\times 10^{-1}$$

$$\therefore \qquad d = 0.2\ \text{m}$$

19. Given, wavelength of light, $\lambda = 620$ nm

$$= 620\times 10^{-9}\text{m}.$$

Distance between slits, $d = 1.5$ mm

$$= 1.5\times 10^{-3}\ \text{m}$$

Distance between slits and screen, $D = 60$ cm

$$= 60\times 10^{-2}\ \text{m}$$

(*i*) As in YDSE,

Fringe separation, $\beta = \frac{D\lambda}{d}$

$= \frac{60 \times 10^{-2} \times 620 \times 10^{-9}}{1.5 \times 10^{-3}}$

$= 24800 \times 10^{-8}$ m

$= 0.248$ mm

(*ii*) Distance of 10th bright fringe,

$y_n = \frac{nD\lambda}{d} = n\beta$

$\therefore \quad y_{10} = 10 \times 0.248$

$= 2.48$ mm

20. Given, wavelength of light, $\lambda = 600$ nm

$= 600 \times 10^{-9}$ m

D = distance between slits and screen = 1.2 m
and d = distance between two slits = 5 mm

$= 5 \times 10^{-3}$ m

(*i*) According to YDSE,

Fringe width, $\beta = \frac{D\lambda}{d} = \frac{1.2 \times 600 \times 10^{-9}}{5 \times 10^{-3}}$

$= 1.44 \times 10^{-4}$

$= 0.144$ mm

(*ii*) Position of 10th bright fringe,

$y_n = n\frac{\lambda D}{d} = n\beta$

$y_{10} = 10 \times 0.144 = 1.44$ mm

21. Given,

Wavelength, $\lambda = 600$ nm $= 600 \times 10^{-9}$m 5th bright fringe observed at distance, $x = 0.48$ mm

$= 0.48 \times 10^{-3}$m

Distance between screen and slits,

$D = 80$ cm $= 80 \times 10^{-2}$m.

(*i*) Distance between two slits, *n*th bright fringe is observed at, $X_n = \frac{nD\lambda}{d}$

$\Rightarrow 0.48 \times 10^{-3} = \frac{5 \times 80 \times 10^{-2} \times 6000 \times 10^{-9}}{d}$

$\Rightarrow d = \frac{5 \times 80 \times 10^{-2} \times 600 \times 10^{-9}}{0.48 \times 10^{-3}} = 5 \times 10^{-3}$m

(*ii*) Fringe width i.e. fringe separation

It is given by, $\beta = \frac{D\lambda}{d}$

$= \frac{80 \times 10^{-2} \times 600 \times 10^{-9}}{5 \times 10^{-3}} = 9.6 \times 10^{-5}$m

22. Given, $\lambda = 630$ nm $= 630 \times 10^{-9}$ m,

$d = 1.8$ mm $= 1.8 \times 10^{-3}$ m,

$D = 80$ cm $= 0.80$m

(*i*) Fringe width is given by $\beta = \frac{\lambda D}{d}$

$= \frac{630 \times 10^{-9} \times 0.80}{1.8 \times 10^{-3}} = 2.8 \times 10^{-4}$m

(*ii*) Distance of 10th bright fringe from the centre,

$x_n = \frac{n\lambda D}{d}$

Here, $n = 10$

$\therefore \quad x_{10} = \frac{10 \times 630 \times 10^{-9} \times 0.80}{1.8 \times 10^{-3}}$

$= 10 \times 2.8 \times 10^{-4} = 2.8 \times 10^{-3}$ m

Common Mistake To obtain the correct answer to the numerical problems, all quantities must be brought to SI system before substituting them in formula.

23. In YDSE, the fringe width depends upon the distance of the screen (D) and slit width (d).

In Young's double slit experiment, the fringe width is given by

$$\beta = \frac{D}{d}\lambda \quad \text{... (i)}$$

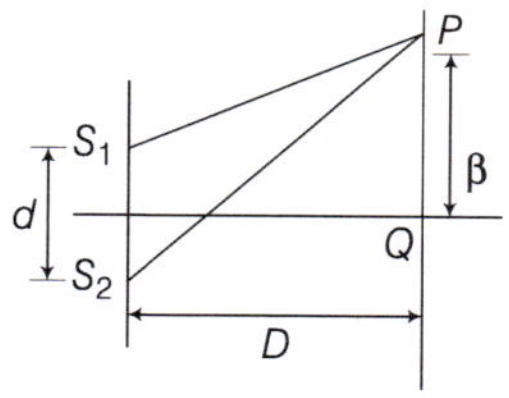

Let the new fringe width be β'.

We can write, $\beta' = \frac{D'}{d}\lambda$ ... (ii)

From Eqs. (i) and (ii), we get

$\beta - \beta' = \Delta\beta = \frac{\lambda}{d}[D - D']$

$= \frac{\lambda}{d}\Delta D$

Given, $\Delta\beta = 3 \times 10^{-5}$ m, $\Delta D = 5 \times 10^{-2}$ m

$d = 10^{-3}$ m, $\lambda = ?$

$\Rightarrow \quad \lambda$ = wavelength of light

$$\text{Now, } 3\times10^{-5}\text{ m} = \frac{\lambda}{10^{-3}\text{ m}}\times5\times10^{-2}\text{ m}$$

$$\lambda = \frac{3\times10^{-5}\times10^{-3}}{5\times10^{-2}} = 0.6\times10^{-6}$$

$$= 6\times10^{-7}\text{ m} \Rightarrow \lambda = 6000\text{ Å}$$

24. According to the question, for the same arrangement of YDSE, the ratio of d/D remains constant.

$$y_n = n\frac{D}{d}\lambda$$

Given, $\lambda_1 = 700$ nm, $n_1 = 10$th bright fringe,

$\lambda_2 = 500$ nm, $n_2 = ?$

We know that, $y = n\dfrac{D\lambda}{d}$

For the same point, x is constant and for same arrangement, then $\dfrac{d}{D}$ is constant.

$$\Rightarrow \quad n_1\lambda_1 = n_2\lambda_2$$

$$\Rightarrow \quad 10\times700 = n_2\times500$$

$$\text{or} \quad n_2 = \frac{10\times700}{500} = 14$$

25. **Fringe width** is the separation between two consecutive bright or dark fringes.

The fringe width, $\beta = \dfrac{\lambda D}{d}$

To increase fringe width (β) without changing source of light, we should

(*i*) increase D (distance between slit and screen)

(*ii*) decrease d (distance between two slits)

26. (*i*) We know that $y_n = n\dfrac{D\lambda}{d}$

where, $n = 0, 1, 2, \ldots$

Here, $y_6 - y_1 = 12.5$ mm

$$y_6 - y_1 = \frac{D\lambda}{d}(6-1) = 5\beta \qquad \left[\because \beta = \frac{D\lambda}{d}\right]$$

$$\text{So, fringe width } (\beta) = \frac{12.5}{5} = 2.5\text{ mm}$$

(*ii*) Since, $\beta = \dfrac{D\lambda}{d}$

Given, $D = 60\text{ cm} = 0.6$ m,

$d = 0.12\text{ mm} = 0.12\times10^{-3}$ m

$$\Rightarrow \quad 2.5\times10^{-3} = \frac{0.6\times\lambda}{0.12\times10^{-3}}$$

$$\lambda = 5\times10^{-7}\text{ m} = 5000\text{ Å}$$

27. **Young's Double Slit Experiment** Suppose S_1 and S_2 are two fine slits, a small distance d apart. They are illuminated by a strong source S of monochromatic light of wavelength λ. MN is a screen at a distance D from the slits.

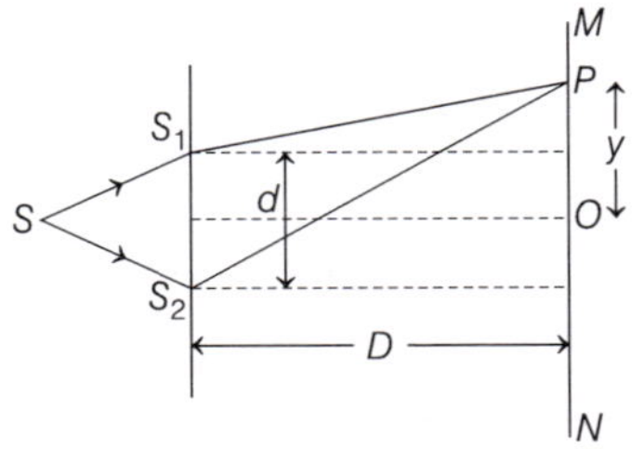

Consider a point P at a distance y from O, the centre of screen.

The path difference between two waves arriving at point P is equal to $S_2P - S_1P$.

Now, $S_2P - S_1P$

$$= \left[D^2 + \left(y+\frac{d}{2}\right)^2\right]^{1/2} - \left[D^2 + \left(y-\frac{d}{2}\right)^2\right]^{1/2}$$

$$= D\left[1 + \frac{(y+d/2)^2}{D^2}\right]^{1/2} - D\left[1 + \frac{(y-d/2)^2}{D^2}\right]^{1/2}$$

$$= D\left[1 + \frac{(y+d/2)^2}{2D^2}\right] - D\left[1 + \frac{(y-d/2)^2}{2D^2}\right]$$

$$= D\left[1 + \frac{(y+d/2)^2}{2D^2} - 1 - \frac{(y-d/2)^2}{2D^2}\right]$$

$$= \frac{D}{2D^2}\left[y^2 + \frac{d^2}{4} + \frac{2yd}{2} - y^2 - \frac{d^2}{4} + \frac{2yd}{2}\right]$$

$$= \frac{1}{2D}[2yd] = \frac{dy}{D}$$

$$\therefore \quad S_2P - S_1P \approx \frac{dy}{D}$$

For constructive interference (Bright fringes)

Path difference $= \dfrac{dy}{D} = n\lambda$,

where, $n = 0, 1, 2, 3, \ldots$

$$\therefore \quad y = \frac{nD\lambda}{d}$$

Hence, for $n = 0$, $y_0 = 0$ at O (central bright fringe)

For $n = 1$, $\quad y_1 = \dfrac{D\lambda}{d}$ (for 1st bright fringe)

For $n=2$, $y_2=\frac{2D\lambda}{d}$ (for 2nd bright fringe)

For $n=n$, $y_n=\frac{nD\lambda}{d}$ (for nth bright fringe)

The separation between two consecutive bright fringes is equal to fringe width given as

$$\beta = y_n - y_{n-1} = \frac{nD\lambda}{d} - \frac{(n-1)D\lambda}{d} = \frac{D\lambda}{d}$$

Concept Enhancer All the bright and dark fringes are of the same width, the angular width of a fringe is $\theta = \frac{\beta}{D} = \frac{D\lambda/d}{D} = \frac{\lambda}{d}$

28. Young's Double Slit Experiment

Suppose S_1 and S_2 are two fine slits, a small distance d apart. They are illuminated by a strong source S of monochromatic light of wavelength λ.

MN is a screen at a distance D from the slits.

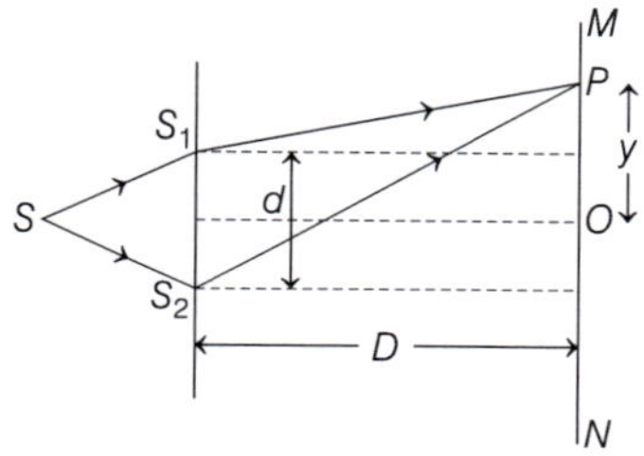

Consider a point P at a distance y from O, the centre of screen.

The path difference between two waves arriving at point P is equal to $S_2P - S_1P$.

Now,

$(S_2P)^2 - (S_1P)^2$

$$= \left[D^2 + \left(y+\frac{d}{2}\right)^2\right] - \left[D^2 + \left(y-\frac{d}{2}\right)^2\right]$$

$$= 2yd$$

Thus, $S_2p - S_1P = \frac{2yd}{S_2p \cdot S_1p}$

But $S_2p + S_1p \approx 2D$

$\therefore$ $S_2p - S_1p \approx \frac{dy}{D}$

For constructive interference (Bright fringes)

Path difference $= \frac{dy}{D} = n\lambda$,

where, $n = 0, 1, 2, 3, \ldots$

$\therefore$ $y = \frac{nD\lambda}{d}$ $[n = 0, 1, 2, 3, \ldots]$

Hence, for $n=0$, $y_0 = 0$ at O (central bright fringe)

The separation between two consecutive bright fringes

$$\beta = \frac{nD\lambda}{d} - \frac{(n-1)D\lambda}{d} = \frac{D\lambda}{d}$$

For destructive interference (Dark fringes)

Path difference $= \frac{dy}{D} - (2n-1)\frac{\lambda}{2}$

Or

$$y = (2n-1)\frac{D\lambda}{2d}, \text{ where } n = 1, 2, 3, \ldots$$

The separation between two consecutive dark fringes is

$$\beta = (2n-1)\frac{D\lambda}{2d} \{2(n-1)-1\}\frac{D\lambda}{2d} = \frac{D\lambda}{d}$$

The distance between two consecutive bright or dark fringes is called fringe width β.

$\therefore$ Fringe width, $\beta = \frac{D\lambda}{d}$

Intensity of the fringes,

$$I_R = I_1 + I_2 + 2\sqrt{I_1 I_2}\cos\phi$$

For a bright fringe, $\phi = 2n\pi$

and $\cos 2n\pi = 1$

So, $I_R = I_{max} = I_1 + I_2 + 2\sqrt{I_1 I_2} = 4I$

(as, $I_1 = I_2 = I$ in YDSE)

$\therefore$ Intensity of a bright fringe $= 4I$

and for a dark fringe, $\phi = (2n-1)\pi$

$\Rightarrow$ $\cos\phi = -1$

So, $I_R = I_{min} = I_1 + I_2 - 2\sqrt{I_1 I_2} = 0$

$\therefore$ Intensity of a dark fringe $= 0$

Distribution of Intensity

The distribution of intensity in Young's double slit experiment is shown below.

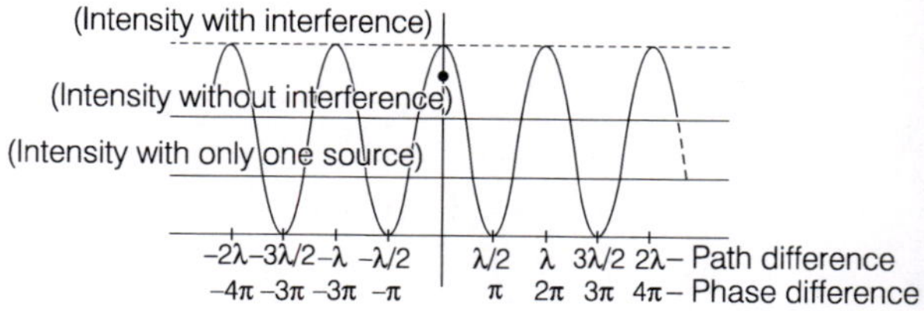

29. Refer to text on pages 228 and 229 (Young's Double Slit Experiment).

30. (*i*) When two or more waves travel simultaneously in a medium, the resultant displacement at each point of medium at any instant is equal to the vector sum of the displacements produced by the two waves separately.

(*ii*) The principle of superposition holds all the waves except the waves of very large amplitude, such as laser waves.

(*iii*) Due to the principle of superposition when we listen an orchestra, the sounds of different musical instruments are produces different characteristics of sound and by the help of this principle we feel that its a pleasure wave (sound).

(*iv*) The principle of superposition holds not only for mechanical waves but also for electromagnetic waves.

(*v*) The sunlight (white light) is the best example of the principle of superposition.

CHAPTER TEST

01 Mark Questions (MCQs)

1 Two waves of equal amplitudes and wavelengths but differing in phases are superimposed. The amplitude of the resultant wave is maximum when phase difference is

(a) zero (b) $\pi / 2$
(c) π (d) $3\pi / 2$

2 For constructive interference to take place between two monochromatic light waves of wavelength λ, the path difference should be

(a) $(2n - 1) \lambda / 4$ (b) $(2n - 1) \lambda / 2$
(c) $n \lambda$ (d) $(2n + 1)\lambda / 2$

where n is an integer.

3 Young's double slit arrangement is contained in a transparent chamber. If the chamber is evacuated, then

(a) fringes will disappear
(b) fringe width will slightly increase
(c) fringe width will slightly decrease
(d) there will be no effect

4 In Young's double slit experiment,sodium lamp is replaced by a blue light lamp. Then,

(a) the fringes will become brighter
(b) the fringes will become fainter
(c) the fringe width will increase
(d) the fringe width will decrease

01 Mark Questions (VSA)

5 What do you mean by principle of superposition?

6 What do you mean by interference of light?

7 Why are coherent sources required to create interference of light?

02 Marks Questions

8 In Young's double slit experiment, derive the condition for constructive interference.

9 Why are coherent sources are necessary for observing a sustained interference pattern? How are two coherent sources obtained in the Young's double slit experiment?

03 Marks Questions

10 What is the effect on the interference fringes to a Young's double slit experiment when

(i) the separation between the two slits is decreased?
(ii) the width of source slit is increased?

11 How does the angular separation of interference fringes change in Young's experiment, if the distance between the slit is increased?

12 In Young's double slit experiment, derive the condition for destructive interference at a point on the screen.

05 Marks Questions

13 (i) Write the conditions for obtaining coherent source of light. Also, for the incoherent source of light.

(ii) What do you mean by Fresnel Biprism? Explain with diagram.

14 In Young's double slit experiment, the two slits 0.15 mm apart are illuminated by monochromatic light of wavelength 450nm. the screen is 1.0m away from the slits.

(i) Find the distance of the second
 (a) bright fringe
 (b) dark central maximum.
(ii) How will the fringe pattern change, if the screen is moved away from the slits?

Answers

1. (a) **2.** (c) **3.** (b) **4.** (d)

14. (i) (a) 6 mm (b) 4.5 mm (ii) $B \propto D$

17

Diffraction of Light

TREND ANALYSIS 4 YEARS

Diffraction of Light

Average No. of Questions Across all Sets

Types of Questions	2024	2023	2020	2019
1 Mark	–	1	–	–
2 Marks	1	–	–	–
3 Marks	–	1	1	–
5 Marks	–	–	–	–

The phenomenon of bending of light around the corners and the spreading of light within the geometrical shadow of the opaque obstacles is called **diffraction of light.**

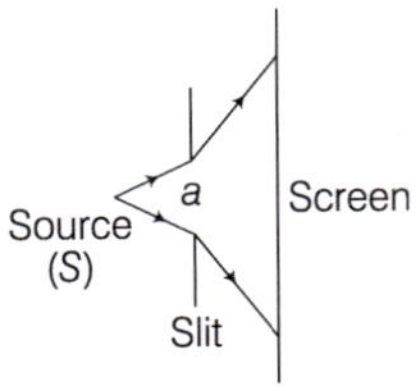

Fresnel diffraction

In this class of diffraction, the source of light and the screen are in general, at a finite distance from the diffracting aperture (slit) as shown below.

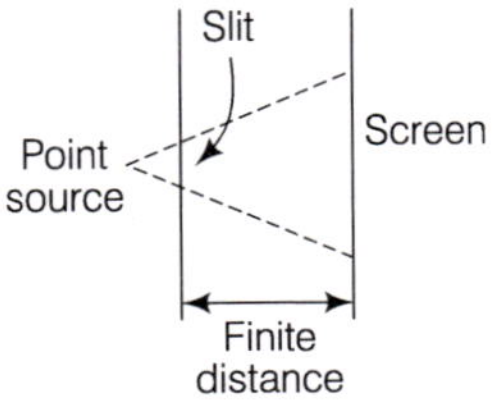

Fraunhofer diffraction

In this class of diffraction, the source and the screen are at infinite distance from the aperture (slit) this condition is achieved by placing the source on the focal plane of a convex lens and placing the screen on the focal plane of another convex lens as shown in the figure.

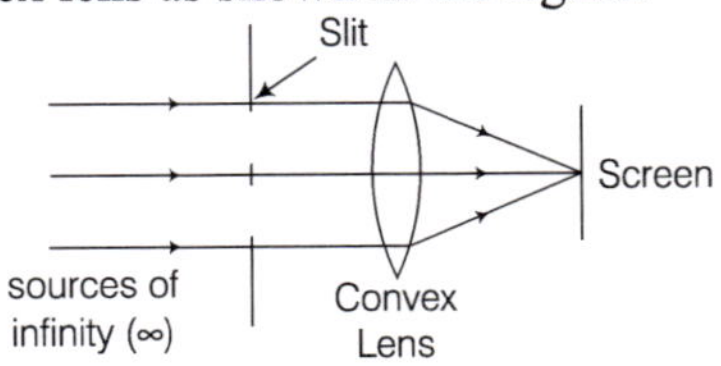

Here, we are mainly concerned with Fraunhofer diffraction.

Diffraction of Light at a Single Slit

A parallel beam of light with a plane wavefront WW' is made to fall on a single slit AB. As width of the slit $AB = d$ is of the order of wavelength of light, therefore, diffraction occurs on passing through the slit.

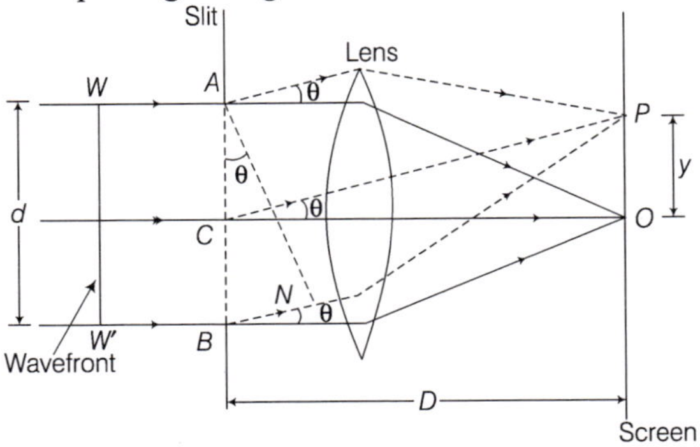

Consider a point P on the screen at which wavelets travelling in a direction, making an angle θ with CO, are brought to focus by the lens. The wavelets from points A and B will have a path difference equal to $BN = d\sin\theta$.

For the nth order of secondary minima, $d\sin\theta = n\lambda$

where, $n = 1, 2, 3, \ldots$, d = width of slit, λ = wavelength of light.

So, nth order of secondary maxima is obtained, when

$$d\sin\theta = (2n+1)\frac{\lambda}{2}$$

where, $n = 0, 1, 2, 3, \ldots$

- Angular separation for nth minima, $\theta_n = \dfrac{n\lambda}{d}$

  where, $n = 1, 2, 3, \ldots$
- Linear separation of nth secondary minima,

$$y_n = \frac{Dn\lambda}{d}$$

[D = distance between screen and slit]

- Angular position of nth order secondary maxima,

$$\theta_n = (2n+1)\frac{\lambda}{2d}$$

where, $n = 0, 1, 2, 3, \ldots$

Width of Central Maxima

The width of central maxima is the distance between the first secondary minima on either side of the central bright fringe.

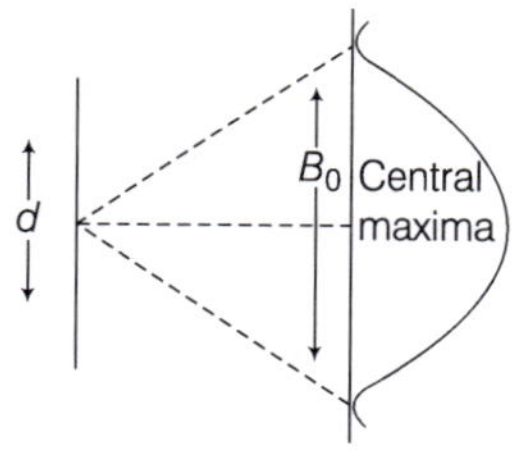

- Angular width of central maxima $= \dfrac{2\lambda}{d}$
- Linear width of central maxima, $\beta_0 = \dfrac{2D\lambda}{d}$
- Angular width of secondary maxima or minima $= \dfrac{\lambda}{d}$
- Linear width of secondary maxima or minima $= \dfrac{D\lambda}{d}$

Diffraction Pattern at a Single Slit due to the Monochromatic Light

Light and White Light

When the source of light is monochromatic, the diffraction pattern consists of alternate bright and dark bands of unequal widths. As **bandwidth ∝ wavelength** λ, therefore, red band with higher wavelength is wider than the violet band.

Distribution of Intensity

Intensity of central maxima is maximum and intensity of the secondary maxima decreases with the increase of their order. The ratio intensities of the secondary maxima with to the intensity of a central maximum are given by

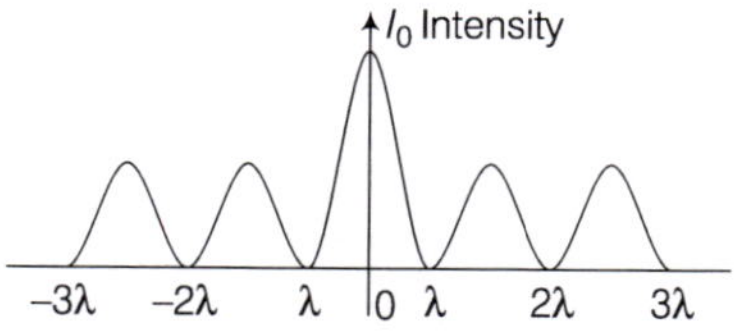

$$1 : \frac{1}{21} : \frac{1}{61} : \frac{1}{121}$$

PYQs Previous Years Questions

1 Mark Questions

1. In a single slit Fraunhofer diffraction experiment, how does the angular width of central maximum change when the slit width is increased? **ISC 2023**

2. State any one difference between interference of light and diffraction of light. **ISC 2015**

3. Fraunhofer diffraction from a single slit of width 1.24×10^{-6} m is observed with the light of wavelength 6200 Å. Calculate the angular width of the central maximum. **ISC 2005**

2 Marks Questions

4. Draw a labelled graph showing the variation in intensity of diffracted light with diffracting angle in a single slit Fraunhofer diffraction experiment. **ISC 2024**

5. (*i*) What is meant by diffraction of light?

   (*ii*) State any one difference between diffraction of light and interference of light. **ISC 2022 Sem-II**

6. (*i*) What is meant by diffraction of light? **ISC 2017**

   (*ii*) In Fraunhofer diffraction, what kind of source of light is used and where is it situated?

7. Monochromatic light of wavelength 650 nm falls normally on a slit of width 1.3×10^{-4} cm and the resulting Fraunhofer diffraction is obtained on a screen. Find the angular width of the central maxima. **ISC 2016**

8. Show graphically, the intensity distribution in Fraunhofer's single slit diffraction experiment. Label the axes. **ISC 2015**

9. What will be the effect on the width of the central bright fringe in the diffraction pattern of a single slit, if

   (*i*) the monochromatic light of smaller wavelength is used.

   (*ii*) slit is made narrower. **ISC 2013**

10. Draw a labelled graph to show the variation in intensity of diffracted light with angular position, in a single slit diffraction experiment. **ISC 2012, 09, 07**

3 Marks Questions

11. (*i*) Calculate the angular width of the central maxima obtained in Fraunhofer single slit diffraction experiment, when a monochromatic light of wavelength 550 nm falls normally on a rectangular slit of width 1.1×10^{-4} cm.

    (*ii*) How will its value change, if the experiment is repeated with monochromatic light of greater wavelength? **ISC SQP 2023**

12. In a single slit diffraction experiment, how does the angular width of the central maxima change when

    (a) screen is moved away from the plane of the slit?

    (b) width of the slit is increased?

    (c) light of larger wavelength is used? **ISC 2022 Sem-II**

13. Draw a labelled graph of intensity variation with angle (θ) in the Fraunhofer diffraction experiment for diffraction. **ISC 2020**

14. (*i*) In Young's double slit experiment, show graphically how intensity of light varies with distance.

    (*ii*) In Fraunhofer diffraction, how is the angular width of the central bright fringe affected when slit separation is increased? **ISC 2018**

15. Determine the angular separation between the central maxima and the first order maxima of the diffraction pattern due to a single slit of width 0.25 mm when light of wavelength 5890 Å is incident on its normally. **ISC 2006, 2000**

4/5 Marks Question

16. Light of wavelength 600 nm, falls normally on a slit of width 1.2 μm producing Fraunhoffer diffraction pattern on a screen. Calculate the angular position of the first minima and the angular width of the central maxima. **ISC 2002**

KEY idea

To know the angular width of the central maxima. First calculate the angular position of the first minima, then apply $\left(\frac{2\lambda}{d}\right)$ to calculate angular width of the central maxima.

Case Based Question
(For Complete Chapter)

17. Direction *Read the passage given below and answer the questions that follows.*

Distribution of Intensity

Intensity of central maxima is maximum and intensity of the secondary maxima decreases with the increase of their order. The diffraction pattern is graphically shown below in the figure. The ratio of intensities of the secondary maxima to the intensity of a central maximum are given by

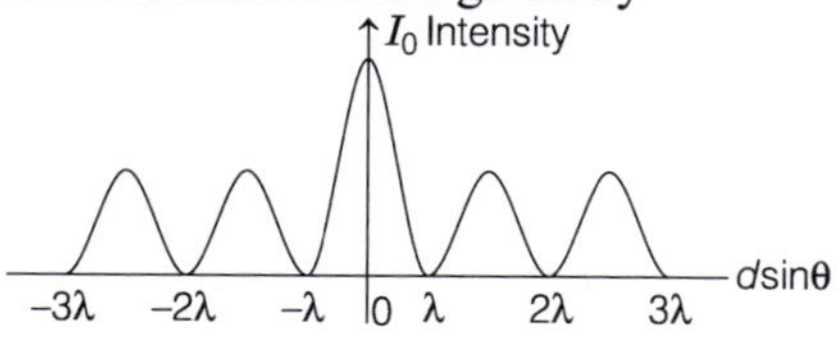

$$1:\frac{1}{21}:\frac{1}{61}:\frac{1}{121}$$

From the given ratio, it is clear that the intensity of secondary maxima is just 4% of that of central maxima.

(*i*) What do you mean by the term distribution of intensity? **(1)**

(*ii*) What is the ratio of the intensity of secondary maxima and central maxima? **(1)**

(iii) What happen when the screen is moved away from the plane of the slit in a single slit diffraction experiment? **(1)**

(*iv*) What happen when the width of the slit is increased in the single slit diffraction experiment? **(1)**

(*v*) What will be the effect on the intensity when the monochromatic light of smaller wavelength is used. **(1)**

Explanations

1. In Fraunhofer diffraction, $b\sin\theta = n\lambda$

where, b in the width of slit, λ is the wavelength of light used.

For central bright fringe, $n=1$

$\Rightarrow \quad b\sin\theta = \lambda$

Thus, angular width of central bright

width $= 2\sin\theta = \dfrac{2\lambda}{b}$

So, angular width of central bright fringe will decrease when the width of slit is increased.

2. The interference pattern has a number of equally spaced bright and dark bands. The diffraction pattern has a central bright maxima, which is twice as wide as the other maxima. The intensity falls, as we go to successive maxima away from the centre on either side.

3. In Fraunhofer diffraction from a single slit, central maxima is given by

$$a\sin\theta = n\lambda$$

where, a = width of a slit,

λ = wavelength of the light.

$$\Rightarrow \quad \sin\theta = \frac{n\lambda}{a} = \frac{6200\times10^{-10}\times1}{1.24\times10^{-6}} = 0.5$$

$$\Rightarrow \quad \theta = 30^\circ$$

$\therefore$ Angular width of the central maxima,

$$2\theta = 2\times30^\circ = 60^\circ$$

4. Variation in intensity with diffracting angle,

$$\sin\theta_n = (2n+1)\frac{\lambda}{2a}$$

Thus, diffraction pattern can be graphically shown as

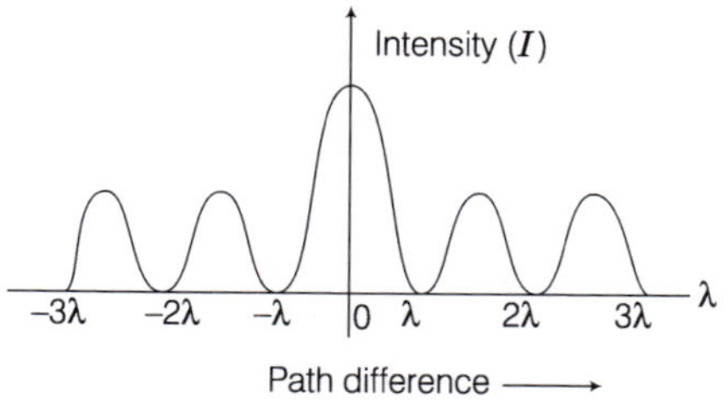

5. (*i*) The phenomenon of bending of light around the edges or the sharp corners and then spreading of light within the geometrical shadow of opaque obstacles is called diffraction of light.

(*ii*) Refer to Sol. 2 on page 242.

6. (*i*) The phenomenon of bending of light around the edges or the sharp corners and then spreading of light within the geometrical shadow of opaque obstacles is called diffraction of light.

(*ii*) **Fraunhofer diffraction**

In this type of diffraction, the source of light is not necessary to be monochromatic or white light but the expression calculated for the central maxima and minima, we considered it to be monochromatic. And the source of light is being placed at large distance from the screen i.e. effectively at infinity.

7. In single slit diffraction, first minimum occurs at

$d \sin\theta = \lambda$ or $\sin\theta = \dfrac{\lambda}{d}$

as $\lambda << d$ so, $\theta = \dfrac{\lambda}{d}$ $\quad (\because \sin\theta = \theta)$

Now, angular width of central maxima,

$$\phi = 2\theta = \frac{2\lambda}{d} = \frac{2 \times 650 \times 10^{-9}}{1.3 \times 10^{-4} \times 10^{-2}} = \frac{13000}{13} \times 10^{-3} = 1 \text{ rad}$$

Thus, the angular width of the central maxima is 1 rad.

8. The graph of variation in the intensity of diffracted light in a single slit experiment is shown in the figure. Here, intensity of the central maxima will be maximum and that of other will gradually decrease.

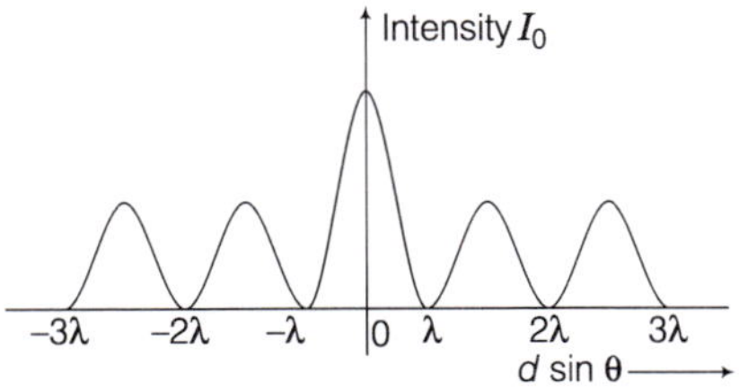

For central bright fringe, $\theta = 0°$

For first dark fringe,

$$d \sin\theta = \pm\lambda \Rightarrow \sin\theta = \pm\frac{\lambda}{d}$$

9. We know that, width of the central bright fringe in the diffraction pattern of a single slit is

$$\beta = \frac{2D\lambda}{d}$$

where, D = distance of the screen
d = width of the slit
λ = wavelength of light

(*i*) As $\beta \propto \lambda$, when λ is smaller, then β decreases.

(*ii*) As $\beta \propto \dfrac{1}{d}$, when slit is made narrower, β increases.

10. Refer to Text 8 on page 240 (Distribution of intensity).

11. (*i*) $\lambda = 550 \text{ nm} = 550 \times 10^{-9}$ m

$$d = 1.1 \times 10^{-4} \text{ cm} = 11 \times 10^{-6} \text{ m}$$

$$\text{Angular width} = \frac{2\lambda}{d} = \frac{2 \times 550 \times 10^{-9} \text{ m}}{11 \times 10^{-6} \text{ m}} = \frac{2 \times 550 \times 10^{-9} \times 10^{6}}{11} = 0.1 \text{ m} = 10 \text{ cm}$$

(*ii*) If the experiment is repeated with monochromatic light of greater wavelength, the angular width of the central maxima obtained in the Fraunhofer single slit diffraction experiment will increase.

Angular width of central maxima $(\theta) \propto \lambda$

If angular width of central maxima increases, then wavelength also increases.

Common Mistake The values of λ and d must be in same units and in SI system.

12. (a) Angular width remains unchanged when the screen is moved away from the plane of the slit.

(b) As, angular width $= \dfrac{2\lambda}{d}$

where, d is the slit width.

If slit width increases, angular width decreases.

(c) If the light of larger wavelength is used than the as per increase in wavelength, the angular width also increases because angular width is directly proportional to the wavelength.

13. Refer to sol. 8 on page 243.

14. (*i*) In Young's double slit experiment, intensity of light varies with distance as given below.

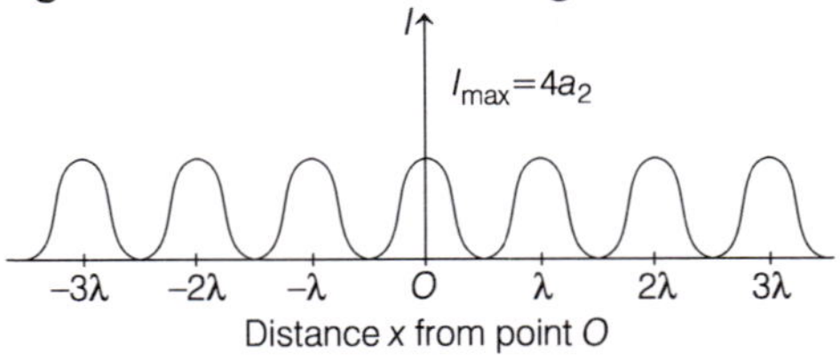

(*ii*) The angular width θ of the central bright fringe in Fraunhofer single slit diffraction experiment is given by $\theta = \dfrac{\lambda}{d}$.

When the slit width or separation d is increased, the angular width θ will decrease.

Concept Enhancer The intensity of the secondary maxima is just 4% of the central maxima in single slit diffraction pattern..

15. To find the angular separation we have to apply condition of maxima for diffraction from a single slit.

The angular separation between the central maxima,

$$d \sin \theta = n\lambda$$

where, symbols have their usual meaning.

For first order maxima, $n = 1$

$$\sin \theta = \frac{5890 \times 10^{-10}}{0.25 \times 10^{-3}}$$

$\Rightarrow$ $\theta \approx \sin \theta = 0.0023$ rad [For small θ]

16. According to the question,

Wavelength, $\lambda = 600 \text{ nm} = 600 \times 10^{-9}$ m

$$d = 1.2 \,\mu\text{m} = 1.2 \times 10^{-6} \text{ m}$$

$\therefore$ Angular position of the first minima,

$$\sin \theta = \frac{\lambda}{d}$$

$\Rightarrow$ $$\sin \theta = \frac{600 \times 10^{-9}}{1.2 \times 10^{-6}}$$

$\Rightarrow$ $$\sin \theta = 0.5 = \frac{1}{2}$$

$\Rightarrow$ $$\sin \theta = \sin 30^\circ$$

$\therefore$ $$\theta = 30^\circ$$

Angular width of the central maxima

$$= \frac{2\lambda}{d} = \frac{2 \times 600 \times 10^{-9} \text{ m}}{1.2 \times 10^{-6}} = 1 \text{ rad}$$

17. (*i*) Intensity of central maxima is maximum and intensity of the secondary maxima decrease with the increase of their order. This whole phenomenon is known as "Distribution of Intensity".

(*ii*) The ratio of the intensity of secondary maxima and central maxima is 4%.

(*iii*) The angular width of central maxima is independent of the distance between slit and screen D. So, angular width remains unchanged. When the screen is moved away from the plane of the slit.

(*iv*) Angular width of central bright fringe will decrease when the width of slit is increased.

(*v*) As, $\beta \propto \lambda$, when λ is smaller, then β decreases.

CHAPTER TEST

01 Mark Questions (MCQs)

1 Light appears to travel in straight lines because:
(a) it is not absorbed by the atmosphere
(b) it is reflected by the upper part of the atmosphere
(c) its wavelength is very small.
(d) its speed is very large.

2 In the diffraction of light of wavelength λ at a single slit of small width *e*, the angle θ between the central maximum and first minimum on either side is
(a) λ / e (b) $\lambda / 2e$ (c) $\lambda / 4e$ (d) $\lambda / 2$

3 Though both light and sound have wave character, yet diffraction is much harder to observe in light because
(a) light can travel in vacuum
(b) light waves are transverse
(c) the speed of light is very large
(d) the wavelength of light is very small

4 Yellow light is used in a single-slit diffraction experiment with slit width of 0.6 mm. If yellow light is replaced by X-rays, then the observed pattern will revel
(a) that the central maximum is narrower
(b) more number of fringes
(c) less number of fringes
(d) no diffraction pattern

01 Mark Questions (VSA)

5 How does the angular separation between the fringes in single slit diffraction experiment change when the distance of separation between the slit and screen is doubled?

6 In Fraunhofer's slit diffraction experiment, how does semi-angular width θ of the central bright fringe depend on slit width?

02 Marks Questions

7 Name the principal used to obtain the diffraction pattern due to a single slit. Show the plot of variation of intensity with angle and state the reason for the reduction in intensity of the secondary maxima compared to central maximum.

8 In what way is diffraction from each slit related to the interference pattern in a double slit experiment?

9 Yellow light ($\lambda = 6000$ Å) illuminates a single slit of width 1×10^{-4} m. Calculate the distance between two dark lines on either side to the central maxima, when the diffraction pattern is viewed on a screen kept 1.5 m away from the slit.

03 Marks Questions

10 In a single slit diffraction experiment, a slit of width *d* is illuminated by red light of wavelength 650 nm. For what value of *d* will
(i) the first minima fall is at an angle of diffraction of 30°?
(ii) the first maxima fall is at an angle of diffraction of 30°?

11 In a single slit diffraction experiment, when a tiny circular obstacle is placed in the path of light from a distance source, a bright spot is seen at the centre of the shadow of the obstacle. Explain why? State two points of difference between the interference pattern obtained in Young's double slit experiment and the diffraction pattern due to a single slit.

05 Marks Question

12 Two wavelengths of sodium light 590 nm and 596 nm are used in turn to study the diffraction taking place at a single slit of aperture 2×10^{-4} m. The distance between the slit and the screen is 1.5 m. Calculate the separation between the positions of the first maxima of the diffraction pattern obtained in the two cases.

Answers

1. (c) **2.** (a) **3.** (d) **4.** (d)

9. 18 mm

10. (i) $d = 1.3 \times 10^{-5}$ m (ii) $d = 1.95 \times 10^{-5}$ cm

12. 6.75×10^{-5} m

18

Photoelectric Effect

TREND ANALYSIS 4 YEARS

Average No. of Questions Across all Sets

	Types of Questions	2024	2023	2020	2019
Photoelectric Effect	1 Mark	–	–	1	1
	2 Marks	–	–	–	1
	3 Marks	1	2	–	–
	5 Marks	–	–	–	–

The phenomenon of emission of photoelectrons from the surface of a metal, when a light of suitable frequency is incident on it, is called **photoelectric effect**.

The emitted electrons are called **photoelectrons** and the current so produced is called **photoelectric current.**

Hertz' Observation

The phenomenon of photoelectric emission was discovered in 1887 by Heinrich Hertz during his electromagnetic wave experiment. In his experimental investigation on the production of electromagnetic waves by means of spark across the detector loop were enhanced when the emitter plate was illuminated by ultraviolet light from an arc lamp.

Lenard's Observation

Lenard observed that when ultraviolet radiation were allowed to fall on emitter plate of an evacuated glass tube enclosing two electrodes, current flows. As soon as, the ultraviolet radiations were stopped, the current flow also stopped. These observations indicate that when ultraviolet radiations fall on the emitter plate, electrons are ejected from it which are attracted towards the positive plate by the electric field.

Terms Related to the Photoelectric Effect

Free electrons In metals, the electrons in the outer shells i.e., valence electrons are loosely bound to the atoms, hence they are free to move easily within the metal surface but cannot leave it. Such electrons are called free electrons.

Electron emission The phenomenon of emission of electrons by giving suitable amount of energy, from the surface of a metal is called electron emission.

Work function (ϕ) The minimum amount of energy of incident radiation required to just eject an electron from the outermost surface of metal is known as work function of the metal. It is given as,

$$\phi_0 = h\nu_0 = \frac{hc}{\lambda_0}$$

Where, ν_0 and λ_0 are the threshold frequency and threshold wavelength, respectively.

Cut-off potential/Stopping potential For a particular frequency of the incident radiation, the minimum negative (retarding) potential V_0 given to the metallic plate so, that the emission of electrons stops or photocurrent becomes zero, is called cut-off or stopping potential. It gives the maximum kinetic energy of an ejected electrons.

i.e.

$$\text{KE}_{\text{max}} = eV_0$$

$\Rightarrow$

$$\frac{1}{2}mv_{\text{max}}^2 = eV_0$$

where v_{max} = velocity of the electron

and V_0 = cut-off potential

Cut-off frequency/Threshold frequency The minimum frequency of the light which can emit photoelectrons from a material is called threshold frequency or cut-off frequency of that material. It is denoted by ν_0. If incident frequency $\nu < \nu_0 \Rightarrow$ No photoelectron emission.

Cut-off wavelength/Threshold wavelength The maximum wavelength of light which can emit photoelectrons from a material is called threshold wavelength or cut-off wavelength of that material. It is denoted by λ_0. If incident wavelength $\lambda > \lambda_0 \Rightarrow$ No photoelectron emission take place.

Effect on Photoelectric current

The following are the effects on photocurrent :

Effect of Intensity of Light on Photoelectric current

For a fixed frequency of incident radiation, the photoelectric current increases linearly with the increase in intensity of the incident light. But the stopping potential V_0 doesn't change. Hence, intensity $\propto$ number of incident photons $\propto$ number of photoelectrons emitted per unit time. The graph is shown in the figure.

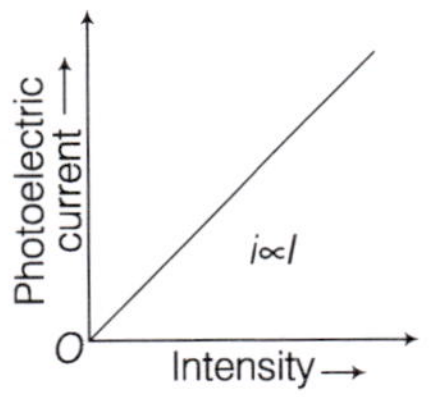

Effect of Potential on Photoelectric Current

For a fixed frequency and intensity of incident light, the photoelectric current increases with increase in the potential applied to the collector plate. When all the photoelectrons reach the plate A, current becomes maximum. It is also known as **saturation current**.

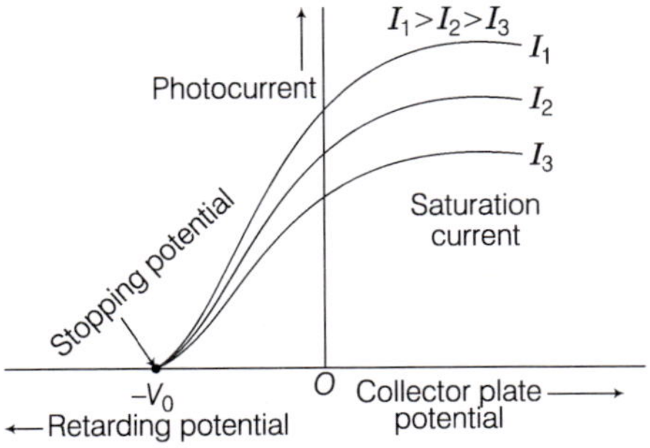

Variation of photoelectric current *versus* potential for different intensities but constant frequency

Effect of Frequency of Incident Radiation on Stopping Potential

We take radiations of different frequencies but of same intensity. For each radiation, we study the variation of photoelectric current against the potential difference between the plates.

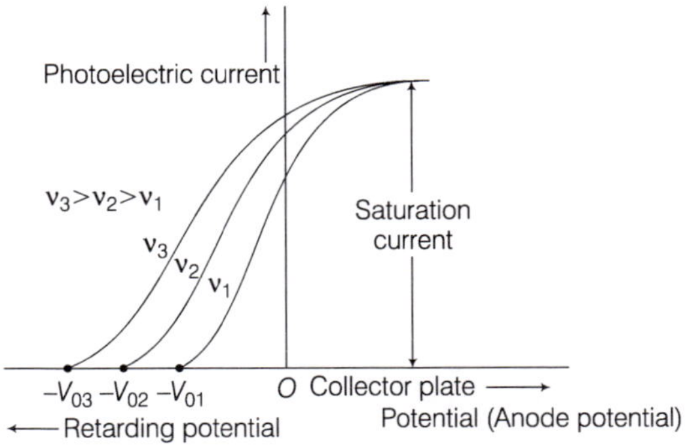

Laws of Photoelectric Emission

(*i*) For a given material and frequency of incident radiation, the photoelectric current or the number of photoelectrons ejected per second is directly proportional to the intensity of the incident light.

(*ii*) For a given material and frequency of incident radiation, saturation current is found to be proportional to the intensity to incident radiation, whereas the stopping potential is independent of its intensity.

(*iii*) For a given material, there exists a certain minimum frequency of the incident radiation below which no emissions of photoelectrons takes place. This frequency is called **threshold frequency**.

Above the threshold frequency, the maximum kinetic energy of the emitted photoelectrons or equivalent stopping potential is independent of the intensity of the incident light but depends only upon the frequency (or wavelength) of the incident light.

(*iv*) The photoelectric emission is an instantaneous process. The time lag between the incidence of radiations and emission of photoelectron is very small, less than even 10^{-9} s.

Quantisation of Radiation

According to the Planck's photon hypothesis, the electromagnetic field comes in discrete particle of energy ($h\nu$) called **photons,** which when falls on metallic surface shows photoelectric effect. This is called quantisation of radiation.

i.e. $$E = h\nu$$

where, h = Planck's constant and its value is 6.63×10^{-34} J-s
and ν = frequency of electromagnetic radiation.

Einstein's Photoelectric Equation

Einstein explained photoelectric equation on the basis of Planck's photon hypothesis or famous quantum theory. Light radiations consist of tiny packets of energy called quanta.

According to Einstein, when a photon is incident on a metal surface, the absorbed energy of the photon is used in two ways,

(*i*) A part is used to overcome the surface barrier, to eject out the electron. This part of energy is work function. It is expressed as $\phi_0 = h\nu_0$.

(*ii*) The remaining part is used to give velocity v to the emitted photoelectron.

According to the law of conservation of energy,

$$h\nu = \phi_0 + \frac{1}{2} m v_{max}^2$$

$$\therefore \quad \frac{1}{2} m v_{max}^2 = K_{max}$$

$$= h(\nu - \nu_0) = h\nu - \phi_0$$

He then gave an equation which is known as Einstein's photoelectric equation. It is given as,

$$\therefore \quad K_{max} = h\nu - \phi_0 \quad \text{and} \quad K_{max} = eV_0$$

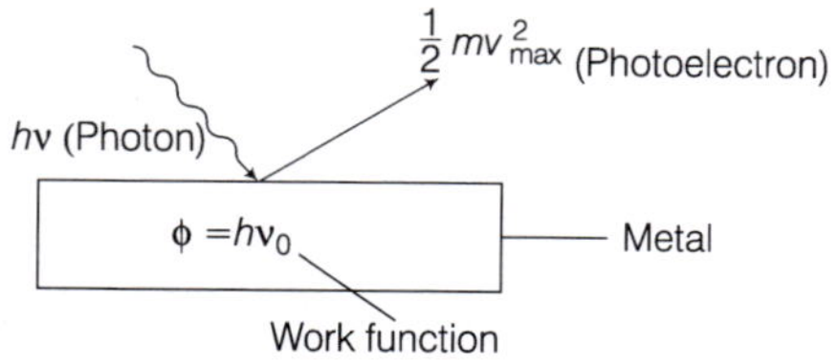

Photoelectric emission

NOTE Photoelectric current is zero whenever no electron or even the fastest photoelectrons is not able to reach the plate *A*. Hence, maximum kinetic energy is given as $K_{max} = eV_0 = \frac{1}{2} mv_{max}^2$, where, m is the mass of photoelectron and v_{max} is the maximum velocity of the emitted photoelectron.

Determination of Planck's Constant

Millikan performed an experiment to verify Einstein's photoelectric equation and to determine the value of Planck's constant h. To calculate the value of h, Millikan measured the maximum kinetic energy of photoelectrons emitted.

As from Einstein's photoelectric equation

$$\frac{1}{2} mv_{max}^2 = h(\nu - \nu_0)$$

As we know that, $$\frac{1}{2} mv_{max}^2 = eV_0$$

So, $$eV_0 = h(\nu - \nu_0)$$

$$V_0 = \frac{h\nu}{e} - \frac{h\nu_0}{e}$$

where, h = Planck's constant, ν = incident frequency,
ν_0 = threshold frequency;
v_{max} = velocity of ejected electrons
and m = mass of electrons.

So, the graph between V_0 and ν is shown alongside

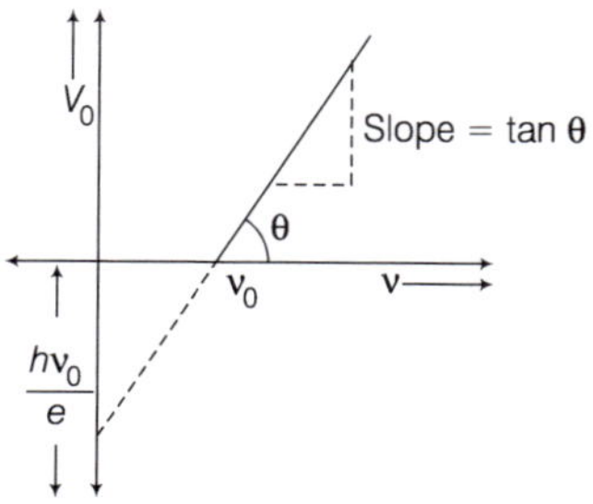

As slope of the graph i.e. $\tan\theta = \frac{h}{e}$, hence, by measuring the slope of the straight line obtained and using the known value of e, the value of h can be calculated.

Energy and Momentum of Photon

Photoelectric effect thus gave evidence that light consists of packets of energy. These packets of energy are called light quantum that are associated with particles named as photon. So, photons confirm the particle nature of light.

Energy of a photon is given by $$E = h\nu = \frac{hc}{\lambda}$$

In electron-volt, $$E(\text{in eV}) = \frac{12400}{\lambda(\text{Å})}$$

where, h is the Planck's constant, ν is the frequency of radiation or photon, c is the speed of light and λ is the wavelength of photon.

The momentum of photon is given by

$$p = \frac{E}{c} = \frac{h\nu}{c} = \frac{h}{\lambda} \text{ kg-ms}^{-1}$$

PYQs Previous Years Questions

1 Mark Questions

1. Which of the following graphs correctly represents the variation of maximum kinetic energy (E_K) of photoelectrons with the frequency (ν) of the incident radiation? **ISC SQP 2022**

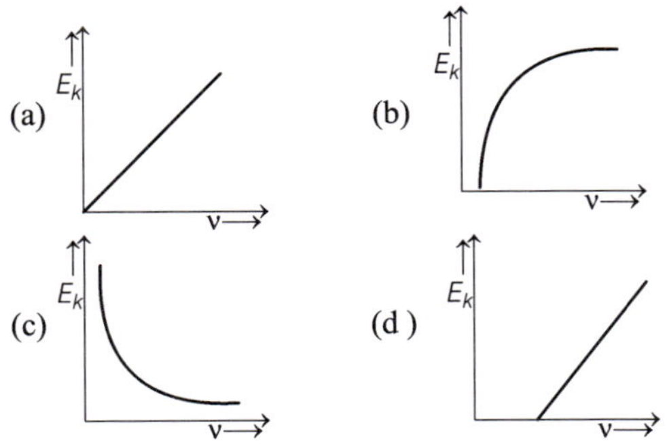

> **KEY idea**
> The above graph is based on ($y = mx + c$) equation.

2. In photoelectric effect, the graph of stopping potential V_s *versus* frequency f of the incident radiaiton is a straight line. Then, slope m of this line, Planck's constant h and elementary charge e are related as follows **ISC 2022 Sem-II**

(a) $h = em$ (b) $m = eh$
(c) $e = mh$ (d) $e = m\pi h$

3. In photoelectric effect experiment, the slope of the graph of the stopping potential *versus* frequency gives the value of **ISC 2020**

(a) $\frac{h}{e}$ (b) h (c) $\frac{e}{h}$ (d) $\frac{hc}{e}$

4. The energy associated with light of which of the following colours is minimum? **ISC 2019**

(a) Violet (b) Red
(c) Green (d) Yellow

5. Einstein's photoelectric equation is, **ISC 2018**

(a) $E_{\max} = h\lambda - \phi_0$ (b) $E_{\max} = \frac{hc}{\lambda} - \phi_0$
(c) $E_{\max} = h\nu + \phi_0$ (d) $E_{\max} = \frac{hc}{\lambda} + \phi_0$

6. Calculate the momentum of a photon of energy 6×10^{-19} J. **ISC 2017**

7. Describe in brief what is observed when moving electrons are allowed to fall on a thin graphite film and the emergent beam falls on a fluorescent screen. **ISC 2017**

8. Two metals A and B have work functions 4 eV and 6 eV, respectively. Which metal has lower threshold wavelength for photoelectric effect? **ISC 2016**

9. With reference to the photoelectric effect, what is meant by threshold wavelength? **ISC 2014**

10. Name the phenomena or experiment which proves particle nature of electromagnetic radiations. **ISC 2013**

11. Threshold frequency of a certain metal for photoelectric emission is 5×10^{14} Hz. Calculate its work function. **ISC 2012, 09**

12. In photoelectric effect, what is meant by the term threshold frequency? **ISC 2011, 01**

13. Give Einstein's equation for photoelectric emission. What do symbol stands for? **ISC 2004**

14. How can the work function of tungsten be increased? **ISC 2007**

2 Marks Questions

15. Threshold wavelength for a certain metal for photoelectric effect is 600 nm.
Calculate its **ISC 2022 Sem-II**

(*i*) threshold frequency
(*ii*) work function

16. Define the following with reference to photoelectric effect. **ISC 2019, 18**

(*i*) Threshold frequency f_0
(*ii*) Stopping potential V_s

17. Monochromatic light of wavelength 198 nm is incident on the surface of a metallic cathode whose work function is 2.5 eV. How much potential difference must be applied between the cathode and the anode of a photocell to just stop the photocurrent from flowing? **ISC 2008**

18. In photoelectric effect, what is meant by the terms **ISC 2008, 01**

(*i*) work function? (*ii*) stopping potential?

3 Marks Questions

19. (i) In an experiment on photoelectric effect, how does stopping potential change, if at all, when intensity of incident monochromatic UV-radiation is increased?

(ii) Ultraviolet light is incident metals P, Q and R, having work functions 8eV, 2eV and 4eV respectively.

(a) Which metal has lowest threshold frequency for photoelectric effect?

(b) For which metal is the value of E_{max} minimum?

(**Note** E_{max} is maximum kinetic energy of the emitted photoelectrons). **ISC 2024**

20. Monochromatic light of wavelength 396 nm is incident on the surface of a metal, whose work function is 1.125 eV. Calculate

(*i*) the energy of an incident photon (in eV) .

(*ii*) the maximum kinetic energy of photoelectrons (in eV). **ISC 2023**

21. Plot a labelled graph of (V_s), where V_s is stopping potential of photoelectrons *versus* frequency ν of incident radiation. How will you use this graph to determine the value of Planck's constant? Explain. **ISC 2023 SQP, 2018, 17, 09**

22. (*i*) Write Einstein's photoelectric equation.

(*ii*) If the frequency of the incident radiation is increased from 4×10^{15} Hz to 8×10^{15} Hz, by how much will the stopping potential for a given photosensitive surface go up? **ISC 2014**

23. Threshold wavelength of certain metal is 792 nm. What is the maximum kinetic energy of photoelectrons emitted by this metal, if it is exposed to ultraviolet light of wavelength 396 nm? **ISC 2010**

24. The work function of sodium is 2.28 eV.

(*i*) What is the minimum energy for a quantum of radiation to cause photoelectric emission from sodium surface?

(*ii*) Calculate the wavelength of this radiation. **ISC 2009**

25. The threshold wavelength of tungsten is 2400 Å when tungsten is illuminated with light of wavelength 1600 Å. Find

(*i*) work function

(*ii*) maximum KE of emitted electron

(*iii*) stopping potential. **ISC 2005**

4/5 Marks Questions

26. What is photoelectric effect? With the help of a suitable graph show the variation of photocurrent with

(*i*) the intensity of incident radiation.

(*ii*) the voltage applied between cathode and anode.

(*iii*) the frequency of incident radiation. **ISC 2004**

(*iii*) the work function of the metal. **ISC 2003, 2000**

KEY idea

In this type of questions, from the given values of h, c and λ, we can calculate the energy incident on metal and then after from the given stopping potential we will calculate maximum kinetic energy of ejected electrons.

Case Based Question
(For Complete Chapter)

27. Direction *Read the passage given below and answer the questions that follows.*

Photoelectric Effect The phenomenon of emission of electrons from a metal surface, when electromagnetic radiations of sufficiently high frequency are incident on it, is called photoelectric emission. The photogenerated electrons called photoelectrons. The wave theory of EM radiation fails to explain some experimentally, observed facts on photoelectric effect effect such as its instantaneous nature, independence of the maximum KE of photoelectrons from intensity of incident radiation, and the existence of threshold frequency for every photoemitter.

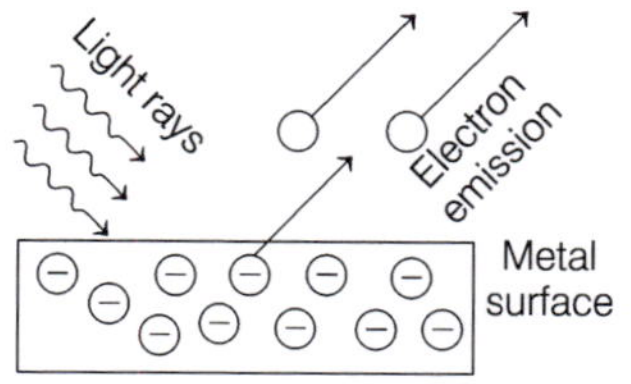

According to the photon picture of radiation, in its interaction with matter, the radiation behaves as if it consists of quanta or small packets of energy, each of energy $h\nu$. This photon picture leads to the Einstein's photoelectric equations: $K_{max} = eV_0 = h\nu - \phi_0$. This equation correctly explains all the experimentally observed features of photoelectric effect.

Answer the following questions from the above passage.

(*i*) What is photoelectrons? **(1)**

(*ii*) What is photon? **(1)**

(*iii*) Which equation tells the relation between kinetic energy and work function? **(1)**

(*iv*) What is the reason behind failure of wave theory of EM radiation? **(2)**

Explanations

1. (d) Maximum kinetic energy of the photoelectrons,

$$E_K = h\nu - \phi$$

where, ν is the frequency of incident radiation.

Thus E_K *versus* ν graph will be straight line having slope $= h$ and intercept $= \phi$ on negative Y-axis, as shown in graph (d).

2. (a) In V_s *versus* f graph, the slope is given by

$$m = \frac{h}{e} \Rightarrow h = em$$

3. (a) From Einstein's photoelectric equation,

$$h\nu = V_0 e + W_0$$

$$\Rightarrow \quad V_0 = \frac{h\nu}{e} - \frac{W_0}{e} \quad \ldots \text{(i)}$$

Equation of line, $y = mx + c$ ...(ii)

By comparing Eqs. (i) and (ii), we get slope $m = \frac{h}{e}$.

4. (b) The energy of light,

$$E = \frac{hc}{\lambda} \text{ or } E \propto \frac{1}{\lambda}$$

Since, red colour has maximum wavelength. So, the energy of light for red colour will be minimum.

Concept Enhancer Energy can also be written in terms of frequency

$$E = h\nu \Rightarrow E \propto \nu$$

5. (b) Einstein's photoelectric equation is given by

$$E_{\max} = h\nu - \phi_0$$

or $$E_{\max} = \frac{hc}{\lambda} - \phi_0 \quad \left[\because \nu = \frac{c}{\lambda}\right]$$

where, ϕ_0 = work function.

6. Given, $E = 6 \times 10^{-19}$ J

Momentum, $p = \frac{E}{c}$

where, c is speed of light.

$$= \frac{6 \times 10^{-19}}{3 \times 10^8} = 2 \times 10^{-27} \text{ J/ms}^{-1}$$

7. When moving electrons are allowed to fall on a thin graphite film, then the electrons from the graphite film will be knocked out, after gaining sufficient energy from the collision with the moving electrons and then this beam of emergent electrons falls on the fluorescent screen, due to which visible radiation will be produced from the screen (i.e. fluorescence), helping in identifying that emission of electrons had been started from the thin film.

8. Given, work function of metal A, $\phi_{0A} = 4$ eV

Work function of metal B, $\phi_{0B} = 6$ eV

Therefore, threshold wavelength of metal A,

$$\lambda_{0A} = \frac{hc}{\phi_{0A}} = \frac{hc}{4} \quad \ldots \text{(i)}$$

Similarly, threshold wavelength of metal B,

$$\lambda_{0B} = \frac{hc}{\phi_{0B}} = \frac{hc}{6} \quad \ldots \text{(ii)}$$

On comparing Eqs. (i) and (ii), we can say that

$$\lambda_{0A} > \lambda_{0B}$$

i.e. Threshold wavelength of metal A is greater than that of metal B.

9. Refer to text on page 247 (Threshold Wavelength).

10. Photoelectric effect is the phenomena which proves particle nature of electromagnetic radiation.

11. Given,

Threshold frequency, $\nu_0 = 5 \times 10^{14}$ Hz

So, work function is given by, $\phi = h\nu_0$

$$\Rightarrow \quad \phi = 6.6 \times 10^{-34} \times 5 \times 10^{14}$$

$$\phi = 3.3 \times 10^{-19} \text{ J}$$

$$\therefore \quad \phi = \frac{3.3 \times 10^{-19}}{1.6 \times 10^{-19}} = 2.06 \text{ eV}$$

12. Refer to text on page 247 (Threshold Wavelength).

13. Refer to text on page 248 (Einstein Photoelectric Equation).

14. Work function of tungsten can be increased by coating it with thorium whose work function is lower than tungsten.

15. Given, threshold wavelength,

$$\lambda = 600 \text{ nm} = 600 \times 10^{-9} \text{ m}$$

(i) Threshold frequency,

$$\nu_0 = \frac{c}{\lambda_0} = \frac{3 \times 10^8}{600 \times 10^{-9}} = 5 \times 10^{14} \text{ Hz}$$

(ii) Work function,

$$\phi = h\nu_0 = 6.63 \times 10^{-34} \times 5 \times 10^{14}$$

$= 33.15 \times 10^{-20}$ J $= 2.07$ eV

Concept Enhancer Work function is also a energy.

$E \text{ (in eV)} = \dfrac{12400}{\lambda \text{ (Å)}}$

16. (i) The lowest frequency of light which can emit photoelectrons from a material is called the threshold frequency f_0.

(ii) The negative potential at which the photoelectric current becomes zero is called stopping potential V_s

17. Given, wavelength, $\lambda = 198$ nm $= 198 \times 10^{-9}$ m

Work function, $\phi_0 = 2.5$ eV

$= 2.5 \times 1.6 \times 10^{-19} = 4 \times 10^{-19}$ J

From Einstein's photoelectric equation, $eV_0 = \dfrac{hc}{\lambda} - \phi_0$

$\therefore$ Stopping potential, $V_0 = \dfrac{1}{e}\left(\dfrac{hc}{\lambda} - \phi_0\right)$

$$= \frac{1}{1.6 \times 10^{-19}} \left(\frac{6.6 \times 10^{-34} \times 3 \times 10^8}{198 \times 10^{-9}} - 4 \times 10^{-19} \right)$$

$$= \frac{1}{1.6 \times 10^{-19}} (0.1 \times 10^{-17} - 4 \times 10^{-19})$$

$$V_0 = \frac{6 \times 10^{-19}}{1.6 \times 10^{-19}} = 3.75 \text{ V}$$

18. (*i*) Refer to text on page 246 (Work Function).

(*ii*) Refer to text on page 246 (Stopping Potential).

19. (i) Stopping potential does not change at all, only photoelectric current increases linearly with intensity of incident monochromatic UV-radiation.

(ii) (a) Threshold frequency is given by $\nu_0 = \dfrac{\phi_0}{h}$

So, $\phi_0 \propto \nu_0$

Thus, metal having less work function will have lowest threshold frequency.

Thus, metal Q has lowest threshold frequency.

(b) According to photoelectric equation,

E_{max} = (Energy of photon) – (Work function of metal)

$= h\nu - h\nu_0 \Rightarrow h(\nu - \nu_0)$

For a particular incident radiation frequency ν, the metal with maximum the value of work function, minimum will be the energy.

Hence, metal P will have E_{max} minimum.

20. (*i*) Given, $\lambda = 396 \text{nm} = 396 \times 10^{-9}$ m

$\phi_0 = 1.125$ eV

Energy of incident photon, $E = hc/\lambda$

$$= \frac{6.6 \times 10^{-34} \times 3 \times 10^8}{396 \times 10^{-9}}$$

$= 0.05 \times 10^{-17} = 5 \times 10^{-19}$ J

$= 5 \times 10^{-19} / 1.6 \times 10^{-19} = 3.125$ eV

(ii) $K_{max} = E - \phi_0 = 3.125 - 1.125$

$K_{max} = 2$ eV

Concept Enhancer The photoelectric equation is given in terms of wavelength as well as frequency.

$E_{max} = h\nu - h\nu_0$ or $E_{max} = \dfrac{hc}{\lambda} - \dfrac{hc}{\lambda_0}$

21. Graph for V_s and ν is as follows

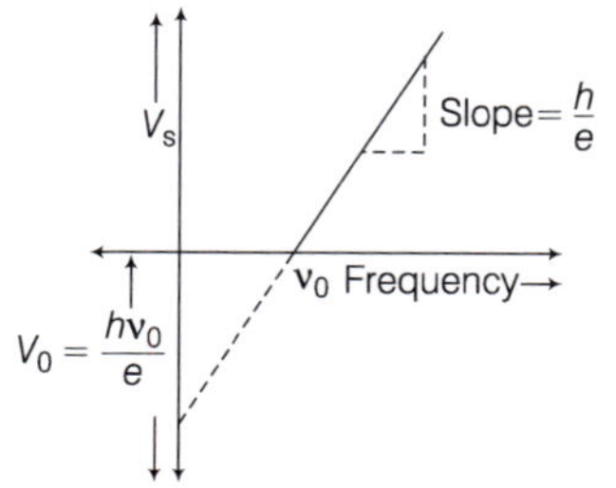

Determination of Planck's constant

As from the graph it is clear that slope of the graph is given by Slope $= \dfrac{h}{e}$

where, h = Planck's constant

and e = charge on an electron.

Now from Einstein's photoelectric equation

$K_{max} = h\nu - \phi \Rightarrow eV_0 = h\nu - \phi$

$\Rightarrow \quad V_0 = \left(\dfrac{h}{e}\right)\nu - \dfrac{\phi}{e}$

Comparing this equation with $y = mx + c$,

Slope of (V_0, ν) graph $= \dfrac{h}{e}$.

So, Planck's constant h = slope (V_0, ν) graph $\times e$.

22. (*i*) Refer to text on page 248 (Einstein Photoelectric Equation).

(*ii*) According to Einstein's photoelectric equation,

$KE_{max} = h\nu - \phi$

where, $h\nu$ = Energy of incident photon,

ϕ = work function.

Now for 1st case,

$KE_1 = h \times 4 \times 10^{15} - h\nu_0$ $[\because \phi = h\nu_0]$

For 2nd case,

$$KE_2 = h \times 8 \times 10^{15} - h\nu_0$$

Change in KE = $KE_2 - KE_1 = h(8 \times 10^{15} - 4 \times 10^{15})$

$$= h \times 4 \times 10^{15}$$

As, $KE_1 = eV_1$ and $KE_2 = eV_2$

So, $eV_2 - eV_1 = h \times 4 \times 10^5$

$$\Rightarrow \quad (V_2 - V_1) = \frac{h}{e} \times 4 \times 10^{15}$$

$$\Rightarrow \quad (V_2 - V_1) = \frac{6.63 \times 10^{-34} \times 4 \times 10^{15}}{1.6 \times 10^{-19}} = 16.5 \text{ V}$$

23. Given, threshold wavelength,

$$\lambda_0 = 792 \text{ nm} = 792 \times 10^{-9} \text{ m},$$

Incident wavelength, $\lambda = 396 \text{ nm}$

$$= 396 \times 10^{-9} \text{ m}$$

So, by Einstein's photoelectric equation,

Maximum kinetic energy

$$KE_{max} = h\nu - \phi_0$$

So, $KE_{Max} = \frac{hc}{\lambda} - \frac{hc}{\lambda_0}$

[ϕ_0 = work function, $h\nu$ = energy]

$$= hc\left[\frac{1}{\lambda} - \frac{1}{\lambda_0}\right] \qquad [\text{as } \nu = c/\lambda]$$

$$= 6.6 \times 10^{-34} \times 3 \times 10^8 \left[\frac{1}{396 \times 10^{-9}} - \frac{1}{792 \times 10^{-9}}\right]$$

$$= 25 \times 10^{-20} \text{ J}$$

24. (*i*) Given, Work function, $\phi_0 = 2.28 \text{ eV}$

So, minimum energy for photocurrent

$$\phi_0 = 2.28 \times 1.6 \times 10^{-19} = 3.648 \times 10^{-19} \text{ J}$$

(*ii*) As we know that, $E = \frac{hc}{\lambda}$

So, $\lambda = \frac{hc}{E} = \frac{6.6 \times 10^{-34} \times 3 \times 10^8}{3.648 \times 10^{-19} \text{ J}}$

$$= 5.428 \times 10^{-7} \text{ m} = 5428 \text{ Å}$$

25. Given,

Threshold wavelength,

$$\lambda_0 = 2400 \text{ Å} = 2400 \times 10^{-10} \text{ m}$$

Wavelength of incident light,

$$\lambda = 1600 \text{ Å} = 1600 \times 10^{-10} \text{ m}$$

(*i*) So, work function $\phi = \frac{hc}{\lambda_0}$

$$= \frac{6.6 \times 10^{-34} \times 3 \times 10^8}{2400 \times 10^{-10}}$$

$$= 8.25 \times 10^{-19} \text{ J} = 5.16 \text{ eV}$$

(*ii*) Maximum kinetic energy

$$KE_{max} = \frac{hc}{\lambda} - \frac{hc}{\lambda_0}$$

[from Einstein photoelectric equation]

$$\Rightarrow KE_{max} = hc\left[\frac{1}{1600 \times 10^{-10}} - \frac{1}{2400 \times 10^{-10}}\right]$$

$$= \frac{hc}{10^{-10}}\left[\frac{2400 - 1600}{1600 \times 2400}\right]$$

$$= \frac{6.6 \times 10^{-34} \times 3 \times 10^8 \times 800}{10^{-10} \times 1600 \times 2400}$$

$$= 4.125 \times 10^{-19} \text{ J} = 2.578 \text{ eV}$$

(*iii*) Stopping potential,

$$KE_{max} = eV_0$$

$$\Rightarrow \quad V_0 = \frac{KE_{max}}{e}$$

$$V_0 = \frac{2.57 \text{eV}}{e} = 2.57 \text{ V}$$

26. When a light of suitable wavelength falls on the metallic surface due to which electrons starts ejecting from that surface is called photoelectric effect.

(*i*) Refer to text on page 247.

(*ii*) Refer to text on page 247.

(*iii*) Variation of photocurrent with frequency of incident radiation

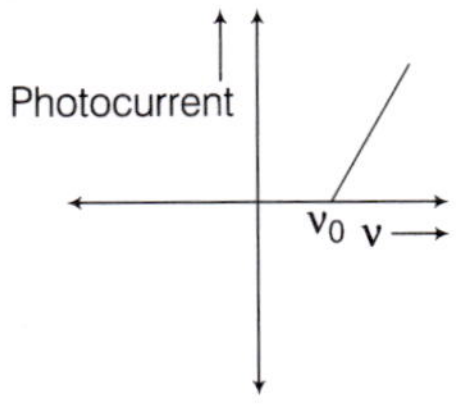

27. (*i*) In photoelectric emission, photogenerated electrons are called photoelectrons.

(*ii*) Photon is quanta or small packets of energy.

(*iii*) The Einstein's photoelectric effect equation gives the relation between kinetic energy and work function.

(*iv*) The wave theory fails to explain the existence of threshold frequency for every photoemitter.

CHAPTER TEST

01 Mark Questions (MCQs)

1 Photoemission with visible light is possible in

(a) alkali metals (b) alkaline earth metals
(c) metalloids (d) semiconductors

2 Monochromatic light of frequency 6.0×10^{14} Hz is produced by a laser. The energy of a photon in the light beam is

(a) 5×10^{-15} J (b) 3.98×10^{-19} J
(c) 2.54×10^{-14} J (d) 5.16×10^{-14} J

3 The wavelength of a photon needed to remove a proton from a nucleus which is bound to the nucleus with 1 MeV energy is nearly

(a) 1.2 nm (b) 1.2×10^{-3} nm
(c) 1.2×10^{-6} nm (d) 1.2×10 nm

4 The phenomenon which shows the quantum nature of electromagnetic radiation is named as

(a) tyndall effect (b) diffraction
(c) photoelectric effect (d) dispersion

01 Mark Questions (VSA)

5 Draw a graph between intensity of light and stopping potential in photoelectric effect.

6 The stopping potential in an experiment on photoelectric effect is 1.5 V. What is the maximum kinetic energy of the photoelectrons emitted?

7 Define intensity of radiation in photon picture of light.

8 The maximum kinetic energy of a photoelectron is 3 eV. What is its stopping potential.

02 Marks Questions

9 Calculate the maximum kinetic energy of photoelectrons emitted by a metal (work function = 1.6 eV) when it is illuminated with light of wavelength 298nm.

10 Monochromatic light of wavelength 200nm is incident on the surface of a metal whose work function is 3eV. Calculate the stopping potential.

11 Two monochromatic radiations; blue and violet, of the same intensity, are incident on a photosensitive surface and cause photoelectric emission. Would the number of electrons emitted per second and the maximum kinetic energy of the electrons be equal in the two cases? Justify your answer.

12 Write Einstein's photoelectric equation. State clearly, the three salient features observed in photoelectric effect, which can be explained on the basis of above equation.

03 Marks Question

13 Ultraviolet light of wavelength 2271 Å from a 100 W mercury source is incident on a photocell made of molybdenum metal. If the stopping potential is 1.3 V, estimate the work function of the metal.

05 Marks Questions

14 A frequency of 2.4×10^{15} Hz is used on magnesium with work function of 3.7 eV.

(i) What is the energy transferred by each photon?
(ii) Calculate
(a) the maximum kinetic energy of ejected electrons,
(b) the maximum speed of electrons and
(c) the stopping potential of the electrons.

15 What is the photoelectric effect? With the help of a suitable graph, show the variation of photocurrent with

(i) the intensity of incident radiation.
(ii) the voltage applied between cathode and anode.
(iii) the frequency of incident radiation.

Answers

1. (a) **2.** (b) **3.** (b) **4.** (c)
6. 2.5×10^{-19} J **8.** 3 V
9. 4.1×10^{-19} J **10.** 3.2 V
13. 4.16
14. (i) 9.92 eV (ii) (a) 6.22 eV (b) 1.35×10^{7} m/s (c) 6.22 V

19

Wave Particle Duality

TREND ANALYSIS 4 YEARS

Wave Particle Duality

Average No. of Questions Across all Sets

Types of Questions	2024	2023	2020	2019
1 Mark	1	2	1	–
2 Marks	–	–	–	–
3 Marks	–	–	–	–
5 Marks	–	–	–	–

Wave particle duality is a theory that proposes that, every elementary particle exhibits the properties of not only particles but also waves. This duality addresses the inability of the classical concepts, particle or wave to fully describe the behaviour of quantum scale objects.

- Electromagnetic radiation are of dual nature, i.e., wave nature as well as of particle nature.
- All the radiations are wave but all the waves are not radiations.

Some Phenomena Based on the Wave Nature

Interference

Interference is a phenomena in which two waves superpose to form a resultant wave of greater or lower amplitude. It usually refer to the interaction of waves that are correlated or coherent with each other.

Diffraction

It refers to the phenomena which occur when a wave encounters an obstacle or a slit and hence, bending of waves takes place around the obstacle (opaque).

Polarisation

It is the phenomenon in which the light waves vibrations (vibrations of electric vector) is being restricted in a particular direction, perpendicular to the direction of wave motion.

Some Phenomena Based on the Particle Nature

Photoelectric Effect

Photoelectric effect is the process of emission of electrons from the metallic surface when a suitable wavelength of radiation falls on it.

Wave Nature of Particles : de-Broglie Hypothesis

According to de-Broglie, a wave is associated with moving material particle which controls the particle in every aspect. The wave associated with the moving material particle is called **matter wave** or **de-Broglie wave** and its wavelength is called **de-Broglie wavelength**. It is expressed as

$$\lambda = \frac{h}{mv}$$

where, m and v are the mass and velocity of the particle and h is Planck's constant.

- According to Planck's quantum theory, the energy of the photon is

$$E = h\nu = \frac{hc}{\lambda} \quad \text{...(i)}$$

- According to Einstein's theory of mass-energy equivalence, the energy of photon can also be considered as,

$$E = mc^2 \quad \text{...(ii)}$$

From Eqs. (i) and (ii), we get

$$\lambda = \frac{h}{mc} \quad \text{or} \quad \lambda = \frac{h}{p}$$

where, p = momentum of photon = mc

- If a material particle of mass (m) is moving with velocity (v), then momentum of the particle $p = mv$ and the equation becomes

$$\lambda = \frac{h}{p} = \frac{h}{mv} = \frac{h}{\sqrt{2mE_K}} \quad \left[\text{as } E_K = \frac{p^2}{2m}\right]$$

where, E_K = kinetic energy of the particle.

If an electron is accelerated through a potential difference V, then wave associated with the electron is given by

$$\lambda = \frac{h}{\sqrt{2meV}}$$

where, e = electron charge, m = mass of electron, which is the expression for de-Broglie wavelength and is named **de-Broglie equation**.

Conclusions of de-Broglie Equations

(*i*) de-Broglie wavelength $\lambda \propto \frac{1}{v}$. If the particle moves faster, then the wavelength will be smaller and *vice-versa*.

(*ii*) If the particle is at rest $(v = 0)$, then the de-Broglie wavelength is infinite $(\lambda = \infty)$. Such a wave cannot be visualised.

(*iii*) de-Broglie waves cannot be electromagnetic in nature, because the electromagnetic waves are produced by accelerated motion of the charged particles.

(*iv*) The wavelength of a wave associated with the moving particles defines a region of uncertainty, within which the position of the particles are unknown.

This facts leads to **Heisenberg's uncertainty principle.** According to this principle, it is not possible to measure both the position and momentum of a particle at the same time exactly. There is always some uncertainty in specification of position (Δx) and some uncertainty in the specification of momentum (Δp). The product of Δx and Δp is of the order of $\hbar$, (with $\hbar = \frac{h}{2\pi}$).

i.e.,
$$\boxed{\Delta x \, \Delta p \approx \hbar = \frac{h}{2\pi}}$$

PYQs Previous Years Questions

1 Mark Questions

1. The de-Broglie wavelength (λ) associated with a moving electron having kinetic energy (E) is given by **ISC 2024**

(a) $\frac{2h}{\sqrt{2mE}}$ (b) $\frac{2\sqrt{2mE}}{h}$

(c) $\frac{h}{\sqrt{2mE}}$ (d) $\sqrt{2mhE}$

2. Matter waves are **ISC 2023**

(a) waves associated with moving particles.

(b) waves associated with stationary particles.

(c) waves associated with any charged particles.

(d) waves associated with electrons only.

3. The graph of de-Broglie wavelength (λ) of a moving electron *versus* its velocity (v) is **ISC SQP 2023**

(a)
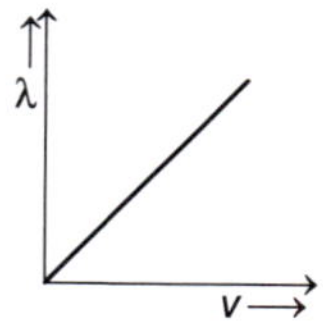

(b)

(c)

(d)
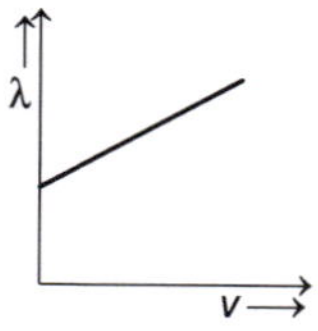

4. de-Broglie wavelength of moving particle is λ. Its momentum is given by **ISC SQP 2018**

(a) $\frac{h\lambda}{c}$ (b) $\frac{h}{\lambda}$ (c) $\frac{hc}{\lambda}$ (d) zero

5. State de-Broglie hypothesis. **ISC 2022 Sem-II , 20, 18**

6. Find the de-Broglie wavelength of electrons moving with a speed of $7 \times 10^6 \text{ms}^{-1}$. **ISC 2017**

7. What is the relation between wavelength and momentum of moving electrons? **ISC 2013**

8. Which one of the following graphs in figure represents variation of de-Broglie wavelength (λ) of a particle having linear momentum (p)? **ISC 2011**

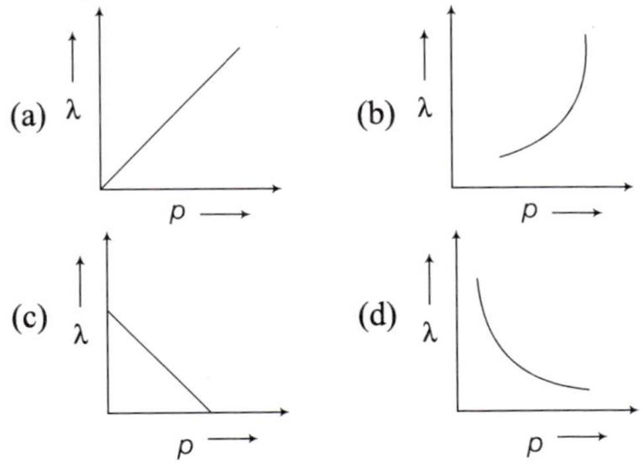

9. de-Broglie wavelength of electrons of kinetic energy E is λ. What will be its value, if kinetic energy of electrons made $4E$? **ISC 2010**

10. Find the momentum of a photon of energy 3.0 eV. **ISC 2009**

11. Calculate the momentum of photon of green light of $\lambda = 500$ nm in SI unit. **ISC 2007**

2 Marks Questions

12. For each of the following, state one phenomenon in which **ISC SQP 2018**

(*i*) particles behave like waves.

(*ii*) waves behave like particles.

13. (*i*) State how de-Broglie wavelength (λ) of moving particles varies with their linear momentum (p).

(*ii*) State anyone phenomenon in which moving particles exhibit wave nature. **ISC 2015**

3 Marks Questions

14. A monochromatic source of light emits light of wavelength 198 nm. Calculate

(*i*) the energy of each photon.

(*ii*) the momentum of photons. **ISC 2011**

15. Electrons initially at rest, are passed through a potential difference of 2 kV. Calculate their

(*i*) final velocity.

(*ii*) de-Broglie wavelength. **ISC 2009**

Case Based Question (For Complete Chapter)

16. **Direction** *Read the passage given below and answer the questions that follows.*

Dual Nature of Matter

Light has dual nature. It manifests itself as a wave in diffraction, interference and polarisation, while it shows up particle nature in photoelectric effect, compton scattering, etc. de-Broglie put forward the bold hypothesis that moving particles (like protons, neutrons, electrons, etc.) of matter should display wave like properties under suitable conditions.

His argument was based on the fact that nature was symmetrical and the two physical quantities-matter and energy must have symmetrical character. If radiation shows due aspect so should matter. The waves associated with the moving particles were called matter waves. The de-Broglie wavelength of a particle of mass m moving with velocity v is given by

$$\lambda = \frac{h}{p} = \frac{h}{mv}, \text{ where } h = \text{Planck's constant}$$

The de-Broglie wavelength is independent of charge and mass of the material particles. It has significant value for sub-atomic particles like electrons, protons, etc., due to their small masses.

(*i*) What are the matter waves? **(1)**

(*ii*) What is relation between de-Broglie wavelength and momentum? **(1)**

(*iii*) Is the de-Broglie wavelength dependent on charge? **(1)**

(*iv*) Is de-Broglie waves same as electromagnetic wave in nature? **(2)**

Explanations

1. (*c*) The de-Broglie wavelength (λ) associated with a moving electron,

$$\lambda = \frac{h}{p} \quad \ldots(i)$$

and kinetic energy, $E = \frac{1}{2}mv^2 = \frac{p^2}{2m}$

$$p = \sqrt{2mE} \quad \ldots(ii)$$

[From Eqs. (i) and (ii)]

So, $\lambda = \frac{h}{\sqrt{2mE}}$

Hence, option (c) is correct.

2. (a) Matter waves are the waves associated with moving particles.

3. (b) As, $\lambda \propto \frac{1}{p}$ or for constant m, $\lambda \propto \frac{1}{v}$

So, the correct graph is

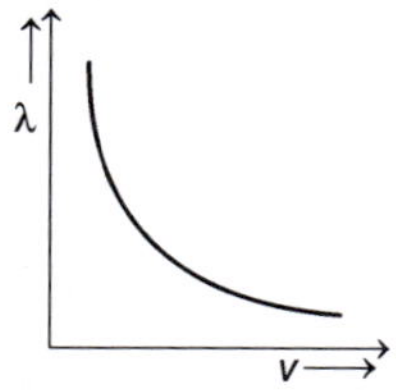

4. (b) According to de-Broglie, wavelength of moving particle is given by

$$\lambda = \frac{h}{mv} = \frac{h}{p} \quad [\because mv = p]$$

Or $p = \frac{h}{\lambda}$ (momentum of particle)

5. Refer to text on page 255 (de-Broglie hypothesis).

6. Given, speed, $v = 7 \times 10^6$ m/s

de-Broglie wavelength is given as, $\lambda = \frac{h}{p} = \frac{h}{m_e v}$

where, m_e = mass of the electron.

$$\Rightarrow \lambda = \frac{6.6 \times 10^{-34}}{9 \times 10^{-31} \times 7 \times 10^6} = 1.0476 \times 10^{-10} \text{m}$$

$$= 10.476 \text{ Å}$$

7. The relation between wavelength and momentum of moving electrons is given by de-Broglie relation,

$$\lambda = \frac{h}{p}$$

where, λ = wavelength,

h = Planck's constant and

$p = mv$ = momentum of electrons

8. (d) As, $\lambda \propto \frac{1}{p}$. The correct graph is

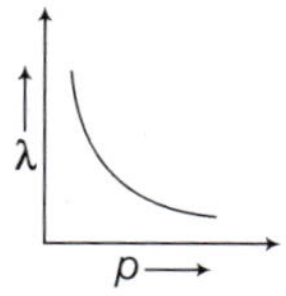

9. As from de-Broglie relation, $\lambda = h/p$

and we know that, $\text{KE} = \frac{p^2}{2m}$

$\therefore \quad p = \sqrt{2m\,\text{KE}}$

Now, $\lambda = \frac{h}{\sqrt{2m\,\text{KE}}} \quad \ldots(i)$

According to the question,

New kinetic energy = 4KE

$\therefore$ New wavelength, $\lambda' = \frac{h}{\sqrt{2m \times 4\,\text{KE}}}$

$$\lambda' = \frac{1}{2}\left(\frac{h}{\sqrt{2m\,\text{KE}}}\right) \quad \ldots(ii)$$

From Eqs. (i) and (ii), we get

$$\lambda' = \frac{1}{2} \times \lambda \Rightarrow \lambda' = \frac{\lambda}{2}$$

So, new wavelength is the half of the first wavelength when kinetic energy of electrons made $4E$.

10. Given, photon of energy = 3.0 eV = $3 \times 1.6 \times 10^{-19}$ J

As we know that,

$$\text{Momentum, } p = \frac{\text{Energy}}{c\,(\text{Velocity of light})}$$

$$= \frac{3 \times 1.6 \times 10^{-19} \text{ J}}{3 \times 10^8 \text{ m/s}}$$

$$= 1.6 \times 10^{-27} \text{ kg ms}^{-1}$$

11. Given wavelength, $\lambda = 500 \text{ nm} = 500 \times 10^{-9}$ m

According to de-Broglie relation,

$$\lambda = \frac{h}{p} \quad [\text{where, } p = \text{momentum}]$$

$$\therefore \quad p=\frac{h}{\lambda}=\frac{6.6\times10^{-34}\text{ J-s}}{500\times10^{-9}\text{ m}}$$
$$=1.32\times10^{-27}\text{ kg ms}^{-1}$$

12. (*i*) Interference of light is the phenomena in which particles behave like waves. In this phenomena, when two or more waves of the same frequency and having zero or constant phase difference are travelling in same direction superimpose on each other.

(*ii*) Photoelectric effect is the phenomena is which waves behaves like particles. In this phenomena, when a suitable frequency of light, falls on the metal surface, electrons are emitted from metal surface.

Concept Enhancer Diffraction and polarisation phenomena also proved that particles behave like waves. Compton effect proved that waves behave like particles.

13. (*i*) According to Planck's quantum theory, the energy of the photon is

$$E=h\nu=\frac{hc}{\lambda} \quad \ldots\text{(i)}$$

According to Einstein's theory, the energy of the photon is $E=mc^2$ ...(ii)

From Eqs. (i) and (ii), we get

$$\lambda=\frac{h}{mc} \text{ or } \lambda=\frac{h}{p}$$

where, p is momentum of a photon.

(*ii*) The phenomenon in which moving particles exhibit wave nature is diffraction.

14. (*i*) Given, wavelength

$$\lambda=198\text{ nm}=198\times10^{-9}\text{ m}$$

As we know that, energy of photon,

$$E=\frac{hc}{\lambda}=\frac{6.6\times10^{-34}\times3\times10^{8}}{198\times10^{-9}}=10^{-18}\text{ J}$$

(*ii*) As wavelength of photon is given by

$$\lambda=\frac{h}{p}$$

$$\Rightarrow \quad p=\frac{h}{\lambda}=\frac{6.6\times10^{-34}\text{ J-s}}{198\times10^{-9}\text{ m}}$$
$$=3.33\times10^{-27}\text{ kg ms}^{-1}$$

15. (*i*) Given,

potential difference, $V=2\text{ kV}=2000\text{ V}$

and we know that, $eV=\frac{1}{2}mv^2$

So, $$v^2=\frac{2eV}{m}$$

$$\Rightarrow \quad v=\sqrt{\frac{2eV}{m}}$$
$$=\sqrt{\frac{2\times1.6\times10^{-19}\times2000}{9.1\times10^{-31}}}$$
$$=\sqrt{\frac{6.4}{9.1}\times10^{15}}=2.65\times10^{7}\text{ m/s}$$

(*ii*) Now, de-Broglie wavelength for electrons is given by

$$\lambda=\frac{12.27}{\sqrt{V}}\text{ Å}=\frac{12.27}{\sqrt{2\times10^{3}}}=0.274\text{ Å}$$

16. (*i*) The waves associated with a moving particle are called matter waves.

(*ii*) The de-Broglie wavelength of a particle is inversely proportional to the momentum and given by the relation.

$$\lambda=\frac{h}{p}, \text{ where } h=\text{Planck's constant.}$$

(*iii*) No, de-Broglie wavelength is independent of charge.

(*iv*) de-Broglie wavelength cannot be electromagnetic wave in nature.

CHAPTER TEST

01 Mark Questions (MCQs)

1 The de-Broglie wavelength λ
(a) is proportional to mass
(b) is proportional to momentum
(c) inversely proportional to momentum
(d) does not depend on momentum

2 de-Broglie wavelength associated with an electron, accelerating through a potential difference of 100 V lies in the region of
(a) Gamma rays (b) X-rays
(c) Ultraviolet (d) Visible region

3 A particle is dropped from a height H. The de-Broglie wavelength of the particle as a function of height is proportional to
(a) H (b) H^0
(c) $H^{1/2}$ (d) $H^{-1/2}$

4 The dependence on the de-Broglie wavelength on temperature is given by
(a) $\lambda \propto \frac{1}{\sqrt{T}}$ (b) $\lambda \propto \sqrt{T}$
(c) $\lambda \propto T^0$ (d) $\lambda \propto T$

01 Mark Questions (VSA)

5 A proton and an electron have same kinetic energy. Which one has greater de-Broglie wavelength and why?

6. Write the relationship of de-Broglie wavelength λ associated with a particle of mass m in terms of its kinetic energy E.

7 Show graphically, the variation of de-Broglie wavelength (λ) with the potential (V) through which an electron is accelerated from rest.

02 Marks Questions

8 An α-particle and a proton are accelerated from rest by the same potential. Find the ratio of their de-Broglie wavelengths.

9 An electron is accelerated through a potential difference of 100 V. What is the de-Broglie wavelength associated with it? To which part of the electromagnetic spectrum does this value of wavelength correspond?

10 For what kinetic energy of a neutron, will the associated de-Broglie wavelength be 1.32×10^{-10} Å? Given that the mass of a neutron $= 1.675 \times 10^{-27}$ kg.

05 Marks Question

11. (i) Determine the de-Broglie wavelength of a proton whose kinetic energy is equal to the rest mass energy of an electron. Mass of a proton is 1836 times to that of electron.
(ii) In which region of electromagnetic spectrum does this wavelength lie?

Answers

1. (c) **2.** (b) **3.** (d) **4.** (a)
9. 1.23 Å **10.** 7.53×10^{-21} J
11. (*i*) 4×10^{-14} m

20

Atomic Structure

TREND ANALYSIS 4 YEARS

	Types of Questions	2024	2023	2020	2019
		Average No. of Questions Across all Sets			
TOPIC 01 Rutherford's Model	1 Mark	–	–	–	–
	2 Marks	–	–	–	–
	3 Marks	–	–	–	–
	5 Marks	–	–	–	–
TOPIC 02 Bohr's Model and Hydrogen Spectra	1 Mark	1	1	–	1
	2 Marks	2	1	–	–
	3 Marks	–	1	1	1
	5 Marks	–	–	–	–

TOPIC 1

Rutherford's Model

All elements consist of very small invisible particles are called atoms. In order to investigate the structure of atom, Rutherford and his two associates Geiger and Marsden studied the scattering of the α-particles over a gold foil.

α-Particles Scattering Experiment

The α-particles from a radioactive source contained in a lead cavity are collimated into a narrow beam with the help of a lead plate having a narrow slit.

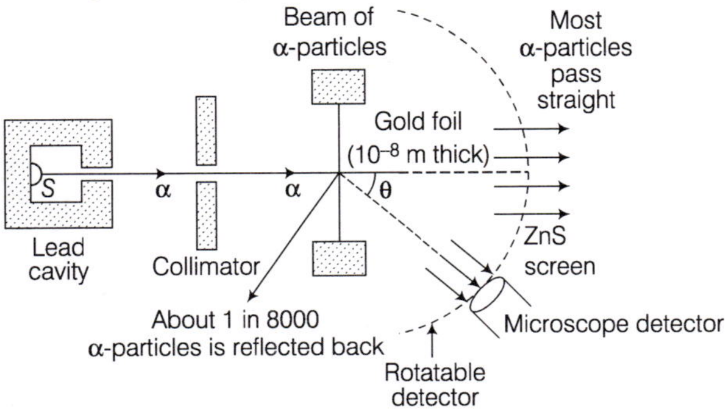

Experimental arrangement of α-particles scattering

The whole chamber is installed inside a vacuum chamber to prevent the loss of α-particles from air molecules.

Observations Drawn by Rutherford

- Most of the α-particle go undeflected.
- Only about 0.14% of incident α-particles scatter by more than 10.
- A small number of α-particles about (1 in 8000) retraced their paths or suffered deflection of more than angle 90°.
- The total number of α-particles scattered at an angle θ by target is given by $N_{(\theta)} = \dfrac{N_i\, nLZ\, K^2 e^4}{4r^2 (\text{KE})^2 \sin^4 (\theta/2)}$

where, N_i = total number of α-particles that strikes the unit area of the scatterer

n = number of target atom/m^3

L = thickness of target

Z = charge on the target nucleus

K = Coulomb's constant

KE = kinetic energy of α-particle

r = distance of screen from the target (i.e. distance between α-particles and the nucleus)

θ = scattering angle.

Conclusions Drawn from Rutherford's Experiment

The following conclusions were drawn from Rutherford's experiment.

- At the centre of atom there is a nucleus of radius approximately 10^{-14} m, in which the entire positive charge and the entire mass of atom are concentrated. The charge on the nucleus is $+Ze$, where Z is the atomic number of the element and e is the charge on one electron.
- Size of nucleus is of the order of 10^{-15} m, which is very small as compared to the size of atom which is a sphere of radius of order of 10^{-10} m.

Rutherford's Atomic Model

- Atomic nucleus is surrounded by certain number of electrons and the total negative charge of electrons is equal to the total positive charge of the nucleus as atom is electrically neutral.
- The electrons do not reside stationary around the nucleus otherwise the electrons due to attractive force of positive charge of nucleus will fall into the nucleus and the atom will become unstable. Hence, Rutherford assumed that the electrons revolve around the nucleus in circular orbits.
- The centripetal force required by electrons for revolution is provided by the electrostatic force of attraction between the electrons and nucleus.

Distance of Closest Approach

At a certain distance r_0 from the nucleus, the whole of the KE of α-particles converts into electrostatic potential energy and α-particle cannot go further close to nucleus. This distance (r_0) is called **distance of closest approach.**

At the distance of closest approach (r_0),

KE of α-particle = Electrostatic potential energy (U)

$$\text{KE} = \frac{1}{4\pi\varepsilon_0}\frac{(Ze)(2e)}{r_0}$$

Since, the charge on α-particle is $+2e$ and charge on nucleus is Ze, where Z is atomic number.

$$\therefore \quad r_0 = \frac{1}{4\pi\varepsilon_0}\frac{2Ze^2}{\text{KE}}$$

or

$$r_0 = \frac{1}{4\pi\varepsilon_0}\frac{2Ze^2}{\left(\frac{1}{2}mv^2\right)}$$

$$\left[\text{as, KE} = \frac{1}{2}mv^2\right]$$

where, m = mass of α-particle

v = initial velocity of α-particle.

Drawback of Rutherford's Model

Rutherford's model had two major drawbacks

(*i*) According to the classical electromagnetic theory, when a charge particle moves around any charge particle it radiates energy.

(*ii*) Regarding explanation of line spectrum, Rutherford's model was unable to explain line spectrum.

PYQs Previous Years Questions

3 Marks Questions

1. What conclusion was drawn by Rutherford based on Geiger Marsden's experiment on scattering of α-particles? **ISC 2012**

2. α-particles having KE of 1.8 MeV each are incident on a thin gold foil from a large distance. Applying the principle of conservation of energy, find the distance of closes approach of the α-particle from the gold nucleus. (Atomic number of gold = 79) **ISC 2009**

3. Why is the classical (Rutherford) model for an atom of electron orbiting around the nucleus not able to explain the atomic structure? **ISC 2007**

4. In the Rutherford scattering experiment, the distance of closest approach for an α-particle is d_0. If α-particle is replaced by a proton, how much kinetic energy in comparison to α-particle will be required to have the same distance of closest approach, d_0. **ISC 2005**

5 Marks Question

5. Draw a schematic arrangement of the Geiger-Marsden's experiment for studying α-particles scattering by a thin foil of gold. Describe briefly by drawing trajectories of the scattered α-particles. How this study can be used to estimate the size of the nucleus? **ISC 2010**

Explanations

1. On the basis of Geiger-Marsden's experiment, Rutherford concluded that
   (*i*) most of space inside the atom is empty .
   (*ii*) at the centre of atom there is a small space, where the whole of positive charges is concentrated.
   (*iii*) the space where only positive charge particle is concentrated is called nucleus.

2. Let the distance of closest approach of the α-particle be r_0.
   So, by principle of conservation of energy,
   Kinetic energy KE = Potential energy PE

$$\Rightarrow \quad \text{KE} = U = \frac{1}{4\pi\varepsilon_0} \cdot \frac{Ze(2e)}{r_0}$$

$$\Rightarrow \quad r_0 = \frac{1}{4\pi\varepsilon_0} \cdot \frac{2Ze^2}{\text{KE}} = \frac{9\times 10^9 \times 2 \times 79 \times (1.6\times 10^{-19})}{1.8 \times 1.6 \times 10^{-13}}$$

$$= 1.264 \times 10^{-13} \text{ m}$$

where, $+Ze$ = charge in nucleus
$+2e$ = charge on α-particle
$\frac{1}{4\pi\varepsilon_0} = K$ = coulomb constant

3. The classical model could not explain the stability of atom as the negatively charged electrons are revolving around the nucleus are accelerated and emits energy as the result, the radius of the electrons on circular paths goes on decreasing. Ultimately, electrons fall into the nucleus, which is not true for an atom.

4. When α-particle is replaced by proton, then there will be a change in atomic number and mass of the particle.
   ∵ For a given distance of closest approach,
   Kinetic energy ∝ Z (charge on particle)

$$\Rightarrow \quad \frac{K_{\text{proton}}}{K_\alpha} = \frac{e}{2e} = \frac{1}{2}$$

[where, e is charge on proton]

$$\therefore \quad K_{\text{proton}} : K_\alpha = 1:2$$

Concept Enhancer The distance of closest approach of α-particle to the nucleus depends on the kinetic energy of α-particle.

5. Given figure shows a schematic diagram of Geiger-Marsden's experiment.

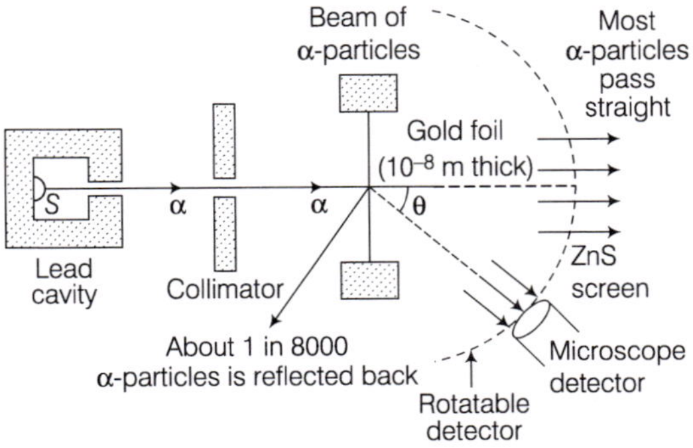

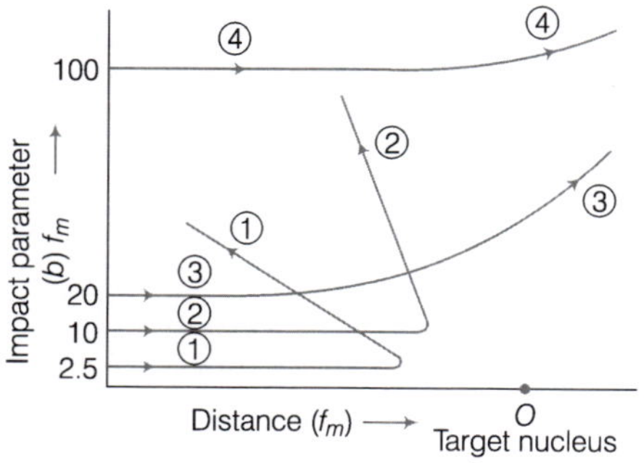

The size of nucleus can be obtained by finding the distance of closest approach, which is given by

$$r_0 = \frac{1}{4\pi\varepsilon_0} \cdot \frac{2Ze^2}{(\text{KE})}$$

where, $+Ze$ = charge in nucleus

$+2e$ = charge on α-particle

$\frac{1}{4\pi\varepsilon_0} = K$ = coulomb constant.

TOPIC 2

Bohr's Model and Hydrogen Spectra

Historical Background

In 1913, Bohr proposed his quantised shell model of the atom to explain how electrons can have stable orbits around the nucleus.

Bohr modified the Rutherford model by considering that the electrons move in orbits of fixed size and energy.

Assumptions of Bohr's Model

- The electron in a hydrogen atom travels around the nucleus in a circular orbit. According to de-Broglie's hypothesis, this electron is also associated with wave characters.
- The energy of the electron in an orbit is inversely proportional to its distance from the nucleus. The farther electron from the nucleus has the more energy.
- Only a limited number of orbits with certain energies are allowed for the revolving electrons. In other words, the orbits are quantised.
- A circular orbit can taken to be a stationary energy state only if it contains an integral number of de-Broglie wavelengths, i.e. $2\pi r = n\lambda$

  but de-Broglie wavelength $\lambda = \frac{h}{mv}$

  $\therefore \quad 2\pi r = \frac{nh}{mv}$
- The only orbits that are allowed must have angular momentum of the electron of an integral multiple of Planck's constant divided by 2π *i.e.* $L = \frac{nh}{2\pi}$.
- Light is absorbed when an electron jumps to a higher energy orbit and emitted when an electron falls into a lower energy orbit.

Bohr's Model of Atom

Bohr combined classical and early quantum concept and gave his theory in the form of three postulates.

These postulates are as follows

(*i*) Bohr's first postulate was that an electron in an atom could revolve in certain stable orbit without the emission of radiant energy, contrary to the predictions of electromagnetic theory.

(*ii*) Bohr's second postulate defines these stable orbits. This postulate states that the electrons revolve around the nucleus only in those orbits for which the angular momentum is an integral multiple of $h/2\pi$, where h is the Planck's constant ($= 6.6 \times 10^{-34}$ J-s). Thus, the angular momentum of the orbiting electron is quantised *i.e.*, $L = \frac{nh}{2\pi}$.

As angular momentum of electron = mvr

$\therefore$ For any permitted (stationary) orbit, angular momentum

$$\boxed{mvr = \frac{nh}{2\pi}}$$

where, n = any positive integer *i.e.*, 1, 2, 3, ...

It is also called **principal quantum number**.

(*iii*) Bohr's third postulate states that an electron migrates from one of its specific non-radiating orbits to another of lower energy.

The frequency of the emitted photon is then given by

$$h\nu = E_i - E_f$$

where, E_i and E_f are the energies of the initial and final states and $E_i > E_f$.

The difference in energy between any two orbits is therefore given by the following equation *i.e.*,

$$\Delta E = E_i - E_f = RhcZ^2\left(\frac{1}{n_1^2} - \frac{1}{n_2^2}\right)$$

As by Planck's equation $E = h\nu = \frac{hc}{\lambda}$

The equation of energy difference becomes

$$\frac{1}{\lambda} = RZ^2\left(\frac{1}{n_1^2} - \frac{1}{n_2^2}\right)$$

where, R = Rydberg constant, n_1 = initial orbit, n_2 = final orbit.

Bohr's Hydrogen Atom

As electrons revolve around the nucleus and the centripetal force is equal to the electrostatic force of attraction between electrons and nucleus.

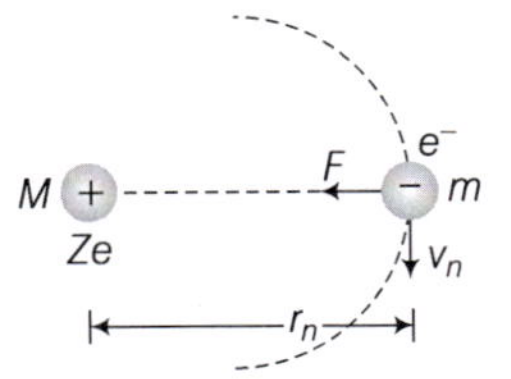

$$\frac{mv_n^2}{r_n} = \frac{1}{4\pi\varepsilon_0}\frac{e^2}{r_n^2} \quad \ldots(i)$$

Angular momentum of stationary orbit

$$\Rightarrow \quad mv_n r_n = \frac{nh}{2\pi} \quad \ldots(ii)$$

where $n = 1, 2, 3$

Radius of Different Orbits

From Eqs. (i) and (ii), we get $r_n = \frac{\varepsilon_0 n^2 h^2}{\pi m e^2}$

where, r_n = radius of nth orbit, n = Planck's constant m = mass of an electron, e = charge on an electron.

For smallest orbit $n=1$, $a_0 = \frac{\varepsilon_0 h^2}{\pi m e^2} = 0.529$ Å $= 5.29$ nm

$$\Rightarrow \quad r_n = n^2 a_0$$

NOTE For hydrogen like atom i.e., He^+, Li^{2+} having one electron the radius of nth orbit is given by

$$r_n = \frac{n^2}{Z}a_0 \qquad \text{[Z is atomic number]}$$

It can be concluded that ratio of radii of stationary orbit is given by $1^2 : 2^2 : 3^2 : 4^2 \ldots$ or $1 : 4 : 9 : 16 \ldots$ i.e., the stationary orbit speed given by Bohr's are not equally speed.

Velocity of Electron Different Orbits

From Eqs. (i) and (ii), we get

$$\boxed{v_n = \frac{e^2}{2\varepsilon_0 nh}}$$

For hydrogen atom and for $Z = 1$ and $n = 1$,

$$v_1 = \frac{e^2}{2\varepsilon_0 h} = \frac{c}{137} = 2.19 \times 10^6 \text{ m/s}$$

where, c = speed of light $= 3 \times 10^8$ m/s

So, velocity of electron in Ist orbit $(v_1) = 2.19 \times 10^6$ m/s

This shows that the velocity of electron is maximum in the lowest orbit $(n = 1)$ and goes on decreasing in higher orbits.

Now for nth orbit velocity of electrons

$$v_n = \frac{v_1}{n}$$

[where, v_n = velocity in nth orbit]

NOTE For hydrogen like atom, $v_n = v_1 \times \frac{Z}{n}$.

Wavelength

The wavelength λ of the emitted radiation is given by

$$\frac{1}{\lambda} = \frac{f}{c} = \frac{me^4}{8\varepsilon_0^2 ch^3}\left(\frac{1}{n_1^2} - \frac{1}{n_2^2}\right)$$

$\frac{1}{\lambda}$ is also called wave number.

$$\therefore \quad \boxed{\frac{1}{\lambda} = R\left(\frac{1}{n_1^2} - \frac{1}{n_2^2}\right)} \qquad \left[\because R = \frac{me^4}{8\varepsilon_0^2 ch^3}\right]$$

NOTE For hydrogen like atom, $\frac{1}{\lambda} = RZ^2\left(\frac{1}{n_1^2} - \frac{1}{n_2^2}\right)$.

Frequency of Electron

It is the number of revolutions completed per second by the electron in a stationary orbit around the nucleus.

$$\because \quad v = r\omega = r \times 2\pi f$$

$$\Rightarrow \quad f = \frac{v}{2\pi r}$$

$\Rightarrow f_n = \frac{v_n}{2\pi r_n}$ substituting values of v_n and r_n

we have, $$f_n = \left(\frac{me^4}{4\varepsilon_0^2 h^3}\right)\frac{1}{n^3}\cdot Z^2$$

Now f_0 = frequency in 1st orbit $= 6.56 \times 10^{15}$ Hz

So, $$f_n = \frac{f_0}{n^3}$$

NOTE For hydrogen like atom, $f_n = \frac{f_0 Z^2}{n^3}$.

Energy of Electron in Different Orbits

The kinetic and potential energies K_n and U_n, respectively of an electron in nth orbit are given by

$$K_n = \frac{1}{2} mv^2 = \frac{me^4 Z^2}{8\varepsilon_0^2 n^2 h^2} = \frac{mZ^2 e^4}{8\varepsilon_0^2 h^2}\left(\frac{1}{n^2}\right)$$

$$U_n = \frac{-1}{4\pi\varepsilon_0}\frac{Ze^2}{r_n} = -\frac{me^4 Z^2}{4\varepsilon_0^2 n^2 h^2}$$

So, total energy of electrons in the stationary orbit is given by

$$E_n = K_n + U_n = \frac{-me^4 Z^2}{8\varepsilon_0^2 n^2 h^2}$$

For first orbit of H-atom, $Z = 1$ and $n = 1$,
Therefore, energy of the first orbit of H-atom,
$E_1 = -13.6\,\text{eV}$

So, energy of nth orbit of the hydrogen atom

$$\boxed{E_n = \frac{-13.6}{n^2}\,\text{eV}}$$

Energy Levels

The energy of an atom is the least, when its electron is revolving in an orbit closest to the nucleus i.e. for which $n = 1$. For $n = 2, 3, \ldots$ the absolute value of energy E ($E_2 = -3.40\,\text{eV}$) is smaller, so the energy is progressively larger in outer orbits.

- The lowest state of the atom is called the ground state, this state has lowest energy. The energy of this state is -13.3 eV.
- It is called ionisation energy of the H-atom. At room temperature, most of the H-atoms are in ground state. When an atom receive some energy (i.e. by electron collisions), the atom may acquire sufficient energy to raise electron to higher energy state.

Energy Level Diagram

It is clear from above expression of energy that energy of different levels depends upon the quantum number (n). The energy level diagram for the stationary state of a hydrogen atom, computed from above expressions of E_n is shown in the figure given below.

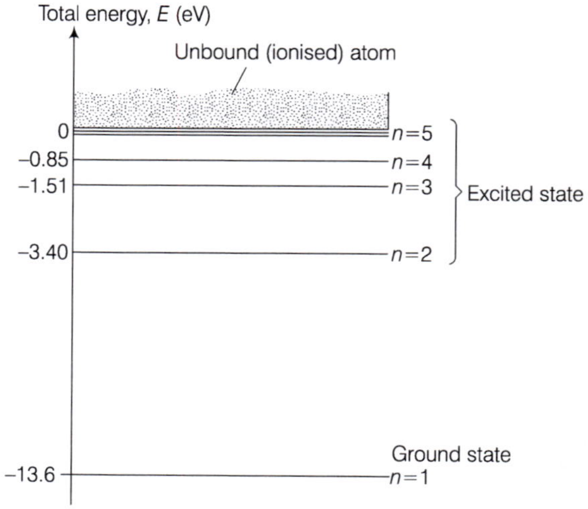

The energy level diagram for the hydrogen atom

NOTE For hydrogen like atom, $E_n = -13.6\text{ eV} \times \frac{Z^2}{n^2}\text{ eV}$

Origin of Spectra

Origin of spectra can be explained on the basis of atomic theory.

An atom consists of a central positive core, called nucleus, which is surrounded by electrons revolving in various orbits, a certain amount of energy is associated with each orbit.

Radiation having energy equal to the difference of energy associated with the two orbits is emitted.

Thus, $$\frac{1}{\lambda} = Z^2 R\left(\frac{1}{n_1^2} - \frac{1}{n_2^2}\right)$$

This is Bohr's formula for hydrogen and hydrogen like atoms ($He^+, Li^{2+}, \ldots\ldots$)

For hydrogen ($Z = 1$), we have

$$\frac{1}{\lambda} = R\left(\frac{1}{n_1^2} - \frac{1}{n_2^2}\right)$$

Emission Spectra

The light emitted by a source of light and resolved into its constituent wavelengths is called emission spectrum.

In emission spectrum, we get bright lines on dark background.

Line Emission Spectrum

Every line spectrum consist of a few isolated bright lines. Each bright line correspond to a particular wavelength.

Band Emission Spectrum

A band emission spectrum is one, which consists of a number of bright bands (group of wavelengths) of light, sharp at one end and fading off at the other end. The band spectrum is emitted by the molecules in gaseous form.

Band spectra is emitted by O_2, N_2, CaF_2 etc.

Absorption Spectrum

When light from a source emitting a continuous range of wavelength is passed through any transparent material (solid, liquid, gas or vapour) and light transmitted is observed in a spectroscope, certain dark regions are seen in continuous spectrum.

Hydrogen Spectrum or Line Spectra of Hydrogen Atom

- Hydrogen spectrum consists of discrete bright lines at dark background and it is specifically known as hydrogen **emission spectrum**.
- There is one more type of hydrogen spectrum exists where we get dark lines on the bright background. It is known as **absorption spectrum**.
- Balmer find an empirical formula by the observation of a small part of this spectrum and it is represented by

$$\frac{1}{\lambda} = R\left(\frac{1}{2^2} - \frac{1}{n^2}\right)$$

[where, $n = 3, 4, 5, \ldots$]

where, R is a constant called **Rydberg constant** having the value of $= 1.097 \times 10^7 \text{ m}^{-1}$.

So, $\frac{1}{\lambda} = 1.522 \times 10^6 \text{ m}^{-1}$

$= 6563$ nm for $n = 3$

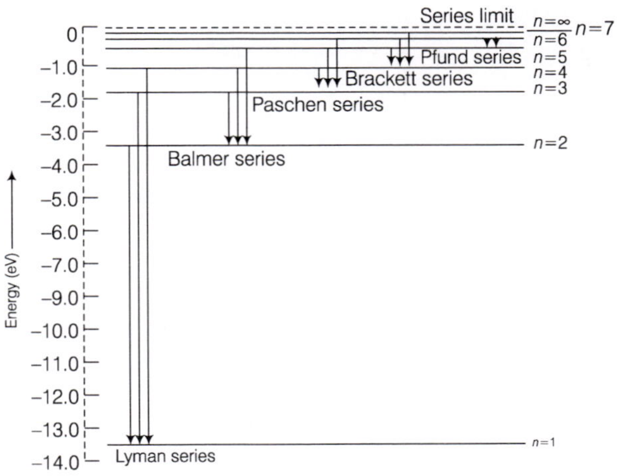

The lines of Balmer series are found in the visible part of the spectrum. Other series were found in the invisible parts of the spectrum. e.g., Lyman series in the ultraviolet region and Paschen, Brackett and Pfund series in the infrared region.

The wavelengths of line in these series can be expressed by the following formula

(i) For Lyman series $\frac{1}{\lambda} = R\left(\frac{1}{1^2} - \frac{1}{n^2}\right)$,

where $n = 2, 3, 4, \ldots$

(ii) For Balmer series $\frac{1}{\lambda} = R\left(\frac{1}{2^2} - \frac{1}{n^2}\right)$,

where $n = 3, 4, 5, \ldots$

(iii) For Paschen series $\frac{1}{\lambda} = R\left(\frac{1}{3^2} - \frac{1}{n^2}\right)$,

where $n = 4, 5, 6, \ldots$

(iv) For Brackett series $\frac{1}{\lambda} = R\left(\frac{1}{4^2} - \frac{1}{n^2}\right)$,

where $n = 5, 6, 7, \ldots$

(v) For Pfund series $\frac{1}{\lambda} = R\left(\frac{1}{5^2} - \frac{1}{n^2}\right)$, where $n = 6, 7, 8, \ldots$

PYQs Previous Years Questions

1 Mark Questions

1. State the Bohr's postulate of angular momentum of an electron. **ISC 2024**

2. How much is the angular momentum of an electron when it is orbiting in the second Bohr orbit of hydrogen atom? **ISC 2023, 11**

3. Angular momentum of an electron orbiting in the 3rd Bohr orbit of a hydrogen atom is **ISC 2022 Sem-II**

(a) $h/2\pi$ (b) $2h/2\pi$
(c) $3h/2\pi$ (d) $4h/2\pi$

4. First line of Balmer series (H_α) in the spectrum of hydrogen is obtained when an electron of hydrogen atom goes from **ISC 2022 Sem-II**

(a) 2nd orbit to 1st orbit (b) 2nd orbit to 3rd orbit
(c) 3rd orbit to 2nd orbit (d) 3rd orbit to 1st orbit

5. Name the series of lines in the hydrogen spectrum which lies in the ultraviolet region. **ISC 2019, 13**

6. In Bohr's model of hydrogen atom, radius of the first orbit of an electron is r_0. Then, radius of the third orbit is **ISC 2018**

(a) $\frac{r_0}{9}$ (b) r_0 (c) $3r_0$ (d) $9r_0$

7. According to Bohr, 'angular momentum of an orbiting electron is quantised'. What is meant by this statement? **ISC 2017**

8. Total energy of an electron in the ground state of hydrogen atom is -13.6 eV. Its total energy when hydrogen atom is in the first excited state, is **ISC 2016**

(a) + 13.6 eV (b) + 3.4 eV
(c) − 3.4 eV (d) − 54.4 eV

9. Calculate angular momentum of an electron in the third Bohr orbit of hydrogen atom. **ISC 2016**

10. If E_P and E_K represent potential energy and kinetic energy respectively of an orbital electron, then according to Bohr's theory **ISC 2015**

(a) $E_K = -E_P/2$ (b) $E_K = E_P$
(c) $E_K = 2E_P$ (d) $E_K = 2E_P$

11. Wavelengths of the first lines of the Lyman series, Paschen series and Balmer series, in hydrogen spectrum are denoted by λ_L, λ_P, and λ_B respectively. Arrange these wavelengths in increasing order. **ISC 2015**

12. White light is passed through sodium vapours contained in a thin walled glass flask and the transmitted light is examined with the help of spectrometer. The spectrum, so obtained is **ISC 2012**

(a) absorption spectrum (b) solar spectrum
(c) band spectrum (d) continuous spectrum

13. Describe absorption spectrum of sodium. **ISC 2009**

2 Marks Questions

14. (*i*) What is the velocity of an electron is the 3rd orbit of hydrogen atom, if its velocity in the 1st orbit is v_0?
(*ii*) Radius of the 1st orbit of hydrogen atom is r_0. What will be the radius of the 4th orbit? **ISC 2024**

15. Figure below is the energy level diagram for hydrogen atom. Study the transitions shown and answer the following questions. **ISC 2024**

(*i*) State the type of spectrum obtained.
(*ii*) Name the series of spectrum obtained.

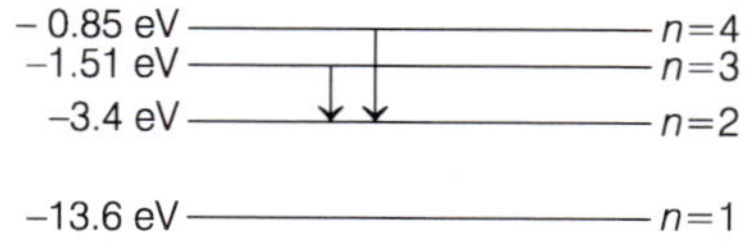

16. Name the series of lines of hydrogen spectrum which lies in the **ISC 2023**

(*i*) ultraviolet region (*ii*) visible region

17. Calculate the minimum wavelength of the spectral line present in Balmer series of hydrogen. **ISC 2018**

18. Draw energy level diagram for hydrogen atom showing at least four lowest energy levels. Show the transitions responsible for emission of Balmer series. **ISC SQP 2018**

19. For Bohr's model of the hydrogen atom, the energy of the electron in ground state is found to be -13.6 eV.
(*i*) Draw energy level diagram for the hydrogen atom and mark the values of energy (in eV at $n=2$ and $n=\infty$).
(*ii*) Obtain the maximum energy of photon emitted by the hydrogen atom in eV. **ISC 2005**

3 Marks Questions

20. Using Bohr's theory of hydrogen atom, obtain an expression for the velocity of an electron in nth orbit of an atom. **ISC 2023**

21. Draw an energy level diagram for hyrogen atom showing four lowest energy levels. On it, show transitions responsible for the emission of lines of **ISC 2022 Sem-II**

(*i*) Balmer series by a continuous line

(*ii*) Lyman series by dotted line.

22. On the basis of Bohr's theory, derive an expression for the radius of the *n*th orbit of an electron of hydrogen atom. **ISC 2022 Sem-II**

23. Draw energy level diagram for hydrogen atom, showing first four energy levels corresponding to $n=1$, 2, 3 and 4. Show transitions responsible for

(i) Absorption spectrum of Lyman series.

(ii) Emission spectrum of Balmer series. **ISC 2020, 16, 08**

24. State any two Bohr's postulate and write the energy value of the ground state of the hydrogen atom. **ISC 2019**

25. (*i*) How are various lines of Lyman series formed? Explain on the basis of Bohr's theory.

(*ii*) Calculate the shortest wavelength of electromagnetic radiation present in Balmer series of hydrogen spectrum. **ISC 2015**

26. On the basis of Bohr's theory, derive an expression for the radius of the *n*th orbit of an electron of hydrogen atom. **ISC 2014**

27. State the postulate of Bohr's regarding

(*i*) angular momentum of an electron.

(*ii*) emission of photon.

(*iii*) total energy of an electron orbiting around the nucleus of an atom is always negative. What is the significance of this? **ISC 2013**

28. Energy levels of H-atom are given by $E_n = \dfrac{-13.6}{n^2}$ eV.

where, $n=$ principal quantum number to calculate the wavelength of electromagnetic radiation emitted by hydrogen atom resulting from the transition $n=2$ to $n=1$. **ISC 2012**

KEY idea

To calculate the wavelength, of emitted electromagnetic radiation, first calculate the energy difference and then calculate the wavelength (λ) by applying $\left(\Delta E = \dfrac{hc}{\lambda}\right)$.

29. (*i*) Name a series of lines of hydrogen spectrum which lies in

(a) visible region, (b) UV region.

(*ii*) Write Bohr's formula to calculate wavelength (λ) of visible light emitted by hydrogen and explain the meaning of each and every symbol used. **ISC 2011**

30. (*i*) What is a continuous emission spectrum? Name one source of light which produces such a spectrum.

(*ii*) Explain in brief why dark lines are observed in the solar spectrum. **ISC 2010**

31. Draw a level diagram of hydrogen, shown by a downward or an upward arrow, a transition which results in

(*i*) emission line of Balmer series.

(*ii*) emission line of Lyman series.

(*iii*) absorption line of Lyman series. **ISC 2010**

32. An electron revolves around the nucleus of hydrogen atom in a circular orbit of radius 5×10^{-11} m. Calculate

(*i*) intensity of electric field of the nucleus of the position of the electron.

(*ii*) electrostatic potential energy of the hydrogen nucleus and electron system. **ISC 2010**

33. Wavelength of 1st line (H_α) of Balmer series of hydrogen is 656.3 nm. Find the wavelength of its 2nd line (H_β). **ISC 2009**

34. Differentiate between line, band and continuous spectra. What type of substances give rise to these spectra? **ISC 2007**

35. From Bohr's energy quantisation formula, determine the target wavelength in the Balmer series of hydrogen atom spectrum. **ISC 2006**

36. In a hydrogen atom, a transition of electrons takes place from 3rd orbit to 2nd orbit. Calculate the wavelength of the emitted photon. To which spectral series will this photon belong? **ISC 2005**

37. Obtain an expression for the kinetic energy of the electron in the Bohr's model of hydrogen atom ($Z=1$). Start from equating the electrostatic force with the centripetal force required and then use the quantisation condition for angular momentum. **ISC 2003**

38. Give the expression for the velocity of electron in the first orbit of hydrogen atom and the radius in the ground state of hydrogen atom. Hence, derive the expression for the magnetic field **(B)** at the centre of the nucleus due to the circular motion of electron. **ISC 2003**

4/5 Marks Questions

39. State the postulate of Bohr's model of hydrogen atom. Hence, derive the expression for the radius of *n*th orbit of electrons. **ISC 2002**

40. The ionisation potential of hydrogen atom is 13.6 eV. Draw the energy level diagram showing four levels. Calculate

(*i*) the energy of the photon emitted when an electron falls from the third orbit to the second orbit.

(*ii*) The wavelength of this photon. **ISC 2000**

> **KEY idea**
>
> To know the wavelength, first calculate the energy of photon when falls form 3rd orbit to the 2nd orbit $(E_3 - E_2)$, then apply $\left(\Delta E = \frac{hc}{\lambda}\right)$.

Case Based Question
(For Complete Chapter)

41. Direction *Read the passage given below and answer the questions that follows.*

In 1909, Geiger and Marsden made a series of measurements on the scattering of α-particles, which led to the discovery of atomic nucleus. Their experimental set up is shown in figure. A beam of high-energy α-particles emitted by a radioactive element polonium was made to fall on a very thin gold foil. The whole arrangement was kept in vacuum, so that there were no collisions of α-particles with air molecules. The particles, while passing through the gold foil were deflected (scattered) through a wide range of angles. The particles scattered in various directions were counted by a scintillation counter. It was found that although most of the particles scattered through angles of the order of 1° or less, but a small number, say about 1 in every 10000, scattered through 90° or even 180°. This large-angle scattering of α-particles could not be at all explained from prevalent ideas about atom at that time.

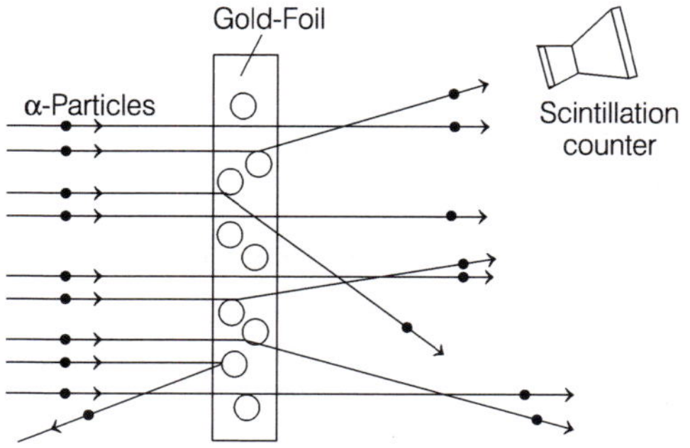

(*i*) Why was 'gold' foil used in α-particle scattering experiment? **(1)**

(*ii*) For scattering of α-particles at large angles, only the nucleus of the atom is responsible, not the electron. Why? **(1)**

(*iii*) Why was 'extremely thin' foil used? **(1)**

(*iv*) The Rutherford's α-particle experiment shows that most of the α-particle pass through almost unscattered while some of them are scattered through large angles. What information does it give about the structure of atom? **(1)**

(*v*) What conclusion was drawn by Rutherford based on Geiger-Marsden's experiment on scattering of α-particles? **(1)**

Explanations

1. Bohr's second postulate states that the electron revolves around the nucleus only in those orbits for which the angular momentum is some integral multiple of $h/2\pi$.

Thus, angular momentum of the orbiting electron is quantised, i.e. $L = \frac{nh}{2\pi}$

$$mvr = \frac{nh}{2\pi}$$

2. Angular momentum of an electron $= mvr$

As, $mvr = \frac{nh}{2\pi}$

For 2nd orbit, $n = 2$

$$mvr = \frac{2 \times 6.6. \times 10^{-34}}{2 \times 3.14} = 2.1 \times 10^{-34} \text{ kg-m}^2/\text{s}$$

3. (c) Angular momentum of an electron orbiting in the *n*th Bohr orbit of a hydrogen atom is given as

$$L = \frac{nh}{2\pi}$$

For 3rd Bohr orbit, $n = 3$

$$L = \frac{3h}{2\pi}$$

4. (b)

5. Lyman series lies in ultraviolet region in hydrogen spectrum.

6. (d) According to the Bohr's model, the radius of third orbit, $r_3 = n^2 r_0$

$$r_3 = (3)^2 r_0 \quad [\because n = 3]$$
$$r_3 = 9r_0$$

7. According to Bohr, 'angular momentum of an orbiting electron is quantised' - it means of all the possible circular orbits, the electrons are permitted to circulate only in those orbits in which the angular momentum of an electron is an integral multiple of $\frac{h}{2\pi}$, h being Planck's constant.

Therefore, for any permitted orbit,

$$L = mvr = \frac{nh}{2\pi}, n = 1, 2, 3, \ldots$$

where L, m and v are the angular momentum, mass and the speed of the electrons, r is the radius of the permitted orbit and n is positive integer called principal quantum number.

Thus, the angular momentum of the orbiting electron is quantised, has certain value $\frac{nh}{2\pi}$.

8. (c) The energy of electron in any state is given by

$$E_n = -\frac{13.6}{n^2}$$

For $n = 2$ (first excited state),

$$E_n = -\frac{13.6}{(2)^2} = -3.4 \text{ eV}$$

9. According to postulate of Bohr's model of hydrogen atom,

Angular momentum of electron in 3rd orbit, $mvr = \frac{nh}{2\pi}$

$$= \frac{(3)\times(6.6\times10^{-34})}{2\times3.14} \quad (\because n = 3)$$
$$= 3.15\times10^{-34} \text{ m}$$

10. Since, according to Bohr's theory, kinetic energy (E_K) is equal to half of potential energy with negative sign.

i.e. $$E_K = -\frac{E_P}{2}$$

11. The arrangement of different series of wavelength in increasing order is that

$$\lambda_P > \lambda_B > \lambda_L$$

12. (a) Absorption spectrum will be observed.

13. When sodium atoms absorb energy. The energy absorbed by sodium atom is equivalent to the corresponding wavelength. Thus, it shows absorption spectrum and it emits a line spectrum of 589.6 nm of wavelength.

14. (*i*) Velocity of 1st orbit, $v_0 = (1)\frac{h}{2\pi mr}$

Velocity in 3rd orbit will be

$$v' = (3)\frac{h}{2\pi mr} = 3(v_0)$$

(*ii*) Radius of 1st orbit of hydrogen atom,

$$r_0 = (1)^2 \frac{h^2\varepsilon_0}{\pi mZe^2}$$

Radius of 4th orbit of hydorgen atom will be

$$r' = (4)^2 \frac{h^2\varepsilon_0}{\pi mZe^2} = (4)^2 r_0 = 16r_0$$

15. (*i*) The type of spectrum obtained is an emission spectrum.

(*ii*) The series of spectrum obtained is the Balmer series.

16. (*i*) Ultraviolet region Lyman series

(*ii*) Visible region Balmer series

17. The wavelength of Balmer series is given by

$$\frac{1}{\lambda} = R\left(\frac{1}{2^2} - \frac{1}{n^2}\right)$$

For minimum wavelength,

$$n = \infty$$

$$\therefore \quad \frac{1}{\lambda} = R\left(\frac{1}{2^2} - \frac{1}{\infty^2}\right)$$

$$\Rightarrow \quad \frac{1}{\lambda} = \frac{R}{4} \Rightarrow \lambda = \frac{4}{R} = \frac{4}{1.097\times10^7}$$
$$= 3.646\times10^{-7} \text{ m}$$
$$= 3646 \text{ Å}$$

This lies in the ultraviolet region.

Concept Enhancer The longest wavelength of this series (for, $n = 3$) is 6563 Å and the shortest wavelength is 3646 Å in Balmer series of H-atom.

18.

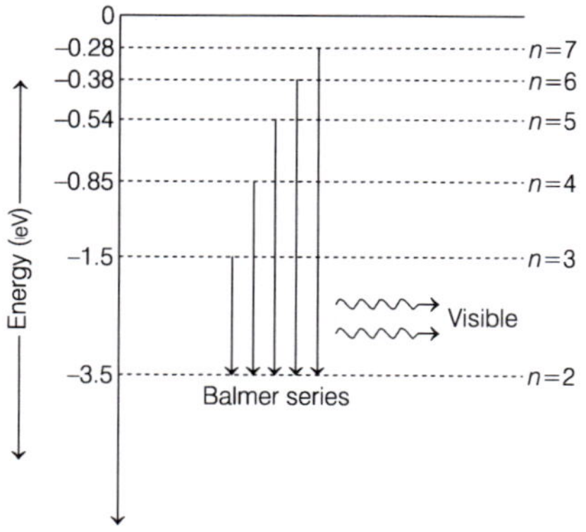

For Balmer series $\bar{\nu} = \frac{1}{\lambda} = R\left[\frac{1}{2^2} - \frac{1}{n^2}\right]$

$$n = 3, 4, 5, \ldots$$

Clearly, when an electron goes from higher energy level to lower energy level, it loses some energy which is released in the form of photons.

19. (*i*) Energy diagram is given as follows

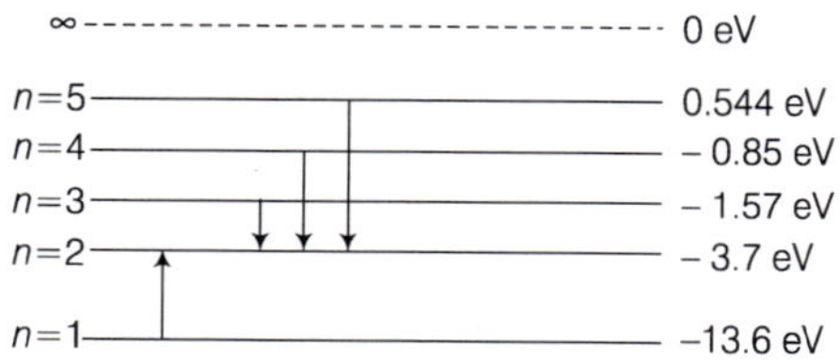

(*ii*) Maximum energy of photon is given by

$$\Delta E = E_\infty - E_1$$

$$\Rightarrow \quad = 0 - (-13.6) = 13.6\text{eV}$$

20. Refer to text on page 265 (Velocity of electron different orbit).

21. According to question, the energy level diagram for hydrogen atom for four lowest energy levels is gives as

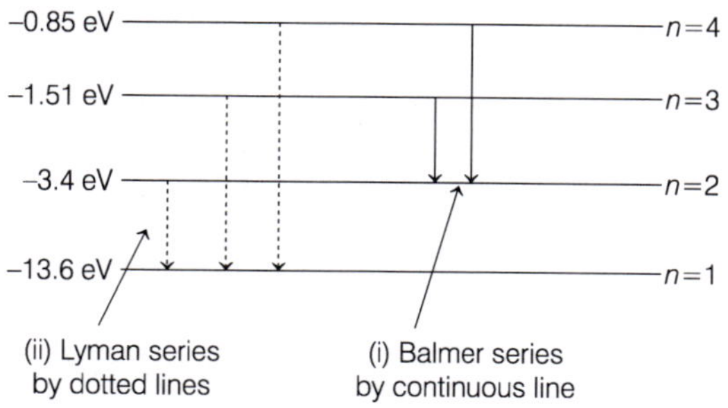

From above energy level diagram, it is clear that transitions are responsible for emission of lines of Balmer series and Lyman series.

22. Refer to text on page 265 (Bohr's hydrogen atom).

23. The energy level diagram of hydrogen atom is shown below. It consists of discrete bright lines in a dark background, known as emission spectrum.

(*i*) The transistors responsible for absorption spectrum of Lyman series can be written from outer orbit to first orbit, hence it is in ultraviolet. Its shown below

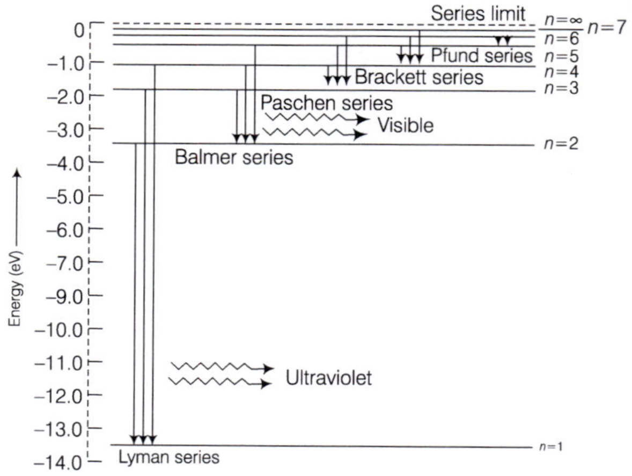

Here, we get dark lines on the bright background.

or **Absorption spectrum of Lyman series** In Lyman series, the electrons jumps from outer orbit to first orbit. So, its absorption spectrum will be

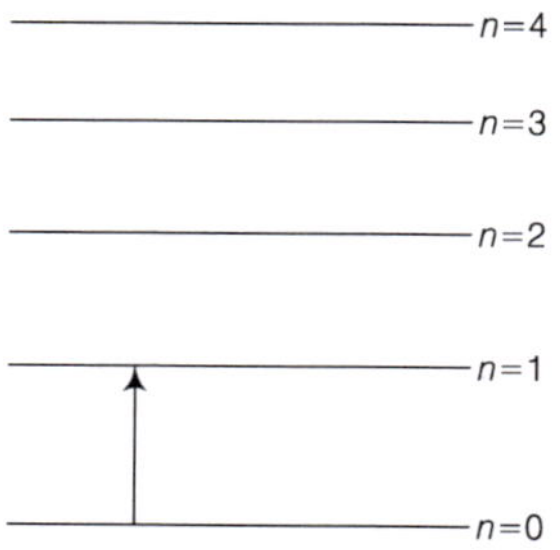

(*ii*) **Emission spectrum of Balmer series** In Balmer series, the electrons jumps from any outer orbit to the second orbit.

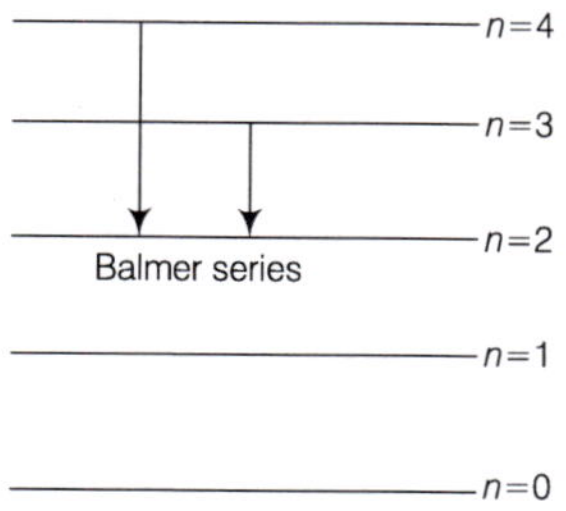

Concept Enhancer The dark regions are due to certain wavelength absorbed by medium. There missing wavelengths constitute the absorption spectrum of medium through which light was passed. Hence in absorption spectrum we get dark lines on bright background.

24. The two postulates are as follows

(i) **Bohr's first postulate** was that an electron in an atom could revolve in certain stable orbits without the emission of radiant energy, contrary to the predictions of electromagnetic theory.

According to this postulate, each atom has certain definite stable states in which it can exist and each possible state has definite total energy. These are called the stationary states of the atom.

(ii) **Bohr's second postulate** states that the electron revolves around the nucleus only in those orbits for which the angular momentum is some integral multiple of $h/2\pi$, where h is the Planck's constant $(=6.63\times10^{-34}$ J-s)

Thus, the angular momentum (L) of the orbiting electron is quantised,

i.e. $$L=\frac{nh}{2\pi}$$

As, angular momentum of electron $= mvr$

$\therefore$ For any permitted (stationary) orbit,

$$mvr=\frac{nh}{2\pi}$$

where, $n=$ any positive integer 1, 2, 3,...

It is also called principal quantum number. The energy value of the ground state of the hydrogen atom, $E=-13.6$ eV.

25. (*i*) Bohr postulated that Lyman series is obtained when an electron jumps to first orbit ($n_1=1$) from any outer orbit ($n_2=2, 3, 4, \ldots$).

Wave numbers of spectral lines of Lyman series can be calculated as

$$\bar{\nu}=R\left[\frac{1}{1^2}-\frac{1}{n_2^2}\right], \text{ where } n_2=2, 3, 4, \ldots$$

(*ii*) The wavelength (λ) of different spectral lines of Balmer series is given by

$$\frac{1}{\lambda}=R\left[\frac{1}{2^2}-\frac{1}{n_2^2}\right]$$

$\because$ For shortest wavelength, $n_2=\infty$.

$$\therefore \quad \frac{1}{\lambda}=1.097\times10^7\left[\frac{1}{2^2}-\frac{1}{\infty}\right]$$

$$\frac{1}{\lambda}=\frac{1.097\times10^7}{4}$$

$$\Rightarrow \quad \lambda=\frac{4}{1.097\times10^7}=3.646\times10^{-7}\text{ m}$$

$$\Rightarrow \quad \lambda=3646\text{ Å}$$

26. A hydrogen-like atom consists of a tiny positively charged nucleus and an electron revolving in a stable circular orbit around the nucleus.

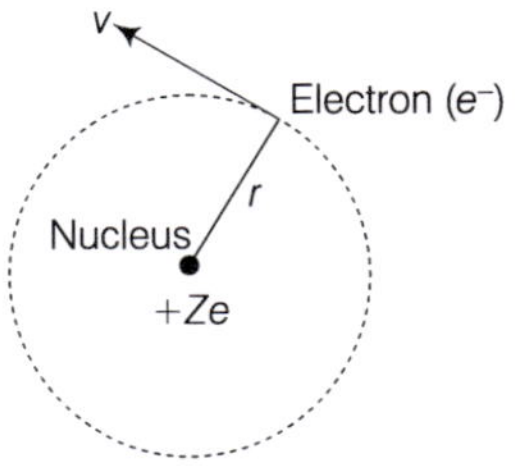

Let e, m and v be respectively the charge, mass and velocity of the electron and r be the radius of the orbit. The positive charge on the nucleus is Ze, where Z is the atomic number. As, the centripetal force is provided by the electrostatic force of attraction, we have

$$\frac{mv^2}{r}=\frac{1}{4\pi\varepsilon_0}=\frac{(Ze)\times e}{r^2} \text{ or } mv^2=\frac{Ze^2}{4\pi\varepsilon_0 r} \quad \ldots\text{(i)}$$

From the second postulate, the angular momentum of the electron is

$$mvr=\frac{nh}{2\pi} \quad \ldots\text{(ii)}$$

where, $n=(1, 2, 3 \ldots\ldots)$ is the principal quantum number.

From Eqs. (i) and (ii), we get

$$r=\frac{n^2h^2\varepsilon_0}{\pi mZe^2}$$

This is the equation for the radii of the permitted orbit.

According to this equation, $r_n=r_1\times n^2$

Since, $n=1, 2, 3\ldots.$

For Bohr radius, $n=1$ and $Z=1$

So, $$r_1=\frac{h^2\varepsilon_0}{\pi me^2}=0.53\text{Å}$$

27. (*i*) The orbit in which electron revolves has fixed angular momentum or it is integral multiple of

$$\frac{h}{2\pi} \quad \text{i.e., } L=mvr=\frac{nh}{2\pi} \; [n=0, 1, 2, 3, 4]$$

(*ii*) The electron can jump from one stationary orbit to other. If it jumps from an orbit from higher energy to lower energy, it emits photons and when it jump from lower energy to higher energy, it absorb photon.

The photon emitted or absorbed is in contrast with the energy difference between the stationary orbits i.e., if E_1 is the energy of stationary orbit, where electron is initially present and E_2 is the energy of stationary orbit to which it has jumped, then

$$E_1 - E_2 = \frac{hc}{\lambda}$$

where, λ is the wavelength of photon.

(*iii*) Total energy of electrons orbiting around nucleus is negative. This signifies that when electron is in free state it has zero energy. In other words, we can say that there is mutual attractive force between electron and nucleus which bind them together.

Concept Enhancer The energy of light emitted or absorbed is exactly equal to the difference between the energies of the orbits.

28. As given in question, $E_n = \frac{-13.6}{2^2}$ eV

So, for $n=2, E_n = \frac{-13.6}{2^2} = -3.4\,\text{eV}$

and for $n=1, E_n = \frac{-13.6}{1^2} = -13.6\,\text{eV}$

So, $E = E_2 - E_1 = [-3.4 - (-13.6)]\,\text{eV}$

As we know that, $\Delta E = \frac{hc}{\lambda} = 10.2\,\text{eV}$

where, λ = wavelength of emitted electromagnetic radiation

$$\Rightarrow \quad \lambda = \frac{hc}{10.2} = \frac{6.6\times10^{-34}\times3\times10^{8}}{10.2\times1.6\times10^{-19}}$$

$$= 1.213\times10^{-7}\text{ m}$$

$$= 1213\text{ Å}$$

29. (*i*) (a) Balmer series of lines of hydrogen spectrum lies in visible spectrum.

(b) Lyman series of hydrogen spectrum lies in UV region.

(*ii*) For hydrogen atom, $\frac{1}{\lambda} = Z^2 R\left(\frac{1}{n_1^2} - \frac{1}{n_2^2}\right)$

where, λ = wavelength

R = Rydberg constant

n_1 = lower energy state

n_2 = higher energy state.

30. (*i*) Continuous spectra contains all the wavelengths from one end to other without any gap. It is due to light from incandescent solid luminous gas flame. The spectrum is unbroken in this case. The colour of band changes from point to point.

(*ii*) Dark lines are observed in solar spectrum due to the absorption of certain wavelength ofmitted radiation by the atmospheric particle.

31. The diagram is given as below.

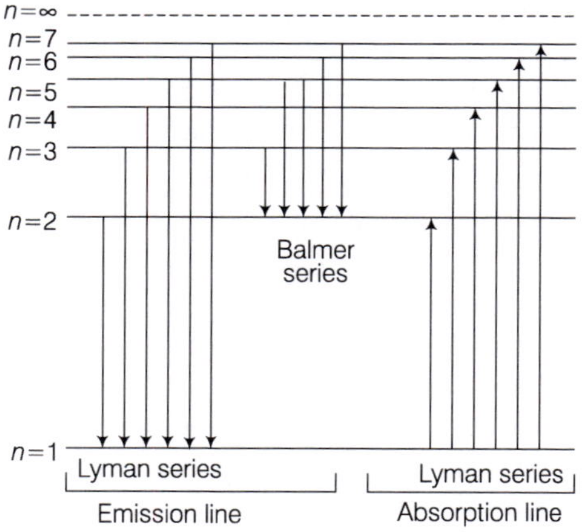

32. As given in question,

(*i*) Radius $r = 5\times10^{-11}$ m, charge $(q) = +e$

So, electric field

$$E = \frac{q}{4\pi\varepsilon_0 r^2} = 9\times10^9\times\frac{1.6\times10^{-9}}{(5\times10^{-11})^2} \quad \left[\text{as } \frac{1}{4\pi\varepsilon_0} = 9\times10^9\right]$$

$$= 5.76\times10^{11}\text{ NC}^{-1}$$

(*ii*) As potential energy of system is given by

$$U = \frac{1}{4\pi\varepsilon_0}\frac{q_1 q_2}{r}$$

$$= \frac{9\times10^9\times(1.6\times10^{-19})\times(-1.6\times10^{-19})}{5\times10^{-11}}$$

$$= -4.608\times10^{-18}\text{ J}$$

33. As we know that, $\frac{1}{\lambda} = Z^2 R\left(\frac{1}{n_1^2} - \frac{1}{n_2^2}\right)$

For Balmer series, first line (H_α)

$n_1 = 2, \quad n_2 = 3, \lambda = 656.3\,\text{nm}$

$$\Rightarrow \quad \frac{1}{656.3\times10^{-9}\text{ m}} = R\left(\frac{1}{2^2} - \frac{1}{3^2}\right) = R\left(\frac{1}{4} - \frac{1}{9}\right)$$

$$\Rightarrow \quad R = 1.09\times10^7$$

For Balmer series 2nd line (H_β)

$n = 2, n_2 = 4$ [given]

$$\frac{1}{\lambda} = R\left(\frac{1}{n_1^2} - \frac{1}{n_2^2}\right)$$

$$\Rightarrow \quad \frac{1}{\lambda} = 1.09\times10^7\left(\frac{1}{4} - \frac{1}{16}\right)$$

$$\therefore \quad \lambda = 4.89\times10^{-7}\text{ m} \quad \text{[approx]}$$

34.

Continuous Spectra	Band Spectra	Line Spectra
It contains all the wavelengths from one end to other without any gap .	It is given by chemical compounds (e.g., by CO_2 or ammonia gas in discharge tube.)	It is formed by light emitted by atoms of elements in vapour phase.
It is due to light from incandescent solid dense luminous gas. The flame spectrum is unbroken.	The large number of luminous band is present. Bands are sharply defined.	It consists of bright lines in different regions. All the lines do not have same intensity.
The colour of band changes from point to point.	Each band consists of a large number of lines being more crowded at the sharp edge and gradually fade away.	It is discontinuous spectrum. Each line corresponds to particular wavelength.

35. As we know that energy is inversely proportional to the wavelength, so for largest wavelength in Balmer series, electron should fall from $n=3$ to $n=2$.

Now, according to the formula to calculate wavelength.

So, $$\frac{1}{\lambda}=R\left(\frac{1}{n_1^2}-\frac{1}{n_2^2}\right) \quad [R = \text{Rydberg constant}]$$

$$\Rightarrow \frac{1}{\lambda}=1.097\times10^7\left(\frac{1}{4}-\frac{1}{9}\right) \quad [\because n_1=2, n_2=3]$$

$$\therefore \lambda=\frac{36\times10^{-7}}{1.097\times5}=6563\times10^{-10}\text{ m}$$

$$=656.3\text{ nm}$$

36. Refer to sol. on Page 274.

37. Assuming mass, charge and velocity of electron are m, e and v, respectively and r will be the radius of Bohr's orbit.

From the given diagram, for circular motion of an electron around nucleus, centripetal force must be equal to electrostatic the attraction.

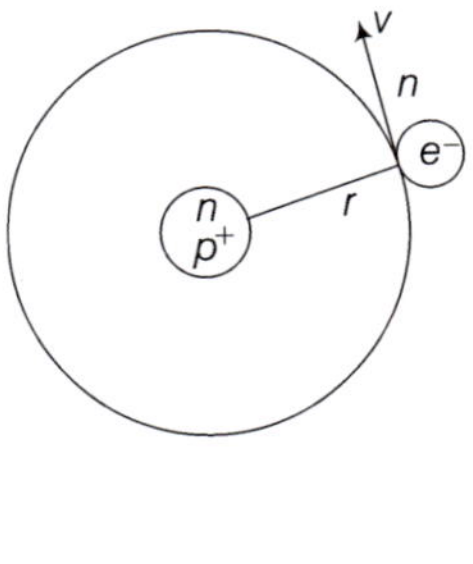

So, $$\frac{mv^2}{r}=\frac{1}{4\pi\varepsilon_0}\frac{Ze\times e}{r^2} \quad \ldots\text{(i)}$$

As we know that,

$$L=mvr=\frac{nh}{2\pi} \quad \ldots\text{(ii)}$$

$L=$ angular momentum [$n=$ quantum number]

From Bohr's postulates of angular momentum of electrons.

Kinetic energy of electrons,

$$K=\frac{1}{2}mv^2 \quad \ldots\text{(iii)}$$

So, from Eqs. (i), (ii) and (iii), we get

$$K=\frac{1}{2}\left(\frac{1}{4\pi\varepsilon_0}\frac{Ze^2}{r}\right)$$

This is the expression for the kinetic energy of the electrons in the Bohr's model of hydrogen.

38. Let the radius of hydrogen atom be r and velocity of electron in this orbit is v.

So, from circular motion electrostatic force of attraction between nucleus and electrons is equal to the centripetal force of electrons.

$$\frac{mv^2}{r}=\frac{1}{4\pi\varepsilon_0}\cdot\frac{q_1q_2}{r^2} \quad \ldots\text{(i)}$$

As we know that, $mvr=\frac{nh}{2\pi}$

$$\Rightarrow v=\frac{nh}{2\pi mr} \quad \ldots\text{(ii)}$$

So, from Eqs. (i) and (ii), we get

$$m\left(\frac{nh}{2\pi mr}\right)^2=\frac{1}{4\pi\varepsilon_0}\frac{e^2}{r}$$

$$\Rightarrow \frac{mn^2h^2}{4\pi^2m^2r^2}=\frac{1}{4\pi\varepsilon_0}\frac{e^2}{r}$$

$$r=\frac{n^2h^2\varepsilon_0}{\pi me^2}$$

For ground state of hydrogen atom $n=1$,

$$r=\frac{h^2\varepsilon_0}{\pi me^2}$$

The velocity of electrons is given by

For first orbit of hydrogen atom $n=1$,

$$v=\frac{nh}{2\pi mr}$$

$$v = \frac{e^2}{2\varepsilon_0 h}$$

(*ii*) Revolving electron are considered as current loop whose magnetic field at centre is given by

$$B = \frac{\mu_0 ni}{2r} = \frac{\mu_0 ne}{2rt} \quad \left[\text{as } i = \frac{e}{t}\right]$$

$$= \frac{\mu_0 nev}{2r \times 2\pi r} \quad \left[\text{as } t = \frac{2\pi r}{v}\right]$$

So, $$B = \frac{\mu_0 ne}{4\pi}\left[\frac{e^2}{2\varepsilon_0 nh} \Big/ \left(\frac{n^2h^2\varepsilon_0}{\pi me^2}\right)^2\right]$$

$$= \frac{\mu_0 \pi m^2 e^7}{8\varepsilon_0^3 h^5 n^4} \text{ Wb/m}^2$$

39. Bohr combined classical and early quantum concepts and gave his theory in the form of three postulates.

These are

(*i*) **Bohr's first postulate** was that an electron in an atom could revolve in certain stable orbit without the emission of radiant energy contrary to the predictions of electromagnetic theory. According to this postulate, each atom has certain definite stable state, which has difinite amount total energy associated with it. These are called the stationary states of the atom.

(*ii*) **Bohr's second postulate** defines these stable orbits. This postulate states that the electrons revolve around the nucleus only in those orbits for which the angular momentum is some integral multiple of $h/2\pi$, where h is the Planck's constant ($=6.6 \times 10^{-34}$ J-s).

Thus, the angular momentum (L) of the orbiting electron is quantised *i.e.*, $L = \frac{nh}{2\pi}$

As angular momentum of electron

$$L = mvr$$

∴ For any permitted (stationary) orbit

$$mvr = \frac{nh}{2\pi}$$

where, n = any positive integer 1, 2, 3, ...

It is also called **principal quantum number.**

(*iii*) **Bohr's third postulate** states that an electron might make a transition from one of its specified non-radiating orbits to another of lower energy. When it does so, a photon is emitted having energy equal to the energy difference between the initial and final states. The frequency of the emitted photon is then given by

$$h\nu = E_i - E_f$$

where, E_i and E_f are the energies of the initial and final states and $E_i > E_f$.

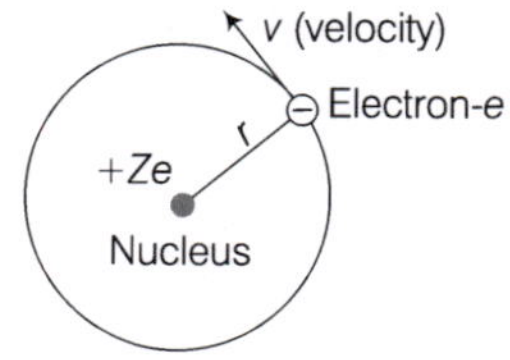

Let e, m and v be the charge, mass and velocity of the electron respectively and r the radius of the orbit.

The positive charge on the nucleus is Ze, where Z is the atomic number (in case of hydrogen atom, $Z = 1$). As the centripetal force is provided by the electrostatic force of attraction.

We have,

$$\frac{mv^2}{r} = \frac{1}{4\pi\varepsilon_0} \cdot \frac{(Ze) \times e}{r^2}$$

or $$mv^2 = \frac{Ze^2}{4\pi\varepsilon_0 r} \quad \text{...(i)}$$

From the first postulate, the angular momentum of the electron is

$$mvr = n\frac{h}{2\pi} \quad \text{...(ii)}$$

where, $n = 1, 2, 3, \ldots$ is the principal quantum number.

From Eqs. (i) and (ii),

$$r = n^2 \frac{h^2\varepsilon_0}{\pi m Z e^2}$$

This is the equation for the radii of the permitted orbits. According to this equation $r_n \propto n^2$.

Since, $n = 1, 2, 3, \ldots$ it follows that the radii of the permitted orbits increase in the ratio $1:4;9:16\ldots$ from the first orbit.

40. The energy level diagram is given by

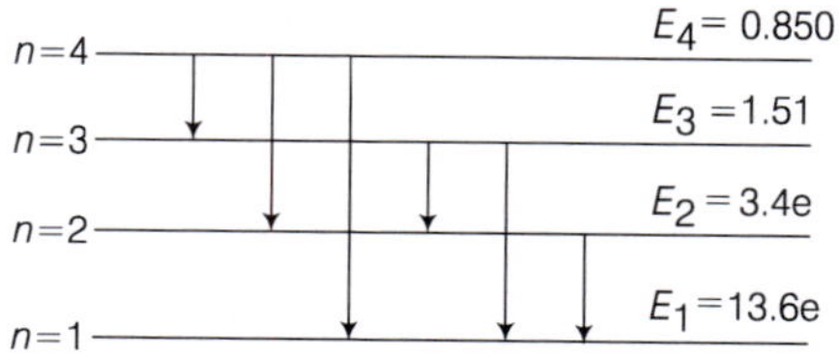

(*i*) Energy of photon when falls from 3rd orbit to the 2nd orbit $= E_3 - E_2$

$$= -1.51\,\text{eV} - (-3.4\,\text{eV}) = 1.9\,\text{eV}$$

(*ii*) So, the corresponding wavelength is given by $\frac{hc}{\lambda}$

$$\Rightarrow \quad \frac{hc}{\lambda} = 1.9\,\text{eV}$$

$$\therefore \quad \lambda = \frac{hc}{1.9\,\text{eV}} = \frac{6.6 \times 10^{-34} \times 3 \times 10^{8}}{1.9 \times 1.6 \times 10^{-19}}$$

$$[1\,\text{eV} = 1.6 \times 10^{-19}\,\text{J}]$$

$$= \frac{12375}{1.9 \times 1.6 \times 10^{-19}} = 651.3\text{ nm}$$

41. (*i*) The gold nucleus is heavy and so it can produce a 'large' deflection in the path of α-particle. Secondly, gold can be beaten into extremely 'thin' foils.

(*ii*) Electron is very light compared to α-particle. Hence, due to conservation of momentum, it cannot scatter the α-particle at large angles.

(*iii*) This was to ensure that an α-particle should be deflected by a 'single' collision.

(*iv*) Most of the inner part of atom is hollow and the positive charge of the atom is concentrated in a very small space (nucleus).

(*v*) The positive charge of an atom was confined to a tiny space at the centre called nucleus of the atom.

CHAPTER TEST

01 Mark Questions (MCQs)

1 If the radius of second electron-orbit in hydrogen atom be r, then the radius of the third orbit will be

(a) $3r$ (b) $2.25r$ (c) $9r$ (d) $r/3$

2 In Bohr's model of hydrogen atom, radius of the first orbit of an electron is r_0. Then, radius of the third orbit is

(a) $\frac{r_0}{9}$ (b) r_0 (c) $3r_0$ (d) $9r_0$

3 Total energy of an electron in the ground state of hydrogen atom is –13.6 eV. Its total energy, when hydrogen atom is in the first excited state, is

(a) +13.6 eV (b) +3.4 eV
(c) –3.4 eV (d) –54.4 eV

4 Classically, the proposed circular path of an electron in the Rutherford's nuclear model of atom would be

(a) circular (b) parabolic
(c) spiral (d) straight

5 In hydrogen atom the minimum angular momentum of the electron in an energy state is

(a) h/π (b) $h/2\pi$
(c) $2\pi/h$ (d) $2h$

6 If l_3 and l_2 represent angular momenta of an orbiting electron in III and II Bohr orbits respectively, then $l_3 : l_2$ is

(a) 3 : 2 (b) 9 : 4 (c) 2 : 3 (d) 4 : 9

01 Mark Questions (VSA)

7 What is the distance of closest approach of an α-particle to the nucleus?

8 When is the (H_α) line of the Balmer series in the emission specturm of hydrogen atom obtained?

9 The ground state energy of hydrogen atom is –13.6 eV. What are the kinetic and potential energies of the electron in this state?

10 Write the expression for Bohr's radius in the hydrogen atom.

02 Marks Questions

11 Explain in brief, why Rutherford's model cannot account for the stability of the atom?

12 The energy of the electron in the ground state of hydrogen atom is –13.6 eV.

(i) What does the negative sign signify?

(ii) How much energy is required to take an electron in this atom from the ground state to the first excited state?

03 Marks Questions

13 (i) In a Geiger-Marsden experiment, calculate the distance of closest approach to the nucleus of $Z = 50$, when an α particle of 8 MeV energy rest and reveres its direction.

(ii) How were the distance of closest approach be affected when the KE of α-particle is doubled?

14 State the basic assumption of the Rutherford's model of the atom. Explain in brief why this model cannot for the stability of an atom?

05 Marks Questions

15 Using postulates of Bohr's theory of hydrogen atom, show that

(i) the radii of orbits increase n^2 and

(ii) the total energy of the electron increases the quantum number of the atom.

16 Using the relevent Bohr's postulates, derive the expression for the

(i) speed of the electron in the nth orbit.

(ii) radius of the nth orbit of the electron in hydrogen atom.

Answers

1. (b) **2.** (d) **3.** (c) **4.** (c) **5.** (b)

6. (a)

9. 13.6 0eV, – 27.2 eV

13. (i) 2.88×10^{-19} m

21

Atomic Mass

TREND ANALYSIS 4 YEARS

Average No. of Questions Across all Sets

	Types of Questions	2024	2023	2020	2019
Atomic Mass	1 Mark	–	–	–	–
	2 Marks	–	1	–	–
	3 Marks	–	–	–	–
	5 Marks	–	–	–	–

Atomic Mass

In every atom, the positive charge and mass are densely concentrated at the centre of the atom forming its nucleus. The radius of the nucleus is smaller than the radius of an atom by a factor of 10^4. More than 99.9% mass of an atom is concentrated in the nucleus.

The unit to express atomic mass is **atomic mass unit** (u).

Atomic mass unit is defined as, $\frac{1}{12}$th of the mass of carbon $^{12}C_6$ atom.

$$1\ \text{u} = \frac{\text{Mass of one atom of } ^{12}C_6 \text{ atom}}{12}$$

$$= \frac{1.992647 \times 10^{-26}}{12}\ \text{kg}$$

$$\boxed{1\ \text{u} = 1.660539 \times 10^{-27}\ \text{kg}}$$

Atomic masses can be measured accurately by using an instrument called **mass spectrometer**.

Electron Volt It is defined as the energy gained by an electron under the potential difference of 1 volt.

$$\boxed{1\text{eV} = 1.602 \times 10^{-19}\ \text{J}}$$

A bigger unit is called MeV.

$1\text{MeV} = 10^6\ \text{eV} = 1.602 \times 10^{-13}\ \text{J}$

The masses of proton, neutron and electron are given below

Mass of proton, $m_p = 1.6726231 \times 10^{-27}\ \text{kg} = 1.00727\ \text{u}$

Mass of neutron, $m_n = 1.6749286 \times 10^{-27}\ \text{kg} = 1.00866\ \text{u}$

Mass of electron, $m_e = 9.1093897 \times 10^{-31}\ \text{kg} = 0.000549\ \text{u}$

According to Einstein's mass-energy relation, $E = mc^2$

The energy equivalence of one amu is given by

$$\boxed{1\ \text{amu} = 931.5\ \text{MeV}}$$

Classification of Nuclei : Isotopes, Isobars and Isotones

The nuclei has been classified on the basis of the number of protons (atomic number) or the total number of nucleons (mass number) in them.

(*i*) **Isotopes** or **Isoprotons** The atoms of element whose nuclei have the same number of protons but different number of neutrons or we can say that they have same atomic number but different mass number are called the 'isotopes' of that element.

The isotopes of some elements are as

Hydrogen : $_1H^1$ (proton), $_1H^2$ (deuterium), $_1H^3$ (tritium)

Oxygen : $_8O^{16}, {}_8O^{17}, {}_8O^{18}$

Neon : $_{10}Ne^{20}, {}_{10}Ne^{21}, {}_{10}Ne^{22}$

Chlorine : $_{17}Cl^{35}, {}_{17}Cl^{37}$

Uranium : $_{92}U^{235}, {}_{92}U^{238}$

(*ii*) **Isobars** The nuclei which have the same number of nucleons (i.e. mass number), but different number of protons and different number of neutrons are called 'isobars'. Their atomic numbers (Z) are different, but mass number (A) is same. The nuclei of isobars belong to the different elements. Some examples of isobars are as

$$_1H^3 \text{ and } {}_2He^3,\ {}_{11}Na^{23} \text{ and } {}_{12}Mg^{23}$$

(*iii*) **Isotones** The nuclei having equal number of neutrons are called 'isotones'. For them, both the atomic number (Z) and the mass number (A) are different, but the value of $(A - Z)$ is same. Some examples of isotones are as

$$_3Li^7 \text{ and } {}_4Be^8,\ {}_{17}Cl^{37} \text{ and } {}_{19}K^{39},\ {}_{11}Na^{23} \text{ and } {}_{12}Mg^{24}$$

Composition of Nucleus

The nucleus was first discovered in 1911 by Lord Rutherford and his associates by scattering of α-particles on atoms. He found that the scattering results could be explained, if atom consists of small, central, massive and positive core surrounded by orbiting negative charge (electrons).

The experimental results indicated that the size of the nucleus is of the order of 10^{-14} m and is thus 10000 times smaller than the size of atom. The study of radioactivity revealed that nucleus is not an elementary body but it is made of nucleons.

The composition of a nucleus can be described using the following terms and symbols.

Atomic Number (Z)

Atomic number of an element is the number of protons present inside the nucleus of an atom of the element. It is also equal to number of electrons revolving in various orbits around the nucleus of the neutral atom.

Atomic number (Z) = Number of protons = Number of electrons [for neutral atom]

Mass Number (A)

Mass number of an element is the total number of protons and neutrons inside the atomic nucleus of the element.

Mass number (A) = Number of protons + Number of neutrons

Size of Nucleus

The size of nucleus has been measured with the help of variety of experiments involving the scattering of particles such as neutrons, protons, electrons, etc. From all these experiments, it is found that the volume of the nucleus is directly proportional to the number of nucleons.

If R is the radius of the nucleus having mass number A, then

$$R \propto A^{1/3} \text{ and } \boxed{R = R_0 A^{1/3}}$$

where, $R_0 = 1.2 \times 10^{-15}$ m is the range of nuclear size.

It is also known as **nuclear unit radius**.

Nuclear Density (ρ)

The density of nuclear matter is the ratio of mass of nucleus and its volume. If m is average mass of a nucleon and A is the mass number of element, then mass of nucleus will be mA. If R is the nuclear radius, then

$$\text{Density of nuclear matter, } \rho = \frac{\text{Mass of nucleus}}{\text{Volume of nucleus}} = \frac{3m}{4\pi R_0^3}$$

Thus, the density of nucleus is constant, independent of A, for all nuclei. Different nuclei are like drop of liquid of constant density. The density of nuclear matter is approximately 2.3×10^{17} kgm^{-3}.

PYQs Previous Years Questions

1 Mark Questions

1. Define 'unified atomic mass unit'. **ISC 2009**

Additional Questions

2. How is the radius of a nucleus related to its mass number?

3. Two nuclei have mass numbers in the ratio 1:8. What is the ratio of their nuclear radii?

4. In a nucleus of ${}_{92}U^{238}$, find the number of protons and the number of neutrons.

2 Marks Questions

5. With reference to Nuclear Physics, answer the following questions

(*i*) What is meant by "Isotopes"?

(*ii*) Define 1u (where u stands for unified atomic mass unit.) **ISC 2023**

Additional Questions

6. Obtain the approximate value of the radius of a nucleus ${}_{92}U^{238}$, R_0 is 1.2×10^{-15}m.

7. How the size of a nucleus is experimentally determined? Write the relation between the radius and mass number of the nucleus. Show that the density of nucleus is independent of its mass number.

8. Obtain an expression for nuclear density in terms of average mass of a neutron.

9. Dictate the following terms.

(*i*) Isotopes

(*ii*) Isobars

(*iii*) Isotones

10. (*i*) Two stable isotopes of lithium ${}^{6}_{3}Li$ and ${}^{7}_{3}Li$ have respective abundances of 7.5% and 92.5%. These isotopes have masses 6.01512u and 7.01600u, respectively. Find the atomic mass of lithium.

(*ii*) Boron has two stable isotopes ${}^{10}_{5}B$ and ${}^{11}_{5}B$. Their respective masses are 10.01294u and 11.00931u and the atomic mass of boron is 10.811u. Find the abundances of ${}^{10}_{5}B$ and ${}^{11}_{5}B$.

Case Based Question (For Complete Chapter)

11. Direction *Read the passage given below and answer the questions that follows.*

The discovery of neutrons by Chadwick, led Heisenberg propose proton-neutron hypothesis in 1932. According to this hypothesis, protons and neutrons are the main building block of all atoms. The protons are positively charged particles while neutrons are electrically neutral. The magnitude of the charge on a proton is equal to that on an electron and can be represented as $(+e)$. The number of protons in the nucleus is called atomic number Z. The total number of protons and neutrons is called mass number A. Hence, $(A - Z)$ gives the number of neutrons and is called neutron number N. A nuclear species or a nuclide is represented as ${}^{A}_{Z}X$, where X is the chemical symbol of the species.

Nuclides with same atomic number Z, but different neutron number N are called isotopes. Nuclides with same mass number A are isobars and those with the same neutron number N are isotones. As most of the element are the mixture of two or more isotopes, the atomic mass of an element is the weighted average of the masses of its isotopes.

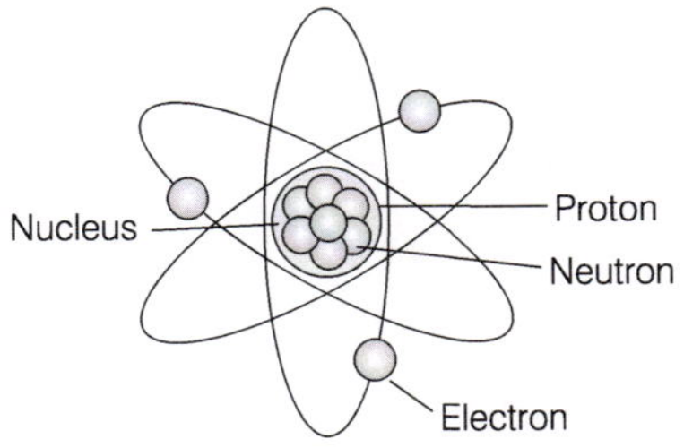

Answer the following questions from the above passage.

(*i*) What is atomic number in the nucleus? **(1)**

(*ii*) What is isotope? Give one example of it. **(1)**

(*iii*) The nuclei having same neutrons number is named as .... **(1)**

(*iv*) In the nucleus of ${}_{8}O^{16}$, calculate the number of protons and neutrons. **(1)**

Explanations

1. Atomic mass unit is defined as one-twelfth of the mass of one carbon atom $({}_6C^{12})$ isotope.

i.e. $$1\,\text{amu} = \frac{1}{12}(\text{mass of a carbon atom})$$

2. Radius of nucleus, $R = R_0 A^{1/3}$

where, R = radius of nucleus,

A = mass number

and $R_0 = 1.2\,\text{Fm} = 1.2 \times 10^{-15}\,\text{m}$

3. Radius of nucleus, $R = R_0 A^{1/3}$

where, R_0 = constant and A = mass number

$$\therefore \quad \frac{R_1}{R_2} = \left(\frac{A_1}{A_2}\right)^{1/3} = \left(\frac{1}{8}\right)^{1/3} = \frac{1}{2}$$

$R_1 : R_2 = 1:2$

4. Number of protons, $Z = 92$

Number of neutrons,
$N = A - Z = 238 - 92 = 146$

5. (*i*) The atoms of element whose nuclei have the same number of protons but different number of neutrons or they have same atomic number but different mass number are called the isotopes.

(*ii*) Refer to text on page 279 (Atomic mass).

Concept Enhancer Isotopes are also known as isoprotons.

6. Given, $A = 238$, $R_0 = 1.2 \times 10^{-15}\,\text{m}$

$$R = R_0 A^{1/3} = 1.2 \times 10^{-15} (238)^{1/3}$$
$$= 7.437 \times 10^{-15}\,\text{m}$$

7. The size of nucleus will increase of mass number. The size of the nucleus is experimentally determined using Rutherford's α-scattering experiment and the distance of closest approach and impact parameter.

The relation between radius and mass number of nucleus is $R = R_0 A^{1/3}$

where, $R_0 = 1.2\,\text{Fm}$
A = mass number
and R = radius of nucleus

Nuclear density, ρ

$$= \frac{\text{Mass of nucleus}}{\text{Volume of nucleus}} = \frac{mA}{\frac{4}{3}\pi(R_0 A^{1/3})^3}$$

where, m = mass of each nucleon

$$\rho = \frac{mA}{\frac{4}{3}\pi R_0^3 A} = \frac{m}{\frac{4}{3}\pi R_0^3} = \text{constant}$$

Common Mistake Sometime students write mass of nucleus as *M* but this will not lead to answer. Write mass of nucelus as *mA*.

8. Refer to text on page 280 (Nuclear density).

9. Refer to text on pages 279 and 280 (Isotopes, Isobars and Isotones).

10. (*i*) Atomic mass of Li

$$= \text{weighted average of the isotopes}$$
$$= \frac{7.5 \times 6.01512 + 92.5 \times 7.01600}{7.5 \times 92.5}$$
$$= \frac{45.1134 + 648.98}{100} = 6.94\,\text{u}$$

(*ii*) Suppose x and y are the abundances of ${}^{10}_{5}\text{B}$ and ${}^{11}_{5}\text{B}$ respectively.

Atomic mass of boron

$$= \text{weighted average of isotopes}$$
$$= \frac{x \times 10.01294 + y \times 11.00931}{100}$$
$$10.811 = \frac{x \times 10.01294 + (100 - x) \times 11.00931}{100}$$
$$[\because y = (100 - x)]$$
$$1081.1 = 10.01294x + 1100.931 - 11.00931x$$
$$0.99637x = 19.831$$
$$\Rightarrow \quad x = 19.90$$
$$y = (100 - x) = 80.1$$
$$x = 19.90\%$$
$$y = 80.1\%$$

11. (*i*) The number of protons in the nucleus is known as atomic number.

(*ii*) Nuclides with same atomic number Z, but different neutron number N are called isotopes.

Example : ${}_1H^1, {}_1H^2, {}_1H^3$

(*iii*) Isotones

(*iv*) In ${}_8O^{16}$

The number of protons, $Z = 8$

The number of neutrons $= A - Z = 16 - 8 = 8$.

CHAPTER TEST

01 Mark Questions (MCQs)

1 As compared to ^{12}C atom, ^{14}C atom has
(a) two extra protons and two extra electrons
(b) two extra protons, but no extra electrons
(c) two extra neutrons and no extra electrons
(d) two extra neutrons and two extra electrons

2 Ratio of mass of nucleus with mass of atom is nearing to
(a) 1 (b) 10 (c) 10^3 (d) 10^{10}

3 What is the value of one atomic mass unit (u) in kg?
(a) 1.660539×10^{-27} kg (b) 1.5382×10^{-27} kg
(c) 1.8096×10^{-27} kg (d) 1.6542×10^{-27} kg

4 The correct option representing the isotopes are
(a) ${}_8O^{16}$, ${}_8O^{17}$ (b) ${}_1H^2$, ${}_2He^4$
(c) ${}_{11}Na^{23}$, ${}_{12}Mg^{23}$ (d) ${}_3Li^7$, ${}_4Be^8$

01 Mark Questions (VSA)

5 What do you understand by term 'isotone'?

6 What is the size of nucleus?

7 What is the definition of 1 atomic mass unit?

8 ${}_2^3He$ and ${}_1^3H$ nuclei have the same mass number. Do they have same binding energy?

9 Why do stable nuclei never have more protons than neutrons?

02 Marks Questions

10 Determine the nuclear radii of (i) ${}_{27}^{60}Co$ and (ii) ${}_{79}^{197}Au$.

11 Check whether the given statement is correct or incorrect, if incorrect then correct it with proper explanation. The order of magnitude of density of nuclear matter is 10^4 kg m^{-3}.

12 Two nuclei have mass numbers in the ratio of 1 : 2. What is the ratio of their nuclear densities?

03 Marks Questions

13 (i) Dictate the following terms
(a) Atomic number
(b) Mass number
(ii) Draw a curve showing variation of radius of a nucleus with its mass number.

14 (i) What is the nuclear density of ${}_{90}^{228}Th$?
(ii) Is the nuclear density of an α-particle (${}_2^4He$) to be greater than, less than or equal ${}_{90}^{228}Th$? Explain.
(iii) Determine the nuclear density of an α-particle.

15 In a periodic table, the average atomic mass of magnesium is given as 24.312u. The average value is based on their relative natural abundance on the earth. The three isotopes and their masses are ${}_{12}^{24}Mg$(23.98504u) and ${}_{12}^{26}Mg$(25.98259u). The natural abundance of ${}_{12}^{24}Mg$ is 78.99% by mass. Calculate the abundances of other two isotopes.

05 Marks Questions

16 Define 'unified atomic mass unit'. Derive it in kilogram. Using Einstein's mass-energy relation express it in terms of MeV.

17 How can you classify the atomic nuclei? Define the term isotope, isobar and isotone. Give two examples of each.

Answers

1. (c) **2.** (a) **3.** (a) **4.** (a)
10. (i) 4.7 fm (ii) 7.0 fm
12. 1
14. (i) 2.3×10^{17} kg m^{-3} (iii) 2.3×10^{17} kg m^{-3}

22

Mass-Energy Equivalence

TREND ANALYSIS 4 YEARS

Average No. of Questions Across all Sets

	Types of Questions	2024	2023	2020	2019
Mass-Energy Equivalence	1 Mark	1	–	1	1
	2 Marks	1	1	1	–
	3 Marks	1	–	–	–
	5 Marks	–	–	–	–

Before, Einstein's theory of mass-energy equivalence, both mass and energy were supposed to be different entity. The total mass of the universe and also the total energy of the universe, were considered to be separately constant. So, mass conservation and energy conservation were supposed to be two independent laws.

Mass-Energy Relation

Einstein showed that mass is the another form of energy and can be converted into energy and other forms of energy.

Einstein's mass-energy equivalence equation is expressed as

$$\boxed{E = mc^2}$$

where, m = mass of the body, c = velocity of the light.

The sun is continuously loosing mass, as a result of which we receive energy in several forms.

Mass Defect of Nucleus

The difference between the sum of the masses of the nucleons constituting a nucleus and the rest-mass of the nucleus is called mass defect (Δm).

Mass defect, Δm = (mass of protons + mass of neutrons) – mass of the nucleus

$$[\{Zm_p + (A-Z)m_n\} - m_N]$$

Binding Energy of Nucleus

The binding energy of a nucleus may be defined as the energy equivalent to the mass defect of the nucleus. If Δm is mass defect, then according to Einstein's mass energy relation.

Binding energy,

$$E_b = \Delta mc^2 = [\{Zm_p + (A-Z)m_n\} - m_N] \cdot c^2$$

where, m_N is the mass of nucleus, m_p is the mass of proton and m_n is the mass of neutron.

This binding energy is expressed in joule if Δm is measured in kg.

If Δm (in amu) $= [\{Zm_p + (A-Z)m_n\} - m_N]$ amu then,

$$\boxed{E_b = \Delta m \times 931.5 \text{ MeV}}$$

Average Binding Energy Per Nucleon of a Nucleus

It is the average energy, we have to spend to remove a nucleon from the nucleus to infinite distance. It is given by total binding energy divided by the mass number of the nucleus.

$$\boxed{\text{Binding energy per nucleon} = \frac{\text{Total binding energy}}{\text{Number of nucleons } (A)}}$$

or

E_b per nucleon, $\boxed{E_{\text{bn}} = \frac{E_b}{A}}$

Binding Energy Curve

It is a plot of the binding energy per nucleon E_{bn} *versus* the mass number A for a large number of nuclei.

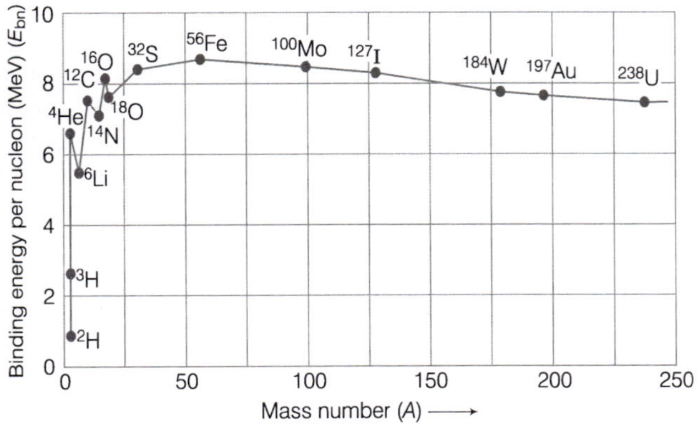

Binding energy per nucleon as a function of mass number

The following are the features of the plot:

(i) Average BE/nucleon for light nuclei like $_1H^1$, $_1H^2$, $_1H^3$ is small.

(ii) For mass numbers ranging from 2 to 20, there are sharply defined peaks corresponding to $_2He^4$, $_6C^{12}$, $_8O^{16}$, etc. The peaks indicate that these nuclei are relatively more stable than the other nuclei in their neighbourhood.

(iii) The BE curve has a broad maximum peak in the range $A = 30$ to $A = 120$, which is practically constant corresponding to average binding energy per nucleon is 8.8 MeV per nucleon for $_{26}Fe^{56}$.

(iv) As, the mass number increases, the BE/nucleon decreases gradually falling to about 7.6 MeV per nucleon for $_{92}U^{238}$. The decrease may be due to Coulomb repulsion between the protons. The heavy nuclei are therefore, relatively less stable.

Pair-production and Pair-annihilation

- The phenomenon in which energy is converted into mass is called **pair-production** and is expressed by the following equation :

$$\underset{(\gamma\text{-photon})}{h\nu} = \underset{(\text{electron})}{_{-1}\beta^0} + \underset{(\text{positron})}{_{+1}\beta^0}$$

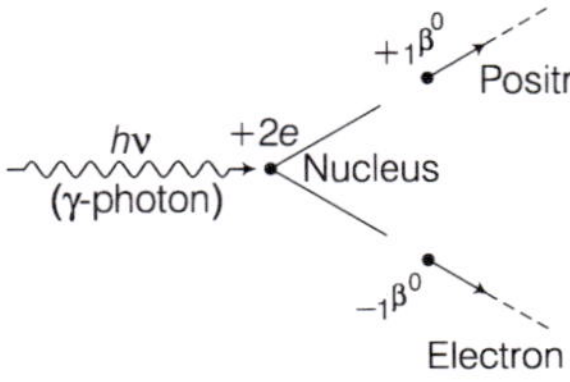

- The phenomenon in which mass is converted into energy is called **pair-annihilation**. It is expressed as

$$_{+1}\beta^0 + _{-1}\beta^0 \rightleftharpoons \underset{(\gamma\text{-photon})}{h\nu} + \underset{(\gamma\text{-photon})}{h\nu}$$

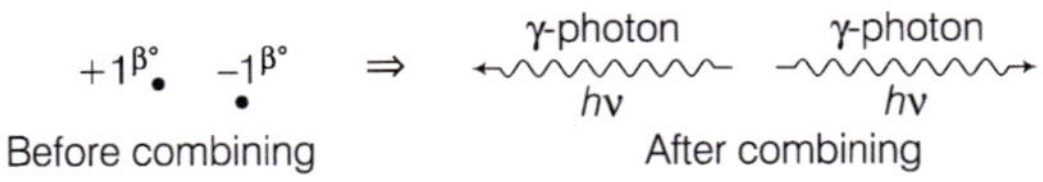

PYQs Previous Years Questions

1 Mark Questions

1. What is pair production? **ISC 2024, 20**

2. What is meant by mass defect? **ISC 2019**

3. What is the minimum energy which a gamma ray photon must possess in order to produce electron-positron pair? **ISC 2017**

2 Marks Questions

4. Calculate the energy released in the following nuclear fusion reaction

$$^2_1H + ^2_1H \longrightarrow ^4_2He + \text{energy}$$

Mass of $^2_1H = 2.014102$ u

Mass of $^4_2He = 4.002604$u **ISC 2024**

5. What is mean by 'binding energy per nucleon' of a nucleus? State its physical significance. **ISC SQP 2023, 18**

6. Calculate the minimum amount of energy which a gamma ray photon should have for the production of an electron and a positron pair. **ISC SQP 2022**

7. Calculate binding energy of oxygen nucleus ($^{16}_{8}O$) from the data given below **ISC 2020**

   Mass of a proton = 1.007825u

   Mass of a neutron = 1.008665u

   Mass of $^{16}_{8}O$ = 15.994915u

8. What is meant by pair annihilation? Write a balanced equation for the same. **ISC 2018**

9. With the help of a suitable example and an equation, explain the term pair production. **ISC 2015**

10. The atomic mass of Uranium $^{238}_{92}U$ is 238.0508 u while that of Thorium $^{234}_{90}Th$ is 234.0436 u and that of Helium $^{4}_{2}He$ is 4.0026 u, Alpha decay converts $^{238}_{92}U$ into $^{234}_{90}Th$ as shown

$$^{238}_{92}U \longrightarrow {}^{234}_{90}Th + {}^{4}_{2}He + \text{energy}$$

Determine the energy released in this reaction. **ISC 2014**

3 Marks Question

11. Calculate mass defect and binding energy of $^{20}_{10}Ne$ nucleus, given

    Mass of $^{20}_{10}Ne$ =19.992397u,

    Mass of $^{1}_{1}H$ = 1.007825u,

    Mass of $^{1}_{0}n$ = 1.008665u. **ISC 2024,17**

Case Based Question
(For Complete Chapter)

12. **Direction** *Read the passage given below and answer the questions that follows.*

An atomic nucleus is composed of protons and neutrons. The measurements using mass spectrometer have revealed that the mass of a stable nucleus is always less than the sum of the masses of its constituent protons and neutrons .The difference in the mass of a nucleus and its constituents is called mass defect, $\Delta m = Zm_p + (A - Z)m_n - M$. Using Einstein's mass energy relation. we express this mass difference in terms of energy as $\Delta E_b = \Delta mc^2$. This energy ΔE_b is called the binding energy of the nucleus. This energy represents the surplus energy which the nucleons give up by virtue of their mutual attraction when they become bound together to form a nucleus. The value of binding energy per nucleon of a nucleus gives a measure of the stability of that nucleus. Greater is the binding energy per nucleon of a nucleus, more stable is the nucleus. In the mass number range $A = 30$ to 170, the binding energy per nucleon is nearly constant, about 8 MeV/nucleon.

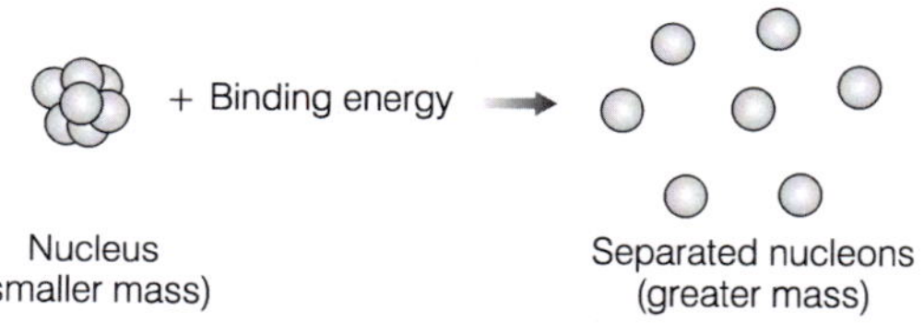

Answer the following questions from the above passage.

(*i*) Which instrument is used for measuring mass of the nuclei? **(1)**

(*ii*) What is mass defect? **(1)**

(*iii*) Why we calculate the binding energy per nucleon of nucleus? **(1)**

(*iv*) The binding energy per nucleon is nearly constant for which mass number range? **(2)**

Explanations

1. Refer to text on page 285 (Pair production and pair annihilation).

2. The sum of the masses of neutrons and protons forming a nucleus is more than the actual mass of the nucleus. This difference of masses is known as mass defect.

3. γ-rays are neutral photons of electromagnetic nature. After an α- or β- decay, the daughter nuclei is usually left in the excited state. It attains the ground state by single or successive transitions by emitting one or more photons. These energies of the order of MeV.

4. Mass of reactants $= 2.014102 \times 2 = 4.028204$ u

   Mass of products $= 4.002604$ u

   Mass defect, $\Delta m =$ Mass loss

   $$= (4.028204 - 4.002604) \text{ u}$$
   $$= 0.0256 \text{ u}$$

   Energy released, $E = \Delta mc^2$

   $$= 0.0256 \times 931 = 23.84 \text{ MeV}$$

5. Binding energy per nucleon is the average energy required to extract one nucleon from the nucleus. It is obtained by dividing the binding energy of the nucleus by the mass number;

   Mathematically,

   BE per nucleon

   $= [Zm_p + (A - Z)m_n - m_N]c^2 / A$ where, m is the mass of nucleus, m_p is the mass of proton and m_n is mass of neutron.

   Physical Significance

   Binding energy per nucleon $\propto$ stability of the nucleus.

   Concept Enhancer Greater the binding energy per nucleon, more stable is that nucleus.

6. Rest mass of electron or positron $= M_0$ (for each)

   From, Einstein's mass-energy equivalence relation,

   $$E = m_0c^2$$
   $$= 9.1 \times 10^{-31} \times (3 \times 10^8)^2$$
   $$= 8.2 \times 10^{-14} \text{J}$$
   $$= \frac{8.2 \times 10^{-14}}{1.6 \times 10^{-19}} \text{ eV} = 0.51 \times 10^6 \text{ eV}$$
   $$= 0.51 \text{ MeV}$$

   For pair production minimum energy

   $$= 2 \times 0.51 = 1.02 \text{ MeV}$$

Common Mistake Here electron and positron are in pair. Do not confuse that they are individual.

7. In the nucleus of ${}^{16}_{8}\text{O}$,

   Number of protons $= 8$

   Number of neutrons $= 16 - 8 = 8$

   Total mass of 8 protons and 8 neutrons

   $$= 8m_p + 8m_n$$
   $$= 8(1.007825) + 8 \times (1.008665)$$
   $$= 8(1.007825 + 1.008665)$$
   $$= 8 \times 2.01649 = 16.13192 \text{ u}$$

   Mass defect, $\Delta m = 16.13192 - 15.994915$

   $$= 0.137005 \text{ u}$$

   Total binding energy $= 0.137005 \times 931.5$

   $$= 127.62 \text{ MeV}$$

8. Refer to text on page 285 (Pair production and pair annihilation).

9. When a photon passes near a massive particle like an atomic nucleus, the photon disappears by creating an electron-positron pair. This process is called pair production. The energy of the photon should be equal to sum of energy of electron and energy of positron. So, a photon must have an energy of at least $2m_0c^2$ to create an electron positron pair, where, m_0 is the rest mass of the electron.

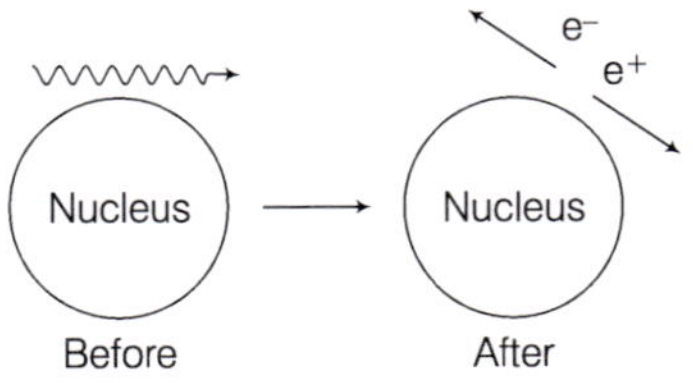

To conserve momentum, the nucleus recoils with very small velocity. Pair production is also known as the materialisation of radiant energy.

10. Mass defect, $\Delta m = 238.0508 - (234.0436 + 4.0026)$

    $$= 0.0046 \text{ u}$$

    As, energy $E = \Delta m \times c^2 = 0.0046 \times 931.5 = 4.28$ MeV

    where, $c =$ velocity of light

11. In a nucleus of ${}^{20}_{10}\text{Ne}$,

    Number of protons $= 10$

    Number of neutrons $= 20 - 10 = 10$

    Total mass of 10 protons and 10 neutrons

    $$= 10m_p + 10m_n = 10(m_p + m_n)$$

$$= 10 \times (1.007825 + 1.008665)$$
$$= 10 \times 2.01649 \text{ u}$$
$$= 20.1649 \text{ u}$$

Mass defect, $\Delta m = 20.1649 - 19.992397$
$$= 0.172503 \text{ u}$$

Total binding energy
$$= 0.17503 \times 931$$
$$= 160.600293 \text{ MeV}$$

$$E_b \text{ per nucleon} = \frac{160.600293}{20}$$
$$= 8.03001465 \text{ MeV/nucleon}$$

12. (*i*) Mass spectrometer is used for measuring mass of nuclei.

(*ii*) The difference in mass of a nucleus and its constituents is known as mass defect.

(*iii*) To know about the stability of the nucleus.

(*iv*) The binding energy per nucleon is nearly constant for mass number range $A = 30$ to 170, it is nearly about 8 MeV / nucleon.

CHAPTER TEST

01 Mark Questions (MCQs)

1 Mass and energy equivalent to 1 amu respectively are
(a) 1.67×10^{-27} kg, 9.30 MeV
(b) 1.67×10^{-27} kg, 931 MeV
(c) 1.67×10^{-27} kg, 1 MeV
(d) 1.67×10^{-34} kg, 1 MeV

2 The relation between nuclear radius and mass number is correctly shown in
(a) $R \propto A$
(b) $R \propto A^2$
(c) $R \propto A^{1/3}$
(d) $R \propto A^3$

3 Binding energy of a nucleus is of the order of
(a) electron volt (eV)
(b) kilo electron volt (KeV)
(c) mega electron volt (MeV)
(d) joule (J)

4 Which nuclei is more stable ?
(a) $_{26}Fe^{56}$
(b) $_{92}U^{238}$
(c) $_1H^1$
(d) $_6C^{12}$

01 Mark Questions (VSA)

5 Give an example where energy is converted into matter.

6 Write the equation representing pair annihilation.

7 Write the equation representing pair production.

02 Marks Questions

8 Can we relate the compressing of a spring with mass-energy relation? How?

9 Calculate the energy released when an electron annihilates a position.

03 Marks Questions

10 What is meant by the mass defect? Draw the binding energy curve and show the variations for light and heavy nucleus.

11 Calculate mass defect and binding energy per nucleon of $^{20}_{10}Ne$, given

Mass of $^{20}_{10}Ne = 19.992397$ u

Mass of $^1_1H = 1.007825$ u

Mass of $^1_0 n = 1.008665$ u

05 Marks Questions

12 Explain why 1 kg of mass is equivalent to an energy as high as 2.5×10^{10} kWh.

13 The energy supplied to Delhi by state electricity board during an average October day was 40 million kilowatt-hour. If this energy could be obtained by the conversion of matter, how much mass would have to be annihilated?

Answers

1. (b) **2.** (c) **3.** (c) **4.** (a)

11. 0.172503 u, 160.6 MeV **13.** 1.6 mg

23

Nuclear Energy

TREND ANALYSIS 4 YEARS

	Average No. of Questions Across all Sets				
	Types of Questions	2024	2023	2020	2019
Nuclear Energy	1 Mark	–	2	1	–
	2 Marks	1	–	–	–
	3 Marks	–	2	2	–
	5 Marks	–	–	–	–

The energy that holds the nucleus of an atom is called **nuclear energy**. Transformation of less stable nuclei into more tightly bound (stable) nuclei can result into releasing of nuclear energy.

Two methods of obtaining nuclear energy are as follow

1. Nuclear Fission 2. Nuclear Fusion

Nuclear Reaction

The process by which the identity of a nucleus is changed when it is bombarded by an energetic particle is called nuclear reaction.

The general expression for the nuclear reaction is as follow

$$\underset{\text{(Parent nucleus)}}{X} + \underset{\text{(Incident particle)}}{a} \longrightarrow \underset{\text{(Compound nucleus)}}{C} \longrightarrow \underset{\text{(Product nucleus)}}{Y} + \underset{\text{(Daughter nucleus)}}{b} \longrightarrow \underset{\text{energy}}{Q}$$

Here, X and a are the reactants, Y and b are the products and Q is the kinetic energy released in the nuclear reaction. a and b may be α-particles (^4_2He), proton (^1_1H or p), neutron (n), γ-ray photon etc.

Conservation laws obeyed by nuclear reaction

(*i*) Mass number and electric charge is conserved

i.e., $\Sigma Z_{\text{initial}} = \Sigma Z_{\text{final}}$

$\Sigma A_{\text{initial}} = \Sigma A_{\text{final}}$

(*ii*) Linear momentum in nuclear reaction are conserved.

(*iii*) Total energy for nuclear reaction are conserved.

Q-value

Q value means the difference between the rest mass energy of initial constituents and the rest mass energy of final constituents of a nuclear reaction.

Q-value of nuclear reaction

As considered, $X + a \longrightarrow Y + b + Q$

where, $Q = U_i - U_f$

Here, U_i = Rest mass energy of initial constituents

U_f = Rest mass energy of final constituents

$= (M_X + M_a - M_Y - M_b).c^2$

If $Q = +\text{ve}$ = reaction is exothermic

and $Q = -\text{ve}$ = reaction is endothermic.

e.g., For α-decay, $_Z X^A \longrightarrow {}_{Z-2}Y^{A-4} + {}_2\text{He}^4$

So, Q-value will be,

$$Q = [m({}_Z X^A) - m({}_{Z-2}Y^{A-4}) - m({}_2\text{He}^4)].c^2$$

which represents the kinetic energy available to the products.

Nuclear Fission

The phenomenon of splitting of heavy nuclei (mass number > 120) into smaller nuclei of nearly equal masses by the bombardment of proton, neutron, α-particle etc. is known as nuclear fission. e.g.,

$$^{239}_{92}\text{U} + ^1_0n \rightarrow ^{141}_{56}\text{Ba} + ^{92}_{36}\text{Kr} + 3\,^1_0n + Q\text{ (energy)}$$

The energy released in U^{235} fission is about 200 MeV or 0.8 MeV per nucleon and on an average 2.5 neutrons are liberated. These neutrons are called fast neutrons and their energy is about 2 MeV (each).

Nuclear Fusion

The phenomenon of conversion of two lighter nuclei into a single heavy nucleus is called nuclear fusion. e.g.,

$$^1_1\text{H} + ^1_1\text{H} \longrightarrow {}_1\text{H}^2 + e^+ + \nu + 0.42\,\text{MeV}$$

$$^2_1\text{H} + ^1_1\text{H} \longrightarrow {}_1\text{He}^3 + \gamma + 5.49\,\text{MeV}$$

$$^3_2\text{He} + ^3_2\text{He} \longrightarrow {}_2\text{He}^4 + {}_2\text{H}^1 + ^1_1\text{H} + 12.86\,\text{MeV}$$

Combining all the reactions, net reaction is

$$4\,^1_1\text{H} + 2e^- \longrightarrow {}_2\text{He}^4 + 2\nu + 6\gamma + 26.7\,\text{MeV}.$$

The energy released during nuclear fusion is known as **thermonuclear energy and nuclear reaction itself is known as thermonuclear reaction**.

Nuclear Chain Reaction

The extra neutrons in turns initiate fission process producing still more neutrons and so on. Thus, a chain of nuclear fission is set up called nuclear chain reaction.

Chain reactions are of two types such as follow

(*i*) **Uncontrolled chain reaction** If a chain reaction is started in a fissionable material having mass greater than certain critical mass. Such a reaction is called uncontrolled chain reaction. It is the underlying principle of atomic bomb.

(*ii*) **Controlled chain reaction** In a chain reaction using some means, the reaction is controlled and only one of the neutrons is emitted in a fission reaction, then energy released is steady. This is called controlled chain reaction.

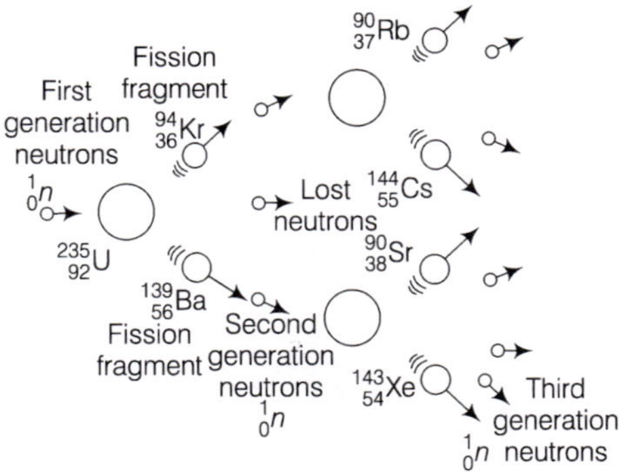

Nuclear chain reaction

Criticality of a Nuclear Reaction

Critical size If the size of the fissionable material is small, the neutrons emitted will escape the fissionable material before they are slowed down, which may jeopardise chain reaction.

The size of the fissionable material should be larger than a critical size.

A chain reaction once started will remain steady, accelerate or retard depends upon neutron reproduction factor or multiplication factor (R) which is defined as

$$R = \frac{\text{Rate of production of neutrons}}{\text{Rate of loss of neutrons}}$$

Nuclear Reactor

A nuclear reactor is a device to initiate and control a sustained nuclear chain reaction.

Principle of operation of a nuclear reactor The principle of operation of a nuclear reactor is based on the nuclear fission reaction. In this process, heavy atomic nucleus is splitted into lighter nuclei releasing tremendous amount of energy.

Main parts of a nuclear reactor are fuel, moderator, control rods, coolant, shield and safety device.

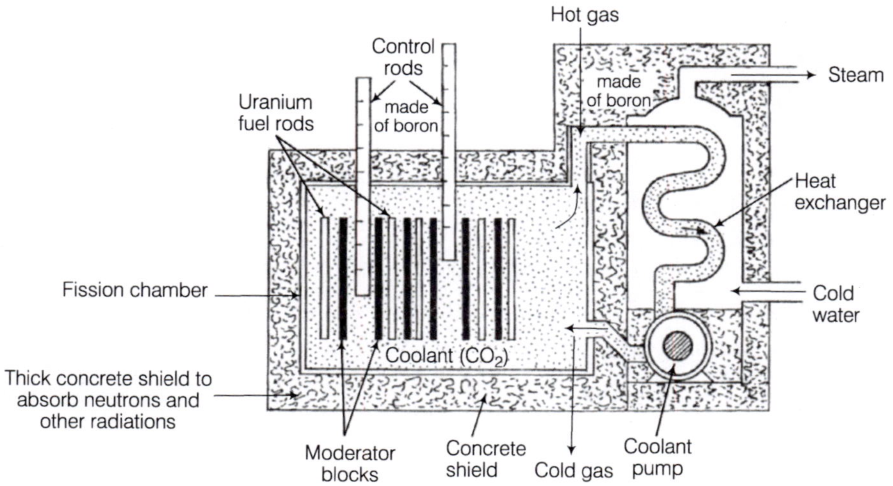

A nuclear reactor

Function of Some Important Parts of Nuclear Reactor

(*i*) **Nuclear Fuel** It is the fissionable material that can be burned by nuclear fission to derive nuclear energy. The common fuels used in reactor are uranium enriched with isotopes or U^{235} or Pu^{239} etc.

(*ii*) **Moderator** It is a medium that slows down the fast moving secondary neutrons. D_2O, graphite, beryllium, etc., are used as a moderator.

(*iii*) **Controlling** Rod Controlling rod is made of cadmium or boron which absorbs the excess neutron so as the rate of fission reactions can be controlled.

(*iv*) **Coolant** It is a liquid or water at high pressure (or metal sodium) used to withdraw the heat produced in the core.

Uses of nuclear reactor 1. In electric power generation.

2. To produce radio isotopes for their use in medical science, agriculture and industry.

Breeder Reactor

A breeder reactor is a special type of nuclear reactor capable of generating more fissile material than it consume. Breeder reactors can utilise nearly 100% of the energy contained in uranium, thorium ores.

Shielding

The whole reactor is protected with concrete walls 2 to 2.5 m thick, so that the radiations emitted during the nuclear reactions may not produce harmful radiations on the people working in the reactor power plant and cause serious health hazards.

Working of nuclear reactor

Neutrons produced by α-particle action on polonium
↓
Neutrons slowed down and start fission of $_{95}U^{235}$
↓
Fast neutrons released slowed down by moderator
↓
Again, the neutrons slown down and hence produces fission of $_{92}U^{235}$, thus chain reactions builds up.

By adjusting control rods, the chain reaction can be controlled. As water is used as coolant as well as moderator. Hence,

Coolant takes up the heat produced in the nuclear fission → Passes to water in heat exchanger
↓
Superheated steam is produced → Drives a turbine coupled with an electric generator
↓
From turbine, low pressure steam cooled → Condensed to water → Forced back to steam generator

Atom Bomb

In the atomic bomb an increasing uncontrolled chain reaction occurs in a very short time when two pieces of Uranium-235 are rapidly brought to form a mass greater than the critical size, by fast neutrons. Atom bomb may consists of P^{239} also. After explosion a temperature of $10^7\,°C$ and a pressure of several million atmosphere is produced.

PYQs Previous Years Questions

1 Mark Questions

1. Name the type of nuclear reaction that takes place in the core of the Sun. **ISC 2023**

2. State the function of a moderator in a nuclear reactor. **ISC SQP 2023**

3. In a nuclear reactor, cadmium rods are used as **ISC 2020**

(a) control rods (b) fuel rods
(c) coolant (d) moderator

4. Name a material which is used in making control rods in a nuclear reactor. **ISC 2018**

5. Name any one material used as a moderator in a nuclear reactor. **ISC SQP 2018**

6. Why nuclear fusion reaction is also called thermo-nuclear reactions? **ISC 2017**

7. In a nuclear reactor, what is the function of a moderator? **ISC 2016**

8. Where in our universe is the thermo- nuclear energy being released naturally? **ISC 2016, 09**

9. Write any one balanced equation representing nuclear fission. **ISC 2015**

10. Write one balanced reaction representing nuclear fusion. **ISC 2014**

11. Consider the following nuclear reaction,

$${}_1^2\text{H} + {}_1^2\text{H} \longrightarrow {}_2^3\text{He} + {}_0^1n$$

What is the name of this reaction? **ISC 2011**

12. Complete the following nuclear reaction,

$${}_0^1n + {}_6^{12}\text{C} \longrightarrow {}_5^{11}\text{B} + \cdots$$ **ISC 2010**

13. What is the source of energy of stars? **ISC 2008**

14. What is the role of control rods in a nuclear reactor? **ISC 2004**

15. What is the function of heavy water in a nuclear reactor? **ISC 2002**

2 Marks Questions

16. In a nuclear reactor, state the use of the following.

(i) Graphite rods **ISC 2024**

(ii) Cadmium rods

17. Write one balanced equation each to show

(*i*) nuclear fission (*ii*) nuclear fusion **ISC 2018**

18. Fission of U-235 nucleus releases 200 MeV of energy. Calculate the fission rate (i.e., number of fissions per second) in order to produce a power of 320 MW. **ISC 2009**

3 Marks Questions

19. Name any two essential parts of a nuclear reactor. State the function of any one of them. **ISC 2023**

20. (i) State any two differences between nuclear fusion and nuclear fission.

(ii) What is the essential difference between the working of a fission bomb and a nuclear reactor? **ISC SQP 2023**

21. In a certain star, three α-particles undergo fusion in a single reaction to form ${}_6^{12}\text{C}$ nucleus. Calculate the energy released in this reaction in MeV.
Given, $m({}_2^4\text{He}) = 4.002604$ u and
$m({}_6^{12}\text{C}) = 12.000000$ u. **ISC 2013**

> **KEY idea**
> To calculate the released energy, first calculate the mass defect.

22. (*i*) Write a balance equation showing nuclear fission of uranium (${}_{92}^{235}\text{U}$) nucleus.

(*ii*) In a nuclear reactor, what is the function of
(a) cadmium rods
(b) graphite rods. **ISC 2010**

Case Based Questions (For Complete Chapter)

23. Direction *Read the passage given below and answer the questions that follows*

India built its first nuclear reactor Apsara at Trombay, Maharashtra in the year 1956. It was used mainly to generate electric power. Nuclear reactors are around to produce radio-isotopes which are used in the fields of research, medicine, agriculture, etc. Unlike thermal power stations, nuclear power stations don't cause atmospheric pollution. Still, there is opposition to installing them as there is an that there may be a radiation leakage which can be harmful to the people living nearby.

(i) In a nuclear reactor, what is the function of cadmium rods? **(1)**

(ii) In a nuclear reactor, which material is used as a moderator? **(1)**

(iii) Give any one balanced equation representing the nuclear fission reaction taking place in a nuclear reactor. **2022 Sem-II (1)**

24. Direciton *Read the passage given below and answer the questions that follow.*

Mr. Ravi had been living in a small town with his family for many years. He decided to shift to a city when he learnt that a nuclear power plant would be built in his town. His son Prakash, who was a science teacher, did not agree with his father's decision.

Prakash explained to his father how mass defect during nuclear fission released energy. He assured his father that the authorities were taking all the possible safety measures to avoid any kind of nuclear mishap. Mr. Ravi understood the scientific explanation given by his son and decided not to shift to another place.

(*i*) What is the cause of energy generation of a nuclear reactor during nuclear fission? **(1)**

(*ii*) Write one nuclear reaction for nuclear fission that takes place in a nuclear reactor. **(1)**

(*iii*) Give the formula for the Energy generation that takes place in the nuclear reactor. **ISC 2022 Sem-II (1)**

Explanations

1. Nuclear fusion reaction takes place in the Sun. The Sun's tremendous pressure and high temperature fuse hydrogen nuclei to form helium through various steps.

2. It is a medium that slows down the fast moving secondary neutrons. D_2O, graphite, beryllium, etc.

3. (a) Cadmium rods are used as control rods in a nuclear reactor because they control the rate of fission of uranium and plutonium.

4. Cadmium or boron is used in making control rods in a nuclear reactor.

5. Heavy water (D_2O).

6. To carry nuclear fusion in a bulk material, the temperature of the material has to be raised to 10^6 K. A high temperature is necessary for the light nuclei to have sufficient kinetic energy so that they can overcome their mutual coulombic repulsion and come closer than the range of nuclear force. Colliding nuclei should have enough energy due to their thermal motion and can penetrate the coulomb barrier. That's why nuclear fusion reaction is also known as thermo-nuclear reaction as it involves lot of heat.

7. In a nuclear reactor, the function of moderator is to slow down the fast moving secondary neutrons produced during the fission.

8. Nuclear reaction takes place at the stars and the sun. Hydrogen get converted to helium.

9. Nuclear fission

$${}_0^1n + {}_{92}^{235}\text{U} \longrightarrow {}_{56}^{144}\text{Ba} + {}_{36}^{89}\text{Kr} + 3\,{}_0^1n$$

10. $4\,{}_1^1\text{H} + 2e^- \rightarrow {}_2^4\text{He} + 2\nu + 6\gamma + 26.7\,\text{MeV}$

11. The given reaction shows that two atoms are combining to form third atom and a neutron released from it. Thus, it is a nuclear fusion reaction.

12. When a neutron reacts with carbon, it gives hydrogen with boron.

$${}_0^1n + {}_6^{12}\text{C} \rightarrow {}_5^{11}\text{B} + {}_1^2\text{H}$$

13. Nuclear fusion reaction takes place at the sun to release tremendous amount of energy.

14. A control rod is used in nuclear reactor to control the rate of fission of uranium and plutonium. They are made of chemical elements capable of absorbing many neutrons, such as boron, cadmium, etc.

15. Heavy water is used as a moderator in a nuclear reactor. It is used to slow the fast moving neutrons being directed at the fissionable material by means of the molecules of the moderator.

16. (i) Graphite rods are used as a moderator. Moderator is a material used in a nuclear reactor to slow down the neutrons produced from fission.

(ii) Controlling rod is made of cadmium or boron which absorbs the excess neutron, so as the rate of fission reactions can be controlled.

17. (i) Refer to sol. 9 and 10 page 294.

(ii) For nuclear fusion

$$_1H^2 + {}_1H^2 \longrightarrow {}_1H^3 + {}_1H^1 + \text{Energy}$$

18. Given, power obtained, $P = 320$ MW $= 320 \times 10^6$ W,

Energy released $= 200$ MeV

$$\text{Power, } P = \frac{E\text{ (energy)}}{t\text{ (time)}}$$

$$320 \times 10^6 = \frac{n \times 200 \times 1.6 \times 10^{-13}}{1}$$

$\therefore$ Number of fissions per second $= n = 10^6 \times 10^{13} = 10^{19}$

Common Mistake The value of *P*, *E* will be must in SI units.

19. Refer to text on page 292 (Function of some important parts of nuclear reactor).

20. (*i*) Refer to text on page 291 (Nuclear fission and Nuclear Fusion)

(*ii*) In a nuclear reactor controlled chain reaction takes place whereas, In a fission bomb uncontrolled chain reaction takes place.

21. Mass of three helium nucleus $_2He^4 = 3 \times 4.002604$ u

$= 12.007812$ u

Mass of $_6C^{12} = 12.000000$ u

Mass defect, $\Delta m = 12.007812 - 12.000000$

$= 0.007812$ u

Energy released, $E = \Delta m \times 931 = 0.007812 \times 931$

$= 7.272972$ MeV

22. (i) The balanced equation showing nuclear fusion of $^{235}_{92}U$ is

$$_{92}U^{235} + {}_0n^1 \rightarrow {}_{56}Ba^{141} + {}_{36}Kr^{92} + 3\,{}_0n^1 + \text{Energy}$$

(ii) (a) Cadmium rods are used to control the rate of nuclear fission as it absorbs the extra neutron.

(b) Graphite rods are used to slow down the fast moving neutrons.

Concept Enhancer Fusion reaction is difficult to initiate as it takes place under the extreme conditions of high pressure and high temperature. So, a fusion bomb is used as ignite of a fusion bomb.

23. (*i*) In a nuclear reactor, cadmium rod is used as control rod. It is used in nuclear reactors to control the rate of fission of uranium and plutonium.

(*ii*) Heavy water (D_2O) is used as moderator in nuclear reactors. Moderator is used to slow down the fast moving neutrons produced during the fission.

(*iii*) Refer to sol. 9 on page 294.

24. (*i*) Nuclear fission can be made a chain reaction that's for the power generation nuclear fission is used.

(*ii*) $_{92}U^{235} + {}_0n^1 \longrightarrow {}_{38}Sv^{94} + {}_{54}Xe^{140} + 2\,{}_0n^1$

(*iii*) The energy released in the fission reaction can be calculated with Einstein's equation, $E = \Delta mc^2$.

CHAPTER TEST

01 Mark Questions (MCQs)

1 What was the fissionable material used in the bomb dropped at Nagasaki (Japan) in the year 1945?
(a) Uranium
(b) Neptunium
(c) Helium
(d) Plutonium

2 The energy of thermal neutrons is of the order of
(a) 1 MeV (b) 1 eV
(c) 10^{-2} eV (d) 10^{-4} eV

3 In a nuclear reactor
(a) moderator is used to control the number of neutrons
(b) moderator is used to slow down the neutrons
(c) controller rods are used to slow down the neutrons
(d) coolant is used to slow down the neutrons

4 The moderator in the nuclear reactor at Trombay is
(a) uranium (b) graphite
(c) heavy water (d) cadmium

5 The controller rods in a nuclear-reactor are made of
(a) cadmium (b) uranium
(c) graphite (d) plutonium

6 Cadmium rods are used in a nuclear reactor to
(a) slow down the neutrons
(b) speed up the neutrons
(c) produce the neutrons
(d) control the fission rate of neutrons

7 During a nuclear fusion reaction
(a) a heavy nucleus breaks into two fragments by itself
(b) a light nucleus bombarded by thermal neutrons breaks up
(c) a heavy nucleus bombarded by thermal neutrons breaks up
(d) two light nuclei combine to give a heavier nucleus and possibly other products

01 Mark Questions (VSA)

8 What do you mean by thermal neutrons?

9 What are the function of heavy water in nuclear reactor?

10 What do you mean by Q-values?

11 What are moderators?

02 Marks Questions

12 Why is it necessary to slow down the neutrons produced through the fission of $^{235}_{92}U$ nuclei (by neutrons) to sustain a chain reaction? What types of materials are (preferably) needed for slowing down fast neutrons?

13 Define the Q-value of a nuclear process. When can a nuclear process not proceed spontaneously?

14 Distinguish between nuclear fission and fusion.

15 Why is it necessary to slow down the neutrons, produced through the fission of $^{235}_{92}U$ nuclei (by neutrons) to sustain a chain reaction?

16 What types of nuclei are (preferably) needed for slowing down fast neutrons?

03 Marks Questions

17 Mass conservation law and energy conservation law were supposed to be different before Einstein's theory of relativity. Why?

18 Define nuclear chain reaction. Explain its different types.

19 Calculate the energy released in MeV in the following nuclear reaction,

$${}_1H^2 + {}_1H^2 \longrightarrow {}_2He^3 + {}_0n^1$$

Given : Mass of ${}_1H^2 = 2.015\,u$

Mass of ${}_2He^3 = 3.017u$

Mass of ${}_0n^1 = 1.009\,u$

05 Marks Questions

20 Define the following terms
(i) Nuclear reaction (ii) Nuclear fission
(iii) Nuclear fusion (iv) Nuclear reactor
(v) Breeder reactor

21 (a) Explain the nuclear reactor with the diagram.
(b) What do you mean by shielding?

Answers

1. (d) 2. (c) 3. (b) 4. (d) 5. (a)
6. (d) 7. (d)

24

Semiconductor Electronics

TREND ANALYSIS 4 YEARS

Average No. of Questions Across all Sets

	Types of Questions	2024	2023	2020	2019
Semiconductor Electronics	1 Mark	–	4	1	–
	2 Marks	–	1	–	–
	3 Marks	–	–	–	1
	5 Marks	–	–	–	–

Material

Material is anything that has mass and occupies space. Mass is a measure of the quantity of matter in a sample of any material.

Types of Material

On the basis of electrical property, material are of three types–conductors, insulators and semiconductors.

Types of Material	Resistivity (ρ)	Conductivity (σ)	Conclusion
(*i*) Conductors (metals)	10^{-2} - $10^{-8}\,\Omega$-m	10^{2} - 10^{8} Sm^{-1}	low resistivity, high conductivity
(*ii*) Insulators	10^{11} - $10^{19}\,\Omega$-m	10^{-11} - 10^{-19} Sm^{-1}	high resistivity, low conductivity
(*iii*) Semiconductor	10^{-5} - $10^{6}\,\Omega$-m	10^{+5} - 10^{-6} Sm^{-1}	resistivity and conductivity intermediate to metals and insulator

Types of Semiconductors

The two types of semiconductors are given below.

(*i*) **Elemental semiconductors** These semiconductors are available in natural form.
e.g. Silicon(Si) and germanium(Ge).

(*ii*) **Compound semiconductors** These semiconductors are made by compounding the metals. e.g. CdS, GaAs, CdSe, InP, Anthracene, polyaniline, etc.

Energy Band in Solids

A solid contains an enormous number of atoms packed closely together. Each atom, when isolated, has a discrete set of electron energy levels named as $1s, 2s, 2p, 3s, 3p, \ldots$. If we imagine all the N (say)-atoms of the solid to be isolated from one another, then they would have completely coinciding sets of energy levels i.e. each of the energy level of this N-atom system would have an N-fold degeneracy. The electrons fill the energy levels in each atom independently.

As, the atoms approach one another to form the soild, a continuously increasing interaction occurs between them which causes each of the levels to split into N distinct level. In practice, however N is very large ($\approx 10^{23}/\text{cm}^3$).

Therefore, the split energy levels become so numerous and so close together that they form an almost continuous energy band.

Figure below shows the formation of energy bands for some of the higher energy levels of isolated sodium atoms whose ground-state configuration $1s^2, 2s^2, 2p^6, 3s^1$ as their interatomic distance decreases.

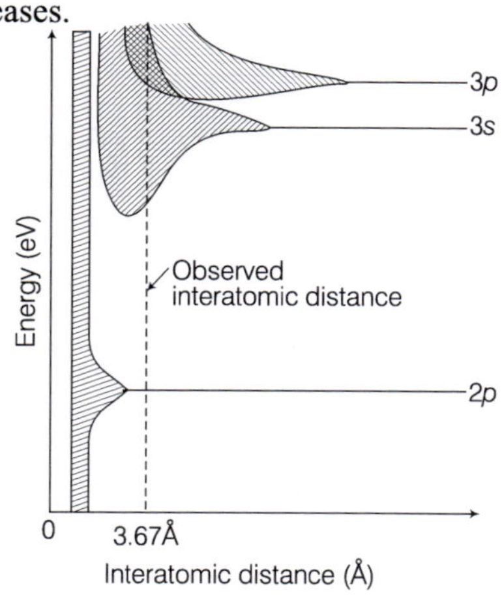

Formation of energy bands

Different Types of Energy Bands

Energy band in a crystal due to the interatomic interaction between valence electrons of one atom are shared by more than one atom in the crystal.

Now, splitting of energy levels take place. The collection of these closely spaced energy levels are called an energy band.

The different types of energy bands are as follows.

(*i*) **Valence band** Valence band is the energy band which includes the energy levels of the valence electrons or in which valence electrons are present (E_v).

(*ii*) **Conduction band** Conduction band is the energy band above the valence band which decides the conductivity of a material (E_c).

(*iii*) **Energy band gap** The minimum energy required for shifting electrons from valence band to conduction band is called energy band gap (E_g).

$$E_g = E_c - E_v$$

(*iv*) **Fermi energy** It is the maximum possible energy possessed by the free electrons of a material at absolute zero temperature, i.e. 0 K. The value of fermi energy is different for different materials.

Difference among Conductor, Insulator and Semiconductor on the Basis of Energy Bands

Conductor (Metal)	**Insulator**	**Semiconductor**
In conductor, either there is no energy gap between the conduction band which is partially filled with electrons and valence band or the conduction band and valence band overlap each other.	In insulator, the valence band is completely filled, the conduction band is completely empty and energy gap is quite large that small energy from any other source cannot overcome it.	In semiconductor, the valence band is totally filled and the conduction band is empty but the energy gap between conduction band and valence band, unlike insulators is very small.
Thus, many electrons from below the fermi level can shift to higher energy levels above the fermi level in the conduction band and behave as free electrons for the conduction of electricity. Therefore, the resistance of conductor or metal is very low.	Thus, electrons are bound to valence band and are not free to move and hence, electric conduction is not possible in this type of material and have high resistivity.	Thus, at room temperature, some electrons in the valence band acquire thermal energy greater than band gap energy and jump over to the conduction band where they are free to move under the influence of even a small electric field and acquire small conductivity.
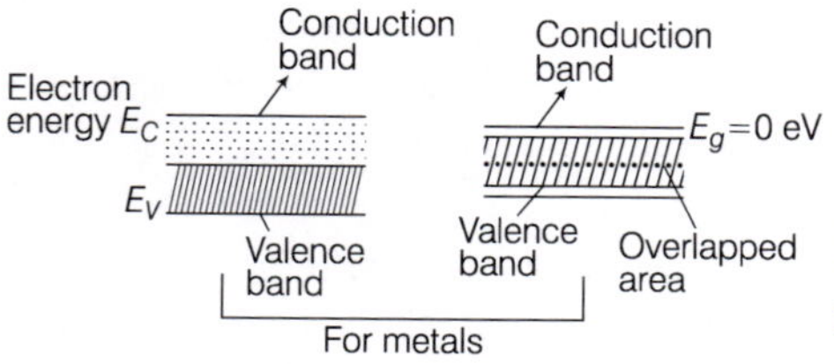	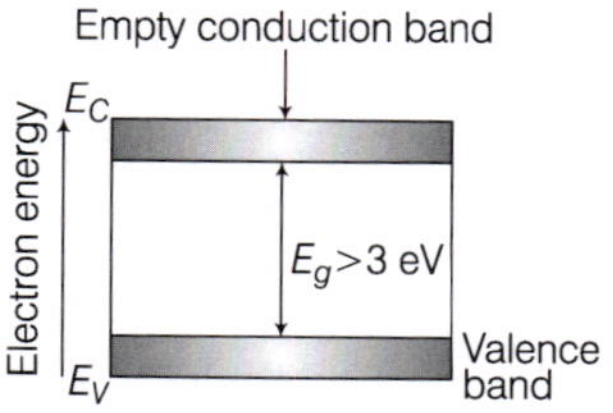	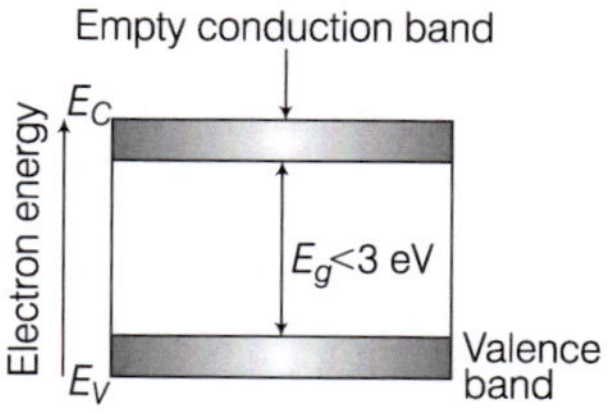

Intrinsic and Extrinsic Semiconductors

On the basis of purity or impurity, semiconductors are of two types

Intrinsic semiconductors

Pure semiconductors in which $n_e = n_h = n_i$

where, n_e and n_h are number densities of electrons and holes respectively and n_i is called intrinsic carrier concentration. An intrinsic semiconductor is also called an **undoped semiconductor** or *i*-type semiconductor. Under the action of electric field, the net current, $I = I_e + I_h$.
where, I_e is current due to the displacement of electrons and I_h is current due to the displacement of holes.

Extrinsic semiconductors

The process of adding impurity to an intrinsic semiconductor in a controlled manner is called **doping**. Doping is done in order to increase the conductivity of a pure semiconductor.

Pure semiconductor, when doped with the impurity it is known as extrinsic semiconductor.

Extrinsic semiconductors are of two types,

(*i*) *n*-type semiconductor (*ii*) *p*-type semiconductor

Note Both *n*-type and *p*-type semiconductors are electrically neutral.

n-type Semiconductor

In *n*-type semiconductor, majority charge carriers are electrons and minority charge carriers are holes, i.e. $n_e > n_h$.

- Formation of *n*-type semiconductor is shown below.

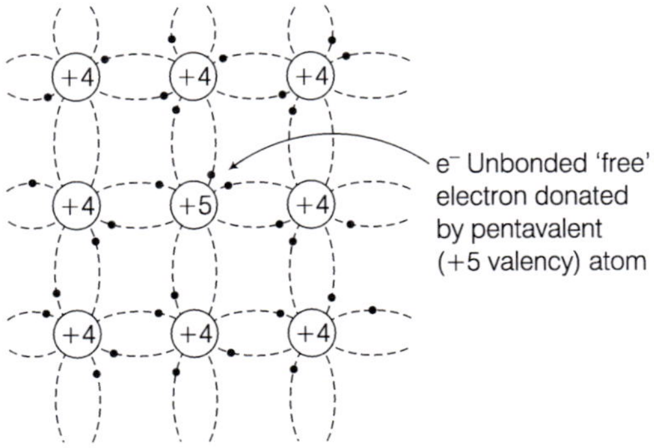

Pentavalent donor atom (As, Sb, P, etc.) doped for pentavalent Si or Ge giving *n*-type semiconductor

p-type semiconductor

In *p*-type semiconductor, majority charge carriers are holes and minority charge carriers are electron, i.e. $n_h > n_e$.

- Formation of *p*-type semiconductor is shown below.

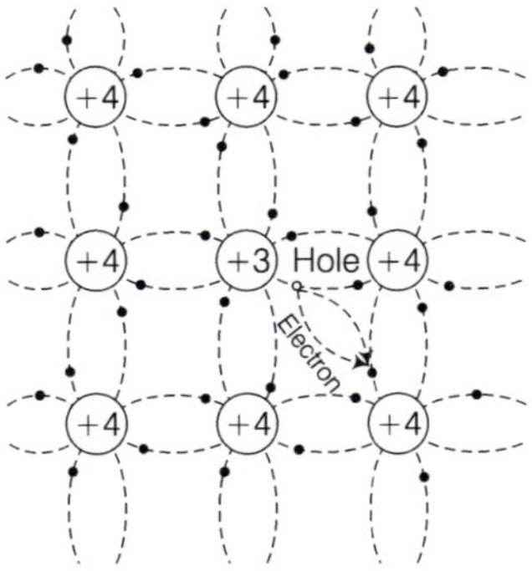

Trivalent acceptor atom (In, Al, B, etc.) doped in tetravalent Si or Ge-lattice giving *p*-type semiconductor

At equilibrium condition, $n_e n_h = n_i^2$

This is known as **mass-action law.**

Under the action of an electric field, holes move towards negative potential giving hole current, I_h and electron towards positive potential giving electron current I_e. The total current is the sum of the electron current I_e and the hole current I_h.

i.e. $$I = I_e + I_h$$

Minimum energy required to create a electron hole-pair,

$$h\nu \geq E_g$$

where, E_g is energy band gap, energy = $h\nu$, ν is frequency of incident radiation.

In Extrinsic Semiconductors

- Current, $I = eA(n_e v_e + n_h v_h)$
  where, A is area of cross-section, while v_e and v_h are speeds of electrons and holes, respectively.
- Mobility of charge carriers, $\mu = \frac{v}{E}$, where E is applied electric field and v is velocity of electron or holes.
  $$\left[\text{where, } \mu_e = \frac{v_e}{E}, \mu_n = \frac{v_h}{E}\right]$$
- Electrical conductivity,
  $$\sigma = \frac{1}{\rho} = e(\mu_e n_e + n_h \mu_h)$$

where, n_e and n_h are concentrations of electrons and holes respectively, μ_e and μ_h are mobilities of electrons and holes, respectively.

Difference between Intrinsic Semiconductor and Extrinsic Semiconductor

Intrinsic Semiconductor	Extrinsic Semiconductor
It is pure semiconducting material and no impurity atoms are added to it.	It is prepared by doping a small quantity of impurity atoms to the pure semiconducting material.
Examples are crystalline forms of pure silicon and germanium.	Examples are silicon and germanium crystals with impurity atoms of arsenic, antimony, phosphorous, etc., or indium, boron, aluminium, etc.
The number of free electrons in conduction band and the number of holes in valence band is exactly equal and very small indeed.	The number of free electrons and holes is never equal. There is excess of electrons in *n*-type semiconductors and excess of holes in *p*-type semiconductors.
Its electrical conductivity is low.	Its electrical conductivity is high.
Its electrical conductivity is a function of temperature alone.	Its electrical conductivity depends upon the temperature as well as on the quantity of impurity atoms doped in the structure.

Differece between *n*-Type Semiconductor and *p*-Type Semiconductor

n-Type Semiconductor	*p*-Type Semiconductor
It is extrinsic semiconductor which is obtained by doping the impurity atoms of Vth group of periodic table to the pure germanium or silicon semiconductor.	It is extrinsic semiconductor which is obtained by doping the impurity atoms of III group of periodic table to the pure germanium of silicon semiconductor.
The impurity atoms added, provide extra electrons in the structure and are called donor atoms.	The impurity atoms added, create vacancies of electrons (i.e. holes) in the structure and are called acceptor atoms.
The electrons are majority charge carriers and holes are minority charge carriers.	The holes are majority charge carriers and electrons are minority charge carriers.
The electron density (n_e) is much greater than the hole density (n_h), i.e. $n_e >> n_h$.	The hole density (n_h) is much greater than the electron density (n_e), i.e. $n_h >> n_e$.
The donor energy level is close to the conduction band and far away from the valence band.	The acceptor energy level is close to the valence band and is far away from the conduction band.
The fermi energy level lies in between the donor energy level and conduction band.	The fermi energy level lies in between the acceptor energy level and valence band.

PYQs Previous Years Questions

1 Mark Questions

1. With an increase in the temperature, electrical conductivity of a semiconductor **ISC 2023**
   (a) decreases
   (b) increases
   (c) does not change
   (d) first increases and then decreases

2. What type of semiconductor is obtained when a crystal of silicon is doped with a trivalent element? **ISC 2023**

3. *n* type semiconductor is that which has **ISC SQP 2023**
   (a) holes as majority carriers
   (b) free electrons as majority carriers
   (c) holes and free electrons equal in number
   (d) trivalent element as an impurity

4. In semiconductors, what is meant by "doping"? **ISC SQP 2023**

5. State how a *p*-type semiconductor will be obtained from a pure crystal of a semiconductor. **ISC 2022 Sem-II**

> **KEY idea**
> *p*-type semiconductor material can be obtained by adding the group III elements.

6. State any one difference between energy band diagram of conductors and that of insulators. **ISC 2020**

7. To convert a pure semiconductor into *n*-type semiconductor, what type of impurity is added to it? **ISC 2013**

8. How can an *n*-type semiconductor be obtained from a pure crystal of germanium? **ISC 2011**

9. In which of the solids (semiconductors, conductors or insulators), do conduction band and valence band overlap? **ISC 2009**

10. What is meant by energy gap in solids? **ISC 2007**

11. Explain why the electrical conductivity of a pure semiconductor increases on heating? **ISC 2005**

12. What are energy bands in solids? **ISC 2002**

2 Marks Questions

13. With reference to semiconductor Physics, answer the following questions.

(*i*) What is meant by "forbidden band" of energy levels?

(*ii*) In which material "forbidden band" is absent? **ISC 2023**

14. Explain the following terms **ISC 2022 Sem-II**

(*i*) Intrinsic semiconductor.

(*ii*) Extrinsic semiconductor.

15. Draw energy band diagrams of conductors, semiconductors and insulators. **ISC 2007, 2000**

3 Marks Questions

16. With reference to semiconductor answer the following. **ISC 2019**

(*i*) What is the change in the resistance of the semiconductor with increase in temperature?

(*ii*) Name the majority charge carriers in *n*-type semiconductor.

(*iii*) What is meant by doping?

17. With reference to a semiconductor diode, define the terms 'depletion region' and 'potential barrier'. How will the width of depletion region change during reverse biasing? **ISC SQP 2018**

18. Draw a labelled energy band diagram for a solid which is an insulator. What is the main difference between this diagram and that of a semiconductor? **ISC 2011**

Case Based Question
(For Complete Chapter)

19. Direction *Read the passage given below and answer the questions that follow.*

Semiconductors Certain materials have the basic crystal structure of an insulator but with a much smaller energy gap (of the order of an electron-volt) between the valence band and the conduction band. Such solids are known as 'semiconductors'. Silicon and germanium having energy gaps of 1.1 eV and 0.7 eV respectively are typical examples of semiconductors.

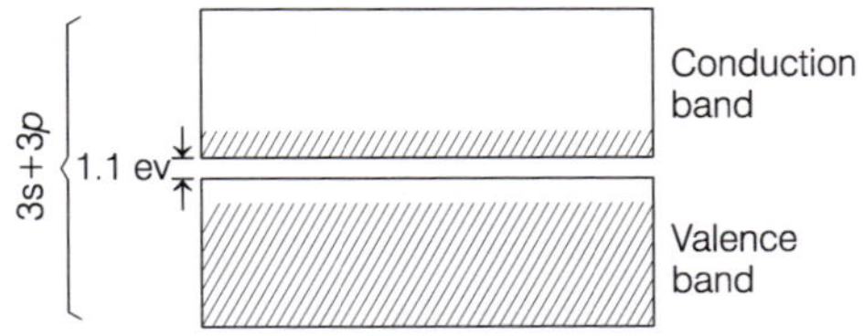

Silicon $1s^2\ 2s^2\ 2p^6\ 3s^2\ 3p^2$

Figure shows the energy bands of silicon. At room temperature, a few of its electrons in the valence band have sufficient kinetic energy of thermal motion to cross the narrow energy gap and enter the conduction band above it. Hence, when an electric field is applied, the few electrons present in the conduction band acquire additional energy to move to the unoccupied levels within the same band. similarly, a few of the many electrons present in the valence band move to the few available unoccupied levels in the same band. Hence, there is a limited flow of current across the crystal. Thus, silicon has an electrical conductivity intermediate between those of conductors and insulators and it therefore a semiconductor.

(*i*) What do you mean by semiconductor? **(1)**

(*ii*) Name the elements having the energy gaps of 1.1 eV and 0.7 eV, respectively. **(1)**

(*iii*) When the electrons are jumped from valence band to conduction band? **(1)**

(*iv*) In which types of materials the free electrons are not able to jump from valence band to conduction band? **(1)**

(*v*) Draw a diagram of valence band as well as the conduction band and their energy gap. **(1)**

Explanations

1. (b) Increases

With rise in temperature the electrical conductivity of intrinsic semiconductor increases.

> **Concept Enhancer** In a intrinsic semiconductor the band gap between the valence band and conduction band is minimum.

2. When a trivalent impurity is doped in an intrinsic semiconductor (silicon), then we get a *p*-type semiconductor.

3. (b)

4. Refer to text on page 299 (Extrinsic Semiconductors).

5. To obtain a *p*-type semiconductor, pure silicon is dopped with a trivalent impurity like indium, aluminium or boron.

6. Refer to text on page 298 (Difference among Conductor, Insulator and Semiconductor on the Basis of Energy Bands).

7. A pentavalent impurity is to be added to form *n*-type semiconductor whose majority carriers are electrons. e.g. Sb, P or As is added to Ge (or Si).

8. An *n*-type semiconductor can be obtained from a pure germanium crystal by adding pentavalent impurity atom to a Ge crystal. Thus increasing number of free electron.

9. In conductors, conduction band and valence band overlap with each other.

10. The energy difference between valence band and conduction band is called energy gap in solids.

i.e. $E_g = E_c - E_v$

11. The conductivity of a semiconductor increases with rise in temperature, because of increase in number of free electrons in conduction band of semiconductor material.

12. On the basis of band theory of solids, there are two energy bands.

(*i*) Conduction band which is responsible for conduction of electricity.

(*ii*) Valence band which is present just below the conduction band and always have electrons.

13. (*i*) Refer to text on page 298. (Energy band gap)

(*ii*) Insulators

[The materials which does not allow the flow of electric current through them are called insulators.]

14. (*i*) Refer to text on page 299 (Intrinsic Semiconductor).

(*ii*) Refer to text on page 229 (Extrinsic Semiconductor).

15.

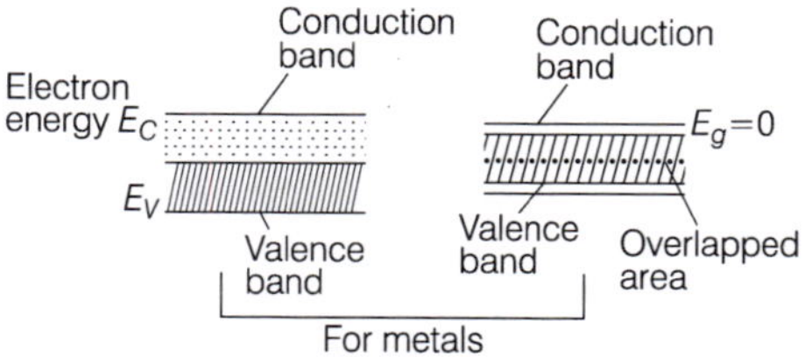

Conductors

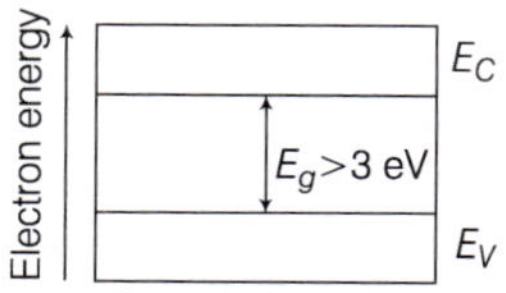

Semiconductors

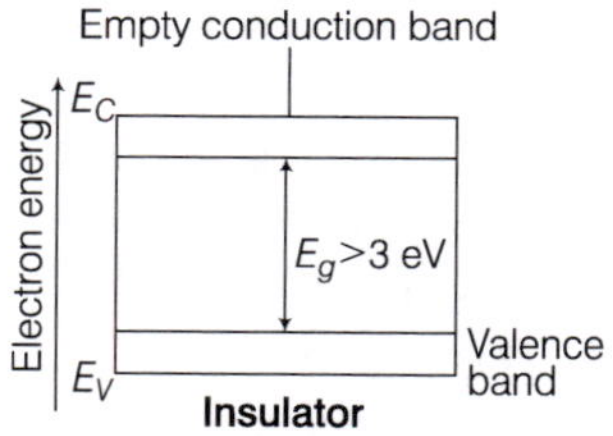

Insulator

16. (*i*) The resistance of semiconductor decreases with rise in temperature.

(*ii*) In *n* - type semiconductor, the electrons are the majority charge carriers.

(*iii*) The process of adding impurity to an intrinsic semiconductor in controlled manner is called doping.

17. **Depletion region** The small region on either side of the junction which is depleted of mobile (free) charge carriers and has only immobile ions is called depletion region.

Potential barrier The accumulation of negative charges in *p*-region and positive charges in the *n*-region set-up a potential barrier i.e., the potential difference across the depletion region. It opposes the diffusion of electron and holes across the junction.

Effect on depletion region during reverse biasing
During reverse biasing, the positive terminal of the external battery attracts electrons from *n*-region and its negative terminal attracts holes from *p*-region.

Due to which, holes in the *p*-region and electrons in the *n*-region are pushed away from the function. Hence, potential barrier and with of the depletion layer increases.

18. In solids, there are two types of energy bands naming conduction band and valence band. Conduction band is of higher energy and hence, less stable.

Energy band diagram for an insulator is shown alongside.

Energy bands of diamond $(1s^2, 2s^2, 2p^2)$.

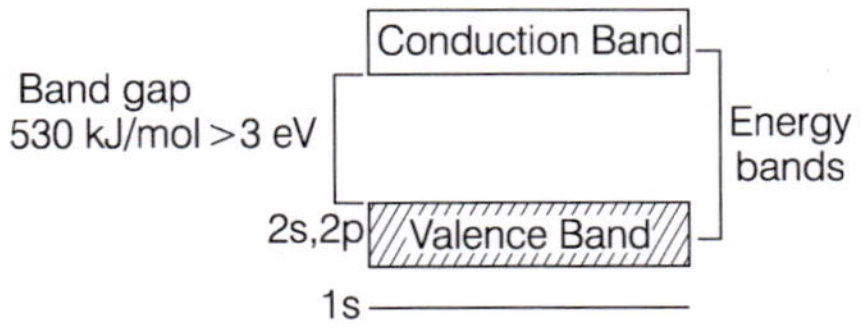

Difference between energy band diagram of insulator and semiconductor

Energy gap between valence band and conduction band is approximately equal to 530 kJ/mol (> 3eV) (very large) in insulators which is much higher than that for a semiconductor. So on giving temperature, electrons can jump from valence band to conduction band and increases its conductivity in case of semiconductors.

19. (*i*) A semiconductor is a substance that has specific electrical properties that enable it to serve as a foundation for computers and other electronic devices.

(*ii*) Silicon and germanium having energy gaps of 1.1 eV and 0.7 eV, respectively.

(*iii*) The electrons which are in valence band have the enough energy to jump to the conduction band.

(*iv*) Insulators are the materials that have no free electrons to jump from valence band to conduction band.

(*v*)

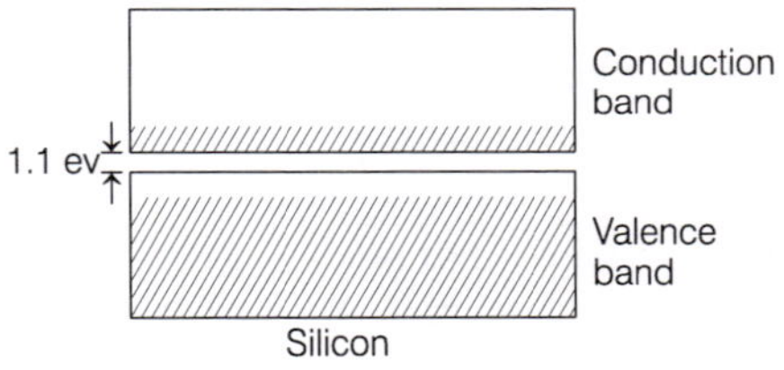

CHAPTER TEST

01 Mark Questions (MCQs)

1 In some substances, charge can flow at ordinary temperature but not at very low temperature. There are called

(a) conductors (b) insulators
(c) semiconductors (d) dielectrics

2 In a semiconductor, the energy gap between the valence and the conduction bands is of the order of

(a) 1 eV (b) 10 eV
(c) 1 keV (d) 1 MeV

3 In an insulator, the energy gap is the order of

(a) 1 eV (b) 10 eV
(c) 1 keV (d) 1 MeV

4 Electric conduction in a semiconductor occur due to

(a) electrons only
(b) holes only
(c) Neither electrons nor holes
(d) Both electrons and holes

5 Germanium and silicon have a valency of

(a) 4 (b) 3
(c) 2 (d) 1

6 An example of *n*-type semiconductor is

(a) pure germanium
(b) pure silicon
(c) arsenic-mixed germanium
(d) boron-mixed germanium

01 Mark Questions (VSA)

7 What do you understand by ''valence band''?

8 Define terms conduction band.

9 What is meant by energy gap in solids?

10 Name the impurities that will make pure Si an extrinic semiconductor.

11 Define the term ''hole''.

02 Marks Questions

12 What do you mean by semiconductor? Draw its energy band diagram and explain it?

13 In an intrinsic semiconductor, define the fermi level.

14 Carbon and silicon both have four valence electrons each, then how are they distinguished?

15 Write two characteristic features to distinguish between *n*-type and *p*-type semiconductors.

16 Pure semiconductor at 300 K has equal electron (n_e) and hole (n_h) concentration of 1.5×10^{16} m^{-3}. By some means hole concentration increases to 3×10^{22} m^{-3}. Calculate n_e in Si.

03 Marks Questions

17 With the help of the energy band diagrams, describe some points in brief to differentiate among conductors, semiconductors and insulators.

18 Distinguish between pure and impure semiconductors.

19 (i) What do you mean by semiconductor with examples.

(ii) Define *n*-type semiconductor and *p*-type semiconductors.

(iii) What do you mean by intrinsic and extrinsic semiconductors.

05 Marks Questions

20 What do you understand by band theory of energy in solids? Define valence band, conduction band and forbidden gap.

21 (i) What do you mean by dopping?

(iii) Explain *p* and *n*-type semiconductors by selecting an element from third and fifth group and also explain acceptor and donar nature of these elements mixed with a pure semiconductor.

Answers

1. (c) **2.** (a) **3.** (b) **4.** (d) **5.** (a)
6. (c)
16. 7.5×10^9 m^{-3}

25

Junction Diode

TREND ANALYSIS 4 YEARS	Average No. of Questions Across all Sets				
	Types of Questions	2024	2023	2020	2019
Junction Diode	1 Mark	1	–	1	–
	2 Marks	2	1	1	–
	3 Marks	–	2	–	2
	5 Marks	–	–	–	–

The basic building blocks of any electronic circuits. The devices in which a controlled flow of electrons can be obtained before the discovery of **semiconductor devices,** such devices were most commonly used as vacuum tubes.

p-n Junction

A *p-n* junction is an arrangement made by a closed contact of *n*-type semiconductor and *p*-type semiconductor.

p-n Junction Diode

A **semiconductor diode** or ***p-n* junction diode** is basically a *p-n* junction with metallic contact provided at the ends for the application of an external voltage. It is a two terminal device.

A *p-n* junction diode is represented by 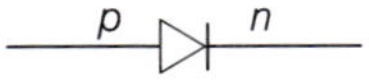.

The direction of arrow indicates the conventional direction of current.

This sets up a potential difference across the junction, which stops further diffusion, when it become strong. The region on either side of junction which becomes depleted (free) of the mobile charge carrier is called **depletion layer/depletion region**.

The potential difference developed across the depletion region is called the **potential barrier**. Due to the positive space charge region on *n*-side and negative space charge region on *p*-side of the junction, an electric field is setup from positive charge to negative charge. Motion of charge carriers due to this electric field is called drift.

Biasing of Junction Diode

The junction diode can be connected to an external battery in two ways, called **forward biasing** and **reverse biasing** of the junction.

(i) Forward Biasing

A junction is said to be forward biased, when the positive terminal of the external battery is connected to the *p* -side and negative terminal to the *n*-side of the diode. As, the direction of applied voltage is opposite to the built in potential or barrier potential, therefore width of depletion layer decreases and hence it offers low resistance.

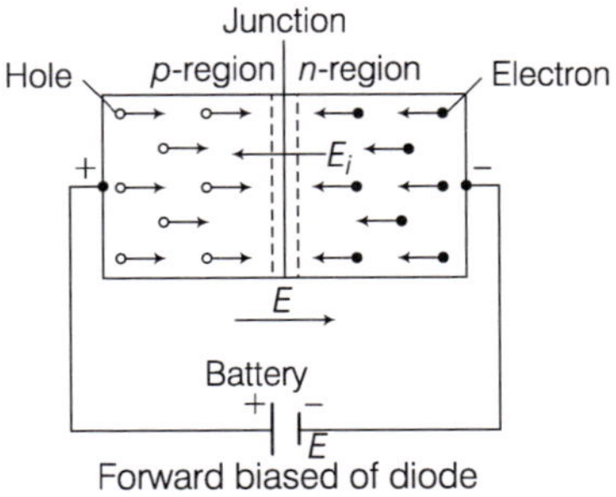

Forward biased of diode

E_i = Voltage due to potential barrier

E = Voltage due to applied voltage

V-I Characteristics of Forward Bias of Diode

The circuit diagram and *V-I* characteristics of a forward biased diode is shown as below.

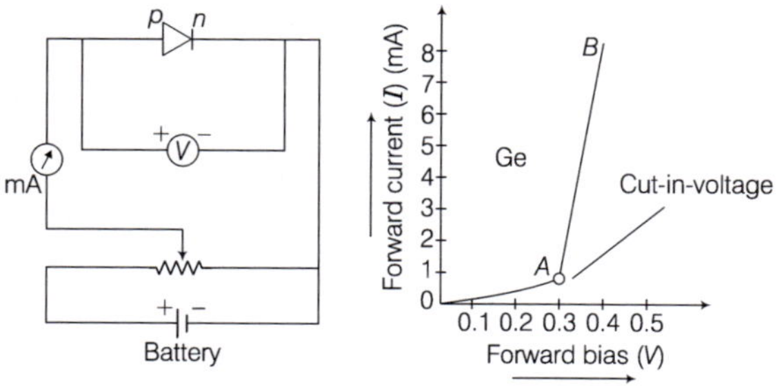

(a) Forward bias circuit (b) Forward bias characteristics

(ii) Reverse Biasing

A junction diode is said to be reverse biased, when the positive terminal of the external battery is connected to the *n*-side and negative terminal to the *p*-side of the diode. As, the direction of applied voltage is in same direction of built in potential or barrier potential of, therefore width of depletion layer increases and hence, it offers high resistance.

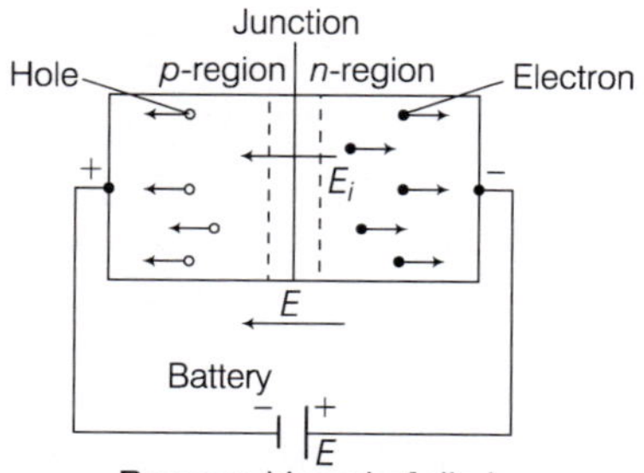

Reverse biased of diode

V-I Characteristics of Reverse Bias of Diode

The circuit diagram and *V-I* characteristics of a reverse biased diode is shown as below.

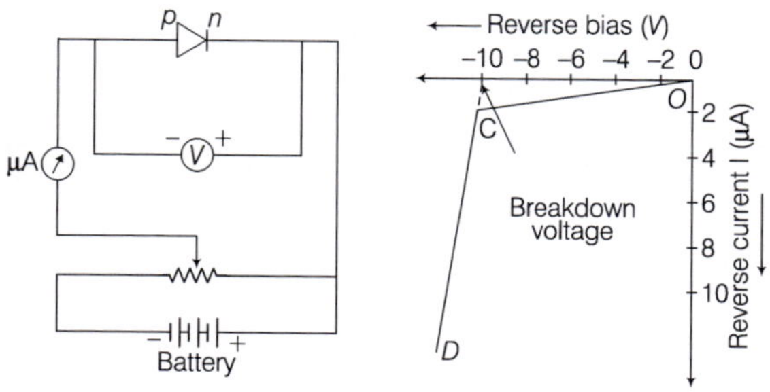

(a) Reverse bias circuit (b) Reverse bias characteristics

- The DC resistance of a junction diode, $r_{DC} = \frac{V}{I}$.
- The dynamic resistance of a junction diode, $r_{AC} = \frac{\Delta V}{\Delta I}$.

Diode as a Rectifier

The process of converting alternating voltage or current into direct voltage or current is called rectification. If an alternating voltage is applied across a diode, the current flows only in that part of the cycle when the diode is forward biased.

There are two ways of using a diode as a rectifier

(*i*) half-wave rectifier

(*ii*) full-wave rectifier

Diode as a Half-Wave Rectifier

During first half cycle of alternating current, diode is forward biased and it allows the current to pass.

When the polarity get reversed, diode becomes reverse biased as it does not allows current to pass through. Thus, we obtained a rectified positive half cycle at each cycle of applied AC.

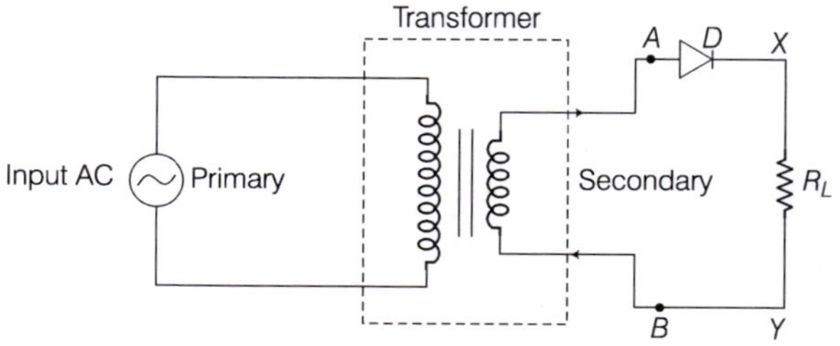

(a) Circuit diagram of half-wave rectifier

The input and output waveforms in half-wave rectifier are shown below.

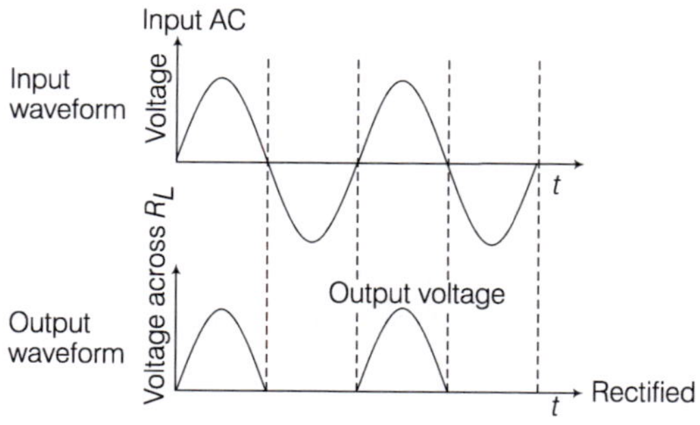

(b) Input and output waveform

Diode as a Full Wave Rectifier

In this case, during first half cycle of AC, one of the diode is forward biased and other is reverse biased and it allows the current to pass.

When the polarity gets reversed during next half cycle, the second diode becomes forward biased and allows the next half cycle of current. Thus, we get full wave rectified voltage.

The circuit diagram of full wave rectifier is shown as below.

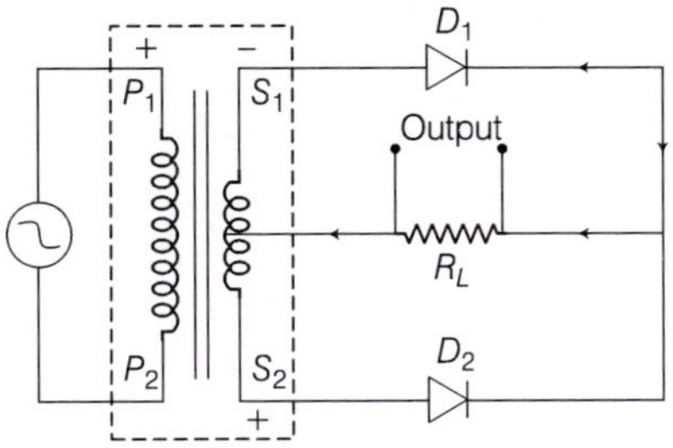

(a) Circuit diagram of full wave rectifier

The input and output waveforms are shown as below.

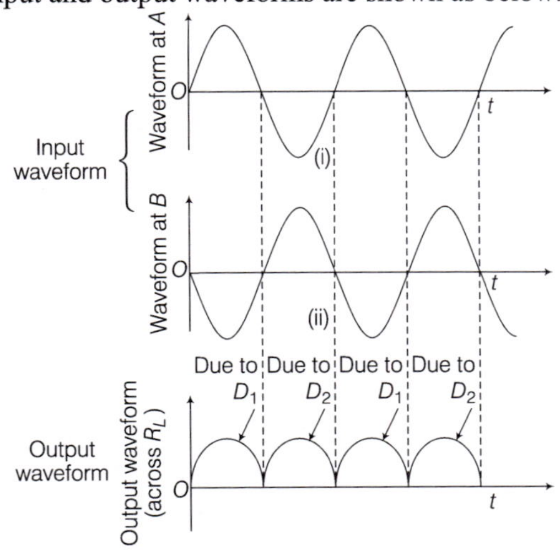

(b) Input and output waveform

Some Special Types of Diodes

Light Emitting Diode (LED)

It is a heavily doped *p-n* junction diode which converts electrical energy into light energy. This diode emits spontaneous radiation under forward biasing. This diode is covered with a transparent cover so, that the emitted light may come out.

Its symbol is given by

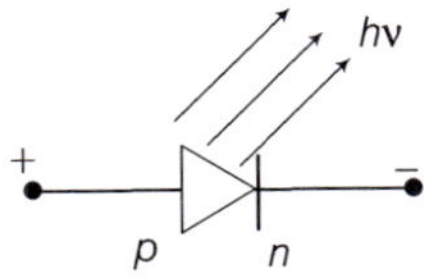

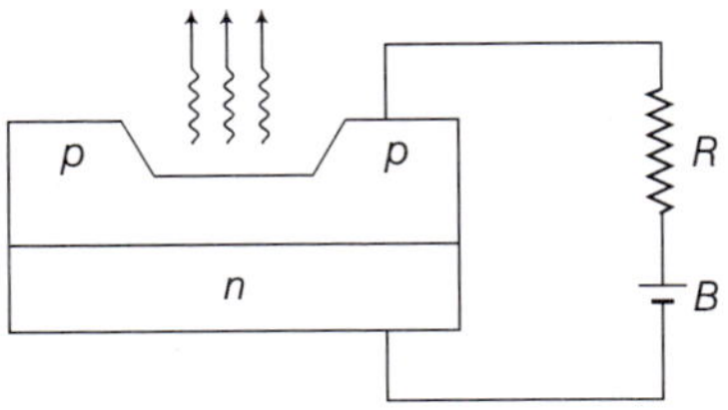

LEDs Advantages over Incandescent Low Power Lamps

It has following advantages over conventional incandescent low power lamps.

(*i*) Fast action and no warm up time required.

(*ii*) The bandwidth of emitted light is from 100 Å to 500 Å. So, it is nearly (not exactly) monochromatic.

(*iii*) Long life and ruggedness.

(*iv*) Low operational voltage and less power consumed.

(*v*) Fast ON-OFF switching capability.

Photodiode

A photodiode is a special type of junction diode used for detecting optical signals. It is a reverse biased *p-n* junction made from a photosensitive material. In photodiode, current carriers are generated by photons through photo excitation.

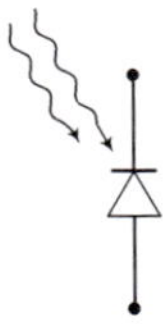

Photodiode symbol

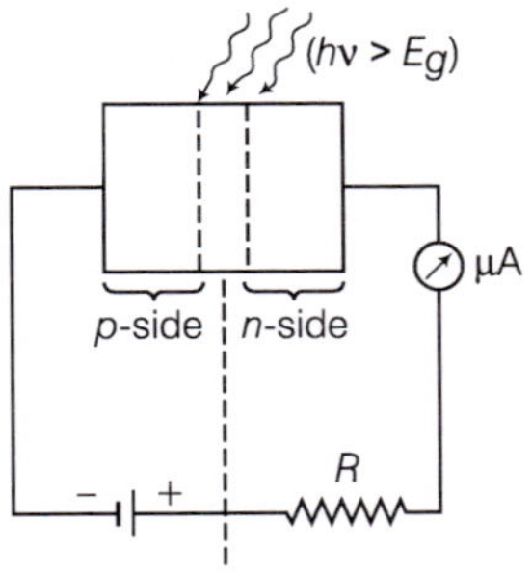

Solar Cell

A solar cell is a *p-n* junction diode, which converts solar energy into electrical energy.

Its symbol is given by

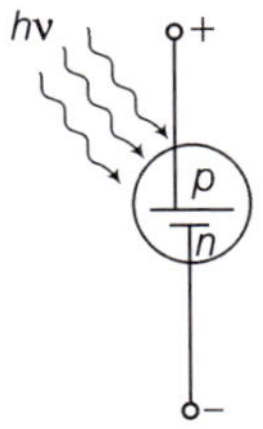

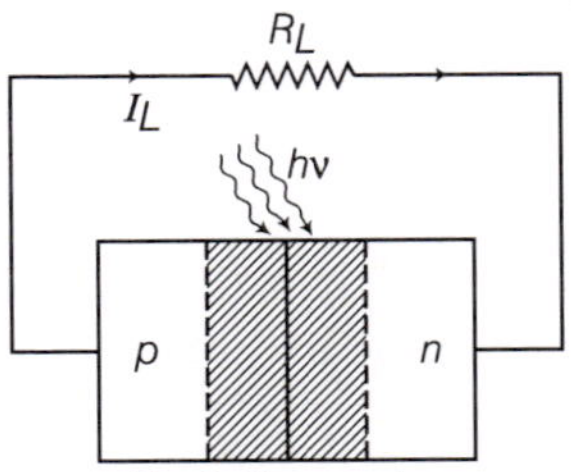

Depletion region

Zener Diode

It is a reverse biased heavily doped *p-n* junction diode.

It is designed to operate in the reverse breakdown voltage continuously without being damaged.

This can be achieved by changing the thickness of the depletion layer to which the voltage is applied. Current through this diode is controlled by an external resistance. It is represented by the symbol

Symbol of Zener diode

V-I Characteristics of Zener Diode

The *V-I* characteristics of Zener diode is shown in the figure. Here, we observe that when the applied reverse voltage (V) reaches the breakdown voltage (V_Z) of the Zener diode, there is a large change in the current.

But after the breakdown voltage V_Z, a large change in the current can be produced by almost insignificant change in the reverse bias voltage.

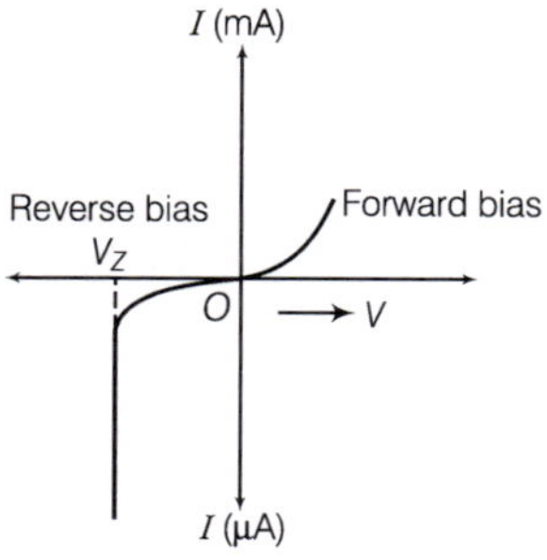

V-I Characteristics of a Zener diode

Zener Diode as a Voltage Regulator

This is the most important application of a Zener diode.

Principle From the above *V-I* characteristic of Zener diode, we can say that, Zener voltage remains constant even though the current through the diode varies over a wide range. If a Zener diode is joined in reverse bias to the fluctuating. DC input voltage through a resistance R, then the constant output voltage is taken across a load resistance connected in parallel with Zener diode.

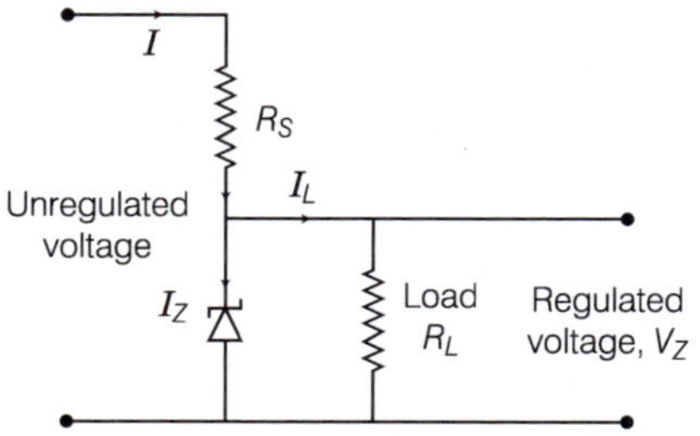

Circuit diagram of Zener diode as a voltage regulator

Working Here, when input DC voltage increases beyond a certain limit, the current through the circuit rises sharply, causing a sufficient increase in the voltage drop across the resistor R_S. Thus, the voltage across the Zener diode remains constant and also the output voltage remains constant at V_Z.

When the input DC voltage decreases, the current through the circuit goes down sharply causing sufficient decrease in the voltage drop across the resistance.

Thus, the voltage across the Zener diode remains constant and also the output voltage across R_L remains constant at V_Z. Hence, the output voltage remains constant in both conditions.

PYQs Previous Years Questions

1 Mark Questions

1. In semiconductor physics, what is the function of a rectifier ? **ISC 2024**
2. What is the advantage of an LED bulb over the filament electric bulb? **ISC 2020**
3. What is meant by a rectifier? **ISC 2014**
4. What is mean by a full wave rectifier? **ISC 2010**
5. Draw the circuit diagram of a half-wave rectifier using a *p-n* junction diode. **ISC 2007**
6. Draw the circuit diagram for reverse biasing of a diode using proper symbol for diode (not rectangular block). **ISC 2002**
7. Draw circuit diagrams to illustrate forward biasing and reverse biasing of a diode. **ISC 2000**

2 Marks Questions

8. With reference to a semiconductor diode, define the following terms **ISC 2024, ISC SQP 2023**
   (*i*) depletion region
   (*ii*) potential barrier

9. (*i*) What is meant by forward biasing of a semiconductor diode ?
   (*ii*) Draw a labelled characteristic curve (*I*-*V* graph) for a semiconductor diode during forward bias. **ISC 2024**

10. With reference to semiconductor physics, define the following terms. **ISC 2022 Sem-II**
    (*i*) Doping (*ii*) Depletion region

11. In a semiconductor diode, what is meant by potential barrier? **ISC 2020**

12. The characteristic curve of a silicon diode is shown below. **ISC SQP 2018**

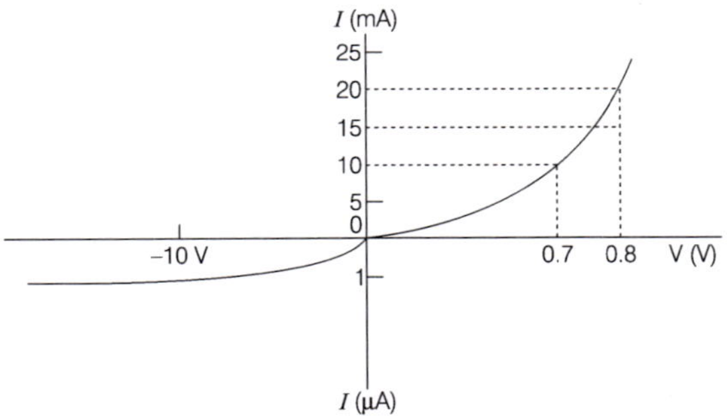

Calculate the resistance of the diode at
(a) $I = 15\,\text{mA}$ and (b) $V = -10\,\text{V}$

3 Marks Questions

13. Draw a labelled circuit diagram of a full wave rectifier. Show graphically how the output voltage varies with time. **ISC 2023**

14. What is meant by reverse biasing of a semiconductor diode? Draw a labelled characteristic curve, i.e *I*-*V* graph for a semiconductor diode during reverse bias. **ISC SQP 2023**

15. (*i*) Answer the following questions.
    (a) Draw the circuit diagram of a full wave rectifier.
    (b) Draw labelled graphs showing the input and output voltages. **ISC 2022 Sem-I**

    Or

    (*ii*) With reference to semiconductor physics,
    (a) Name the diode that emits spontaneous radiation when forward biased.
    (b) Draw a labelled energy band diagram for a semiconductor.
    (c) Name the process that causes depletion region in a *p*-*n* junction.

16. (*i*) Answer the following questions.
    (a) Draw a labelled circuit diagram of a half-wave rectifier
    (b) Show graphically, how output voltage varies with time in case of a half wave rectifier when an AC voltage is fed to it from the mains.

    Or

    (*ii*) With reference to semiconductor physics, answer the following questions.
    (a) Show how a junction diode can be forward biased.
    (b) Draw a labelled *V*-*I* characteristic curve of a junction diode during forward bias. **ISC 2019**

17. Draw a labelled circuit diagram of a half-wave rectifier and give its output waveform. **ISC 2019**

18. Draw a labelled diagram of a full wave rectifier. Show how output voltage varies with time if voltage is a sinusoidal voltage. **ISC 2015**

19. Show by drawing labelled diagram, the nature of output voltage in case of
    (*i*) a half-wave rectifier. (*ii*) a full wave rectifier.
    Circuit diagrams of these devices are not required. **ISC 2013**

20. Draw a labelled diagram of a full wave rectifier circuit. Explain briefly the functions of its components and sketch the input and output waveforms. **ISC 2001**

21. Draw the circuit diagram of a half-wave rectifier using a semiconductor diode. Explain briefly the functions of each component. **ISC 2000**

4/5 Marks Question

22. (*i*) The forward characteristic curve of a junction diode is shown in figure below

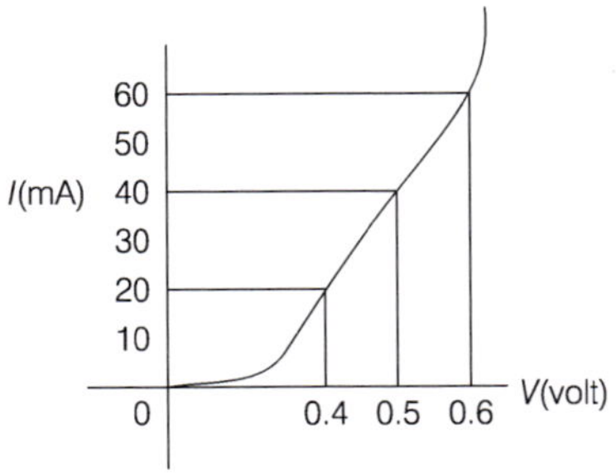

Calculate the resistance of the diode at

I. $V = 0.5\,V$ II. $I = 60\,mA$

(*ii*) Draw separate energy band diagrams for conductors, semiconductors and insulators and label each of them.

ISC 2018

KEY idea

To find the resistance from the graph problem, we have to find the linear slope of the graph.

Case Based Question
(For Complete Chapter)

23. Direction *Read the passage given below and answer the questions that follows.*

It is an important light source used in optical communication, and is based on the principle of conversion of biasing electricity into light. It is a specially designed forward-biased *p-n* junction diode which emits light spontaneously when energised.
Principle When a *p-n* junction diode is forward biased, the electrons in *n*-region and the holes in *p*-region both move towards the junction.
As they cross the junction, the electrons and the holes recombine and energy is released at the junction in the form of light. Since energy is required to generate an electron-hole pair, the same energy is released when electron and hole recombine. In case of Si and Ge diodes, the energy released is infrared radiation, and hence of no use. If however, the diode is made of gallium phosphide (GaP) or gallium-arsenic phosphide (Ga As P), the energy released is visible light (figure). The diode is then called a Light Emitting Diode (LED). By a proper choice of the semiconducting material, light in any desired wavelength range may be obtained.

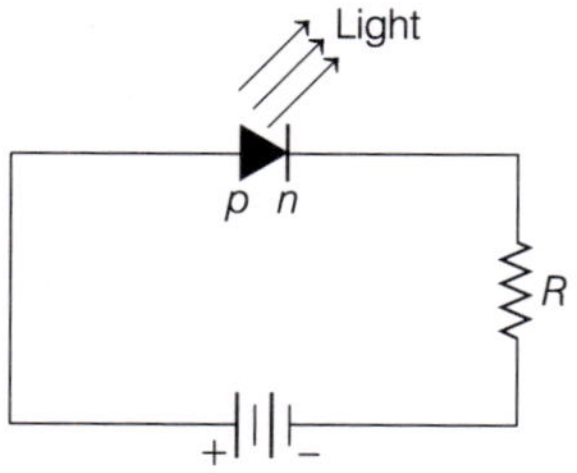

(*i*) What do you mean by LED? **(1)**

(*ii*) Describe the working principle of LED in short. **(1)**

(*iii*) Write the applications of LED. **(1)**

(*iv*) Draw the circuit diagram of LED. **(1)**

(*v*) Write the advantages of LED. **(1)**

Explanations

1. The process of converting alternating voltage/current into direct voltage/current is called rectification. Diode is used as a rectifier for converting alternating current/voltage into direct current/voltage.
2. LED's are small, solid light bulbs which are extremely energy efficient and long lasting, so these devices are more rugged and durable than traditional filament electric bulbs.
3. Rectifier is a semiconductor device used to convert Alternating Current (AC) to Direct Current (DC).
4. A full wave rectifier is a device which converts both the halves (negative and positive) of an AC input voltage into a unidirectional pulsating output voltage.
5. Refer to text on page 306 (Half-wave Rectifier).
6. Refer to text on page 306 (Reverse Biasing).
7. Refer to text on pages 305 and 306 (Forward Biasing and Reverse Biasing).
8. (*i*) The region on either side of the junction with becomes depleted (free) from the mobile charge carriers is called depletion region or depletion layer. The width of depletion region is of the order of 10^{-6} m.

   (*ii*) The potential difference developed across the depletion region is called the potential barrier. It depends on dopant concentration in the semiconductor and temperature of the junction.
9. (*i*) A junction diode is said to be forward biased when the positive terminal of the external battery is connected to the p-side and negative terminal to n-side of the diode.

   (*ii*)

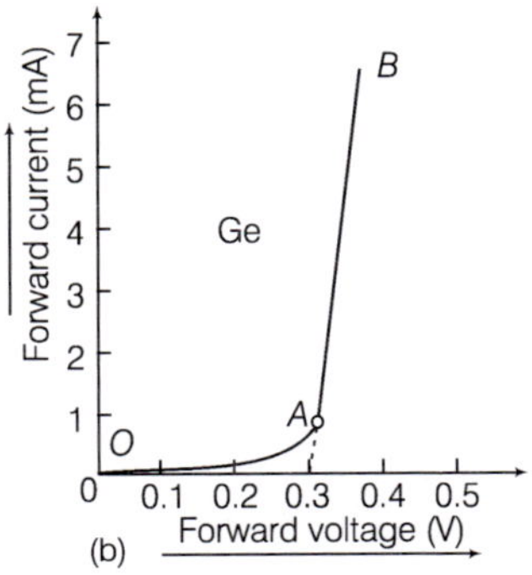

(b)

10. (*i*) **Doping** The process of adding impurity to an intrinsic semiconductor in a controlled manner is called doping.

    (*ii*) **Depletion region** The region on either side of the junction which becomes depleted (free) from the mobile charge carriers is called depletion region.
11. Refer to text on page 305 (p-n Junction Diode).
12. (a) From the graph, at

$$R = \frac{\Delta V}{\Delta I}$$

$$= \frac{(0.8 - 0.7)}{(20 - 10) \times 10^{-3}}$$

$$= 10\,\Omega$$

    (b) From the graph, at

$$\Rightarrow \quad R = \frac{\Delta V}{\Delta I}$$

$$= \frac{(-10 - 0)}{(-1 - 0) \times 10^{-6}} = 10^{7}\,\Omega$$

Common Mistake Take in mind that unit conversion is important to solve the problem accurately.

13. Refer to text on pages 306 and 307. (Diode as a Full Wave Rectifier)
14. Refer to text on page 306 (Reverse Biasing and V-I characteristics of Reverse bias of Diode).
15. (*i*) (a) Refer to text on pages 306 and 307 (Diode as a full wave Rectifier) .

    (b) Refer to text on page 307. (Diode as a full wave Rectifier)

Or

    (*ii*) (a) Light Emitting Diode (LED) emits spontaneous radiation when forward biased.

    (b)

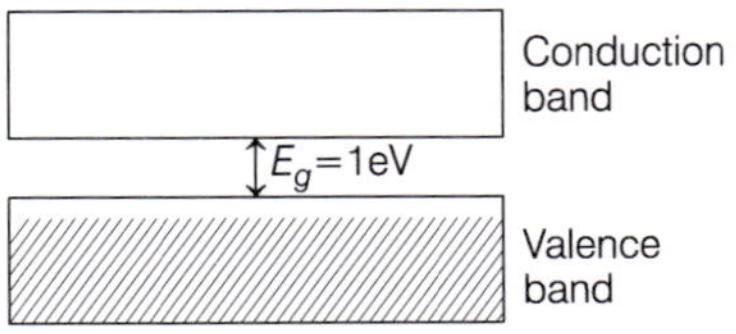

(c) The depletion layer of a *p-n* junction diode is due to doping of the materials and diffusion of charge carriers.

16. (*i*) (a) Refer to text on page 306 (Diode as a half wave rectifier).

(b) Refer to text on page 306 (Diode as a half wave rectifier).

Or

(*ii*) (a) When *p*-type is connected with positive terminal of the battery and *n*-type is connected with the negative terminal of the battery, then junction diode is in forward biased. It is shown below

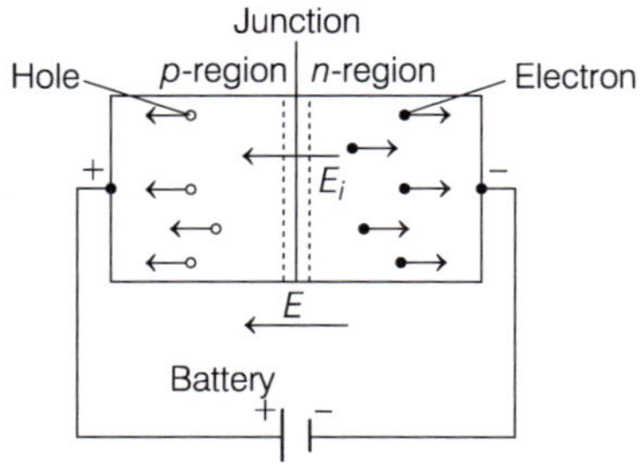

Forward biasing of a diode

(b) Refer to on page 306 (*V-I* characteristics of forward bias of diode).

17. Refer to text on page 306 (Diode as a half-wave rectifier).

18. Refer to text on pages 306 and 307 (Diode as a full wave rectifier).

19.

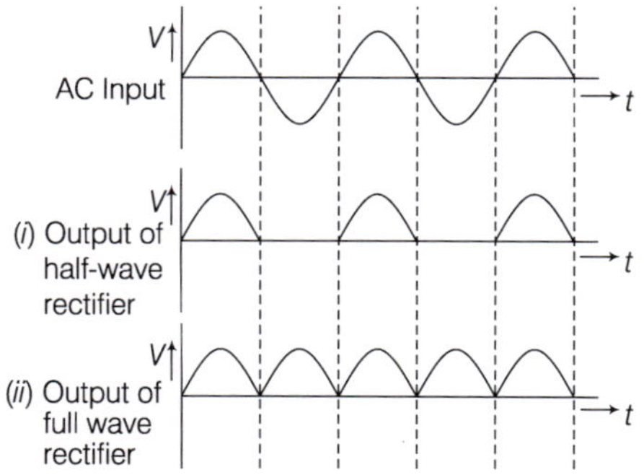

20. The diagram of full wave rectifier circuit is given as below.

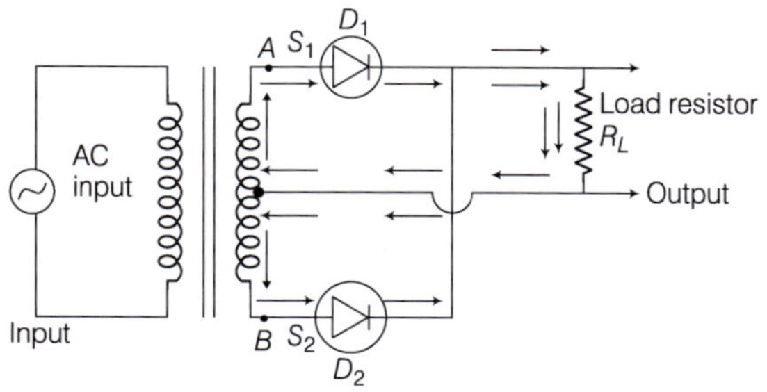

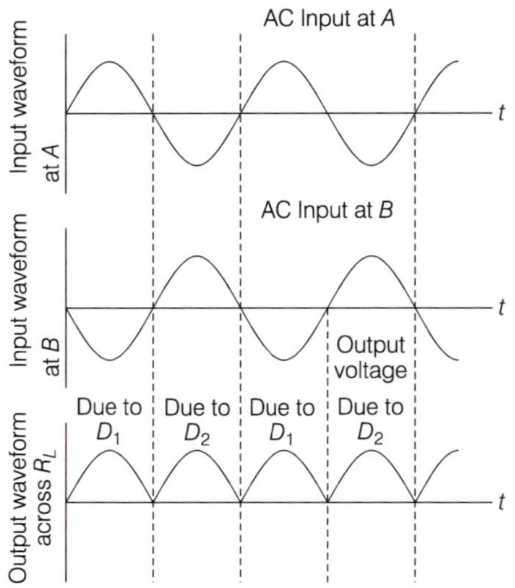

In a full wave rectifier, an unidirectional pulsating output current is obtained for both halves of the AC input voltage. The two junction diodes rectify the input.

During the first half cycle of input voltage (AC), the terminal S_1 is positive while terminal S_2 is negative. In this situation, diode D_1 is forward biased, while diode D_2 is reverse biased.

Therefore, D_1 conducts and D_2 does not. The conventional current flows through diode D_1, load R_L and the upper half of the secondary windings, as shown by the solid arrows. During the second half cycle of the input voltage, S_1 is negative and S_2 is positive, which implies D_1 as reverse biased and does not conduct while D_2 is forward biased which conducts. The current now flows through D_2.

It may be seen that the current in the load R_L flows in the same direction for both the half cycles of the AC input voltage. Thus, the output current is a continuous series of unidirectional pulses. However, it can be made fairly steady by means of smoothing filters.

21. The diagram below shows a semiconductor diode used as a half-wave rectifier.

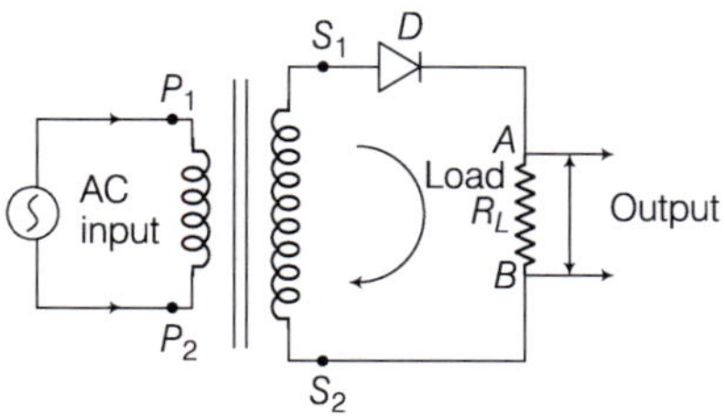

The figure shows an AC input voltage is applied across the primary coil P_1P_2 of transformer and $S_1\,S_2$ is the secondary coil of the same transformer. During first half cycle, the end S_1 of the transformer is positive with respect to the end S_2. The diode is then in forward bias condition hence, current flows through it. In the load R_L, the current flows from A to B. During second half cycle, S_1 is negative with respect to S_2, then the diode is said to be in reverse biased and is non-conducting.

Hence, current through load R_L is zero.

Thus, the output current flows in one direction only. The lower half part of the AC is cut-off, only the upper half part constitutes current. Thus, a semiconductor diode acts as a half-wave rectifier. The wave diagram is shown as below.

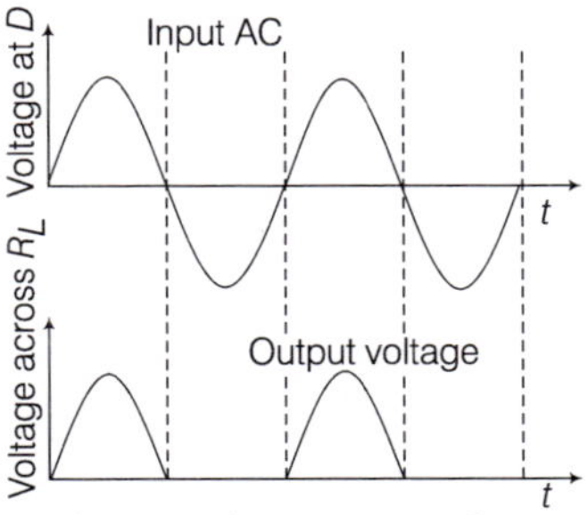

Input and output waveform

22. (*i*) I. At $V = 0.5$ V, the current is 40 mA from the figure.

$\therefore$ Diode resistance,

$$R_d = \frac{\Delta V}{\Delta I} = \frac{(0.5 - 0.4)}{(40 - 20) \times 10^{-3}} = 5\,\Omega$$

II. At $I = 60$ mA, the voltage is 0.6 V from the figure.

Voltage, $V = 0.6$ V, $I = 60 \times 10^{-3}$ A

$\therefore$ Diode resistance,

$$R_d = \frac{\Delta V}{\Delta I} = \frac{(0.6 - 0.5)}{(60 - 40) \times 10^{-3}} = 5\,\Omega$$

(*ii*) I. Energy band gap diagram for insulator.

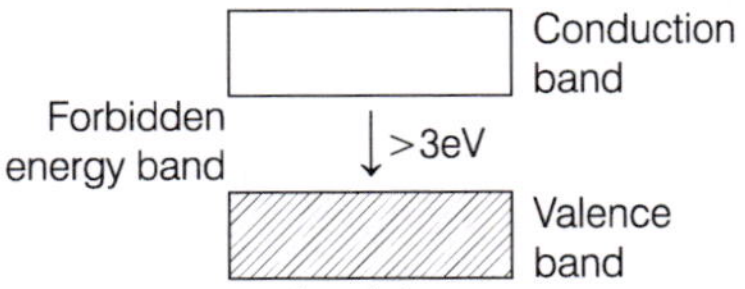

Insulator

II. Energy band gap diagram for conductor.

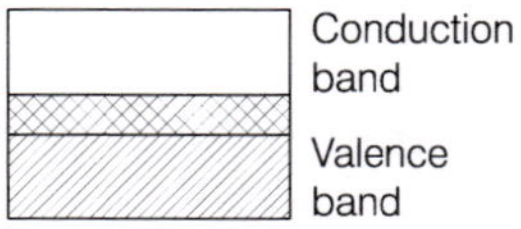

III. Energy band gap diagram for semiconductor.

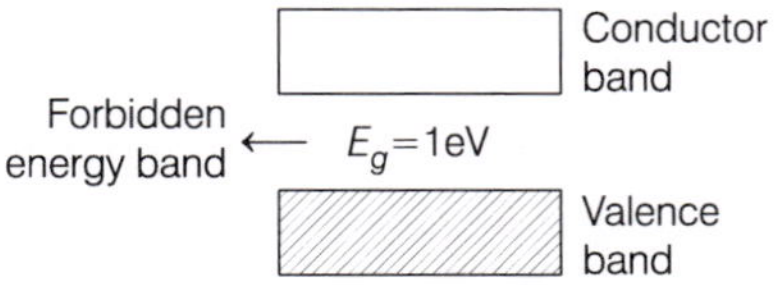

23. (*i*) A Light Emitting Diode (LED) is a semiconductor device, which can emit light when an electric current passes through it.

(*ii*) An electrical current passes through a microchip which illuminates the tiny light sources we call LEDs and the result is visible light.

(*iii*) LED's have a number of applications.

(a) LED's produces visible light.

(b) It is also used in solid-state circuits.

(c) The infrared LED is a potential source for optical fibre communication.

(*iv*)

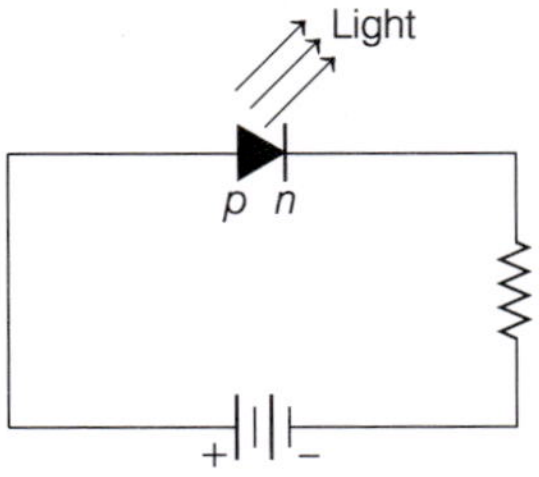

(*v*) Following are the advantages of LED.

(a) LEDs need a very low input power.

(b) They are very fast in action, requiring no heating time.

(c) Their ON-OFF switching is very fast.

(d) They are small in size and light in weight.

(e) They are quite safe against mechanical shocks.

CHAPTER TEST

01 Mark Questions (MCQs)

1 In an unbiased *p-n* junction, holes diffuse from *p*-region to *n*-region because

(a) free electrons in the *n*-region attract them

(b) they move across the junction by the potential difference

(c) hole concentration in *p*-region is more compared to *n*-region

(d) All of the above

2 When a forward bias is applied to a *p-n* junction, it

(a) raises the potential barrier

(b) reduces the majority carrier current to zero

(c) lowers the potential barrier

(d) None of the above

3 In the following figure, the diodes which are forward biased are

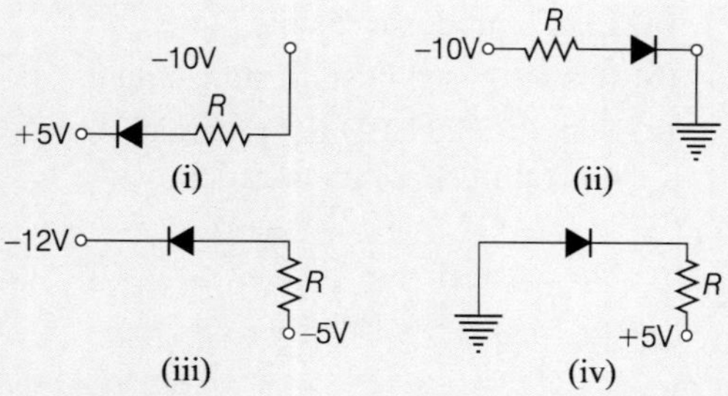

(a) (ii) and (iv) (b) (i), (ii) and (iv)

(c) (iii) only (d) (iii) and (i)

4 The order of magnitude of the barrier potential in a *p-n* junction is

(a) 0.01 V (b) 0.05 V (c) 0.1 V (d) 1.0 V

01 Mark Questions (VSA)

5 Why cannot we take one slab of *p*-type semiconductor and physically join it to another slab of *n*-type semiconductor to get *p-n* junction?

6 Figure shows the *V-I* characteristics of a given device. Name the device and write where it is used.

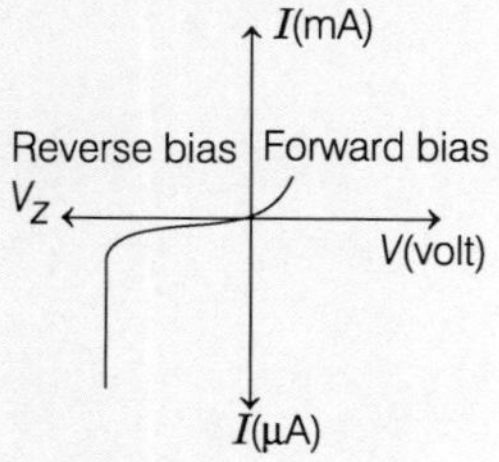

02 Marks Questions

7 Mention the important considerations required while fabricating a *p-n* junction diode to be used as a Light Emitting Diode (LED). What should be the order of band gap of an LED, if it is required to emit light in the visible range?

8 How is forward biasing different from reverse biasing in a *p-n* junction diode?

9 The current in the forward bias is known to be more (~ mA) than the current in the reverse bias (~ μA). What is the reason to operate the photodiode in reverse bias?

03 Marks Questions

10 (i) Why is a photodiode operated in reverse bias mode?

(ii) For what purpose is a photodiode used?

(iii) Draw its *V-I* characteristics for different intensities of illumination.

11 (i) Why are Si and GaAs preferred materials for solar cells?

(ii) Describe briefly with the help of a necessary circuit diagram, the working principle of a solar cell.

05 Marks Questions

12 Draw *V-I* characteristics of a *p-n* junction diode. Answer the following questions giving reasons.

(i) Why is the current under reverse bias almost independent of the applied potential upto a critical voltage?

(ii) Why does the reverse current show a sudden increase at the critical voltage?

(iii) Name any semiconductor device, which operates under the reverse bias in the breakdown region.

13 Draw a labelled diagram of a full wave rectifier circuit. State its working principle. Show the input-output waveforms.

Answers

1. (c) **2.** (c) **3.** (c) **4.** (c)

6. *p-n* junction diode

7. 1.8 eV-3.1 eV

ISC

CHAPTERWISE - TOPICWISE

QUESTION BANK

ISC Sample Paper (1-3)

ISC Unsolved

SAMPLE PAPER 01

Time : 3 hrs
Marks : 70

Physics
Paper 1

General Instructions

1. This paper is divided into four **Sections- A, B, C** and **D**. Answer all questions.
2. **Section A** consists of one question having sub-parts of one mark each.
3. **Section B** consists of seven questions of two marks each.
4. **Section C** consists of nine questions of three marks each.
5. **Section D** consists of three questions of five marks each.
6. Internal choices have been provided in two questions each in Section B, Section C and Section D.

Section-A **[14 Marks]**

1. A. In questions (i) to (vii) given below, choose the correct alternative (a), (b), (c) or (d) for each of the questions given below.

(i) A current i is flowing through a resistance connected to a primary cell. Now, the resistance is reduced to half, the new current through the resistance is **[1]**

(a) i (b) $2i$ (c) $< 2i$ (d) $> 2i$

(ii) For the graph of collector plate potential *versus* photoelectric current shown below **[1]**

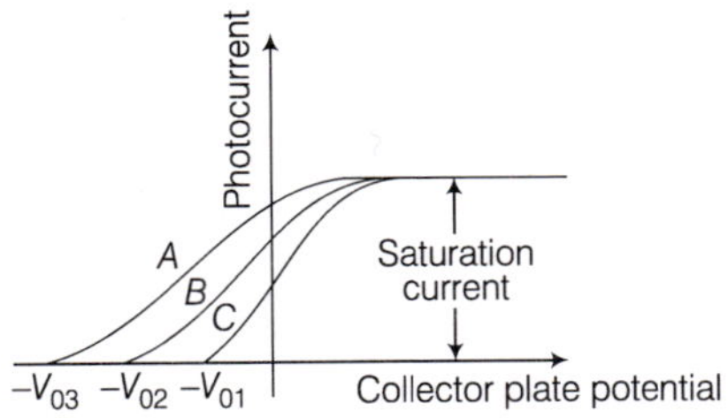

If I denotes intensity of incident radiation, then

(a) $I_A > I_B > I_C$
(b) $I_A < I_B < I_C$
(c) $I_A = I_B = I_C$
(d) $I_B > I_A$ and $I_B < I_C$

(iii) **Assertion** A ray of light incident along the normal to the plane mirror retraces its path after reflection from the mirror.

Reason A ray of light along the normal has angle of incidence as $\frac{\pi}{2}$. **[1]**

(a) Both Assertion and Reason are correct and Reason is the correct explanation for Assertion.
(b) Both Assertion and Reason are correct but Reason is not the correct explanation for Assertion.
(c) Assertion is true and Reason is false.
(d) Assertion is false and Reason is true.

(iv) An electron is projected with uniform velocity along the axis of a current carrying long solenoid. Which of the following is true? **[1]**

(a) The electron will be accelerated along the axis.
(b) The electron path will be circular about the axis.
(c) The electron will experience a force at 45° to the axis and hence, execute the helical path.
(d) The electron will continue to move with uniform velocity along the axis of the solenoid.

(v) **Assertion** The magnetic field produced by a current carrying solenoid is independent of its length and cross-sectional area.

Reason The magnetic field inside the solenoid is uniform.

(a) Both Assertion and Reason are correct and Reason is the correct explanation for Assertion.
(b) Both Assertion and Reason are correct but Reason is not the correct explanation for Assertion.
(c) Assertion is true and Reason is false.
(d) Assertion is false and Reason is true.

(vi) The simple Bohr's model cannot be directly applied to calculate the energy levels of an atom with many electrons. This is because **[1]**
(a) of the electrons not being subjected to a central force
(b) of the electrons colliding with each other
(c) of screening effect
(d) the force between the nucleus and an electron will no longer be given by Coulomb's law

(vii) The areas of cross-section of three magnets of same lengths are $A, 2A$ and $6A$ respectively, the ratio of their magnetic moments will be **[1]**
(a) 6 : 2 : 1 (b) 1 : 2 : 6
(c) 2 :6 : 1 (d) 1 : 1 : 1

B. Answer the following questions briefly.

(i) State the condition in which terminal voltage across a secondary cell is equal to its emf. **[1]**
(ii) Define emf. **[1]**
(iii) An electron does not suffer any deflection while passing through a region of a uniform magnetic field. What is the direction of the magnetic field? **[1]**
(iv) How are de-Broglie wavelength and kinetic energy of a particle related? **[1]**
(v) Write down the name of the phenomenon which certifies the particle nature of light. **[1]**
(vi) Find an expression for the width of interference fringes obtained in Young's double slit experiment. **[1]**
(vii) Write down the names of few moderators used in nuclear reactor. **[1]**

Section-B [14 Marks]

2. (i) Two wires are placed parallel to each other at the distance of 2.5 cm and current passing through them in same direction. Determine the force on 10 cm length of each wire. **[2]**

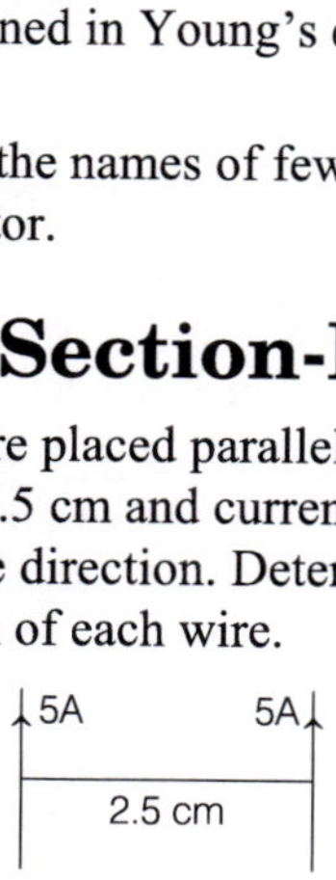

Or

(ii) 2A current is passing through a long straight wire. An electron is moving with velocity 4×10^4 m/s parallel to the wire at a distance 0.1 m. Determine the force experienced by the electron.

3. (i) Write down the relation between potential difference of conductor and drift velocity of free electron. **[1**
(ii) What do you mean by non-ohmic resistance? **[1**

4. A straight wire of mass per unit length 4×10^{-3} kg/m is placed in a uniform magnetic field at right angle to it. Find the maximum strength of magnetic field which can support the wire against its weight, when a current of 4A flows through the wire. **[2]**

5. (i) What is the effect of temperature on extrinsic semiconductors? **[2]**

Or

(ii) Explain with the help of a circuit diagram the working of a photodiode. Write briefly, how it is used to detect the optical signals?

6. (i) Explain the meaning of photoelectric work function of a metal. **[1]**
(ii) How does the value of work function affect the kinetic energy of the liberated photoelectrons? **[1]**

7. What is an ideal inductor? Why inductors are made of copper? **[2]**

8. With reference to nuclear physics, answer the following questions.
(i) What is meant by pair production? **[1]**
(ii) Mention any two characteristics of nuclear force. **[1]**

Section-C [27 Marks]

9. Derive an expression for electric field due to electric dipole in its equatorial position. **[3]**

10. (i) In the circuit E, F, G and H are cells of emf 2, 1, 3 and 1 V and their internal resistances are 2, 1, 3 and 1 Ω, respectively. Calculate the potential difference between B and D. **[3]**

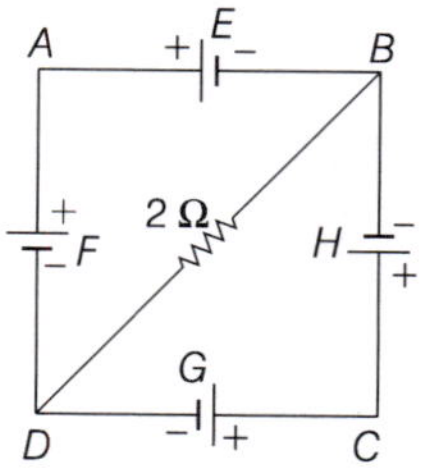

Or

(ii) A heater is designed to operate with a power of 1000 W in a 100 V line. It is connected to two resistances of 10 Ω and R Ω as shown in the figure. If the heater is now operating with a power of 62.5 W. Calculate the value of R.

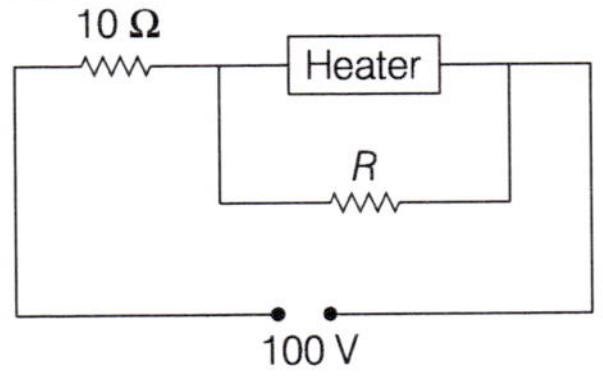

11. Obtain an expression for equivalent capacitance when three capacitors are connected in series. **[3]**

12. Derive the law of reflection using Huygen's wave theory. **[3]**

13. (i) Define dispersive power of an optical medium and obtain a formula for the dispersive power of the material of a prism in terms of refractive indices. **[3]**

Or

(ii) For any spherical surface, write formula for refraction of light and with the help of this establish the formula for lens.

$$\frac{1}{f}=(n-1)\left(\frac{1}{R_1}-\frac{1}{R_2}\right)$$ **[3]**

14. (i) Write down condition for interference of light.

(ii) What do you mean by diffraction of light? **[3]**

15. In Young's double slit experiment, the two parallel slits are made 2 mm apart and a screen is placed 2 m away.

(i) Calculate the fringe separation when a monochromatic radiation of wavelength 500 nm is used.

(ii) What will be fringe width, if the entire apparatus is immersed in a liquid of refractive index 1.33? **[3]**

16. State any two Bohr's postulates and write the energy value of the ground state of the hydrogen atom. **[3]**

17. (i) Deduce the relation between current I flowing through a conductor and drift velocity v_d of the electrons.

(ii) Figure shows a plot of current I flowing through the cross-section of a wire *versus* the time t. Use the plot to find the charge flowing in t_2 second through the wire. **[3]**

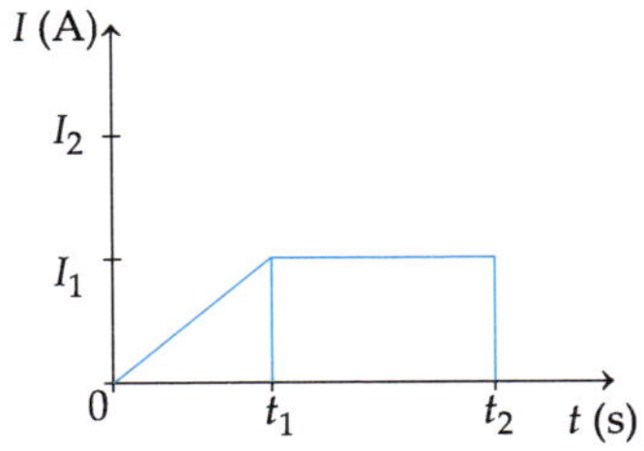

Section-D **[15 Marks]**

18. (i) In an AC circuit inductance, capacitance and resistance are connected in series. The voltage and current equations are represented by

$$V=200\sin\left(314t+\frac{\pi}{6}\right)$$

$$I=5\sin(314t-\pi/6)$$

Determine current,

(a) frequency of AC source

(b) phase difference between V and I

(c) impedance of circuit **[5]**

Or

(ii) (a) In the given circuit, the voltage measured by AC voltmeter across component of the circuit are V_L, V_C and V_R respectively and their values are 20 V, 11 V and 12 V. Determine resultant voltage and phase difference between resultant voltage and current in the circuit.

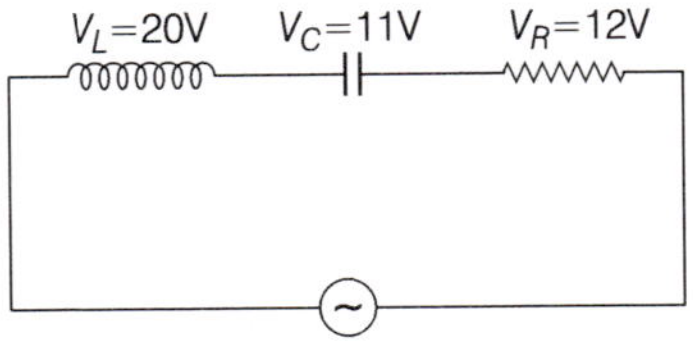

(b) A lamp of 20 V and 5 W has to be lit up by AC source of 200 V and frequency 50 Hz. For this purpose, what will be the value of choke coil to be placed in series with the lamp? **[5]**

19. (i) (a) An alternating emf of 200V, 50Hz is applied to an L-R circuit, having a resistance R of 10 Ω and an inductance L of 0.05H connected in series. Calculate

I. impedance.

II. current flowing in the circuit.

(b) State any two characteristics of resonance in an *L-C-R* series circuit.

(c) With reference to semiconductor, answer the following.

I. What is the change in the resistance of the semiconductor with increase in temperature? **[5]**

II. Name the majority charge carriers in *n*-type semiconductor.

Or

(ii) (a) Explain the Huygen's theory of wave propagation using the concept of wavefronts, explain reflection of light at plane surfaces.

(b) In Young's double slit experiment using monochromatic light of wavelength λ, the intensity of light a point on the screen, where path difference is λ, is k units.

What is the intensity of light at a point, where path difference is $\frac{\lambda}{3}$? **[5]**

20. Spherical mirror is a mirror whose reflecting surface is a part of a hollow sphere.

Spherical mirrors are of two types

I. Concave spherical mirror

II. Convex spherical mirror.

Concave mirror is used as a reflector in search light, head light of vehicles, etc, and convex mirror is used as rear view mirror in vehicles, because it has a wider field of view.

The mirror formula is given by $\frac{1}{f} = \frac{1}{u} + \frac{1}{v}$

where, u = object distance, v = image distance and f = focal length.

(i) Write the relation between focal length and radius of curvature.

(ii) How can the real image of an object be obtained with a convex mirror?

(iii) Find out the position of image of an object placed at f distance form a convex mirror of focal length f. **[5]**

Answers

1. A. (i) (c) (ii) (c) (iii) (c) (iv) (d) (v) (b) (vi) (a) (vii) (b)

2. (i) 2×10^{-5} N or (ii) 2.56×10^{-20} N

4. 10^{-2} T

10. (i) 0.154 V (ii) 5Ω

15. (i) 5×10^{-4} m (ii) 3.75×10^{-4} m

18. (i) (a) 50 Hz (b) $\pi/3$ rad (c) 40 Ω

Or (ii) (a) 15 V, 36.86°(b) 2.54 H

19. (i) (a) I. 18.614 Ω (a) II. 10.744 A

Or (ii) (b) $\frac{k}{4}$

20. (i) $\frac{R}{2}$ (ii) $\frac{f}{2}$

ISC **Unsolved**

SAMPLE PAPER 02

Time : 3 hrs
Marks : 70

Physics
Paper 1

General Instructions

1. This paper is divided into four **Sections- A, B, C** and **D**. Answer all questions.
2. **Section A** consists of one question having sub-parts of one mark each.
3. **Section B** consists of seven questions of two marks each.
4. **Section C** consists of nine questions of three marks each.
5. **Section D** consists of three questions of five marks each.
6. Internal choices have been provided in two questions each in Section B, Section C and Section D.

Section-A [14 Marks]

1. A. In questions (i) to (vii) given below, choose the correct alternative (a), (b), (c) or (d) for each of the questions given below.

(i) P and Q are two square plates of copper having the same thickness. The current is flowing through them as shown in the figure. If the side of Q is twice than the side of P, then **[1]**

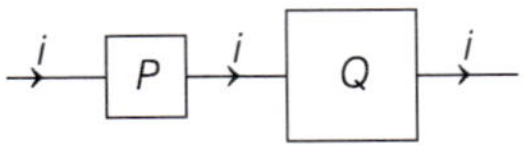

(a) the resistance of P is twice that of Q
(b) the resistance of P is half that of Q
(c) both have equal resistances
(d) the resistance of P is one-fourth that of Q

(ii) The graph of de-Brogile wavelength (λ) of a moving electron *versus* its velocity (v) is **[1]**

(a)

(b)
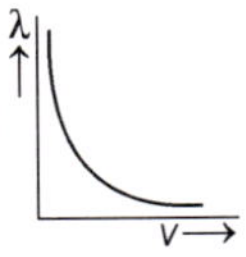

(c)
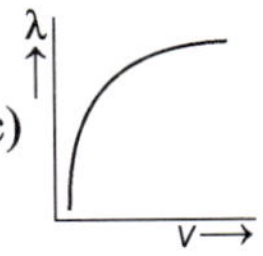

(d)
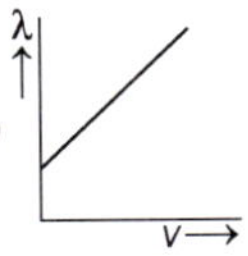

(iii) **Assertion** An α-particle enters a uniform magnetic field perpendicularly along with a proton with same speed, proton has half the rotation time of the α-particle.

Reason The period of revolution of a charged particle in a magnetic field is directly proportional to the mass and inversely proportional to charge of particle. **[1]**

(a) Both Assertion and Reason are correct and Reason is the correct explanation for Assertion.
(b) Both Assertion and Reason are correct but Reason is not the correct explanation for Assertion.
(c) Assertion is true and Reason is false.
(d) Assertion is false and Reason is true.

(iv) **Assertion** (A) At resonance, L - C-R series circuit have a zero current.

Reason (R) At resonance, in L - C-R series circuit the current and emf are 180° out of phase with each other.

(a) Both Assertion and Reason are correct and Reason is the correct explanation for Assertion.
(b) Both Assertion and Reason are correct but Reason is not the correct explanation for Assertion.

(c) Assertion is true and Reason is false.
(d) Both Assertion and Reason are false.

(v) A radio transmitter operates on a wavelength of 1500 m at a power of 400 kW. The energy of the radio photons will be **[1]**

(a) 1.32×10^{-28} J (b) 4.32×10^{-28} J
(c) 1.32×10^{-29} J (d) 4.32×20^{-29} J

(vi) The ratio of minimum to maximum wavelength in Balmer series is **[1]**

(a) 5 : 9 (b) 5 : 36
(c) 1 : 4 (d) 3 : 4

(vii) Those substances which at room temperature retain their ferromagnetic property for a long period of time are called **[1]**

(a) permanent magnets
(b) electromagnets
(c) ferromagnets
(d) paramagnet

B. Answer the following questions briefly.

(i) Is the direction of emf in a cell dependent on the direction of current within the cell? **[1]**

(ii) How will you convert a moving coil galvanometer into an ammeter? **[1]**

(iii) A charged particle moving in a straight line enters a uniform magnetic field B at an arbitrary angle with the field direction. What will be its path? **[1]**

(iv) State the law that gives the polarity of the induced emf. **[1]**

(v) Both proton and electron have same kinetic energy. Which particle will have greater de-Broglie wavelength? **[1]**

(vi) What is interference of light waves? **[1]**

(vii) Define nuclear fission with an example. **[1]**

Section-B [14 Marks]

2. (i) Two long parallel, straight wires A and B carrying currents of 0.8 A and 0.5 A in the same direction are placed 4.0 cm apart. Estimate the force on a 10 cm section of wire A. **[2]**

Or

(ii) Calculate the magnetic field at a point 10 cm from a north pole of strength 10 A-m.
$(\mu_0 = 4\pi \times 10^{-7}$ N-A$^2)$

3. (i) What do you mean by magnetism? **[1**

(ii) Give some properties of magnetic lines of force. **[1**

4. What is the effect of temperature on the resistivity of alloys? Draw a graph between voltage and resistance, if the current supplied to a variable resistor is constant **[2**

5. (i) An electric current I flows through an infinitely long conductor as shown in the figure given below. Write an expression and direction for the magnetic field at point P. **[2]**

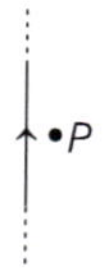

Or

(ii) An electric current I flows through a circular loop as shown in the figure given below. Write an expression and direction for the magnetic field at the centre of the loop at point P.

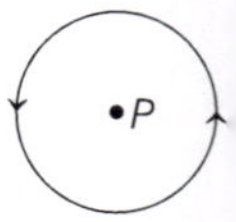

6. (i) Define ampere in terms of force between two current carrying conductors. **[1]**

(ii) What is an ideal transformer? **[1]**

7. What is the nature of image formed by a concave mirror, when object is placed at the centre of curvature? **[2]**

8. With reference to ray optics, answer the following questions.

(i) Write the necessary conditions for the phenomenon of total internal reflection to occur. **[1]**

(ii) Write the relation between refractive index and critical angle for a given pair of optical media. **[1]**

Section-C [27 Marks]

9. Using Gauss theorem, obtain an expression for electric field intensity at a point due to two parallel sheets of charge with charge densities σ and $-\sigma$. **[3]**

10. (i) A parallel plate capacitor is charged by a battery,. which is then disconnected. A dielectric slab having dielectric constant (relative permittivity) K, is now introduced between its two plates in order to occupy the space completely. **[3]**

State, in terms of K, its effect on the following.

(a) the capacitance of the capacitor.

(b) the potential difference between its plates.

(c) the energy stored in the capacitor

Or

(ii) Using Kirchhoff's law, calculate the value of currents in the various arms of the network shown below.

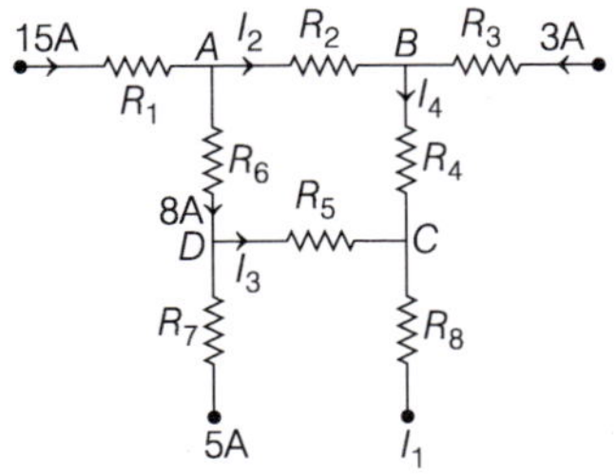

11. Obtain an expression for magnetic flux density B at the centre of a current carrying circular coil. **[3]**

12. Using Bohr's theory of hydrogen atom, obtain an expression for the radius of the nth orbit of an electron in an atom. **[3]**

13. (i) Discuss the action of a prism, a convex lens and a concave mirror, when a plane wavefront is incident on each of them. **[3]**

Or

(ii) Derive the relation $\frac{1}{f}=\frac{1}{v}-\frac{1}{u}$ for a biconvex lens.

How is the approximate value of the focal length of such a lens estimated in the laboratory?

14. (i) Draw a schematic arrangement of a reflecting telescope (cassegrain) showing how rays coming from a distant object are received at the eyepiece.

(ii) Draw a diagram showing the formation of primary rainbow and explain at what angles the primary rainbow is visible. **[3]**

15. In Young's experiment, what will be the phase difference and path difference between the light waves reaching

(i) third bright fringe and

(ii) third dark fringe from the central fringe.

(Take, $\lambda = 5000 Å$) **[3]**

16. What is a thermonuclear reaction? Define with example. **[3]**

17. (i) For a coherent source, initial phase difference between two sources must have same finite value. Justify.

(ii) Write the expression for intensity of interference and show

$$I_R = I_1 + I_2 + 2\sqrt{I_1 I_2}\cos\phi$$ **[3]**

Section-D **[15 Marks]**

18. (i) Determine following parameters in the given circuit

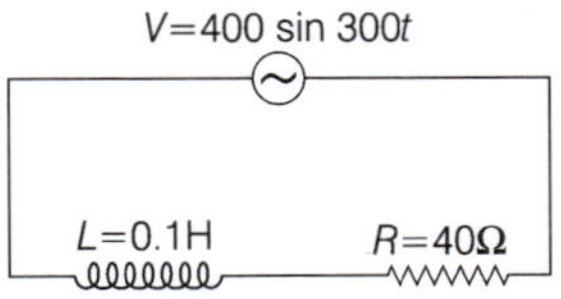

(a) Maximum current flowing in the circuit.

(b) Root mean square value of current in the circuit.

(c) Phase difference between voltage and current. **[5]**

Or

(ii) An inductor of 0.2 H inductance and resistance of 100 Ω are connected in series with an AC voltage source $V = 6\sin(500t)$.

Determine

(a) phase difference between current and voltage. **[5]**

(b) average power used in the circuit.

19. (i) (a) State the postulate of Bohr's theory regarding

I. Quantisation of angular momentum of an electron.

II. Emission of energy by an atom.

(b) Maximum torque acting on ideal dipole of dipole moment 3×10^{-29} C-m in a uniform electric field E is 6×10^{-25} N-m. Find the value of E.

(c) In a hydrogen atom, a transition of electrons takes place from 3rd orbit to 2nd orbit. Calculate the wavelength of the emitted photon . To which spectral series will this photon belong? **[5]**

Or

(ii) (a) Write down the Huygen's wave theory of light.

(b) Write down the definition of plane of vibration or phase of a wavefront. **[5]**

20. Specific resistance or resitivity of the materials of a conductor is defined as the resistance of a unit length with unit area of cross-section of the material of the conductor. The unit of resistivity is ohm-metre.

The resistivity of conductor depends on the nature of the material and resistivity of conductor changes with temperature.

(i) What is the conductivity?

(ii) Name one material whose resistivity decreases with rise in temperature.

(iii) Write the formula of resistivity of the material. **[5]**

Answers

1. A. (i) (a) (ii) (b) (iii) (a) (iv) (d) (v) (a) (vi) (a) (vii) (a)

2. (i) 2×10^{-7} N towards B or (ii) 2×10^{-4} T

5. (i) $B = \frac{\mu_0 I}{2\pi r}$ or (ii) $B = \frac{\mu_0 I}{2a}$

10. (ii) $I_1 = 13$ A, $I_2 = 7$ A, $I_3 = 3$ A, $I_4 = 10$ A

15. (i) 6π, 15000Å (ii) 5π, 12500Å

18. (i) (a) 8A, (b) $4\sqrt{2}$ A, (c) 36.86° (ii) (a) $\frac{\pi}{4}$, (b) 0.09 W

19. (i) (b) 2×10^4 V/m

ISC Unsolved

SAMPLE PAPER 03

Time : 3 hrs
Marks : 70

Physics
Paper 1

General Instructions

1. This paper is divided into four **Sections- A, B, C** and **D**. Answer all questions.
2. **Section A** consists of one question having sub-parts of one mark each.
3. **Section B** consists of seven questions of two marks each.
4. **Section C** consists of nine questions of three marks each.
5. **Section D** consists of three questions of five marks each.
6. Internal choices have been provided in two questions each in Section B, Section C and Section D.

Section-A [14 Marks]

1. A. In questions (i) to (vii) given below, choose the correct alternative (a), (b), (c) or (d) for each of the questions given below.

(i) The polarity of cell Y in the circuit is reversed, so that the two cells now oppose each other. The new terminal voltage of Y is **[1]**

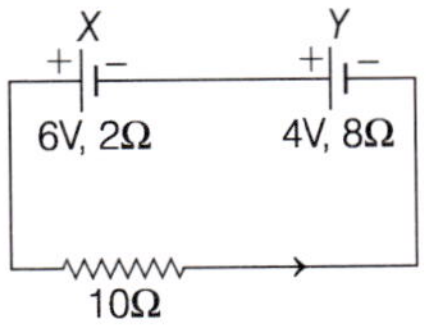

(a) 2.8 V (b) 3.8 V (c) 4.8 V (d) 5.8 V

(ii) If the angular momentum of an electron of mass m, charge e, revolving in a circular orbit is L, then its magnetic moment is **[1]**

(a) eLm (b) eL/m (c) $\frac{eL}{2m}$ (d) $\frac{2eL}{m}$

(iii) **Assertion** Emitted radiations lie in visible region when electrons jump from higher level to $n=2$ in hydrogen.

Reason Balmer series radiations belong to visible range in H-atoms. **[1]**

(a) Both Assertion and Reason are correct and Reason is the correct explanation for Assertion.

(b) Both Assertion and Reason are correct but Reason is not the correct explanation for Assertion.

(c) Assertion is true and Reason is false.

(d) Assertion is false and Reason is true.

(iv) The electrons may come out of a metal surface, when the frequency of incident light is **[1]**

(a) half of the threshold frequency

(b) one-third of the threshold frequency

(c) a bit less than threshold frequency

(d) more than threshold frequency

(v) In an astronomical telescope of refracting type, the **[1]**

(a) eyepiece has greater focal length.

(b) objective has greater focal length.

(c) objective and eyepiece have equal focal length.

(d) eyepiece has greater aperture than the objective.

(vi) **Assertion** When radius of a circular loop carrying current is doubled, its magnetic moment becomes four times.

Reason Magnetic moment depends on the area of the loop **[1]**

(a) Both Assertion and Reason are correct and Reason is the correct explanation for Assertion.
(b) Both Assertion and Reason are correct but Reason is not the correct explanation for Assertion.
(c) Assertion is true and Reason is false.
(d) Both Assertion and Reason are false.

(vii) Choose the correct option of : The Biot-Savart's law in vector form is [1]

(a) $d\mathbf{B} = \frac{\mu_0}{4\pi}\frac{dl\,(I \times r)}{\mathbf{r}^3}$ (b) $d\mathbf{B} = \frac{\mu_0}{4\pi}\frac{I\,(dl \times \mathbf{r})}{\mathbf{r}^3}$

(c) $d\mathbf{B} = \frac{\mu_0}{4\pi}\frac{\mathbf{I}\,(\mathbf{r} \times dl)}{\mathbf{r}^3}$ (d) $d\mathbf{B} = \frac{\mu_0}{4\pi}\frac{I\,(dl \times r)}{\mathbf{r}^2}$

B. Answer the following questions briefly.

(i) In a potentiometer balance point is obtained at length 339.4 cm for a cell of emf 1.0182 V. Find the potential gradient of the potentiometer. [1]

(ii) What do you understand by current sensitivity? [1]

(iii) Two parallel wires carry currents in (a) same direction and (b) opposite directions.

What is the nature of force between them in each case? [1]

(iv) Define coefficient of mutual induction and give one practical example of it. [1]

(v) Define mass-energy equivalence. [1]

(vi) Why are coherent sources necessary to produce a sustained interference pattern? [1]

(vii) Name the absorbing material used to control the reaction rate of neutrons in a nuclear reactor. [1]

Section-B [14 Marks]

2. (i) An electron is moving in a circular path of radius 0.60 cm with velocity 10^7 m/s in the magnetic field 10^{-2} Wb/m^2. Determine the specific charge (*e*/*m*) of electron. [2]

Or

(ii) An electron is moving with 3×10^6 m/s uniform velocity on a circular path of radius 2×10^{-10} m. Calculate the magnetic field at the centre of the circular path.

3. (i) To which part of the electromagnetic spectrum does a wave of frequency 5×10^{11} Hz belong?.

(ii) The charging current for a capacitor is 0.25 A. What is the displacement current across its plates? [2]

4. A convex lens with focal length 12 cm is kept in contact with concave lens of focal length 36 cm. Find the nature, location and magnification of image formed by an object placed 27 cm away from this combination. [2]

5. (i) Explain critical mass and controlled chain reaction with reference to nuclear reactor. [2]

Or

(ii) What is the difference between nuclear fission and nuclear fusion?

6. (i) Name the part of an electromagnetic spectrum of wavelength 10^{-2} m and mention its one application.

(ii) Which part of electromagnetic spectrum has larger penetrating power? [2]

7. (i) What do you understand by the magnifying power of microscope?

(ii) How does the magnifying power of a microscope affect the level of details visible in the magnified image? [2]

8. With reference to wave optics, answer the following questions.

(i) What is meant by wavefront?

(ii) State one condition for obtaining sustained interference of light. [2]

Section-C [27 Marks]

9. Deduce the expression. for capacitance of a parallel plate capacitor partially filled with dielectric substance. [3]

10. (i) A spherical conductor of radius 12 cm has a charge of 1.6×10^{-8} C distributed uniformly on its surface.

What is the electric field

(a) inside the sphere

(b) just outside the sphere [3]

Or

(ii) A conductor carrying a current *I* is of types as shown below. Find the magnetic field induction at the common centre *O* of all the three arcs.

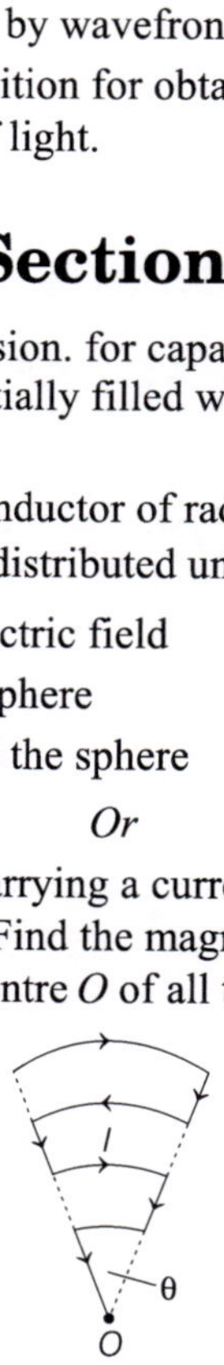

11. (i) Write formula for colour dispersion power of any optical medium.

(ii) Is colour dispersion power is dependent on prism angle? [3]

12. Show that maximum intensity in interference pattern is four times the intensity due to each slit.

Hence, show that interference involves only redistribution of energy. **[3]**

13. (i) *ABCDEF* is a regular hexagon formed by six equal wires, each of resistance $r\,\Omega$, as shown in the figure.

The corners have been joined at the centre of hexagon by wires of the same resistance. Find the equivalent resistance between the corners *A* and *D* using Kirchhoff's rules. **[3]**

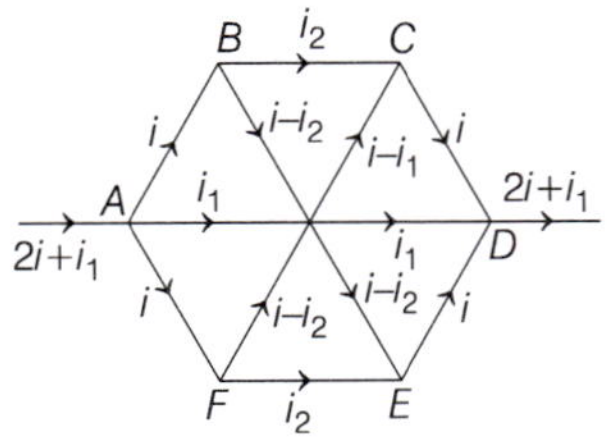

Or

(ii) A heating coil of 2000 W is immersed in an electric kettle. How much time will it take in raising the temperature of 1L of water for 4°C to 100°C? Only 80% part of the thermal energy produced is used in raising the temperature of water.

14. (i) Two insulated charged copper spheres *A* and *B* have their centres separated by a distance of 50 cm. What is the mutual force of electrostatic repulsion, if the charge on each is 6.5×10^{-7} C and the radii of *A* and *B* are negligible compared to the distance of separation?

(ii) What is the force of repulsion, if each sphere is charged double the above amount and the distance between them is halved? **[3]**

15. An electric dipole is placed at angles θ from the direction of uniform electric field *E*. Find

(i) net translational force acting on dipole.

(ii) torque acting on dipole. **[3]**

16. What are differences between interference and diffraction? **[3]**

17. Starting from the expression for the energy, $W = \frac{1}{2} LI^2$, stored in a solenoid of self-inductance *L* to build up the current *I*, obtain the expression for the magnetic energy in terms of the magnetic field *B*, area *A* and length *l* of the solenoid having *n* number of turns per unit length. Hence, show that the energy density is given by $B^2/2\mu_0$. **[3]**

Section-D [15 Marks]

18. (i) In an AC circuit an inductance coil of 1H, a capacitance of 0.2 μF and resistance of 3000 Ω are connected in series with AC voltage source of 200 V and frequency $\frac{1000}{2\pi}$ cycles/sec. Determine

(a) impedance of circuit.

(b) phase difference between voltage and current.

(c) the voltage across coil, capacitor and resistance. **[5]**

Or

(ii) (a) When an alternating emf $e = 310 \sin(100\pi t)$ V is applied to a series *L-C-R* circuit, current flowing through it is $i = 5 \sin(100\pi t + \pi/3)$ A.

I. What is the phase difference between the current and the emf ?

II. Calculate the average power consumed by the circuit.

(b) A 400 Ω resistor, a 3H inductor and a 5μF capacitor are connected in series to a 220 V, 50 Hz AC source. Calculate the

I. impedance of the circuit.

II. current flowing through the circuit.

19. (i) (a) Draw a schematic sketch of an AC generator describing its basic elements. State briefly its working principle. Show a plot of variation of

I. magnetic flux.

II. alternating emf *versus* time generated by a loop of wire rotating in a magnetic field.

(b) With reference to alternating current, state difference between resistance and the reactance.

(c) With reference to a semiconductor diode, explain the terms

I. Depletion region.

II. Potential barrier or barrier potential difference. **[5]**

Or

(ii) (a) Explain the working of a solar cell with circuit diagram.

(b) What is LED? Show its (*V-I*) characteristics by drawing its circuit diagram.

20. Nuclear energy is the energy released during the transformation of nuclei with less total binding energy to nuclei with greater binding energy.

Nuclear fission and nuclear fusion are the two distinct way of obtaining energy from nucleus.

Nuclear fission is the phenomenon of splitting of a heavy nucleus into two or more lighter nuclei by the bombardment of proton, neutron, α-particle, etc. Nuclear fusion is the phenomenon of fusing two or more lighter nuclei forming a single heavy nucleus.

(i) Consider the following nuclear reaction,

$${}_1H^2 + {}_1H^2 \longrightarrow {}_2He^3 + {}_0n^1$$

What is the name of this reaction?

(ii) What is the source of energy of stars?

(iii) Define the nuclear chain reaction. **[5]**

Answers

1. A. (i) (c) (ii) (c) (iii) (a) (iv) (d) (v) (b) (vi) (a) (vii) (b)

B. (i) 0.3 V/m

2. (i) 1.66×10^{11} C/kg or (ii) 1.2 T

3. (i) Infrared radiation (ii) $I_d = 0.25$ A

4. 54 cm and – 2

10. (i) (a) zero, (b) 1×10^5 N/C

13. *Or* (ii) 250.8 s

14. (i) 1.521×10^{-2} N, (ii) 0.24 N

18. (i) (a) 5000 Ω, (b) 53.13° (c) 40V, 200 V, 120 V

Or (ii) (a) I. 60°, II. $P_{av} = 387.5$ W

(b) I. 503.1 Ω, II. 0.437 A

ISC

CHAPTERWISE - TOPICWISE
QUESTION BANK

Latest Specimen Question Paper

ISC

Latest Specimen Question Paper 2025

Time : 3 hrs
Marks : 70

Physics
Paper 1

General Instructions

1. This paper is divided into four **Sections- A, B, C** and **D**. Answer all questions.
2. **Section A** consists of one question having sub-parts of one mark each.
3. **Section B** consists of seven questions of two marks each.
4. **Section C** consists of nine questions of three marks each.
5. **Section D** consists of three questions of five marks each.
6. Internal choices have been provided in two questions each in Section B, Section C and Section D.

Section-A [14 Marks]

1. A. In questions (i) to (vii) below, choose the correct alternative (a), (b), (c) or (d) for each of the questions given below:

(i) Figure below shows a circuit containing an ammeter A, a galvanometer G and a plug key K. When the key is closed, • *Analysis* [1]

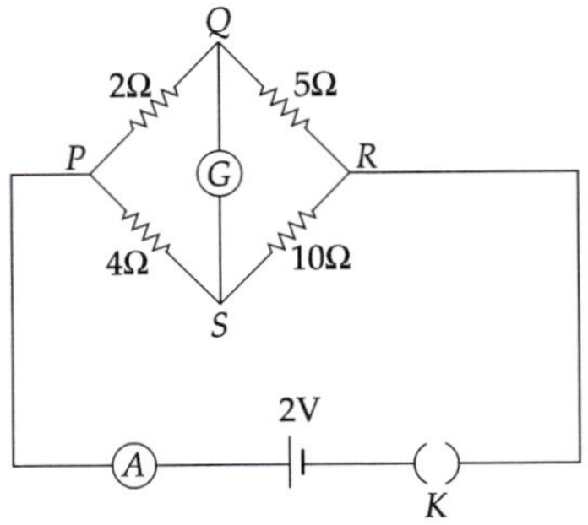

(a) both G and A show deflections
(b) neither G nor A shows deflection
(c) G shows deflection but A does not
(d) A shows deflection but G does not

(ii) A circular coil having N turns of radius R carrying a current I is used to produce a magnetic field B at its centre O. If this coil is opened and rewound such that the radius of the newly formed coil is $2R$ carrying the same current I, what will be the magnetic field at the centre O? • *Analysis* [1]

(a) $2B$ (b) B (c) $\frac{B}{2}$ (d) $\frac{B}{4}$

(iii) Magnetic susceptibility of a diamagnetic substance • *Recall* [1]
(a) decreases with the increase in its temperature
(b) is not affected by the change in its temperature
(c) increases with increase in its temperature
(d) first increases, then decreases with increase in its temperature

(iv) The de-Broglie wavelength of an electron in the first Bohr's orbit of hydrogen atom is equal to • *Understanding* [1]
(a) diameter of the first orbit
(b) circumference of the first orbit
(c) radius of the second orbit
(d) $\frac{h}{2\pi}$

(v) An ideal p-n junction diode offers • *Recall* [1]
(a) zero resistance in forward as well as reverse bias
(b) infinite resistance in forward as well as reverse bias
(c) zero resistance in forward but infinite resistance in reverse bias
(d) infinite resistance in forward but zero resistance in reverse bias

(vi) Given below are two statements marked Assertion and Reason. Read the two statements and choose the correct option.

Assertion An astronomical telescope has an objective lens having large focal length.

Reason Magnifying power of an astronomical telescope varies directly with focal length of the objective lens. • *Understanding* [1]

(a) Both Assertion and Reason are true and Reason is the correct explanation for Assertion.

(b) Both Assertion and Reason are true but Reason is not the correct explanation for Assertion.

(c) Assertion is false and Reason is true.

(d) Both Assertion and Reason are false.

(vii) Given below are two statements marked, Assertion and Reason. Read the two statements and choose the correct option.

Assertion If critical angle of glass-air pair ($\mu_g = 3/2$) is θ_1 and that of water-air pair ($\mu_w = 4/3$) is θ_2, then the critical angle for the water-glass pair will lie between θ_1 and θ_2.

Reason A medium is optically denser, if its refractive index is greater. • *Analysis* [1]

(a) Both Assertion and Reason are true and Reason is the correct explanation for Assertion.

(b) Both Assertion and Reason are true but Reason is not the correct explanation for Assertion.

(c) Assertion is false and Reason is true.

(d) Both Assertion and Reason are false.

B. Answer the following questions briefly.

(*i*) Current I flowing through a metallic wire is gradually increased. Show graphically how heating power (P) developed in it varies with the current (I). • *Application* [1]

(*ii*) Explain why core of a transformer is always laminated? • *Recall* [1]

(*iii*) Why does a car driver use a convex mirror as a rear-view mirror? • *Recall* [1]

(*iv*) Represent diagrammatically how the incident planar wavefronts of wavelength λ pass through an aperture of size d, when d is approximately equal to λ ? • *Understanding* [1]

(*v*) What is meant by "Dual nature of matter"? • *Recall* [1]

(*vi*) What happens when an electron collides with a positron? • *Recall* [1]

(*vii*) What energy conversion takes place in a solar cell? • *Recall* [1]

Section-B

[14 Marks]

2. (i) A dielectric slab of dielectric constant K and thickness t is introduced between the two plates of a capacitor of plate- separation d ($> t$) and common area A. The capacitance of this system is given as

$$C = \frac{\varepsilon_0 A}{(d-t) + \left(\frac{t}{K}\right)}$$

How does the capacitance C modify in each of the following cases? • *Application* [2]

(a) The dielectric slab covers half the distance of separation between the two plates.

(b) The whole space between the plates is filled with the dielectric.

Or

(ii) In given figure, the current-voltage graphs for a conductor are given at two different temperatures T_1 and T_2. • *Analysis* [2]

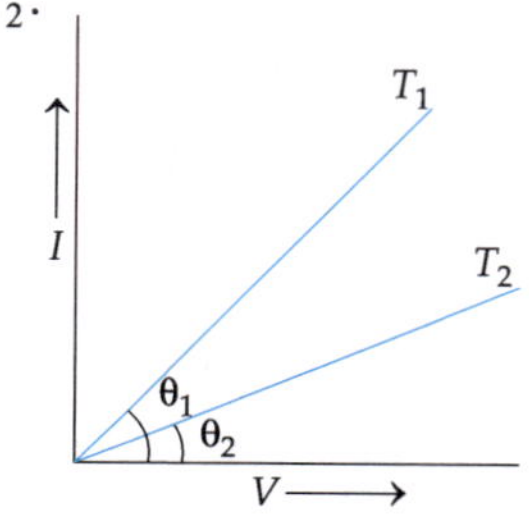

(a) At which temperature T_1 or T_2 is the higher resistance ?

(b) Which temperature T_1 or T_2 is higher?

3. Arrangement of an oxygen ion and two hydrogen ions in a water molecule is shown in figure. Calculate electric dipole moment of water molecule. Express your answer in terms of e (charge on hydrogen ion), l and θ. • *Application* [2]

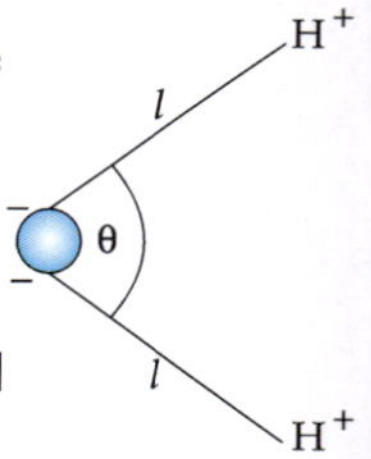

4. (i) Figure below shows a part of an electric circuit. • *Application* [2]

(a) Apply Kirchhoff's junction rule to the junction A to find current flowing through the 5 Ω resistor.

(b) Apply Kirchhoff's loop rule to the loop $ABDA$ to find current flowing through the 7Ω resistor.

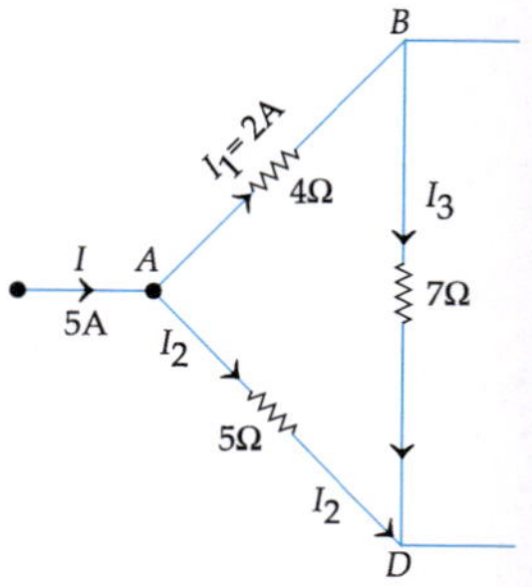

Or (ii) In a potentiometer, a cell is balanced against 110 cm when the circuit is open. A cell is balanced at 100

cm when short-circuited through a resistance of 10 Ω. Find the internal resistance of the cell.

• *Application* [2]

5. Figure below are two long, parallel wires carrying current in the same direction such that $I_1 < I_2$.

• *Recall* [2]

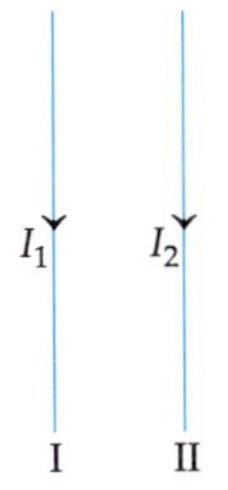

(i) In which direction will wire I_1 move?

(ii) If the direction of the current I_2 is reversed, then in which direction will the wire I_1 move now?

6. (i) The focal length of a double convex lens is equal to the radius of curvature of either surface. What is the refractive index of its material?

• *Application* [1]

(ii) What is meant by a thin prism? • *Recall* [1]

7. (i) Name the electromagnetic radiation that has been used in obtaining the image below • *Recall* [1]

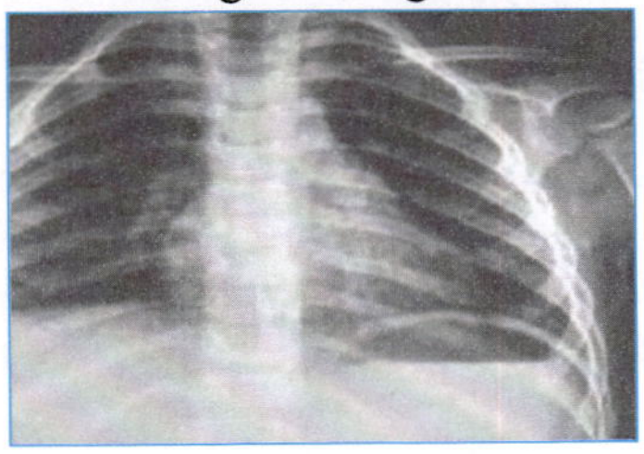

(ii) What is the wavelength range of electromagnetic radiation used in radio broadcast? • *Recall* [1]

8. How does stopping potential in photoelectric emission vary, if

(i) the intensity of the incident radiation increases?

• *Recall* [1]

(ii) the frequency of incident radiation decreases?

• *Understanding* [1]

Section-C

[27 Marks]

9. "A uniformly charged conducting spherical shell for the points outside the shell behaves as if the entire charge of the shell is concentrated at its centre". Show this with the help of a proper diagram and verify this statement. • *Recall* [3]

10. (i) Study the two circuits shown in figure below. The cells in the two circuits are identical to each other. The resistance of the load resistor R is the same in both circuits.

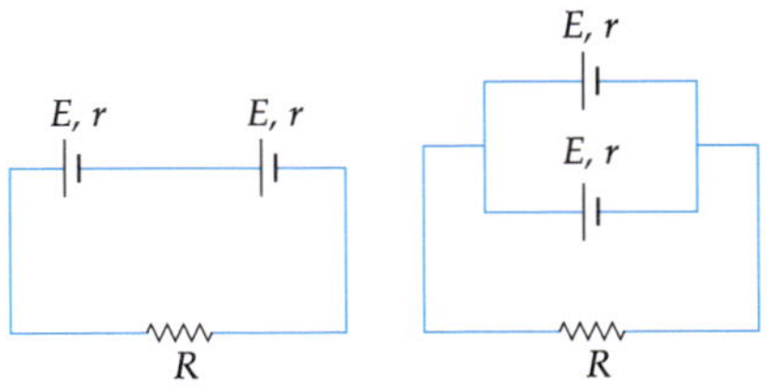

If the same current flows through the resistor R in both circuits, calculate the internal resistance of each cell in terms of the resistance of resistor R. Show your calculations. • *Application* [3]

Or (ii) The drift velocity of electrons in a conductor connected to a battery is given by

$v_d = -e\frac{E\tau}{m}$, where e is the charge of the electron, E is the electric field, τ is the average time between collisions and m is the mass of the electron.

Based on this, answer the following • *Analysis* [3]

(a) How does the drift velocity change with a change in the potential difference across the conductor?

(b) A copper wire of length l is connected to a source. If the copper wire is replaced by another copper wire of the same area of cross-section but of length $4l$, how will the drift velocity change? Explain your answer.

11. A galvanometer of resistance 100 Ω gives a full-scale deflection for a potential difference of 200 mV.

• *Application* [3]

(i) What must be the resistance connected to convert the galvanometer into an ammeter of the range 0-200 mA?

(ii) Determine resistance of the ammeter.

12. (i) A student records the following data for the magnitudes (B) of the magnetic field at axial points at different distances x (as shown in figure below) from the centre O of a circular coil of radius a carrying a current I. Verify (for any two) that these observations are in good agreement with the expected theoretical values of B. • *Application* [3]

x	$x=0$	$x=a$	$x=2a$	$x=3a$
B	B_0	$\frac{B_0}{2\sqrt{2}}$	$\frac{B_o}{5\sqrt{5}}$	$\frac{B_0}{10\sqrt{10}}$

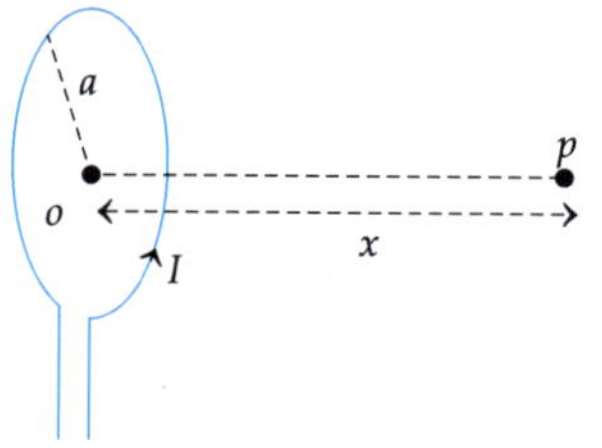

Or (*ii*) An electron moving along positive X-axis with a velocity of $8\times10^{-7}\,\text{ms}^{-1}$ enters a region having uniform magnetic field $B = 1.3\times10^{-3}$ T along positive Y-axis. • *Application* [3]

(a) Explain why the electron describes a circular path.

(b) Calculate the radius of the circular path described by the electron.

13. With the help of a neatly drawn labelled diagram, prove the law of reflection on the basis of Huygens' wave theory. • *Recall* [3]

14. A lens of focal length f is divided into two equal parts and then these parts are put in a combination as shown in figure . • *Application* [3]

(*i*) What is the focal length of L_1?

(*ii*) What is the focal length of the final combination?

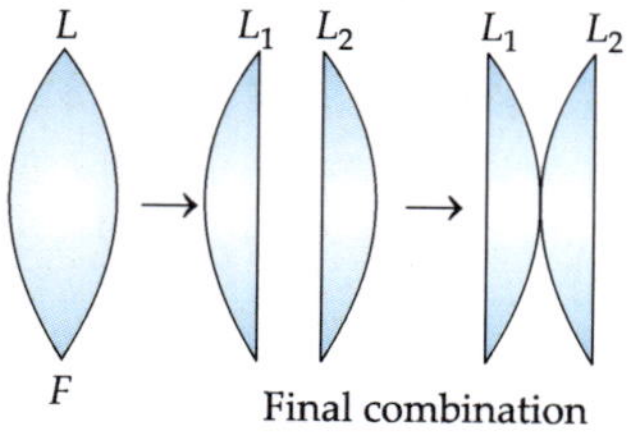

15. In Young's double slit experiment, how is interference pattern affected when the following changes are made • *Understanding* [3]

(i) Slits are brought closer to each other.

(*ii*) Screen is moved away from the slits.

(*iii*) Red coloured light is replaced with blue coloured light.

16. (*i*) A virologist studies details of a virus with the help of an instrument. Name the instrument used by him. • *Recall* [1½]

(*ii*) Draw a labelled ray diagram of an image formed by this instrument, assuming • *Recall* [1½]

(a) a small upright object.

(b) image lies at least distance of distinct vision

17. The graphs below show the variation of the stopping potential V_S with the frequency (ν) of the incident radiations for two different photosensitive materials M_1 and M_2.

Express work function for M_1 and M_2 in terms of Planck's constant (h) and threshold frequency and charge of the electron (e).

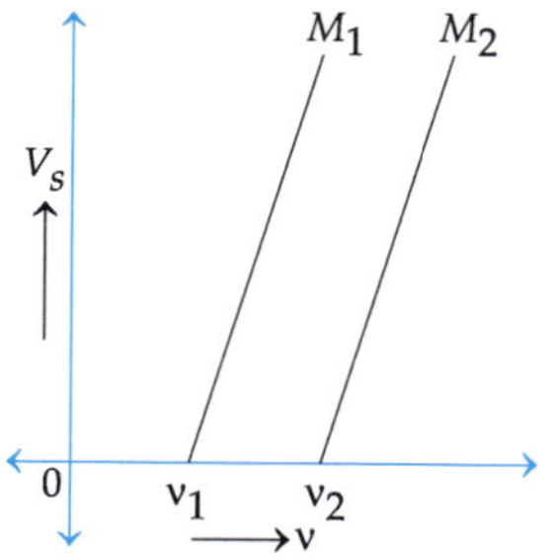

If the values of stopping potential for M_1 and M_2 are V_1 and V_2 respectively, then show that the slope of the lines equals to $\frac{V_1 - V_2}{\nu_1 - \nu_2}$ for a frequency, $\nu > \nu_2$ and also $\nu > \nu_1$. • *Analysis* [3]

Section-D

[15 Marks]

18. (i) The magnetic field through a single loop of wire, 12 cm in radius and 8.5 Ω resistance, changes with time as shown in graph below. The magnetic field is perpendicular to the plane of the loop. **[5]**

(a) Find the induced emf for the time intervals 0 to 2.0 s, 2.0 to 4.0 s and 4.0 to 6.0 s. • *Application*

(b) Hence, plot induced current as a function of time. • *Application*

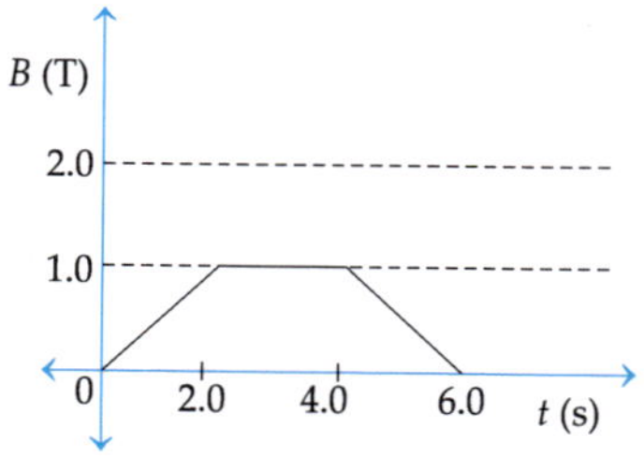

Or (ii) Three students, X, Y and Z performed an experiment for studying the variation of AC, with frequency in a series L-C-R circuit and obtained the graphs as shown below. They all used

(I) an AC source of the same emf and

(II) inductance of the same value. **[5]**

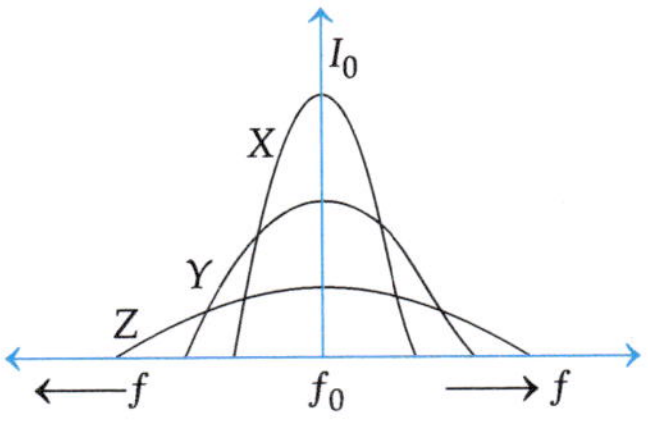

(a) Who used minimum resistance? • *Analysis*

(b) In which case will the quality Q factor be maximum? • *Analysis*

(c) What did the students conclude about the nature of impedance at resonant frequency (f_0)? • *Analysis*

(d) An ideal capacitor is connected across 220 V, 50 Hz and 220 V, 100 Hz supplies. Find the ratio of current flowing through it in the two cases. • *Application*

19. (i) (a) Find the binding energy per nucleon of ^{235}U based on the information given below.

	Mass (u)
Mass of neutral $^{235}_{92}U$	235.0439
Mass of a proton	1.0073
Mass of a neutron	1.0087

(b) Find the energy released during the following fission reaction.

$$^{235}_{92}U + {}^1_0n \rightarrow {}^{236}_{92}U \rightarrow {}^{90}_{36}Kr + {}^{143}_{56}Ba + 3\,{}^1_0n$$

	Mass (u)
^{235}U	235.0439
^{90}Kr	89.9195
^{143}Ba	142.9206
^1n	1.0087

• *Application*

(c) During Rutherford's gold foil experiment, it was observed that most of the α-particles did not deflect. However, some showed a deflection of 180°. What hypothesis was made to justify the deflection of α-particle by 180°? • *Recall* [5]

Or

(ii) (a) Define unified atomic mass unit. • *Recall*

(b) Calculate its energy equivalent. • *Application*

(c) In an atom X, electrons absorb the energy from an external source. This energy "excites" the electrons from a lower-energy level to a higher energy level around the nucleus of the atom. When electrons return to the ground state, they emit photons.
Figure below is the energy level diagram of atom X with three energy levels,
$E_1 = 0.00$ eV, $E_2 = 1.78$ eV and $E_3 = 2.95$ eV.
The ground state is considered 0 eV for reference. The transition of electrons takes place between levels E_1 and E_2.

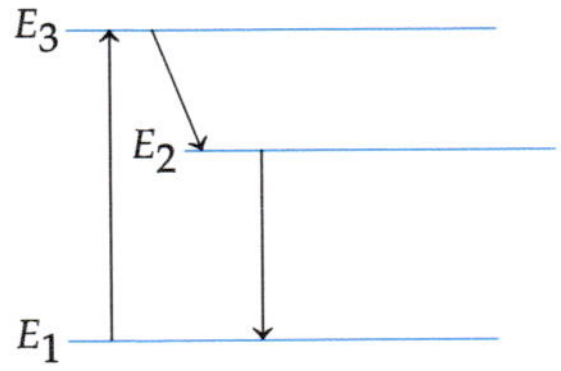

I. What wavelength of radiation is needed to excite the atom to energy level E_2 from E_1? • *Application*

II. Suppose the external source has a power of 100 W. What would be the rate of photon emission? • *Application* [5]

20. Sanya performed an experiment of obtaining characteristic curves of a junction diode. When she forward biased it, she found that beyond forward voltage $V = V_k$, the conductivity is very high. When she reverse biased the diode, she found that a very small current (of about a few microamperes) flows in the diode. It remained constant even though she varied the voltage. **[5]**

(i) In given figure, which one of the diodes is forward biased? • *Recall*

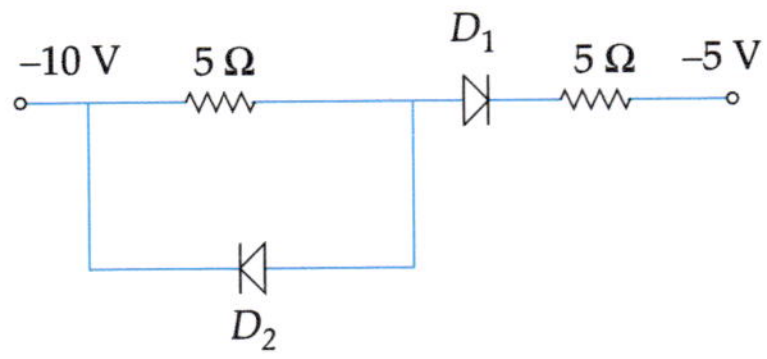

(ii) What is meant by a saturation current? • *Application*

(iii) When applied voltage during forward bias is small, why does no current flow in the diode? • *Recall*

(iv) The circuit shown in the figure below contains two diodes, each with a forward resistance of 50 Ω and with infinite resistance during reverse bias. If the battery voltage is 6V, then calculate the current through the 100 Ω resistance. • *Application*

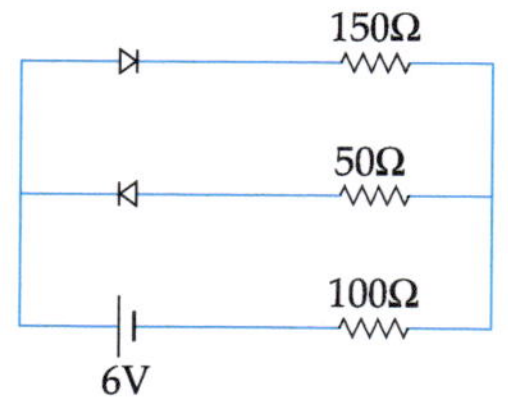

Useful constants and Relations

Planck's constant	h	=	6.6×10^{-34} J-s
Speed of light in vacuum	c	=	$3\times10^{8}\,ms^{-1}$
Charge of a proton = Charge of an electron	e	=	$\pm1.6\times10^{-19}$C
Mass of an electron	m	=	9.1×10^{-31} Kg
One electron volt	1 eV	=	1.6×10^{-19} J
Unified atomic mass unit	1 u	=	931.5 MeV

Explanations

1. A. (i) (*d*) *A* shows deflection but *G* does not. When key is closed, the galvanometer is connected in parallel with a very low resistance, it will not show any deflection because most of the current by passes the galvanometer and flows through the low resistance.

The ammeter will show a deflection as it measures the current flowing through the circuit.

(ii) (*d*) The initial length, $C = 2\pi RN$

New length, $C' = 2\pi(2R)N'$

Since, new length and old length are equal, we have $N' = \frac{N}{2}$

Old magnetic field, $B = \frac{\mu_0 NI}{2R}$

New magnetic field, $B' = \frac{\mu_0 N'I}{2R'}$

On substituting values N' and R', we get

$$\therefore \quad B' = \frac{\mu_0 NI}{4R\cdot 2} \qquad \left[\because B = \frac{\mu_0 NI}{2R}\right]$$

$$B' = \frac{B}{4}$$

(iii) (*b*) The paired spins of electrons remains unaffected due to increase in temperature, hence diamagnetism is independent of temperature.

(iv) (*b*) According to the de-Broglie's hypothesis, the wavelength λ of a particle is given by

$$\lambda = \frac{h}{p}$$

The de-Broglie wavelength of the electron in the first orbit is equals to the circumference of that orbit, i.e. $2\pi r_1$, where r_1 is the radius of the first Bohr orbit. This ensures that the electron's wave fits exactly into the orbit, forming a standing wave with an integer number of wavelengths around the circle.

(v) (*c*) When the diode is forward biased, it allows current to flow freely with no voltage drop and when the diode is reverse biased, it does not allow any current to flow, behaving like an open circuit. Thus, in forward bias, the resistance is effectively zero and in reverse bias, it is infinite.

(vi) (*a*) Both A and R are true and R is the correct explanation for A.

The magnifying power of an astronomical telescope is given by $M = \frac{f_o}{f_e}$

From the above relation, it can be said that the magnifying power is directly proportional to the focal length of the objective lens, not the focal length of the eyepiece.

(vii) (*c*) The critical angle for the water-glass pair (θ_{wg}) is less than both θ_1 and θ_2 and will not lie not between them.

Also, a medium is optically denser, if its refractive index is greater. Hence, Assertion is false and Reason is true.

B. (i)

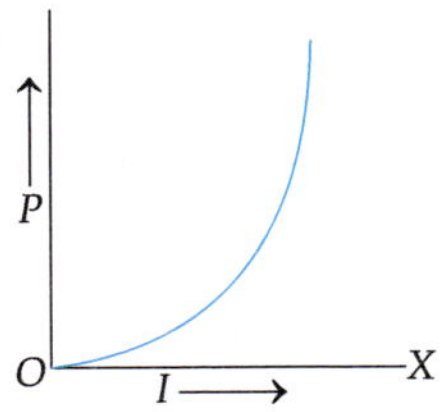

(ii) The core of a transformer is always laminated to reduce energy losses due to eddy currents. Laminations increase the electrical resistance of the core, minimising these currents and thus improving efficiency.

(iii) A car driver uses a convex mirror as a rear view mirror because it forms diminished image and hence provides a wider field of view, allowing the driver to see more area behind the vehicle.

(iv)

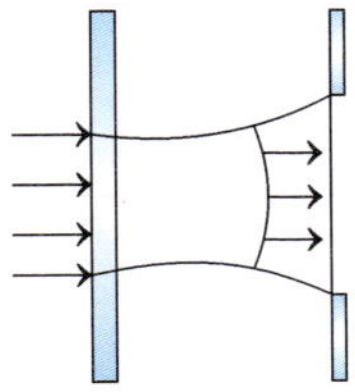

(v) The dual nature of matter refers to the concept that particles, such as electrons and photons, exhibit both wave-like and particle like nature.

(vi) When an electron collides with a positron, they annihilate each other, producing gamma ray photons.

(vii) In a solar cell, light energy is converted into electrical energy.

2. (i) (a) Substitute $t = \frac{d}{2}$ in the following equation,

$$\therefore \quad C = \frac{\varepsilon_0 A}{(d-t) + \frac{t}{k}} \quad \text{...(i)}$$

$$C = \frac{\varepsilon_0 A}{\left[\left(d - \frac{d}{2}\right) + \frac{d}{2k}\right]} = \frac{2\varepsilon_0 AK}{[d(k+1)]}$$

(b) Substitute, $t = d$

So, $$C = \frac{k\varepsilon_0 A}{d}$$

Or (ii) (a) The slope of the *I*-*V* graph gives the conductance,

$$R = \frac{V}{I} = \frac{1}{\tan\theta}$$

$$\therefore \quad \theta_1 > \theta_2$$

$$\tan\theta_1 > \tan\theta_2$$

So, resistance at T_1 < resistance at T_2.

(b) The resistance of a conductor rises with temperature, therefore $T_2 > T_1$.

3. Electric dipole moment is given by

$$p = q \times l \quad \text{...(i)}$$

where, q is charge and l is distance between two charges.

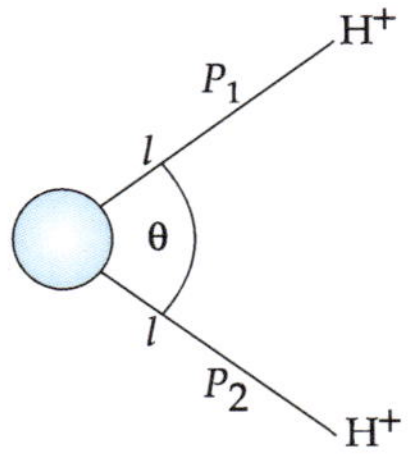

Using Eq. (i), we get

$$p_1 = p_2 = e \times l$$

Net dipole moment, $p' = 2p\cos\alpha = 2e \times l\cos\left(\frac{\theta}{2}\right)$

4. (i) (a) According to the Kirchhoff's junction rule to the junction *A*,

$$I = I_1 + I_2$$
$$5 = 2 + I_2$$
$$I_2 = 5 - 2 = 3\text{A}$$

(b) Apply Kirchhoff's loop rule to the loop *ABDA*,

$$I_1 \times 4 + I_3 \times 7 = I_2 \times 5$$
$$2 \times 4 + I_3 \times 7 = 3 \times 5$$
$$8 + 7I_3 = 15$$
$$I_3 = \frac{15-8}{7}$$

Hence, $I_3 = 1\text{A}$

Or

(ii) Given, resistance, $R = 10\ \Omega$

$$l_1 = 110 \text{ cm}$$
$$l_2 = 100 \text{ cm}$$

Internal resistance, $r = ?$

$$r = R\left(\frac{l_1}{l_2 - 1}\right) = 10\left(\frac{110}{100-1}\right) = 11.11\ \Omega$$

5. (i) Two long parallel wires carrying current in the same direction attract each other, therefore, it will move towards I_2.

(ii) Two long, parallel wires carrying current in the opposite direction repel each other, therefore it will move away from I_2.

6. (i) Focal length of a lens is given by

$$\frac{1}{f}=(\mu-1)\left(\frac{1}{R_1}+\frac{1}{R_2}\right)$$

By the given information, we have

$$R_1=R_2=f$$

$$\frac{1}{f}=(\mu-1)\left(\frac{1}{f}+\frac{1}{f}\right)$$

$$(\mu-1)=\frac{1}{2}$$

So, $\mu=1.5$

(ii) A thin prism is a transparent, triangular prism which has a very small refracting angle, i.e. less than 4°.

7. (i) X-rays

(ii) Greater than 1m

8. (i) The stopping potential is independent of the intensity of the incident photon.

(ii) The stopping potential will change with the frequency of the incident photon.

9. A uniformly charged spherical shell of radius R carrying charge density σ.

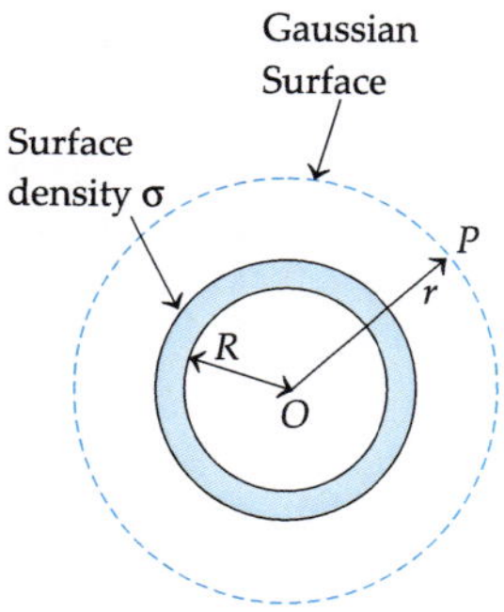

According to the Gaussian surface, a sphere of radius $r>R$ and with centre O, passing through P.

E and ΔS (area vector) at every point are parallel.

Hence, flux through each of the area element,

$$\Delta\phi=E\cdot\Delta S$$

Summing over all ΔS,

$$\Delta\phi=E\cdot 4\pi R^2$$

The charge enclosed is $\sigma\times 4\pi R^2$.

By Gauss's law, $E\times 4\pi r^2=\dfrac{q}{\varepsilon_0}=\dfrac{\sigma\times 4\pi R^2}{\varepsilon_0}$

$$E=\frac{\sigma R^2}{\varepsilon_0 r^2}=\frac{q}{4\pi\varepsilon_0 r^2}$$

According to the coulomb's law, this formula is exactly similar to the field produced by a point charge q placed at the centre O.

10. (i) $I=\dfrac{E}{(R+r)}$

where, $E=$ the emf of the cell

and $r=$ internal resistance of the cell.

In circuit 1, the cells are in series.

$\therefore\quad E_{eq}=2E$ and $r_{eq}=2r$

Hence, $I=\dfrac{2E}{(R+2r)}$ ...(i)

In circuit 2, the cells are in parallel.

$\therefore\quad E_{eq}=E$ and $r_{eq}=\dfrac{r}{2}$

$\therefore\quad I=\dfrac{E}{\left(R+\dfrac{r}{2}\right)}$ ...(ii)

From Eqs. (i) and (ii), we get

$$\frac{2E}{(R+2r)}=\frac{E}{\left(R+\dfrac{r}{2}\right)}$$

$$2\left(R+\frac{r}{2}\right)=R+2r$$

$$2R+r=R+2r$$

$\therefore\quad r=R$

Or

(ii) (a) If the potential difference across the conductor is increased, the electric field inside the conductor increases. So, $v_d\propto E$, drift velocity also increases with an increase in potential difference.

(b) We know that,

$$V_d\propto E$$

But $E=\dfrac{V}{l}$

Hence, when length increases to $4l$, drift velocity becomes $\left(\dfrac{1}{4}\right)$th of the original value.

11. (i) Given, galvanometer of resistance, $G=100\,\Omega$

Potential difference, $V_g=200\,\text{mV}$

$I=200\,\text{mA}$

Resistance to be connected to the galvameter to convert to an ammeter.

$$S=I_gG/(I-I_g)$$

Here, $I_g = V_g / G = 200/100 = 2$ mA

$\therefore \quad S = 2\times10^{-3}\times100/(0.2-0.002) = 1.01\,\Omega$

(ii) The resistance of the ammeter,

$$\frac{1}{R} = \frac{1}{100} + \frac{1}{1.01} = 0.999\,\Omega$$

12. (i) The expression for B at an axial point of a circular coil carrying current is

For N turns $\quad B = \frac{\mu_0}{4\pi}\frac{2NI(\pi a^2)}{r^3}$

For $N = 1$ turn $\quad B = \frac{\mu_0}{4\pi}\frac{2I(\pi a^2)}{r^3}$

At the centre, $x = 0$; $B = \frac{\mu_0}{2}\frac{I}{a}$

At $x = a$; $B = \frac{B_0}{2\sqrt{2}}$

At $x = 2a$; $B = \frac{B_0}{5\sqrt{5}}$

At $x = 3a$; $B = \frac{B_0}{10\sqrt{10}}$

Or (ii) (a) The electron describes a circular path because force exerted by the magnetic field is always perpendicular to its velocity, hence it provides the necessary centripetal force to the electron.

(b) Given, $v = 8\times10^{-7}\ \text{ms}^{-1}$

$$B = 1.3\times10^{-3}\ \text{T}$$

We know that, $\frac{e}{m} = \frac{v}{Br}$

$$\frac{1.6\times10^{-19}}{9.1\times10^{-31}} = \frac{8\times10^{-7}}{1.3\times10^{-3}\times r}$$

$$r = \frac{8\times10^{-7}\times9.1\times10^{-31}}{1.6\times10^{-19}\times1.3\times10^{-3}}$$

So, $\quad r = 0.35$ m

13. Let 1, 2, 3 be the incident rays and $1', 2', 3'$ be the corresponding reflected rays.

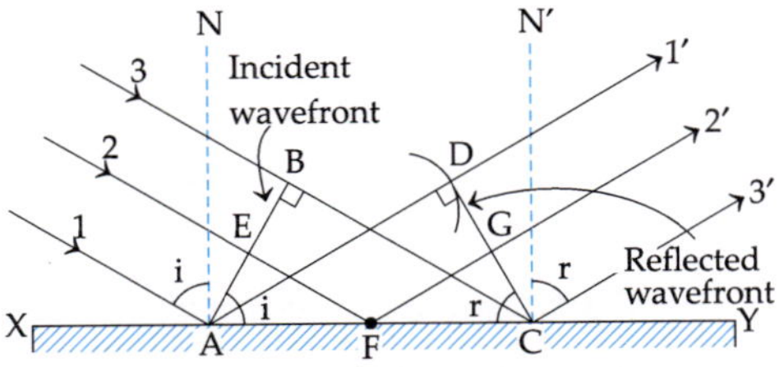

If c is the speed of the light, t is the time taken by light to go from B to C or A to D or E to G through F, then

$$t = \frac{EF}{c} + \frac{FG}{c} \quad \text{...(i)}$$

In ΔAEF, $\sin i = \frac{EF}{AF}$

In ΔFGC, $\sin r = \frac{FG}{FC}$ or $t = \frac{AF\sin i}{c} + \frac{FC\sin r}{c}$

$$\Rightarrow t = \frac{AC\sin r + AF(\sin i - \sin r)}{c} \quad [\because FC = AC - AF]$$

For rays of light from different parts on the incident wavefront, the values of AF are different. But light from different points of the incident wavefront should take the same time to reach the corresponding points on the reflected wavefront.

So, t should not depend upon AF. This is possible only, if

$$\sin i - \sin r = 0$$

i.e. $\quad \sin i = \sin r$

or $\quad \angle i = \angle r \quad$ ...(ii)

which is the **first law of reflection.**

Further, the incident wavefront AB, the reflecting surface XY and the reflected wavefront CD are all perpendicular to the plane of the paper. Therefore, incident ray, normal to the mirror XY and reflected ray all lie in the plane of the paper. This proves the **second law of reflection**.

14. (i) The focal length of L_1,

$$\frac{1}{f} = (\eta - 1)\left(\frac{2}{R}\right)$$

(ii) The focal length of the final combination,

$$\frac{1}{f_1} = (\eta - 1)\left(\frac{1}{R}\right)$$

$$f_1 = 2f$$

$$\frac{1}{f_2} = (\eta - 1)\left(\frac{2}{R}\right)$$

$$f_2 = f$$

15. (i) Fringe width is given by

$$\beta = \frac{\lambda D}{d}$$

where, λ is the wavelength of light, D is the distance between the slits and the screen and d is the distance between the slits.

If d decreases, β increases.

(ii) If the screen is moved away from the slits (i.e., D increases) the fringe width β will increase. This means the fringes will be farther apart.

(iii) When red light is replaced by blue light, λ decreases and thus β decreases.

16. (i) The instrument used by a virologist to study details of a virus is a compound microscope.

(ii)

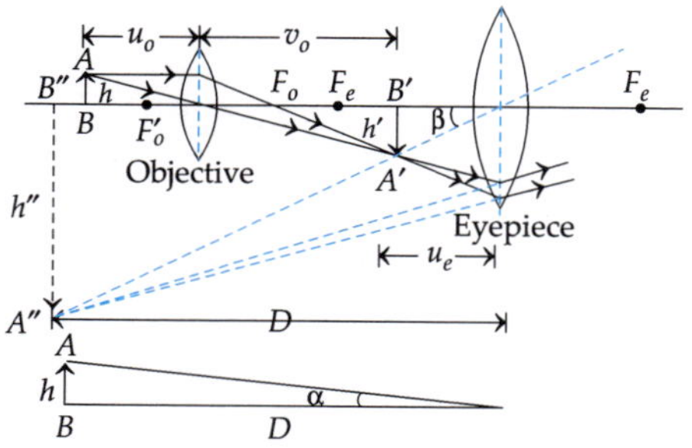

17. Work function for metals M_1 and M_2,

$$W_{01} = \frac{h\nu_{01}}{e} \text{ and } W_{02} = \frac{h\nu_{02}}{e}$$

Stopping potential of metal 1 and 2 are

$$V_1 = \left[\frac{h}{e}\right]\nu - \left[\frac{h}{e}\right]\nu_1$$

$$V_2 = \left[\frac{h}{e}\right]\nu - \left[\frac{h}{e}\right]\nu_2$$

$$\therefore \quad V_1 - V_2 = \left[\frac{h}{e}\right](\nu_1 - \nu_2)$$

$$\left[\frac{h}{e}\right] = \frac{V_1 - V_2}{\nu_1 - \nu_2}$$

18. (i) (a) Area of the circular loop $= \pi r^2$

$$= 3.14 \times (0.12)^2 \text{ m}^2 = 4.5 \times 10^{-2} \text{ m}^2$$

$$E = \frac{-d\phi}{dt} = -\frac{d}{dt}(BA)$$

$$= -A\frac{dB}{dt} = -A \cdot \frac{B_2 - B_1}{t_2 - t_1}$$

For $0 < t < 2$ s,

$$E_1 = -4.5 \times 10^{-2} \left\{\frac{1-0}{2-0}\right\}$$

$$= -2.25 \times 10^{-2} \text{ V}$$

$$\therefore \quad I_1 = \frac{E_1}{R} = \frac{-2.25 \times 10^{-2}}{8.5}$$

$$= -2.6 \times 10^{3} \text{A}$$

$$= -2.6 \text{ mA}$$

For $4\text{s} < t < 6$ s,

$$I_3 = \frac{-4.5 \times 10^{-2}}{8.5} \times \left(\frac{0-1}{6-4}\right) \text{A} = 2.6 \text{ mA}$$

(b)

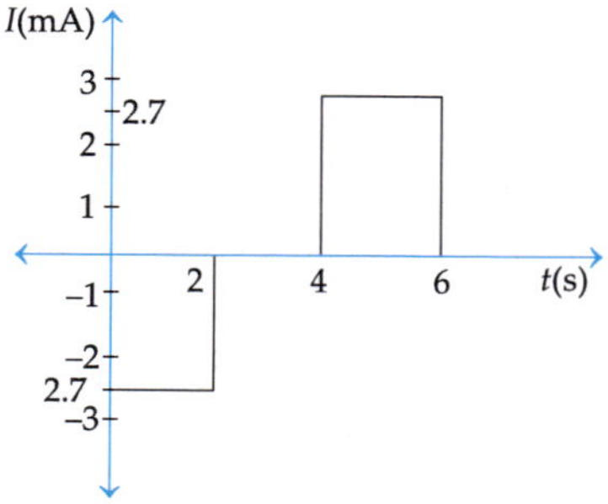

Or

(*ii*) (a) From the graph, the sharper the peak, the lower the resistance is, therefore, student X's graph is minimum.

(b) The quality factor will be maximum for student X's.

(c) At resonant frequency, the impedance is equal to ohmic resistance.

(d) Given, $I = V \cdot \omega C$

where, $\omega = 2\pi f$

For 50 Hz : $I_1 = V \cdot 2\pi \times 50 \times C$

For 100 Hz : $I_2 = V \cdot 2\pi \times 100 \times C$

$$\text{Ratio of current } \frac{I_1}{I_2} = \frac{V \cdot 2\pi \cdot 50}{V \cdot 2\pi \cdot 100}$$

$$= \frac{50}{100} = \frac{1}{2}$$

The ratio of current flowing through it in the two cases is $1:2$.

19. (i) (a) Given,

Mass of $^{235}U_{\text{nucleus}} = 235.0439$

Number of protons $(Z) = 92$

Number of neutrons $(N) = 235 - 92 = 143$

Mass of a proton $= 1.0073$ u

Mass of a neutron $= 1.0087$ u

Total mass of proton and neutron

$$= 92 \times 1.0073 + 143 \times 1.0087$$

$$= 92.6716 + 144.2441$$

$$= 236.9157 \text{ u}$$

Mass defect,

$$\Delta m = \text{Total mass} - \text{Mass of } {}^{235}U$$

$$= 236.9157 - 235.0439$$

$$= 1.8718 \text{ u}$$

Convert mass defect to energy

1 atomic mass unit (u) $= 931.5$ MeV

Binding energy $= \Delta m \times 931.5 = 1.8718 \times 931.5$

$$= 1743.58$$

$$\text{Binding energy per nucleon} = \frac{1743.58}{235}$$

$$= 7.49 \text{ MeV}$$

(b) $^{235}_{92}U + ^{1}_{0}n \longrightarrow ^{236}_{92}U \longrightarrow ^{90}_{36}Kr + ^{143}_{56}Ba + 3^{1}_{0}n$

Given, masses

$^{235}U = 235.0439$

Neutron = 1.0087 u

$^{90}Kr = 89.9195$ u

$^{143}Ba = 142.9206$ u

Total mass before the reaction

$= 235.0439 + 1.0087$

$= 236.0526$ u

Total mass after the reaction

$= 89.9195 + 142.9206 + 3(1.0087)$

$= 235.8662$ u

Mass defect (Δm) =

$236.0526 - 235.8662 = 0.1864$ u

$\theta = \Delta m \times 931.5$ MeV

$= 0.1864 \times 931.5$ MeV

$= 173.63$ MeV

(c) Rutherford hypothesised that the atom has a small, dense, positively charged nucleus that cause the deflection of α-particles by 180°.

Or

(*ii*) (a) A standard unit of mass that quantifies mass on a atomic or molecular scale.

(b) The value of E can be calculated (in MeV)

$$1 \text{ amu} = \frac{1}{12} \times \text{mass of one carbon atom}$$

$$= \frac{1}{12} \times \frac{12}{N}$$

$$1 \text{ amu} = \frac{1}{N} \text{ gram}$$

$$1 \text{ u} = \frac{1}{6.0221 \times 10^{23}}$$

$$= 1.6605 \times 10^{-24} \text{ g}$$

$$1 \text{ u} = 1.6605 \times 10^{-27} \text{kg}$$

$$E = mc^2$$

$$= 1.6605 \times 10^{-27} \times (3.0 \times 10^8)^2$$

$$= \frac{1.4924 \times 10^{-10}}{1.6022 \times 10^{-13}} \text{ MeV}$$

$$= 931.5 \text{ MeV}$$

(c) I. The wavelength of radiation is needed to excite the atom to energy level E_1 to E_3 are

$$\lambda = \frac{hc}{\Delta E} = 1.24 \times 10^{-6}/2.95 = 420.3 \text{ nm}$$

When the laser transition takes place between E_1 and E_2.

$\therefore$ The wavelength of the beam of laser produced will be

$$\lambda = \frac{hc}{\Delta E} = 1.24 \times 10^{-6}/1.78 = 696.6 \text{ nm}$$

II. Energy of photon = 1.78 eV

$= 1.78 \times 1.602 \times 10^{-19}$ J

$= 2.8516 \times 10^{-19}$ J

Photons emitted per second = power (energy emitted per second)/energy of each photon

$= 100 \text{ W} / 2.8516 \times 10^{-19}$ J

$= 3.506 \times 10^{20}$

20. (i) D_2 is forward biased because in D_2, p-side is connected to higher voltage, than n-side.

(ii) Saturation current is that current which remains constant even on increasing the potential difference.

(iii) Due to the potential barrier or barrier potential difference, no current flows in the diode when applied voltage during forward bias is small.

(iv)

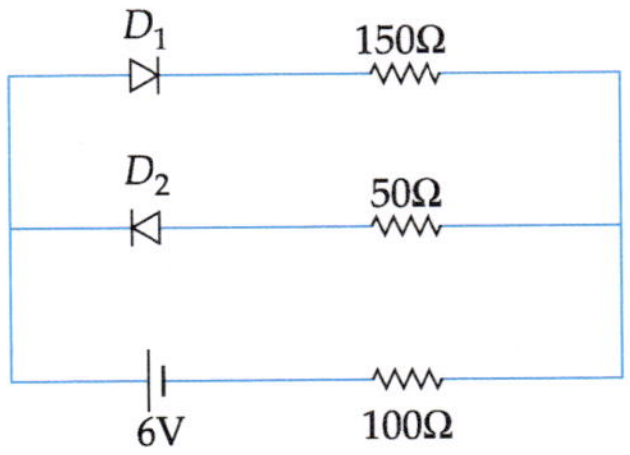

Ignoring 50 Ω because D_2 is reverse biased and offers infinite resistance. By Ohm's law,

$$I = \frac{V}{R} = \frac{6}{(50 + 150 + 100)}$$

$$= \frac{6}{300} = 0.02 \text{ A}$$

ISC

CHAPTERWISE - TOPICWISE

QUESTION BANK

ISC Examination Paper
2025

Examination Paper 2025 Physics (Full Solved)

Time : 3 hrs
Marks : 70

Physics
Paper 1

General Instructions

1. This paper is divided into four Sections- A, B, C and D. Answer all questions.
2. **Section A** consists of one question having sub-parts of one mark each.
3. **Section B** consists of seven questions of two marks each.
4. **Section C** consists of nine questions of three marks each.
5. **Section D** consists of three questions of five marks each.
6. Internal choices have been provided in two questions each in Section B, Section C and Section D.

Section-A [14 Marks]

1. (A) In questions (i) to (vii) given below, choose the correct alternative (a), (b), (c) or (d).

(i) When a battery is connected between the terminals P and Q, as shown in figure below, it is found that no current flows through 5 Ω resistor. Then, the value of resistor X is **[1]**

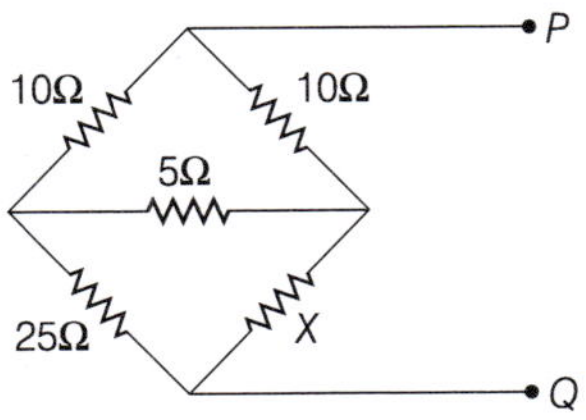

(a) 10 Ω (b) 20 Ω
(c) 25 Ω (d) 45 Ω

(ii) The relative permeability of substance X is slightly less than one and that of substance 'Y' is slightly more than one. Then, **[1]**
(a) X is paramagnetic and Y is ferromagnetic.
(b) X is diamagnetic and Y is ferromagnetic.
(c) X is paramagnetic and Y is diamagnetic.
(d) X is diamagnetic and Y is paramagnetic.

(iii) If kinetic energy of moving electrons is made four times, then their de-Broglie wavelength becomes **[1]**
(a) eight times (b) four times
(c) two times (d) half

(iv) A student has made connections, as shown in figure below, so that the wires MN and ST repel each other. But it is observed that they are attracting each other. What change should the student make for the wires to repel each other? **[1]**

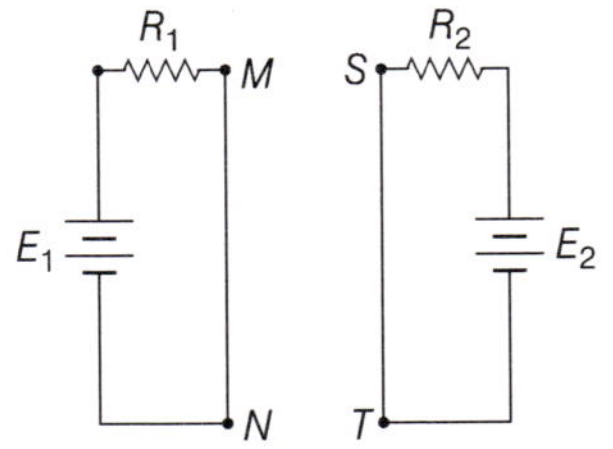

(a) Reverse the terminals of batteries E_1 and E_2.
(b) Reverse the terminals of battery E_1 or E_2.
(c) Choose supply voltage such that $E_1 = E_2$.
(d) Add key and ammeter to the circuit.

(v) n-type semiconductor is that which has **[1]**
(a) majority of holes as charge carriers
(b) majority of free electrons as charge carriers
(c) trivalent element added as an impurity
(d) An equal number of holes and free electrons

(vi) Given below are two statements marked, Assertion and Reason. Read the two statements and choose the correct option. **[1]**

Assertion When a convex lens made of glass is completely immersed in water, its focal length increases.

Reason Refractive index of glass with respect to water is greater than that of glass with respect to air.

(a) Both Assertion and Reason are true and Reason is the correct explanation for Assertion.

(b) Both Assertion and Reason are true but Reason is not the correct explanation for Assertion.

(c) Assertion is true and Reason is false.

(d) Both Assertion and Reason are false

(vii) Given below are two statements marked, Assertion and Reason. Read the two statements and choose the correct option. **[1]**

Assertion Diffraction of light is difficult to observe in everyday situations but can be observed in laboratory conditions.

Reason To produce diffraction of waves, size of an obstacle must be comparable to the wavelength of the waves.

(a) Both Assertion and Reason are true and Reason is the correct explanation for Assertion.

(b) Both Assertion and Reason are true but Reason is not the correct explanation for Assertion.

(c) Assertion is true and Reason is false.

(d) Both Assertion and Reason are false.

(B) Answer the following questions briefly.

(i) How does the resistance of a semiconductor crystal vary with its temperature? **[1]**

(ii) Figure below shows an ideal transformer. Explain why current flowing through secondary coil is greater than that in primary coil.

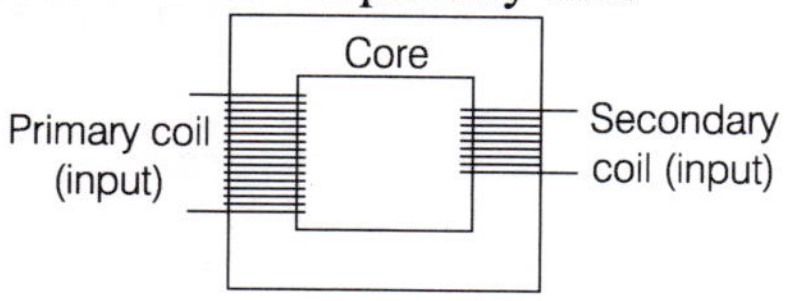

[1]

(iii) State any one difference between a primary rainbow and a secondary rainbow. **[1]**

(iv) Hubble telescope employs a large parabolic mirror as an objective. State any one advantage of using a mirror in place of a lens in such a telescope. **[1]**

(v) Name any one phenomenon where moving particles behave like waves. **[1]**

(vi) What is the minimum energy a gamma ray (γ) photon should possess to produce an electron-positron pair? **[1]**

(vii) In an energy band diagram of a certain material, forbidden band is absent. Identify this material. **[1]**

Section-B

[14 Marks]

2. (i) (a) What is the effect on capacitance of a parallel plate capacitor if the distance between its plates is increased?

(b) How will capacitance of a capacitor change if a dielectric slab is introduced between its plates? **[2]**

Or

(ii) Figures (a) and (b) represent the combination of two identical cells having negligible internal resistance.

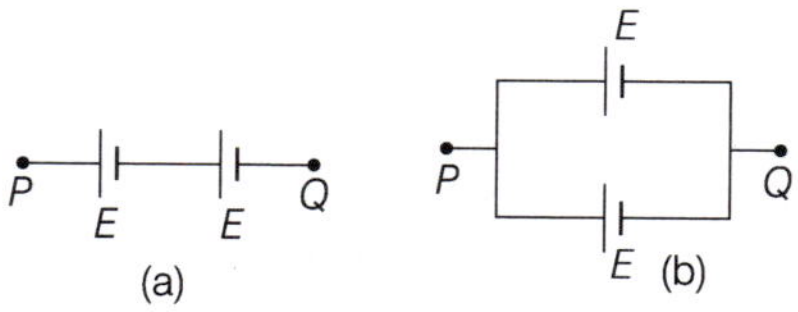

(a) In which of the two combinations, emf of the battery is greater?

(b) When a resistor R is connected between the terminals P and Q, I_1 and I_2 are the currents flowing through R in figure (a) and figure (b) respectively. Obtain the ratio $\frac{I_1}{I_2}$. **[2]**

3. In case of a short electric dipole

(i) What is the locus of a point having zero potential?

(ii) If electric field intensity at a point in axial position is E_1 and at an equidistant point in equatorial position is E_2. What is the ratio $\frac{E_1}{E_2}$? **[2]**

4. (i) Figure below shows an electric circuit. **[2]**

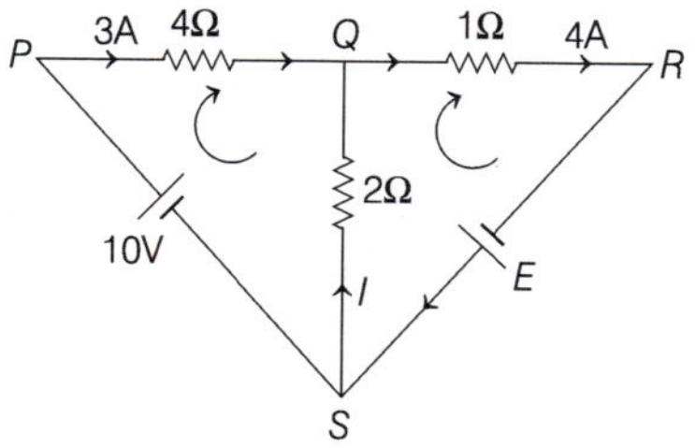

Apply Kirchhoff's laws to calculate

(a) current I flowing through the $2\,\Omega$ resistor.

(b) emf of the cell E.

Or

(ii) In a potentiometer experiment, a cell of emf 1.25V gives a balance point at 35 cm mark of the wire. If this cell is replaced by another cell, the balance point is at 63 cm mark. Calculate the emf of the second cell. **[2]**

5. Magnetic field at the centre of a circular coil is B. Calculate the magnetic field at the same point when each of the current, number of turns of the coil and its radius is doubled. **[2]**

6. The objective of a telescope consists of two lenses kept in contact. One lens has an optical power of $+2.0$ D, whereas the other lens has an optical power of -1.5 D. Calculate focal length of the objective. **[2]**

7.

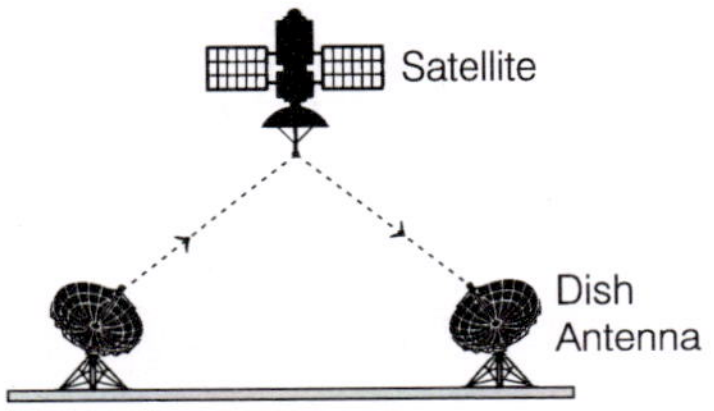

(i) Name the electromagnetic wave travelling from the satellite to the dish antenna shown in the image above. **[2]**

(ii) If the wavelength of an electromagnetic wave is 6 nm, what is its frequency?

8. With reference to photoelectric effect, define the terms

(i) Threshold frequency **[2]**

(ii) Work function

Section-C [27 Marks]

9. An infinite plane metallic sheet having surface charge density $+\sigma$ is placed in vacuum. P is a point at a small distance r to its right.

(i) Write an expression for intensity of electric field at point P.

(ii) Now, an identical charged sheet having surface charge density $-\sigma$ is placed parallel to the first sheet such that the point P is to its left at the same distance r. (The point P lies between the two plates.) **[3]**

(a) What is the resultant intensity of electric field at point P?

(b) What is its direction?

10. (i) Harry sets up a circuit as shown in figure below. He measures potential difference V across the variable resistor R with an instrument Y. He also measures current I flowing through R with another instrument X. **[3]**

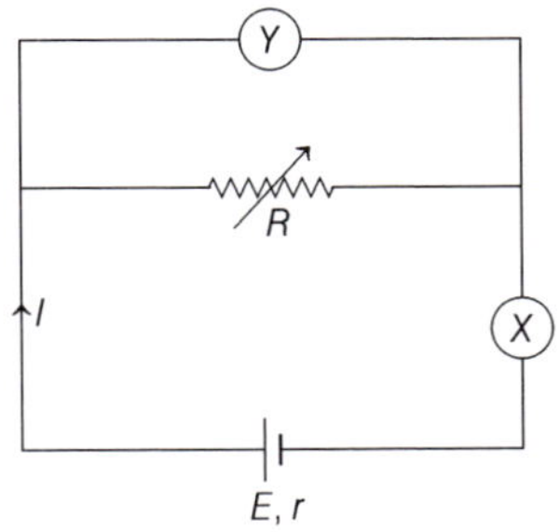

(a) Identify the instruments X and Y.

(b) Using the graph of V against I shown below, calculate

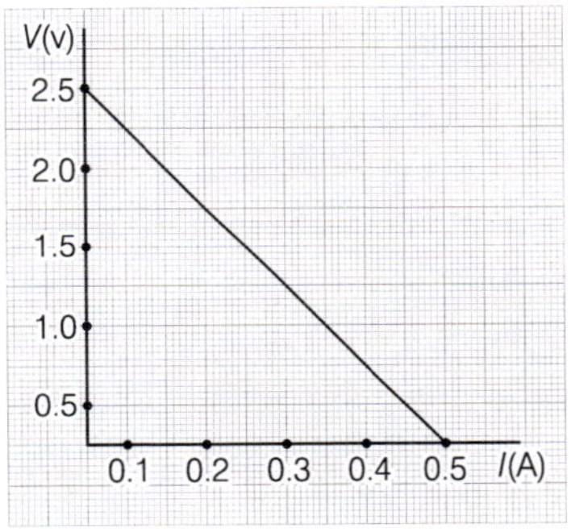

1. emf (E) of the cell.
2. Internal resistance (r) of the cell.

Or

(ii) The graph below shows the variation of current density (J) with electric field (E) applied to two different metallic wires A and B. **[3]**

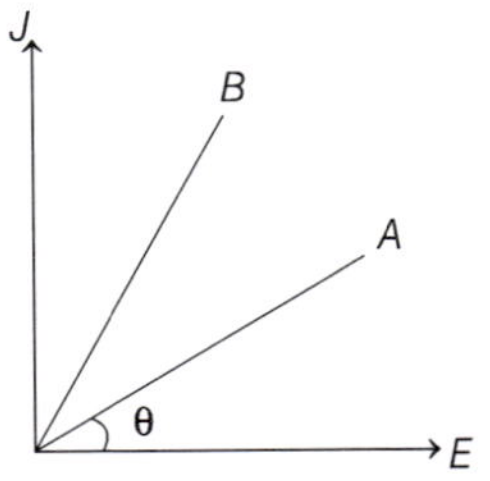

(a) Which one of the wires, A or B, has higher resistivity?

(b) For a certain value of electric field (E), in which wire A or B is drift velocity greater? Give a reason for your answer.

11. A galvanometer having a resistance of 20 Ω shows a full scale deflection with a current of 1 mA. How can it be converted into a voltmeter with a range of 0-10 V? **[3]**

12. (i) Two infinitely long straight wires PQ and RS carrying currents I_1 and I_2 respectively are kept 10 cm apart in vacuum. Calculate magnetic field (B) at the point X shown in figure below.

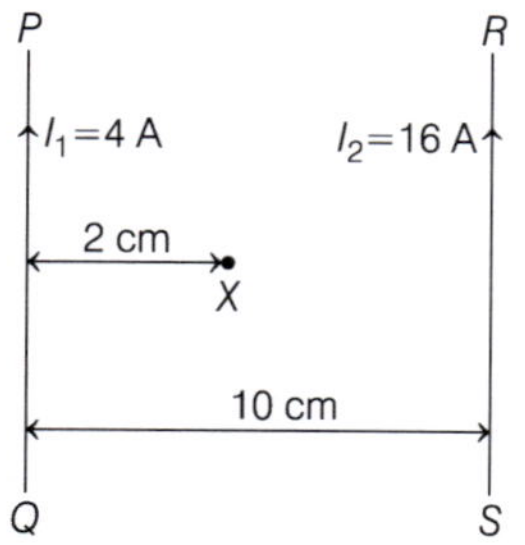

[3]

Or

(ii) An electron and a proton are moving along the $+X$ axis. If an external magnetic field $B = 0.314$ T is applied along $-Z$ axis.

(a) What is the path followed by the electron due to the magnetic field?

(b) Calculate the frequency of revolution of the proton. **[3]**

13. A convex lens having small focal length is to be used as a magnifying glass (simple microscope) to obtain an image of a small diamond. If the image lies at least distance of distinct vision (D)

(i) Where will you keep the diamond to obtain its image at D?

(ii) State any two characteristics of the image formed by the magnifying glass.

14. A parallel beam of light is travelling obliquely from an optically rarer medium to an optically denser medium. **[3]**

(i) Draw a labelled diagram showing incident and refracted wavefronts. Mark angle of incidence as i and angle of refraction as r.

(ii) Use Huygen's wave theory to prove Snell's law.

15. For any prism, show that refractive index n of its material is given by **[3]**

$$n = \frac{\sin\left(\frac{A+\delta_m}{2}\right)}{\sin\left(\frac{A}{2}\right)}$$

where the terms have their usual meaning.

16. Two identical rectangular slits 5 mm apart are illuminated with a monochromatic light of wavelength 600 nm. The screen is kept 1.2 m away from the slits.

(i) Calculate the distance between the 5th bright fringe (band) on one side and the 3rd bright fringe on the other side of the central bright band.

(ii) What will be the change in the interference pattern if the given light is replaced with monochromatic light of wavelength 500 nm? **[3]**

17. (i) Plot a labelled graph of stopping potential (V_s) *versus* frequency (f) of incident UV-radiation.

(ii) State how the value of Planck's constant can be determined from this graph. **[3]**

Section-D

[15 Marks]

18. (i) (a) Figure shows a metallic rod MN length $l = 3$ m moving in an external uniform magnetic field, $B = \left(\frac{1}{\pi}\right)$ T which is directed into the plane of this paper.

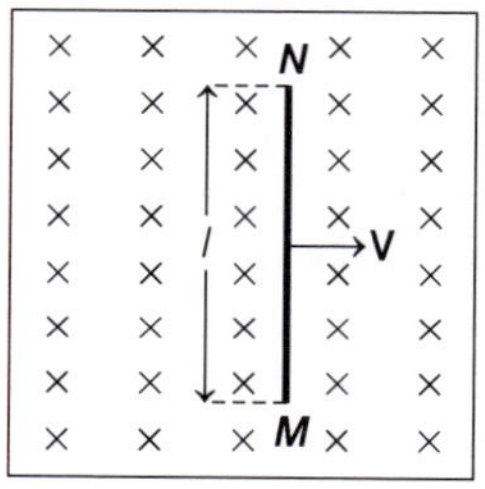

If the position of the rod changes with time as $x = \pi t$, where x is in metre and t is in second, then

1. Calculate the motional emf developed in the rod.
2. Name the law used to find the direction of induced current.

(b) When current flowing through a solenoid decreases from 15 A to 0 in 0.2 s, an emf of 30 V is induced in it. Calculate the coefficient of self-inductance of the solenoid. **[5]**

Or

(ii) An alternating emf $E = 5.0 \sin(314t)$ V is applied to a circuit containing a resistor connected in series with an unknown component X.

The current in the circuit is found to be **[5]**

$$I = 3.0 \sin\left(314t - \frac{\pi}{3}\right) \text{A}$$

(a) Identify the component X.

(b) Calculate rms value (I_{rms}) of the current flowing through the circuit.

(c) Find the frequency of the source.

(d) Calculate power factor.

(e) Find the impedance (Z) of the circuit.

19. (i) (a) Show that radius (r_n) of the nth Bohr orbit varies directly with square of the principal quantum number (n) of the orbit. **[5]**

(b) 1. Where does nuclear fusion reaction take place continuously in the Universe?

2. What is meant by "mass defect" of a nucleus?

Or

(ii) (a) A group of students went on an educational tour of Bhabha Atomic Research Centre, Mumbai. They visited various nuclear reactors like Apsara, Cirus, Zerlina and Dhruv and observed that Apsara was a swimming pool type reactor. The teacher explained how water slows down fast moving neutrons and absorbs the heat produced in the reactor.

1. What is the use of a nuclear reactor?
2. What is the name given to a material which slows down fast moving neutrons?
3. State how a nuclear reactor can be shut down in case of an emergency.

(b) 1. What is meant by the statement "Angular momentum of an orbiting electron is quantised"? **[5]**

2. What is the physical significance of the fact that total energy of an orbiting electron is negative?

20. When a television set (scientifically known as a television receiver) is opened, components like semiconductor diodes, transistors, capacitors, resistors, etc. can be observed on its motherboard. There are different types of diodes like photodiode, Zener diode, LED etc. found in the TV set. With the help of these components, a television receives audio as well as video signals. **[5]**

(i) A semiconductor diode has two types of semiconducting materials: p type and n type. What is the difference between them?

(ii) Draw a labelled diagram of a full wave rectifier. Show graphically how its output voltage varies with time.

(iii) What type of diode can be used as a voltage regulator?

Useful Constants and Relations

1.	Speed of light in vacuum	c	=	$3 \times 10^8 \text{ ms}^{-1}$
2.	Charge of a proton	e	=	$1.6 \times 10^{-19}\text{C}$
3.	Mass of a proton	m_p	=	1.67×10^{-27} kg
4.	Permeability of vacuum	μ_0	=	$4\pi \times 10^{-7}\text{Hm}^{-1}$
5.	1 nm		=	10^{-9}m
6.	π		=	3.14

Explanations

1. (A) (i) (c) Since the circuit is in balanced Wheatstone bridge condition as no current slows through the 5 Ω resistor, so

$$\frac{10}{25} = \frac{10}{X}$$

$$\Rightarrow \quad X = 25\,\Omega$$

(ii) (d) Relative permeability of a diamagnetic substance is slightly less than one and it is slightly more than one for a paramagnetic substance.

(iii) (d) de-Broglie wavelength of an electron is given as $\lambda = \frac{h}{p}$, where h is the Planck's constant and p is the momentum of the electron.

Now, $p = \sqrt{2mK}$, where K is the kinetic energy of electron.

$$\Rightarrow \quad \lambda \propto \frac{1}{\sqrt{K}}$$

⇒ If K increases four times, then λ decreases by two times.

∴ The wavelength becomes half.

(iv) (b) For the wires to repel each other, the direction of currents through MN and ST should be opposite.

(v) (b)

(vi) (c) Refractive index of glass with respect to water (1.2) is less than the refractive index of glass with respect to air (1.5).

(vii) (a) Both Assertion and Reason are true and Reason is the correct explanation of Assertion because when the obstacle is manually made to be comparable to the wavelength of the light wave used to observe diffraction, only then it can be observed.

(B) (i) The resistance of a semiconductor decreases with the increase in temperature.

(ii) In the step-down transformer shown in the figure, the voltage across the primary coil is greater than that of the secondary coil, So to maintain power balance ($P = VI$), the current across the secondary coil is greater than that of the primary coil.

(iii) Primary rainbows have one total internal reflection in the rain droplet and secondary rainbows have two total internal reflections in the rain droplet.

(iv) Mirrors can be made parabolic in shape which helps in reducing spherical aberration which is not possible in case of lenses.

(v) Davisson and Germer experiment, in which the wave nature of the electron is verified.

(vi) The minimum energy a gamma ray photon should possess to produce an electron-positron pair is 1.022 MeV.

(vii) The material is a conductor.

2. (i) (a) As we know that, $C = \frac{\varepsilon_0 A}{d}$, where A is the area of the capacitor plates and d is the distance between the plates.

Therefore if the distance between the plates is increased, the capacitance will decrease.

(b) If a dielectric of dielectric constant K is introduced between the capacitor plates, the capacitance increases by a factor of K.

Or

(ii) (a) In figure (a) the effective emf of the battery is $2E$ and in figure (b) the emf is E.

∴ Emf is greater for figure (a).

(b) $I_1 = \frac{2E}{R}$ and $I_2 = \frac{E}{R}$

$$\therefore \quad \frac{I_1}{I_2} = \frac{2}{1} = 2$$

3. (i) The locus of a point having zero potential for a small dipole is the equatorial line.

(ii) For a dipole having dipole moment **p**,

$\mathbf{E}_1 = \mathbf{E}_{\text{axial}} = \frac{2\mathbf{p}}{4\pi\varepsilon_0 x^3}$, where x is the distance of the point on the axis of the dipole from its centre.

Similarly,

$\mathbf{E}_2 = \mathbf{E}_{\text{equatorial}} = \frac{-\mathbf{p}}{4\pi\varepsilon_0 x^3}$, where x is the distance of a point on the equatorial line along the dipole.

$$\Rightarrow \quad \frac{|\mathbf{E}_1|}{|\mathbf{E}_2|} = \frac{2}{1} = 2$$

4. (i)

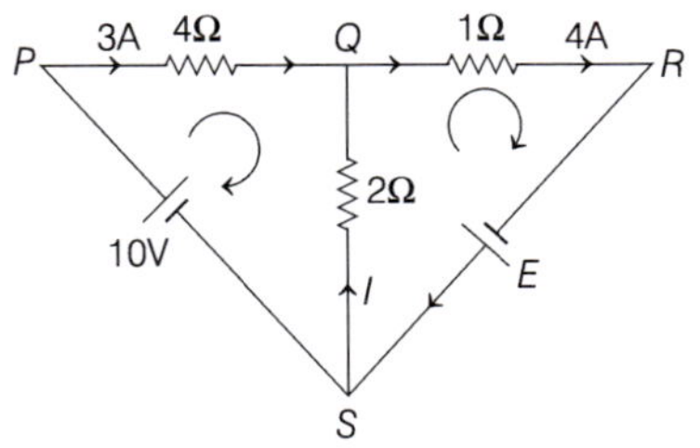

(a) Applying KVL in the loop *PQS*, we get

$10 - 3 \times 4 + 2 \times I = 0. \Rightarrow I = 1\text{ A}.$

(b) Again, applying KVL in the loop *SQR*, we get

$$E - 2I - 4 \times 1 = 0.$$

$$\Rightarrow \quad E = 2 \times 1 + 4 \times 1 = 6\text{ V}$$

Or (ii) For a potentiometer,

$$\frac{E_1}{E_2} = \frac{l_1}{l_2}$$

Here, $E_1 = 1.25$ V, $l_1 = 35$ cm, $E_2 = ?$ and $l_2 = 63$ cm.

$$\Rightarrow \quad \frac{1.25}{E_2} = \frac{35}{63}$$

$$\Rightarrow \quad E_2 = \frac{1.25 \times 63}{35} = 2.25\text{ V}$$

∴ The emf of the 2nd cell is 2.25 V.

5. Magnetic field at the centre of a circular coil *B* is given as

$$B = \frac{\mu_0 NI}{2R}$$

where, *N* is the number of turns of the coil, *I* is the current through the coil and *R* is the radius of the coil.

Now, when all the parameters are doubled, the magnetic field becomes,

$$B' = \frac{\mu_0 (2N)(2I)}{2(2R)} = 2\left(\frac{\mu_0 NI}{2R}\right)$$

$$\therefore \quad B' = 2B$$

∴ The magnetic field gels doubled.

6. The combined power of the two lenses is given as

$$P = +2D + (-1.5)D = +0.5D$$

∴ Focal length of the combination of lens is

$$f = \frac{1}{P} = \frac{1}{0.5} = 2\text{ m} = 200\text{ cm}$$

7. (i) Infrared waves.

(ii) We know that, $c = f\lambda$, where *c* is the speed of an EM-wave, *f* is its frequency and λ is its wavelength.

$$\therefore \quad f = \frac{c}{\lambda} = \frac{3 \times 10^8\text{ ms}^{-1}}{6 \times 10^{-9}\text{ m}} = 0.5 \times 10^{17}\text{ s}^{-1}$$

$$= 5 \times 10^{16}\text{ Hz}$$

8. (i) Refer to text on page 247.

(ii) Refer to text on page 246.

9. (i) The intensity of electric field at point *P* is

$$E = \frac{\sigma}{2\varepsilon_0}$$

(ii) (a) The resultant intensity of electric field at point *P* is

$$E_R = 2 \times \left(\frac{\sigma}{2\varepsilon_0}\right) = \frac{\sigma}{\varepsilon_0}$$

(b) The direction of the field is from the positively charged plate towards the negatively charged plate.

10. (i) (a) *X* is an ammeter, *Y* is a voltmeter.

(b) (1) We know that, the terminal potential difference (*V*) of a cell is related to the emf (*E*) of the cell as

$$V = E - Ir$$

where, *r* is the internal resistance of the cell.

When the current passing through the cell is zero, $E = V$.

$$\therefore \quad E = 2.5\text{ V}$$

2. $V = E - Ir.$

For point 2.0 V on the *V*-axis the corresponding current on the *I*-axis is 0.1 A.

$$\therefore \quad 2 = 2.5 - 0.1 \times r$$

$$\Rightarrow \quad r = \frac{2.5 - 2}{0.1} = 5\,\Omega$$

Or (ii) (a) We know that $J = \sigma E$, where σ is the conductivity of a substance which is the reciprocal of resistivity.

∴ For a greater slops, the resistivity of the substance will be less. So, *A* will have a higher resistivity.

(b) Also, $J = nev_d$, So, $J \propto v_d$.

∴ For a particular value of *E*, v_d will be greater for wire *B*, since *J* is greater for wire *B*.

11. To convert a moving coil galvanometer into a voltmeter, a higher resistance *R* should be connected in series with the galvanometer.

where, $R = \dfrac{V}{I_g} - G$

Here, *V* is the voltage across the galvanometer terminals which must be obtained.

G is the resistance of the galvanometer, and I_g is the full scale deflection current.

$$\therefore\ R = \frac{10}{1\times10^{-3}} - 20 = (10000-20)\,\Omega \Rightarrow R = 9980\,\Omega$$

12. (i) Magnetic field at point - X due to the infinitely long wire PQ is

$$B_{PQ} = \frac{\mu_0 I_1}{2\pi\, r_{PQ}} = \frac{\mu_0}{2\pi}\,\frac{4}{(2\times10^{-2})} = \left(\frac{\mu_0}{2\pi}\times200\right)T$$

The direction of the field B_{PQ} is into the page. Similarly, the magnetic field at X due to the wire RS is

$$B_{RS} = \frac{\mu_0 I_2}{2\pi\, r_{RS}} = \frac{\mu_0}{2\pi}\,\frac{16}{(8\times10^{-2})} = \left(\frac{\mu_0}{2\pi}\times200\right)T$$

The direction of the field B_{RS} is out of the page.
∴ The resultant field at point X is

$$B_R = B_{RS} - B_{PQ} = \frac{\mu_0}{2\pi}[200-200] = 0$$

Or

(ii) (a) The electron will follow a circular path along the XY- plane.

(b) The time period of revolution of the proton is given as

$$T = \frac{2\pi\, m_p}{q_p\, B}$$

$$\Rightarrow\quad f = \frac{1}{T} = \frac{q_p\, B}{2\pi\, m_p}$$

$$\Rightarrow\quad f = \frac{1.6\times10^{-19}\times0.314}{2\times3.14\times1.67\times10^{-27}} = 4.8\times10^{6}\text{ Hz}$$

13. (i) We know that, for a thin lens, $\frac{1}{v} - \frac{1}{u} = \frac{1}{f}$.

It is given that $v = -D$.

$$\Rightarrow\quad \frac{1}{u} = -\frac{1}{D} - \frac{1}{f} = -\left(\frac{D+f}{Df}\right).$$

∴ The object has to be kept at a distance,

$u = \frac{Df}{D+f}$ to the left of the lens of the simple microscope.

(ii) The two characteristics of the image formed are
(a) The image is erect and virtual.
(b) The image is magnified.

14. (i) Refer to figure on page 222.

(ii) Refer to theory on page 221 (Laws of refraction at a plane surface).

15. Refer to text on page 179 (Prism Formula).

16. (i) Distance of the nth bright fringe for a double - slit experiment is given as $Y_n = \frac{nD\lambda}{d}$

where, D is the distance between the slits and the screen, λ is the wavelength of the light used and d is the separation between the slits.

Here, $D = 1.2$ m, $\lambda = 600\times10^{-9}$ m,

$d = 5\times10^{-3}$ m.

∴ For the 5th bright fringe, the distance from the central band is

$$Y_5 = \frac{5\times1.2\times600\times10^{-9}}{5\times10^{-3}} = 7.2\times10^{-4}\text{ m} = 0.72\text{ mm}.$$

For the 3rd bright fringe, the distance from the central band is

$$Y_3 = \frac{3\times1.2\times600\times10^{-9}}{5\times10^{-3}} = 4.32\times10^{-4}\text{m}$$

$$= 0.432\text{ mm}.$$

∴ The distance between the 5th bright fringe on one side and the 3rd bright fringe on the other side is

$$Y = (0.72+0.432)\text{mm} = 1.152\text{ mm}$$

(ii) If the given light is changed to a wavelength 500 nm then the fringe width (β) will decrease, as $\beta\propto\lambda$.

17. (i) Refer to the graph (Variation of stopping potential *versus* frequency) on page 248.

(ii) As, $h\nu = h\nu_0 + \frac{1}{2}mv^2$ or $h = h\nu_0 + eV_0$

$$\therefore\quad eV_0 = h(\nu-\nu_0) \Rightarrow V_0 = \frac{h}{e}(\nu-\nu_0)$$

Comparing with straight line equation

$y = mx + c$, we see that

Slope $m = \frac{h}{e}$ and

Intercept $c = \frac{-h\nu_0}{e}$

So, the value of h can be determined if either the slope or the intercept is known.

18. (i) (a) (1) Velocity of the rod is given as

$$v = \frac{dx}{dt} = \pi\text{ m/s}.$$

The emf induced in the rod is given as

$$e = Blv$$

where, $B = \frac{1}{\pi}T$, $v = \pi$ m/s and $l = 3$ m

$\therefore \quad e = \frac{1}{\pi} \times 3 \times \pi = 3\text{ V}$

2. Faraday's second law of electromagnetic induction.

(b) Coefficient of self-inductance is given as $L = \frac{-e}{\frac{\Delta I}{\Delta t}}$,

where e is the emf.

Here, $e = 30\text{ V}$

$$\frac{\Delta I}{\Delta t} = \frac{-15}{0.2}$$

$$\therefore \quad L = \frac{30}{30} = 1\text{ H}$$

Or

(ii) (a) The component X is an inductor.

(b) From the given data, we know

$$I_0 = 3\text{ A}$$

$$\therefore \quad I_{\text{rms}} = \frac{I_0}{\sqrt{2}} = \frac{3}{\sqrt{2}} = 2.121\text{ A}$$

(c) From the given data, we know

$$\omega = 314\text{ rad/s}$$

$\therefore$ Frequency of the source is

$$f = \omega / 2\pi = \frac{314}{2 \times 314} = 50\text{ Hz}$$

(d) The power factor is $PF = \cos\phi$, where $\phi = \frac{\pi}{3}$

$$\therefore \quad PF = \cos\frac{\pi}{3} = \frac{1}{2}$$

(e) We know, $I_0 = \frac{E_0}{Z}$, where Z is the impedence of the circuit

$\therefore \quad Z = E_0 / I_0 = (5/3)\,\Omega = 1.67\,\Omega$

19. (i) (a) Refer to theory on page 264 (Bohr's Theory).

(b) 1. In the sun and other stars.

2. Refer to theory on page 284 (Mass defect).

Or (ii) (a) 1. Nuclear reactor is a device that can initiate a self-sustaining controlled chain reaction of a fissionable material.

2. Moderator

3. In case of an emergency, a special set of control rods, known as 'shut-off rods' enter the reactor automatically. They immediately absorb the neutrons so that the chain reaction stops entirely.

(b) 1. Refer to text on page 264 (Bohr's second postulate)

2. The negative total energy of an electron signifies that the electron is bound to the nucleus of the atom.

20. (i)

p-type Semiconductor	*n*-type Semiconductor
Formed by doping a pure semiconductor (like silicon) with a trivalent impurity (e.g., boron, aluminium).	Formed by doping a pure semiconductor with a pentavalent impurity (e.g., phosphorus, arsenic).
Has holes (positively charged carriers) as the majority charge carriers.	Has electrons (negatively charged carriers) as the majority charge carriers.
Minority charge carriers are electrons.	Minority charge carriers are holes.
Creates a deficiency of electrons, making it positively charged.	Has excess electrons, making it negatively charged.

(ii) Refer to theory on page 306. (Diode as a full wave rectifier).

(iii) Zener diode